Sixties Spotting Days Around The Western Region

Strathwood

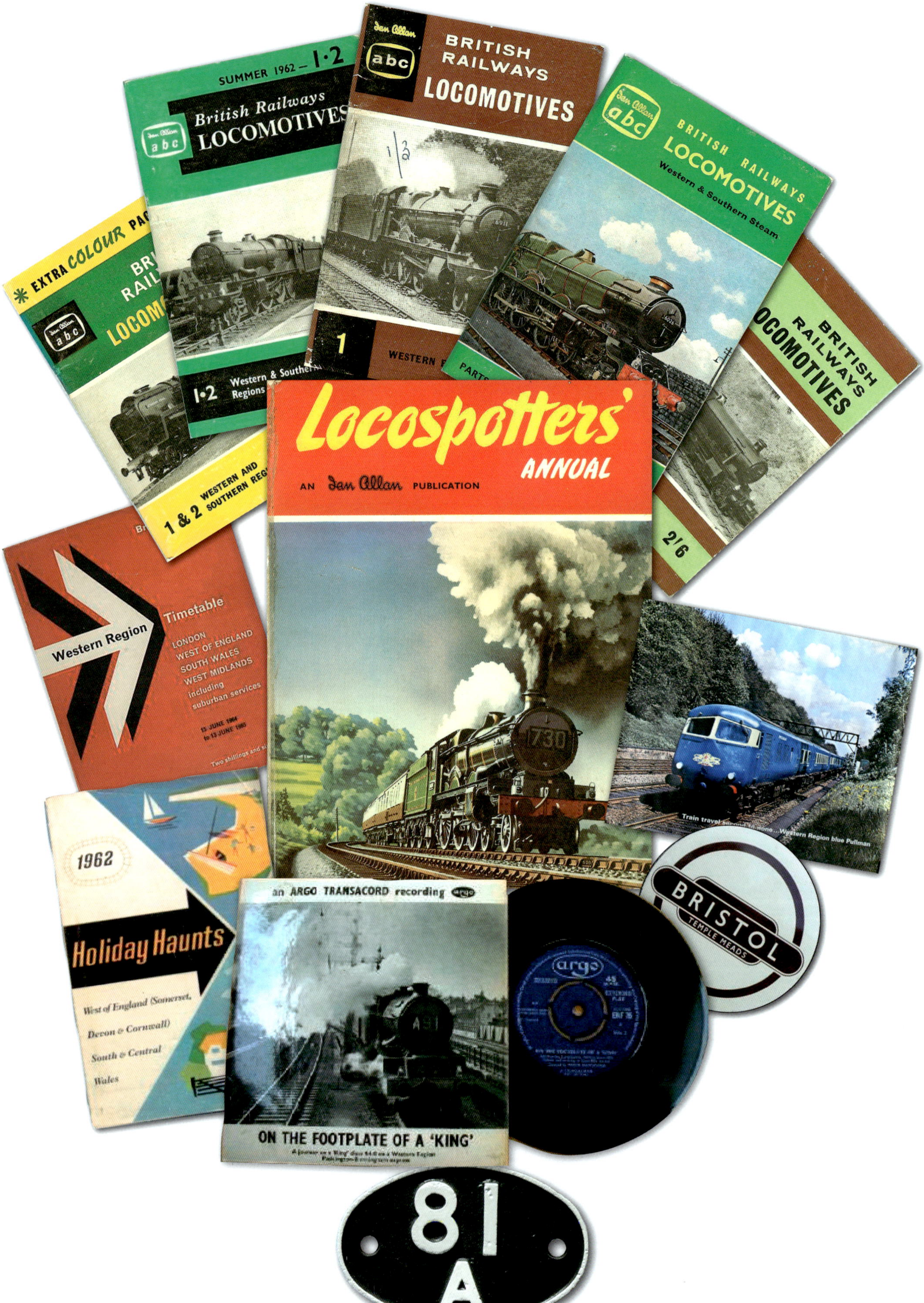
SUMMER 1962 – 1·2
British Railways
LOCOMOTIVES
1·2 Western & Southern Regions
Ian Allan
abc
BRITISH RAILWAYS
LOCOMOTIVES
1
WESTERN
BRITISH RAILWAYS
LOCOMOTIVES
Western & Southern Steam
BRITISH RAILWAYS
LOCOMOTIVES
2/6
EXTRA COLOUR PAGES
1 & 2 WESTERN AND SOUTHERN REGIONS
Locospotters' ANNUAL
AN Ian Allan PUBLICATION
730
Western Region
Timetable
LONDON
WEST OF ENGLAND
SOUTH WALES
WEST MIDLANDS
including
suburban services
15 JUNE 1964
to 13 JUNE 1965
Western Region blue Pullman
1962
Holiday Haunts
West of England (Somerset, Devon & Cornwall)
South & Central Wales
an ARGO TRANSACORD recording
argo
ON THE FOOTPLATE OF A 'KING'
BRISTOL
TEMPLE MEADS
81
A

Sixties Spotting Days Around The Western Region

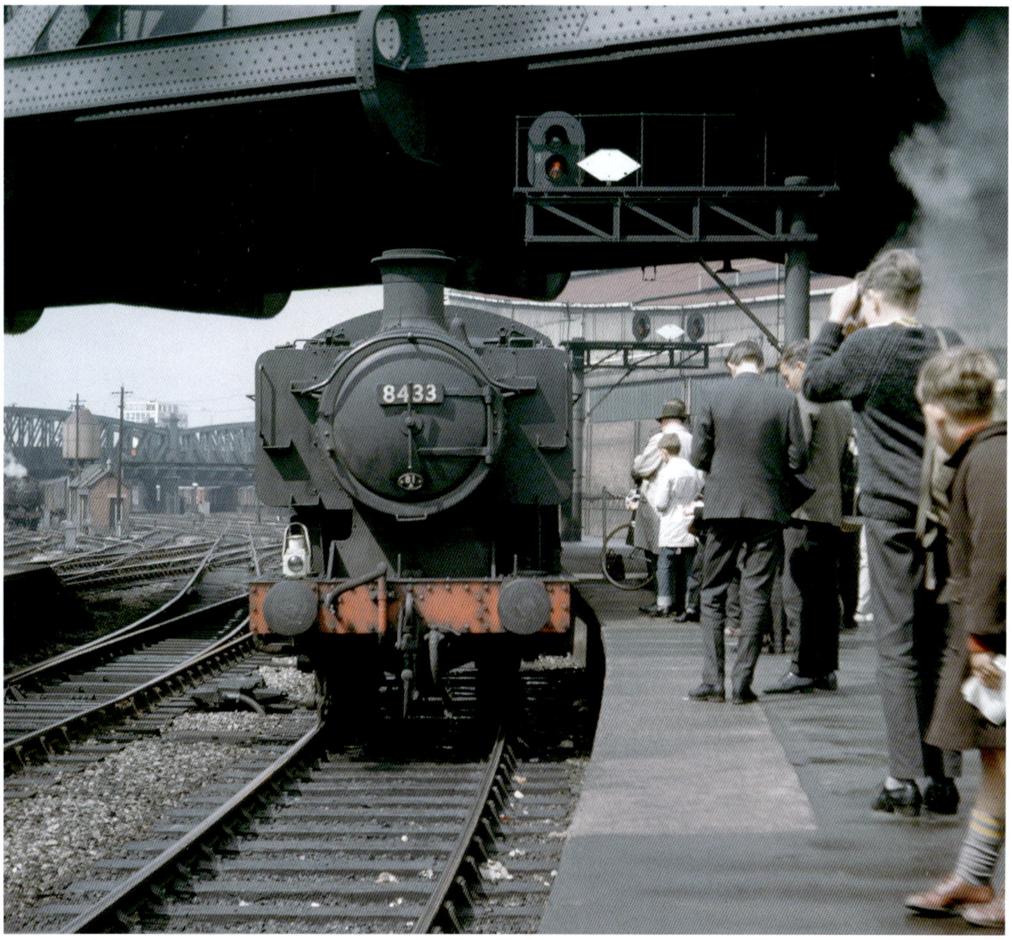

Front cover: Hawksworth Pannier Tank 8433 entertains the crowds of spotters at Paddington on 31 August 1963. ***Peter Coton***

Kevin Derrick

Strathwood

Sixties Spotting Days Around The Western Region

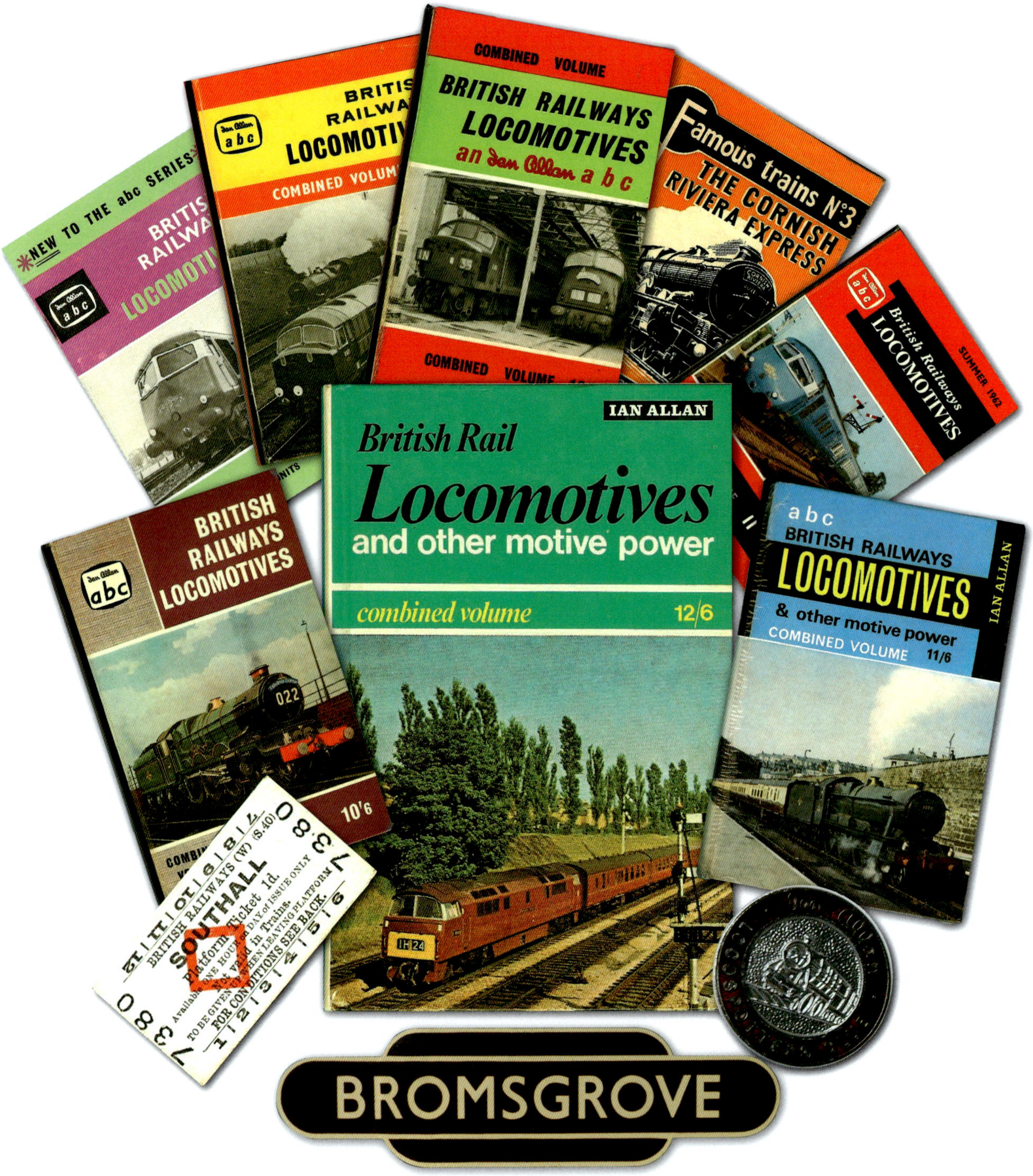

First published 2010

ISBN 1-905276-17-6
ISBN 978-1-905276-17-2

Published by Strathwood Ltd, Glenavon House, Kinchurdy Road, Boat of Garten, Inverness-shire, PH24 3BP. Tel 01479 831139

Contents **Page**

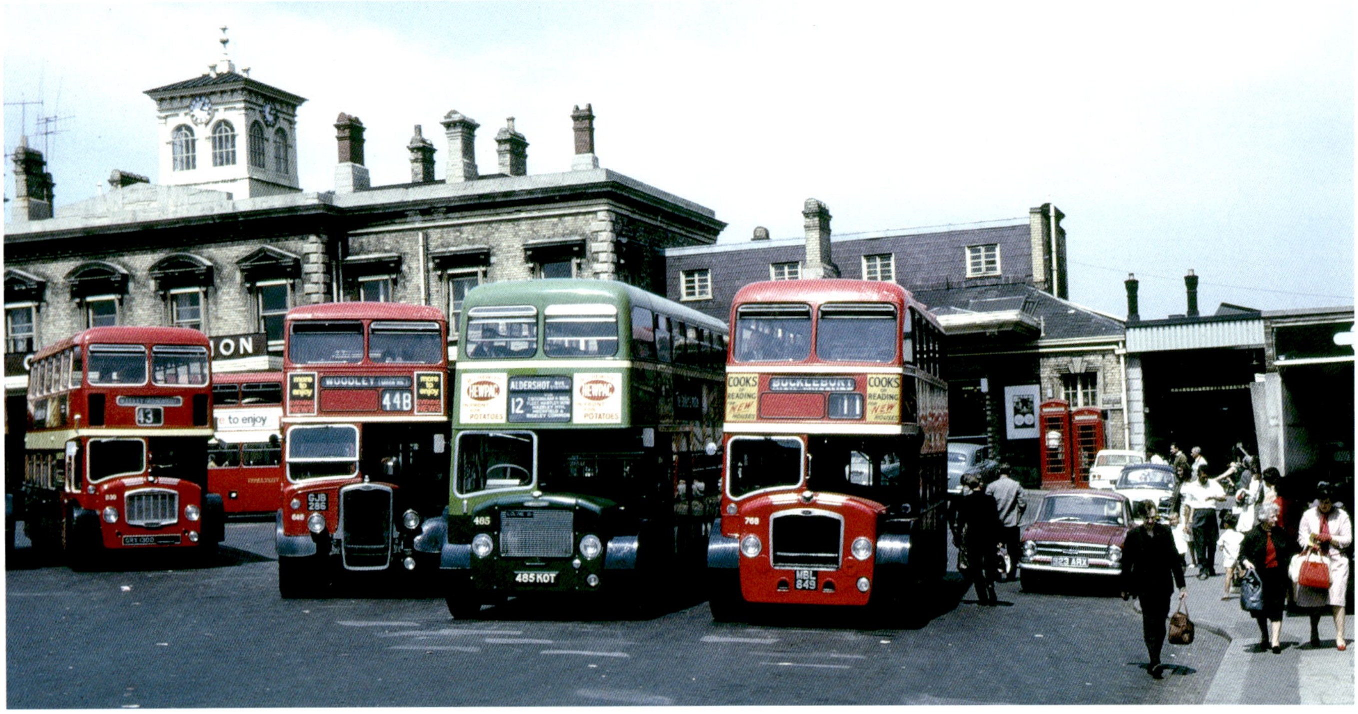

The importance of road transport and interchange traffic was recognised very early by the Great Western Railway. It is just a quirk of politics that the forward thinking of the Directors of the company could not have been taken full advantage of by within the nationalised railway. This was the scene outside Reading General station in June 1966. ***Strathwood Library Collection***

Introduction

Why is is he starting a book for railway enthusiasts with two photographs of buses you may well ask? The answer is simple, the Great Western Railway recognised before the other companies within the Big Four railway that the value of the motor bus to either replace or compliment rail traffic would become increasingly more important in the the developing world. Hence the Great Western Railway had their own fleet of motor buses before the outset of World War Two.

It seems their forward thinking was confused a little in the post war era, as a Labour government firstly and then Conservative governments identified opportunities for their parties supporters to receive favours with policy decisions as to how the United Kingdom's transport network was progressed. The two photographs selected reflect the attitude of the all powerful and one time influential Great Western Railway who many years before saw the sense in an integrated transport system, long before the advent of the family motor car.

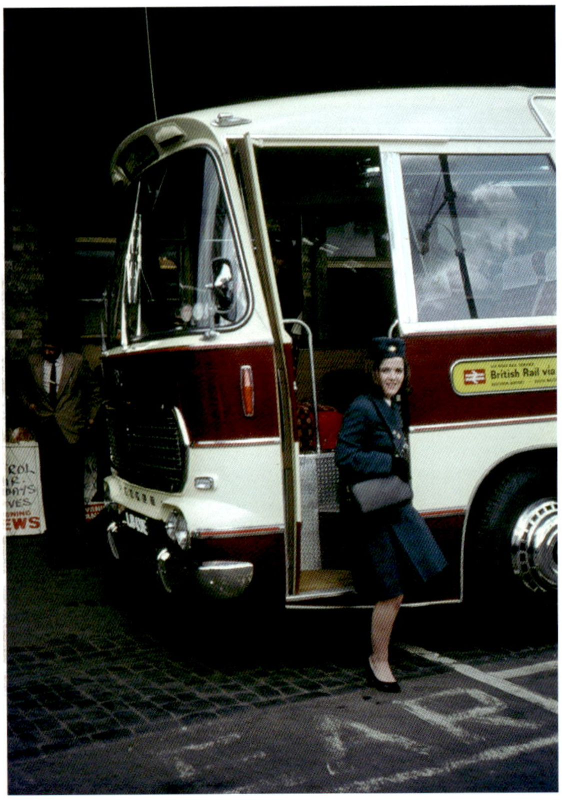

So when you hear of politicians waffling on about such subjects please reflect back upon the past of our once evolutionary public transport system and consider that much is to be learnt from history by a wise man.

Politics aside lets us take another look back at how life was during the 1960s within the growing Sixties Spotting Days series. If like us you enjoy a little bit of nostalgia join us in a good wallow again back in time within both the Sixties and Seventies Spotting Days series and enjoy a link back through a time warp to our youth.

Kevin Derrick
Boat of Garten 2010

The importance of connecting traffic with airports was observed as long ago as the 1960s in this publicity photograph of the then new Rail-Air connections with Gatwick and Heathrow Airports from Reading General. ***Strathwood Library Collection***

Reading Bound

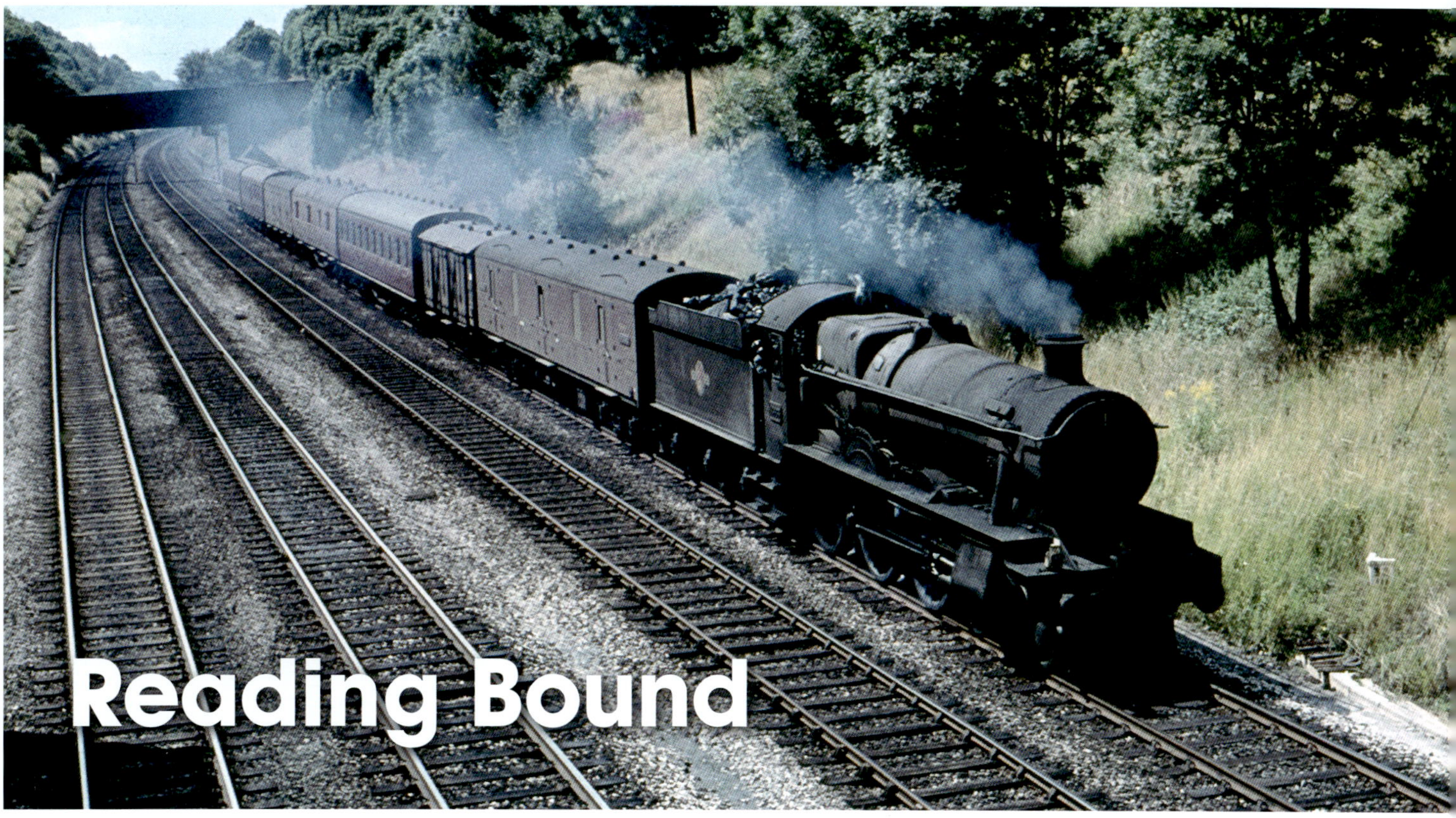

What would become a fortunate engine being saved for preservation ultimately was 6998 Burton Agnes Hall, seen heading a varied rake of vehicles, including redundant coaching stock displaced by recent DMU deliveries, now finding use as parcels stock near Sonning in 1960. ***Strathwood Library Collection***

Hardly a testing load the same day for 5987 Brocket Hall which was built ten years earlier than 6998 in 1939 during the first months of the Second World War at Swindon. The arrival of Warships during the late 1950s started the Western Region's rampant plans to be the first to be free of steam. ***Strathwood Library Collection***

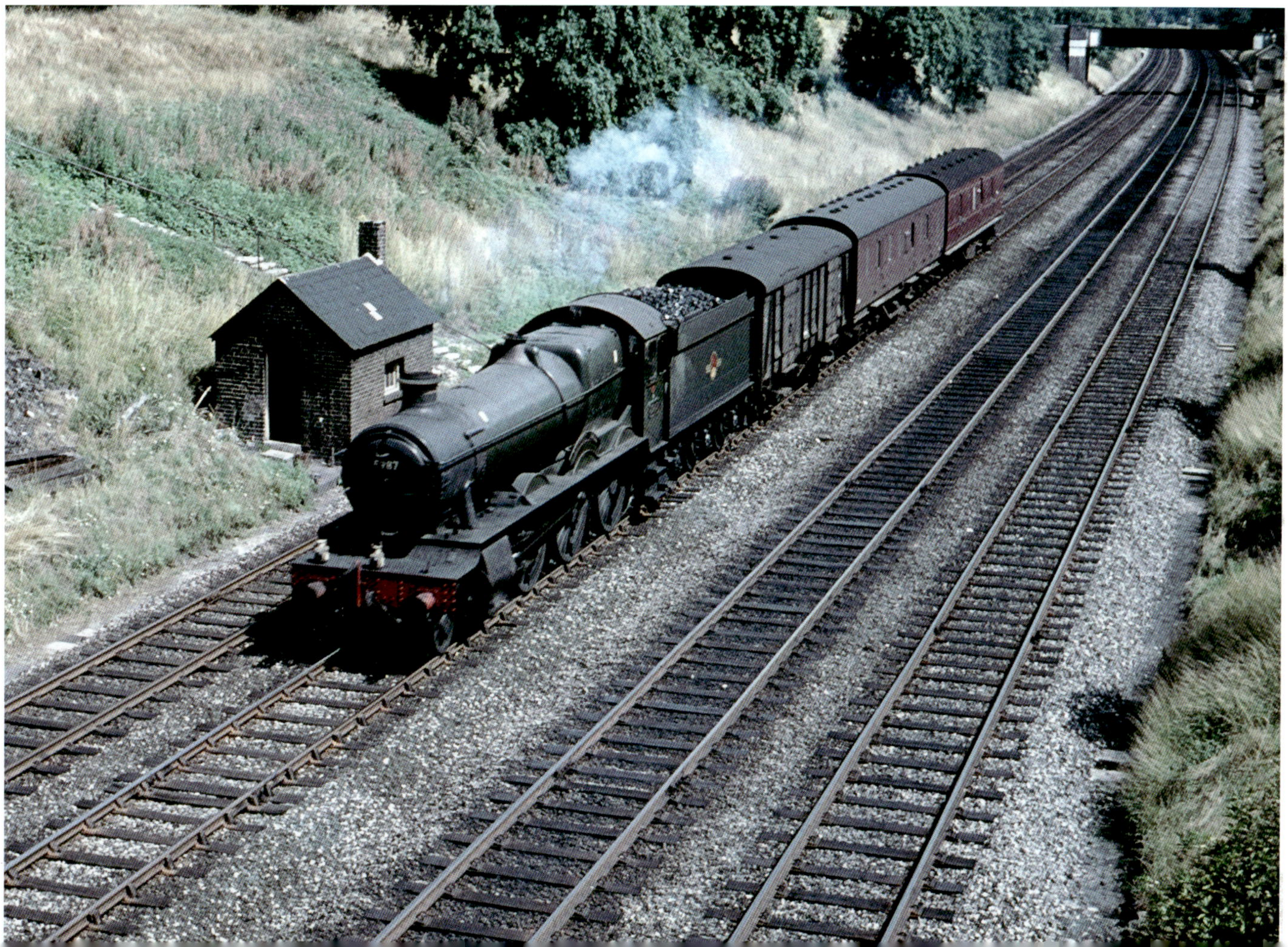

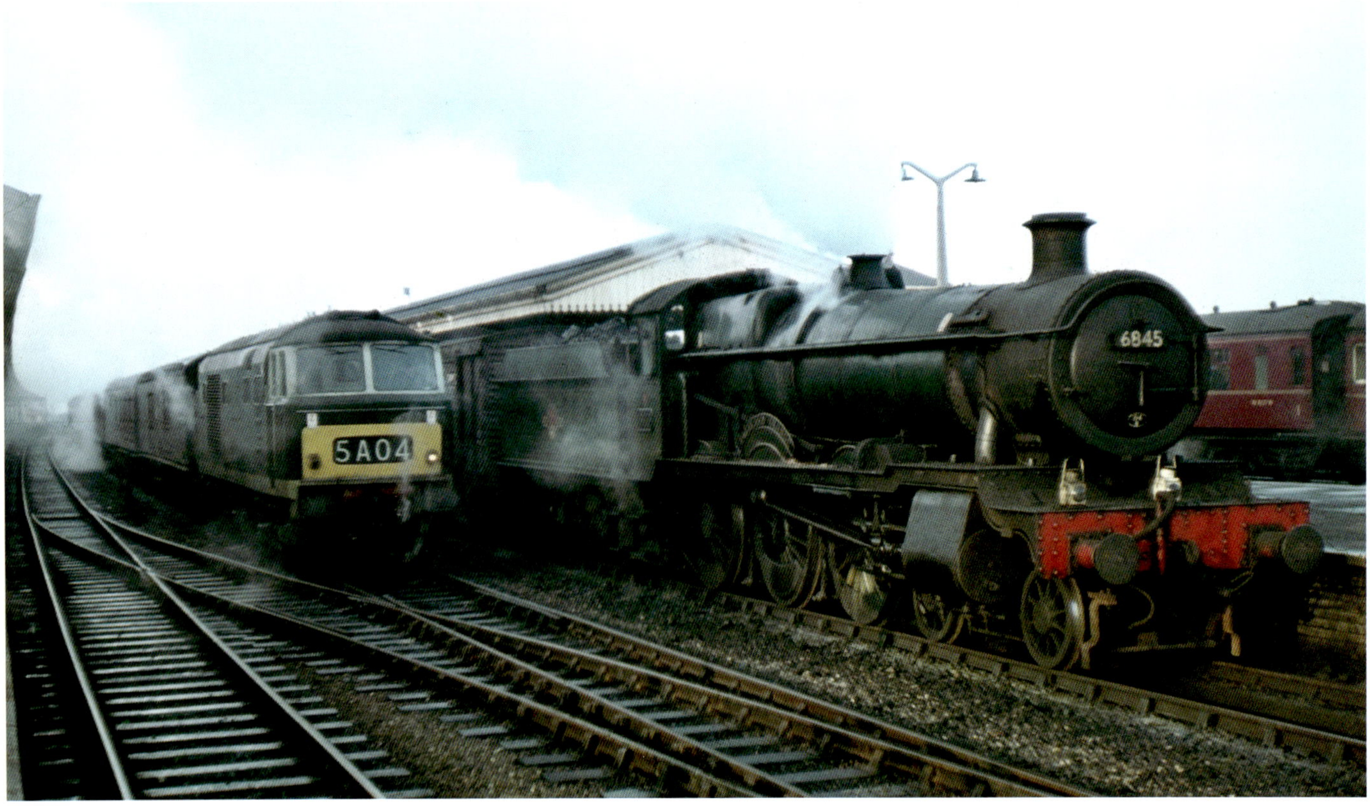

Hymeks started appearing on the region in May 1961, this one D7027 arriving in April 1962 has another parcels working coming through the centre road at Reading General overtaking 6845 Paviland Grange on a similar duty just three days before Christmas of 1962, no doubt filled with seasonal traffic once carried almost exclusively by the railways. ***Richard Icke***

Also employed with some parcels work is West Country 34002 Salisbury, awaiting the off from one of the bays at the western end of Reading General station around 1964. ***Douglas Paul***

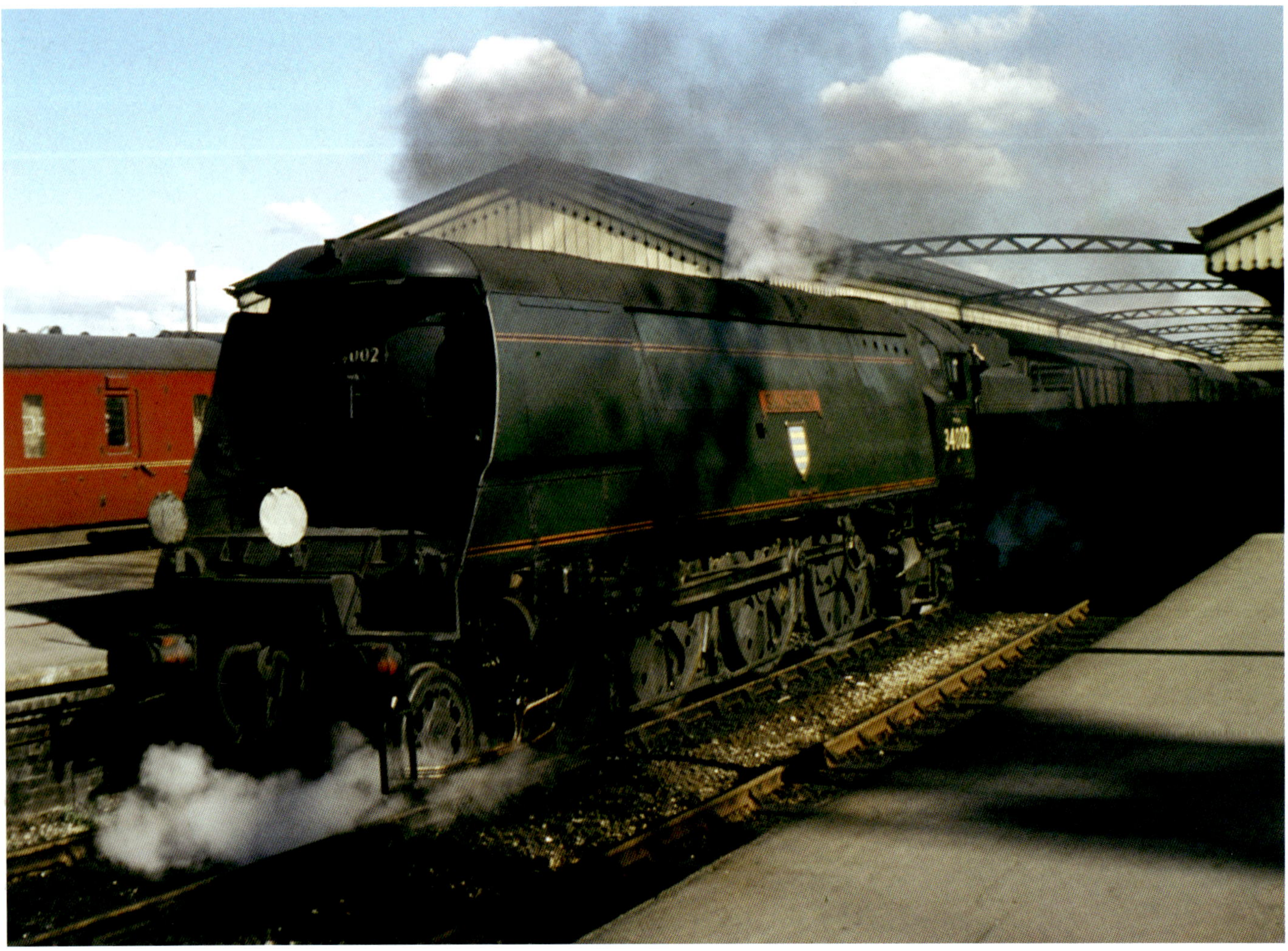

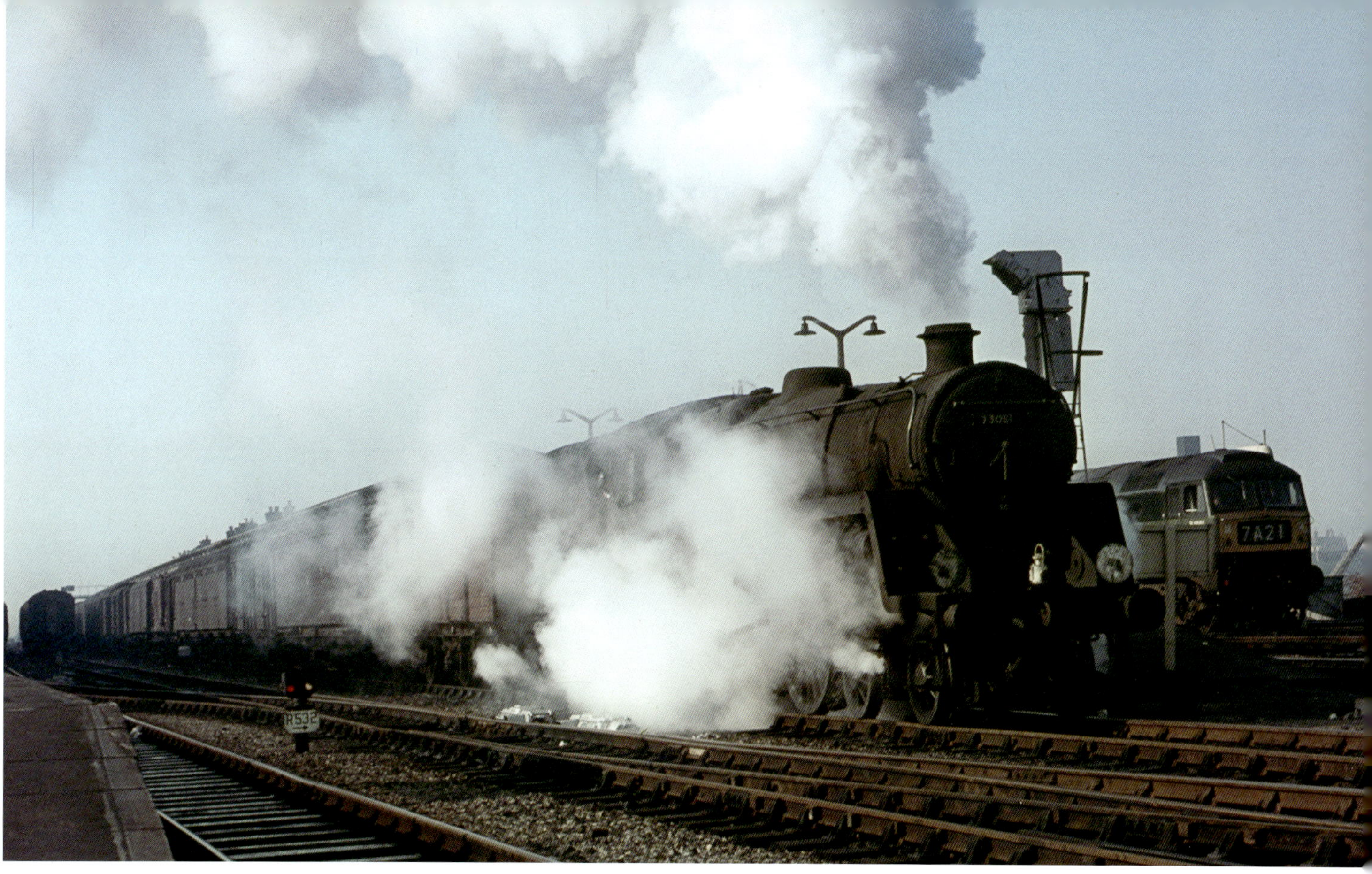

It seems we cannot get away from this once abundant traffic with Standard Class 5MT 73081 once named Excalibur during 1964, just two years away from the end of itís short eleven year life. Deliveries of Brush Type 4s had begun in 1962 with the first batches destined for the Eastern Region, however by late 1963 with both Crewe and Loughborough building locomotives the Western Region started taking their first batches of this all conquering class. ***Bob Treacher/Alton Model Centre***

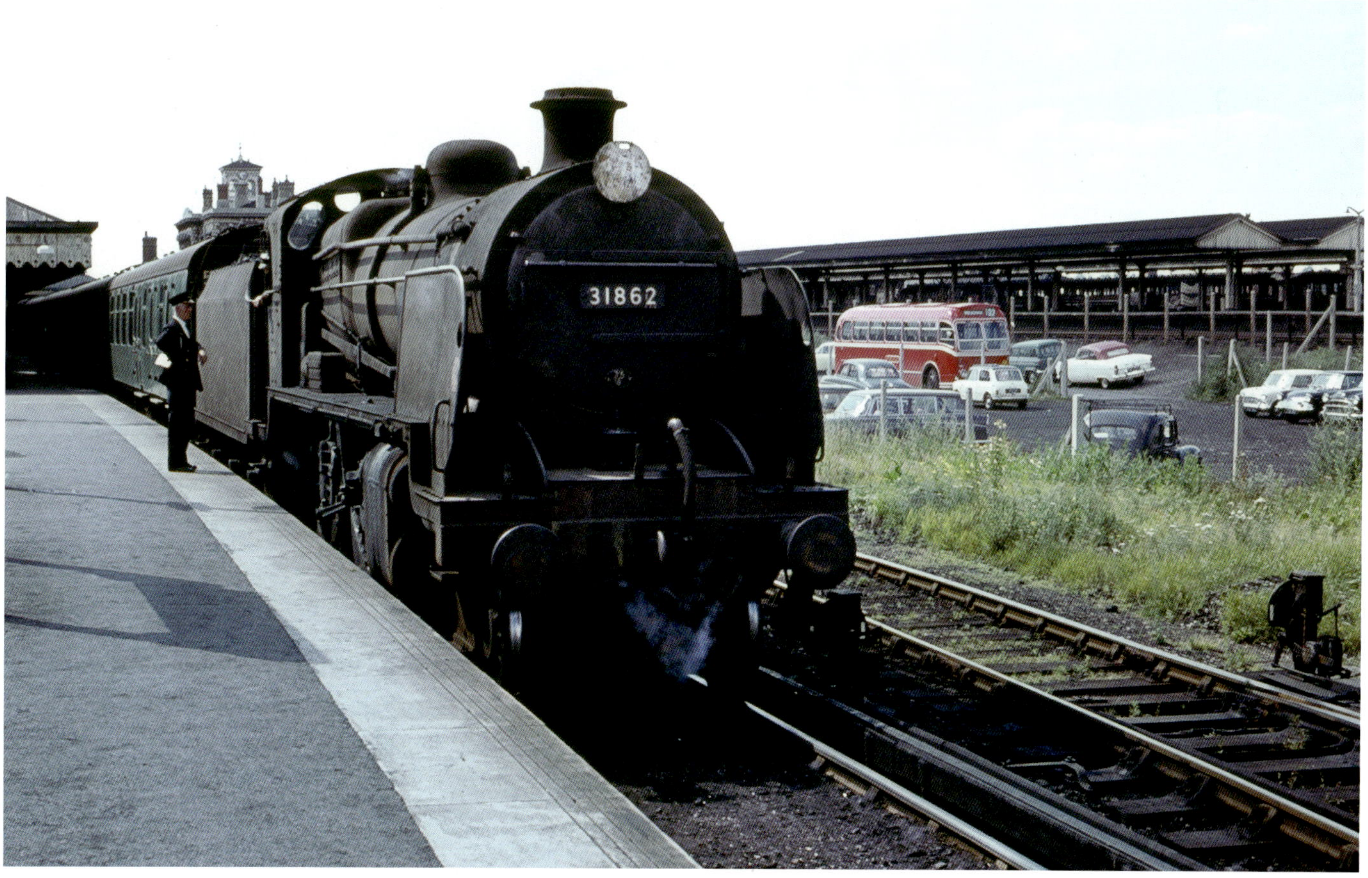

In the summer of 1964 the pace of change that would come at the adjoining Reading Southern station had not taken effect yet, in this peaceful scene as Maunsell N Class 31862 is ready for departure towards Redhill. ***Strathwood Library Collection***

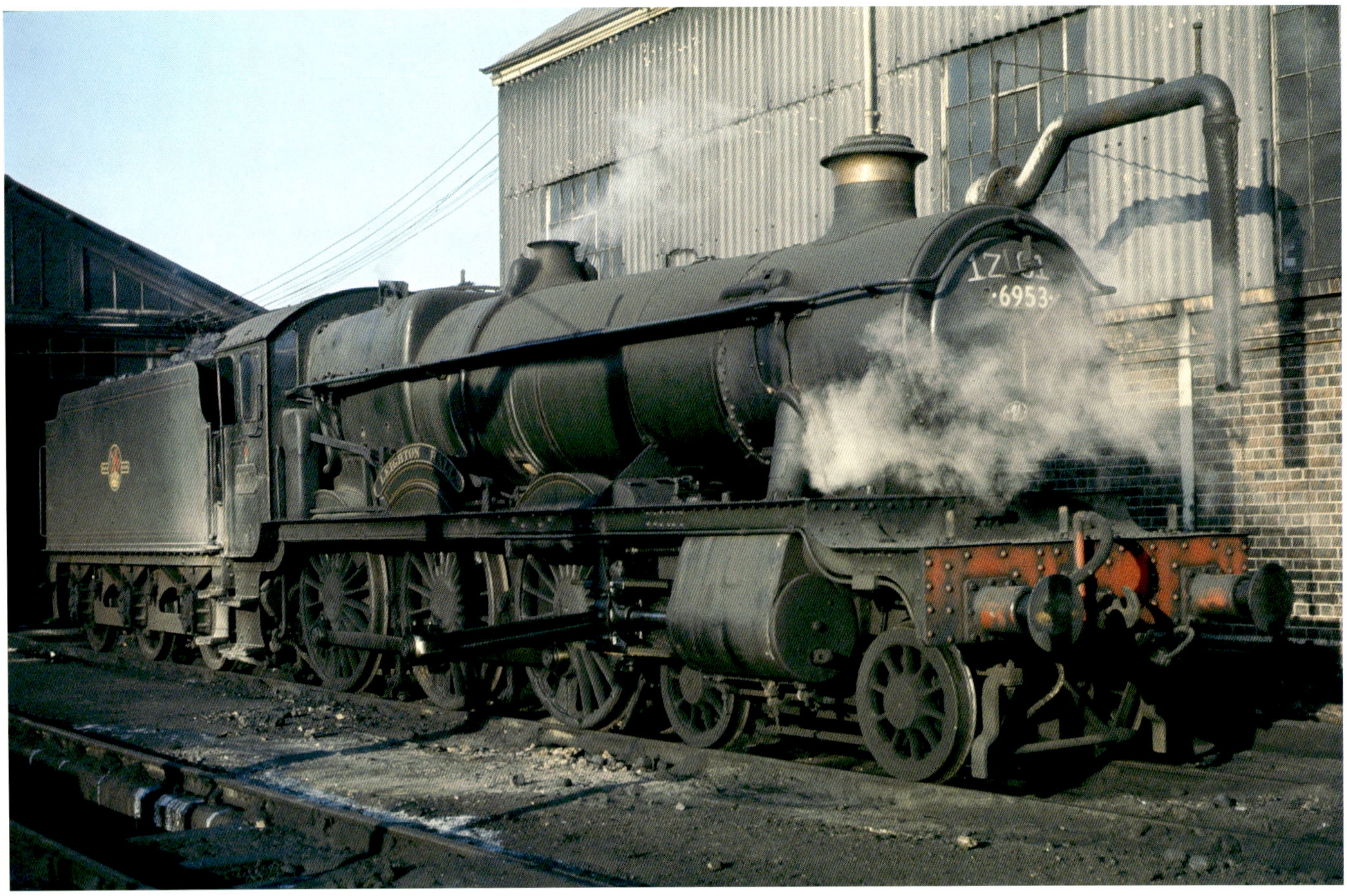

A ten minute walk from Reading General station to the Western Region shed rewards us with one of Collett's Halls 6953 Leighton Hall in the crisp morning sunshine in early 1964. ***Bob Treacher/Alton Model Centre***

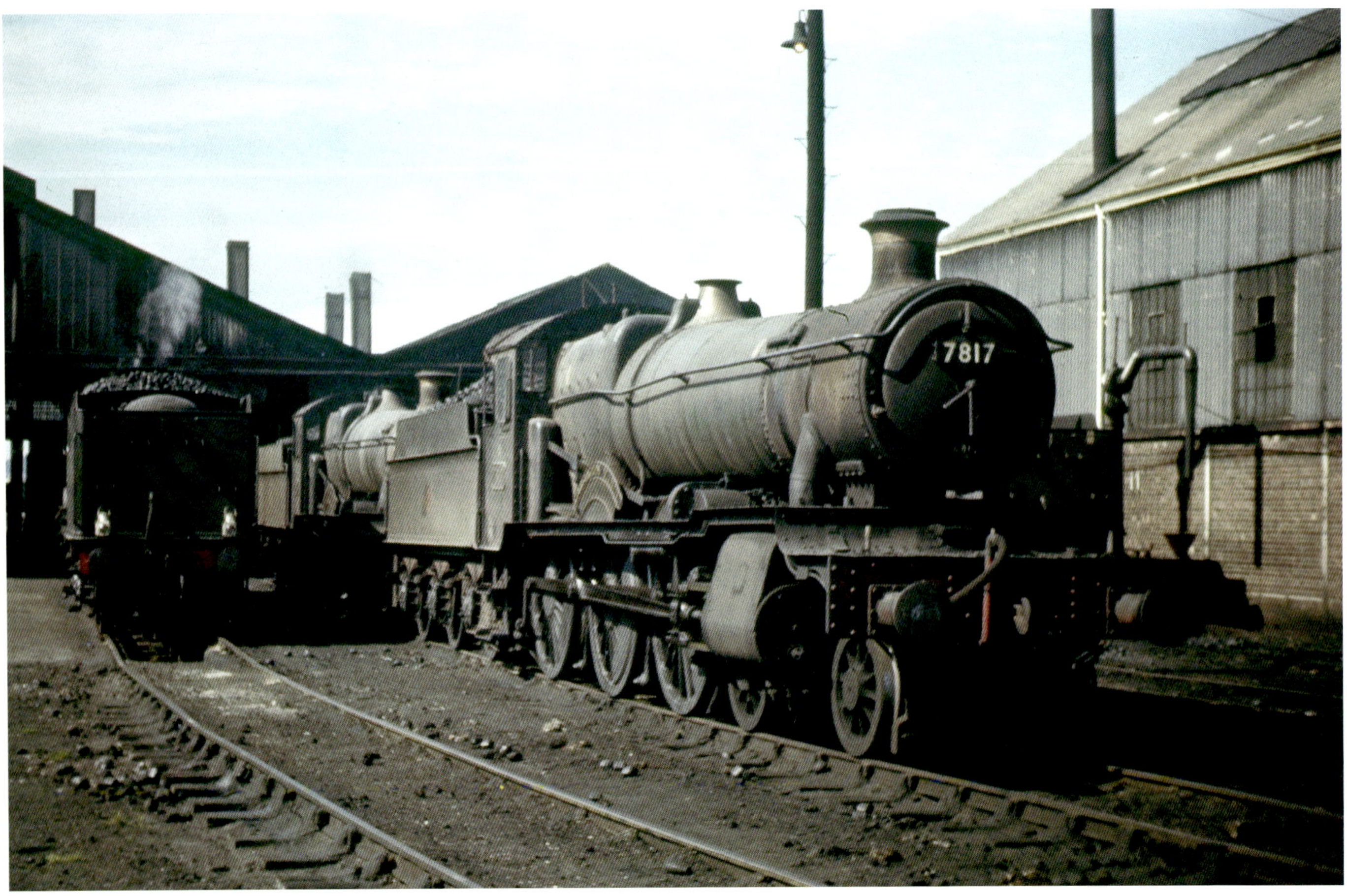

Another visit brings us 7817 Garsington Manor on shed the year before, unfortunately this engine would be withdrawn in June 1964 just as the South African judiciary was sentencing Nelson Mandela to a lifetime prison sentence. ***Len Smith***

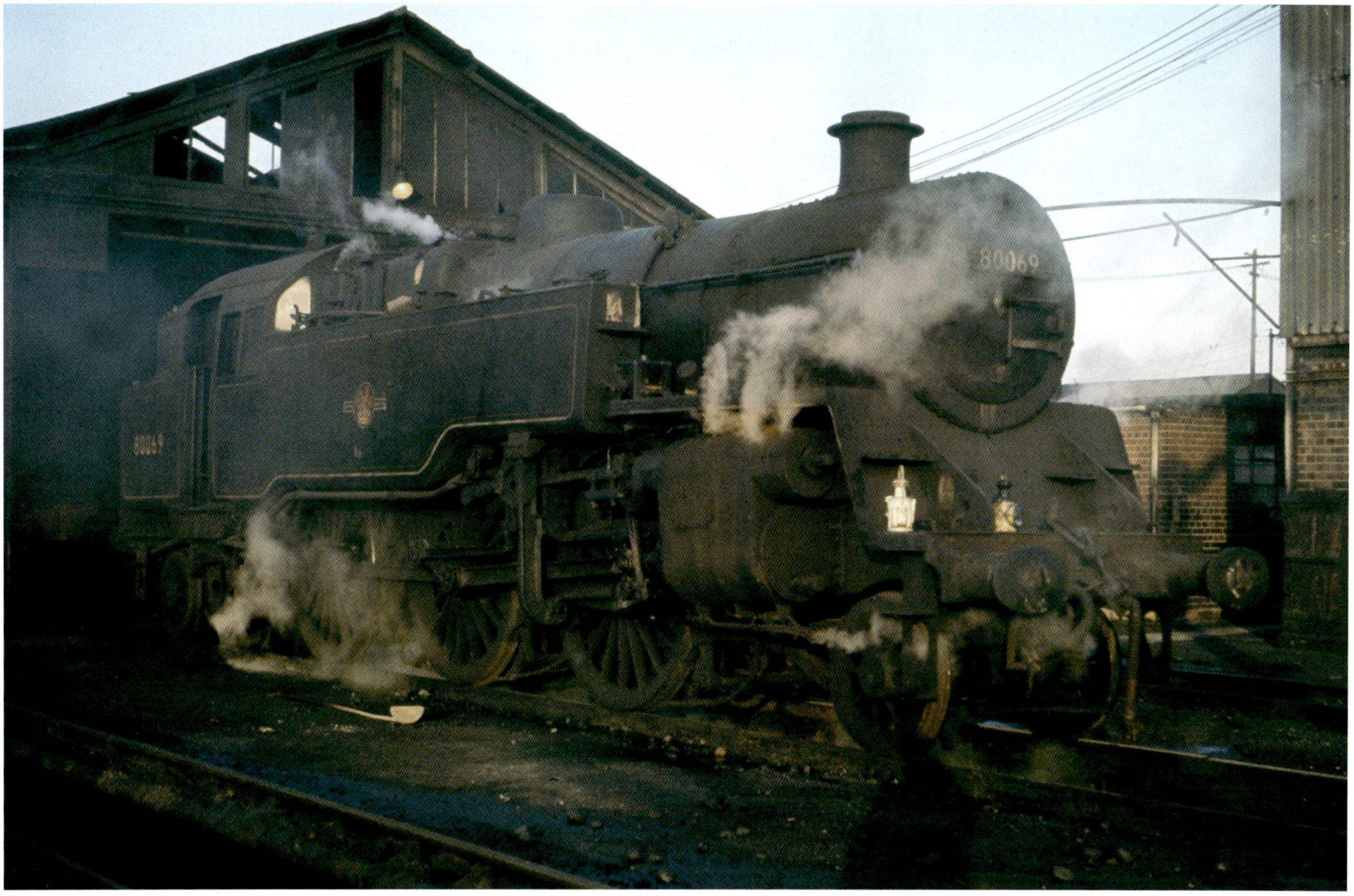

When Reading's Southern Region shed closed on 6 April 1964 it fell to the Western Region shed 81D to service locomotives such as Standard 4MT 80069 from the Southern Region. ***Bob Treacher/Alton Model Centre***

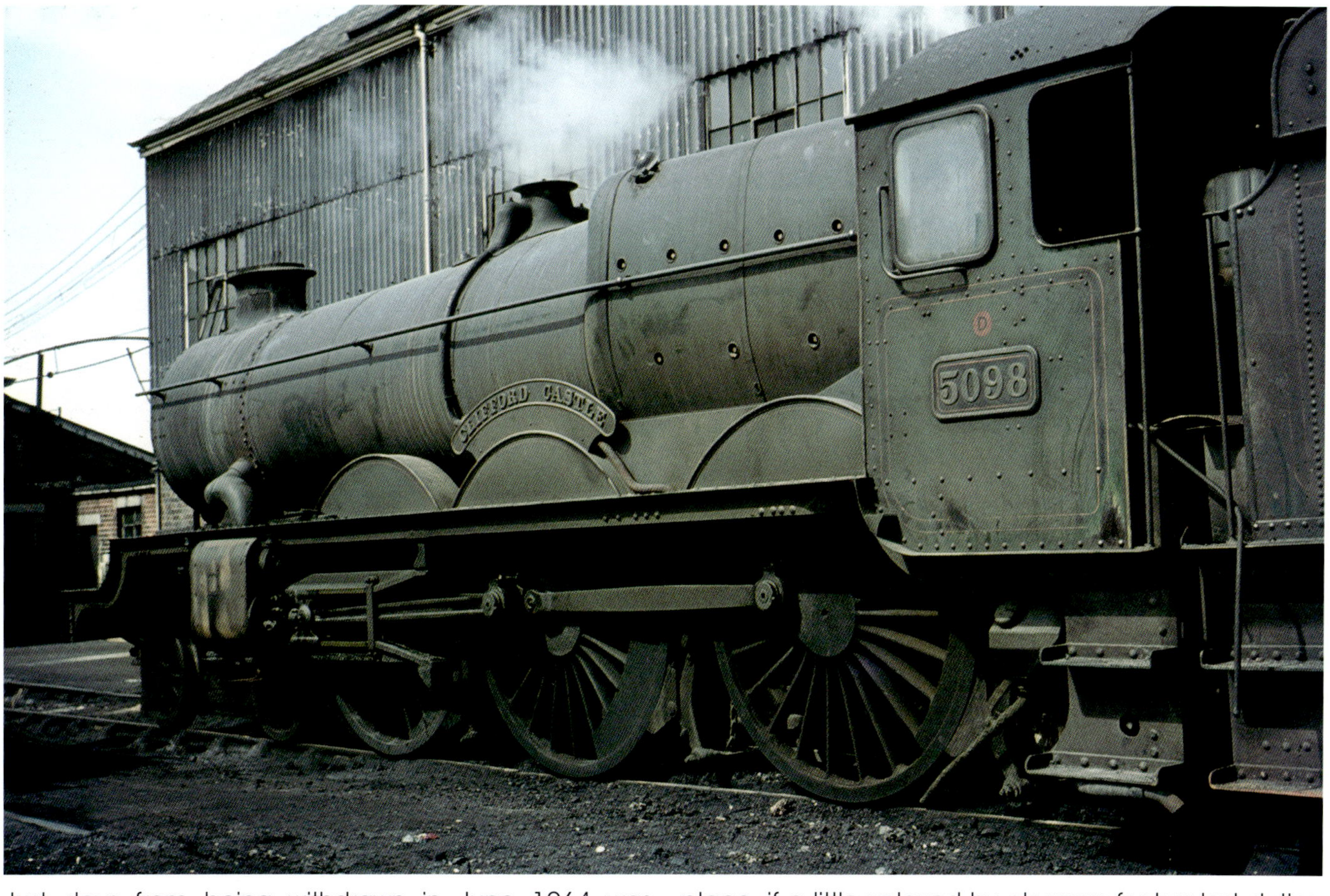

Just days from being withdrawn in June 1964 was 5098 Clifford Castle thankfully with all her plates in place, if a little unloved by cleaners for her last duties. ***Bob Treacher/Alton Model Centre***

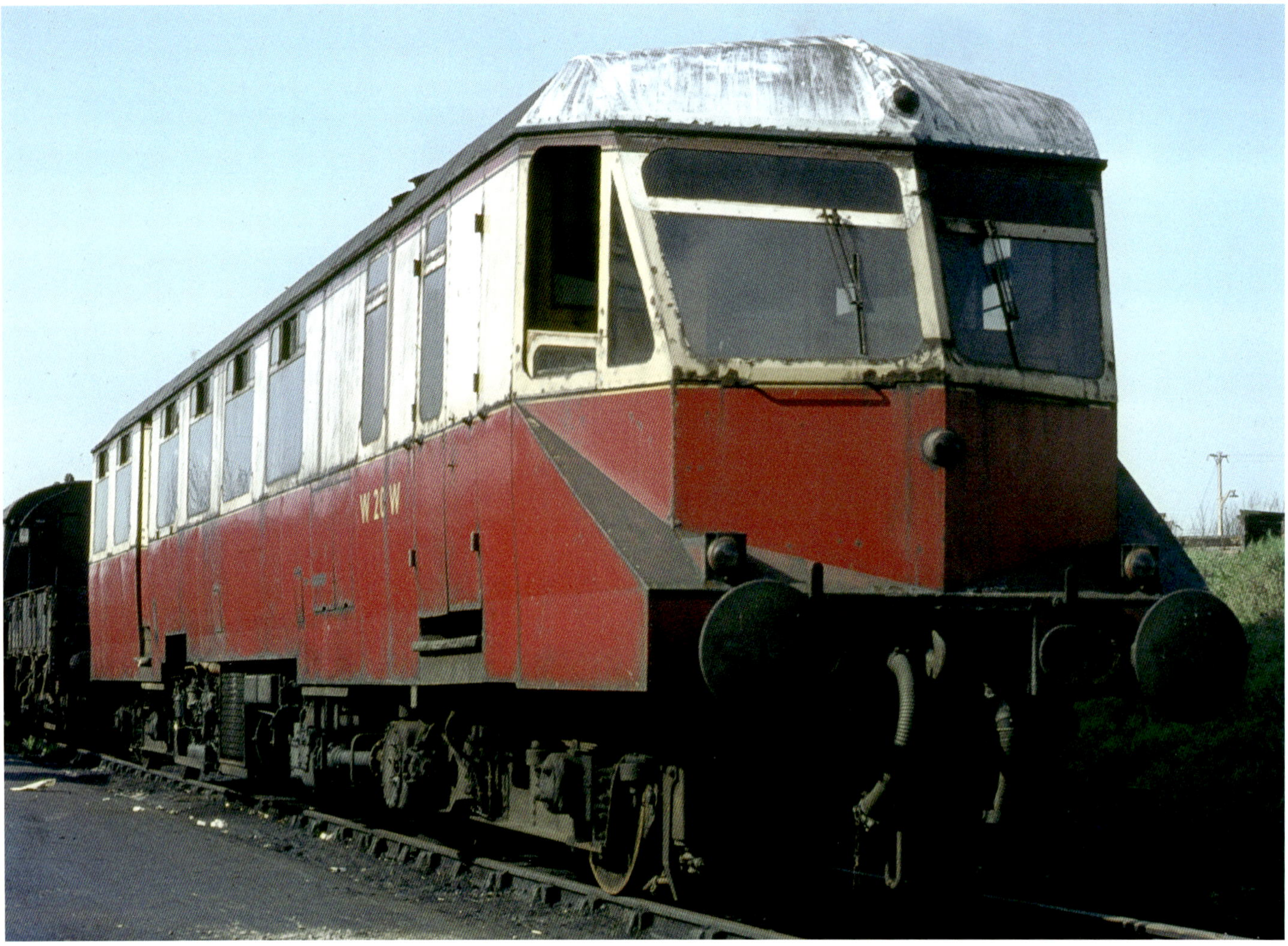

Already cast aside and awaiting disposal from Reading shed was W20W, the deliveries of the then modern new DMUs to the region had spelt the end for these AEC built prototypes for this mode of traction once pioneered by the Great Western Railway. ***Bob Treacher/Alton Model Centre***

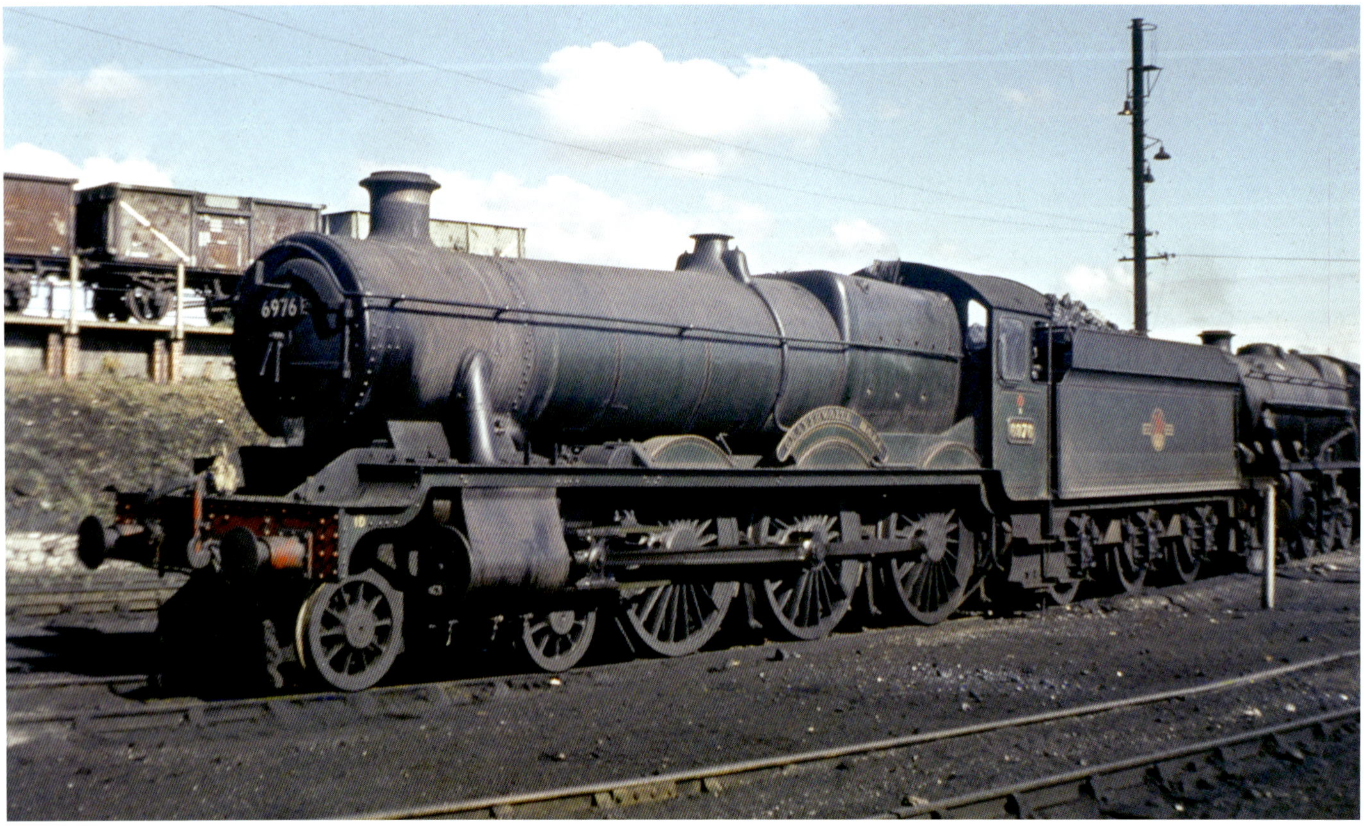

Stabled in front of a Stanier 8F on this visit in 1964 was one of Hawksworth's Modified Halls 6976 Graythwaite Hall which would be among the last of her class withdrawn towards the end of 1965. ***Douglas Paul***

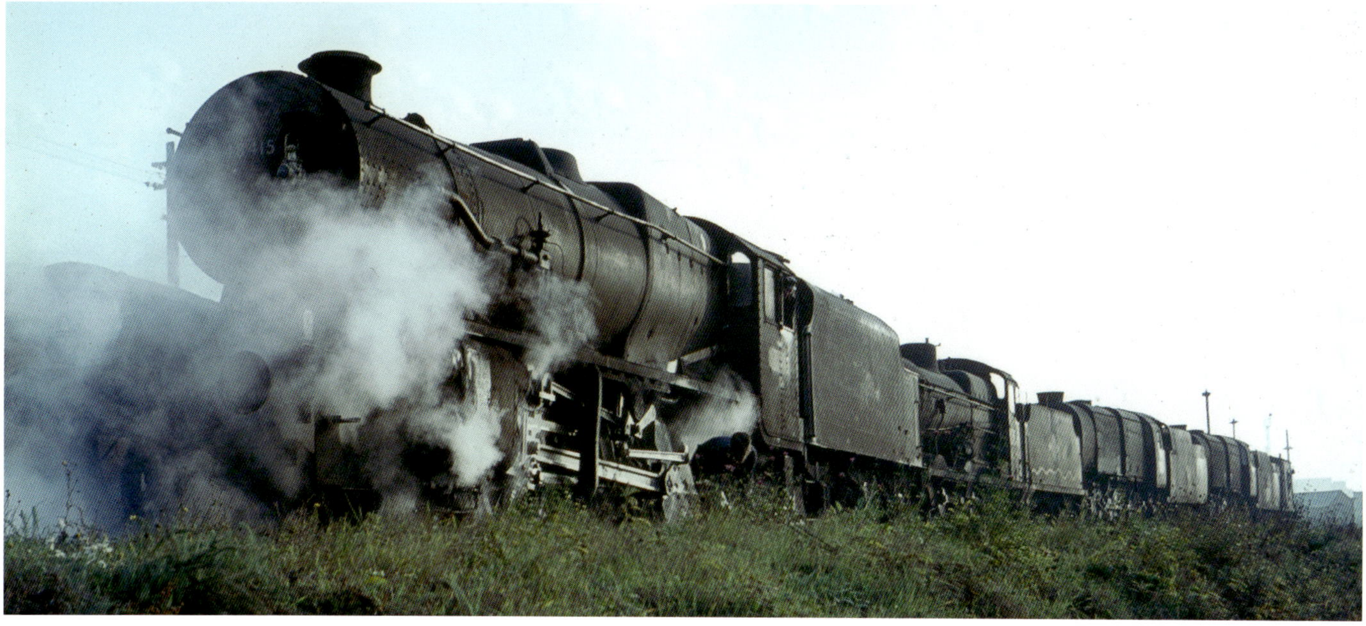

Melancholy work for another Stanier 8F as 48415 drags away a rake of redundant Southern engines in the direction of South Wales and hungry scrap dealers in 1965.

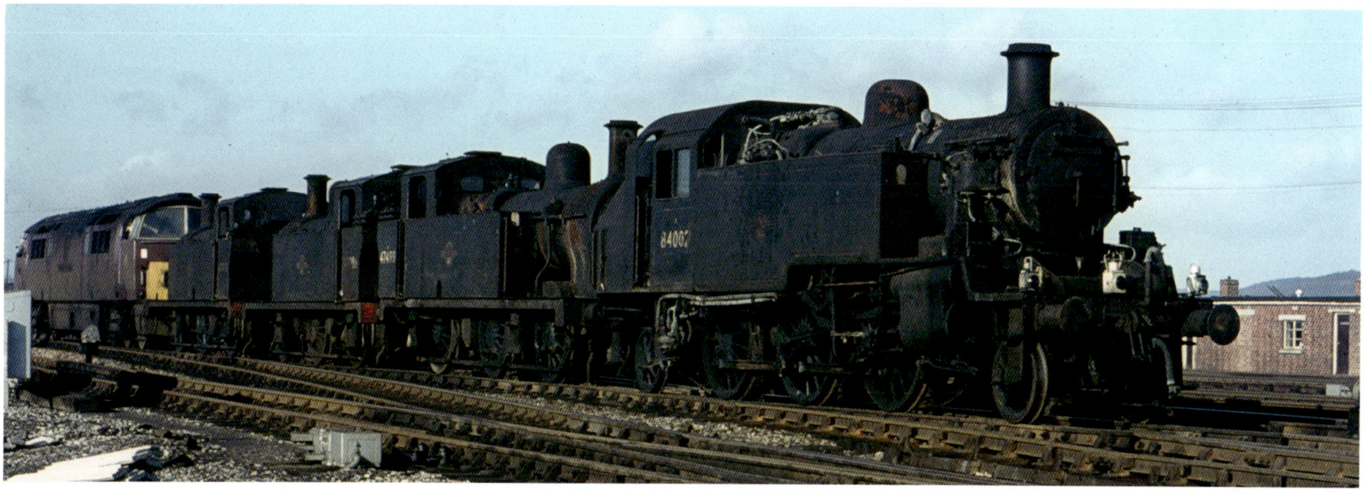

Standard 2MT 84002 has three Jinties for company as it makes its way west behind D1017 Western Warrior.

Below: Visiting Black Five 45070 makes its way off shed towards the busy yards at Reading to take over a train back to the London Midland Region again in 1965. ***All Bob Treacher/Alton Model Centre***

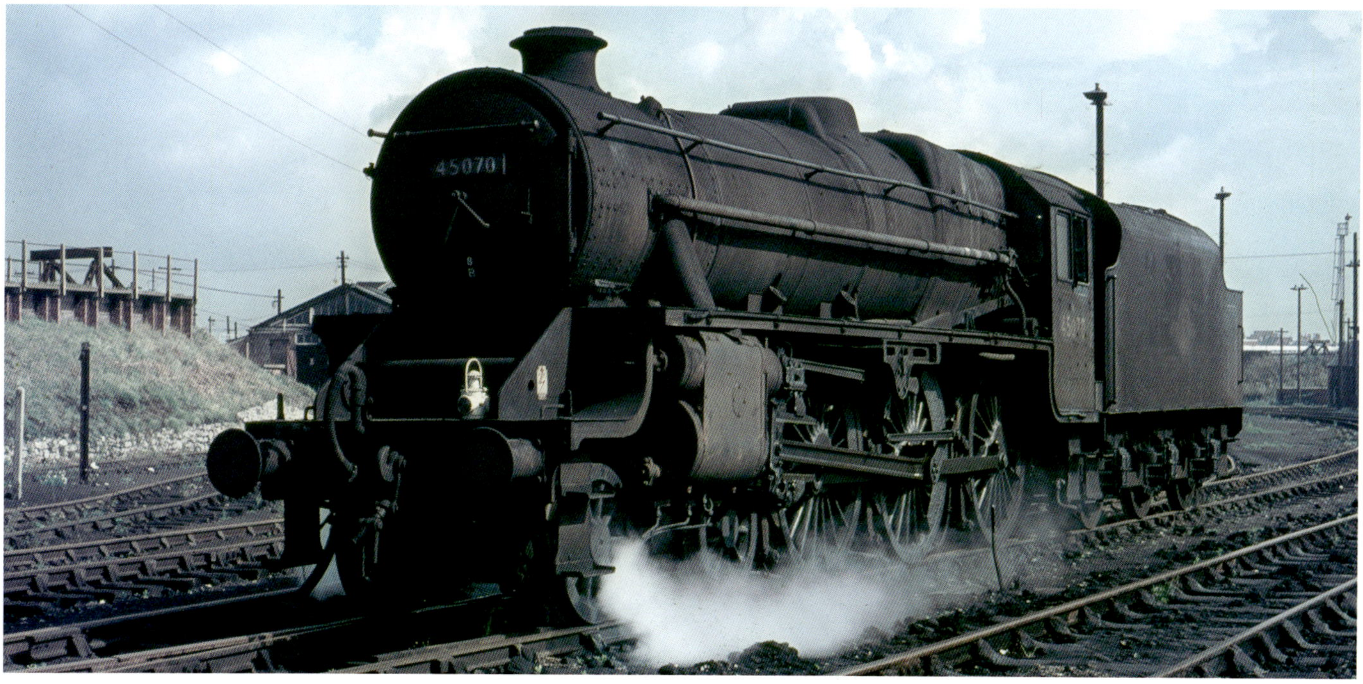

Lickey Interlude

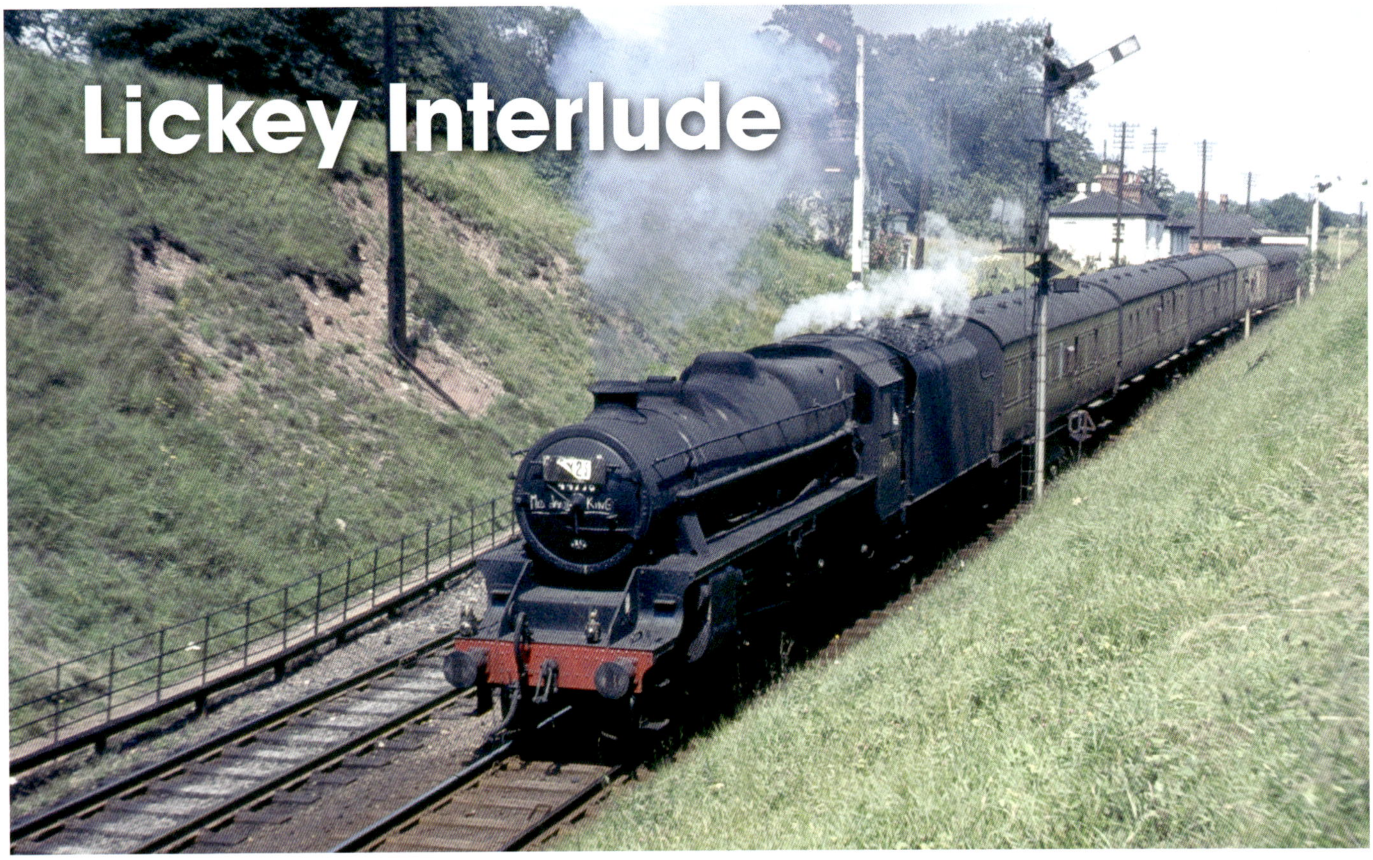

Running southbound on the Lickey incline on 27 July 1963 was Black Five 44776 in charge of what looks like a pigeon extra. ***Peter Simmonds***

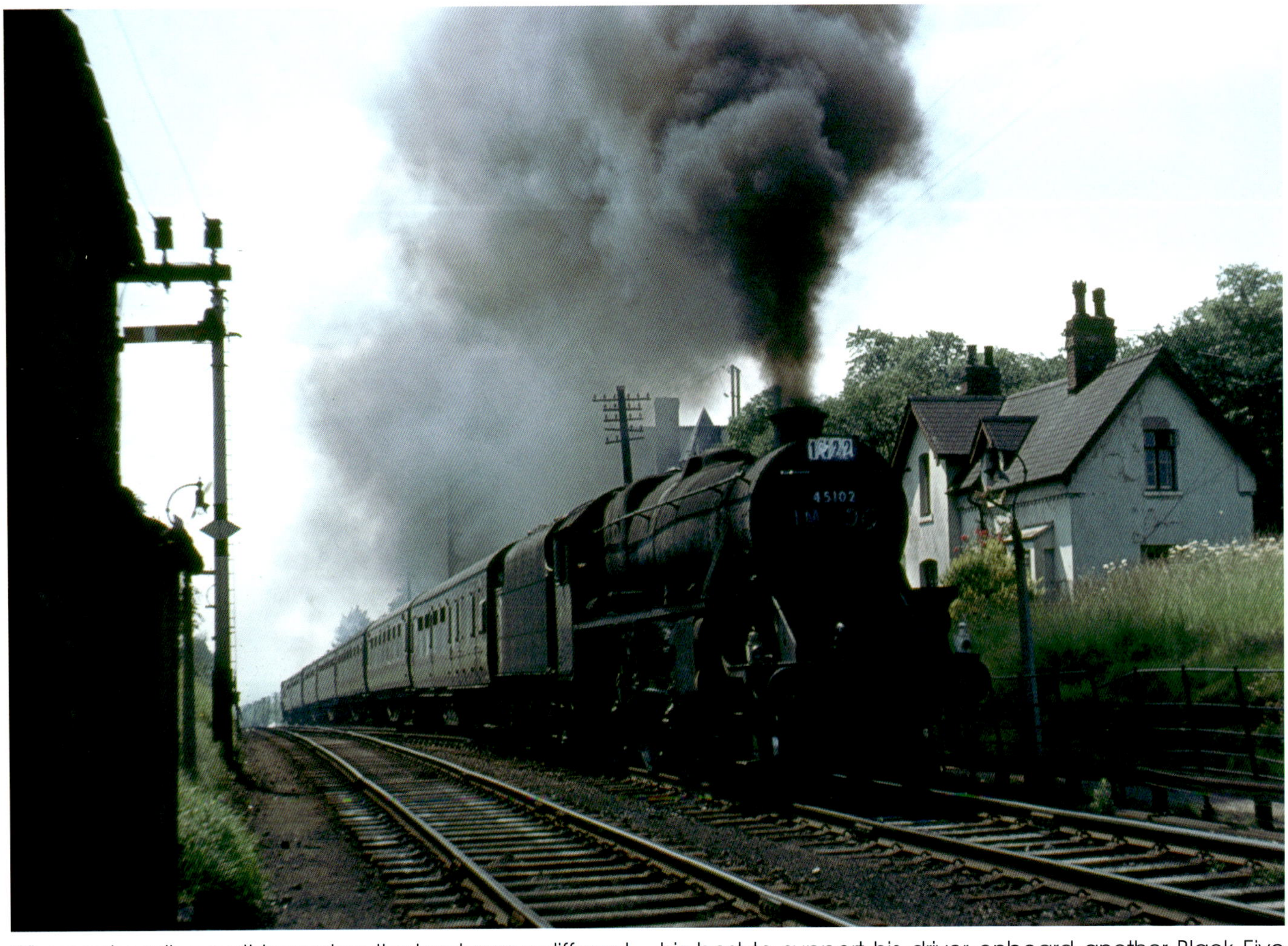

Whereas heading northbound up the bank was a different proposition for the engine crew with the fireman doing his best to support his driver onboard another Black Five 45102 the same day. ***Peter Simmonds***

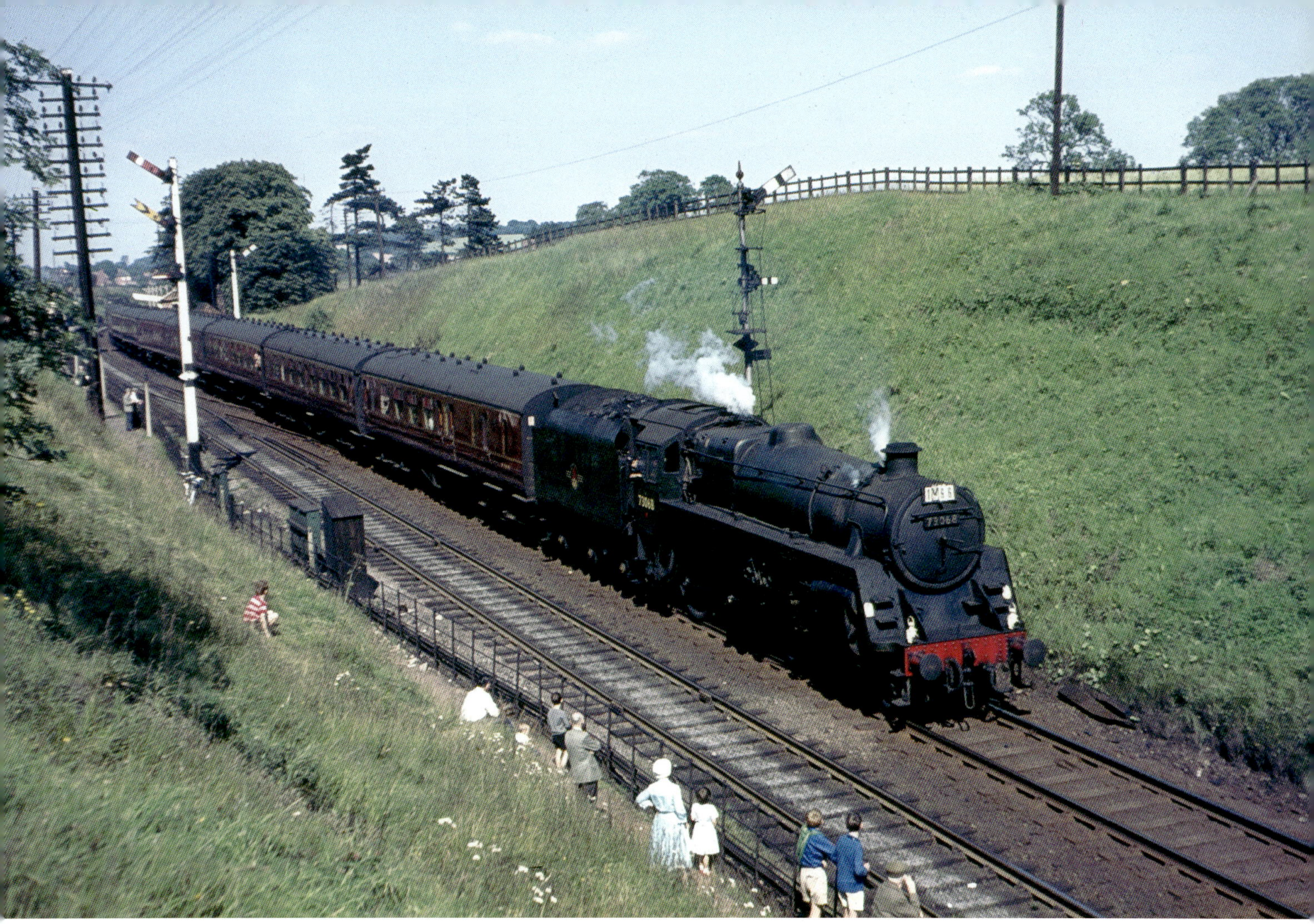

The footpath alongside the line near the summit provides a perfect vantage point for both locals and visitors alike to watch the procession of trains on a summer Saturday at Blackwell as Standard 5MT 73068 heads southbound. ***Peter Simmonds***

The Beatles performed a week of concerts at the Odeon Cinema in Weston-super-Mare between Monday 22 to Saturday 27 July 1963, on the morning of this last concert of the week for the Fab Four a pairing of Hawksworth's Panniers give assistance to a northbound working at Blackwell. ***Peter Simmonds***

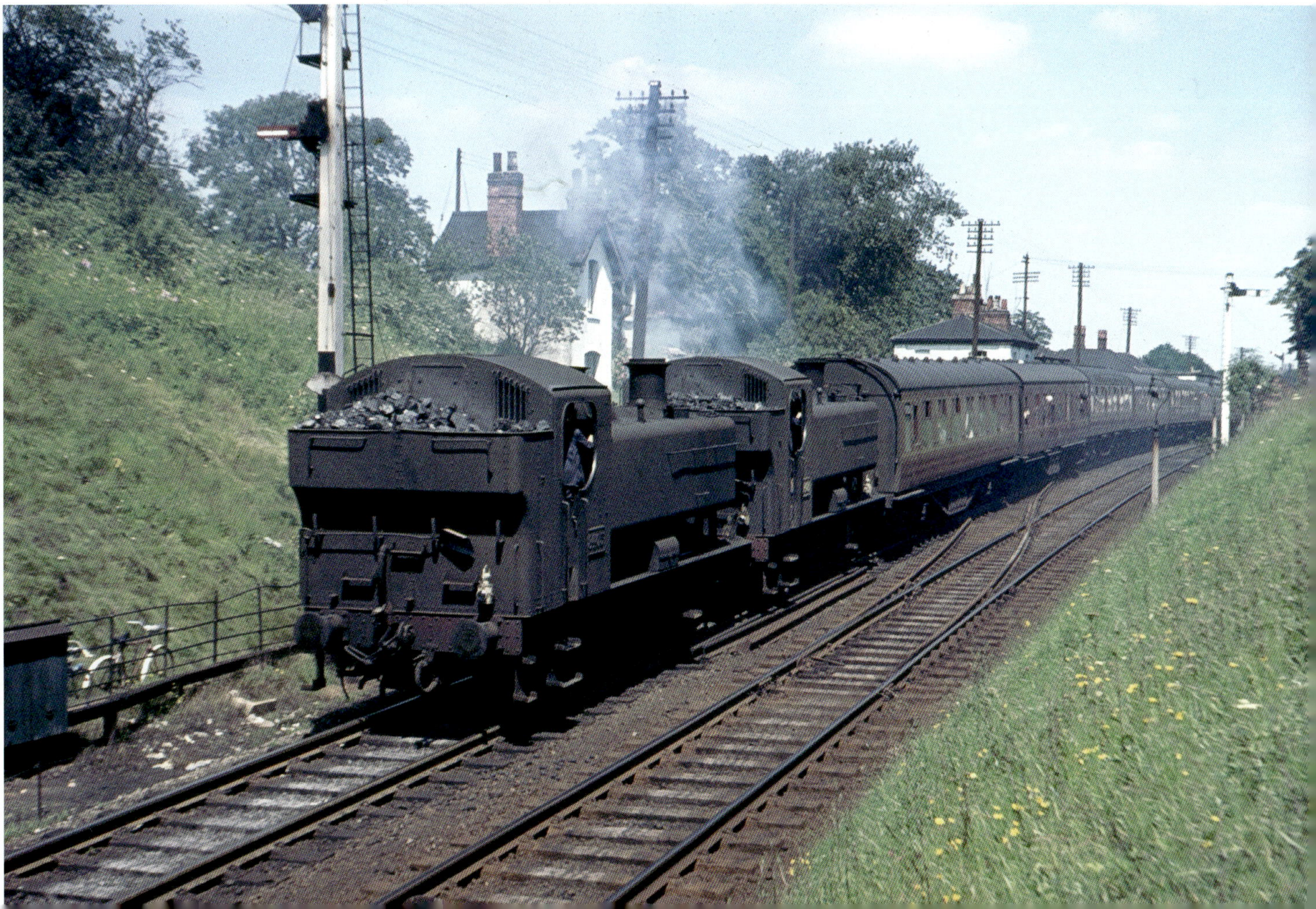

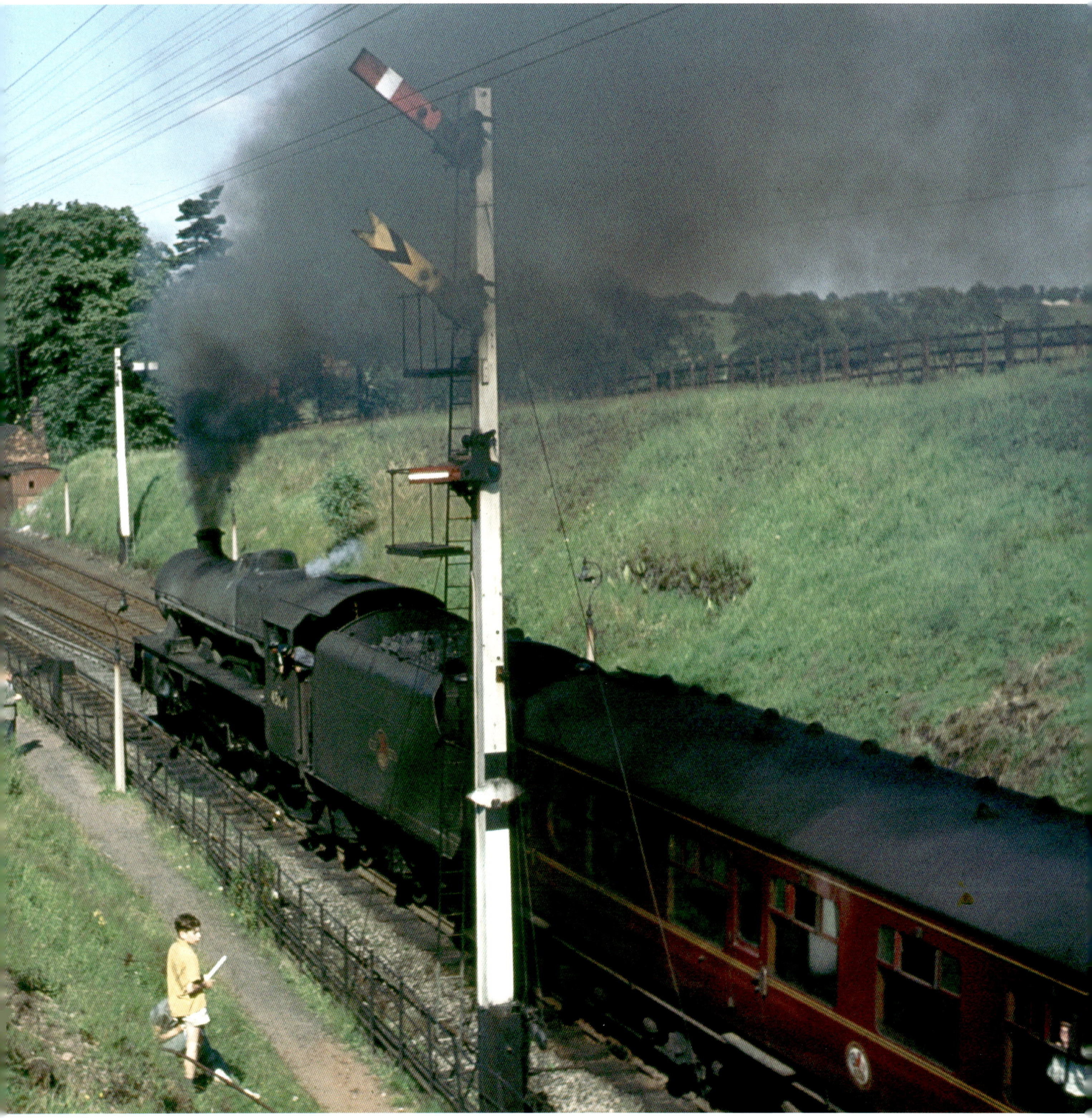

Finally on that same glorious summer Saturday fellow spotters watch the triumphant assault on the climb of Jubilee 45694 Bellerophon as the driver sees clear signals for his fine steed. If you had gone for a night out at your local cinema at the time you may have had the choice between Billy Liar starring Julie Christie, Tom Courtney and Wilfred Pickles or you could have opted for Summer Holiday and Cliff Richard with Una Stubs, Melvyn Hayes and The Shadows. ***Peter Simmonds***

Westward Ramblings

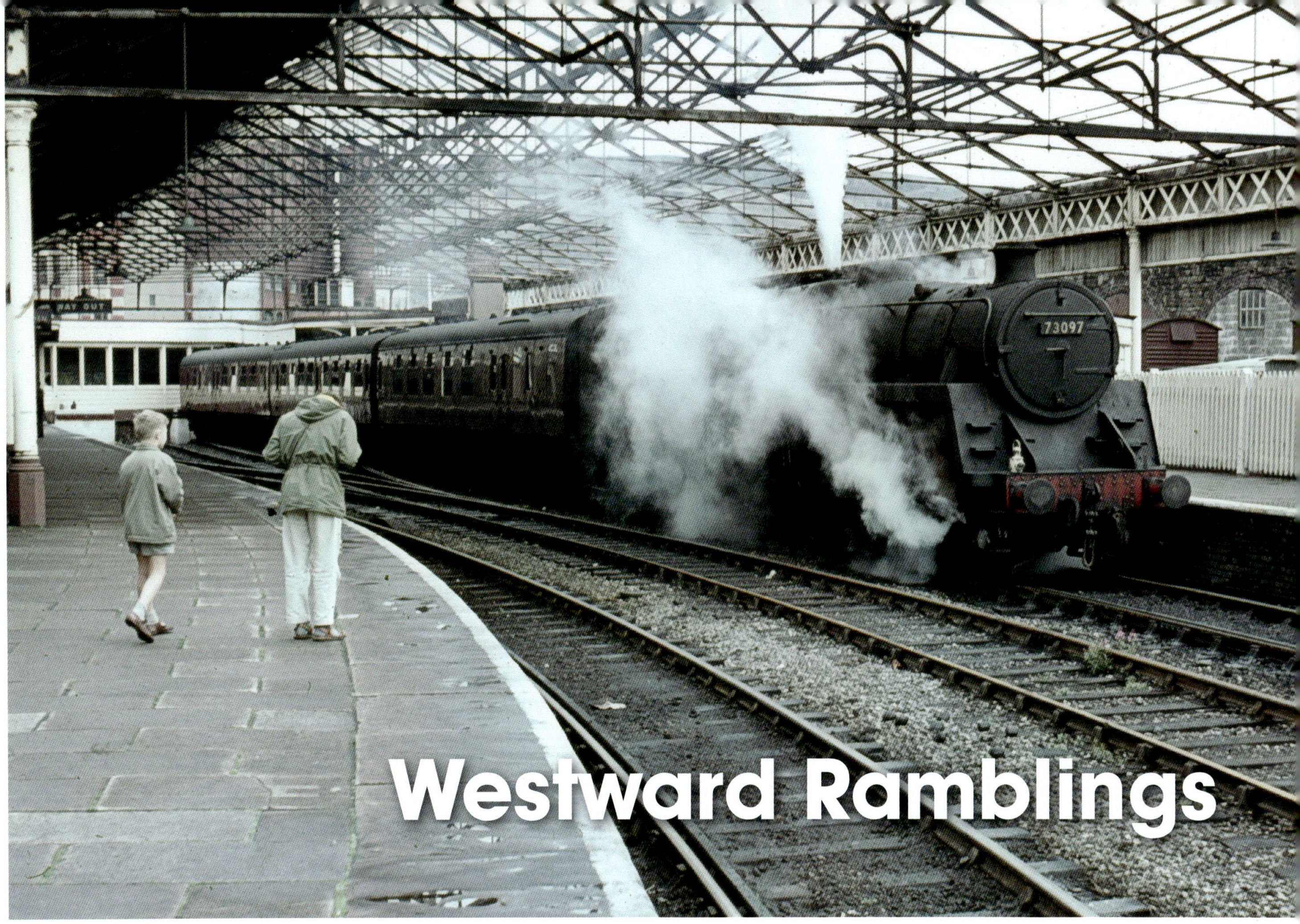

Two youthful spotters record the number of Standard 5MT 73097 as she makes plenty of steam before departure from Swansea Victoria in 1963. ***Strathwood Library Collection***

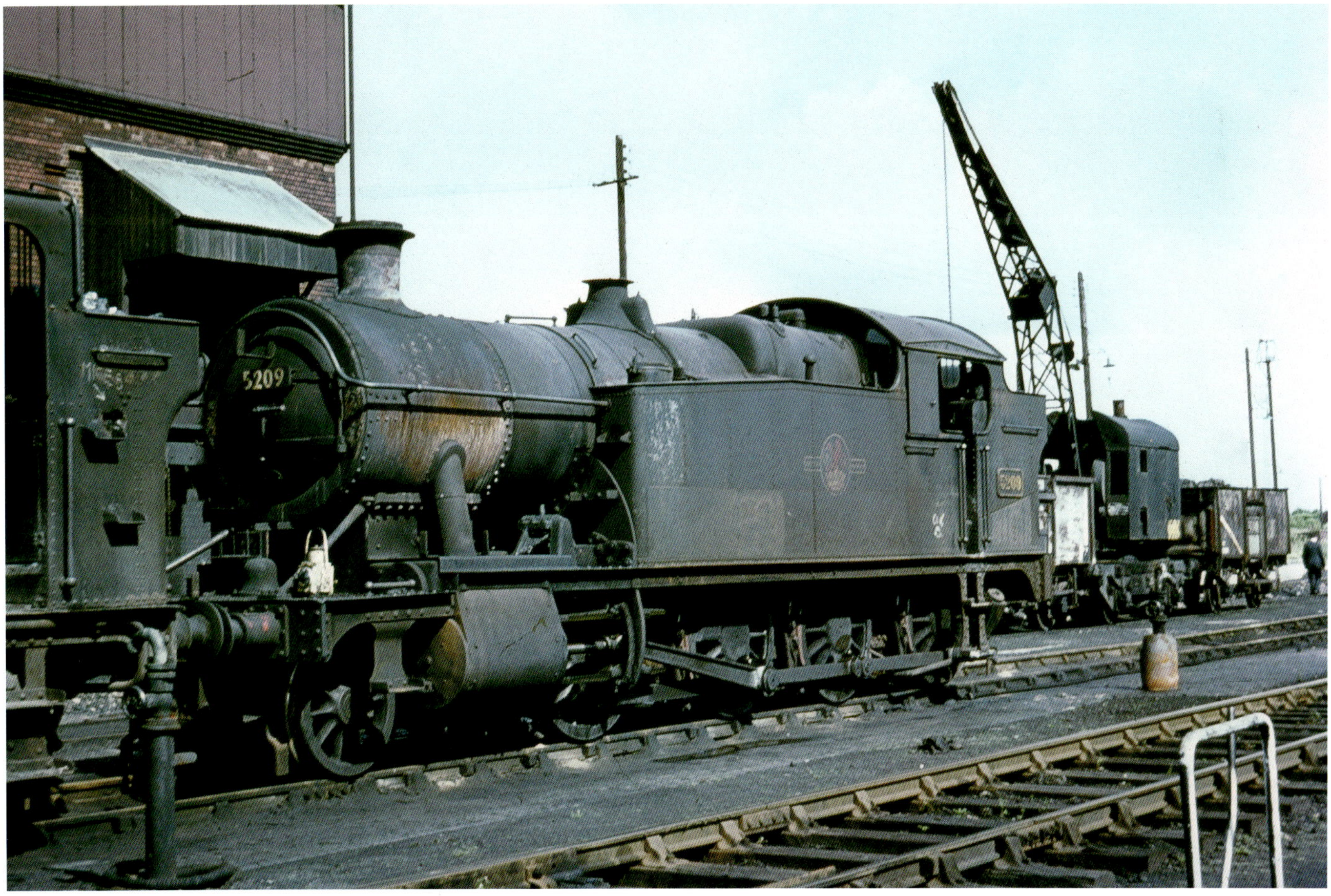

Just taken out from service on 27 July 1965 was Collett's 2-8-0T 5209 at Ebbw Junction, she had been the last of her series to be withdrawn. ***Frank Hornby***

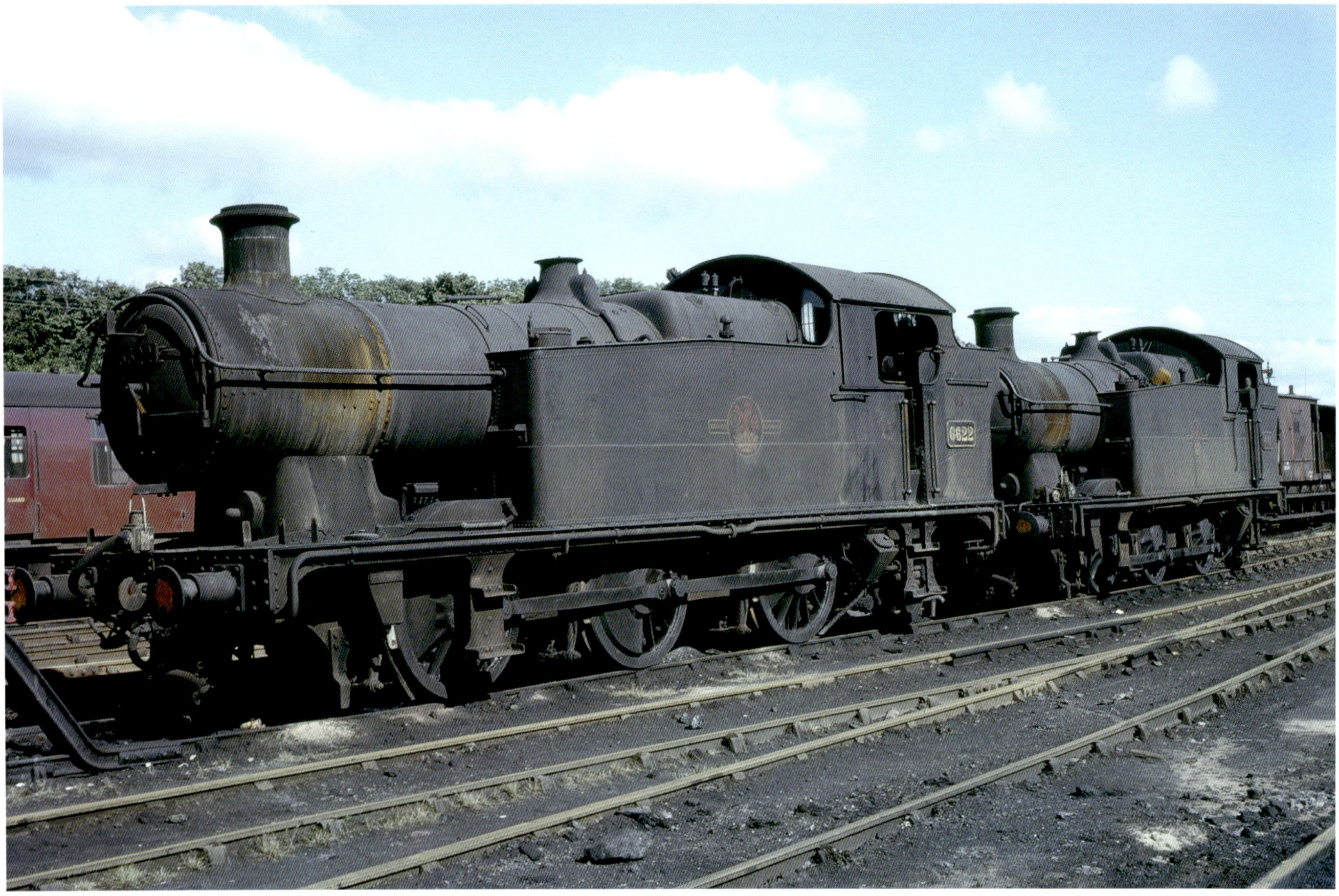

Another Collett design synonymous with South Wales sheds were his 5600 Class, although by the summer of 1964 many had been either withdrawn of set aside into open storage as English Electric Type 3s were taking over the duties once performed by 6622 out of Rhymney shed. ***Win Wall/Strathwood Library Collection***

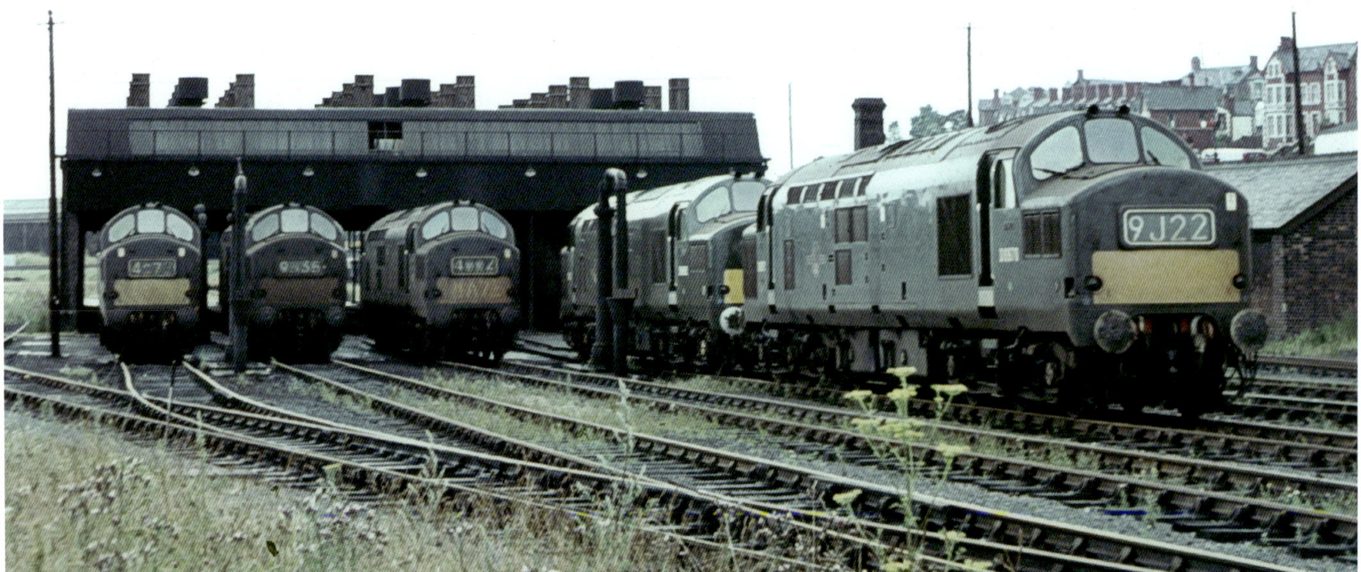

The ex Barry Railway 0-6-2Ts had been long replaced around the time of Nationalisation by Collett's 0-6-2Ts and Panniers, they in turn gave way to a fleet of these Vulcan Foundry built Type 3s from English Electric as they swept most of South Wales steam before them by 25 July 1965 as witnessed outside Barry shed. ***Frank Hornby***

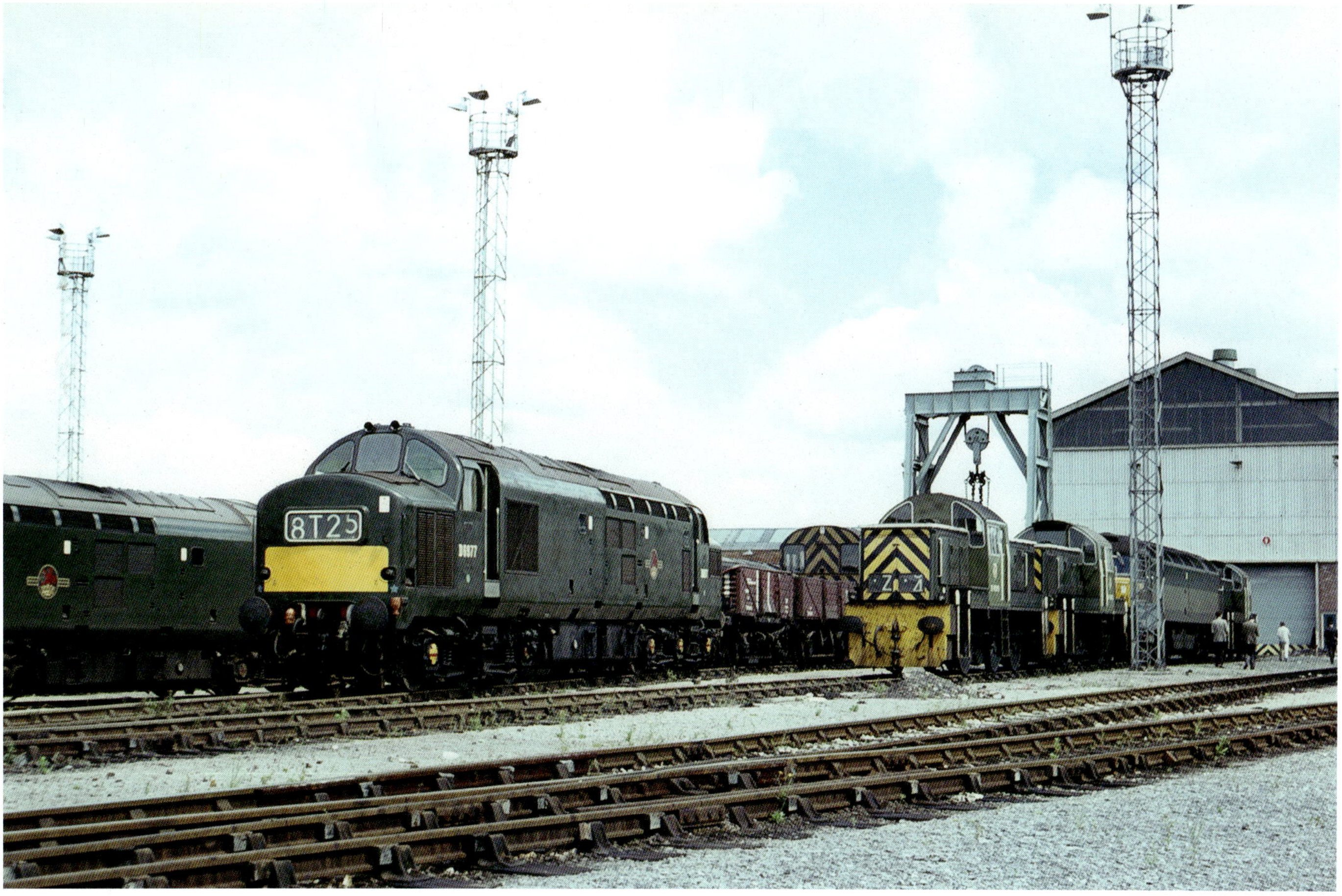

A tour of the modernised Landore shed the same day brought about more of the Type 3s along with early examples of what would later become Class 14s that had begun work on duties once carried out more efficiently by a large fleet of Pannier tanks using locally mined coal. ***Frank Hornby***

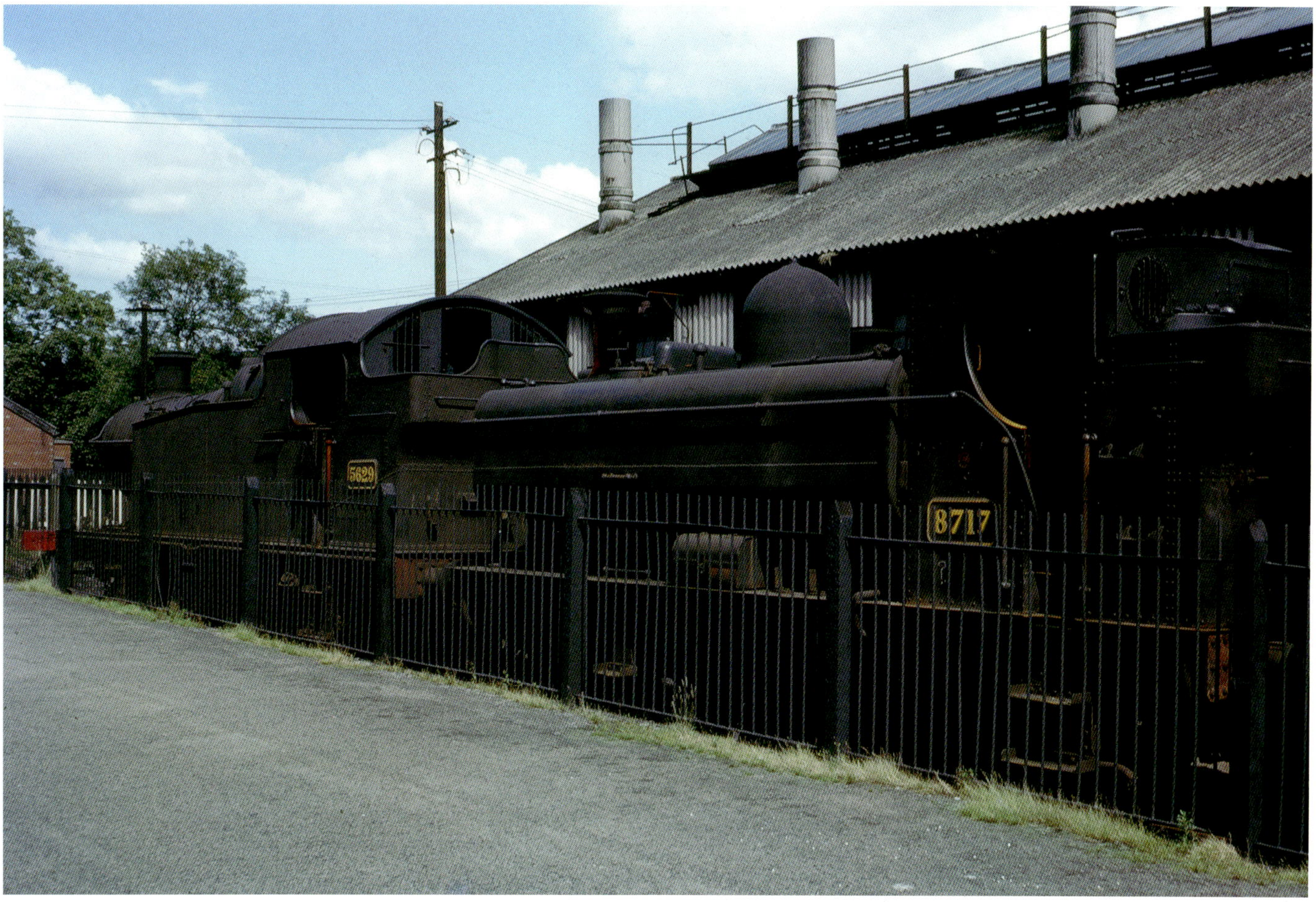

With the scrap yards throughout South Wales engaged in the mass disposal of so many locomotives this pairing of 5629 and 8717 alongside the shed at Abercynon in July 1964 would be quickly catered for. ***Win Wall/Strathwood Library Collection***

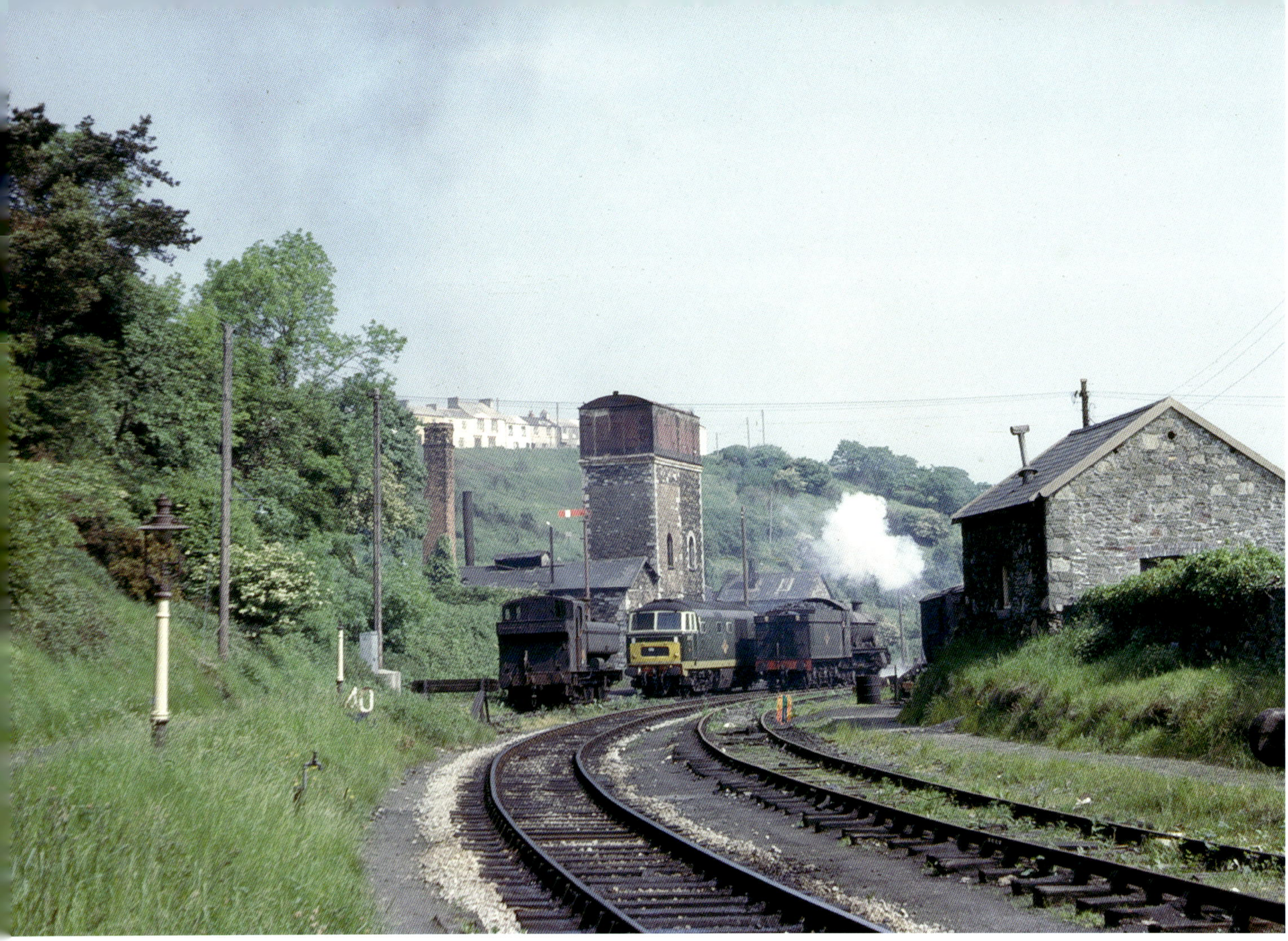

Go west young man and explore the shed at Neyland on 5 June 1963, already the drone of a Hymek can be heard in the distance. Coded 87H, Neyland shed would close completely on 8 September 1963. The following day the legendary driver Jim Clark became the then youngest ever World Champion Formula 1 racing driver aged 27. ***Frank Hornby***

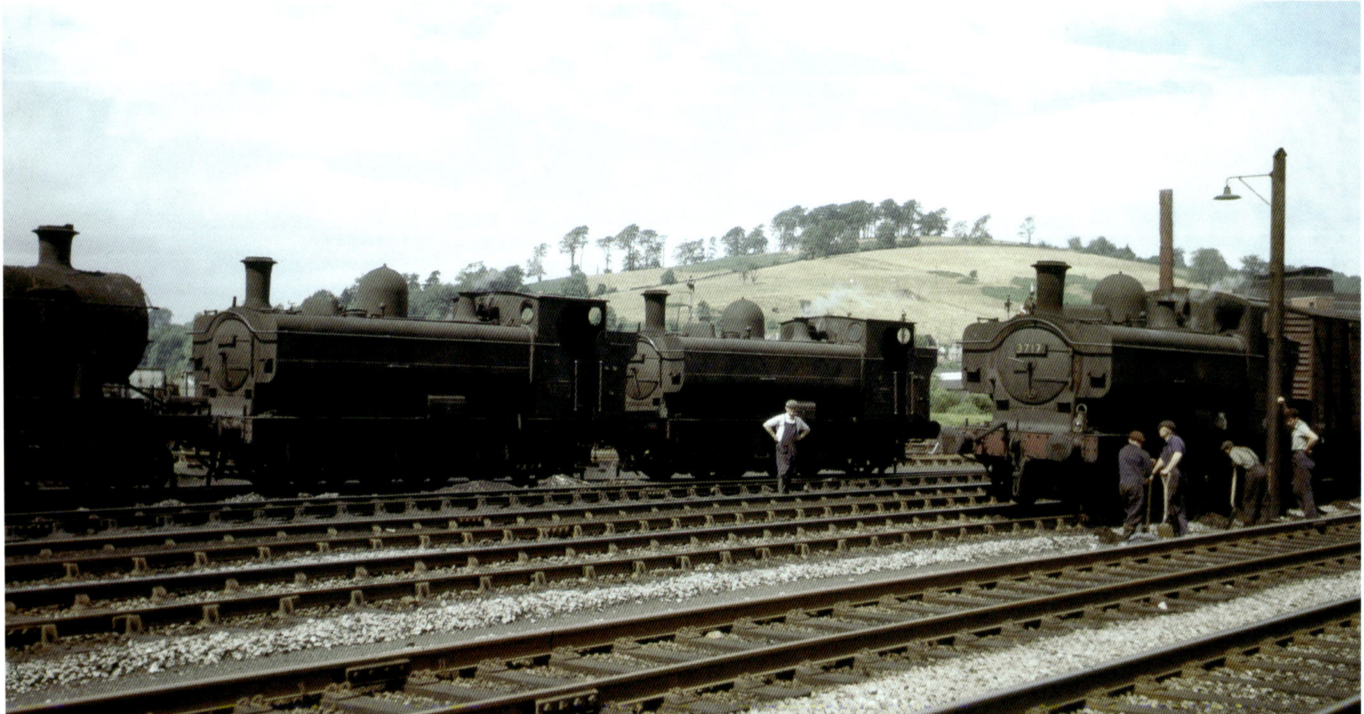

Pannier and trackside activity at Pontypool Road on 15 August 1962 with 5775, 8716 and 3717 on show. The former has led a charmed life since this picture was taken as 5775 became L89 in the London Transport fleet the following year and remained in use in London until 1969. Then is passed into preservation in Yorkshire on the Keighley & Worth Valley Railway who put it into a fictitious brown livery for a starring role in the Railway Children film. ***Strathwood Library Collection***

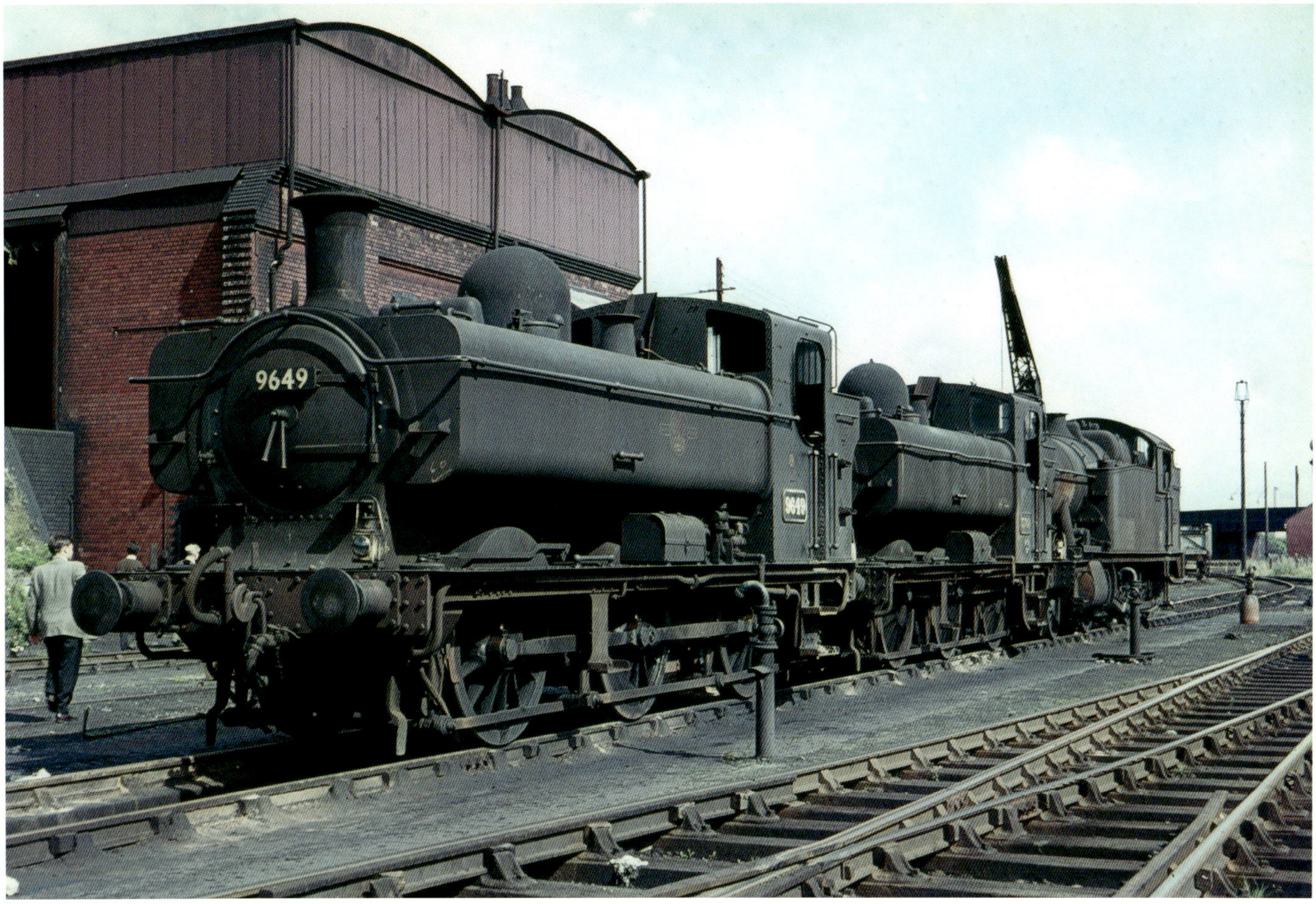

No chance of fame for withdrawn Pannier Tank 9649 at Newport Ebbw Junction on 25 July 1965 as she would be tuned into scrap the following month. ***Frank Hornby***

During 1960 Esso built the first oil refinery at Milford Haven which began a rapid expansion of traffic to the town. In this view from 5 June 1963 a rake of the company's oil tanks can be seen alongside the station. ***Frank Hornby***

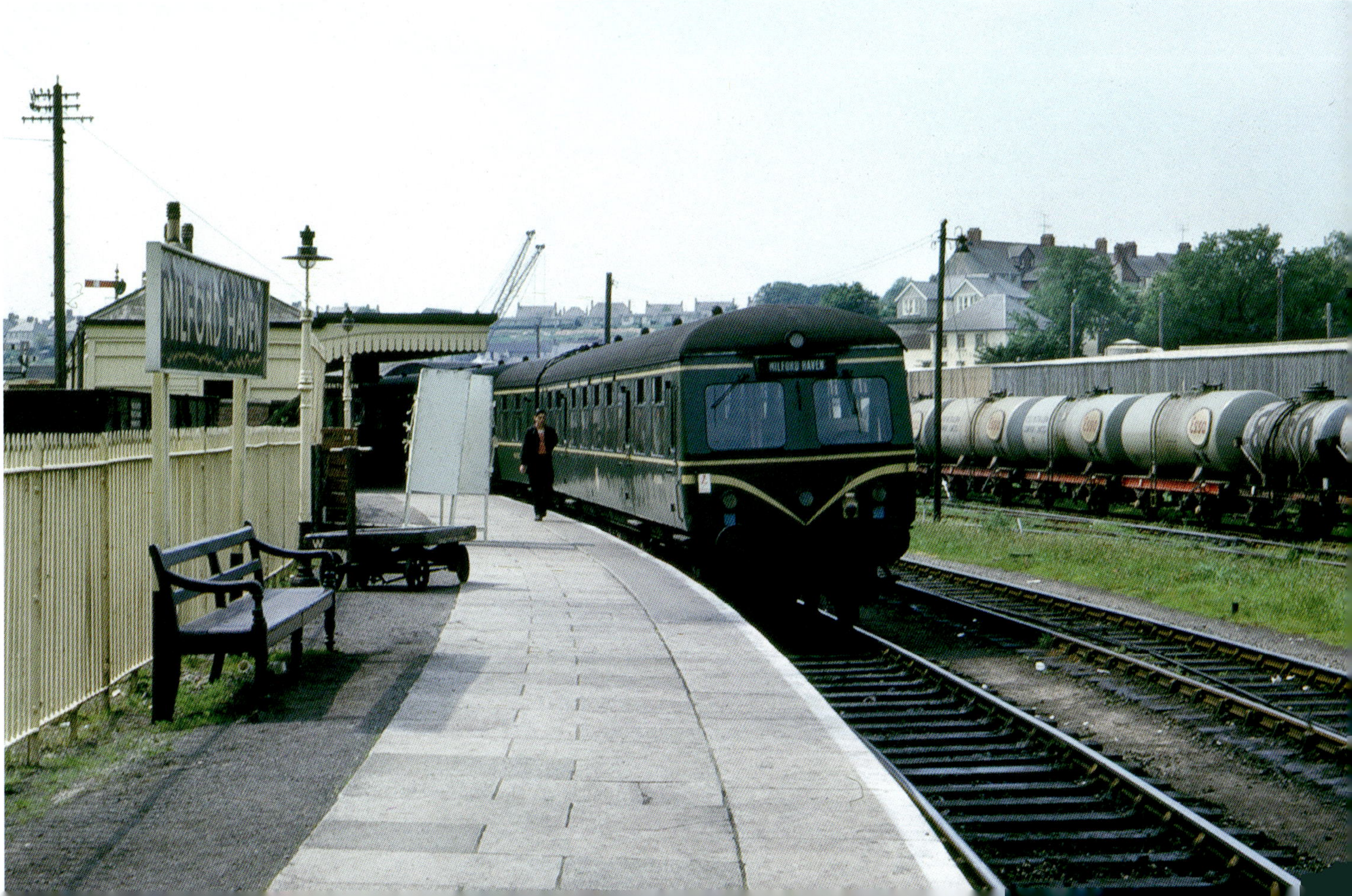

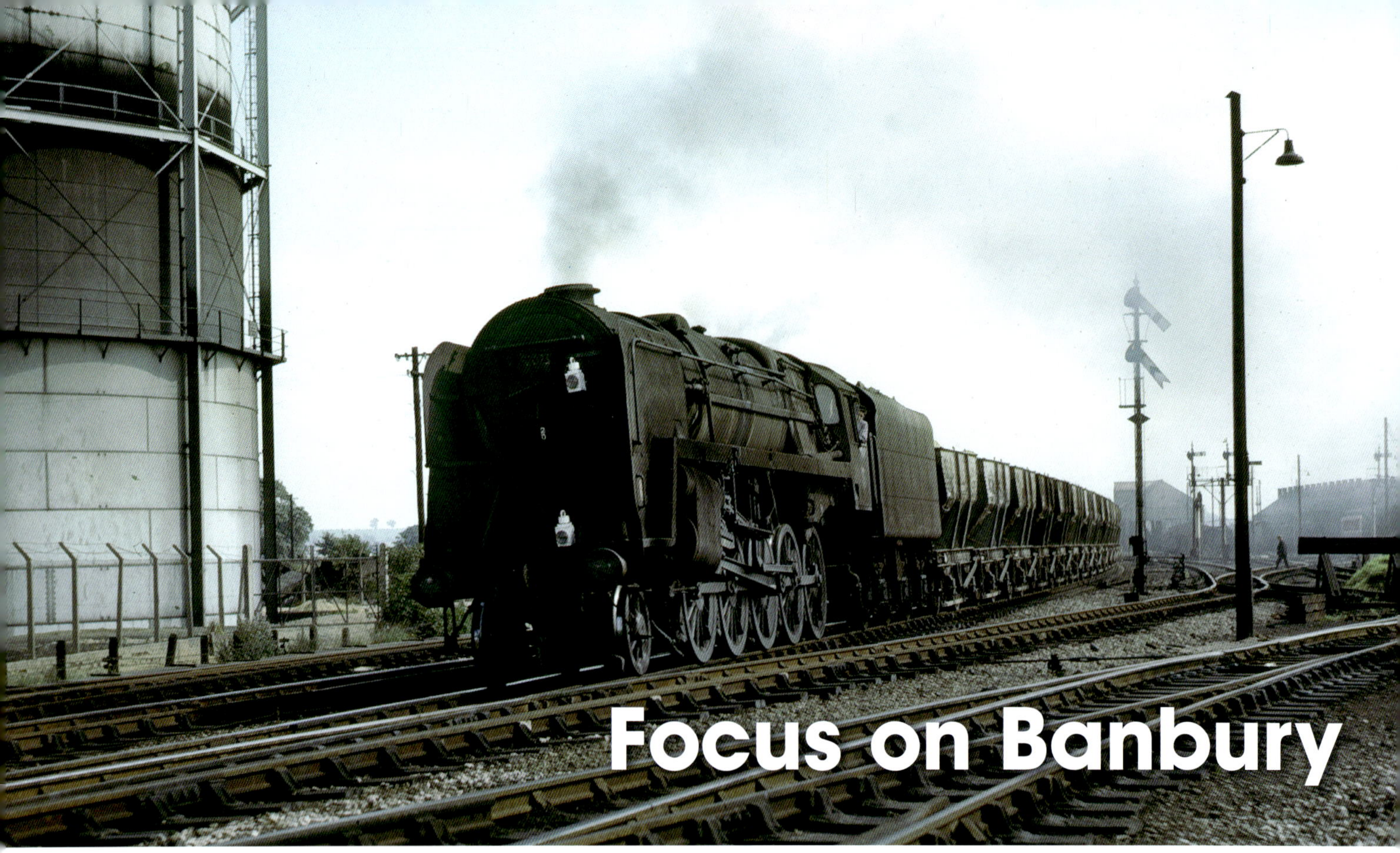

Focus on Banbury

Sweeping past the shed and our cameraman under clear signals on 3 September 1966 was Standard 9F 92073 at the head of an empty iron ore train. ***Aldo Delicata***

Banbury shed had been coded 2D within the London Midland Region since 9 September the previous year to this visit in March 1964, although clues to its previous coding of 84C could still be found with a trio of Swindon built 4-6-0s on shed including 6951 Impney Hall and 7912 Little Linford Hall. ***Win Wall/Strathwood Library Collection***

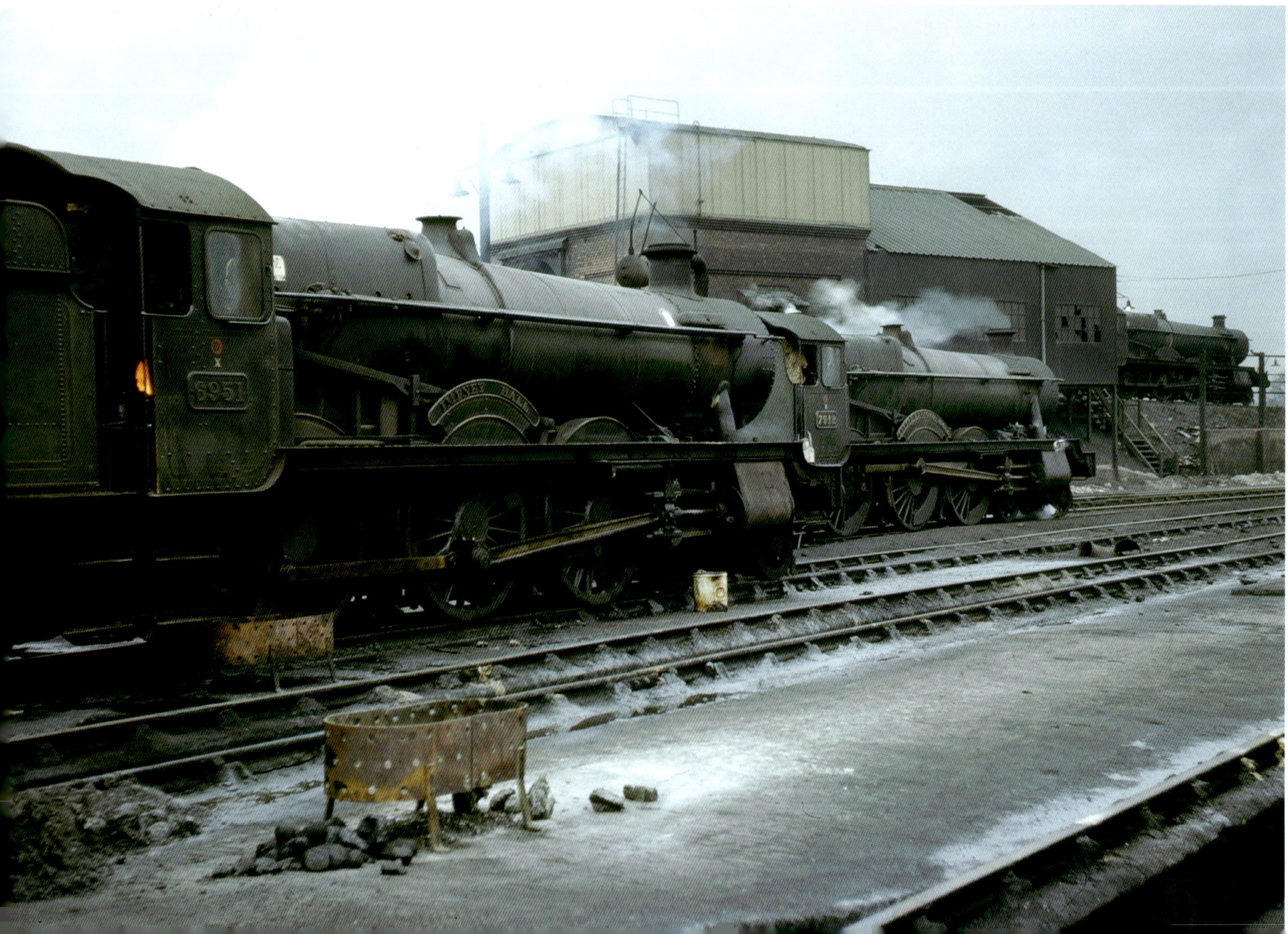

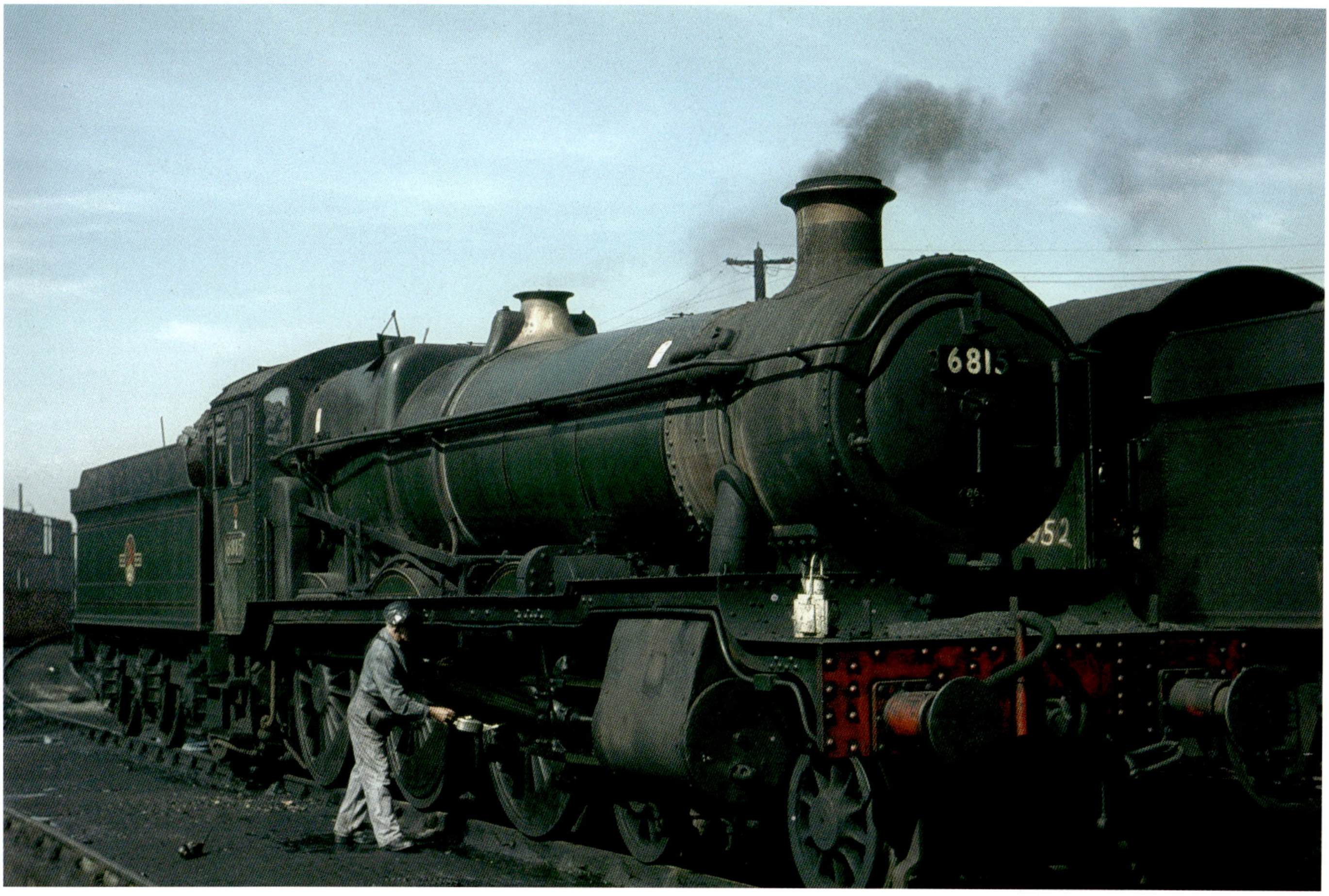

The nameplates off 6815 Frilford Grange have been removed for 'safe keeping' when seen on shed in September 1965 two months away from being taken out of traffic. ***Strathwood Library Collection***

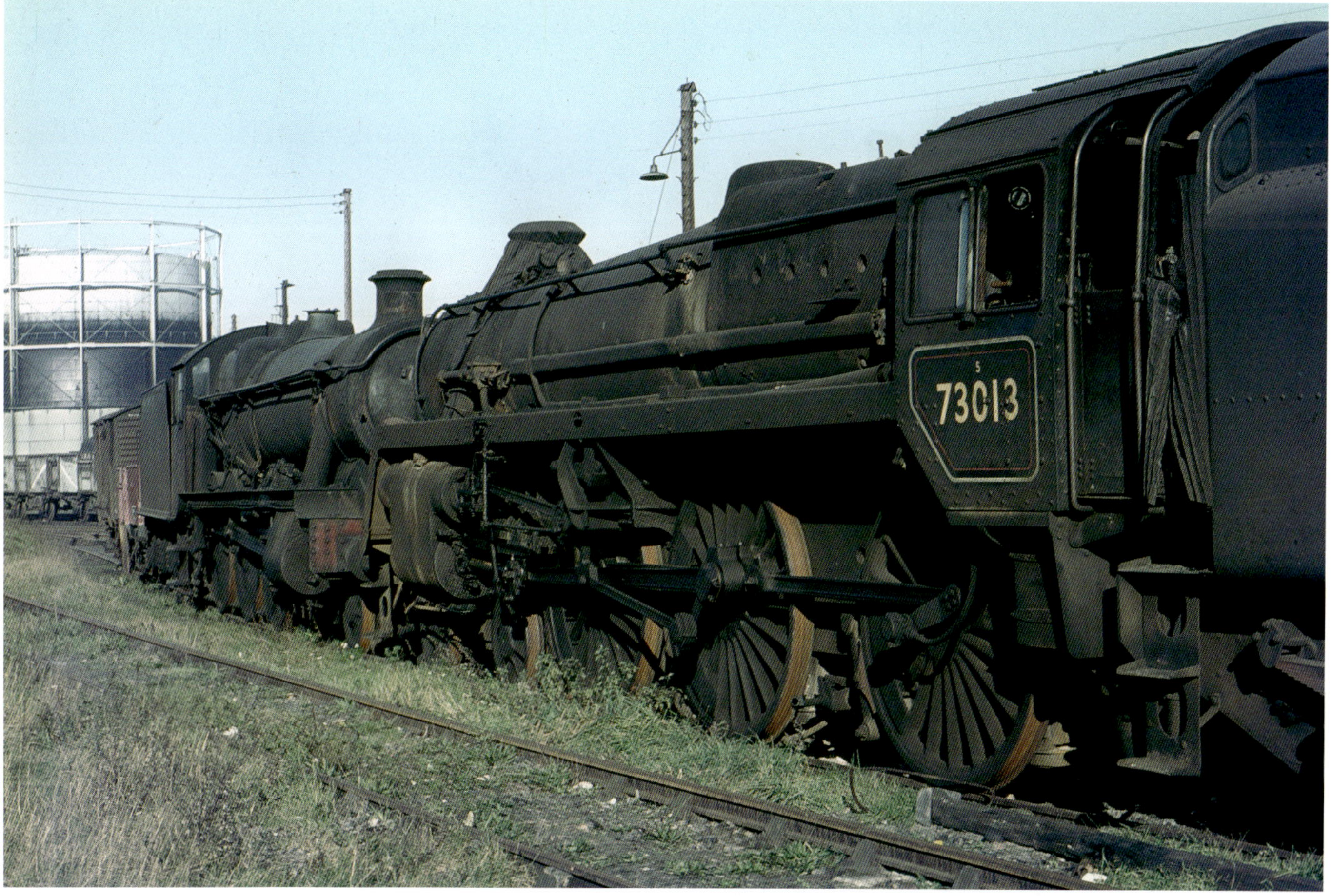

In the summer of 1966 Standard 5MT 73013 had its chimney sacked over in the forlorn hope she might see further use, but was now on the scrap road at Banbury with an equally unfortunate Modified Hall. ***Bob Treacher/Alton Model Centre***

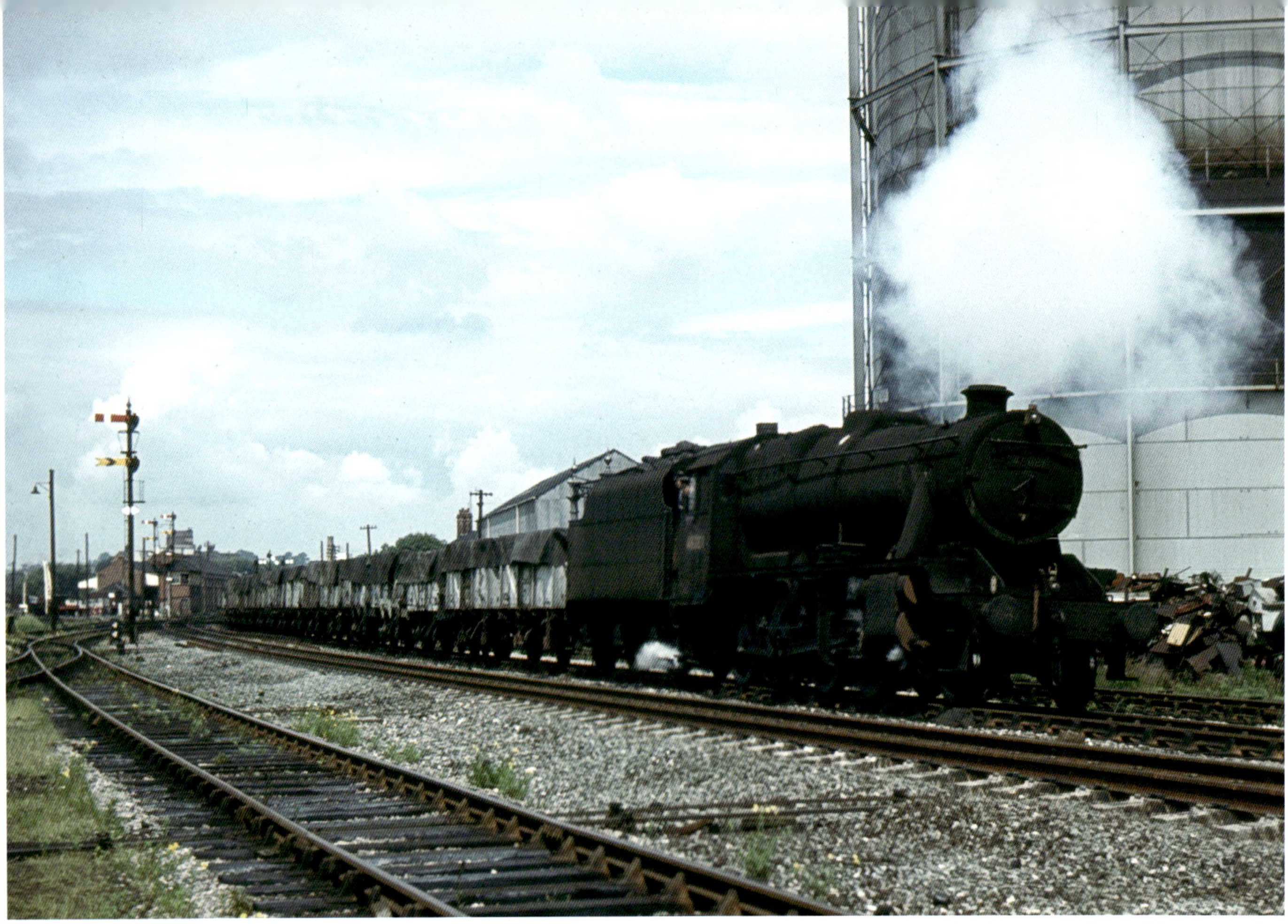

Rattling a rake of trucks past the gasworks in July 1963 was Stanier 8F 48621. The top television programmme at the time was the ever present Coronation Street, beating the likes of comedy shows such as Morecambe and Wise and Steptoe and Son in the ratings of the day. ***Strathwood Library Collection***

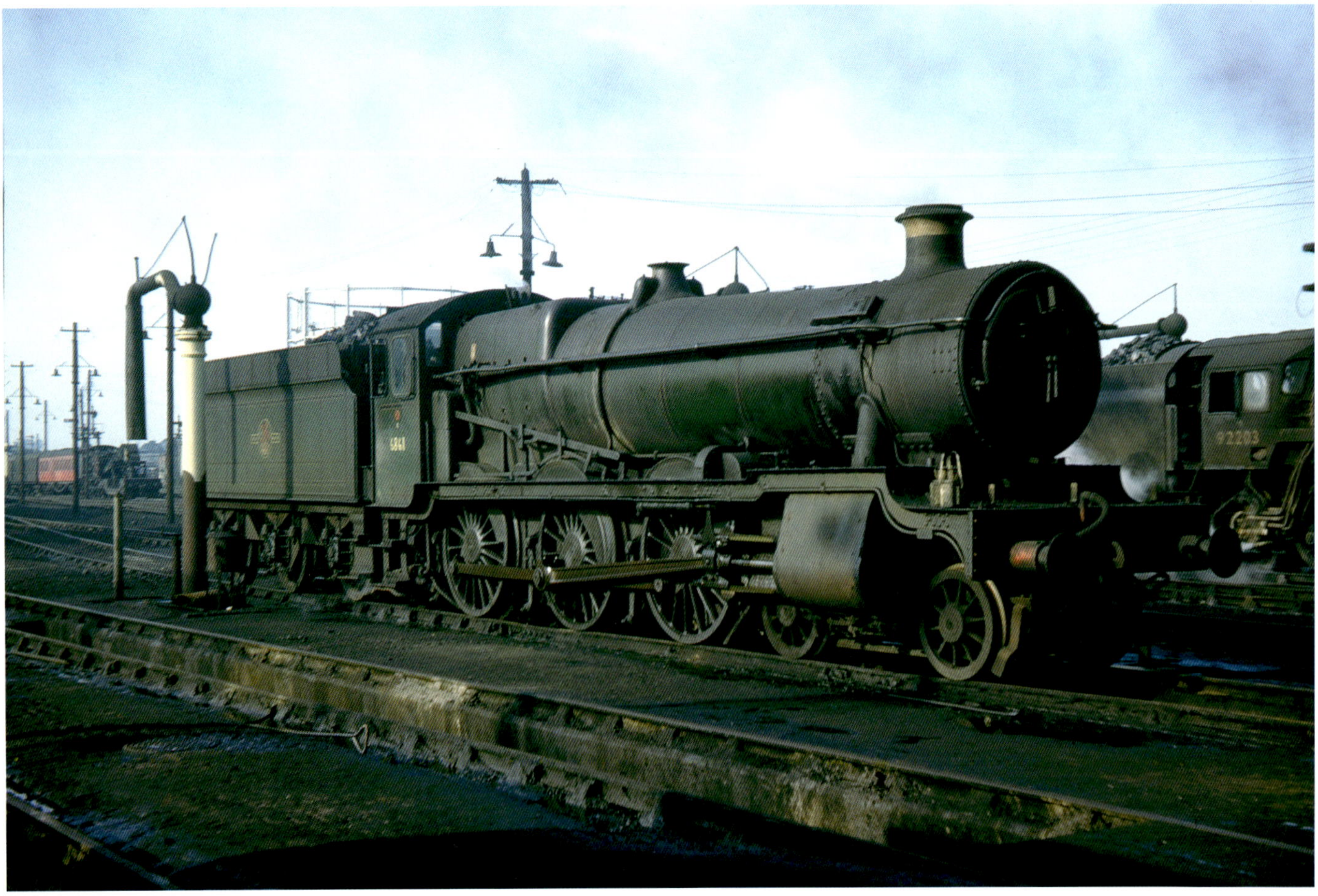

All the plates from 6861 Crynant Grange have disappeared although the tender is fully coaled perhaps for that final run to the breakers when seen in the yard at Banbury on 9 October 1965. ***Michael Beaton***

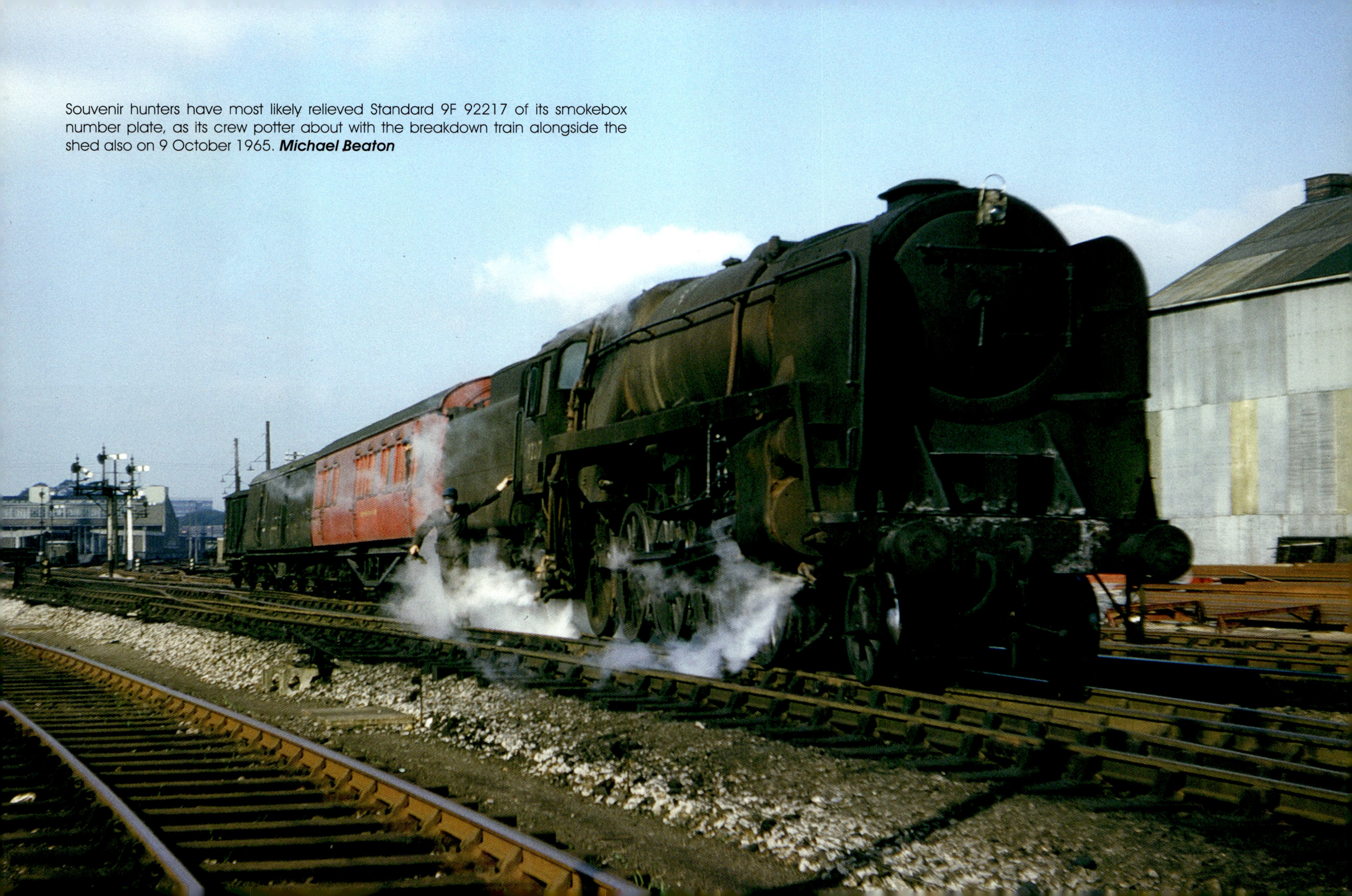

Souvenir hunters have most likely relieved Standard 9F 92217 of its smokebox number plate, as its crew potter about with the breakdown train alongside the shed also on 9 October 1965. ***Michael Beaton***

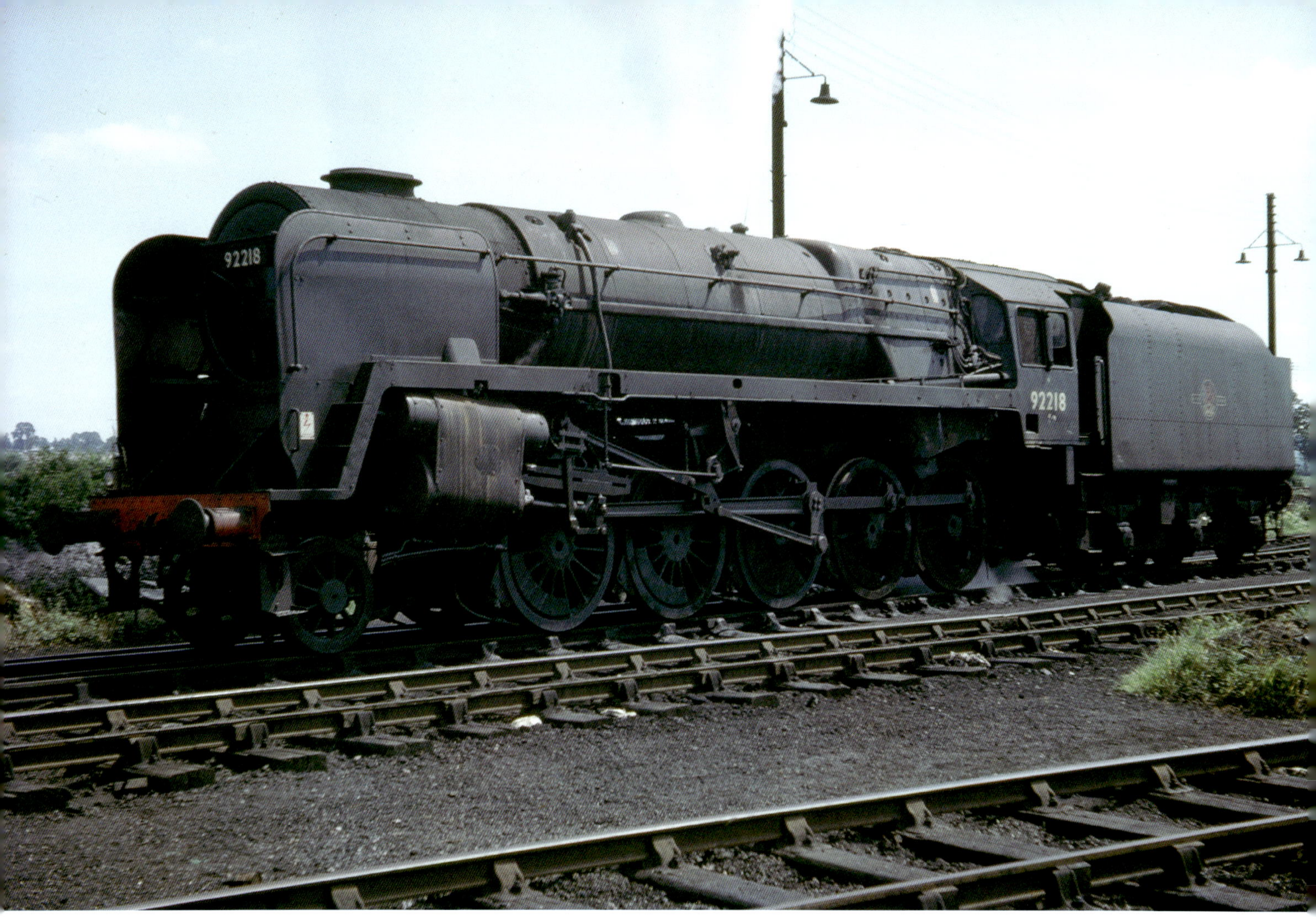

Much more presentable was 9F classmate 92218 on the shed in July 1966 paired to a BR1C tender.
Michael Beaton

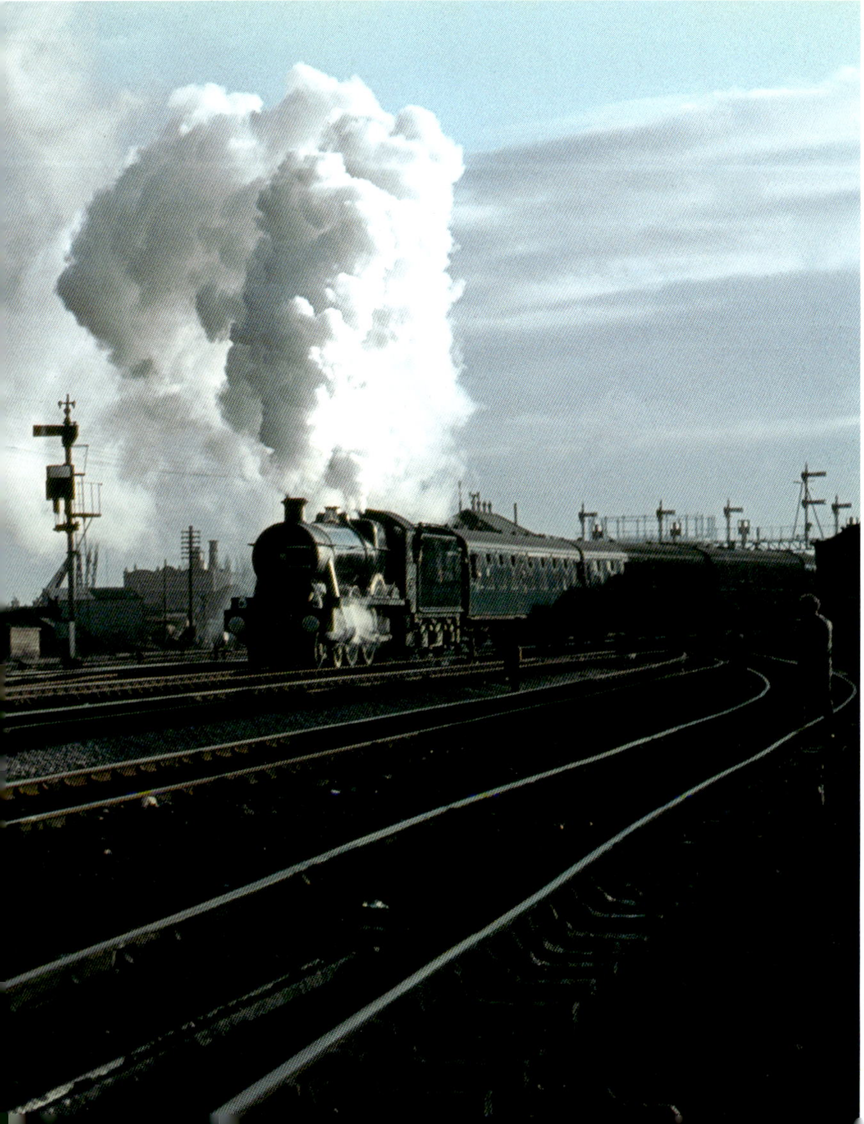

One of the Hawksworth design of tenders is coupled to Modified Hall 6998 Burton Agnes Hall seen departing Banbury on 3 January 1966. The newly formed Great Western Society acquired the locomotive shortly after this and moved the engine to their base at Didcot the following year.
Bob Treacher/Alton Model Centre

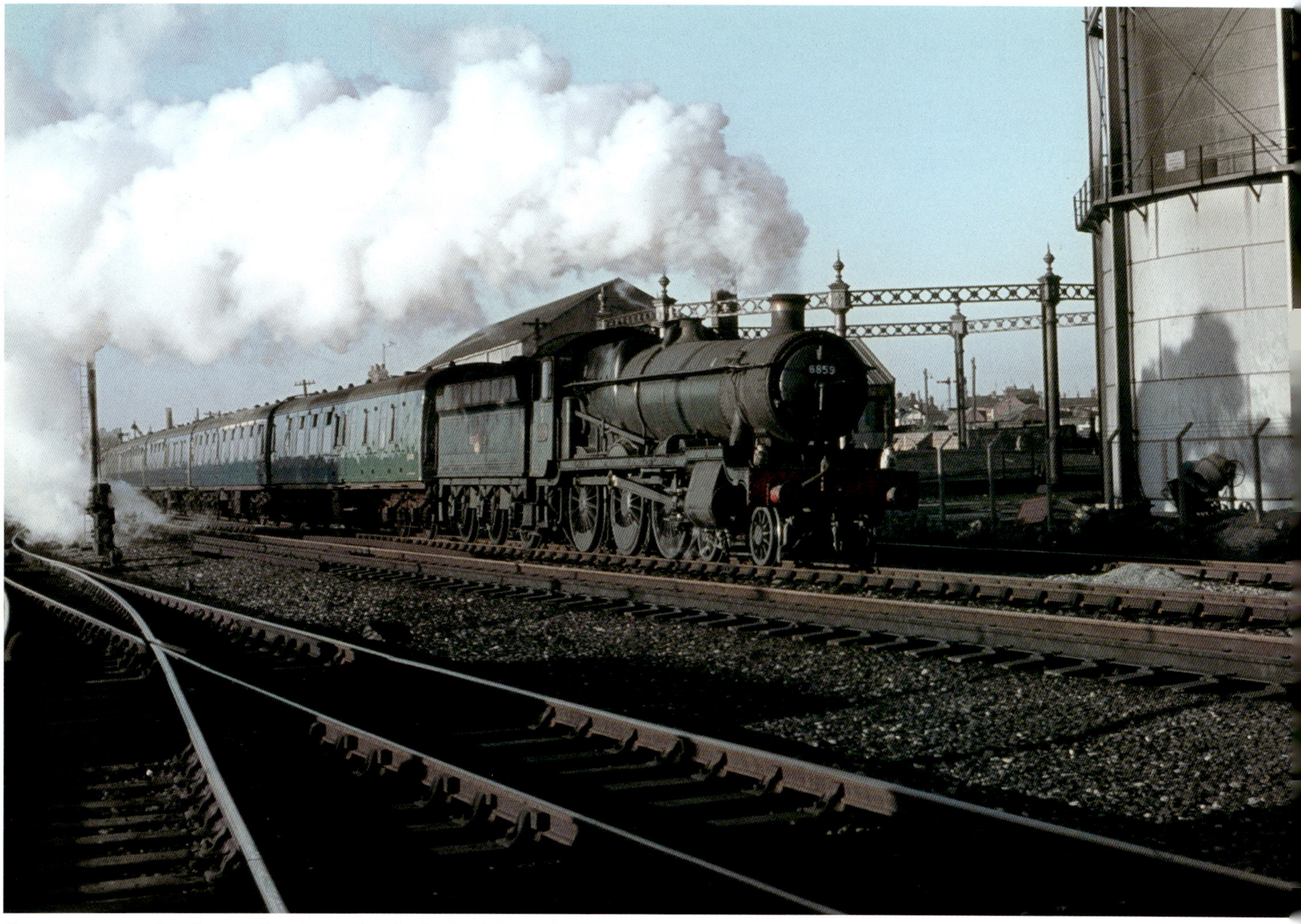

Once more Southern Region stock is behind 6859 Yeiwsley Grange making a comfortable start away from Banbury in 1965. ***Bob Treacher/Alton Model Centre***

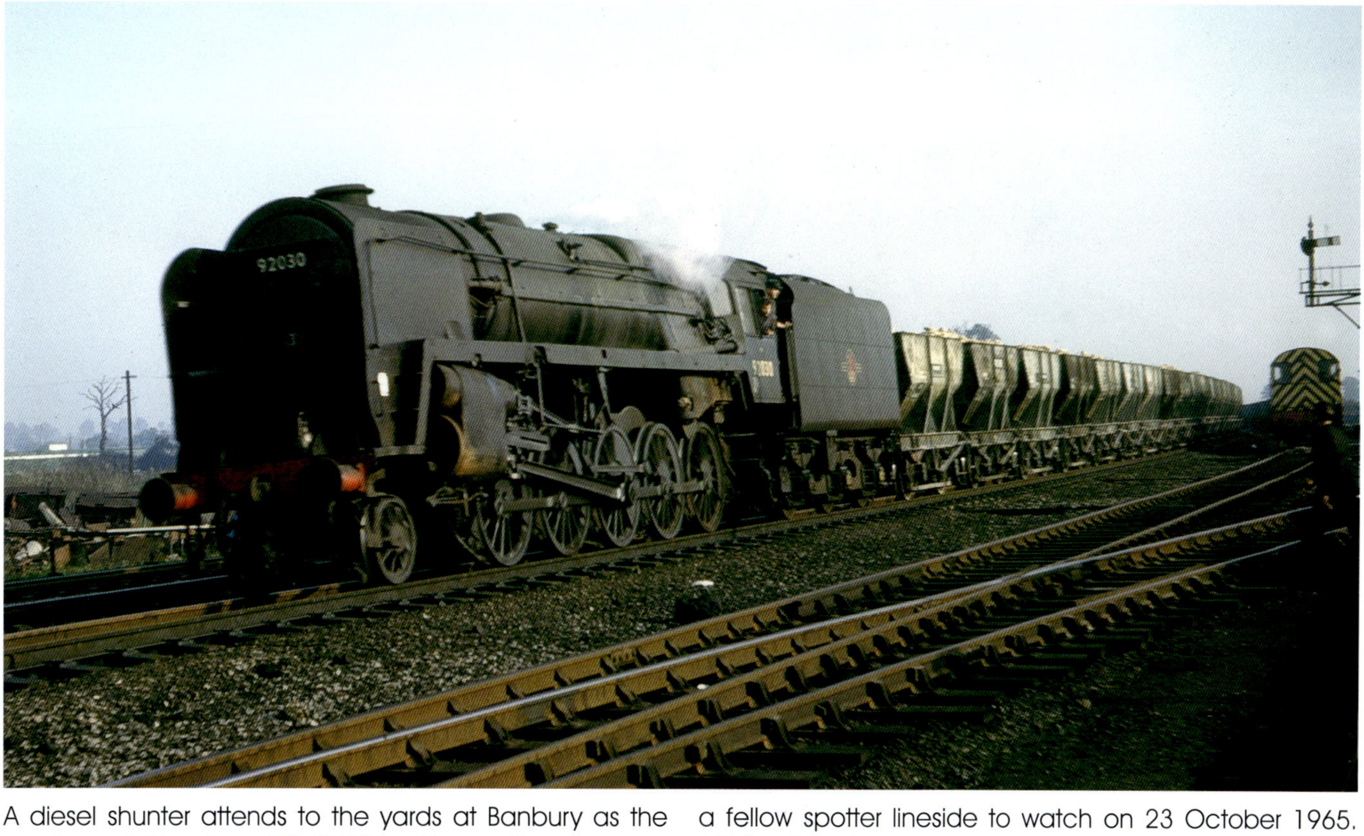

A diesel shunter attends to the yards at Banbury as the passing of Standard 9F 92030 with another iron ore working for the once busy minefields in Oxfordshire brings a fellow spotter lineside to watch on 23 October 1965. ***Michael Beaton***

Salvation

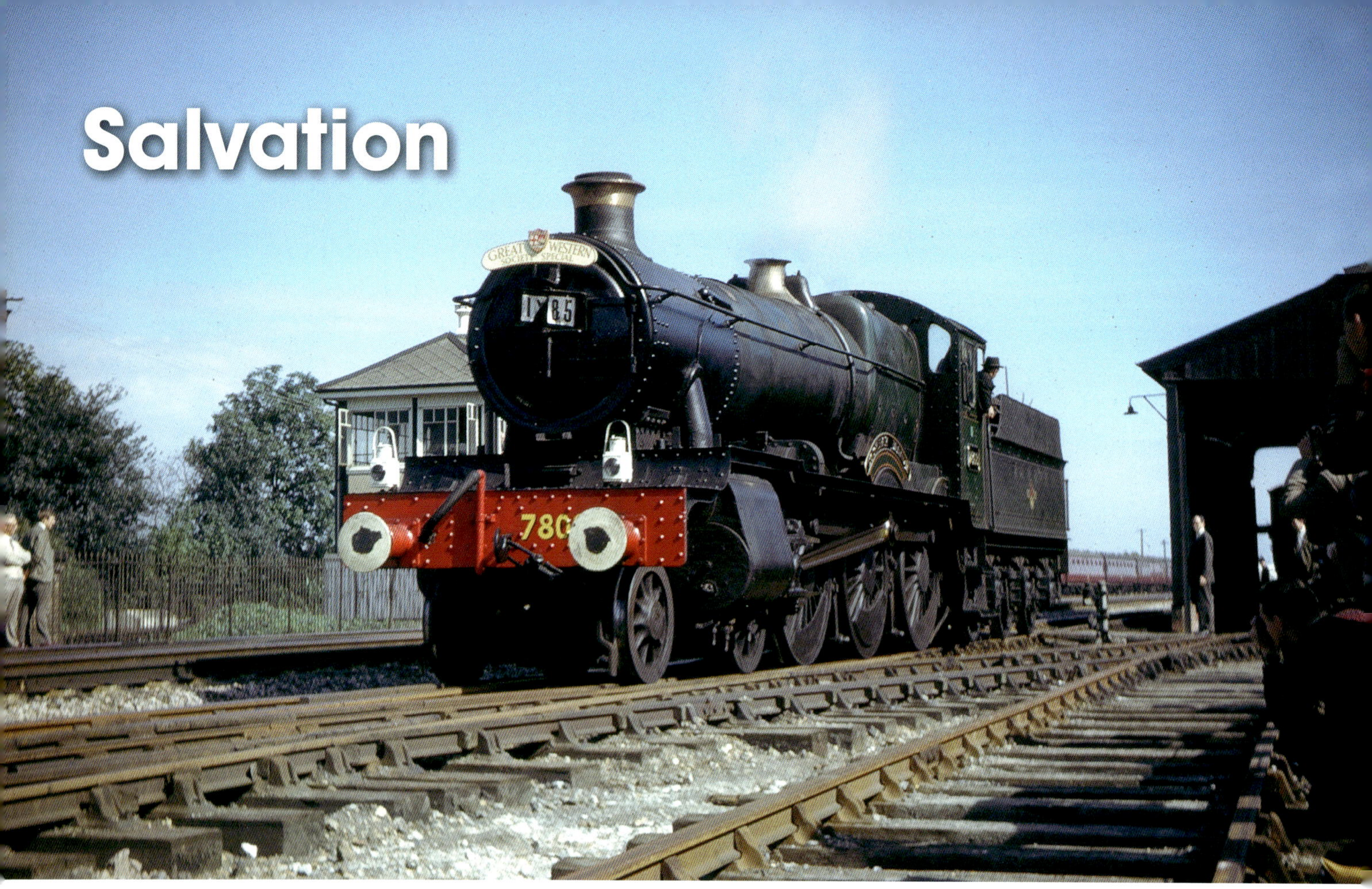

Although seven more of her classmates stood at Barry on 17 September 1966, we thought at the time that it would only be the likes of 7808 Cookham Manor attending the Open Day at Taplow that would ever steam again. ***Edward Dorricott***

Also present this day was the Great Western Society's Large Prairie 6106 coupled to an Ocean Saloon. ***Strathwood Library Collection***

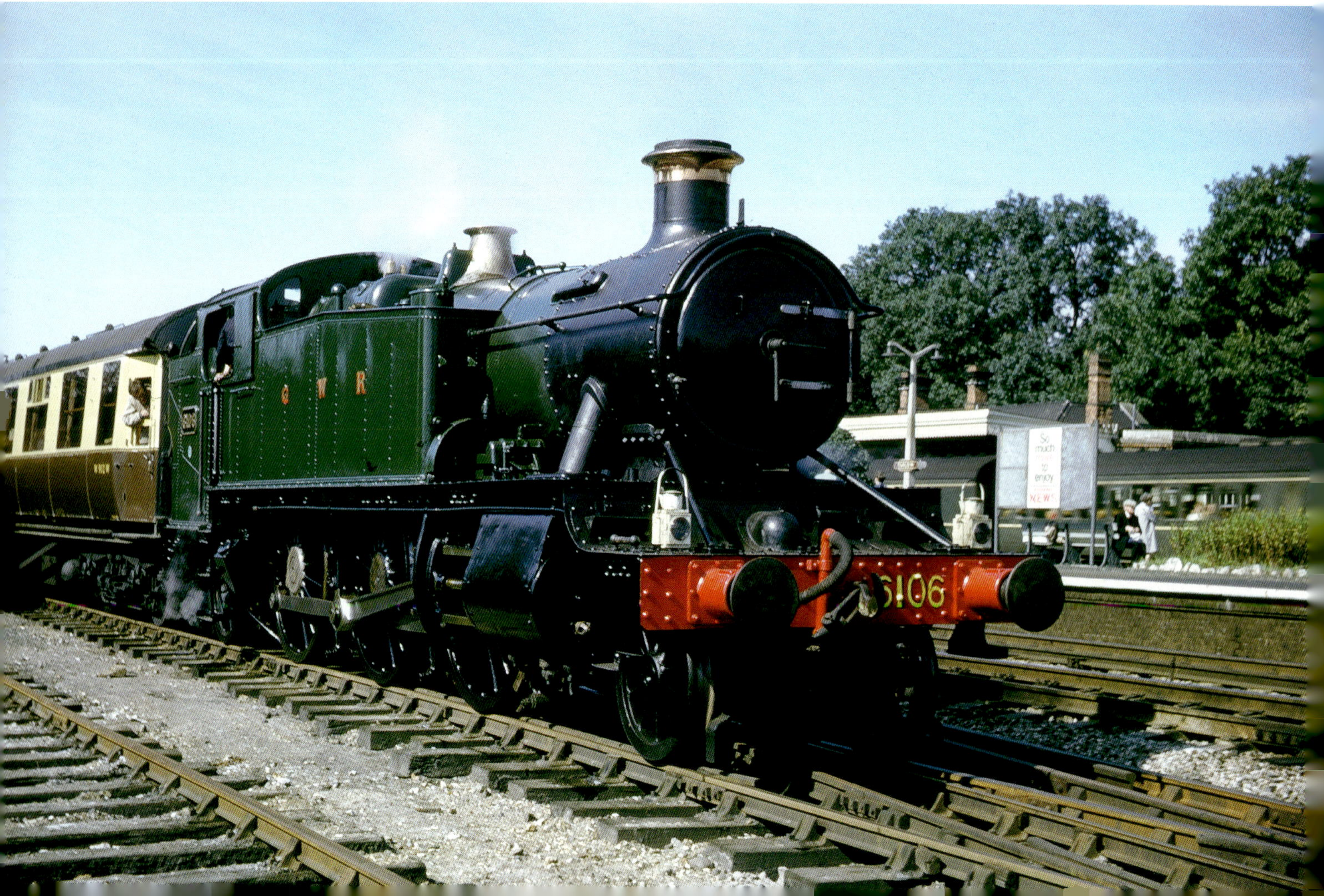

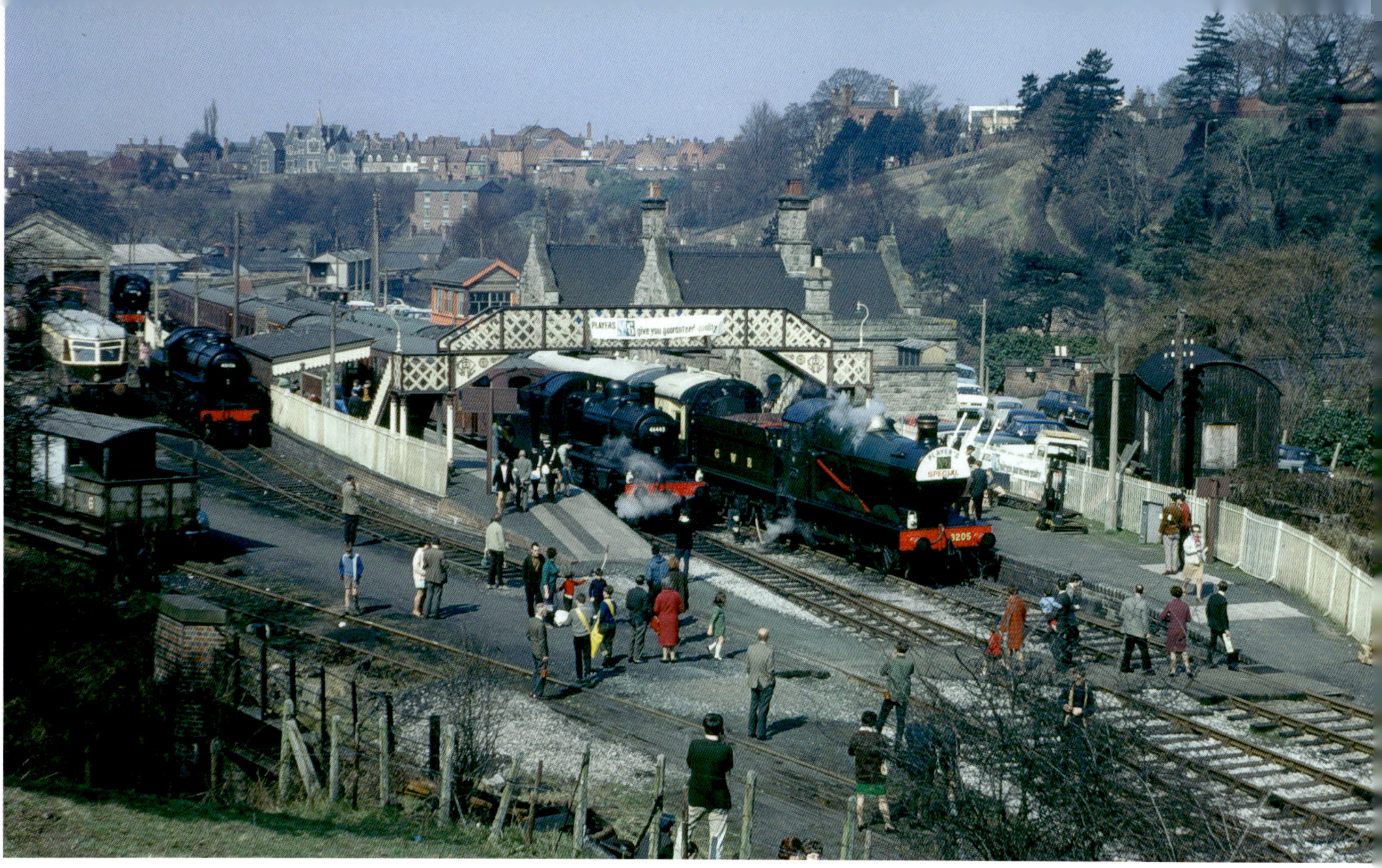

Back then the Severn Valley Railway were much more relaxed as indeed we all were about passengers and enthusiasts around the lineside on 5 April 1969 at Bridgnorth as Collett 0-6-0 3205 shares duties with Ivatt 2-6-0 46443. ***Jerry Beddows***

The once familiar use of 1400 Class locomotives on the region's branches inspired the running of the Great Western Society's 1466 from Wallingford to Cholsey and return on 21 September 1968. ***Aldo Delicata***

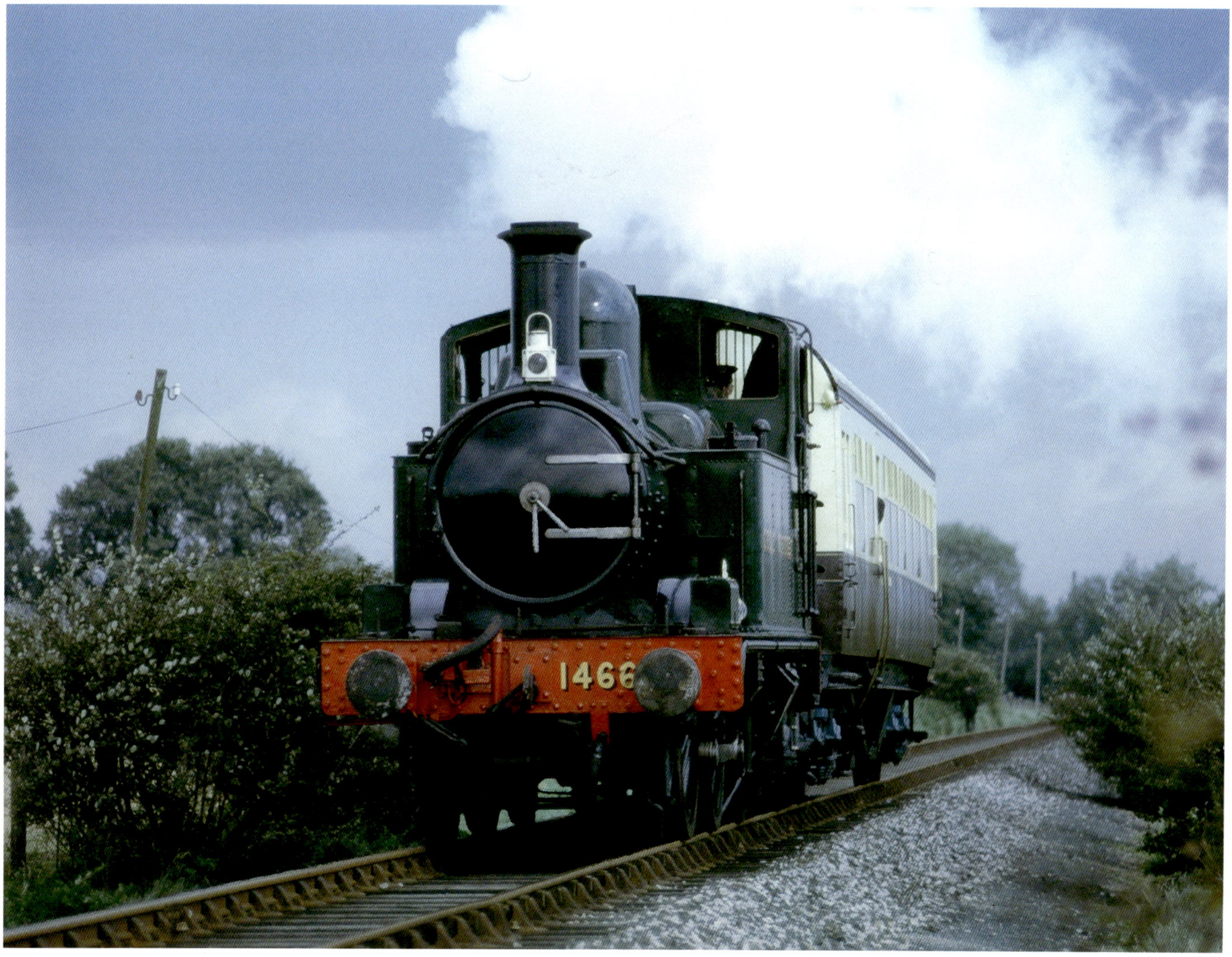

Heading for Devon and Cornwall

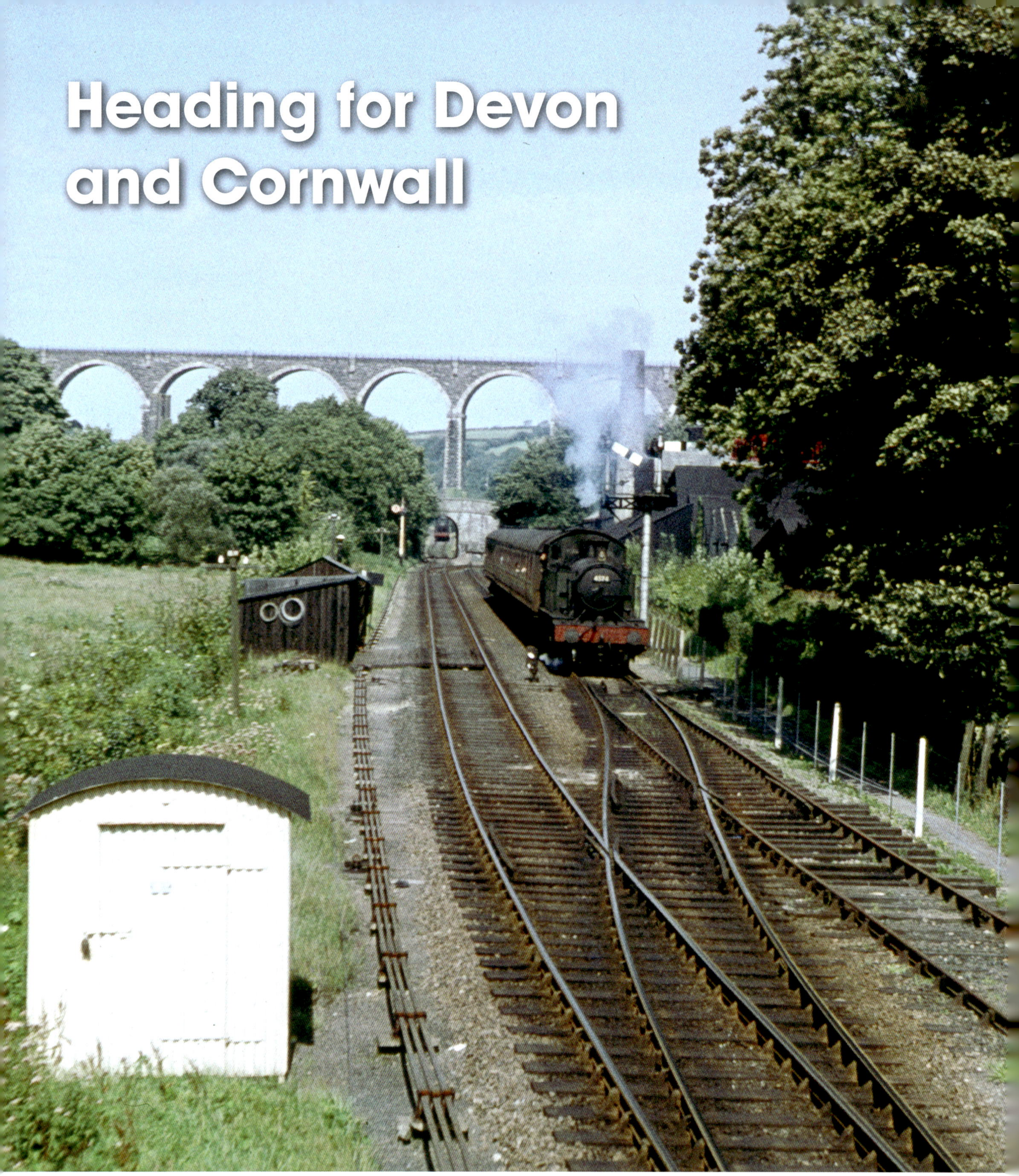

Another Prairie can be glimpsed in the distance as 4564 negotiates Coombe Junction in August 1961 whilst the mainline viaduct dominates the background. The branch from the Cornish mainline at Liskeard snaked down to almost sea level over eight miles to Looe. Shortly after this view was taken DMUs appeared on the branch. It was considered for closure and 5 October 1966 was to have been the last day for the branch, however a reprieve was granted and it survives to this day. ***Strathwood Library Collection***

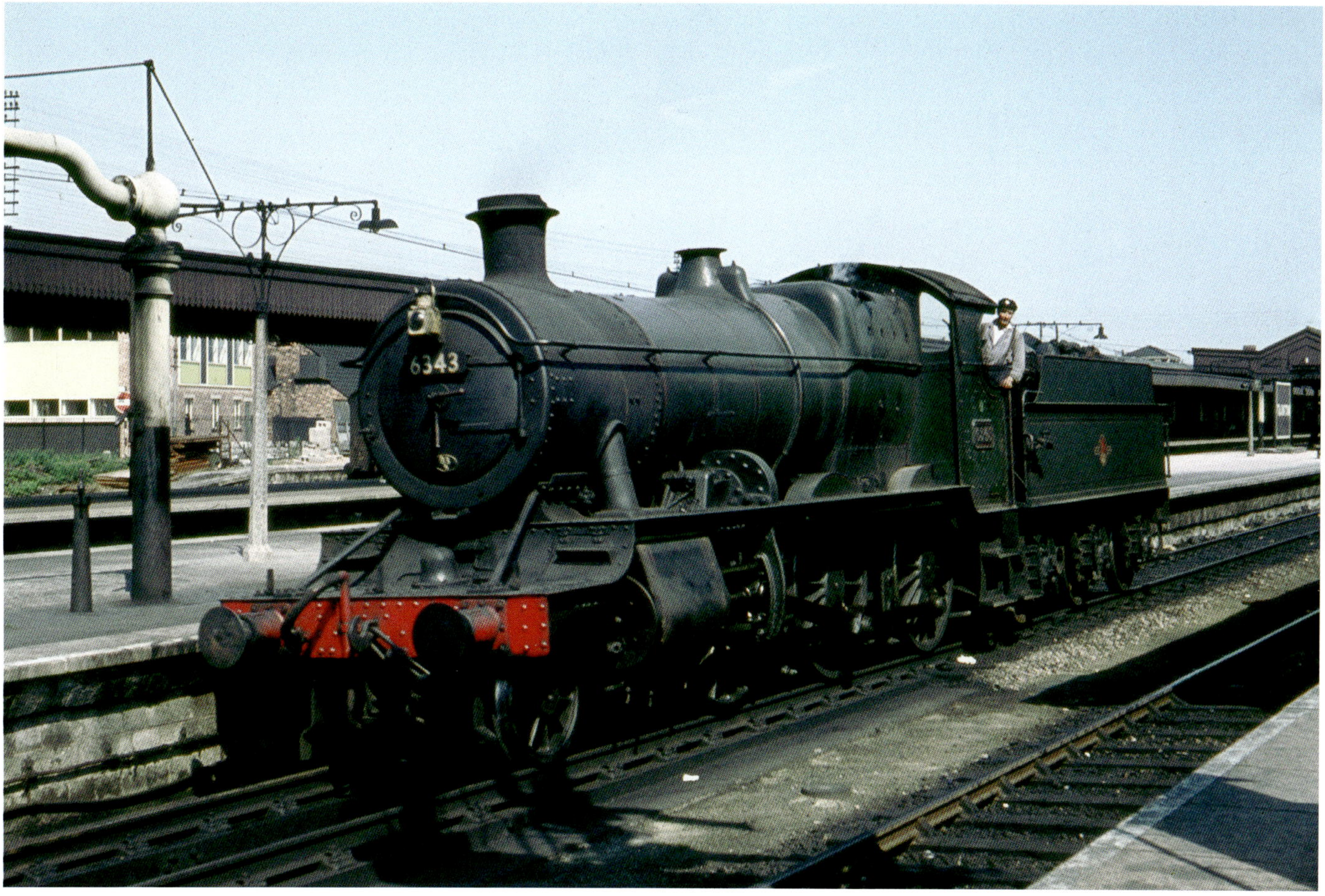

Running light through Taunton's station in 1960 was Churchward Mogul 6343 which would have been engaged on traffic for the line to Barnstaple Junction. The Bristol and Exeter Railway first brought the railway to the Somerset town in 1842. ***Strathwood Library Collection***

The line onwards to Exeter St. Davids was completed and opened on 1 May 1844 where we find a smartly presented Pannier 3794 during1960. ***Strathwood Library Collection***

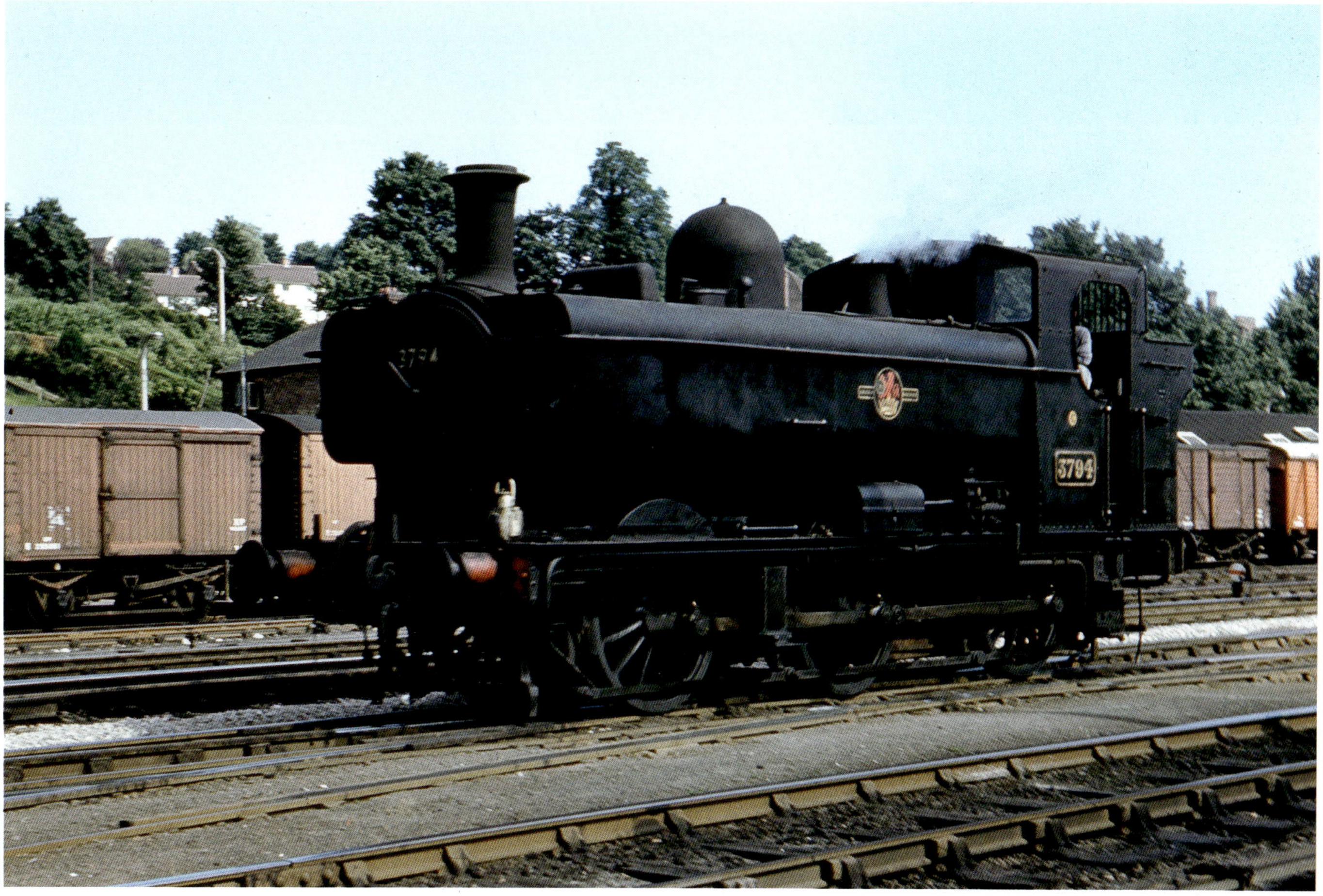

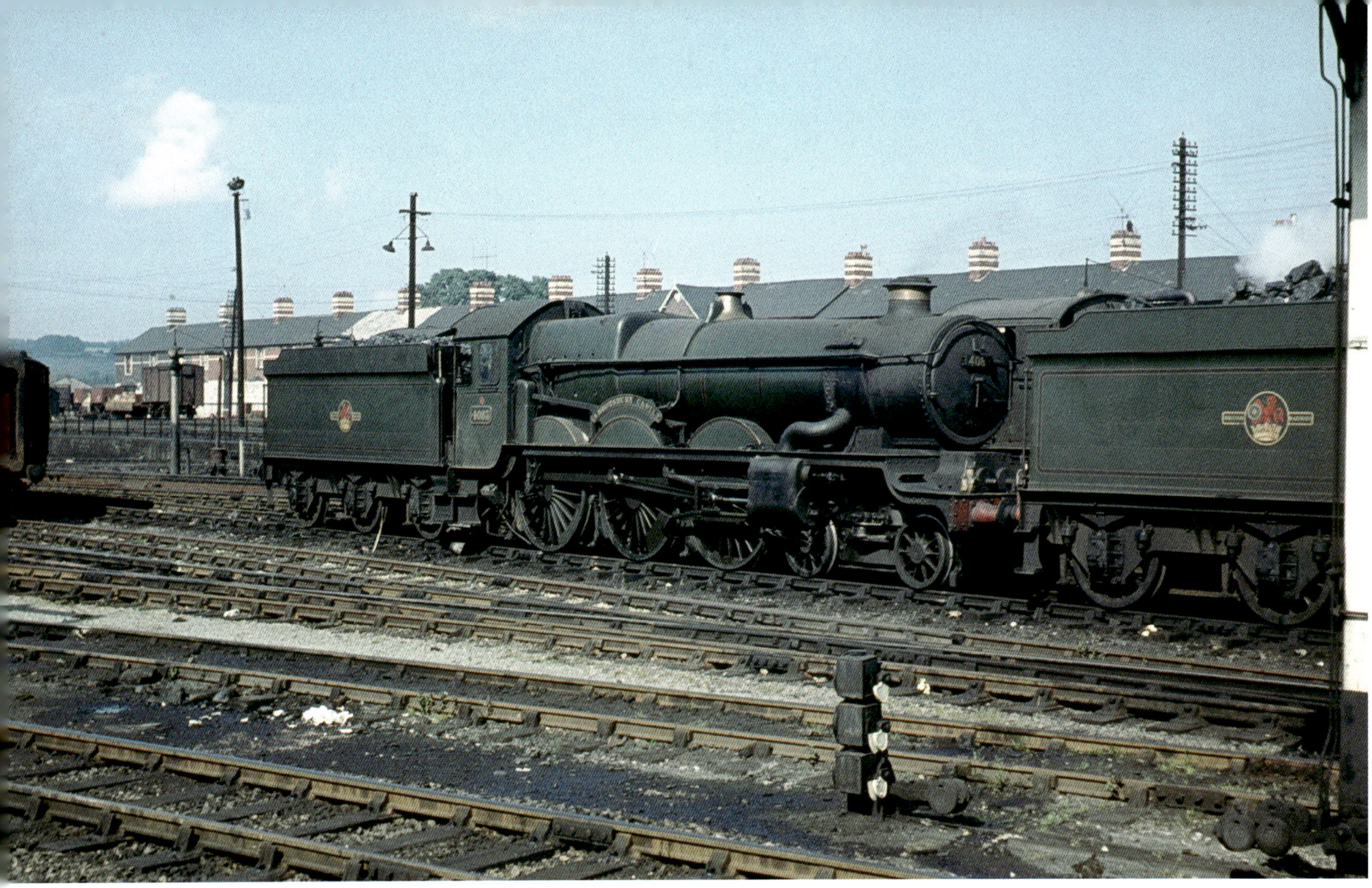

Among the locomotives laying over at Newton Abbot the same year was 4083 Abbotsbury Castle which had begun its thirty six year career emerging from Swindon Works in May 1925 being withdrawn and cut up at its birthplace in December 1961. ***Alan Pike OBE***

Ivatt and Riddles influences alongside the coaler at Laira on 13 December 1963 in the shape of 41316 and 73044. ***Dave Down***

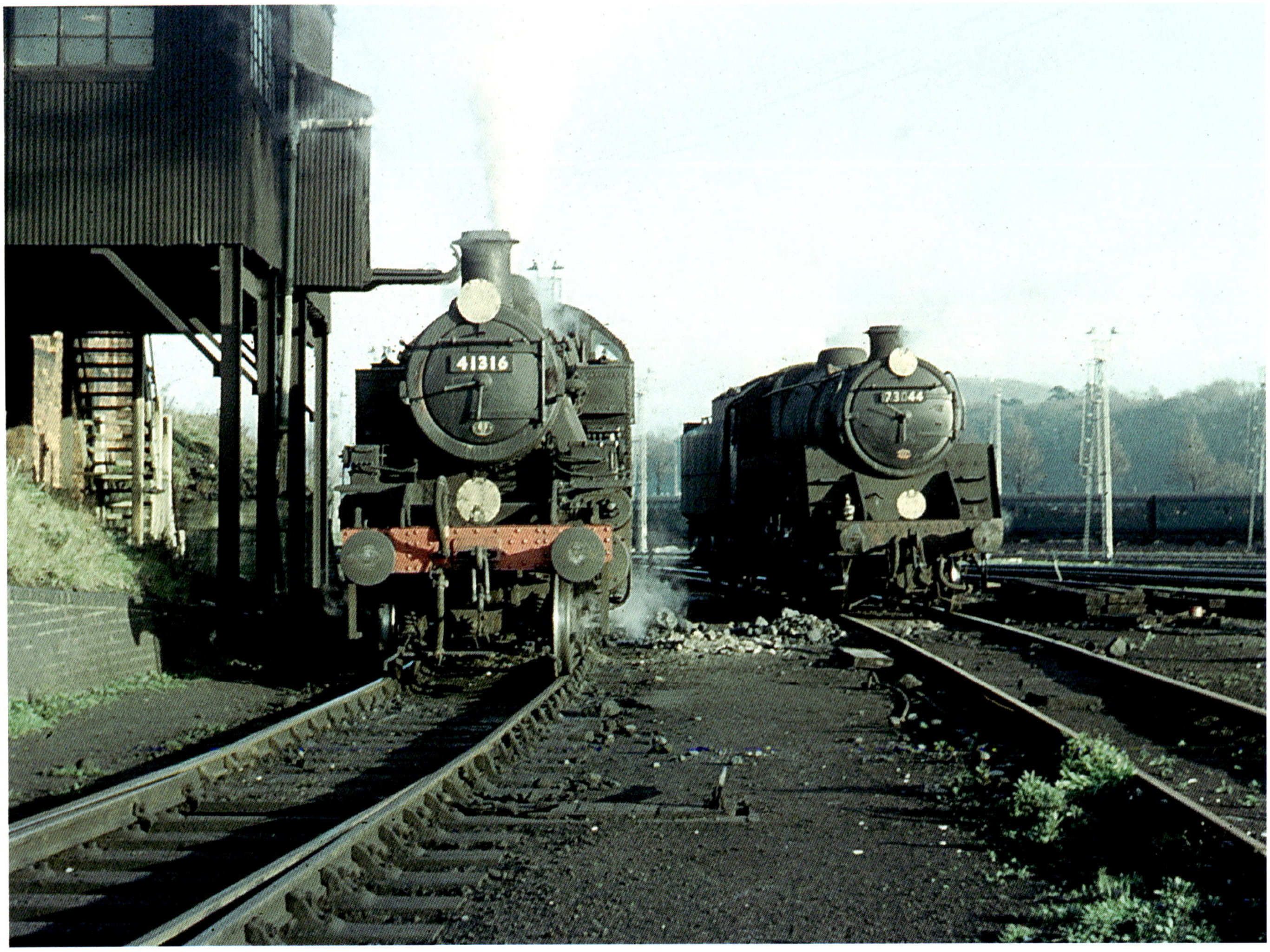

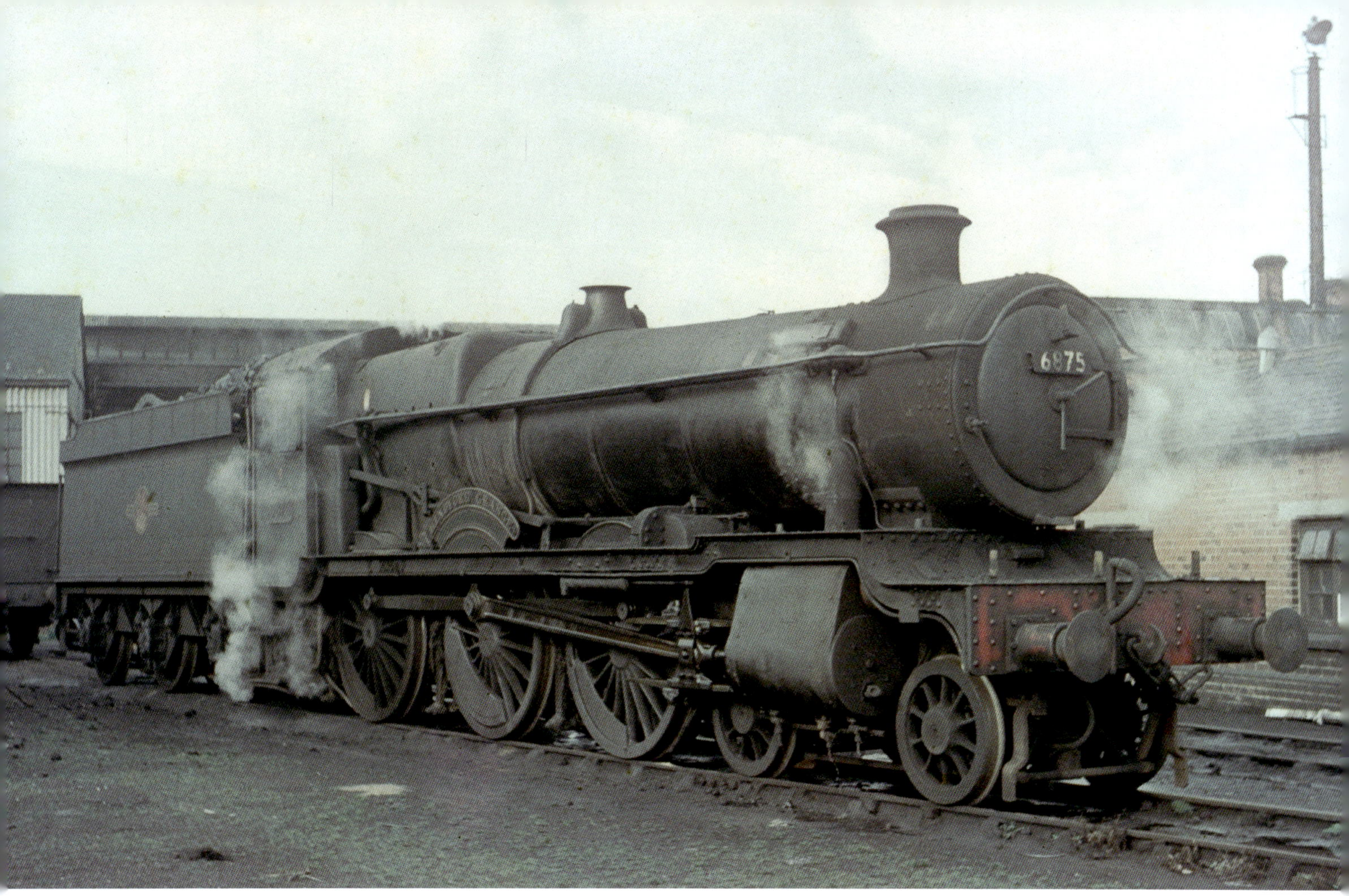

Percolating nicely in the cold air of 12 January 1960 outside the shed at Laira was 6875 Hindford Grange. ***Dave Down***

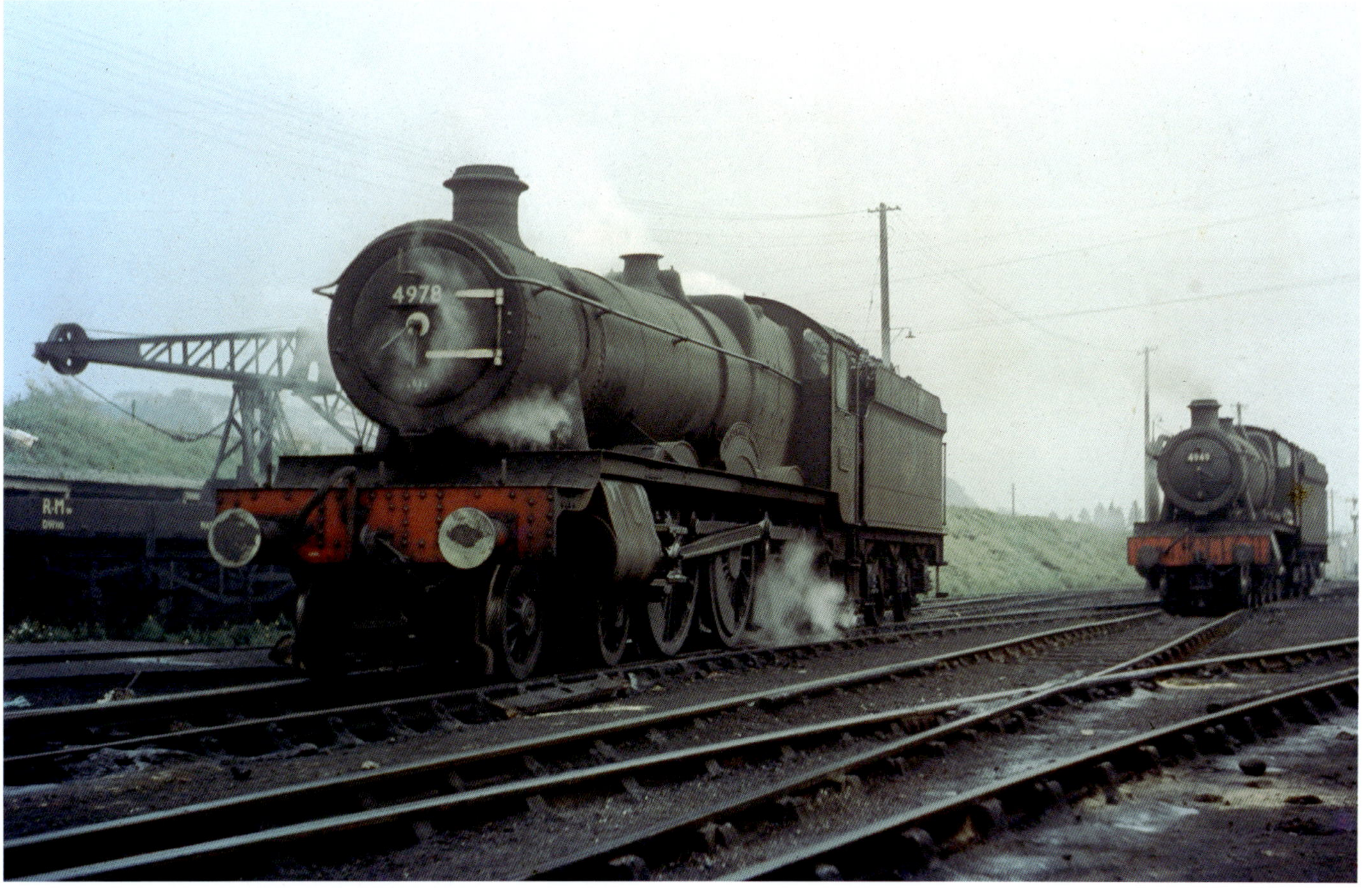

On 27 October 1963 it is a pair of Halls that grab our attention with 4978 Westwood Hall and sister 4949 Packwood Hall on shed at Laira which had changed codes from 83D to the more familiar to our younger readers 84A the previous month. ***Dave Down***

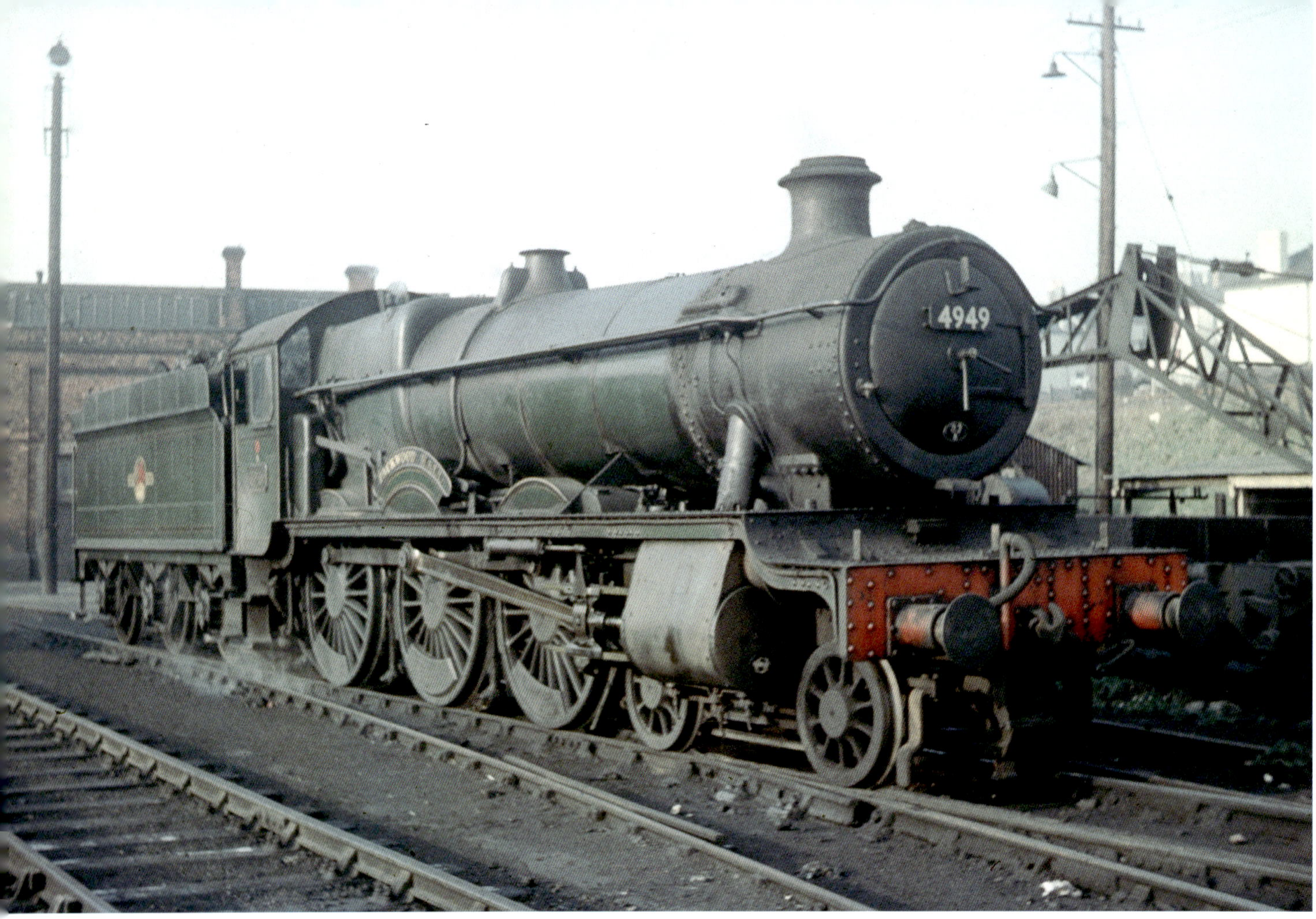

Back on shed again at Laira on 8 December 1963 was 4949 Packwood Hall allowing a solo portrait to be taken just before the locomotive entered its last year in service as the region would be taking deliveries of more Western diesels into 1964. ***Dave Down***

New Years day in 1964 provides 6984 Owsden Hall catching the milky winter sunshine at Laira. ***Dave Down***

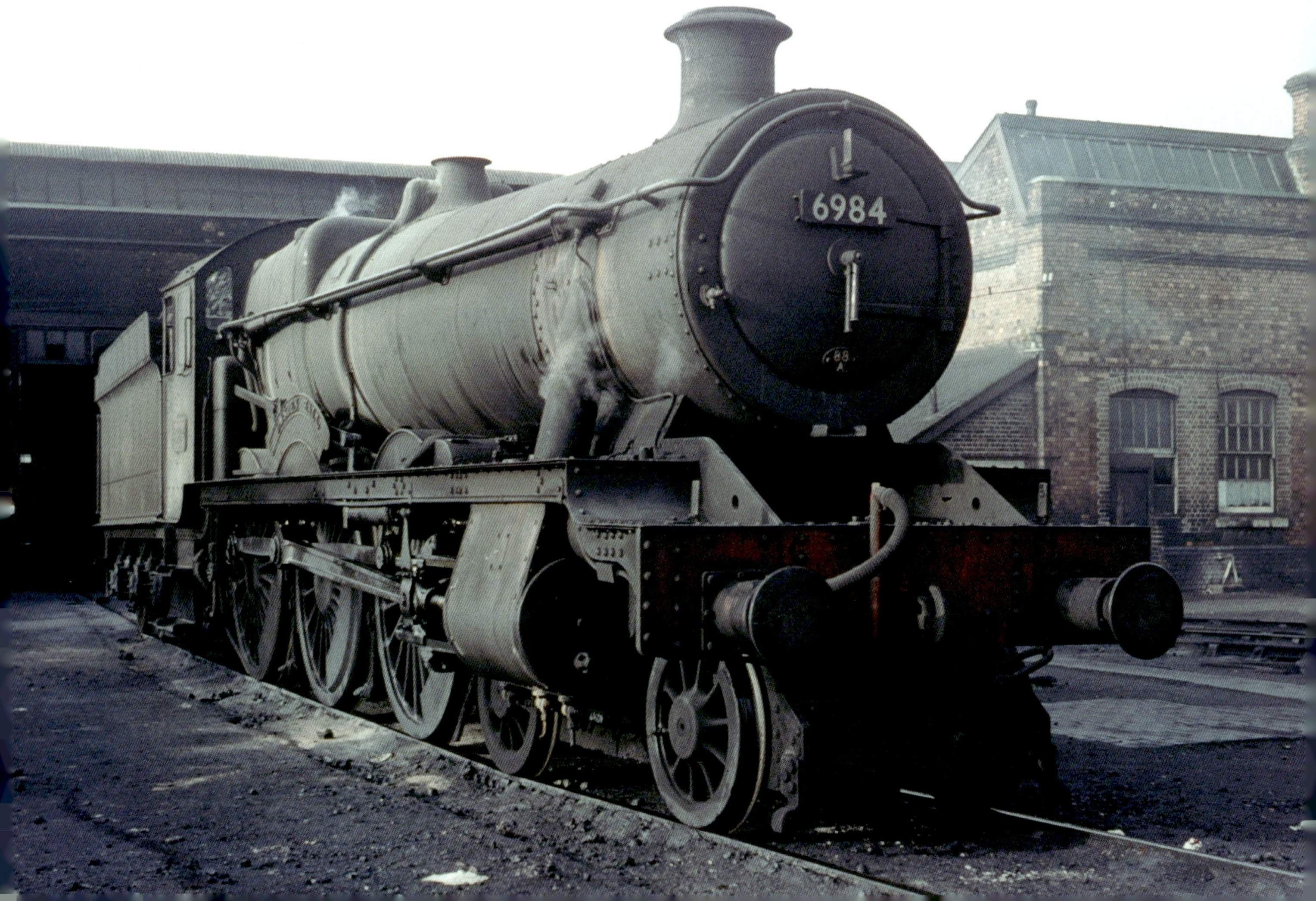

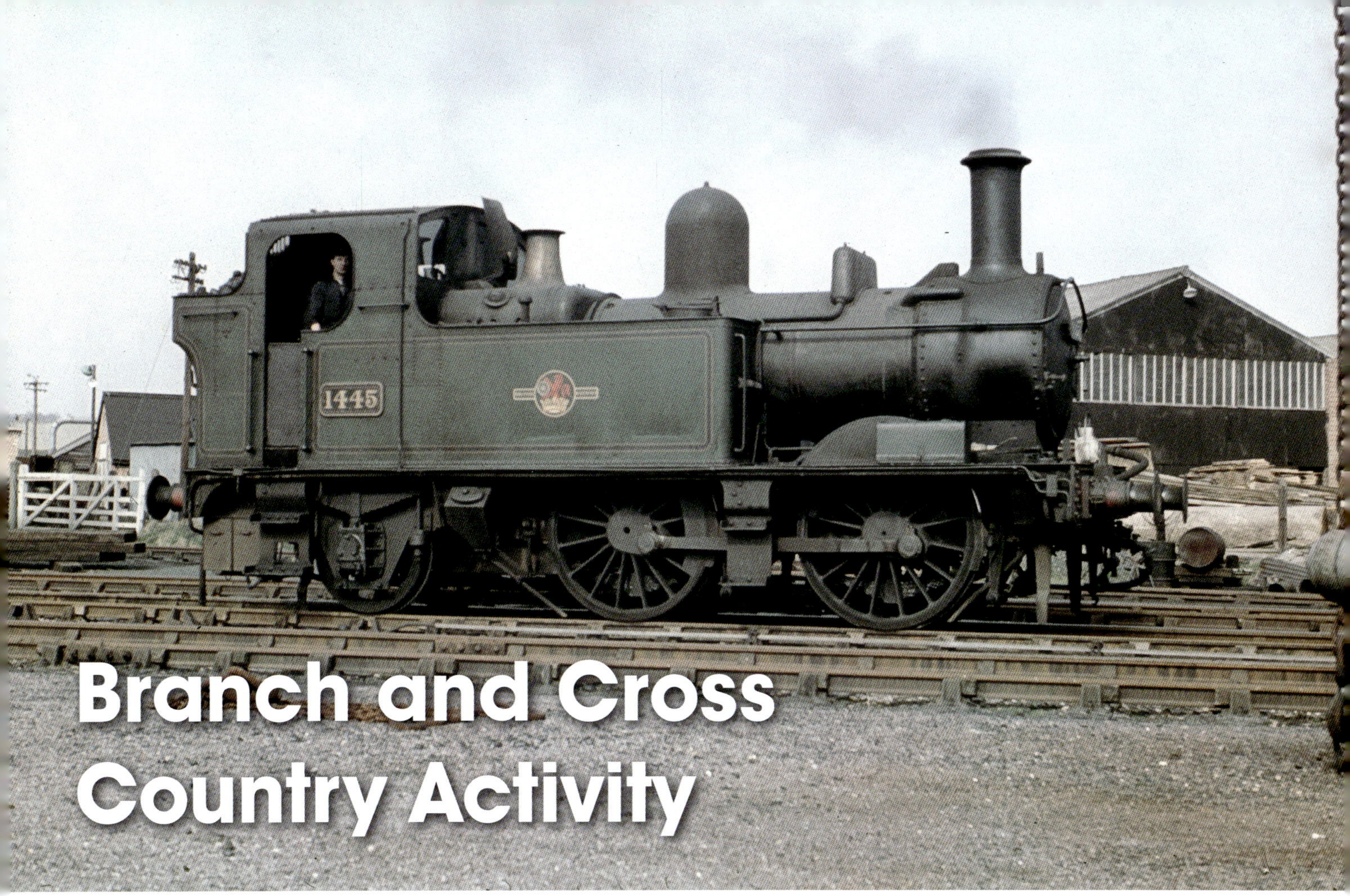

Branch and Cross Country Activity

Seen light engine at Marlow on 25 August 1962 was 1445, which poses a question was it standing in for a failed DMU railcar, as they had taken over the previous month? The meaty looking ball and hook of the goods yard's crane is neatly tethered into the anchor point. ***Strathwood Library Collection***

The 09.34 service from Chard Central to Chard Junction waits to get away behind 7436 in 1960, and appears to be running as a mixed today. ***Strathwood Library Collection***

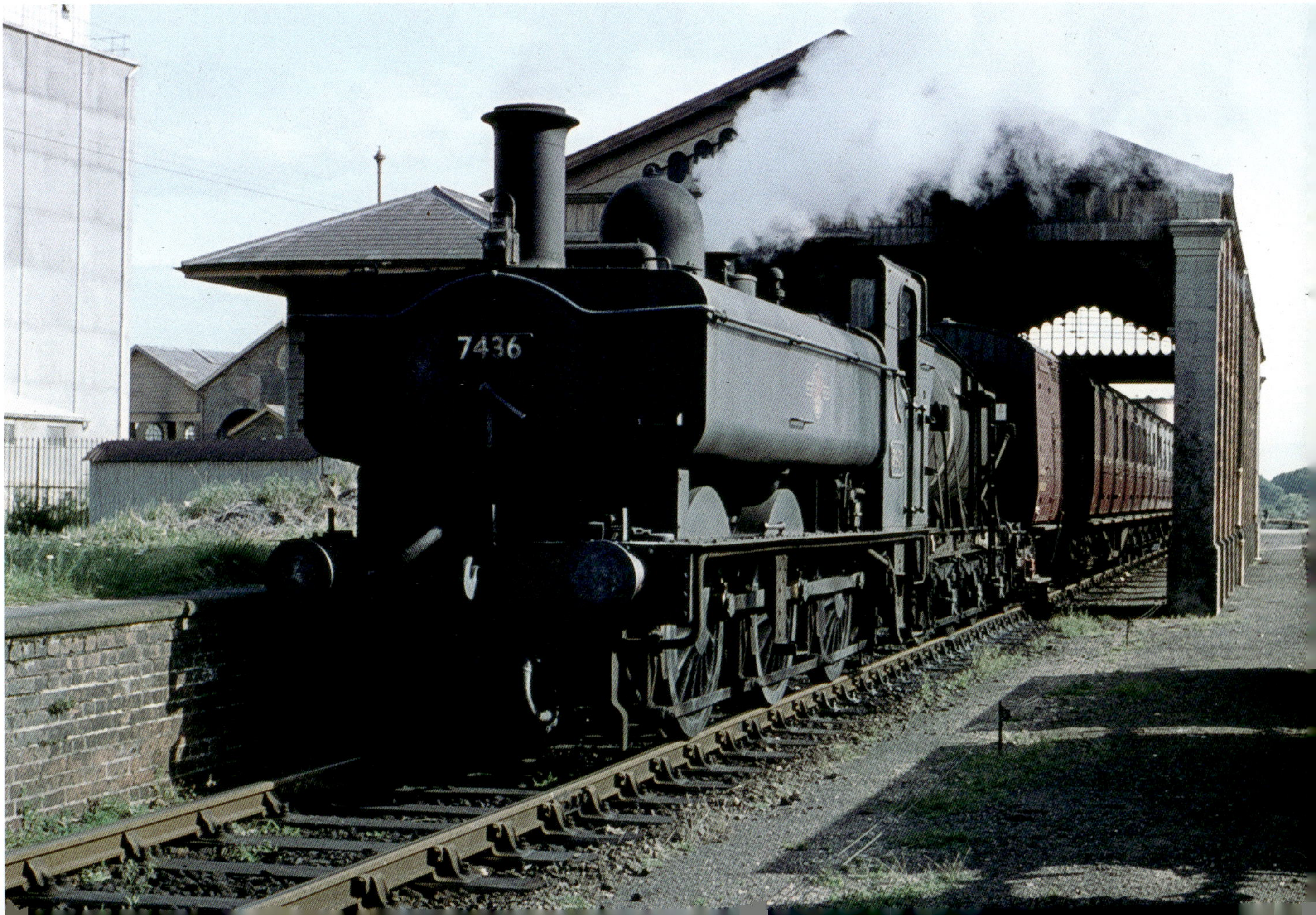

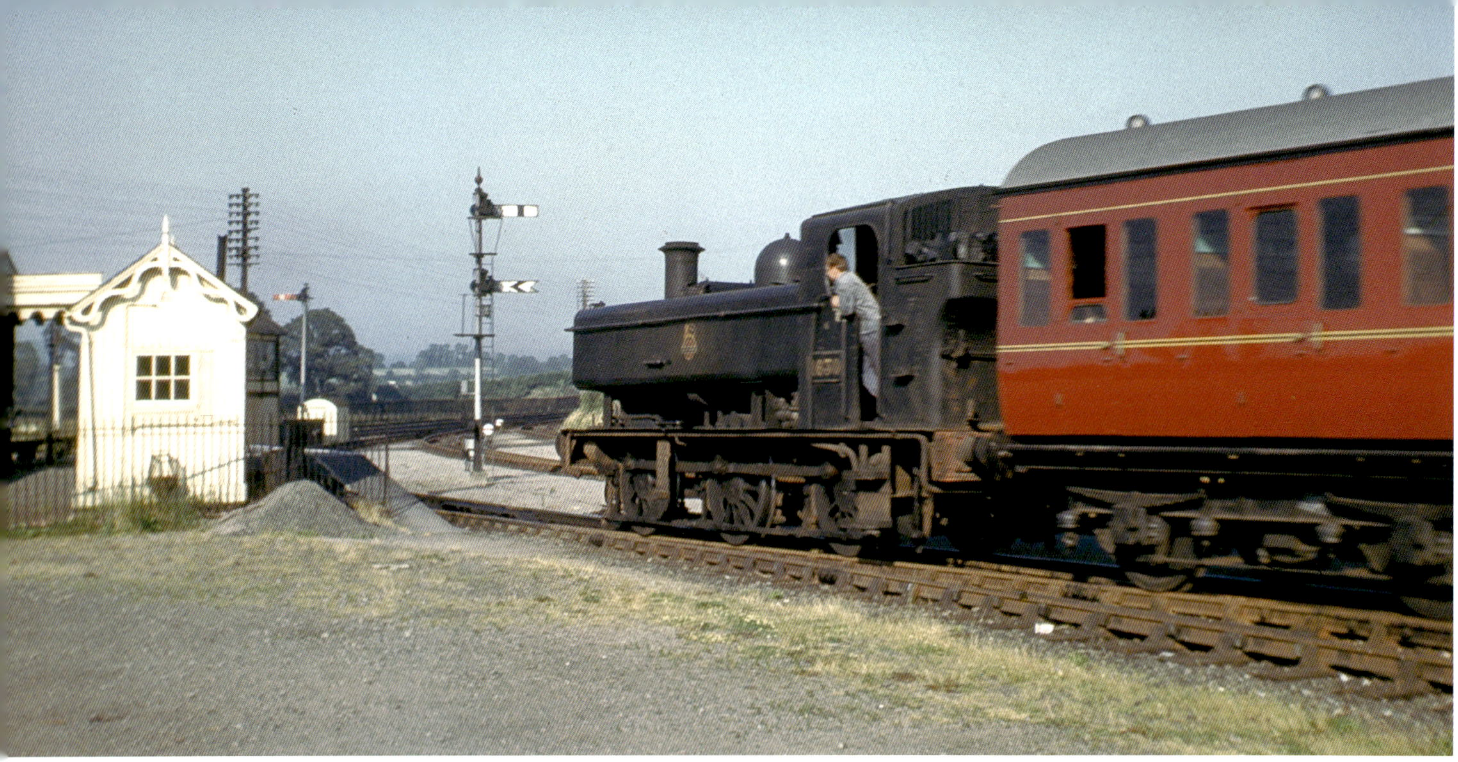

A recently overhauled compartment coach rides behind Hawksworth designed Pannier Tank 1630 at Coaley from Dursley during 1962. ***Gerald Peacock***

Whereas the two Autocoaches coupled behind 1471 arriving at Tiverton with an Exeter to Dulverton train on 22 June 1963 appear less salubrious. ***Peter Simmonds***

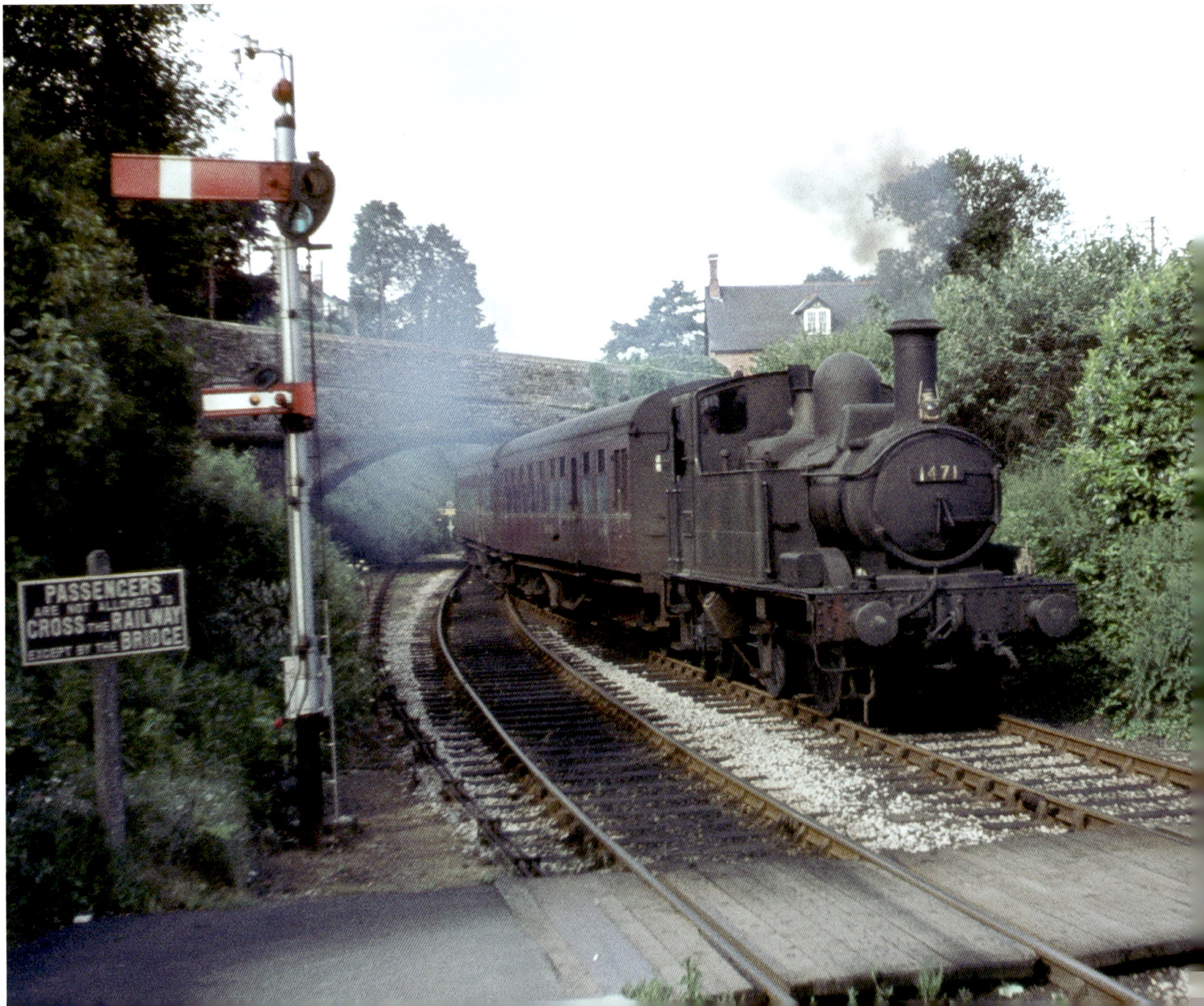

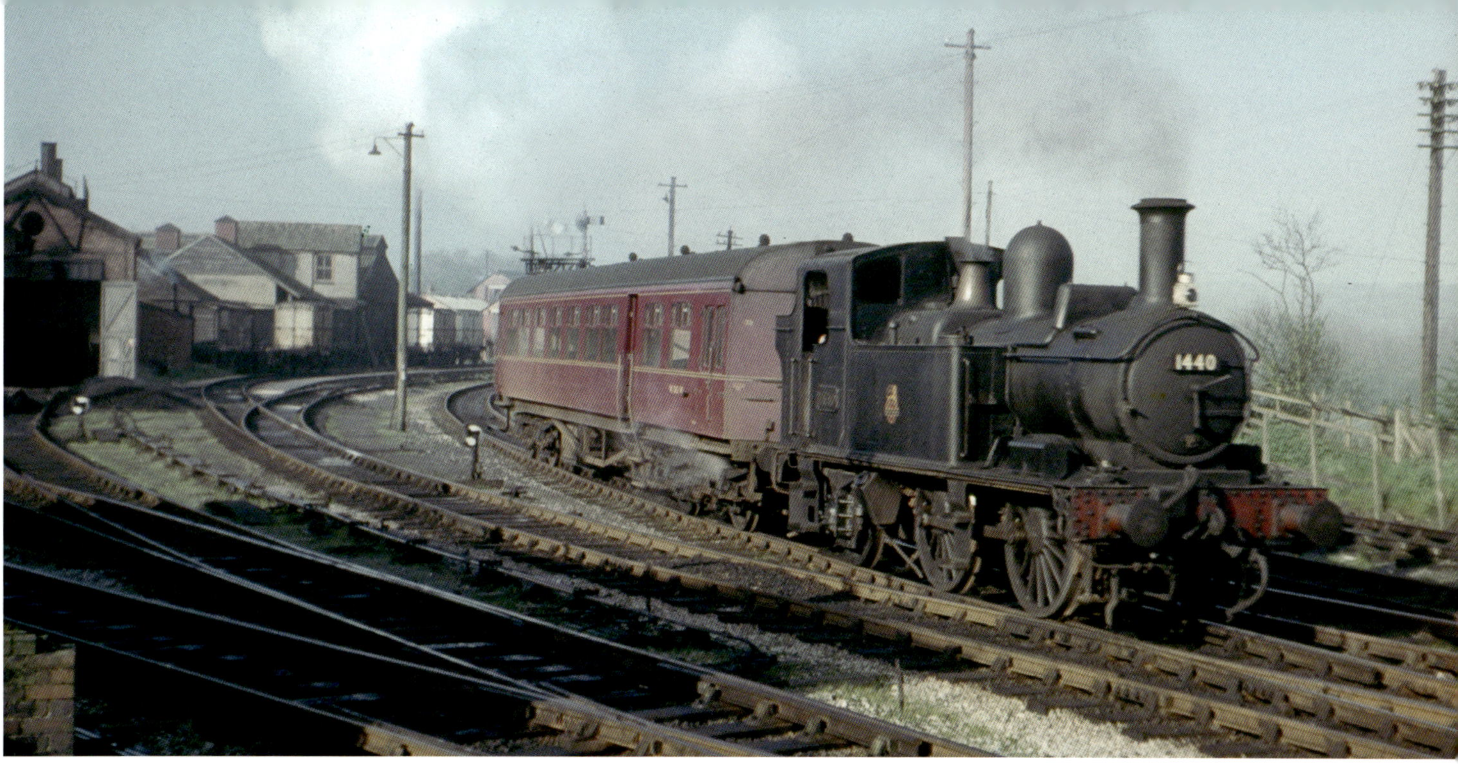

Arriving at Tiverton Junction during April 1961 was just a single Autocoach behind 1440, perhaps the crew can be forgiven for not cleaning this ensemble so thoroughly either as we have just come away from the cold winter months. The Russians had just won the Space Race as Major Yuri Gagarin made a 108 minute flight orbiting the earth at 17,000 miles an hour. The cosmonaut became an international icon but was disappointed to be banned from more space missions because the Soviet state considered him too valuable a propaganda asset to risk his life. In 1968 he was killed in a plane crash just outside Moscow in what some people believed were suspicious circumstances. ***Strathwood Library Collection***

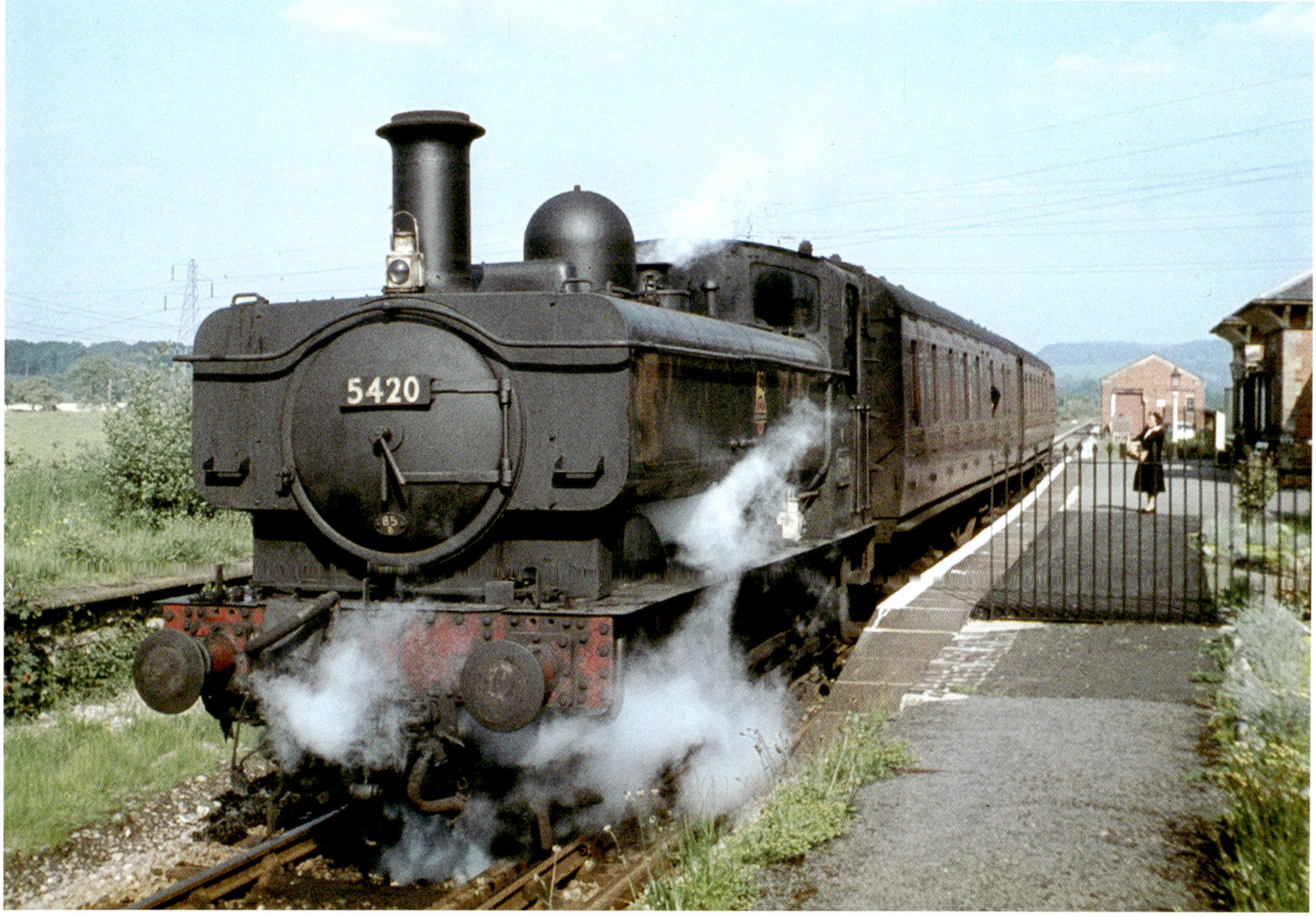

The lined green livery of Collett's auto fitted 5420 shows more pride in the job from the staff around Berkeley Road during 1962. ***Gerald Peacock***

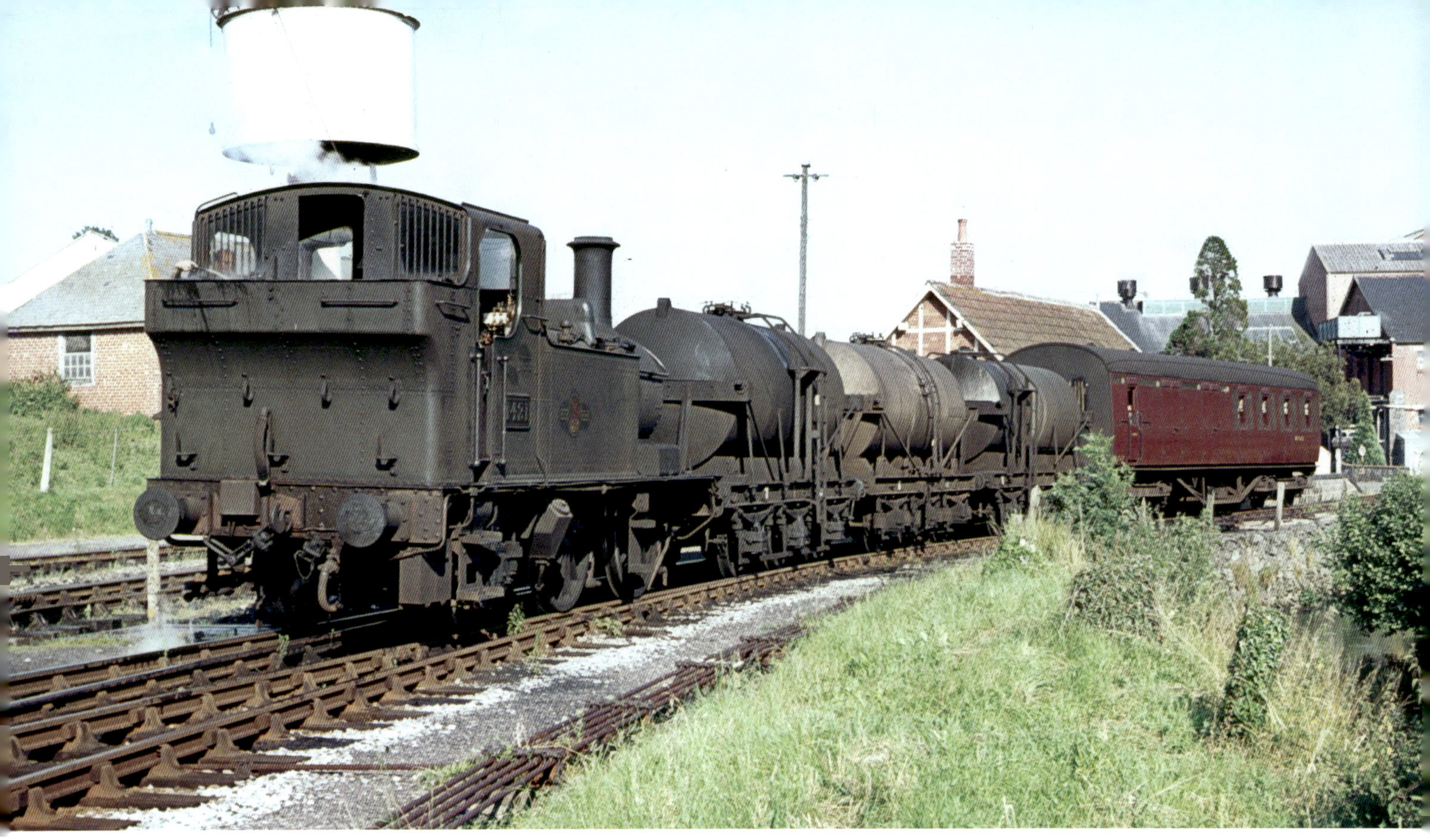

Another mixed working, this time behind 1421 at Hemyock during May 1963 the milk tanks would have been shunted out from the creamery seen in the background. ***Strathwood Library Collection***

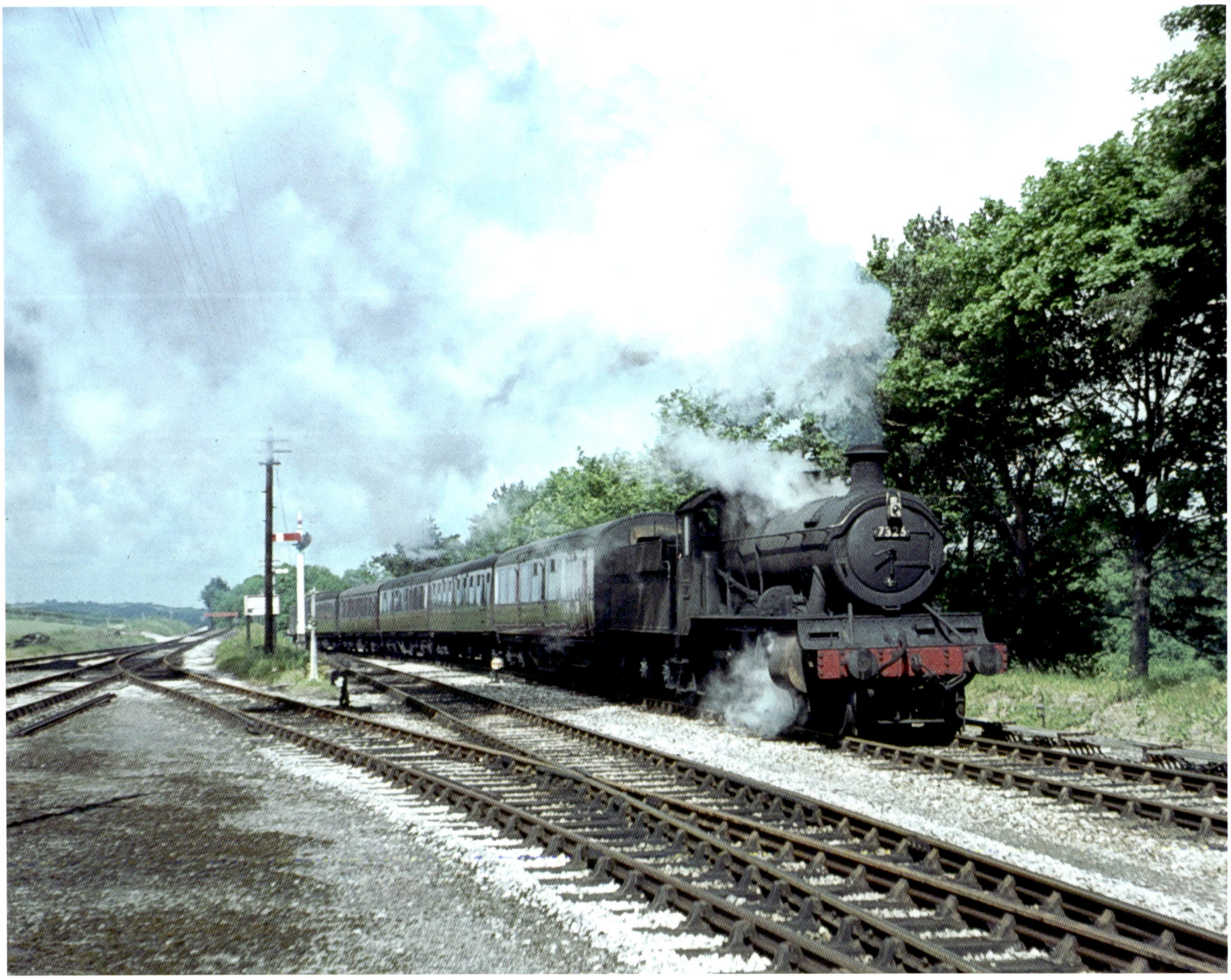

Arriving at East Anstey with a Taunton service on 22 June 1963 was Churchward Mogul 7326. ***Peter Simmonds***

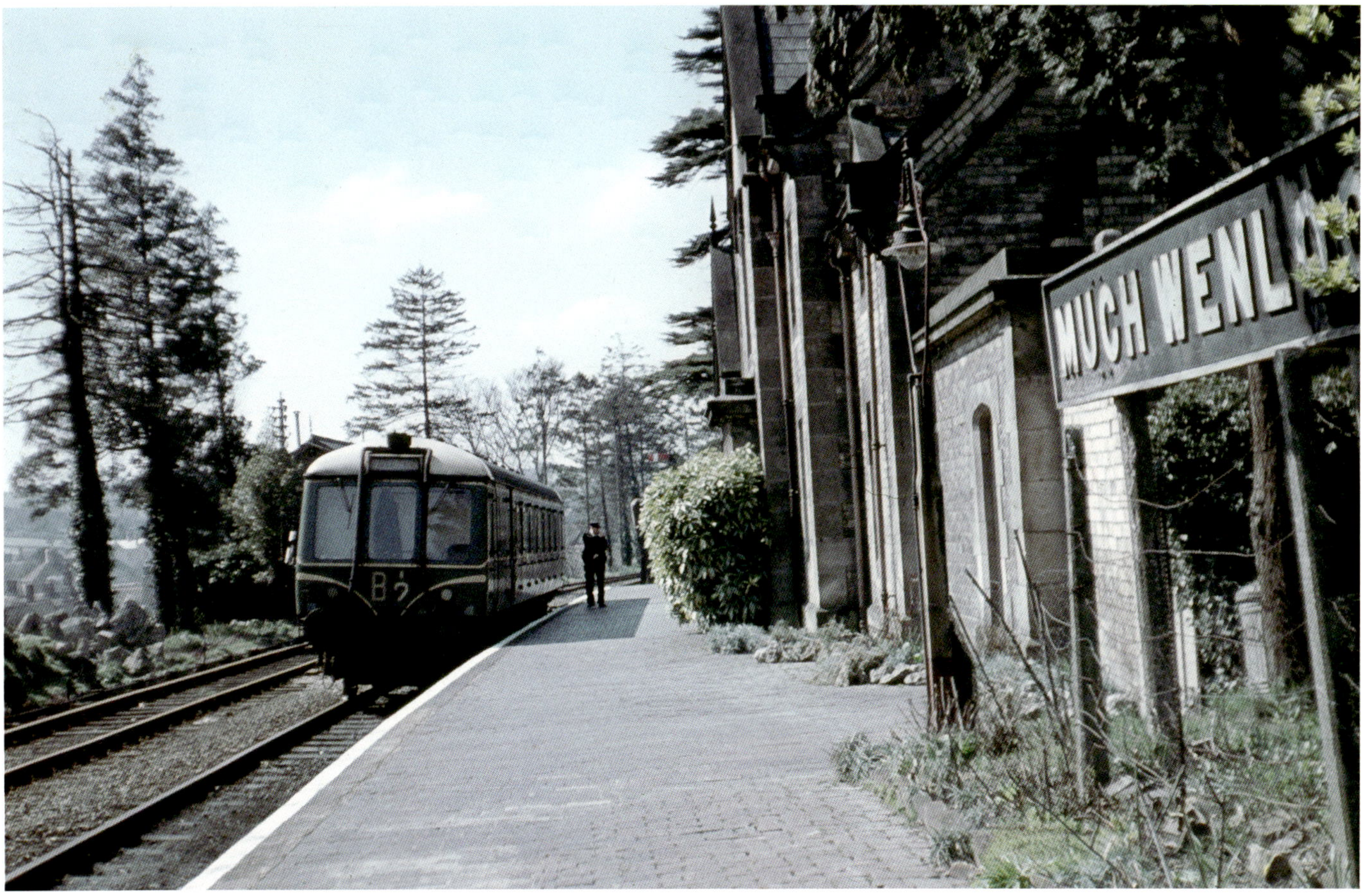

A single car Gloucester Carriage & Wagon Co. built DMU suffices for the last days of passenger services to Much Wenlock when seen on 23 April 1962. ***Richard Icke***

Recently overhauled A.C. Cars built railbus W79977 is put back to work at Kemble on 28 March 1964 with a service for Cirencester Town. ***Frank Hornby***

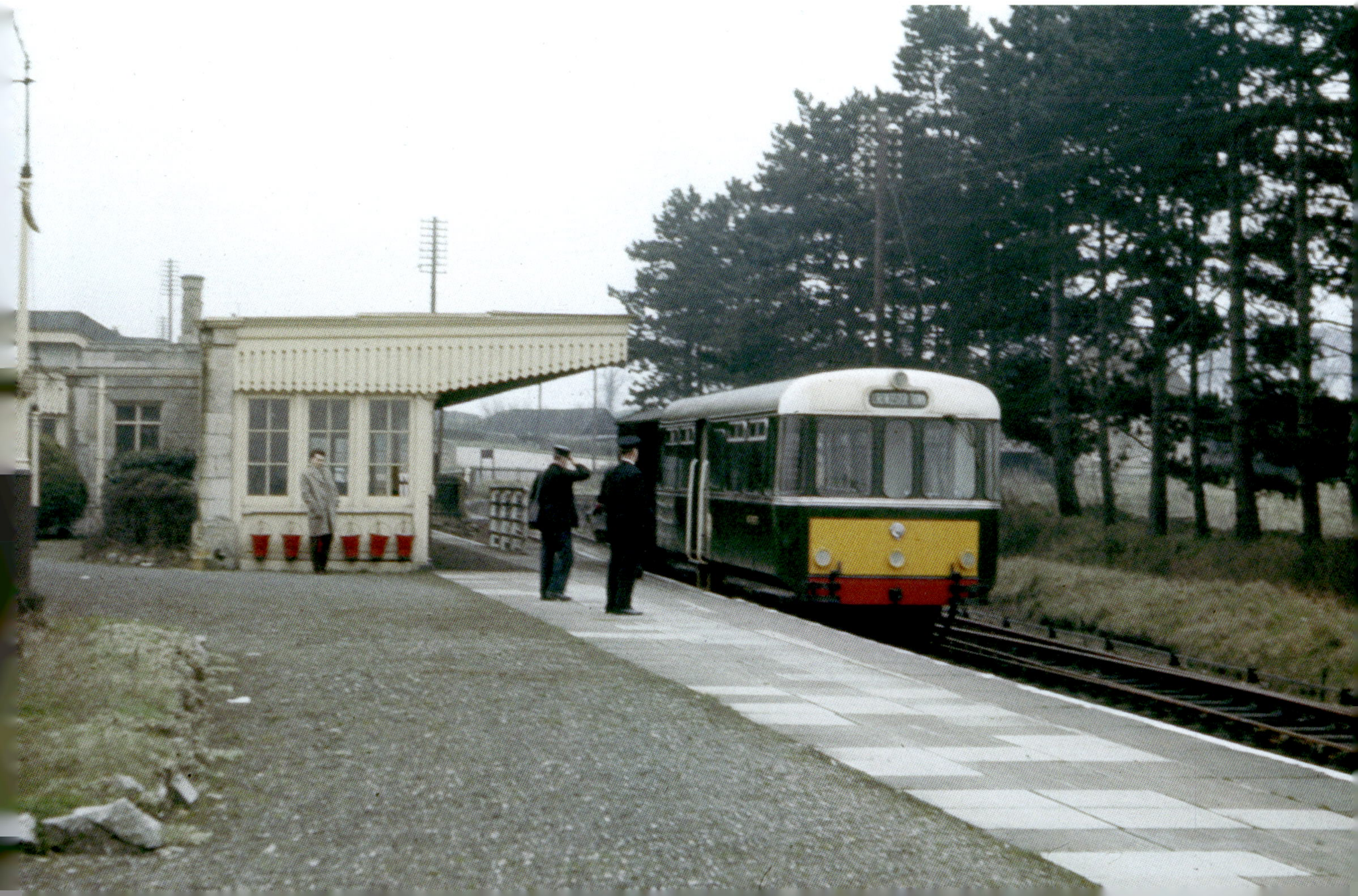

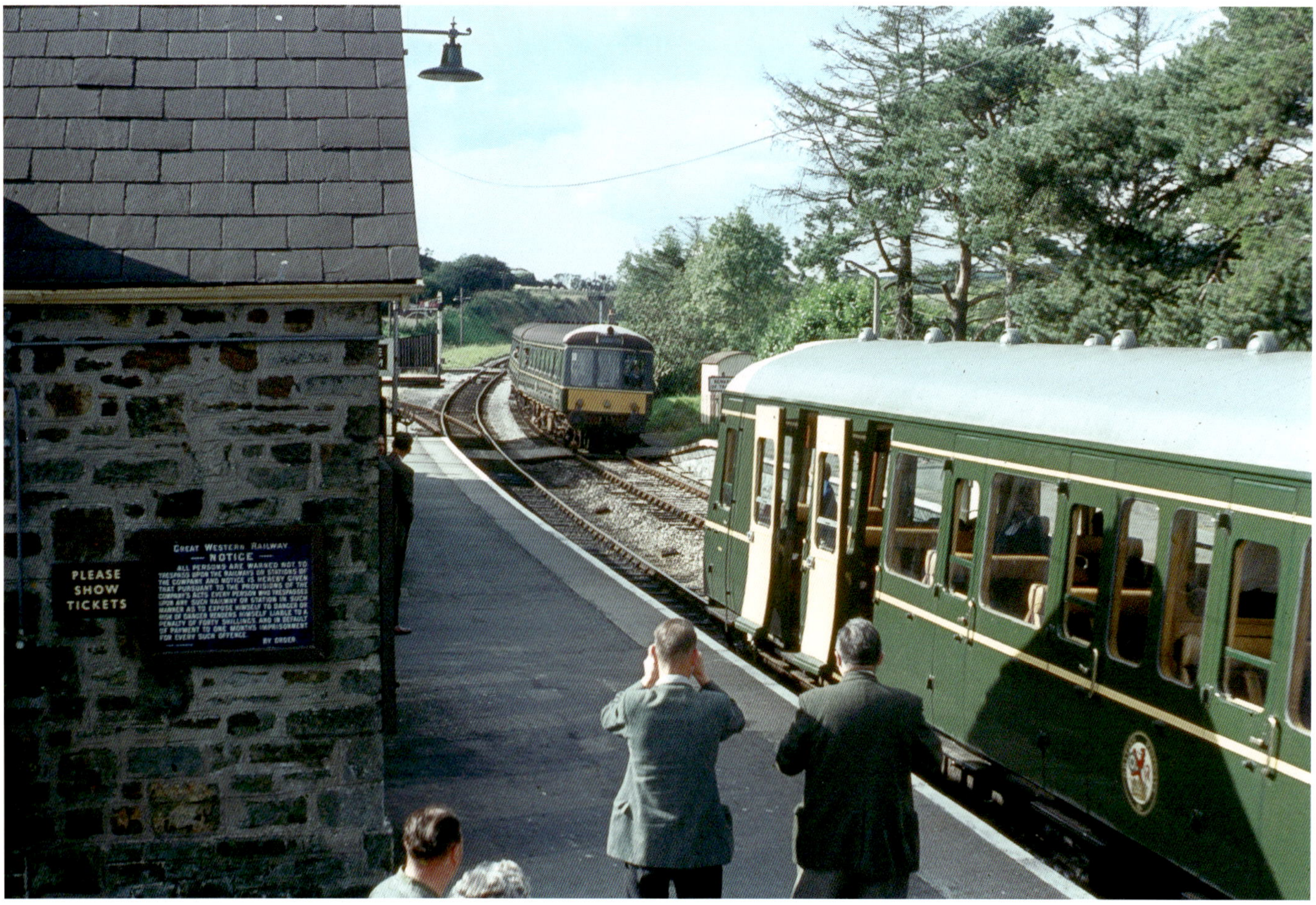

The last days at South Molton on 17 September 1966 with the chance for enthusiasts to disembark from their chartered DMU special as a Taunton DMU hauled service train comes off the single line. ***Strathwood Library Collection***

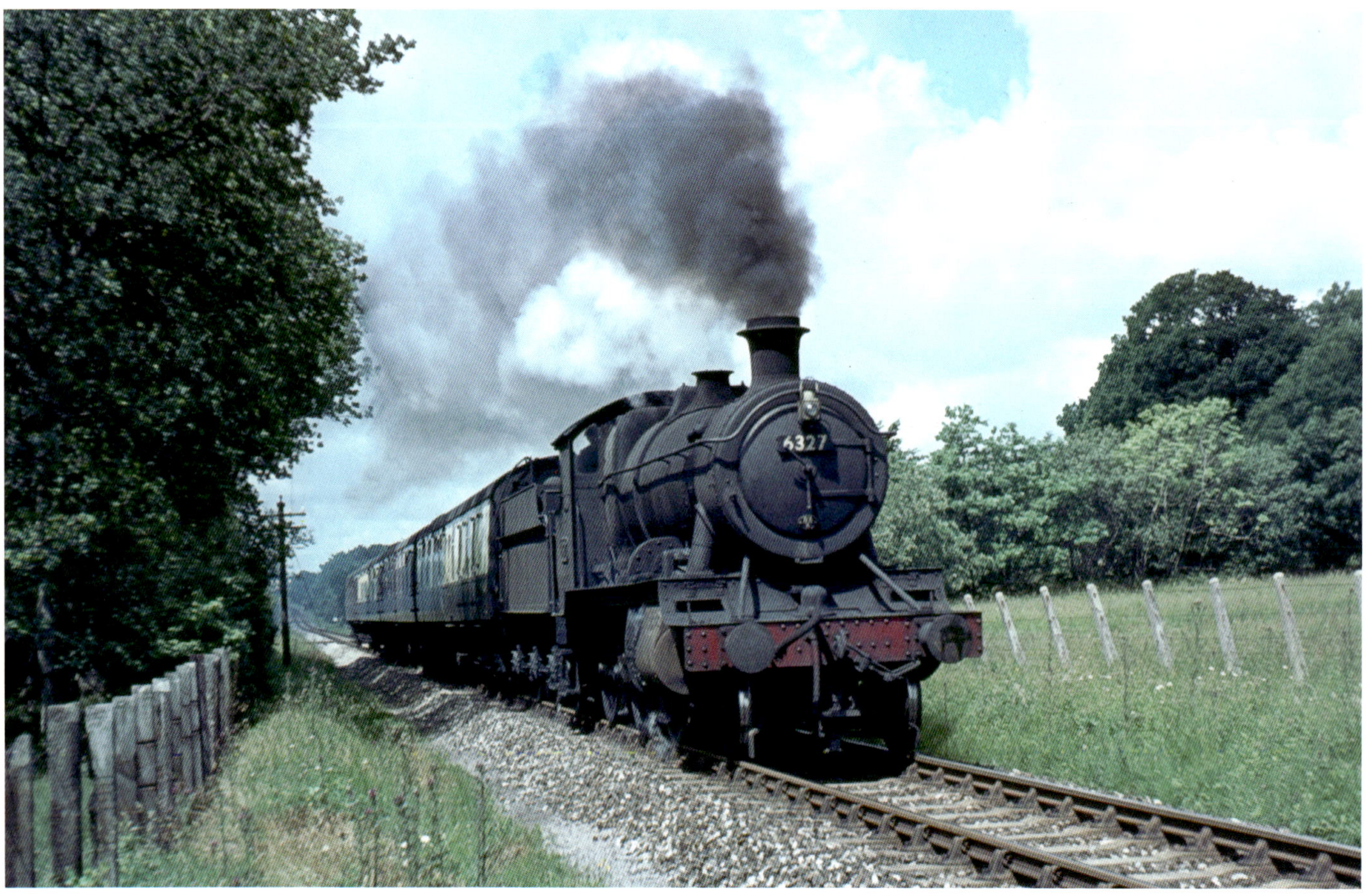

Three years before and Churchward Moguls were the route's regulars with 6327 nearing South Molton with another Taunton service on 22 June 1963. ***Peter Simmonds***

Oxfordshire Memories

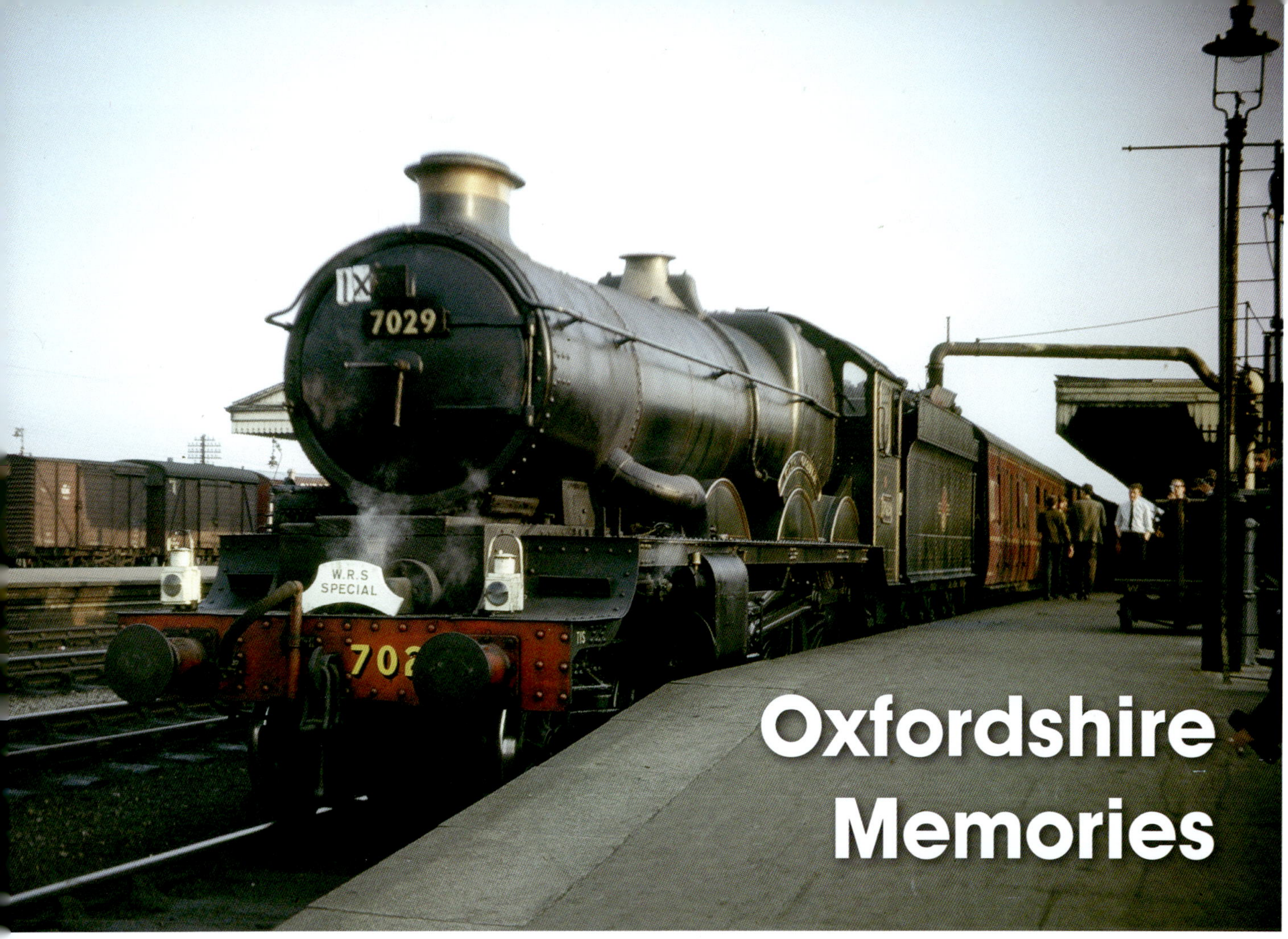

On 3 April 1965 the Warwickshire Railway Society ran their special from Birmingham Snow Hill to Swindon Works behind 7029 Clun Castle which was stopped for water at Oxford on the return journey. ***Edward Dorricott***

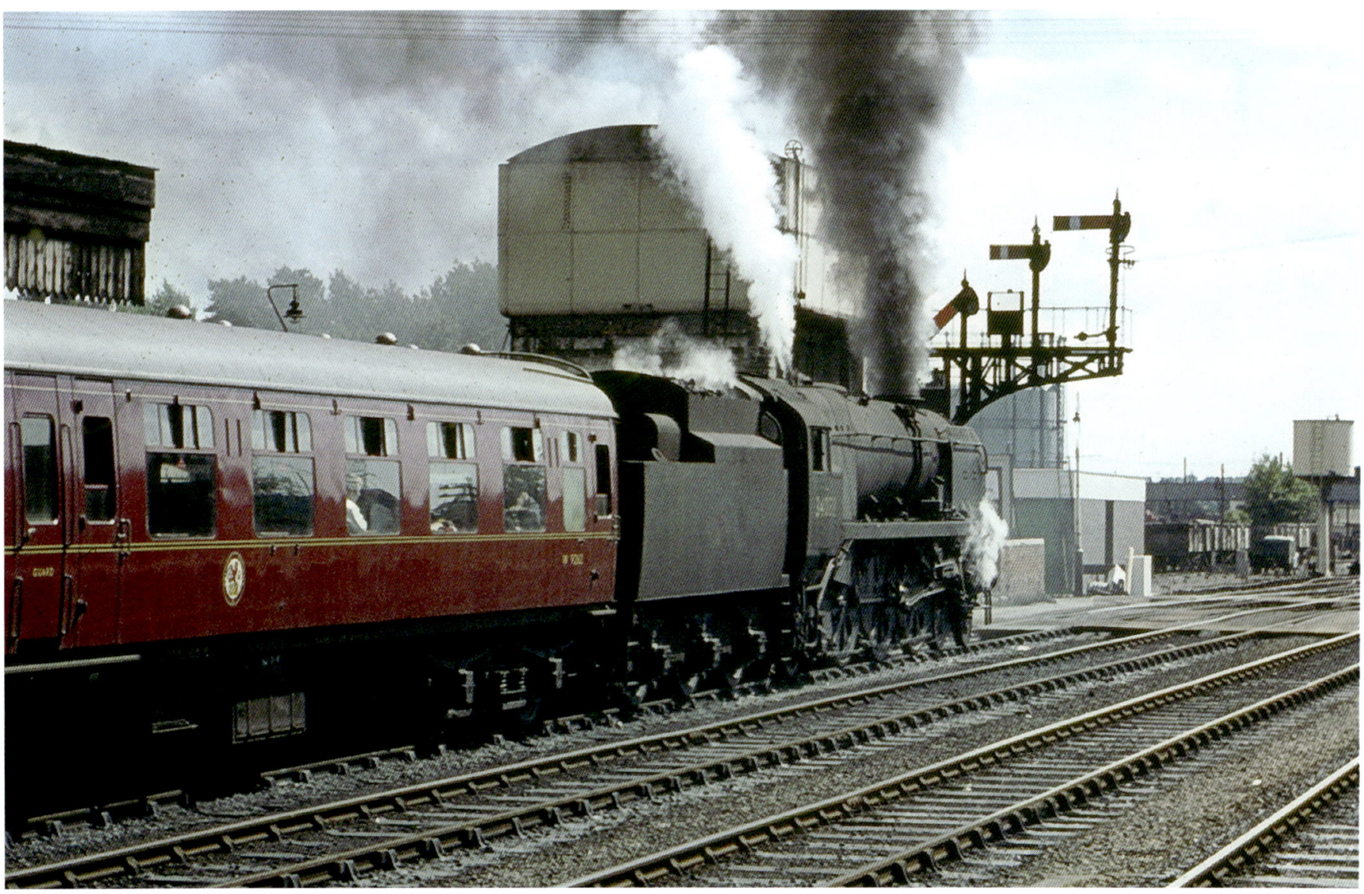

Devoid of its 213 Squadron nameplates rebuilt Battle of Britain 34088 has been signalled away from Oxford with the up Pines express on 7 August 1965. ***Strathwood Library Collection***

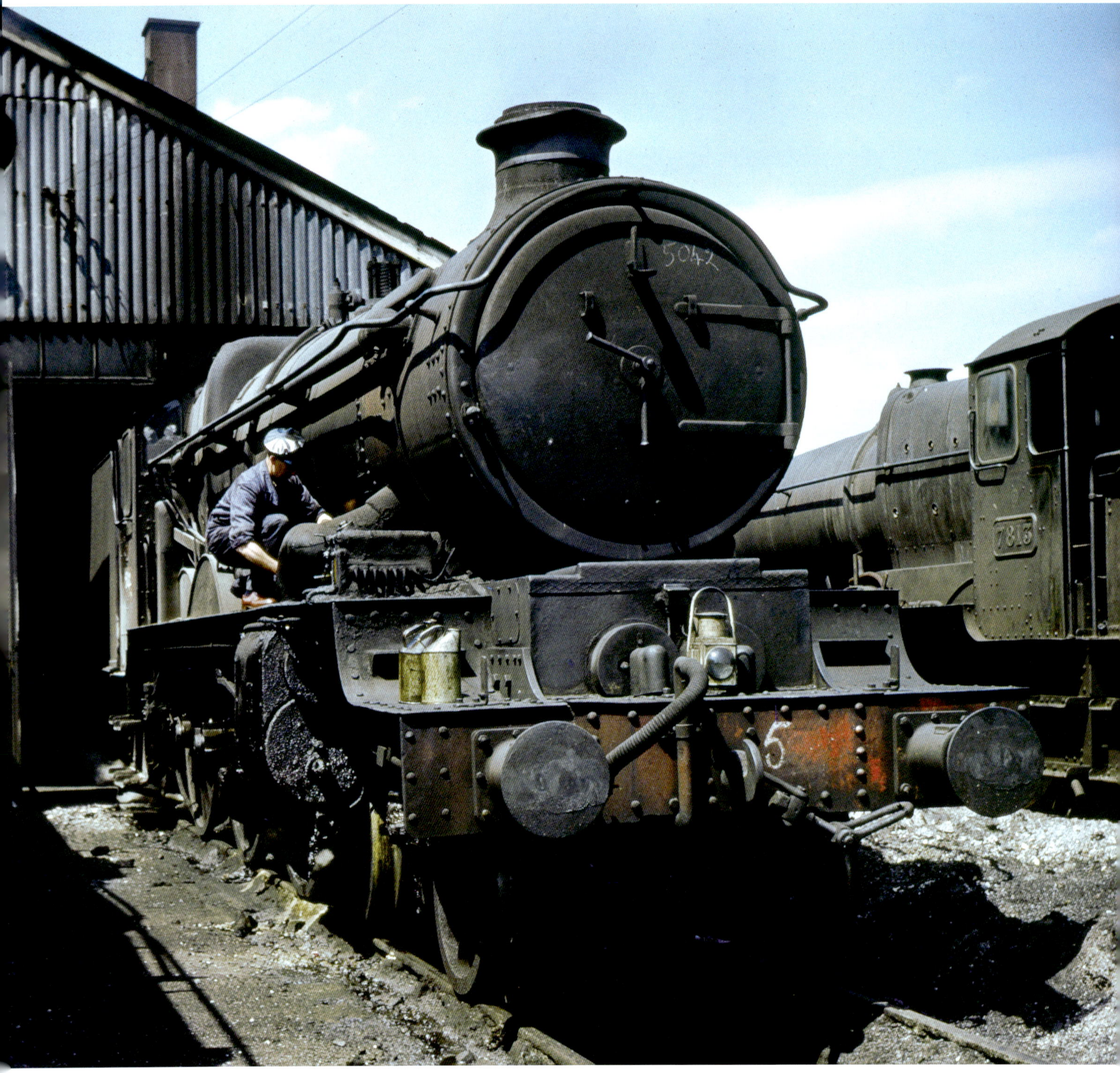

Much of the dignity has been stripped from the once splendid 5042 Winchester Castle by the early summer of 1965 as her driver sets about preparation duties in the sunshine at Didcot. Coded as 81E the shed here was officially closed on 14 June 1965 and then saw use as a stabling point where Hymeks and shunters could often be found. In 1967 the Great Western Society took on a long term lease of the site, progressively developing their collection of locomotives as funds allowed. Always popular with enthusiasts were the open days which in the late sixties and early seventies also drew British Rail diesels as exhibits as well for the many visitors. ***Bob Treacher/Alton Model Centre***

Snow has fallen across the Chilterns in February 1963 which has brought our cameraman out in the winter sunshine to record 7813 Freshford Manor on a goods working at Saunderton. From the start of the year the pop charts were dominated by The Shadows or their former members. Starting the year at Number 1 was the double A side The Next Time and Bachelor Boy with three weeks at the top spot for Cliff Richard and the Shadows, toppled by The Shadows own hit Dance On for one week. Then three weeks followed as former Shadows Jet Harris and Tony Meehan outsold everyone else with their single Diamonds. With Foot Tapper and Summer Holiday also at Number 1 before mid April it was a golden time for their music. ***Both John Newman***

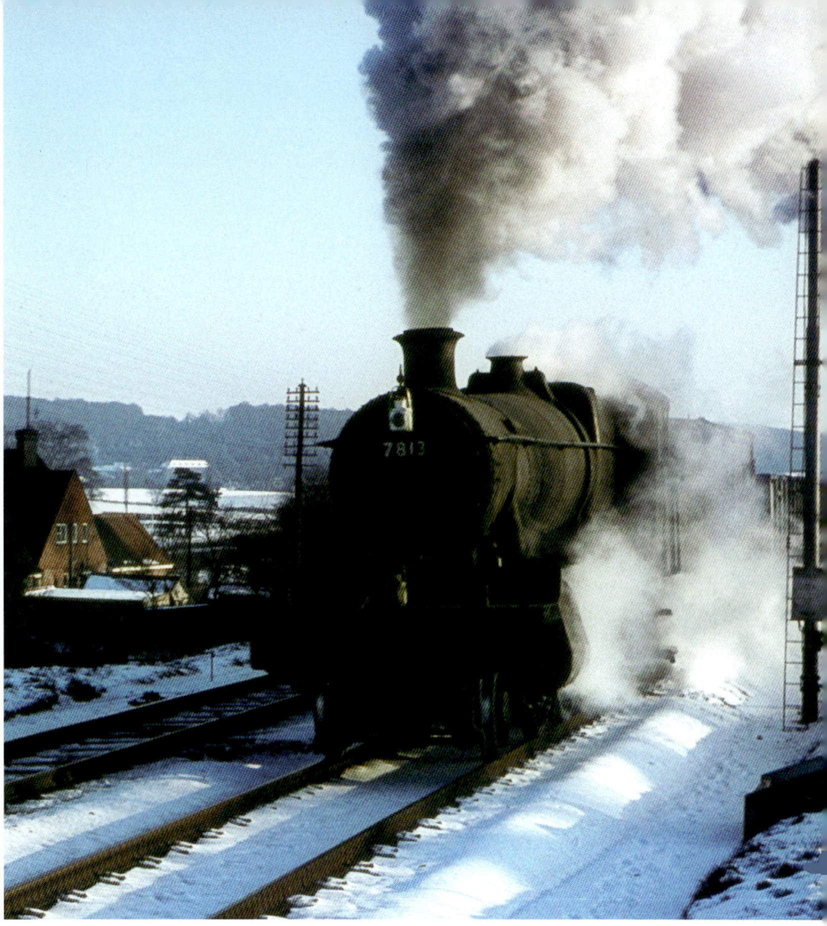

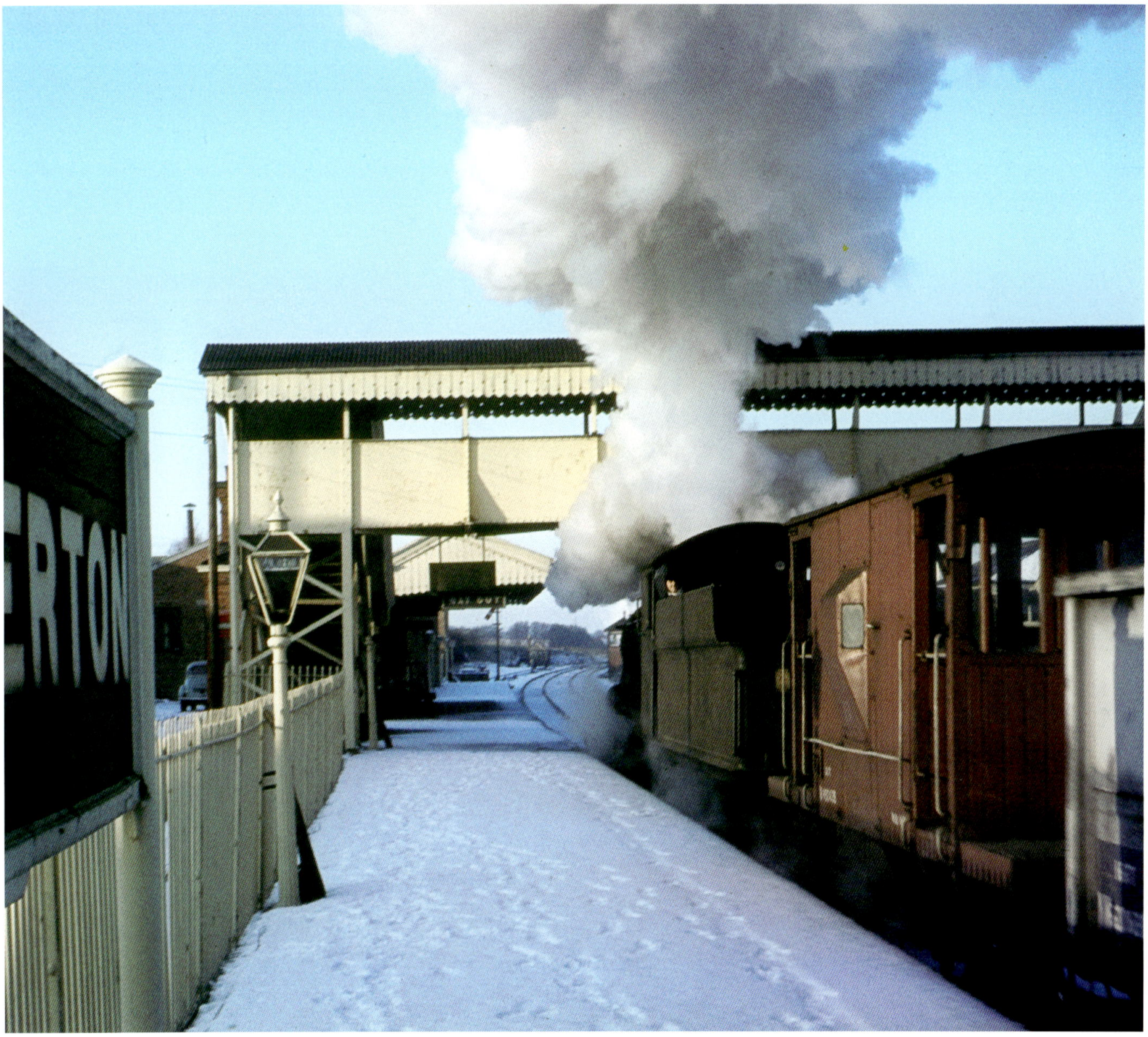

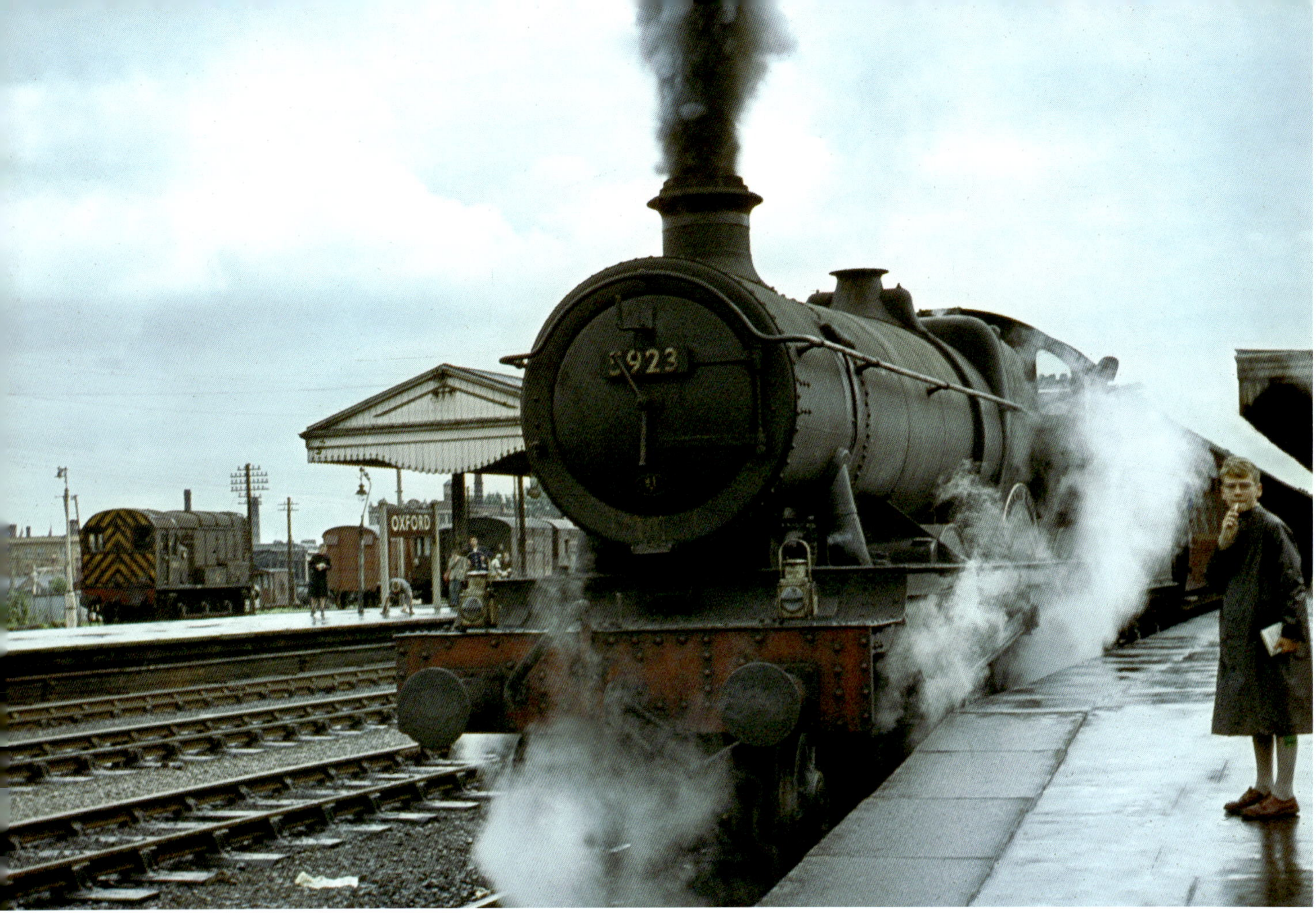

It is rain that greets this visit to the platform ends at Oxford in 1963 with 5923 Colston Hall ready for the off. ***John Newman***

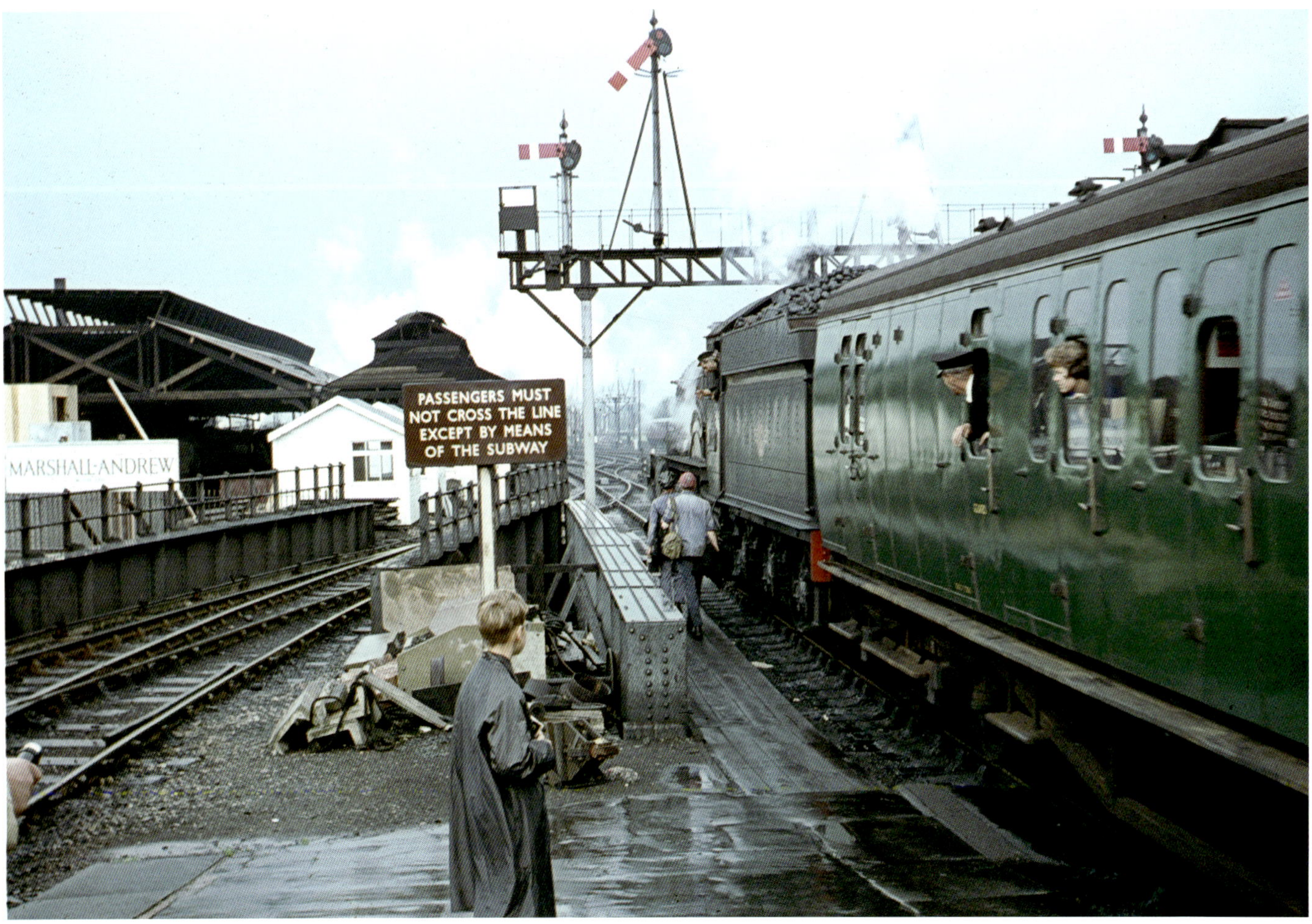

The same day sees an unknown Castle head northwards with an inter regional train from the Southern Region as a engine crew make their way towards the shed at Oxford. ***John Newman***

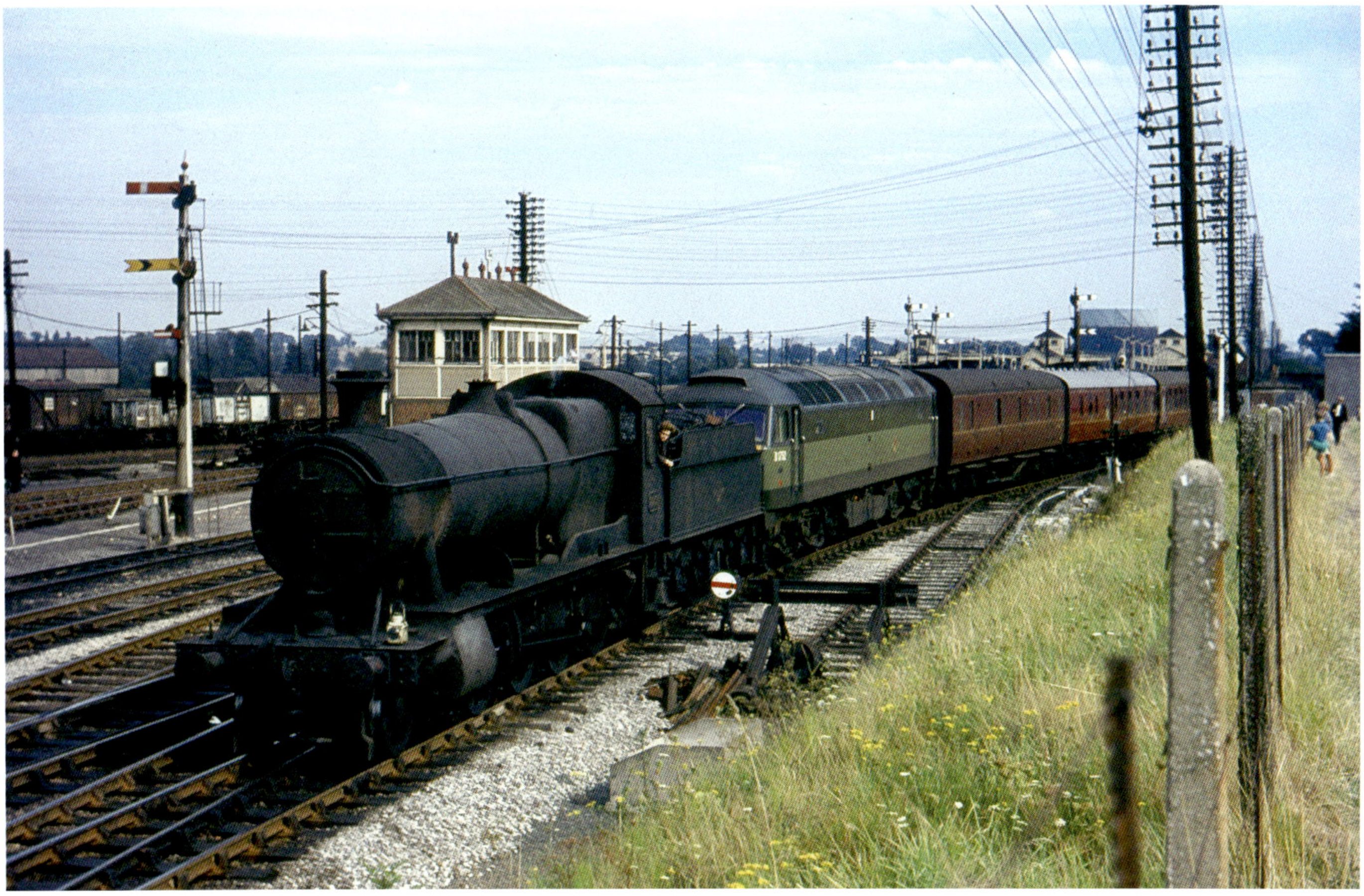

Several young spotters are on hand by the fence at Didcot to see one of the modified 2800 Class 2-8-0s 3859 hastily removed from a freight to pilot a failed D1752 onwards towards Bristol in August 1964. One wonders how the large goods engine got on with some express timings? ***Strathwood Library Collection***

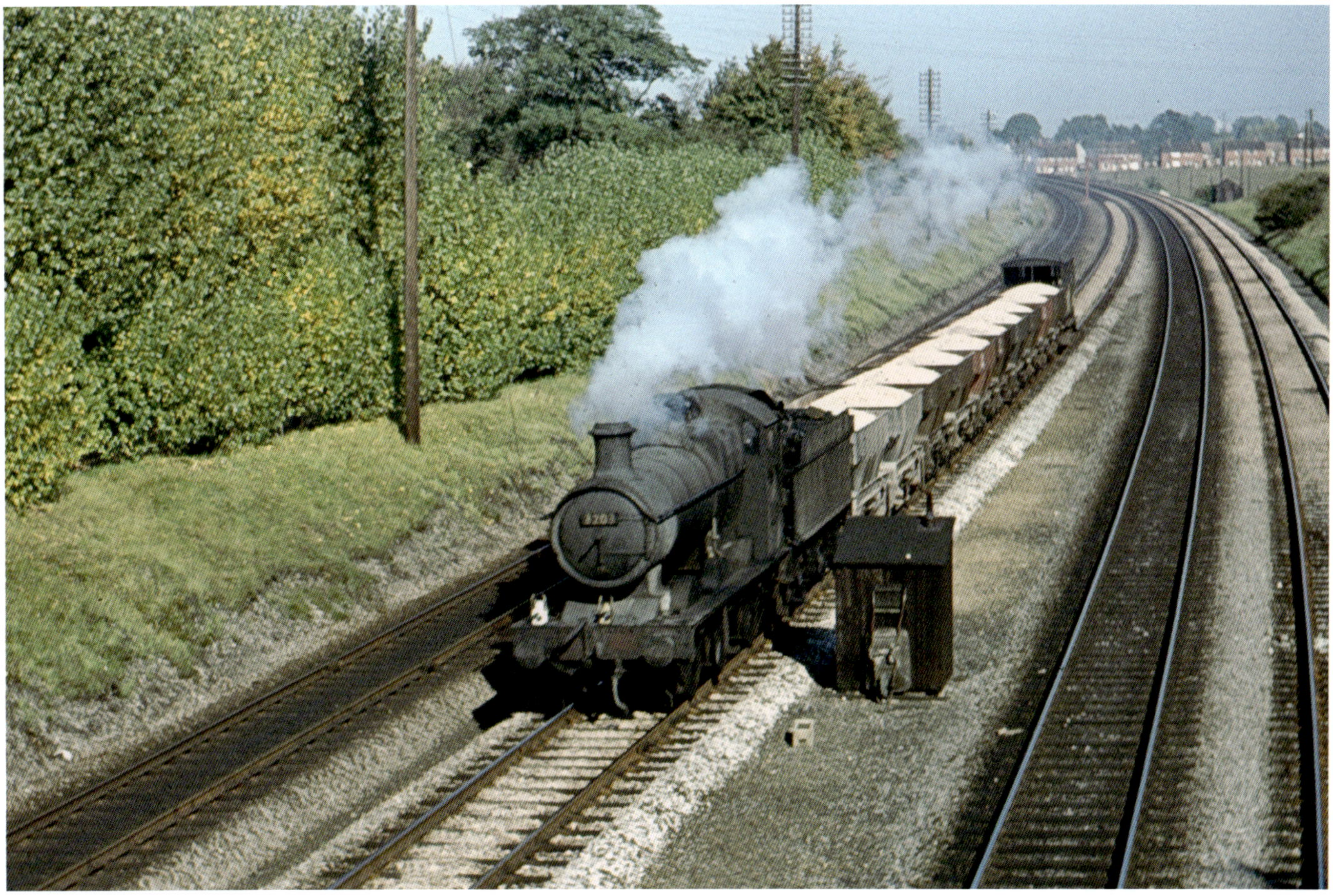

A fresh load of ballast is being brought smartly along behind Collett 0-6-0 3203 near Goring on 12 October 1963. ***John Newman***

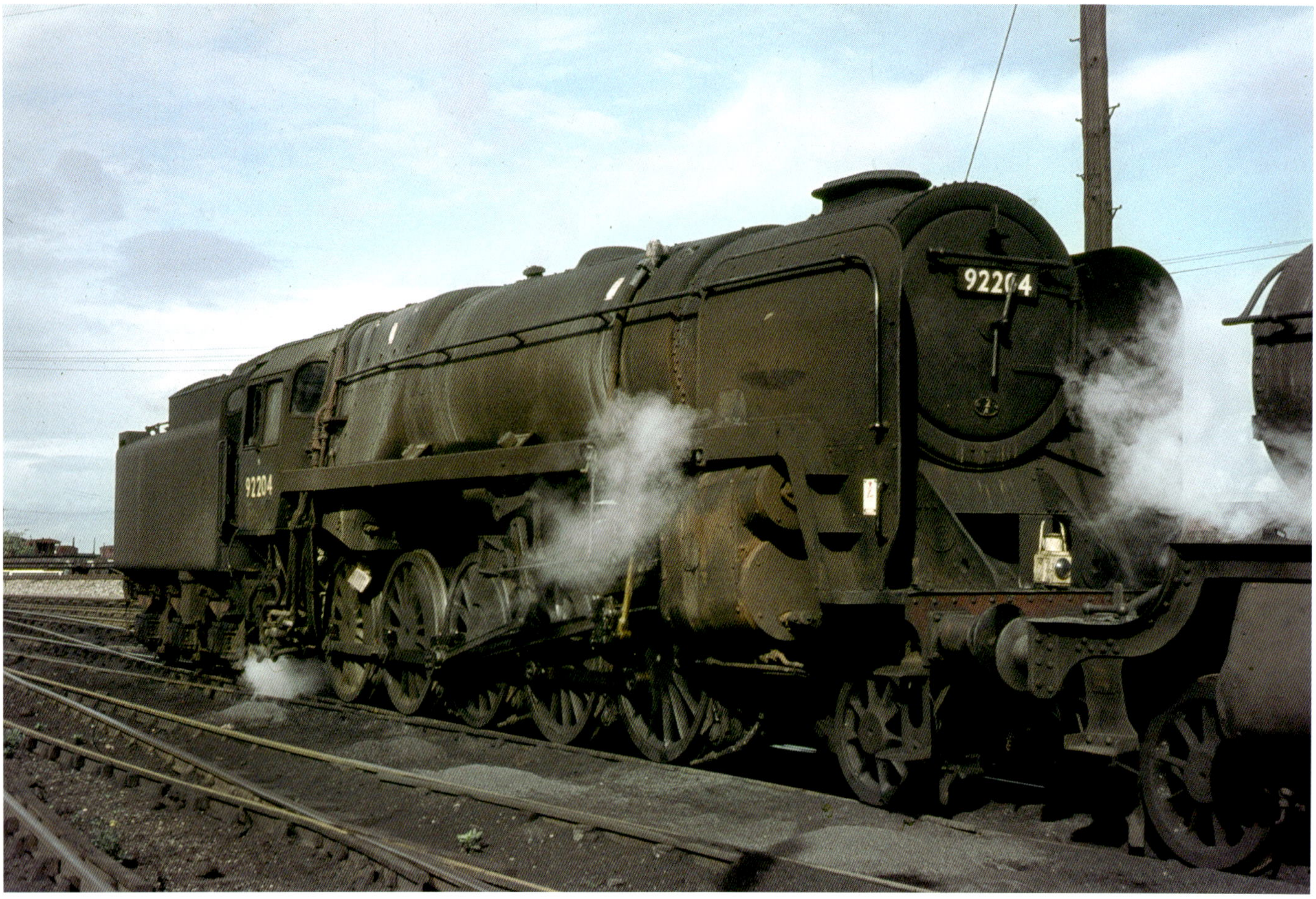

Packing considerably more punch would be Standard 9F 92204 standing in the shed yard at Oxford in typical workaday condition during 1965 among the steam survivors. ***Bob Treacher/Alton Model Centre***

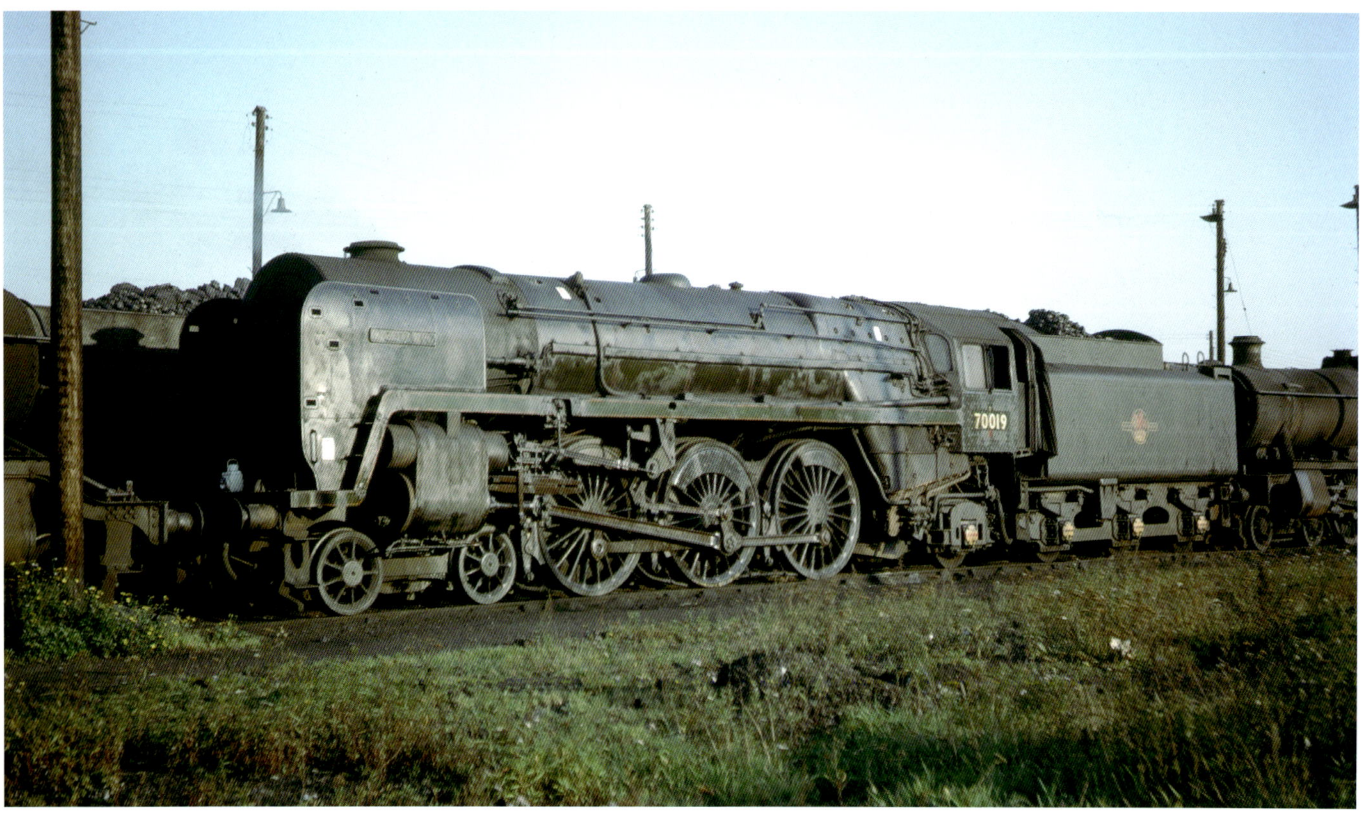

A modest attempt by the cleaners to restore some shine to Britannia 70019 Lightning on 12 October 1963 among the lines of more traditional but shabbily presented Western Region types at Oxford. ***Stewart Blencowe Collection***

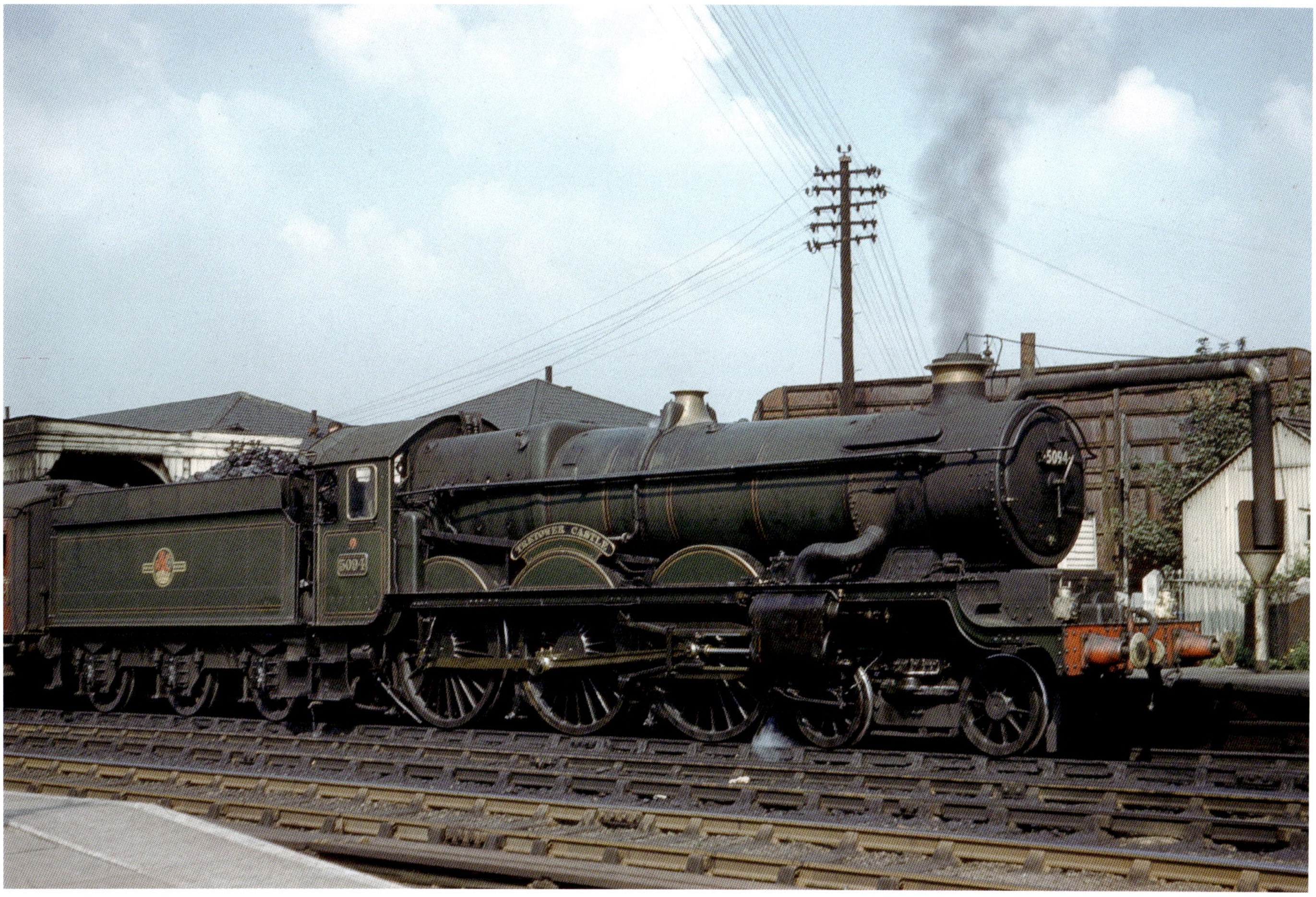

The scene early in 1960 at Oxford was one of the former Great Western Railway's pride in the shape of a clean 5094 Tretower Castle. ***Frank Hornby***

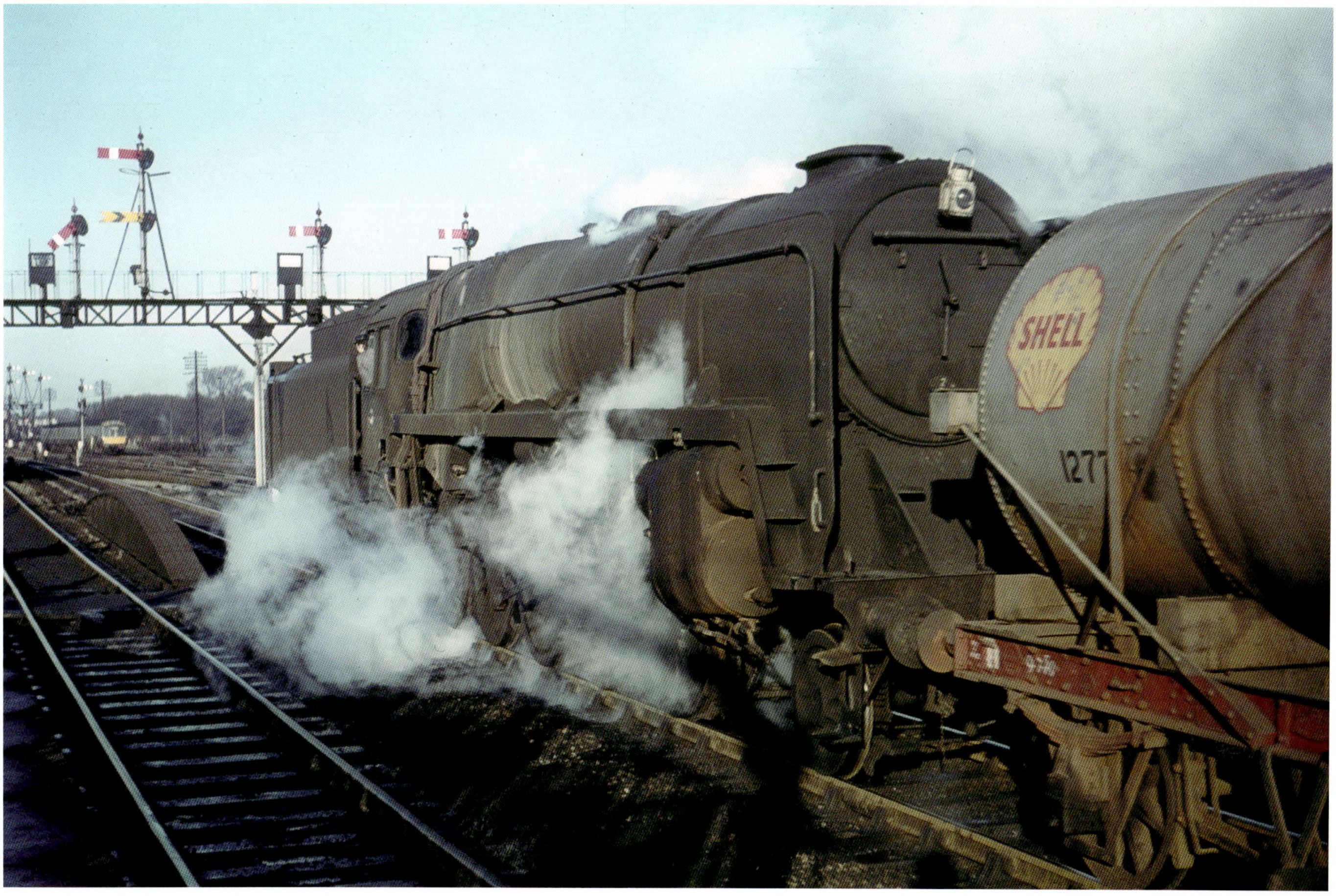

By 30 December 1965 the DMU in the background is clearly a better enticement to passengers than a run down looking Standard 9F 92218 working tender first through Oxford. ***Strathwood Library Collection***

London Sheds

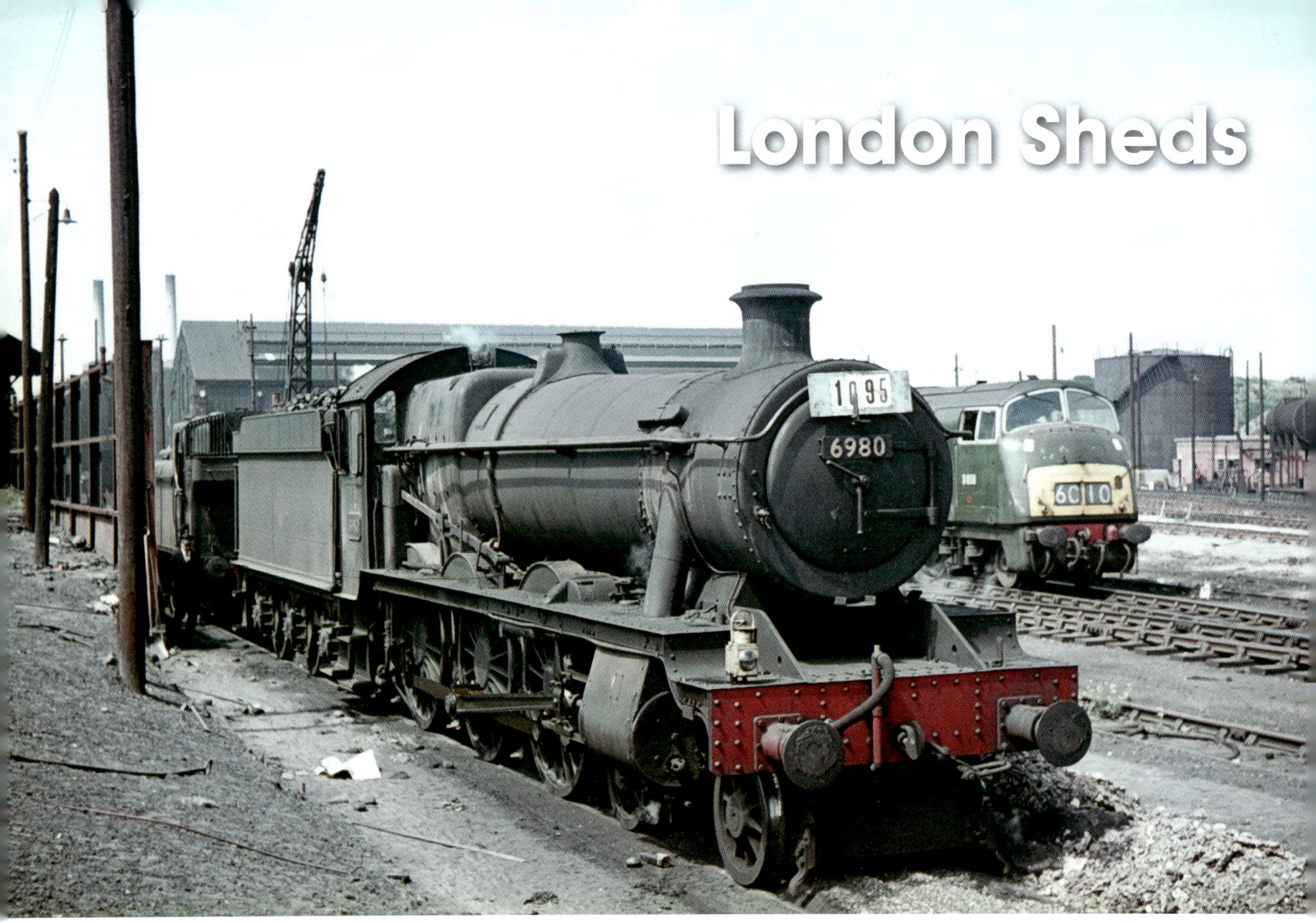

Old Oak Common was being made ready for the servicing of the diesel fleet by the beginning of August 1964, standards of cleanliness around the shed had fallen as witnessed while Modified Hall 6980 Llanrumney Hall keeps company with a condensing Pannier and a Warship. ***Peter Coton***

Alongside the improved office block at Old Oak Common in 1962 was a much smarter 5932 Haydon Hall. ***Strathwood Library Collection***

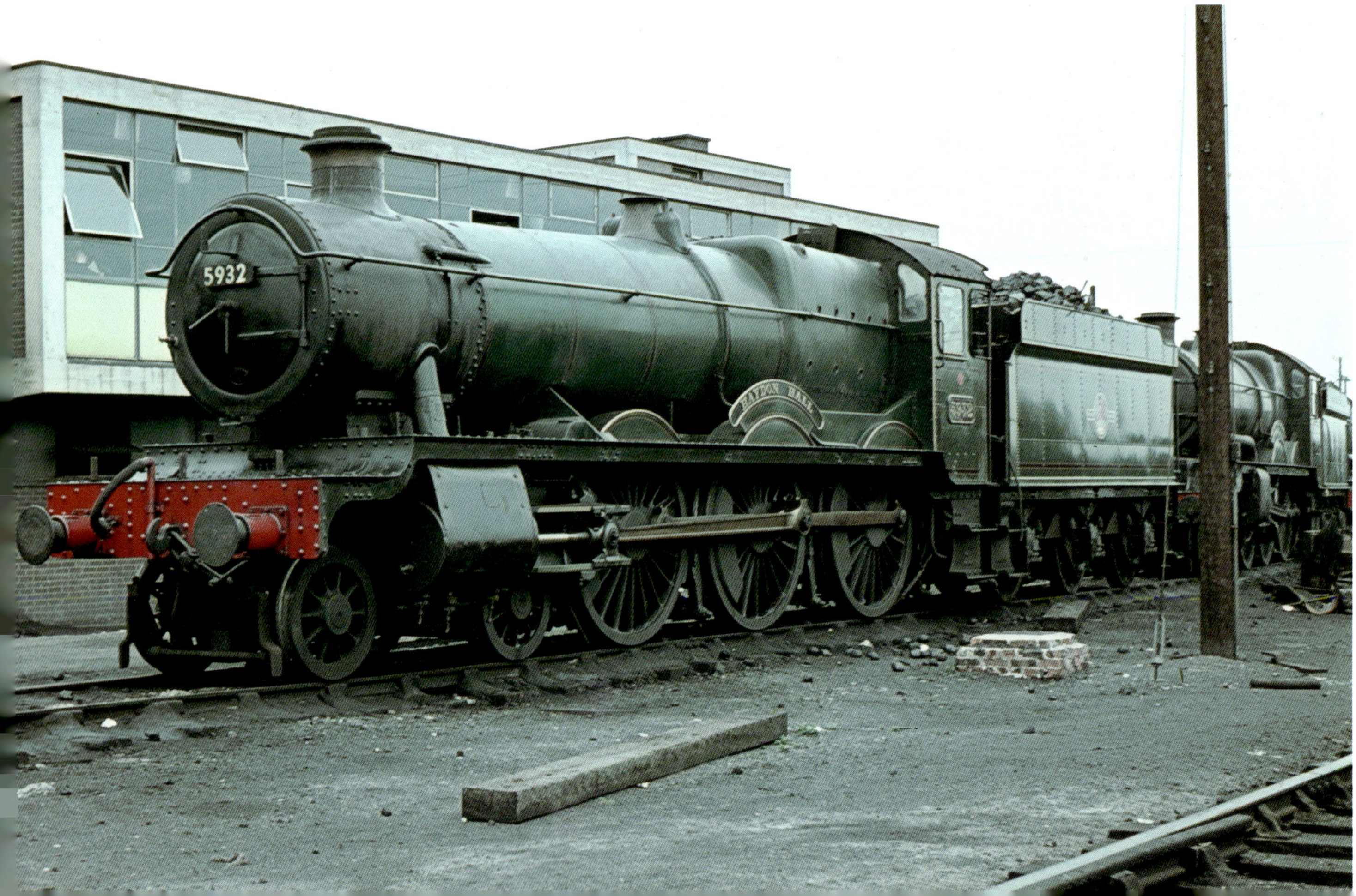

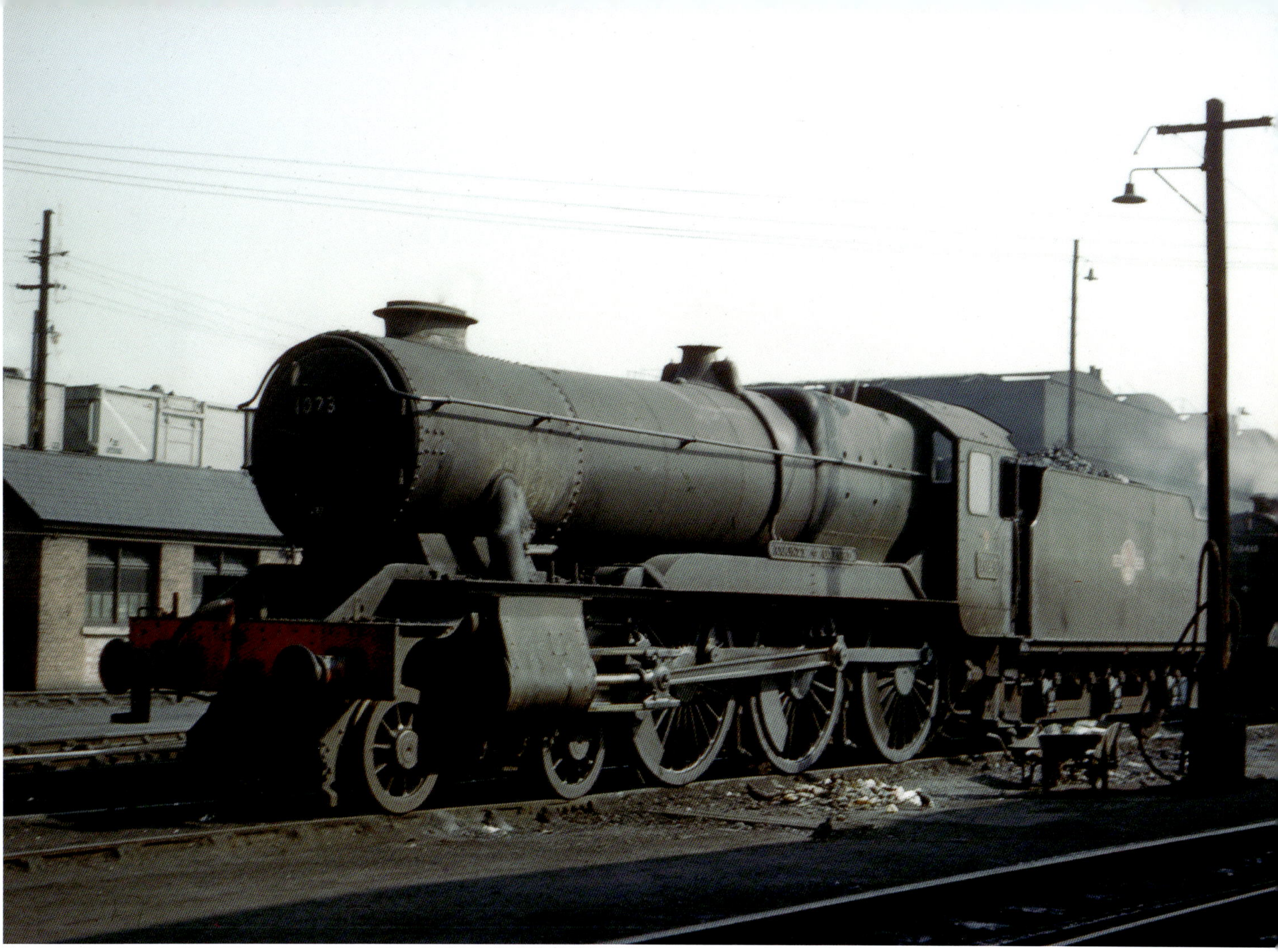

It is Sunday 20 March 1960 and 1023 County of Oxford looks work stained in front of a Stanier 8F out by the coaler at Old Oak Common. Perhaps macabre but the severed head of Oliver Cromwell, Lord Protector of the Commonwealth of England, Scotland and Ireland from 1653 to 1658, was reburied in an undisclosed location at the other great varsity city Cambridge within Sidney Sussex College later that week. ***Frank Hornby***

Showing at least some sign of a wipe over with an oily rag during 1962 was 5034 Corfe Castle between turns also at Old Oak Common. ***Strathwood Library Collection***

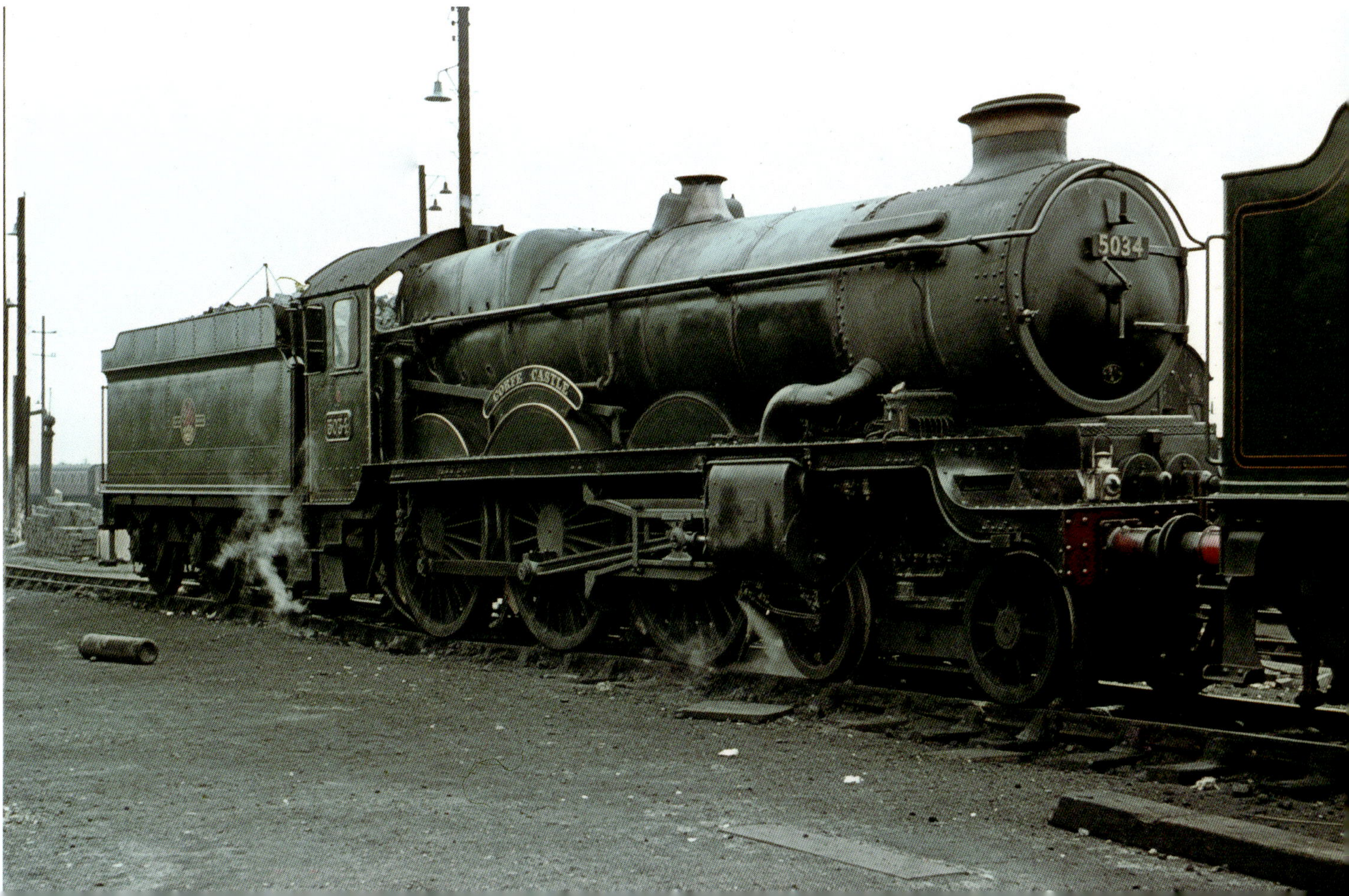

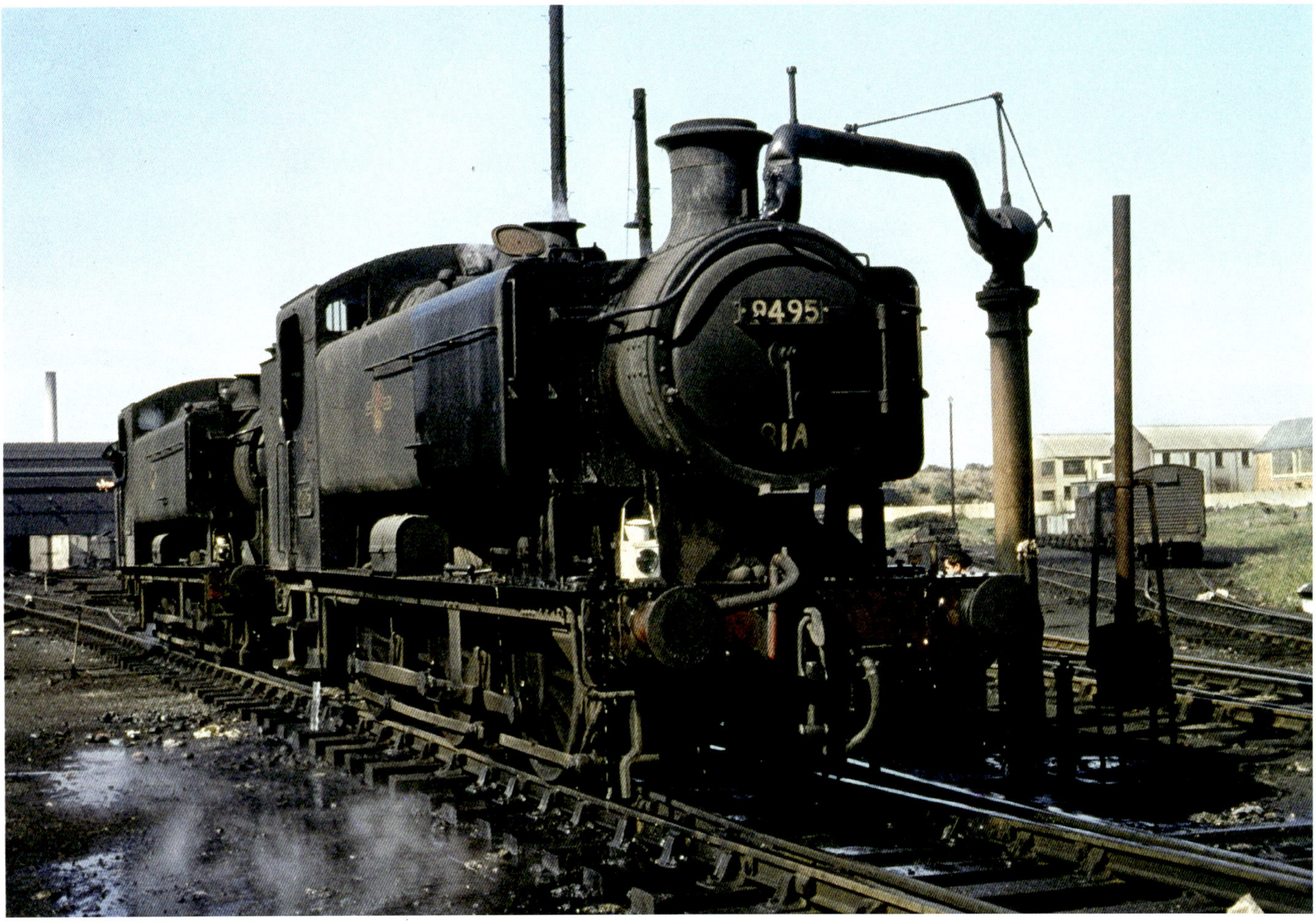

Hawksworth Panniers led by 9495 first in line for a top up of water at Old Oak Common on 21 September 1964. ***Dave Down***

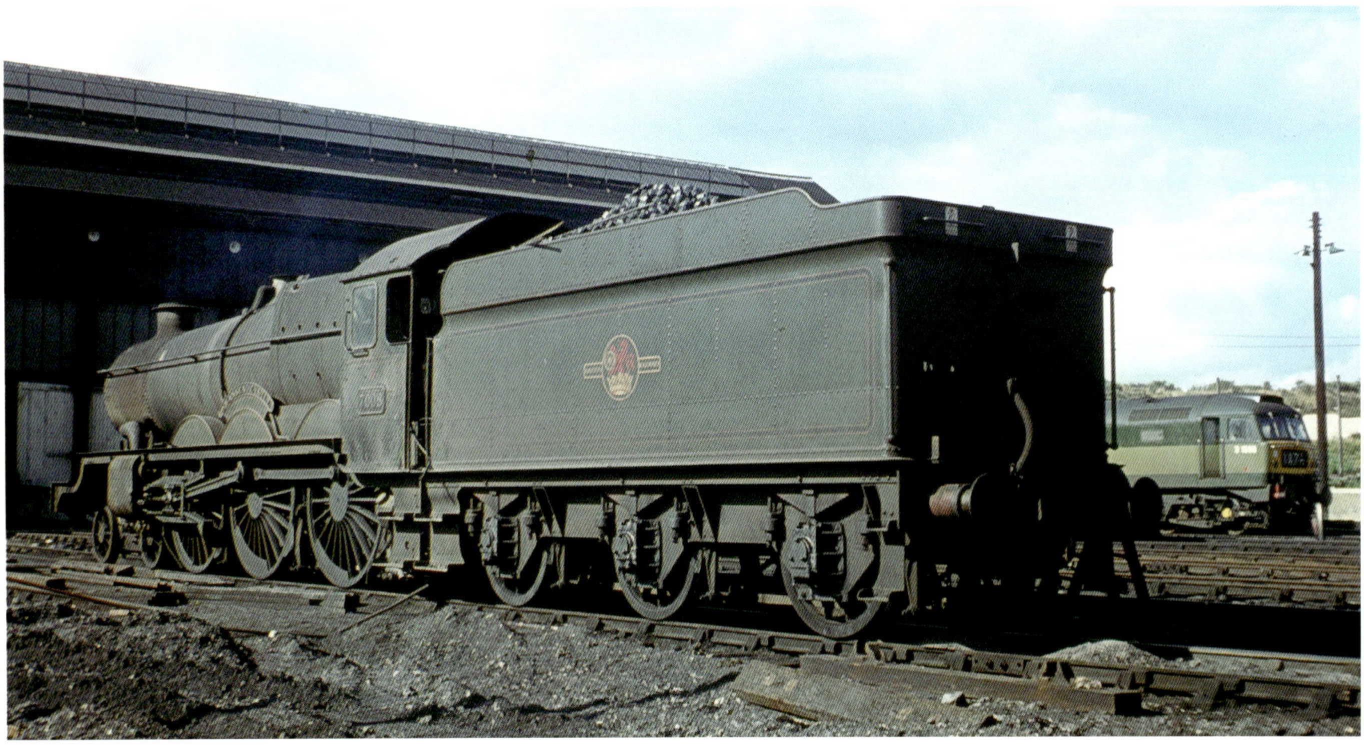

Taken about the same time was this shot of 7008 Swansea Castle which entered service in May 1948 and was posted as withdrawn in September 1964. Also taken out of service the same month were the last eighteen of that former Great Western man Sir William Stanier's Coronation Pacifics. ***Strathwood Library Collection***

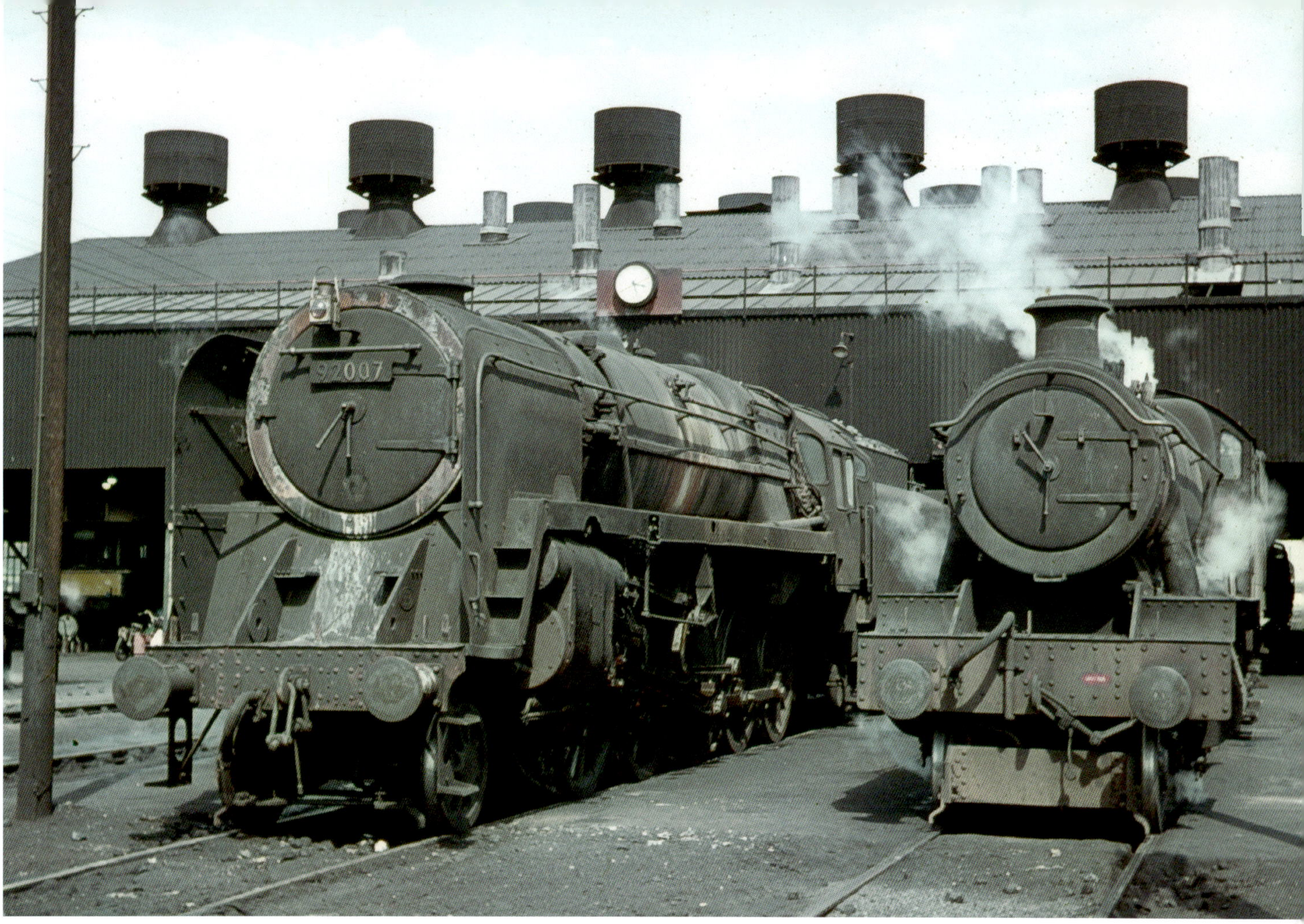

The other major engine shed in London during the decade was 81C Southall, although it was progressively turned over to use for the considerable fleet of DMUs for local services out of Paddington. Four months away from being closed to steam Standard 9F 92007 kept company with Modified Hall 7914 Lleweni Hall on 15 May 1965. ***Peter Coton***

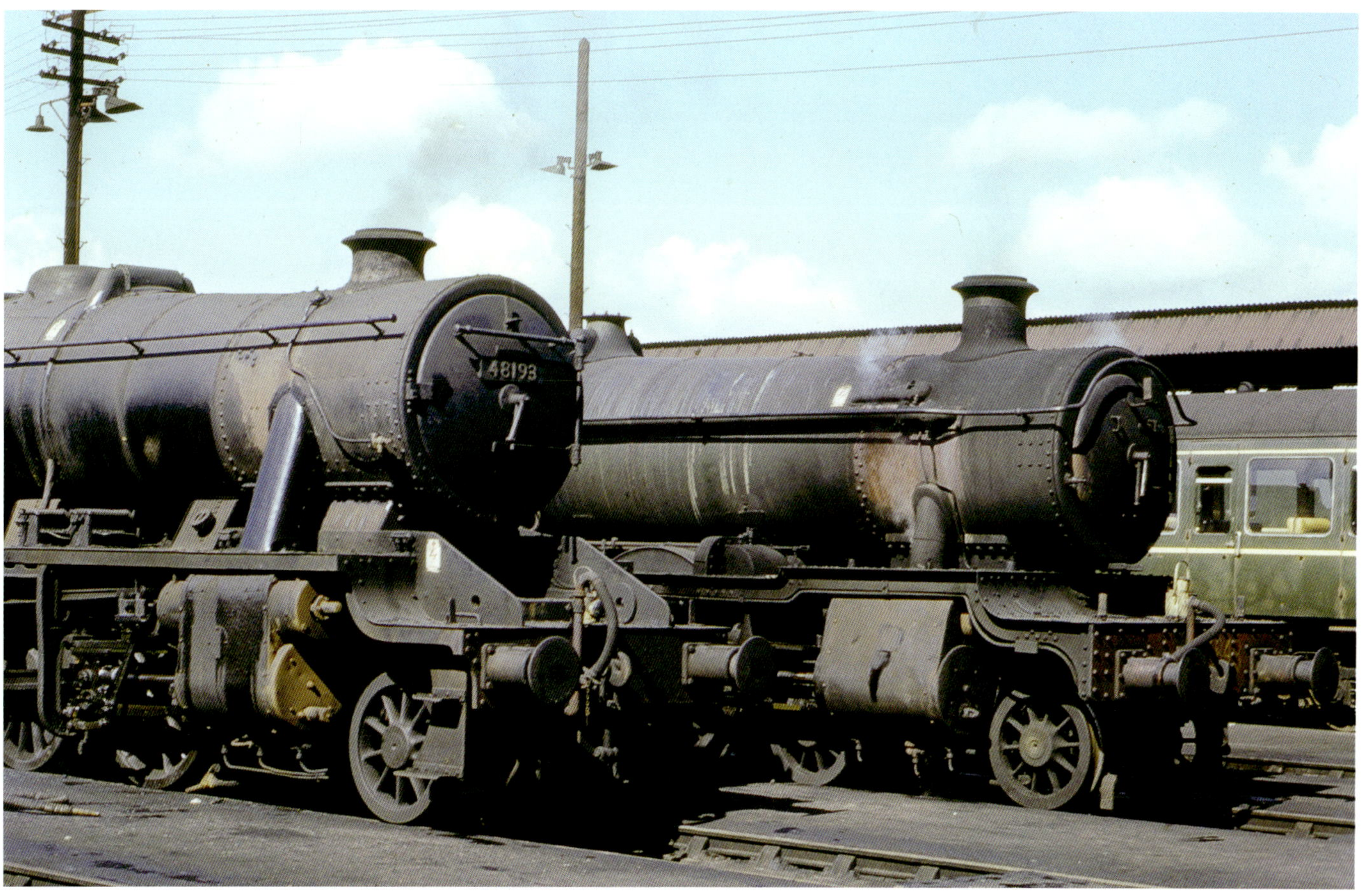

Standing alongside an anonymous Grange just before closure to steam in September 1965 was Stanier 8F 48193. Although a few of the 8Fs were built at Swindon during the war and a number ran as Western Region locomotives, this specimen was built by North British in Glasgow during May 1942. ***Win Wall/Strathwood Library Collection***

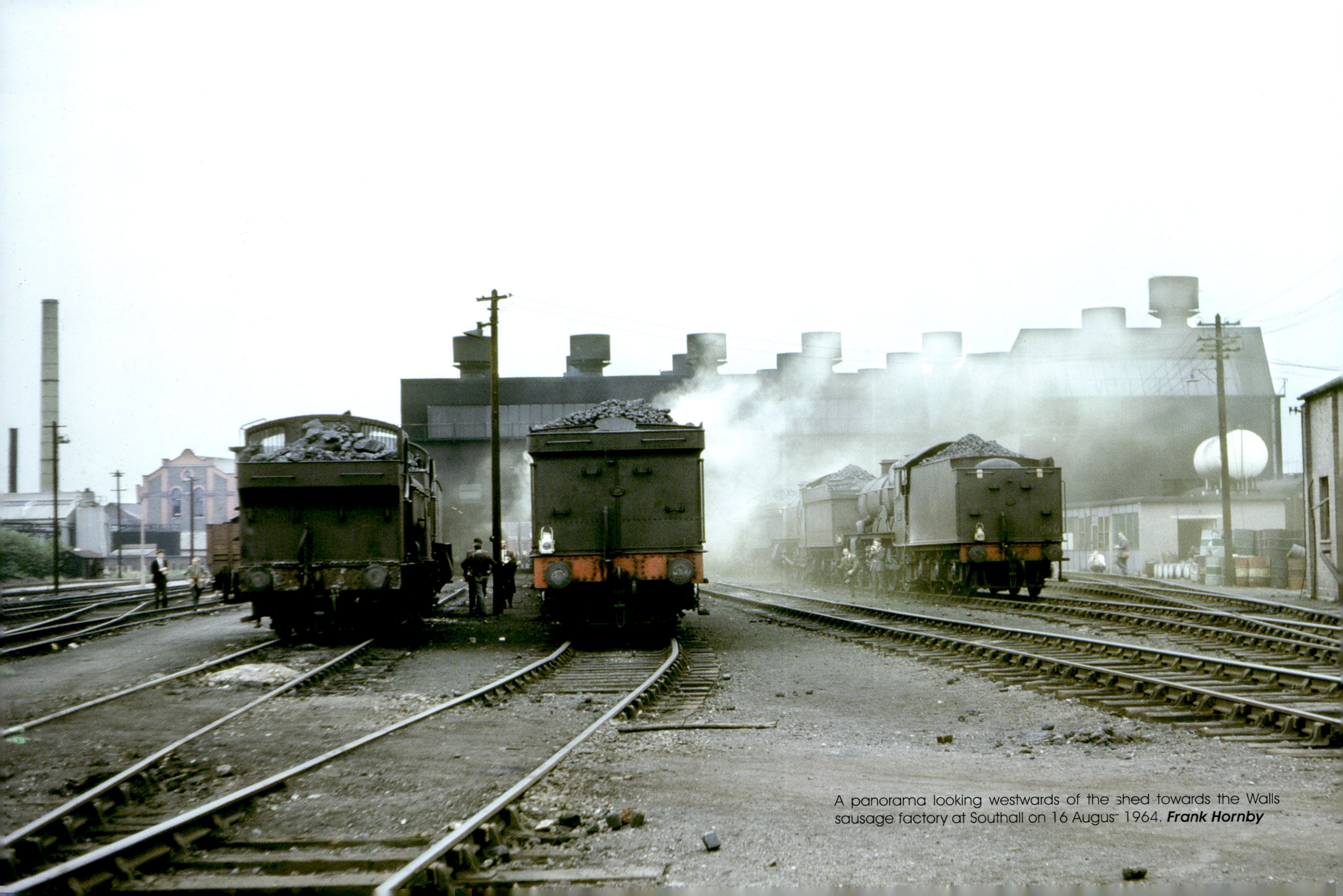

A panorama looking westwards of the shed towards the Walls sausage factory at Southall on 16 August 1964. ***Frank Hornby***

The Heart of the Region

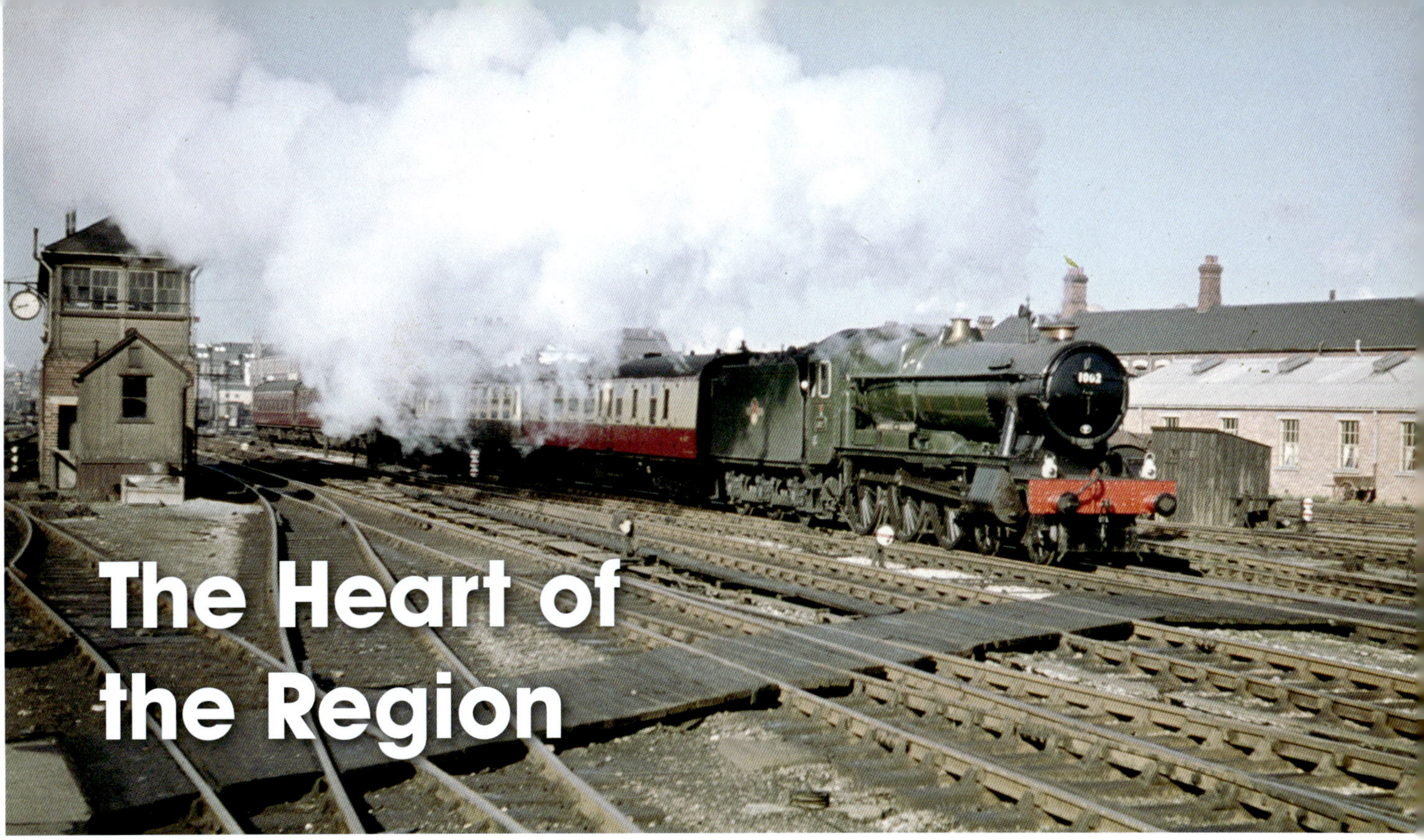

Speeding through Swindon with a short five coach rake in 1960 was a recently ex works 1002 County of Berks. ***Strathwood Library Collection***

Waiting in the bay at Swindon on 31 March 1962 was 1658 which will form the stock for a special arranged by the Gloucester Railway Society to traverse the Highworth, Malmesbury and Faringdon branches. ***Richard Icke***

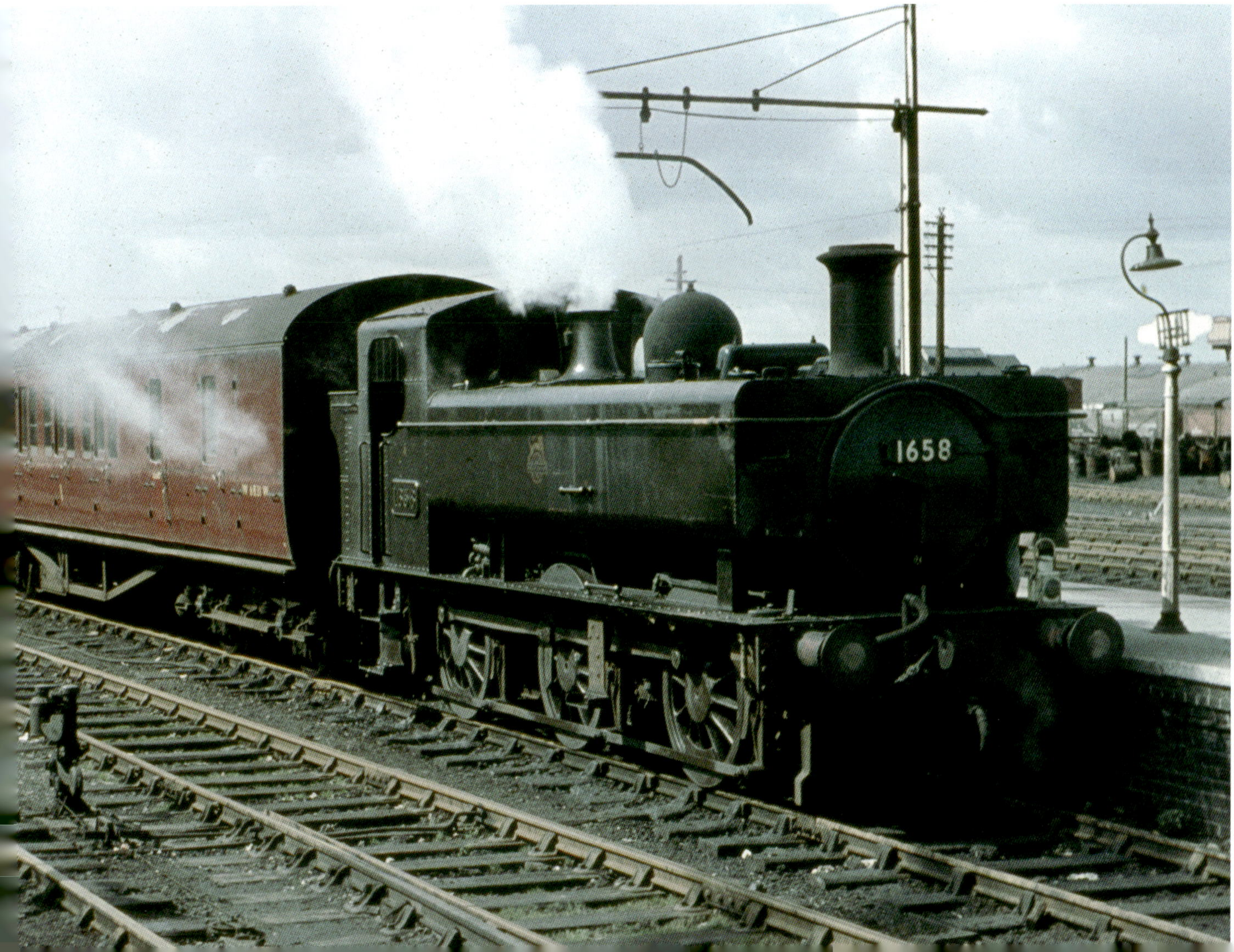

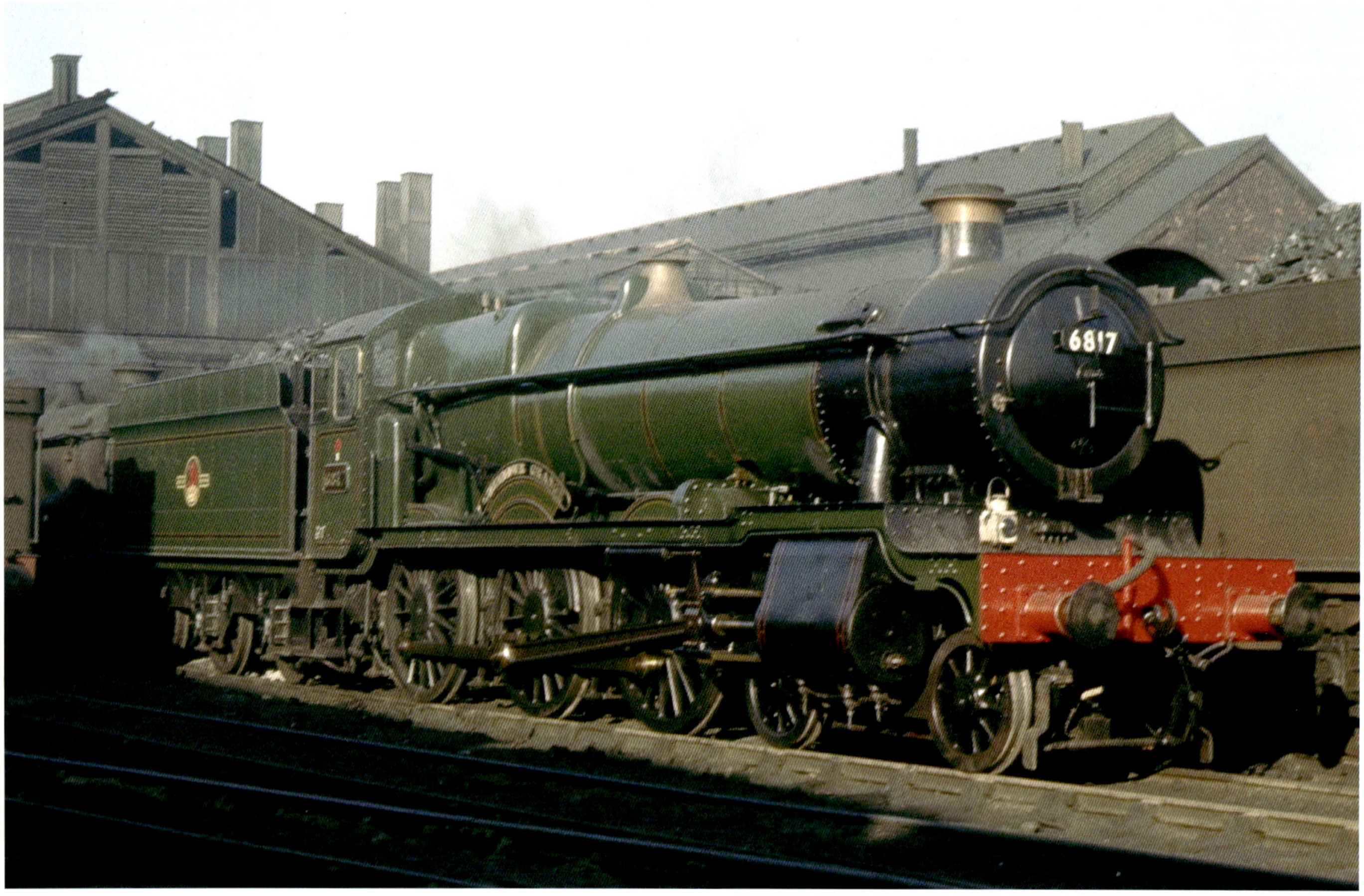

Swindon shed would often host recently ex works locomotives employed on running in turns before they returned to their home sheds. On 8 February 1960 6817 Gwenddwr Grange has recently seen works attention. In the news this month was the engagement of Princess Margaret to the commoner, but albeit posh Anthony Armstrong Jones, an event that would carry much more of a shock factor then, than today in court circles. ***Frank Hornby***

Seen again at Swindon in recently ex works condition was 1002 County of Berks, this time around 1962. Just a year from before being taken out of service. ***Strathwood Library Collection***

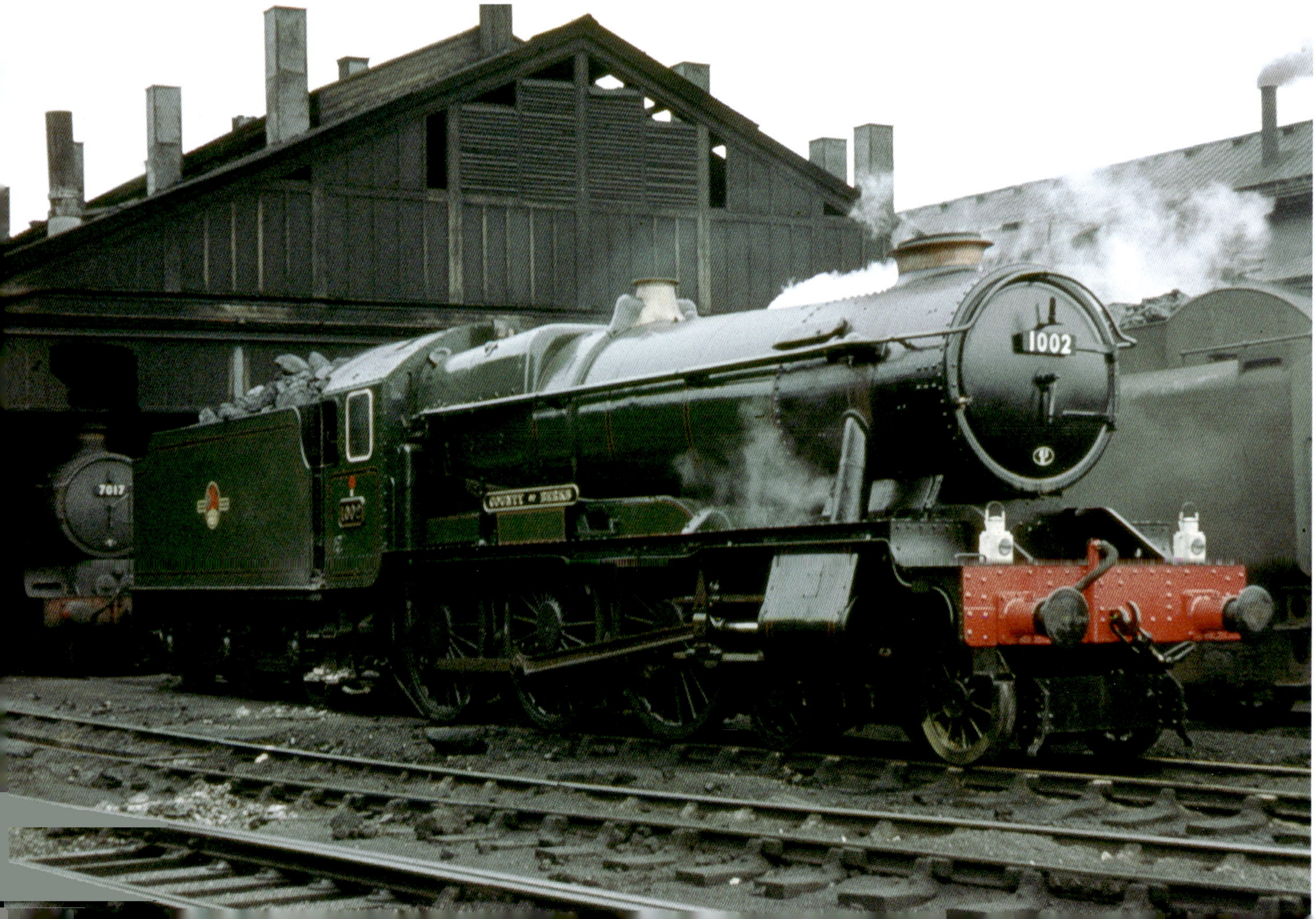

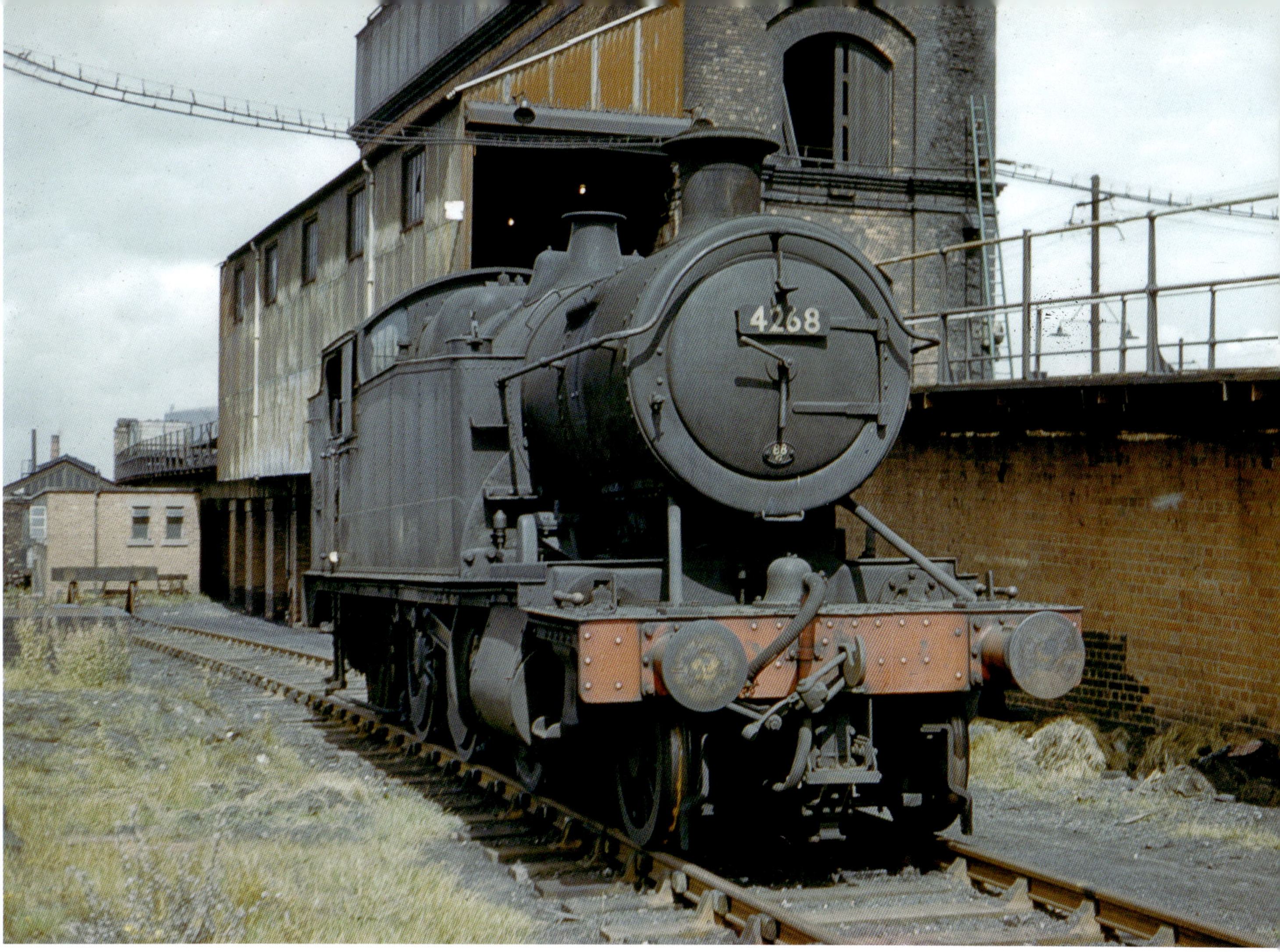

Although a number of her class were withdrawn before 12 August 1962, 4268 has come to Swindon for a works visit and would go back into traffic for a further three years. ***Frank Hornby***

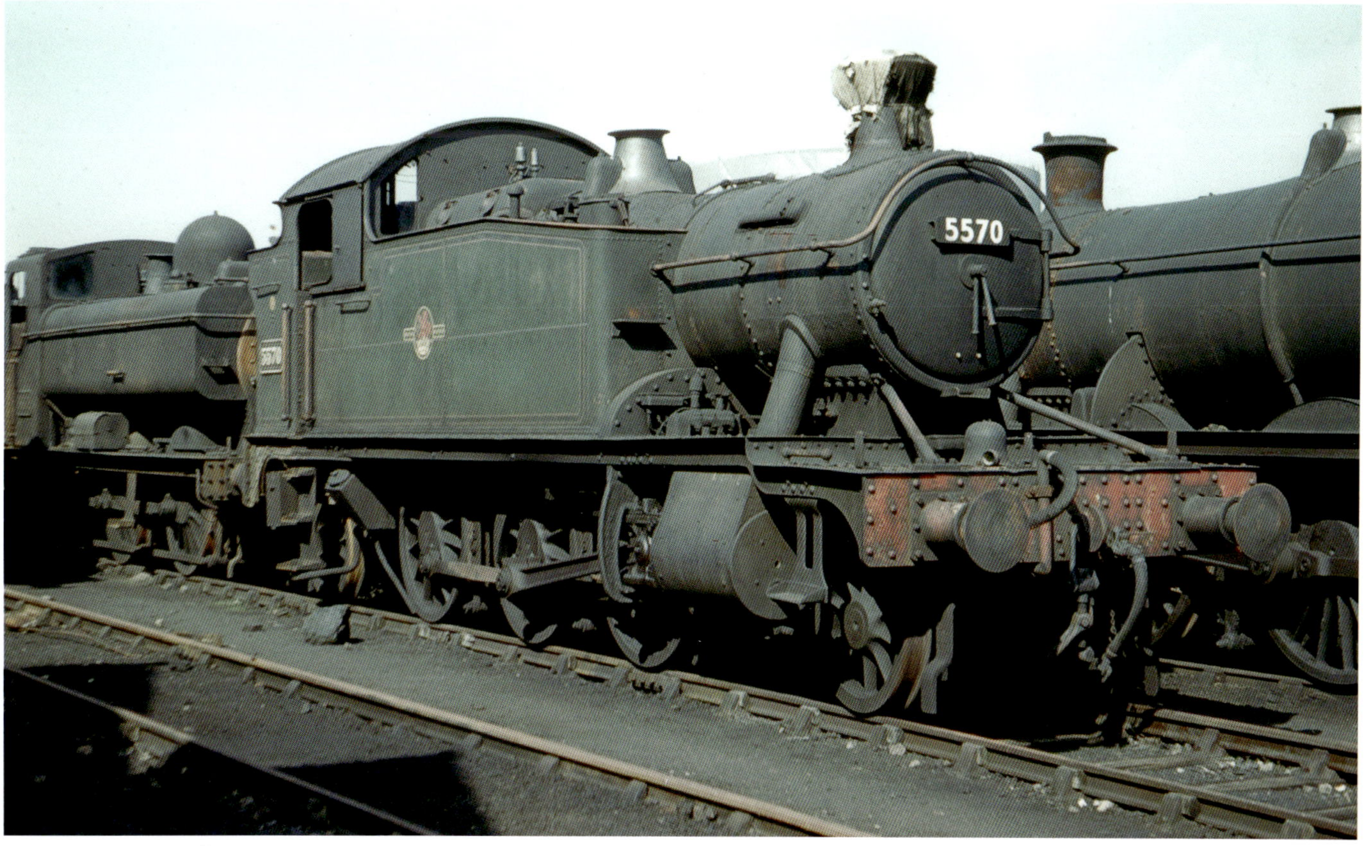

Not so fortunate was small Prairie 5570 amongst the lines in the Gas Works sidings on 24 March 1963 although the books show she was not withdrawn officially until December that year. ***Frank Hornby***

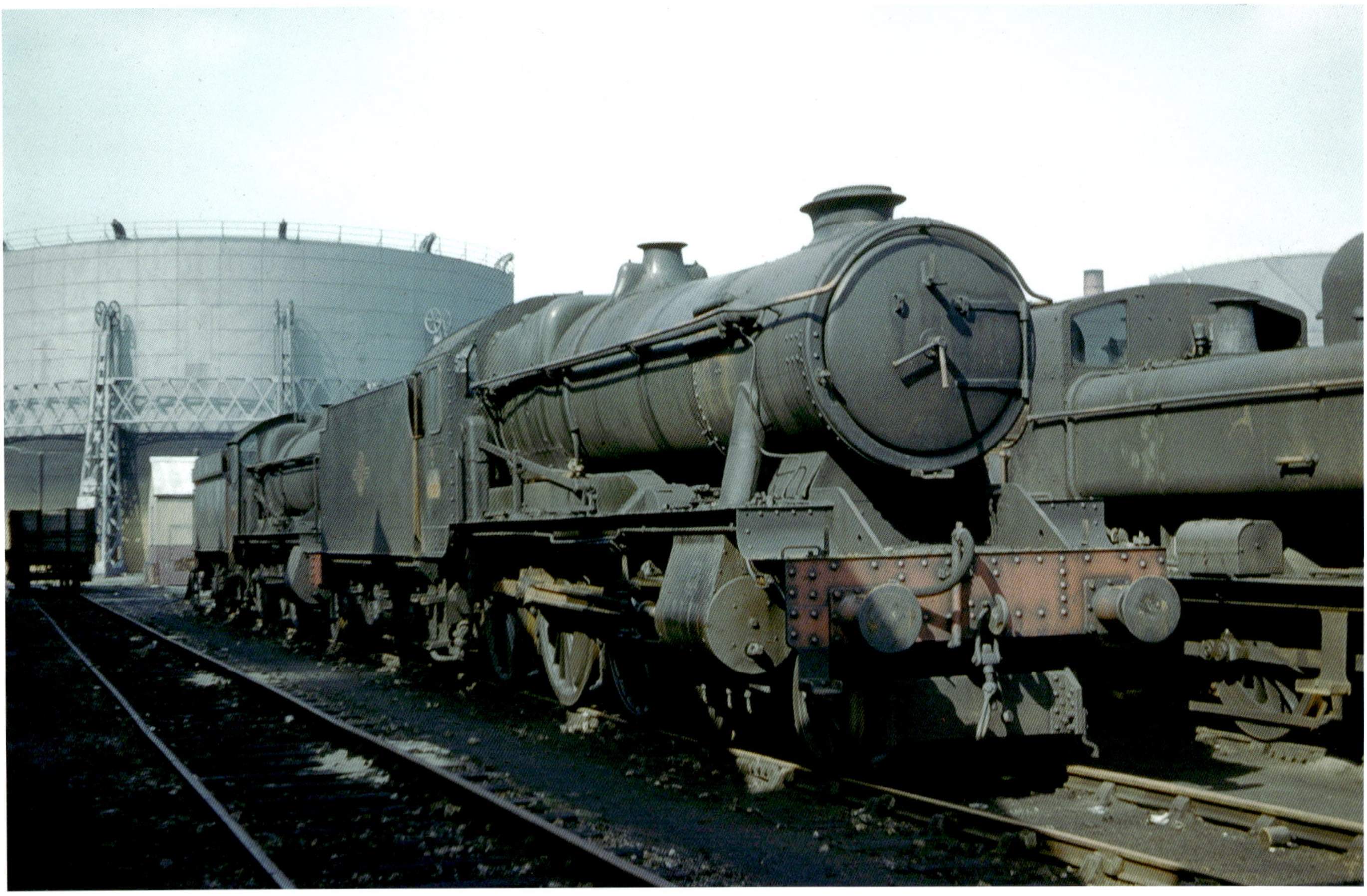

Also to be found not far away the same day was the already condemned 1029 County of Worcester which had been booked as withdrawn four months before. ***Frank Hornby***

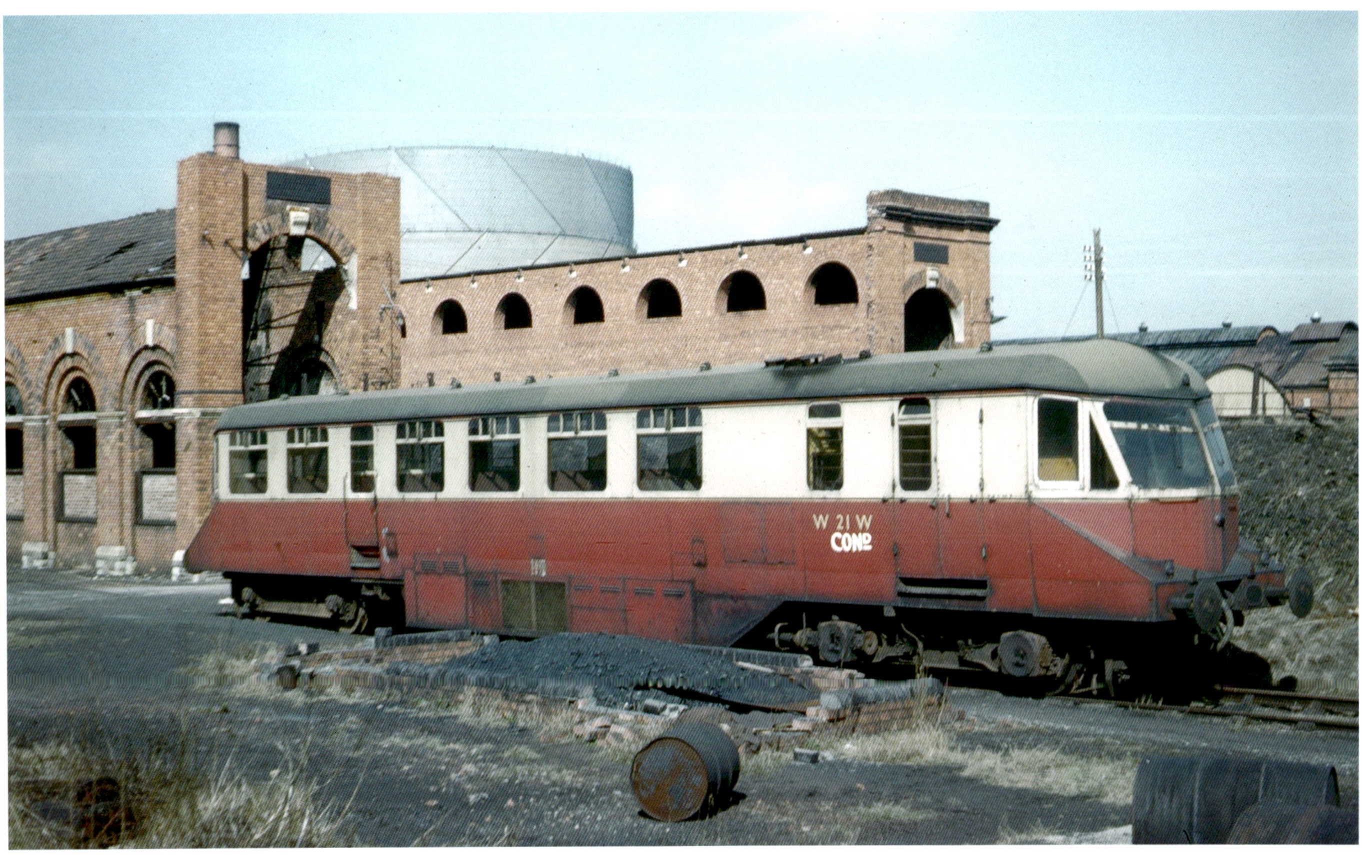

Hidden among the former retort houses of the gas works was the doomed railcar W21W once again on 24 March 1963. ***Frank Hornby***

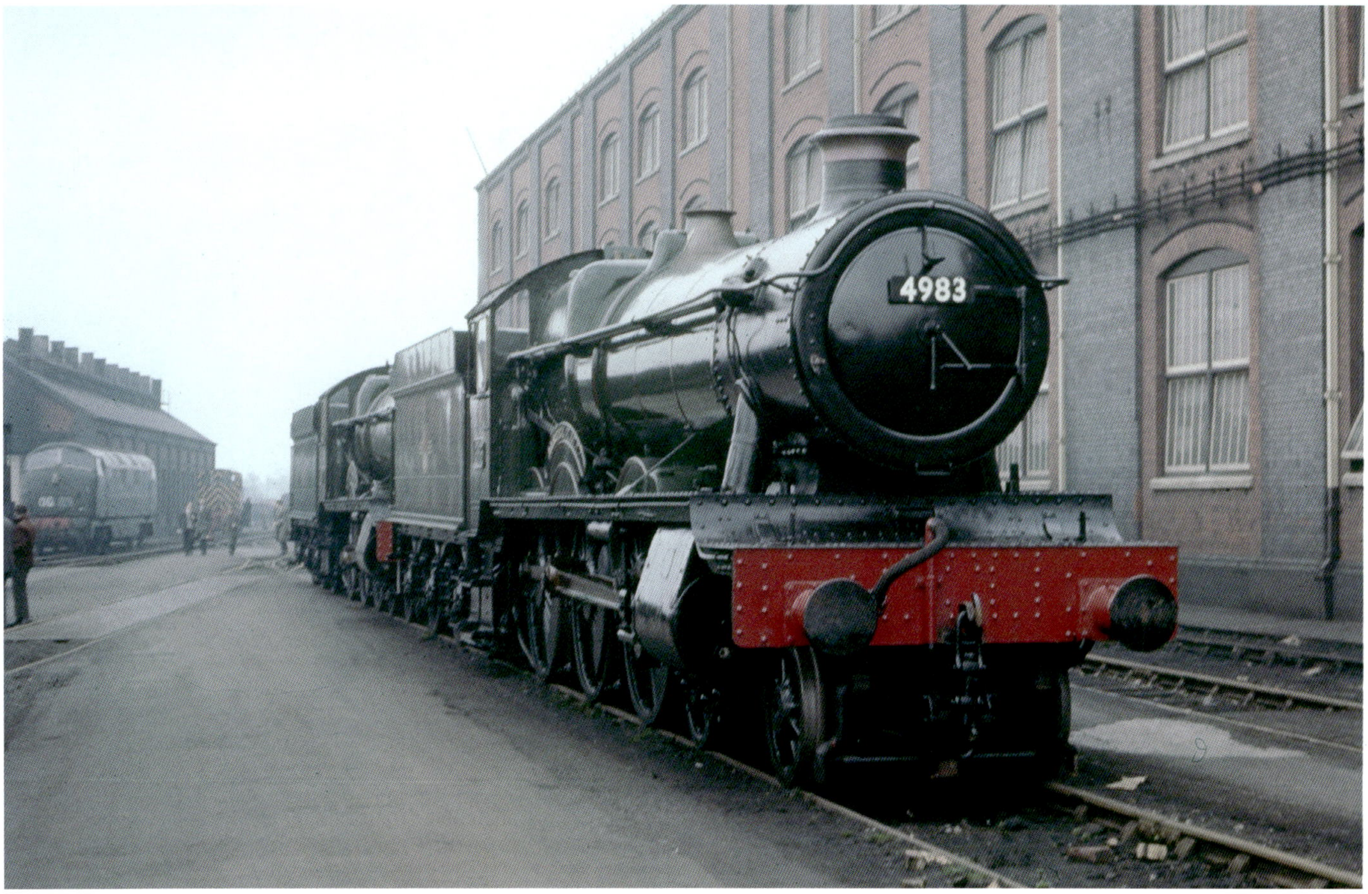

Awaiting a chance to be steamed again outside the workshops on 9 April 1961 was 4983 Albert Hall as the visiting party of spotters get split up walking around the Works, no doubt under the watchful eyes of a guide. ***Frank Hornby***

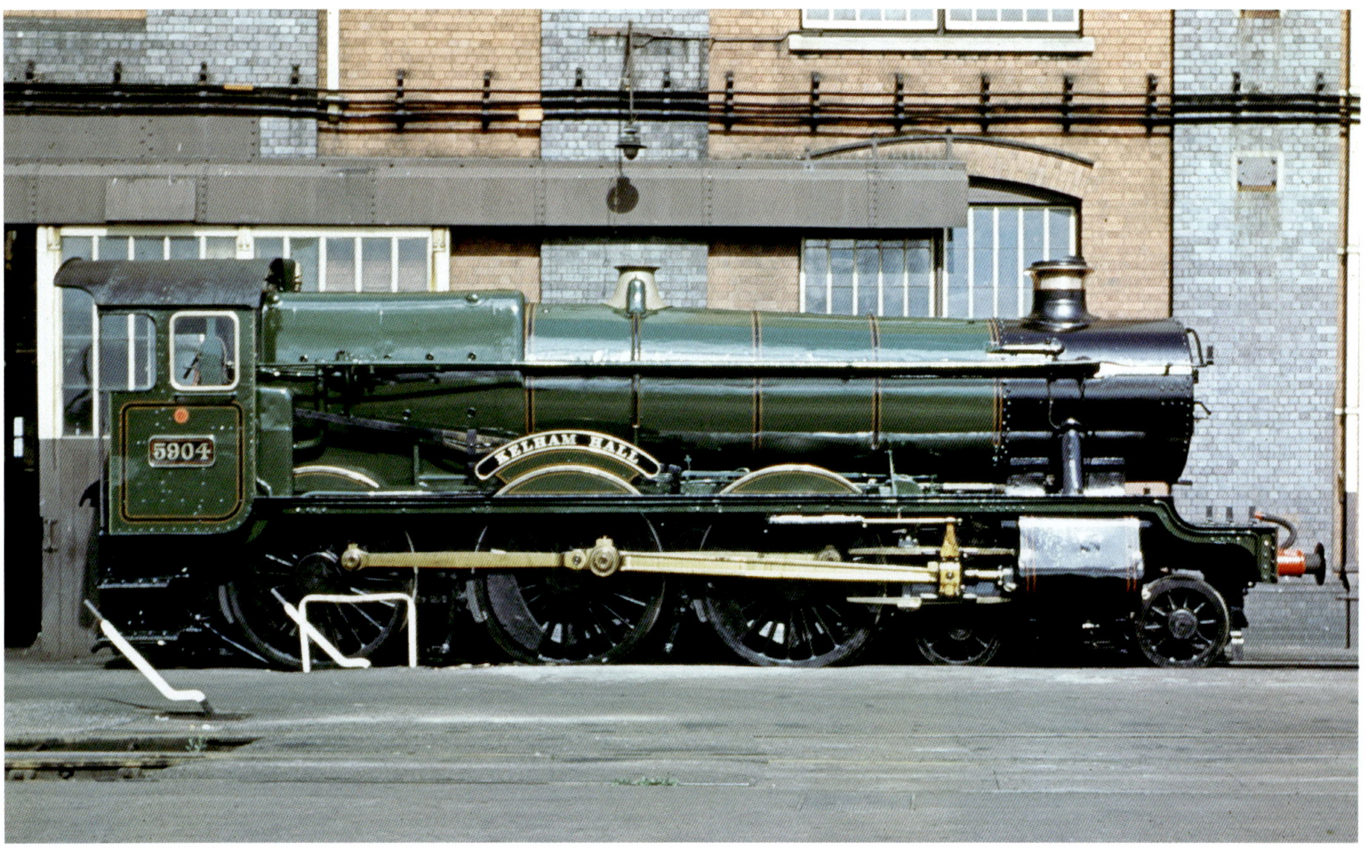

Outside the works awaiting matching with a suitable tender was 5904 Kelham Hall around 1962, this locomotive had previously spent some time paired with the experimental eight wheel tender. ***John Gill***

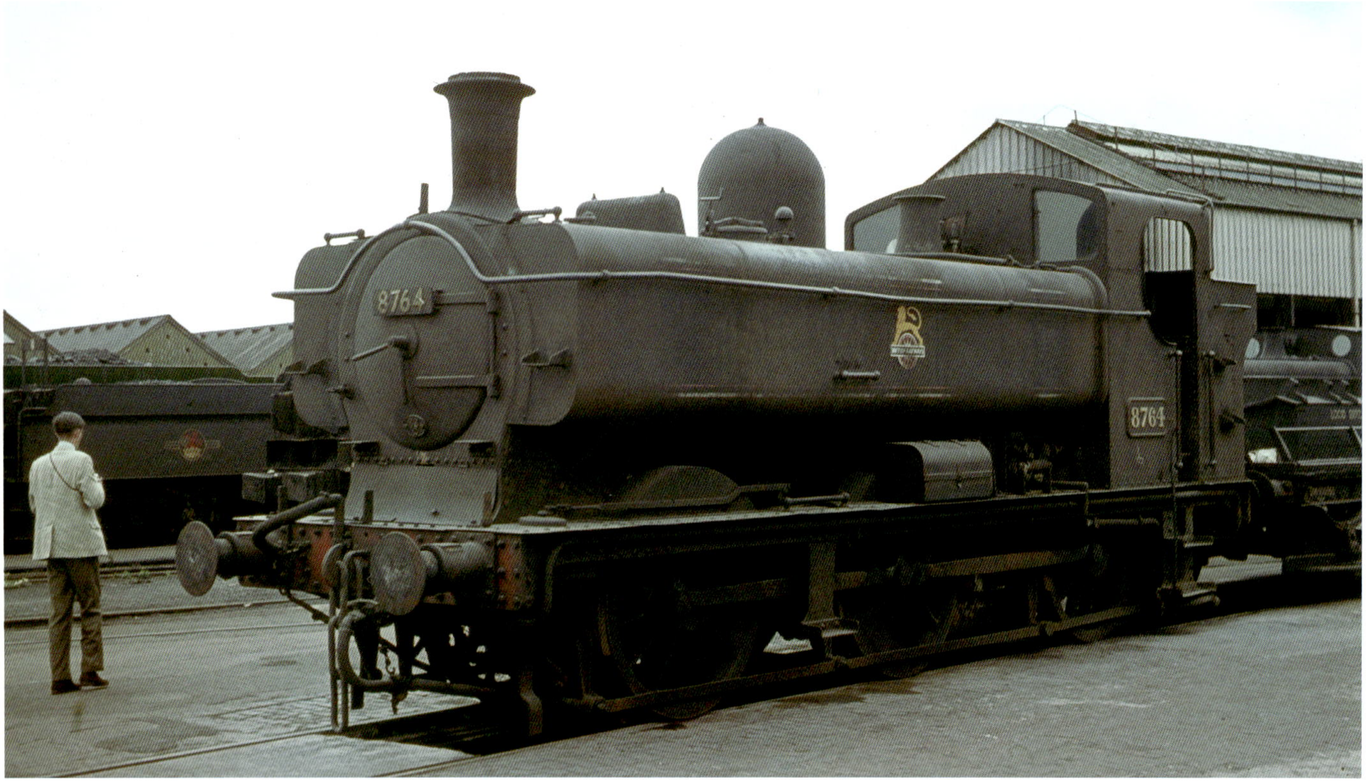

Signs of her unusual previous lined mixed traffic black livery can still be seen on 8764 now withdrawn in 1962, but a once proud resident of Old Oak Common. ***Strathwood Library Collection***

Another sad gathering of scrap has arrived at the works in April 1965 with a Modified Hall at its head. Both Leeds United and Liverpool had long runs in the FA Cup this year, with the silkverware journeying back to Merseyside after the final. ***Edward Dorricott***

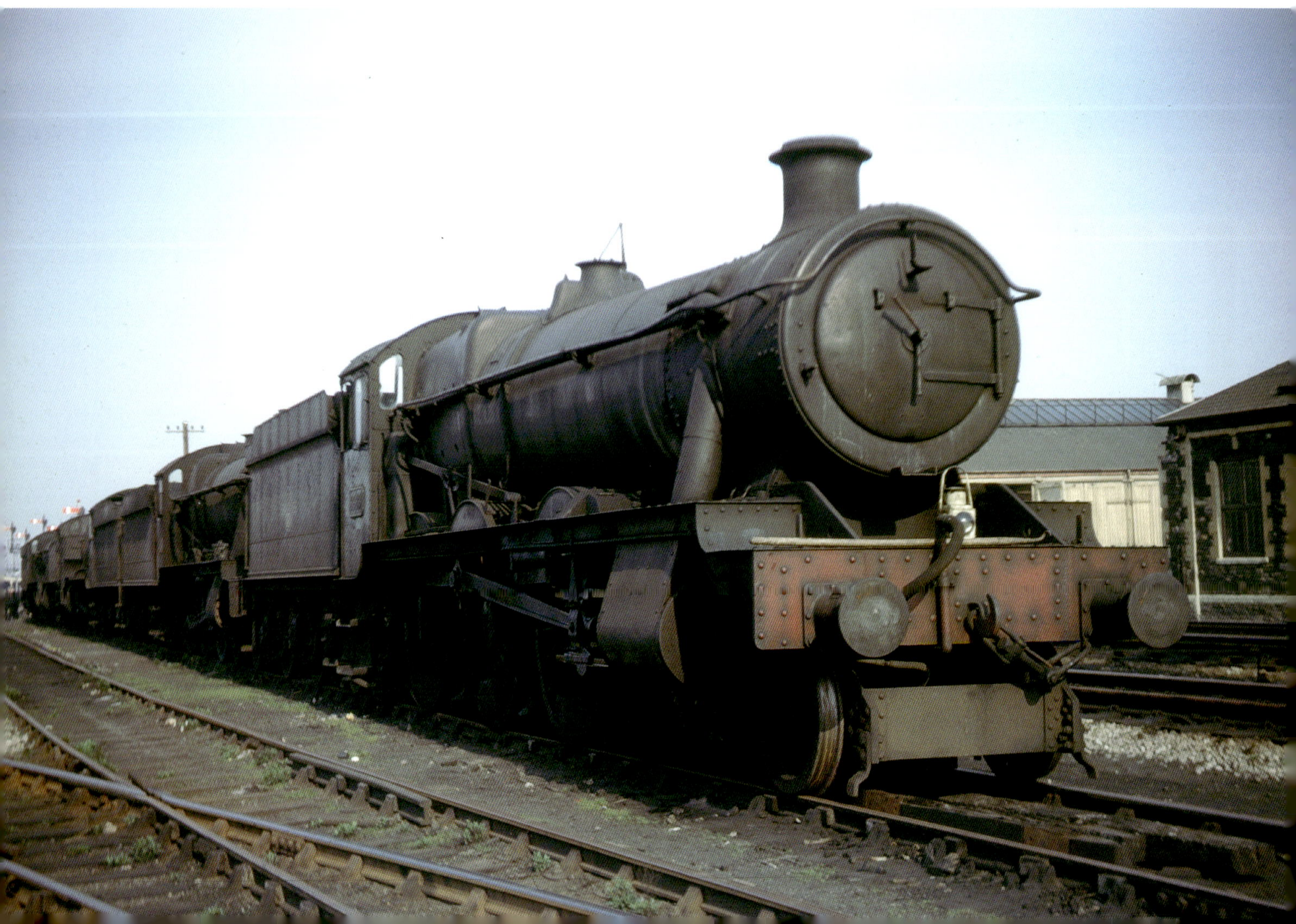

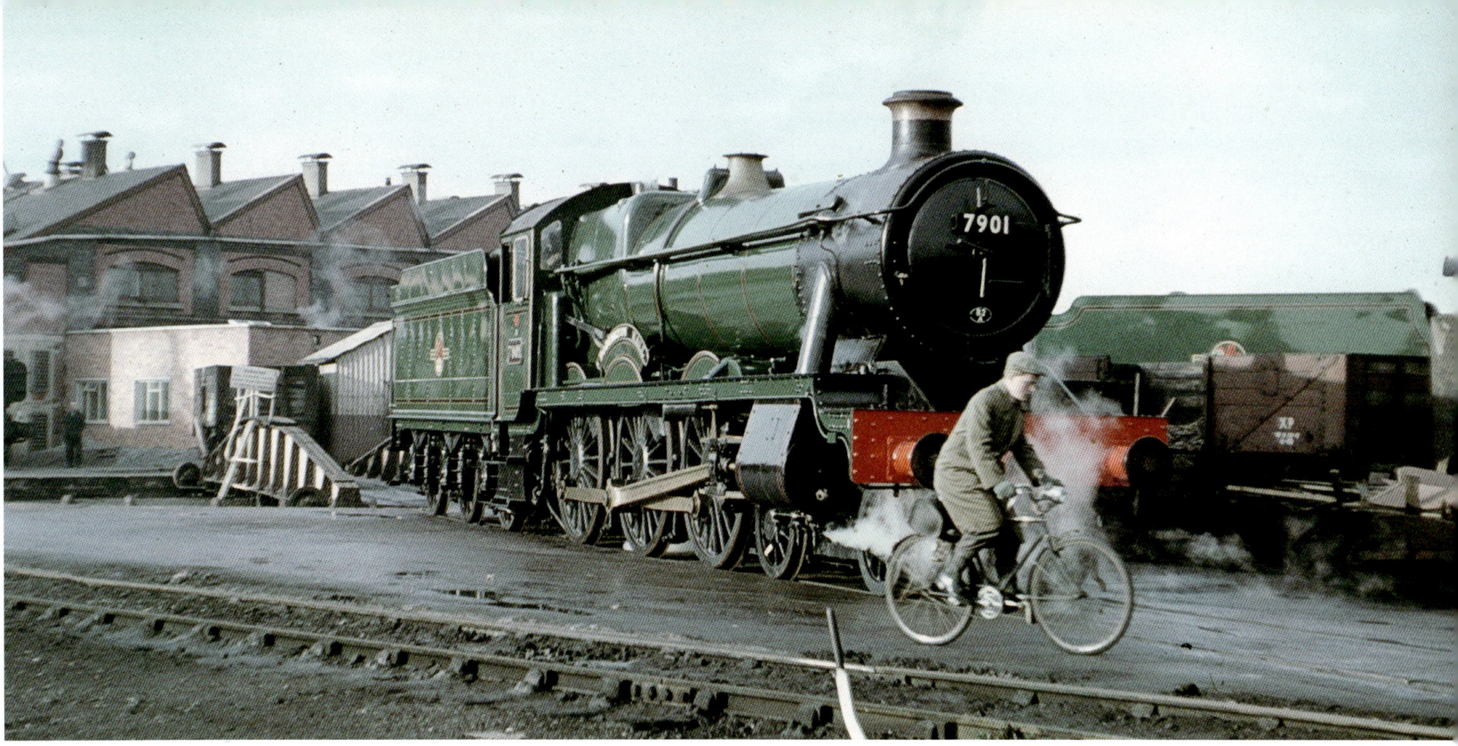

Its either knocking off time at the works or this is the best way to get from one office to another within this once huge complex on 9 January 1961. Meanwhile shining in the background 7901 Doddington Hall stands on a turntable road in the works yard prior to running in turns and a return to regular traffic. ***Richard Icke***

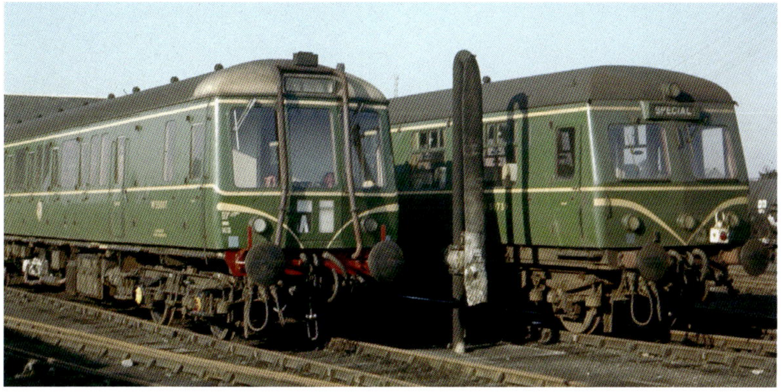

Overhauls within the large DMU and coach repair facilities have brought this pair to the works on 8 February 1960. ***Frank Hornby***

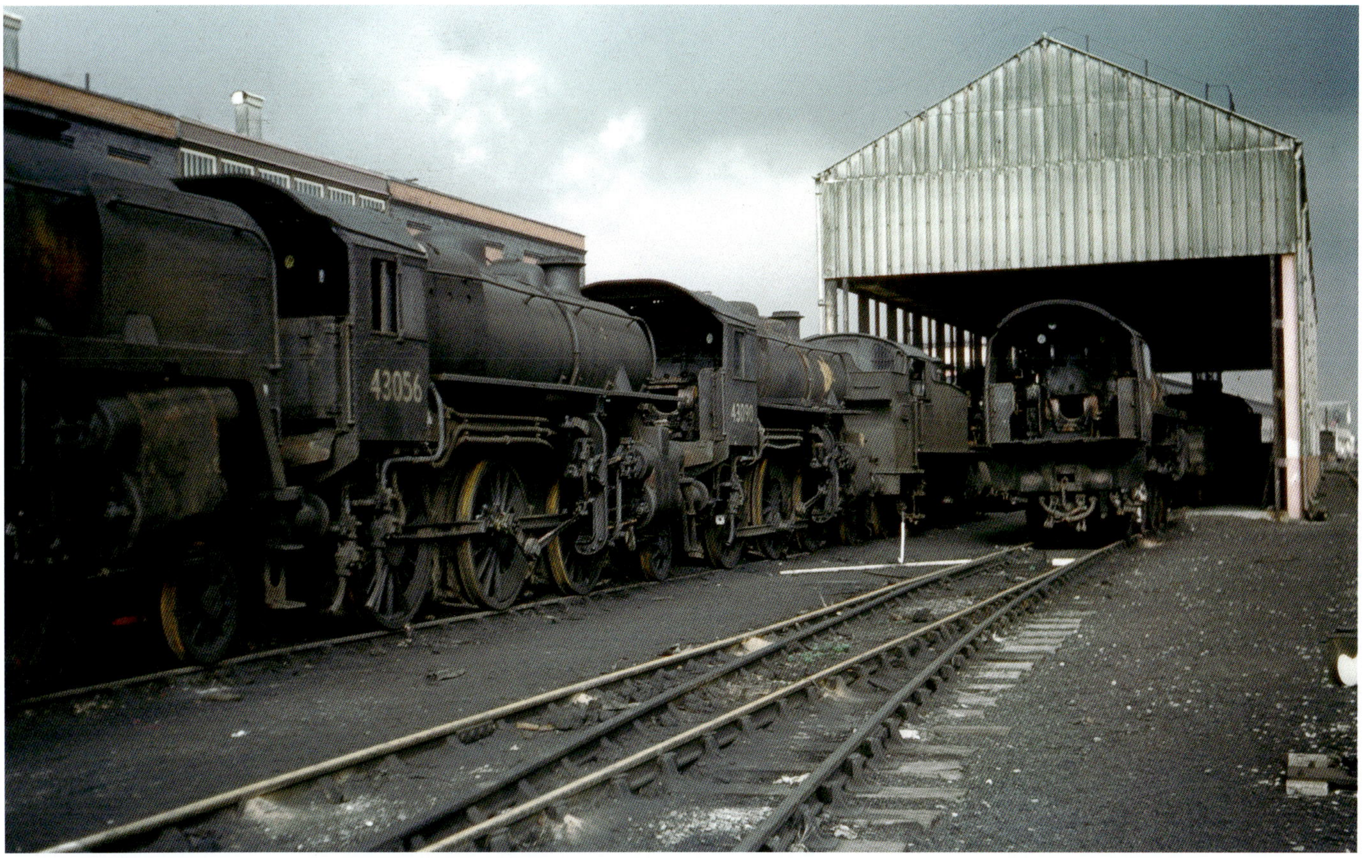

Repairs to a number of the Ivatt designed Moguls such as 43056 and 43090 were made during the early months of 1964 giving them a brief respite in the tide of withdrawals sweeping the country and keeping the works busy. ***Late Norman Browne/Strathwood Library Collection***

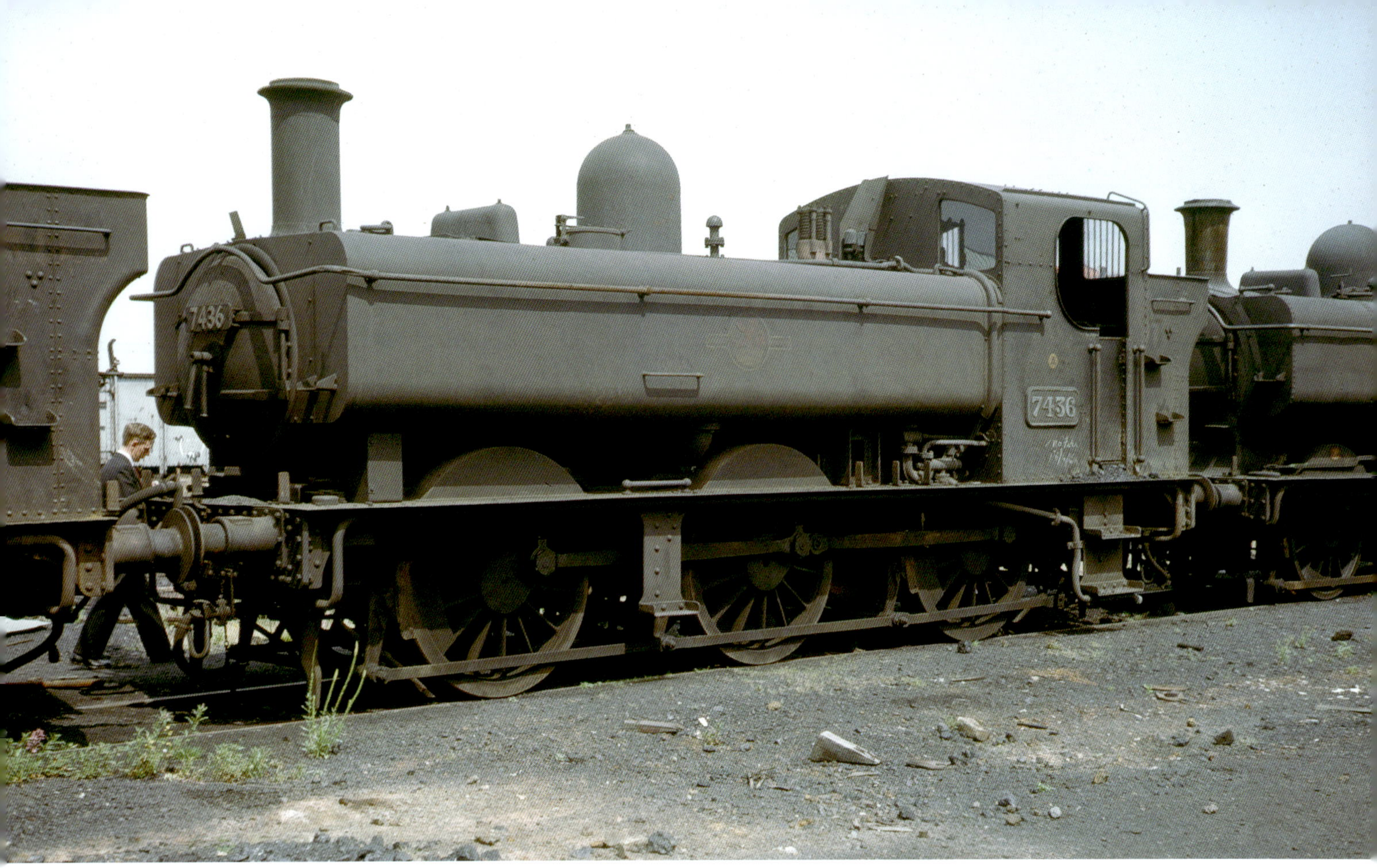

Many readers will recall walking through the long lines of withdrawn locomotives in the yards at Swindon. This small Collett Pannier, 7436 seen in August 1964 was used as the stationary boiler in St. Phillips Marsh roundhouse until a few weeks previously before arrival here. ***Late Norman Browne/Strathwood Library Collection***

This works visit for Large Prairie 8109 on 24 March 1963 will afford the engine another three years use and make her the last of her ten sub class in service when withdrawn in June 1965. ***Strathwood Library Collection***

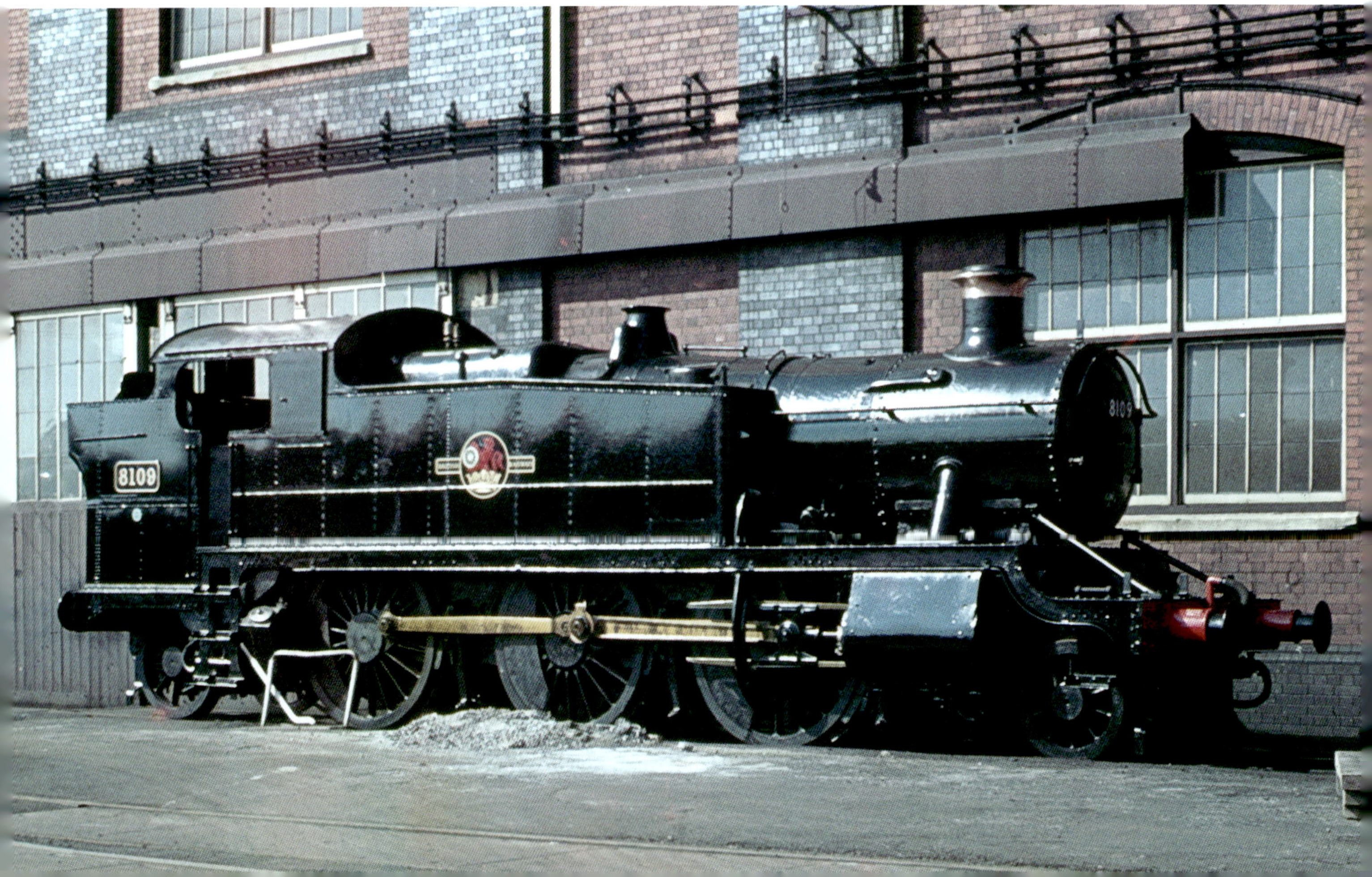

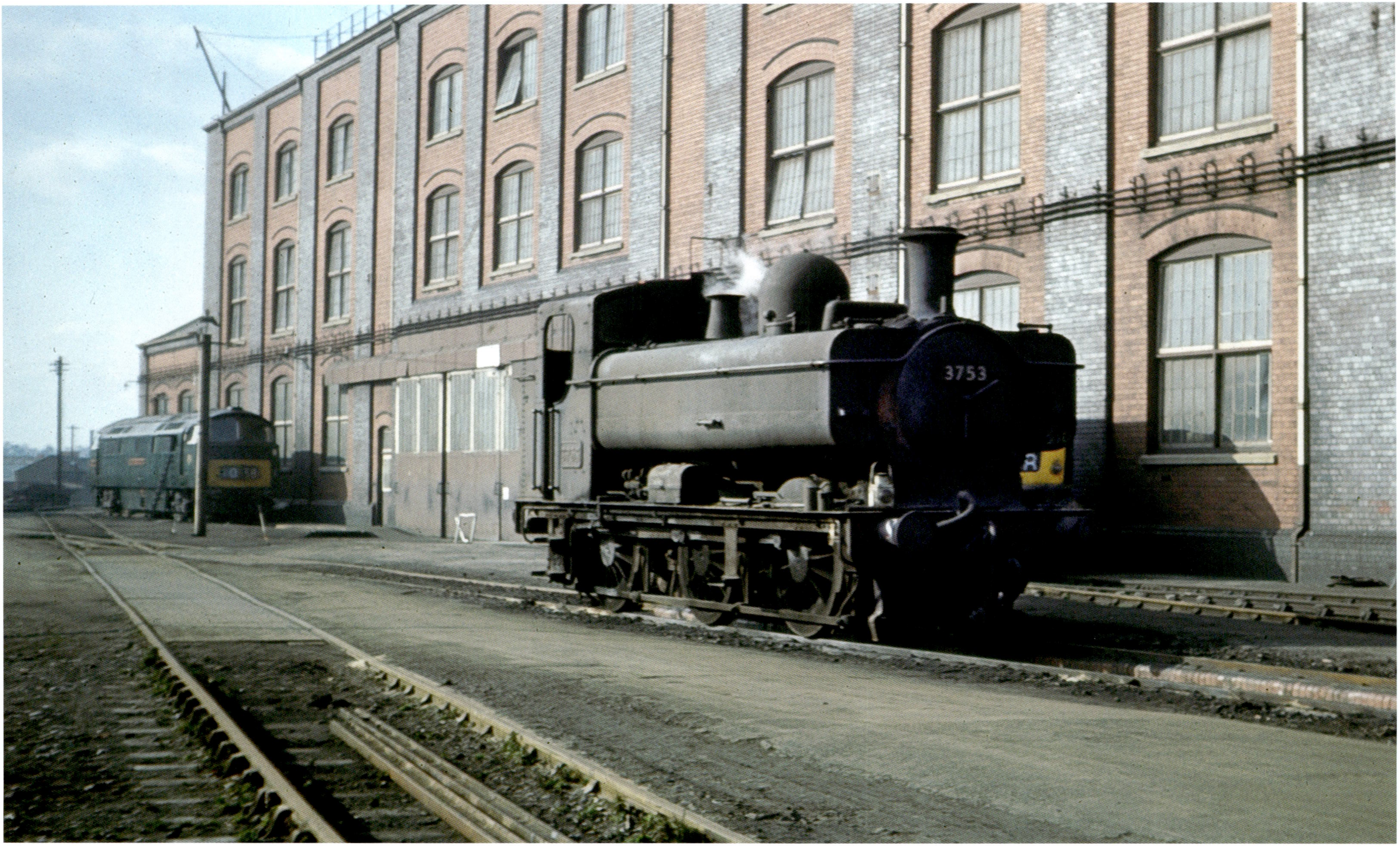

One of the few green liveried Westerns, D1038 Western Sovereign is in the distance whilst a Hymek hides behind Pannier 3753 during a visit around 1965. The 0-6-0PT had been built within the works as part of a large batch during 1937 being among seven released during November alone that year from Swindon for service with the Great Western Railway. ***Len Smith***

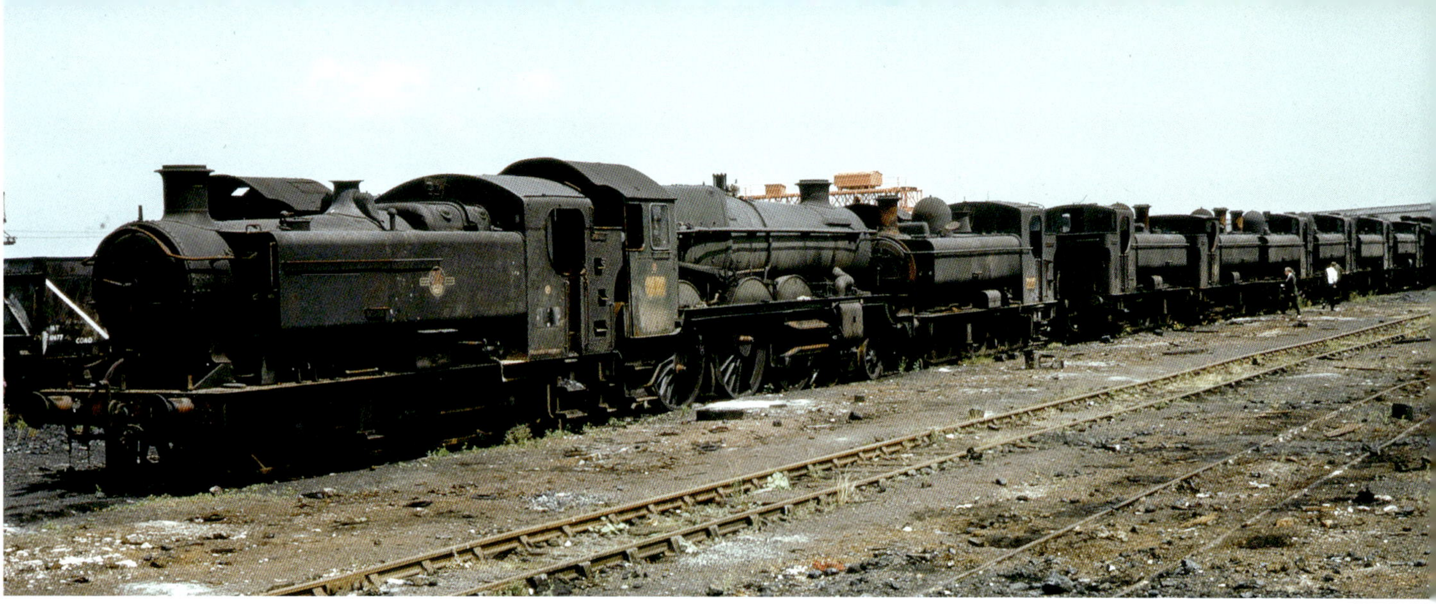

On the dump in August 1964 were a collection of ten Panniers and one Castle. ***Late Norman Browne/Strathwood Library Collection***

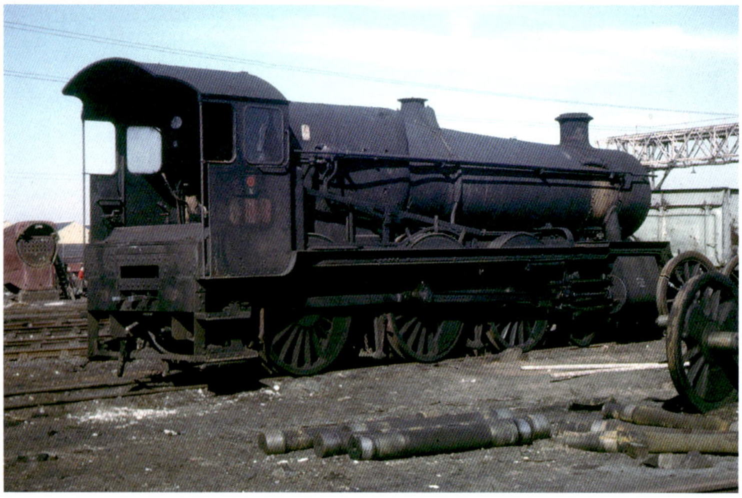

An unknown Grange will be dealt with soon by the cutters in April 1965. ***Edward Dorricott***

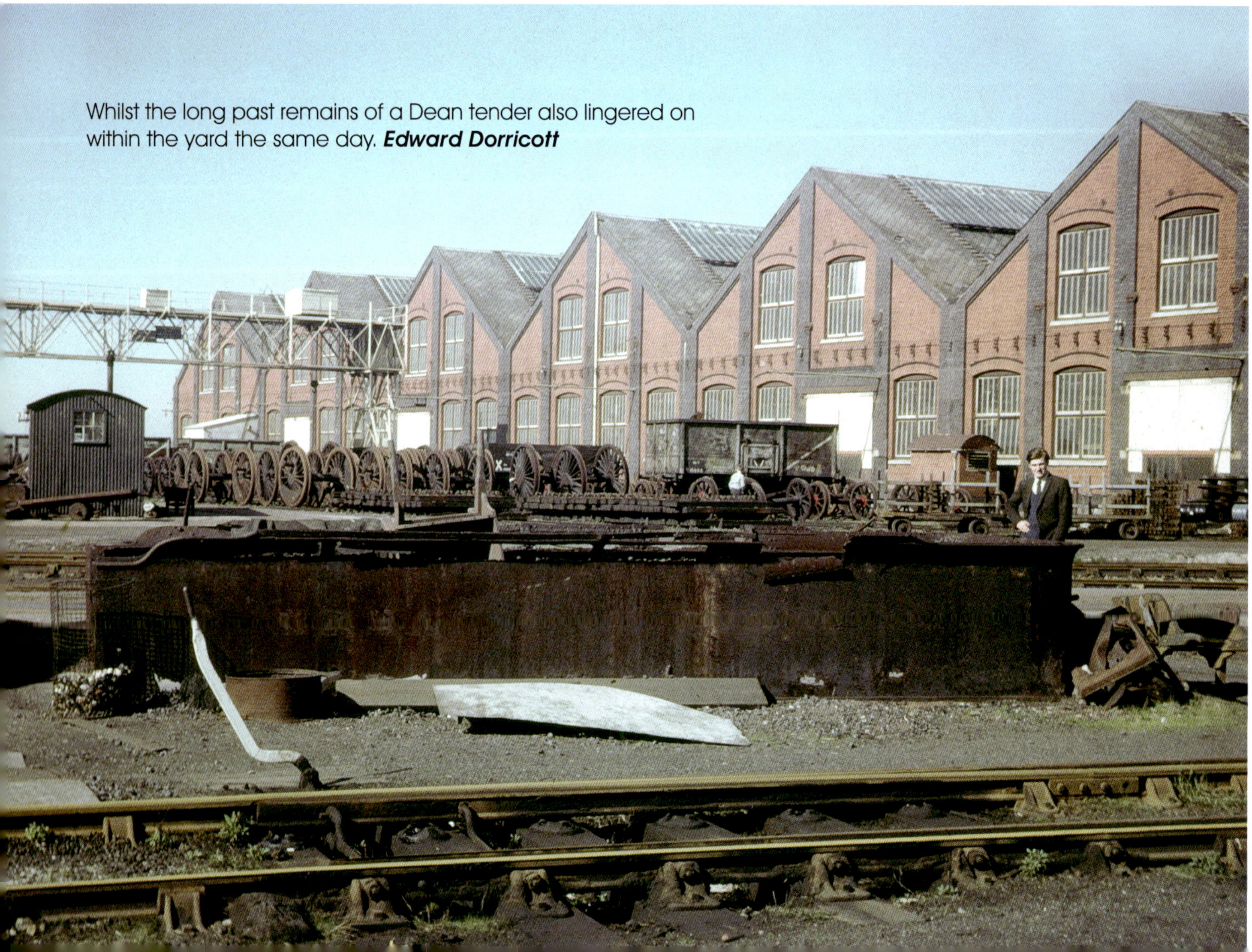

Whilst the long past remains of a Dean tender also lingered on within the yard the same day. ***Edward Dorricott***

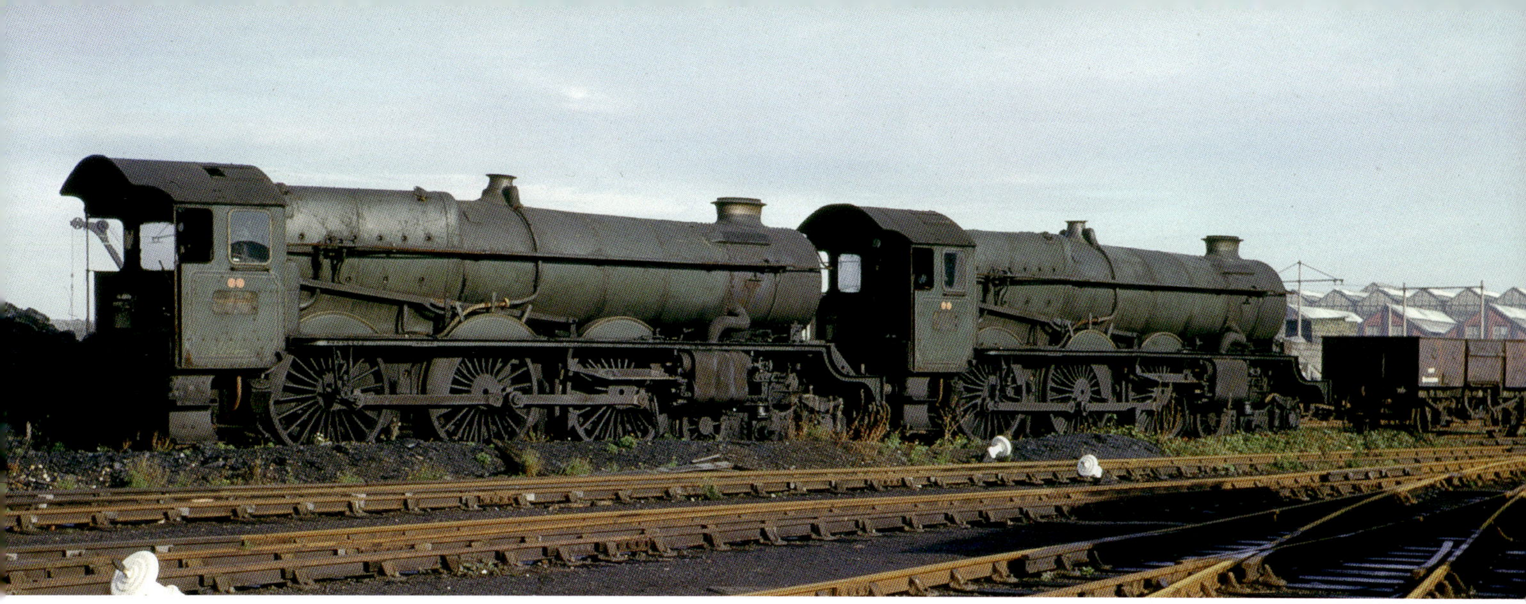

Two once proud Kings await their last rites within the yard during 1963.

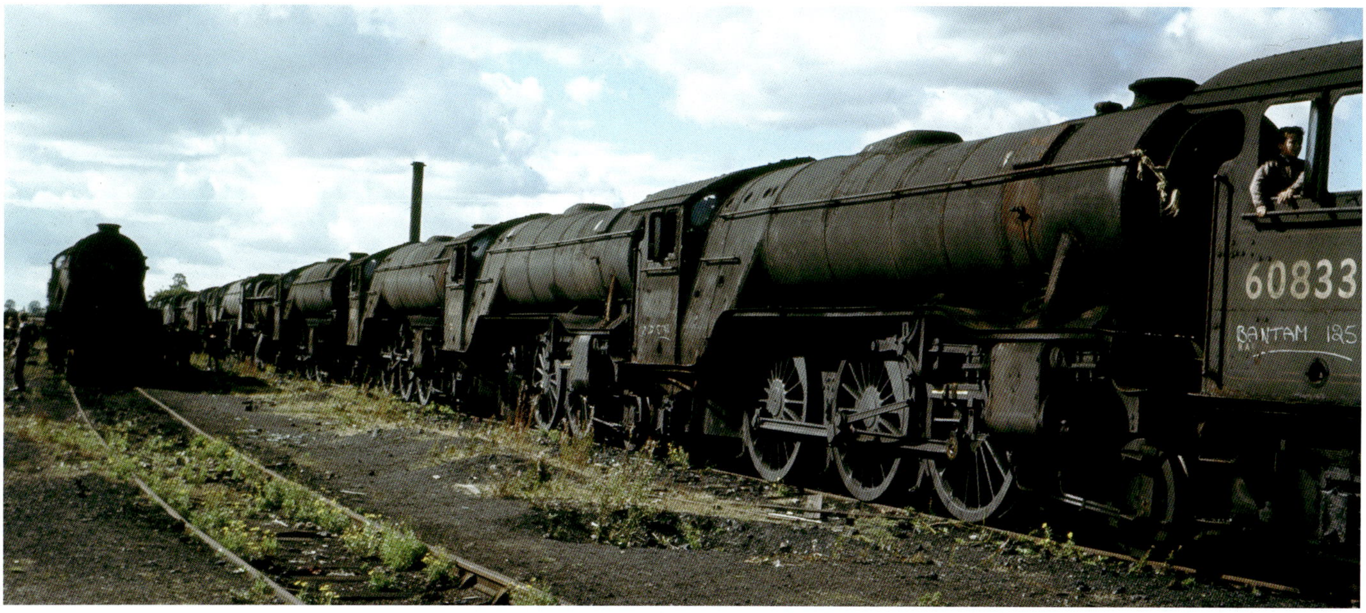

Several of Gresley's V2s found their way here too for disposal.

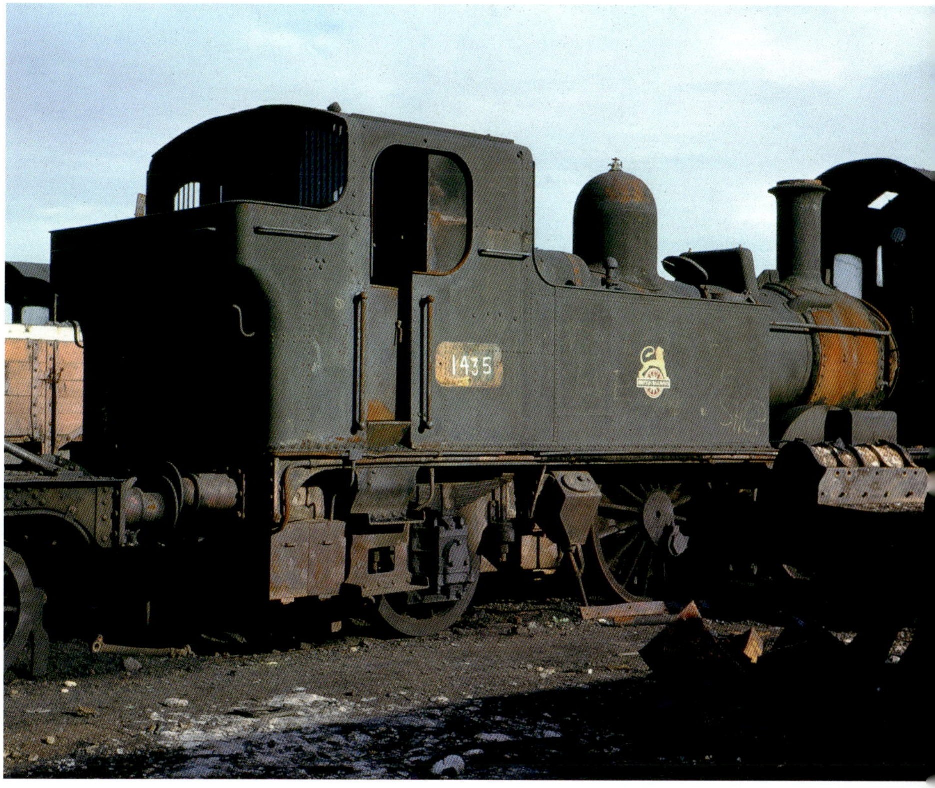

Also tucked away among much larger engines was 1435 awaiting it's destiny with the scrapmen. ***All by John Gill***

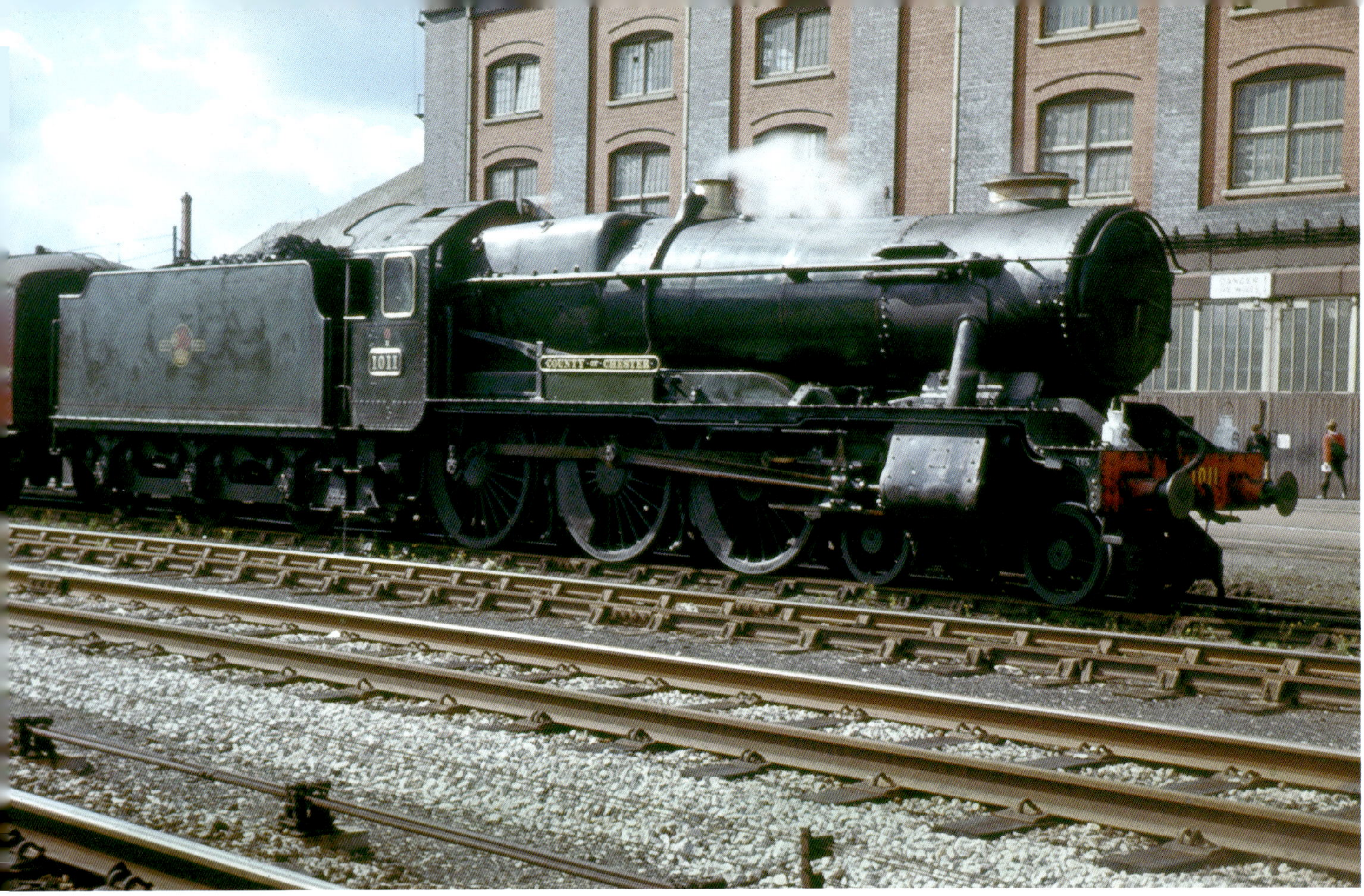

An enthusiasts tour train has brought 1016 County of Hants into the works to allow participants to disembark for a tour of the works and to rejoin their train alongside the main erecting shops. ***John Gill***

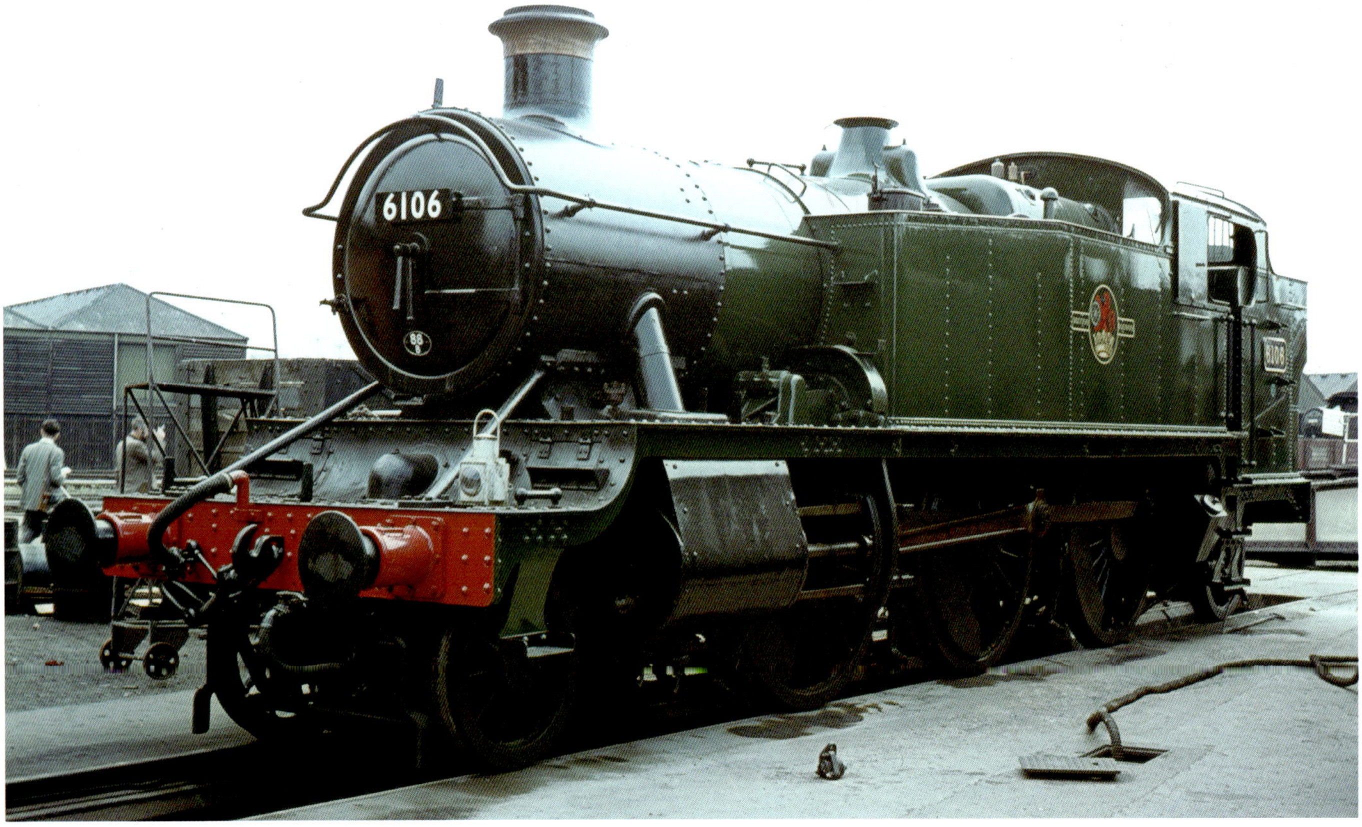

This would be her last official works visit for the later to be preserved Large Prairie 6106 in 1964 repainted into a more economic un-lined green livery for its last eighteen months in service before purchase by the Great Western Society. ***Noel Marrison***

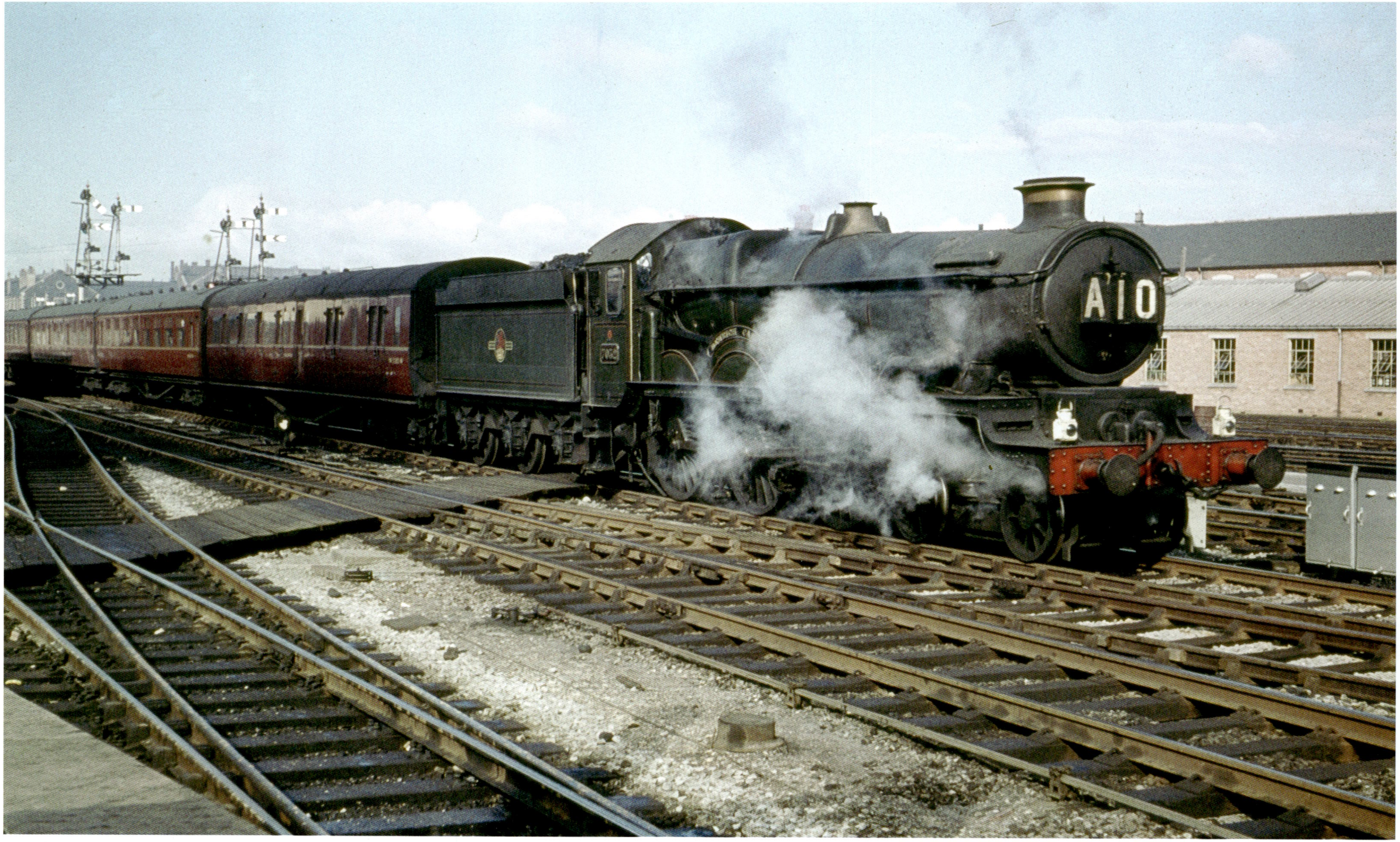

Making its way into the station at Swindon in 1960 was 7032 Denbigh Castle with express headlamps and the once often used train reporting number system in place for the benefit of signalling and station staff. ***Strathwood Library Collection***

Bristol City Rover

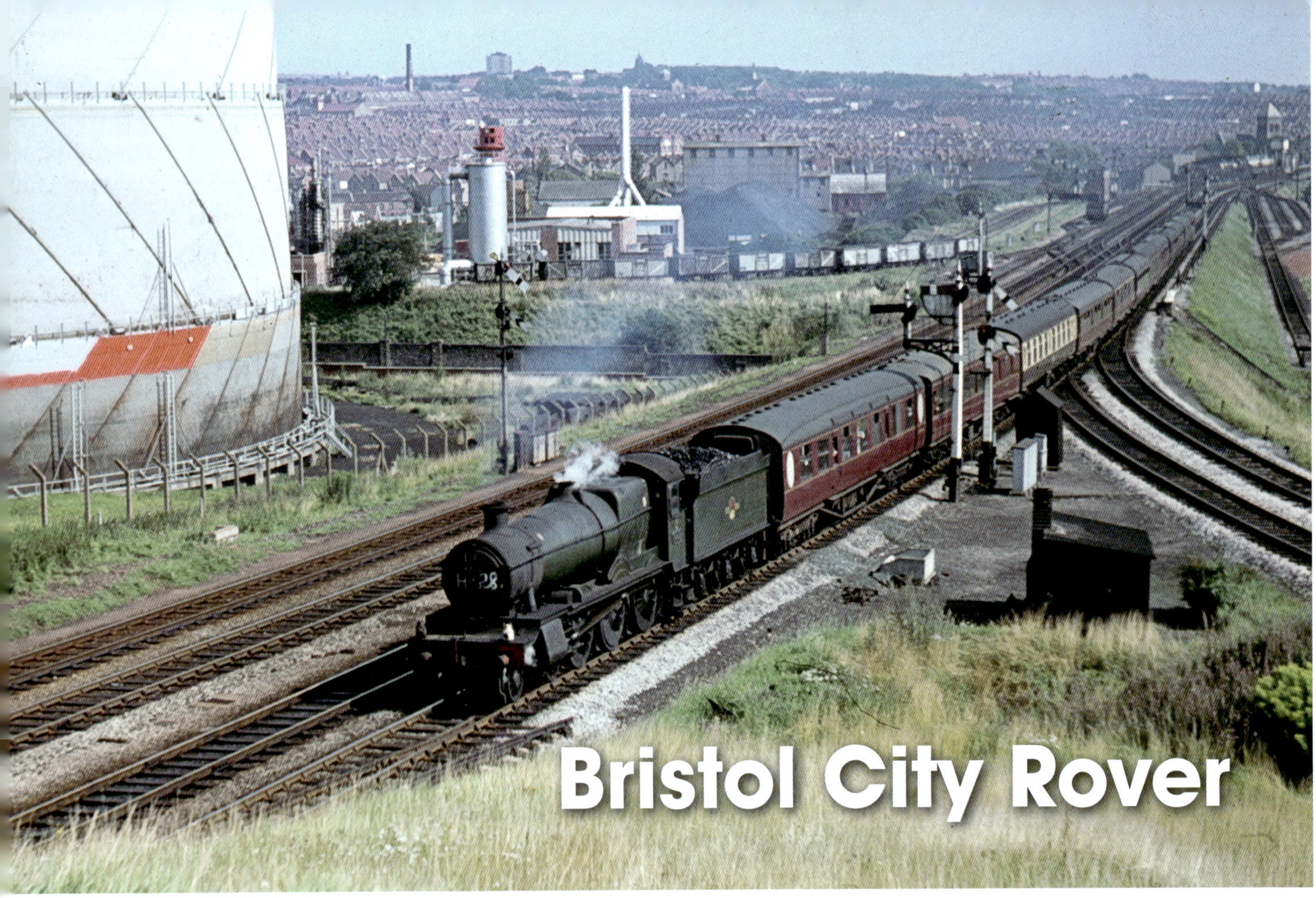

An inter regional express makes its way past Narroways Junction with 6862 Derwent Grange at the helm in 1964.
Strathwood Library Collection

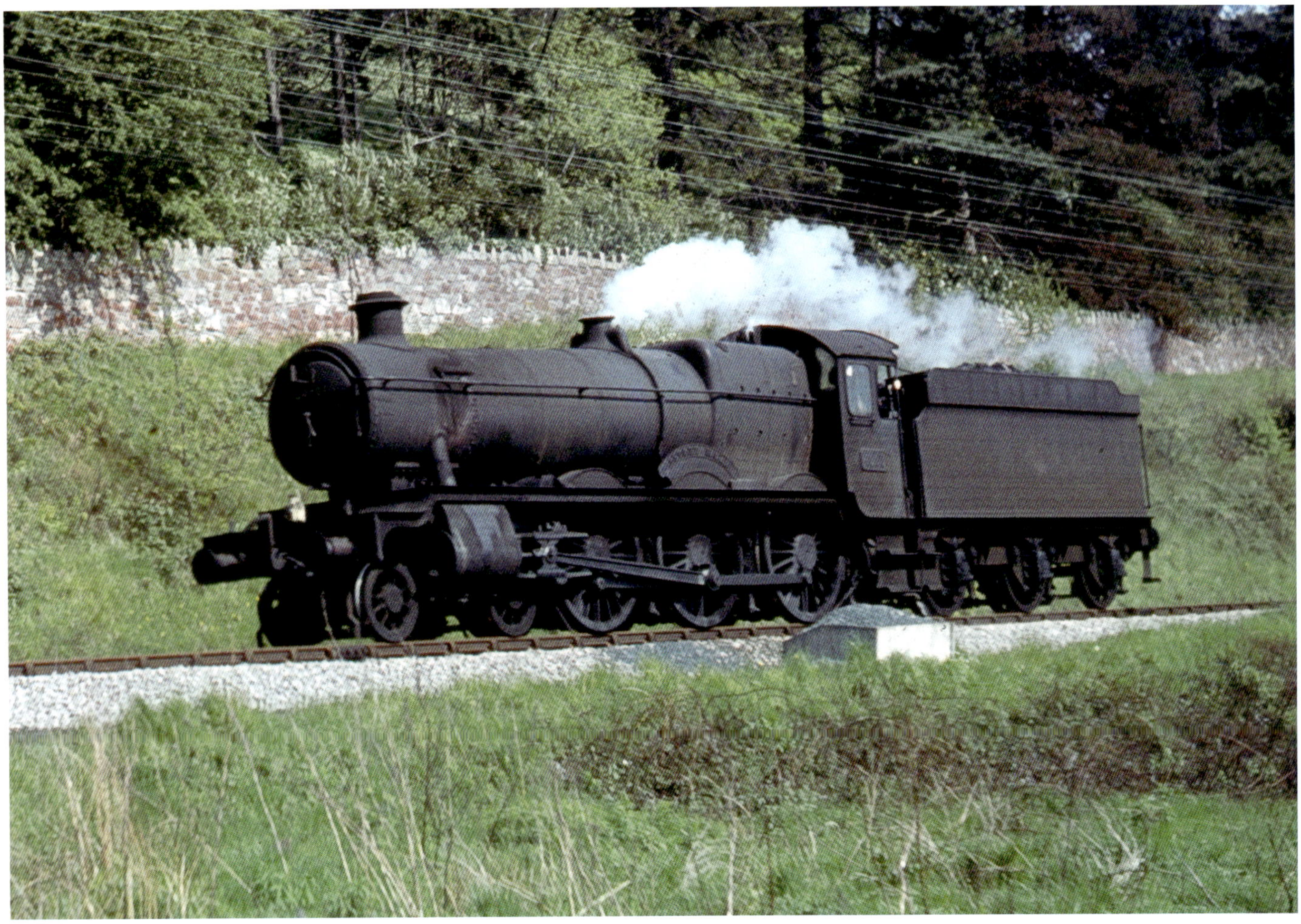

Running briskly as a light engine near Twerton also in 1964 was 4903 Astley Hall long past the care of any cleaners at its home shed or anywhere else for that matter. ***Strathwood Library Collection***

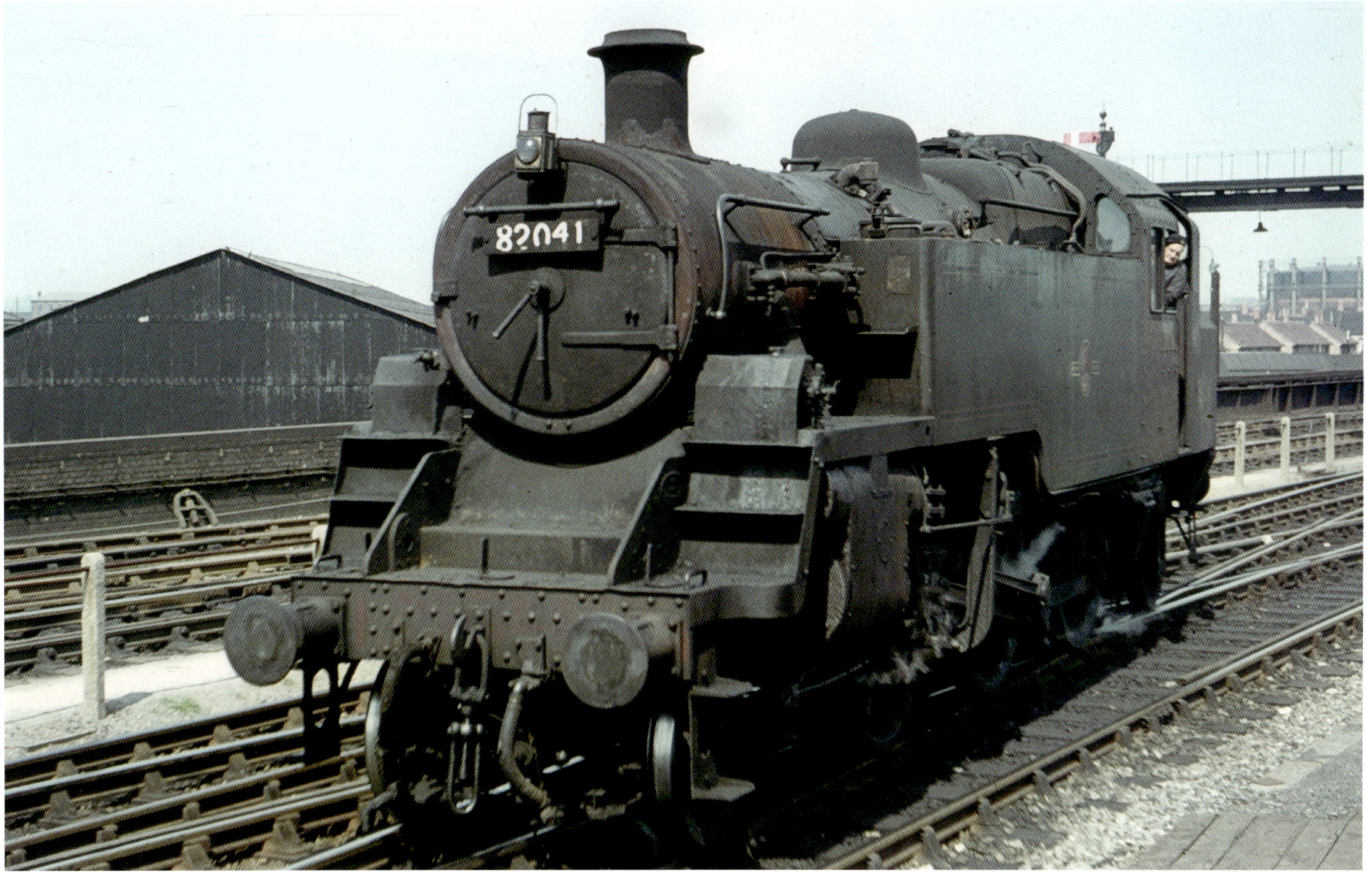

The Western Region's preference for painting a number of Standard locomotives into lined green is borne out with Class 3MT 82041 shuffling around Temple Meads during 1965 whilst a number of its classmates had to make do with lined black livery. ***Strathwood Library Collection***

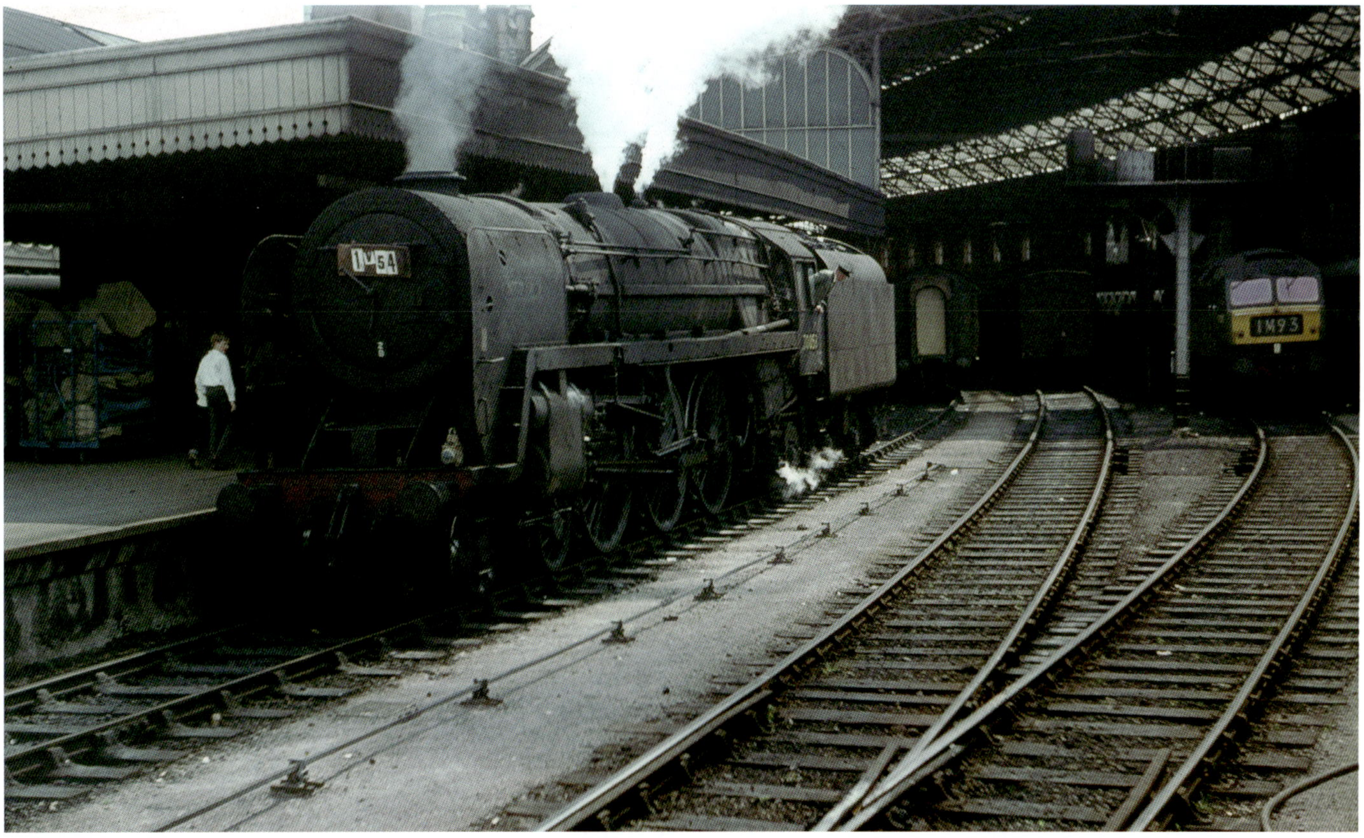

Whereas the lined green livery of woebegone Britannia 70053 Moray Firth is almost academic when allowed to deteriorate to this level also at Temple Meads the same day. ***Strathwood Library Collection***

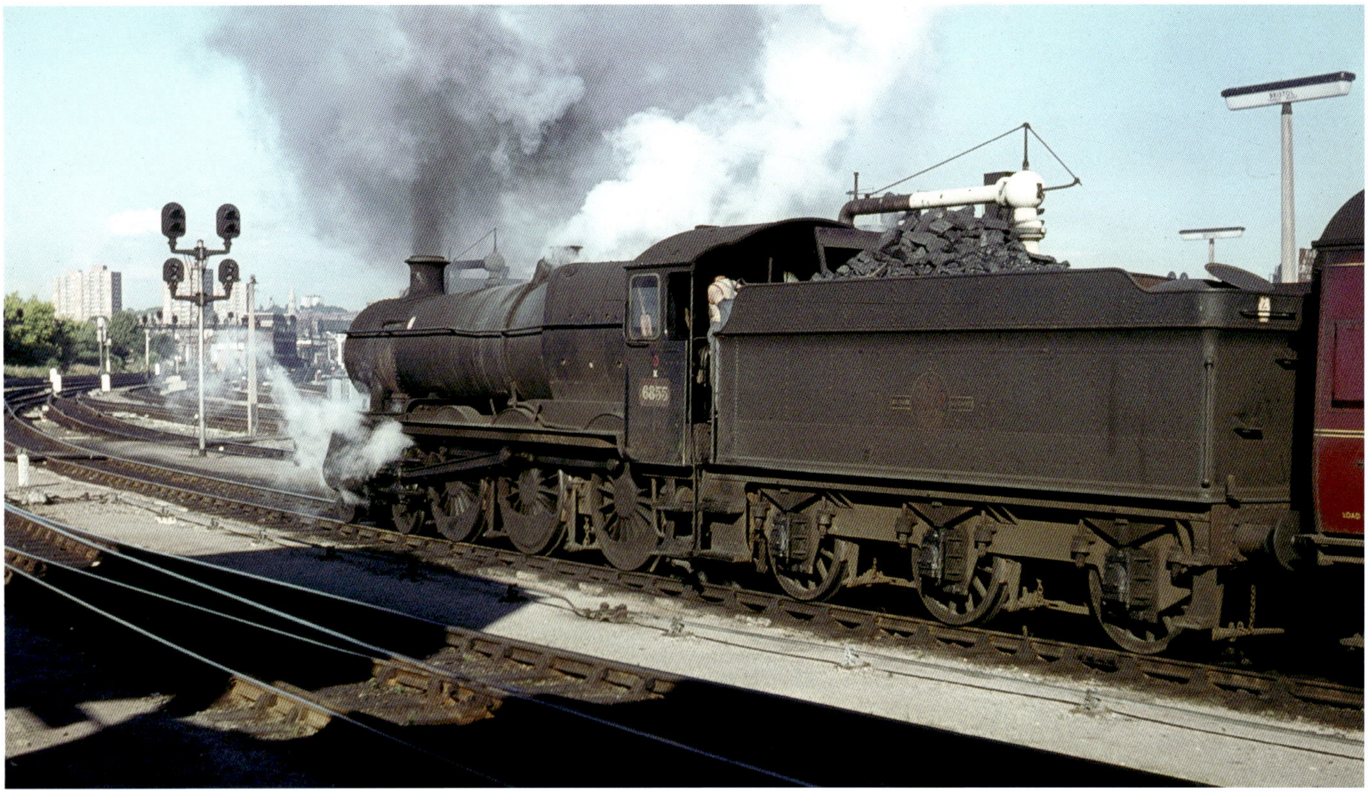

They may have been run down but locomotives such as 6855 Saighton Grange could still provide some drama, such as here powering out of Temple Meads in the summer of 1965. ***Strathwood Library Collection***

However just a few years before in 1962 sights such as 5072 Hurricane with headboard still applied having just been taken off the Cornishman whilst a Warship lurks in the distance the other side of the Bath Road bridge could be savoured. ***Gerald Peacock***

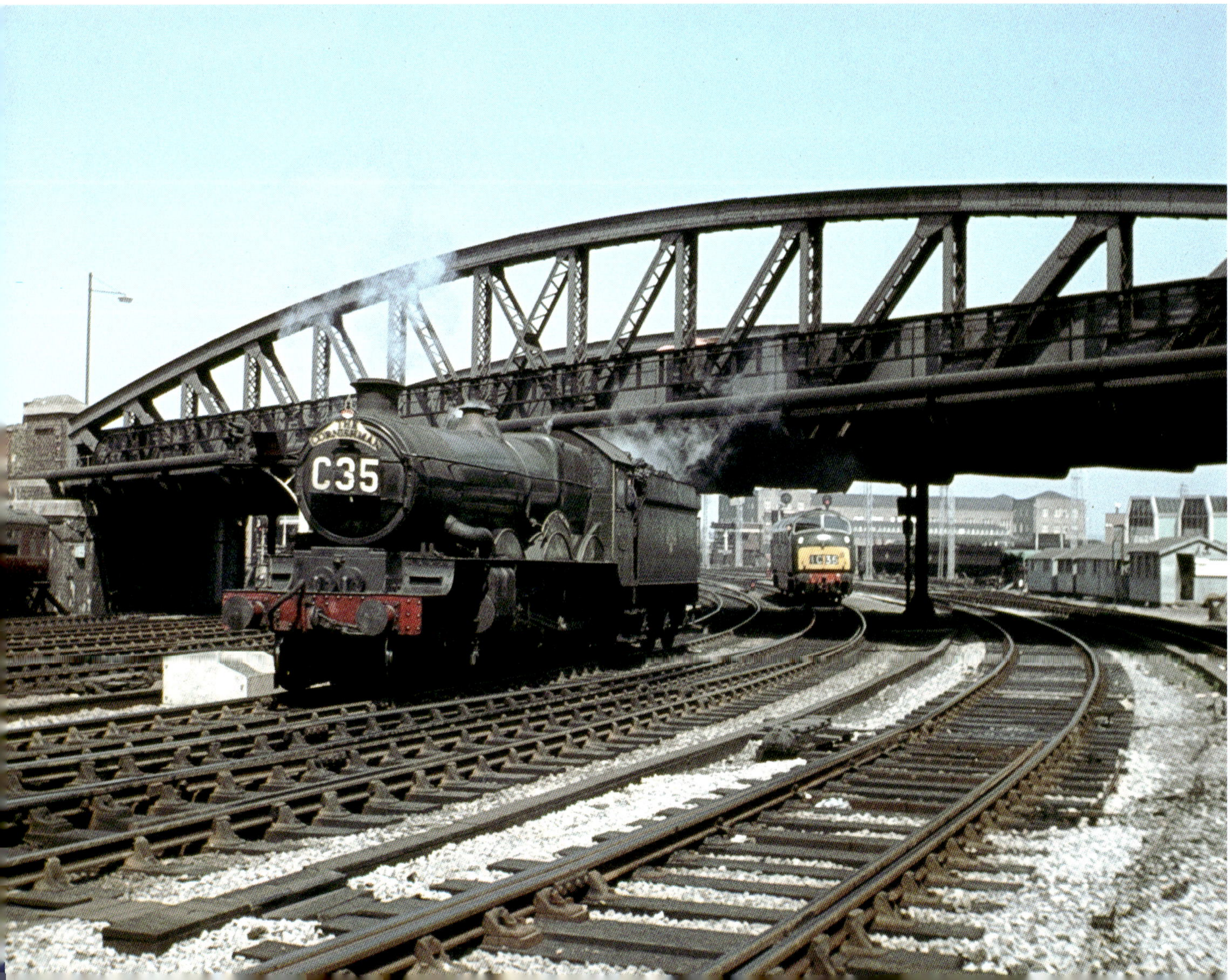

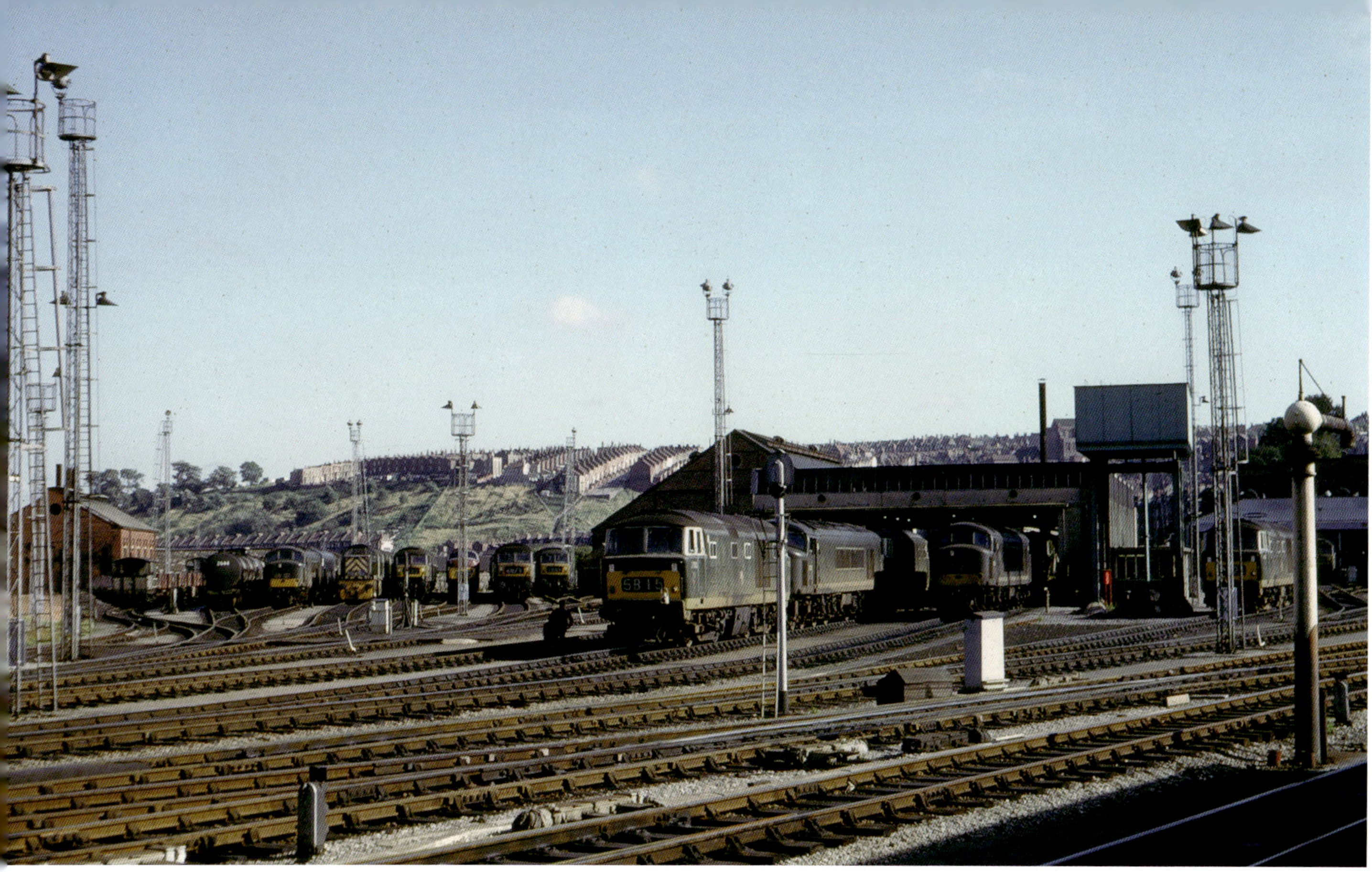

This is the kind of vista that would greet a spotter alighting at Temple Meads of 82A Bath Road, now wholly dealing with diesels, with a fine mix of classes to be enjoyed on 4 September 1966. ***Frank Hornby***

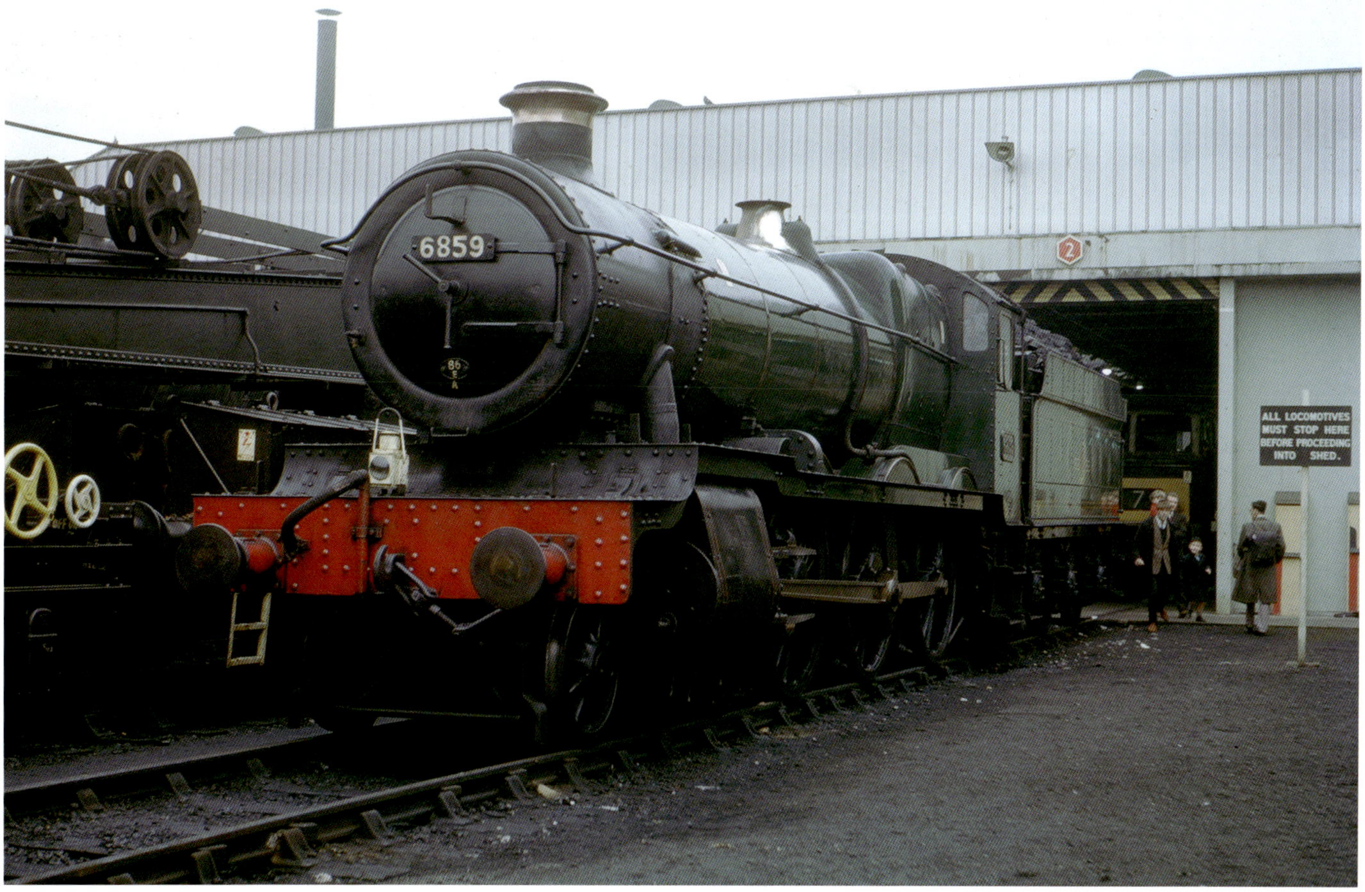

British Rail arranged an Open Day at Bath Road for 23 October 1965 and put some effort into cleaning up a few locomotives for display such as 6859 Yiewsley Grange, although it seems the nameplates were no longer to be found. ***Strathwood Library Collection***

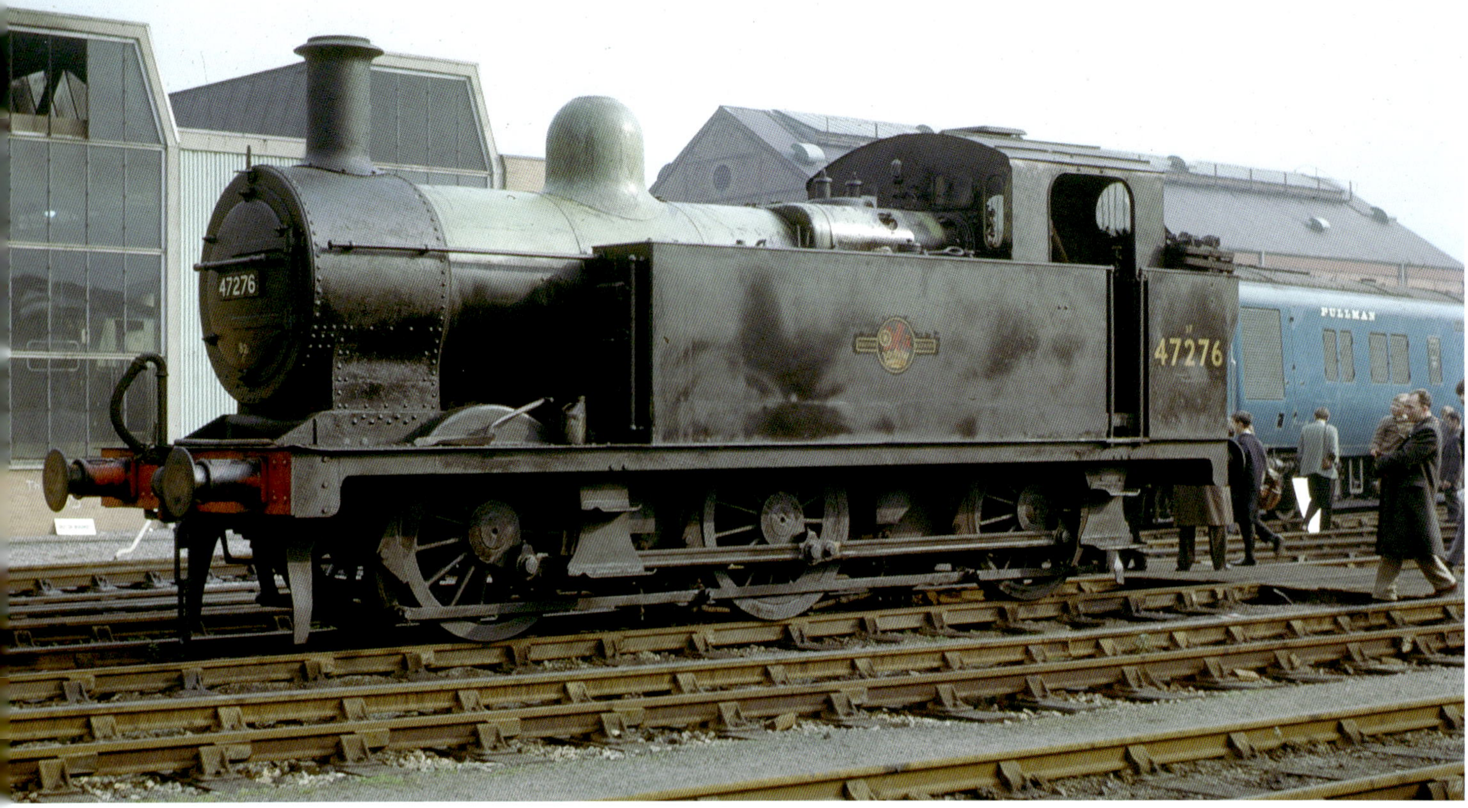

Among the steam exhibits that day was this Jinty 47276 parked up close to one of the region's Blue Pullman sets. If you had been home in time that Saturday evening you could have watched William Hartnell as Doctor Who, or perhaps Danger Man starring Patrick McGoohan on television. ***Late Bill Potter/Strathwood Library Collection***

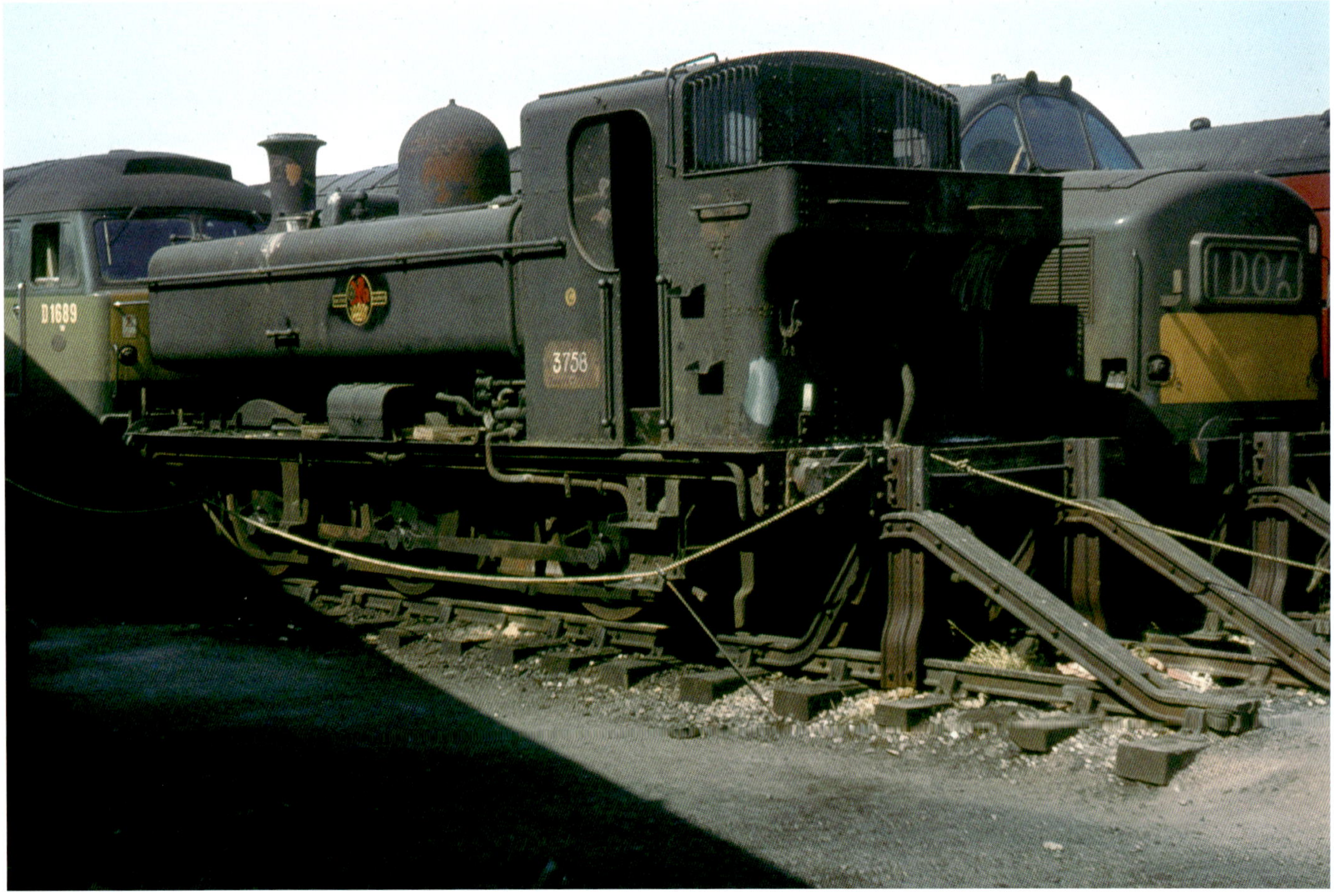

Tucked around the back for those exploring the depot 3738 could be found among the diesels. As luck would have it this Pannier would be sent to Barry, spending eight and half years there before finding sanctuary with the Great Western Society at Didcot. ***Strathwood Library Collection***

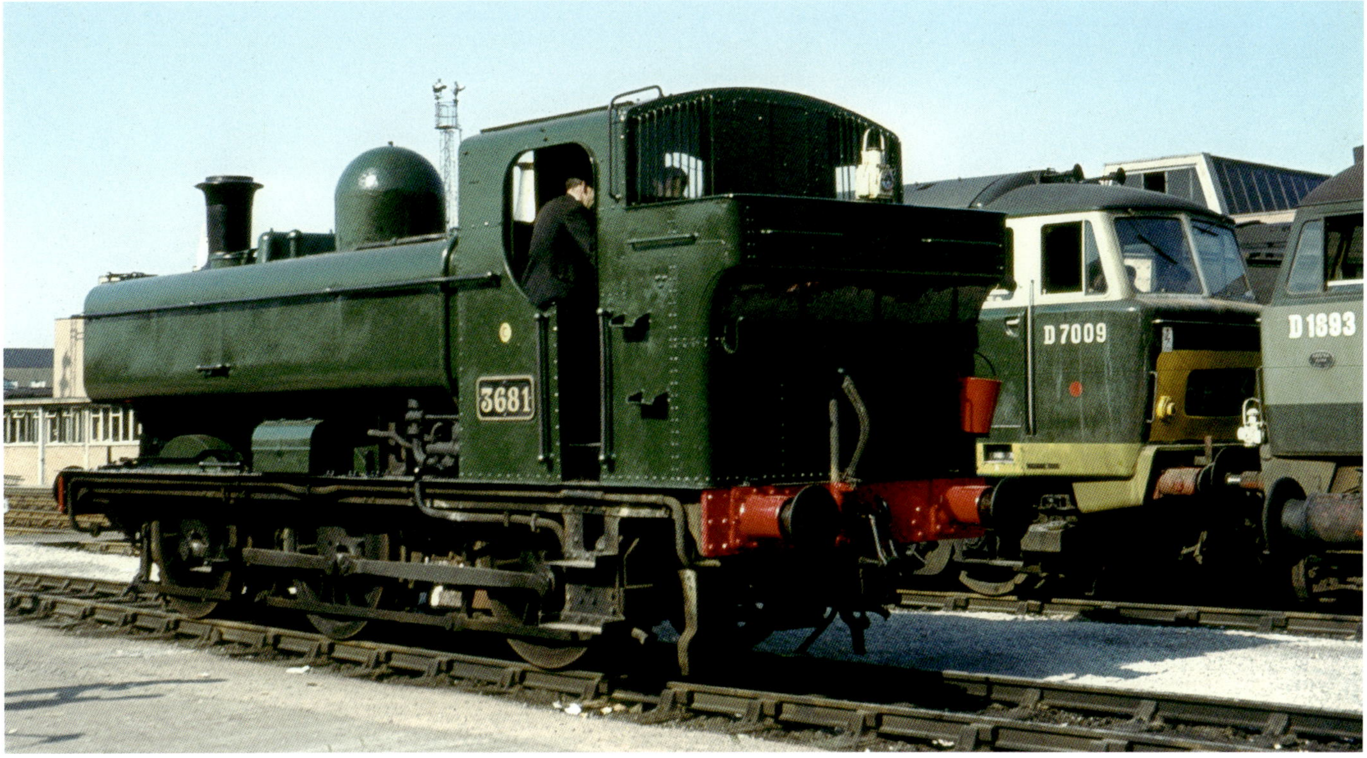

Ironically sister Pannier 3681 had been repainted and set aside at the depot for a preservation project along with 3758, however the local scheme stalled and failed and the pair were sold to Cashmores for scrap. ***Strathwood Library Collection***

Also to be found among the then new D9500 diesels, later Class 14s was 6141 which still looked to be in very serviceable condition although it was withdrawn six weeks later. ***Strathwood Library Collection***

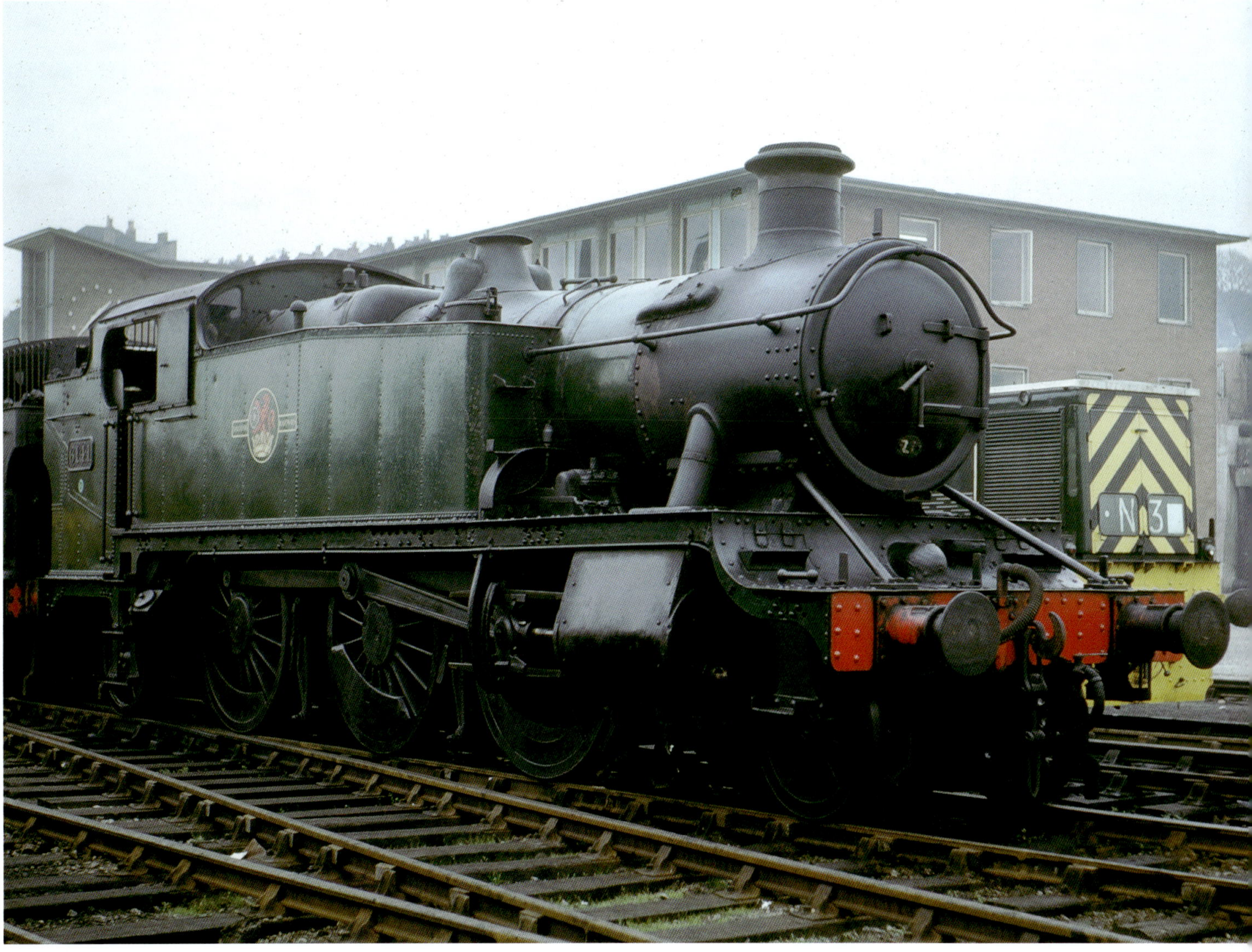

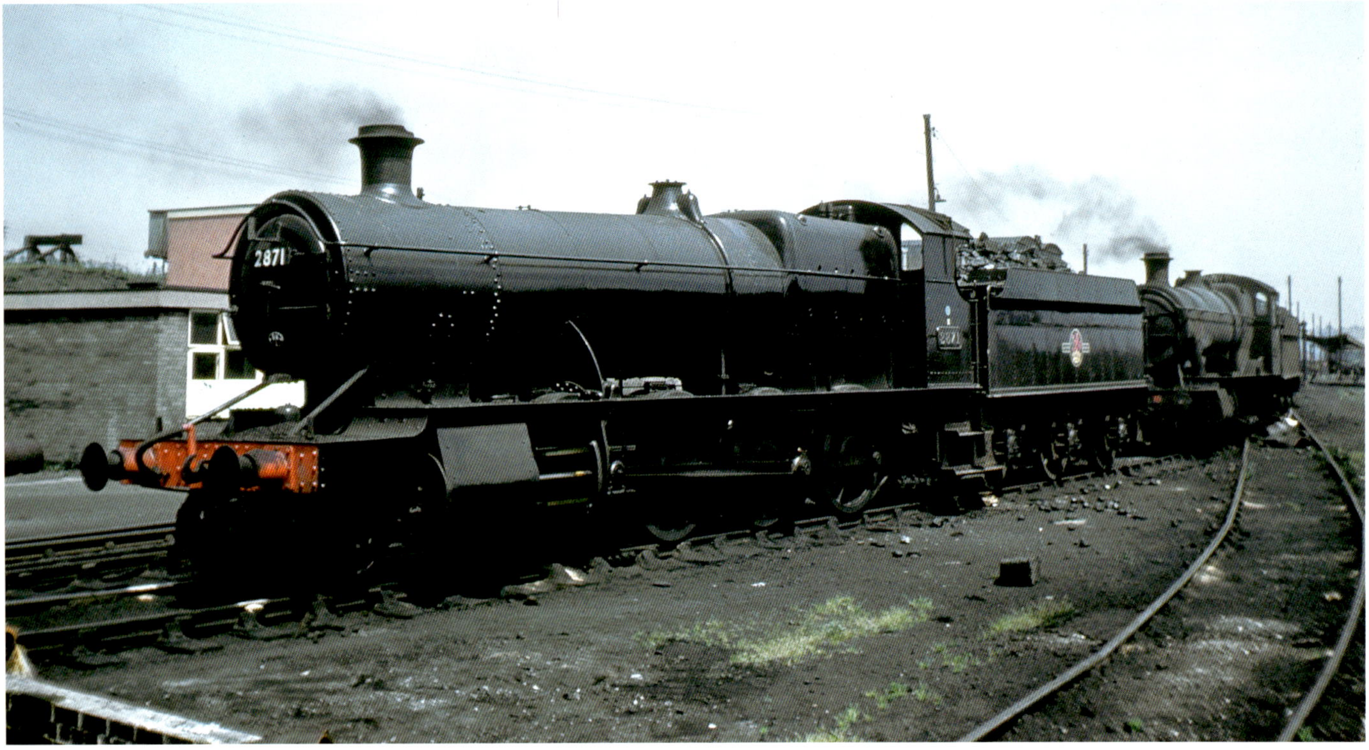

Coded as a large sub shed to Bristol Bath Road was 82B St.Phillips Marsh where we come across a recently ex works 2871 which in 1960 had given the railways forty two years service and would manage another three before being declared withdrawn. ***Gerald Peacock***

The scene inside the roundhouse here was certainly ethereal, and this was just three days before closure on 13 June 1964. On the radio that day you may have tuned into Juke Box Jury hosted by David Jacobs whose guests were Adam Faith and Zsa Zsa Gabor! ***Dave Down***

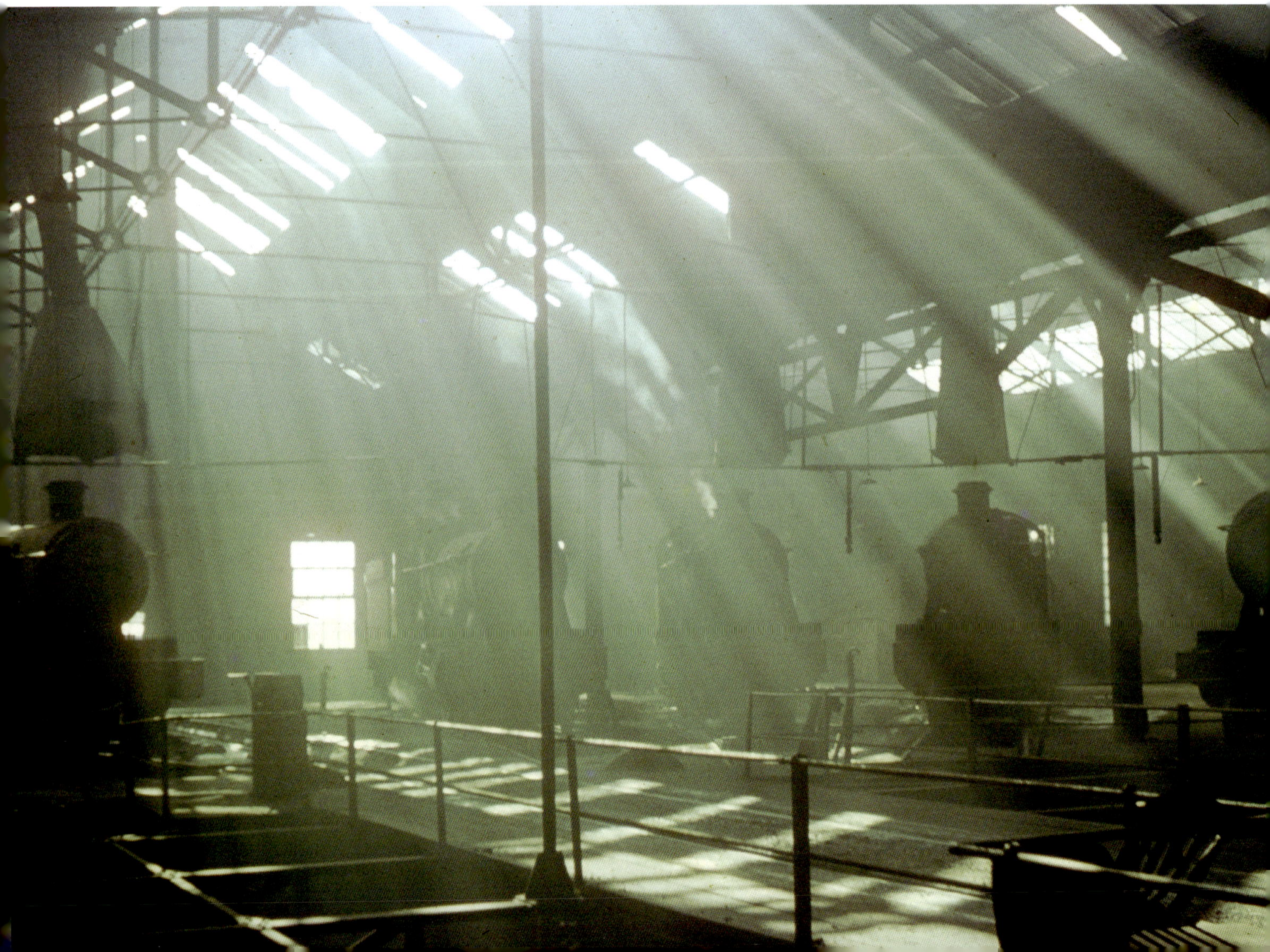

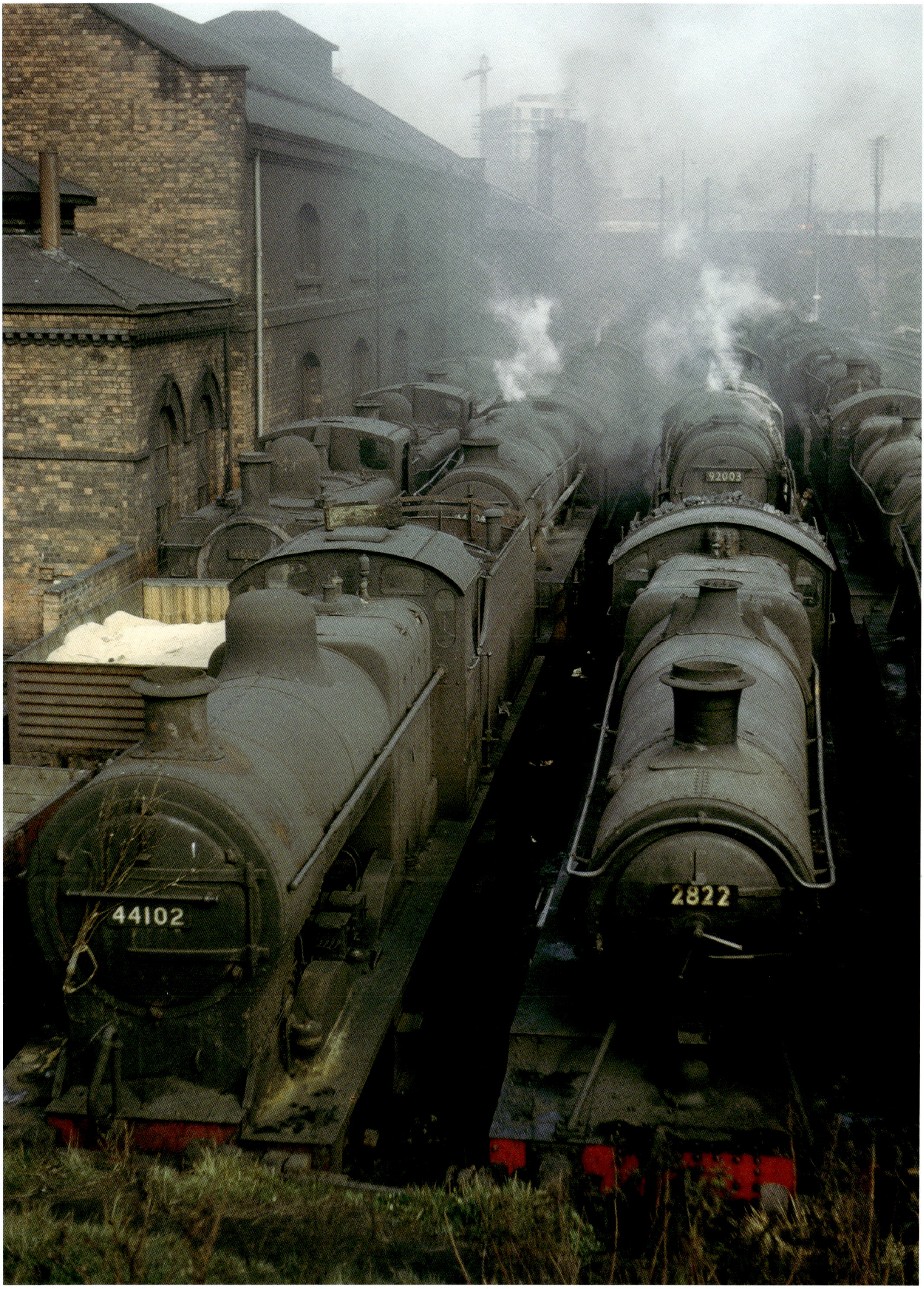

Bristol also boasted another engine shed coded 82E at Barrow Road which had a Midland Railway provenance from their routes to the city. It had been part of the London Midland Region from Nationalisation coded 22A until taking over the former Yeovil Pen Mill shed code and falling within the Western Region's boundaries from February 1958. It certainly looked full on 25 October 1964. ***Colin Rogers/Strathwood Library Collection***

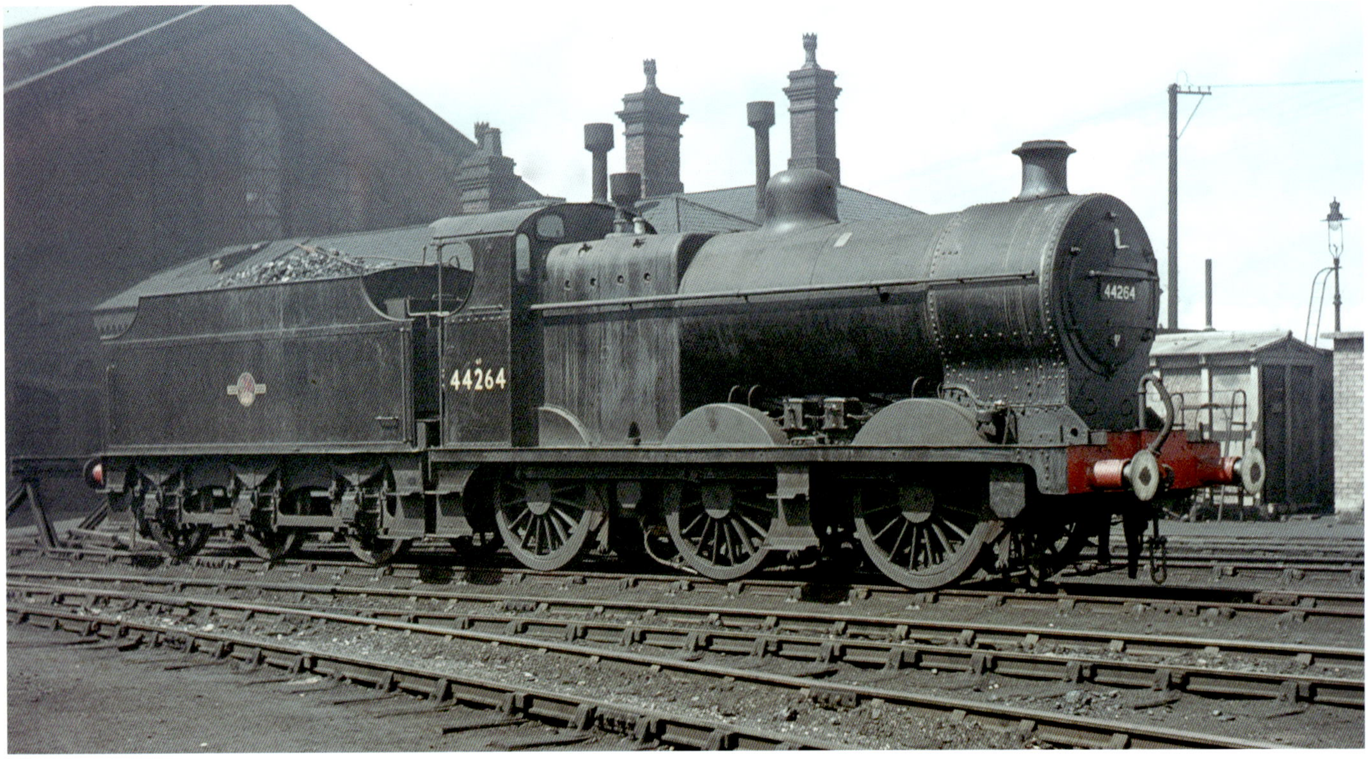

Well turned out on the shed in 1965 was 44264, this Fowler 4F had seen recent use on an enthusiast's special, hence its condition. ***Strathwood Library Collection***

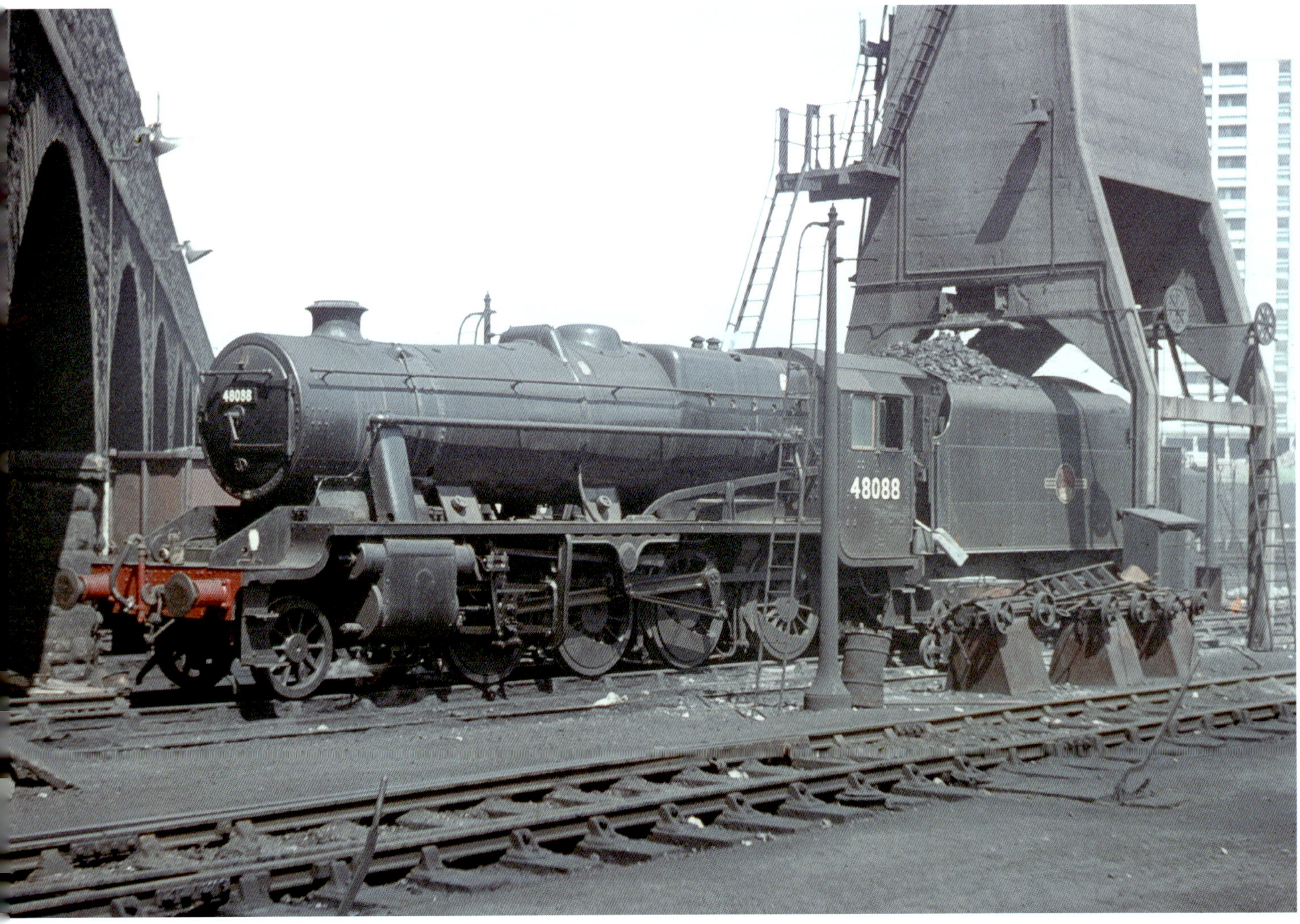

Having just taken on a healthy charge of fresh coal in her tender Stanier 8F 48088 is ready for the road again in 1965. This was the last year for Barrow Road as the shed closed as of 21 November. ***Strathwood Library Collection***

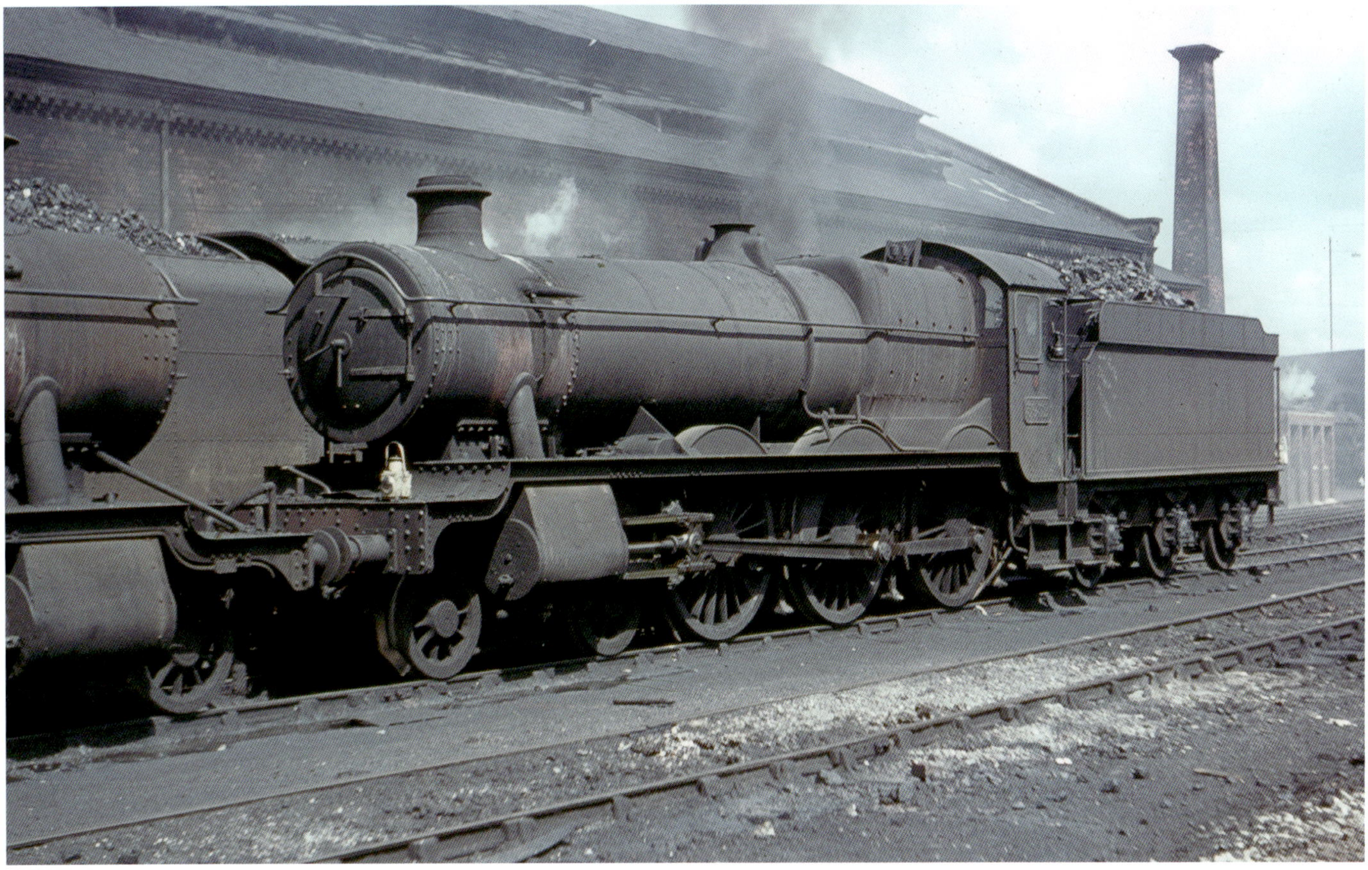

An all too familiar scene as 5932 has lost a number of it's plates by 1965. Named as Haydon Hall when built in 1933 it was just days away from being taken out of service here in the late summer sunshine. The locomotive had been sent when new to the city being based at Bath Road. During the 1950s it was a regular out of Old Oak Common, returning to Bristol and being allocated here at Barrow Road when withdrawn. For scrapping it was sent across the other side of the River Severn to Cashmore's yard in Newport. ***Strathwood Library Collection***

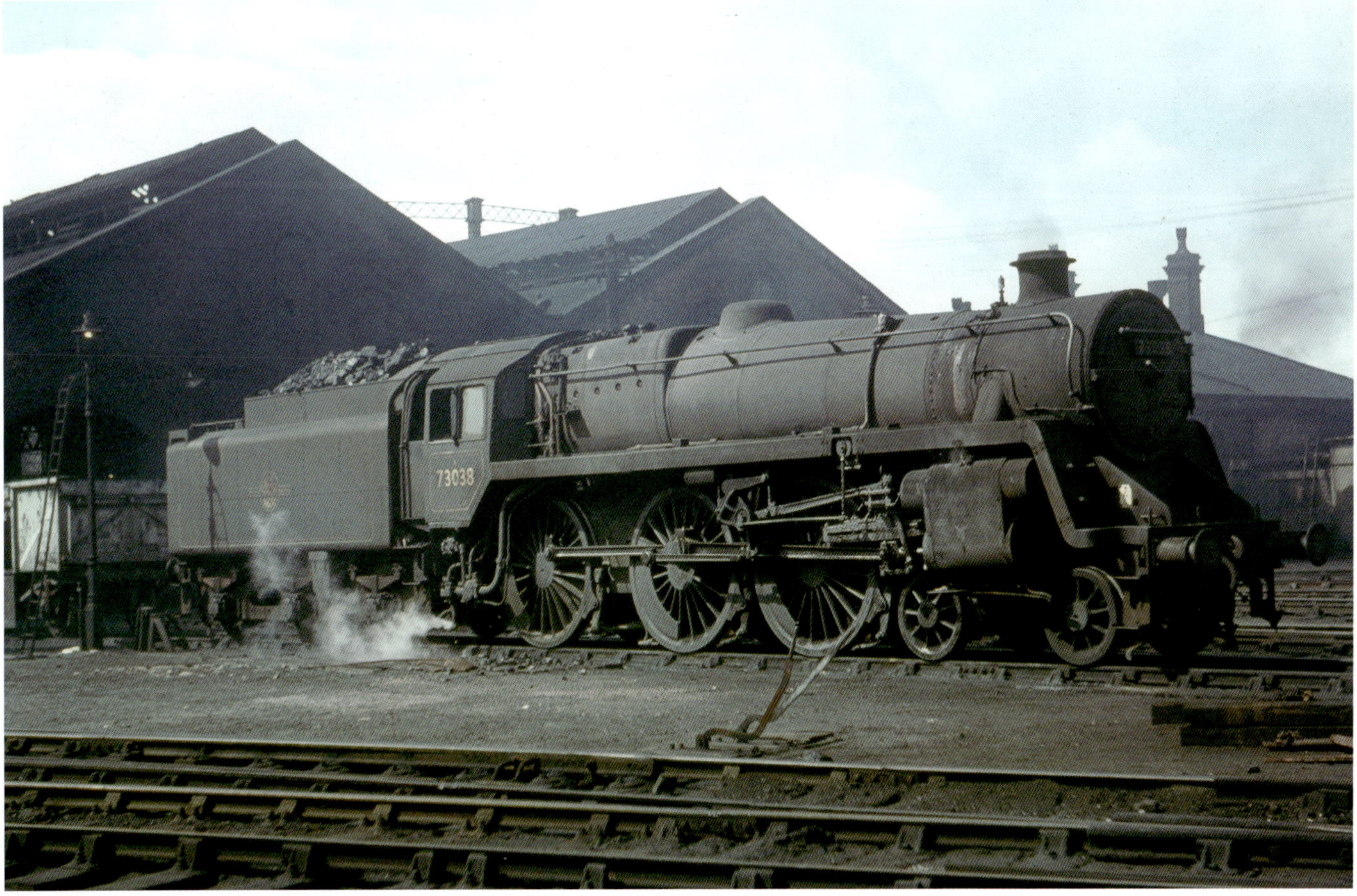

Also ready for her next duty that day was Standard 5MT 73038 which was a product of Derby Works being one of four released to traffic in September 1953. ***Strathwood Library Collection***

Tunnel Vision

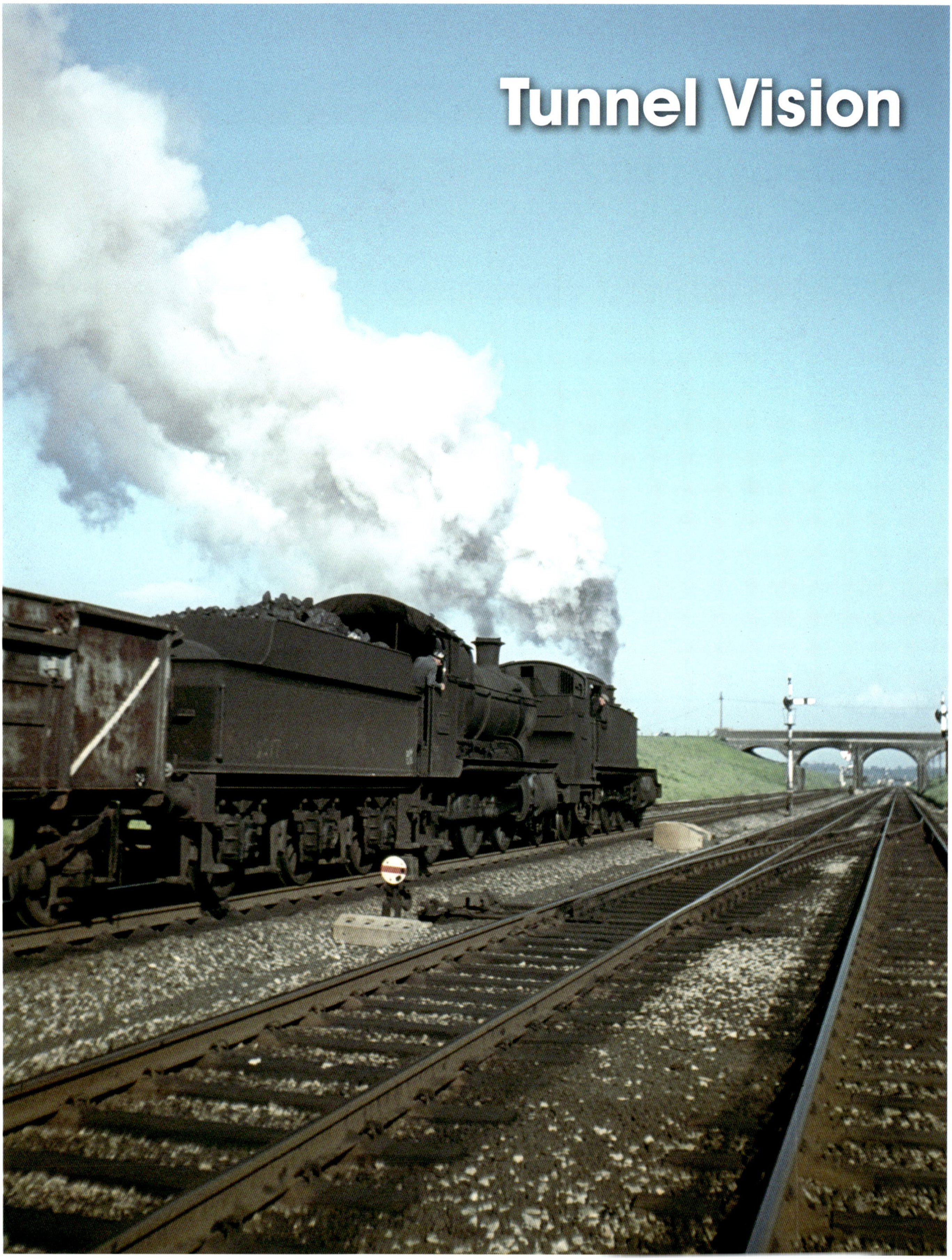

The use of pilots and banking engines for freights going through the Severn Tunnel was commonplace, as it was hardly a spot where engine crews or railway management would want trains to get into difficulties. In 1963 this Prairie and Churchward Mogul combination were not hanging about near Aust Road. ***Gerald Peacock***

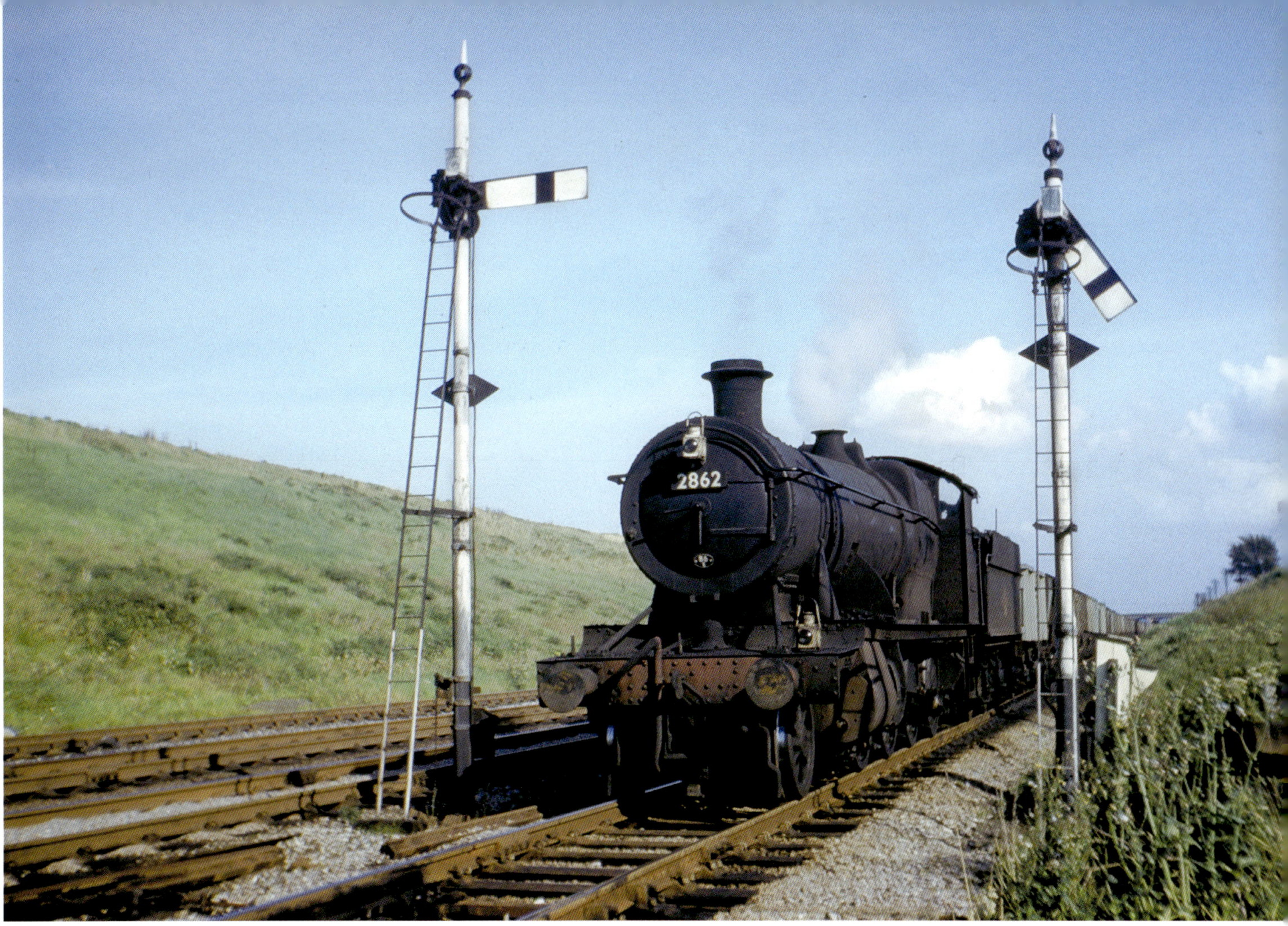

The Western Region retained a preference for lower quadrant semaphore signals which had been the choice of the Great Western before them. On the approaches to the tunnel under the River Severn 2862 has just been signalled away with a down freight in 1963. ***Gerald Peacock***

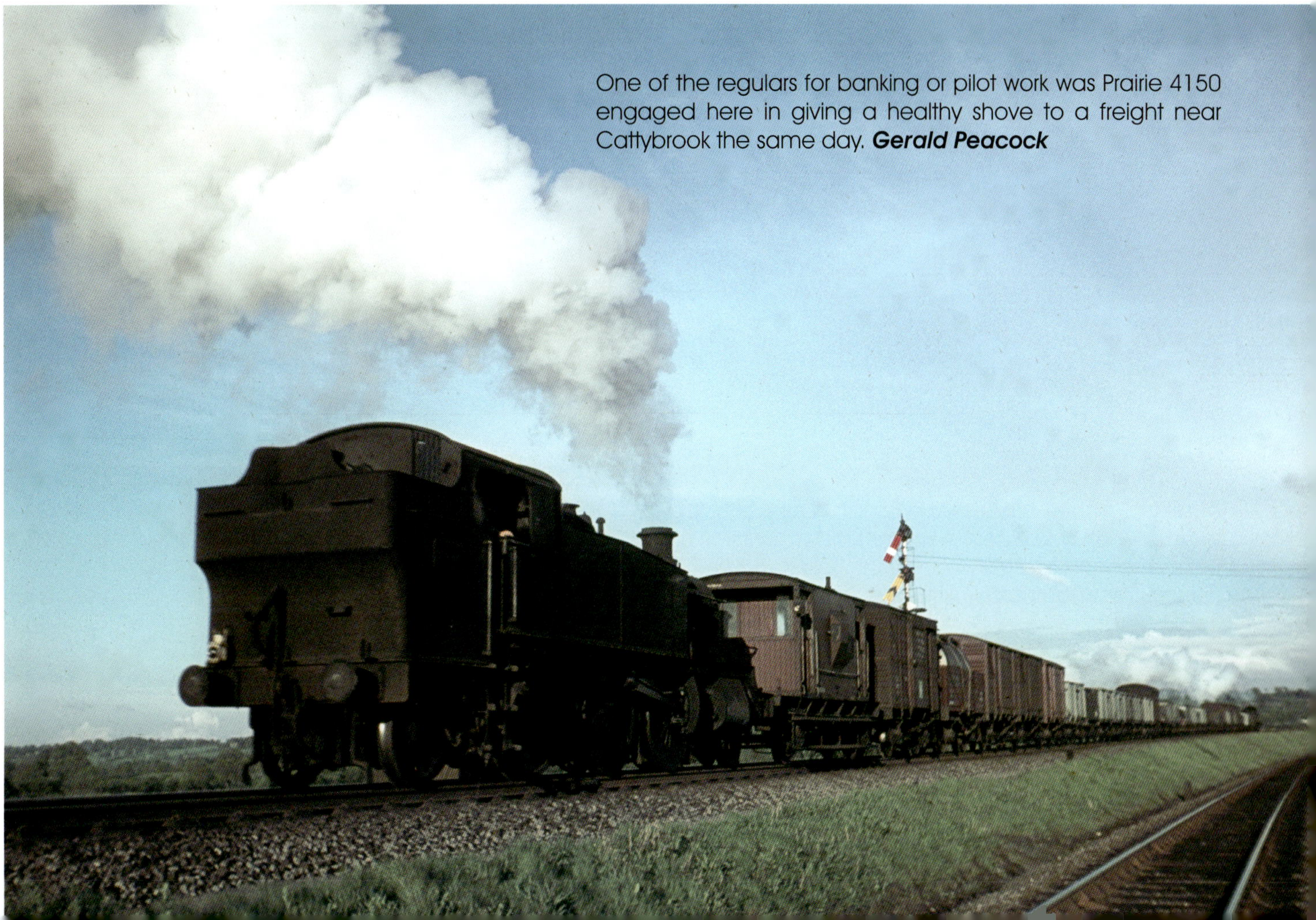

One of the regulars for banking or pilot work was Prairie 4150 engaged here in giving a healthy shove to a freight near Cattybrook the same day. ***Gerald Peacock***

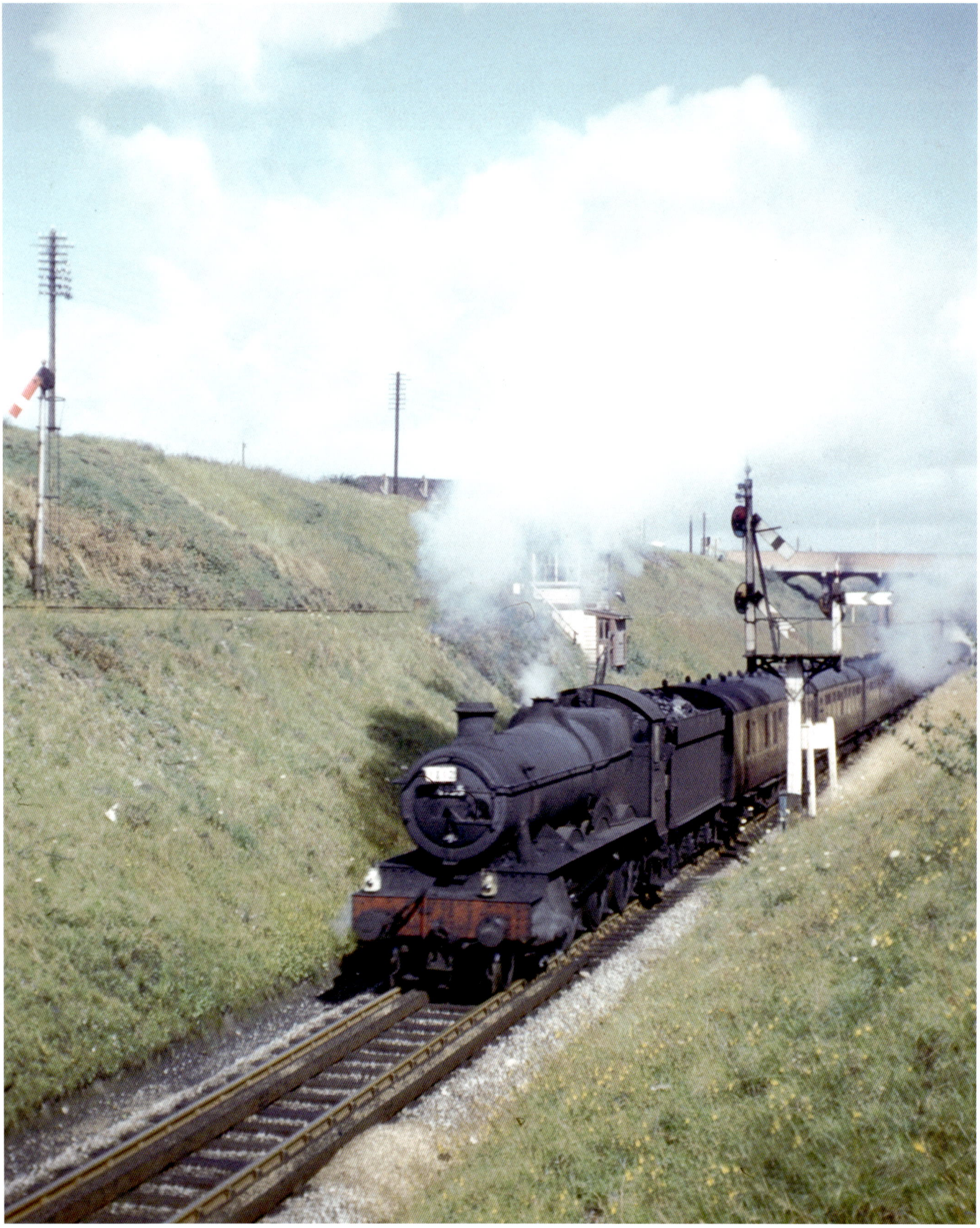

An up passenger train has 4955 Plaspower Hall at Patchway in 1963 which would be the engine's last year of traffic. Just like the locomotive the real Hall at Plas Power has been lost, it once stood near Wrexham and close to Offa's Dyke. It was once an important coal and iron smelting area with trees from the estate being used to provide charcoal for the processing. ***Gerald Peacock***

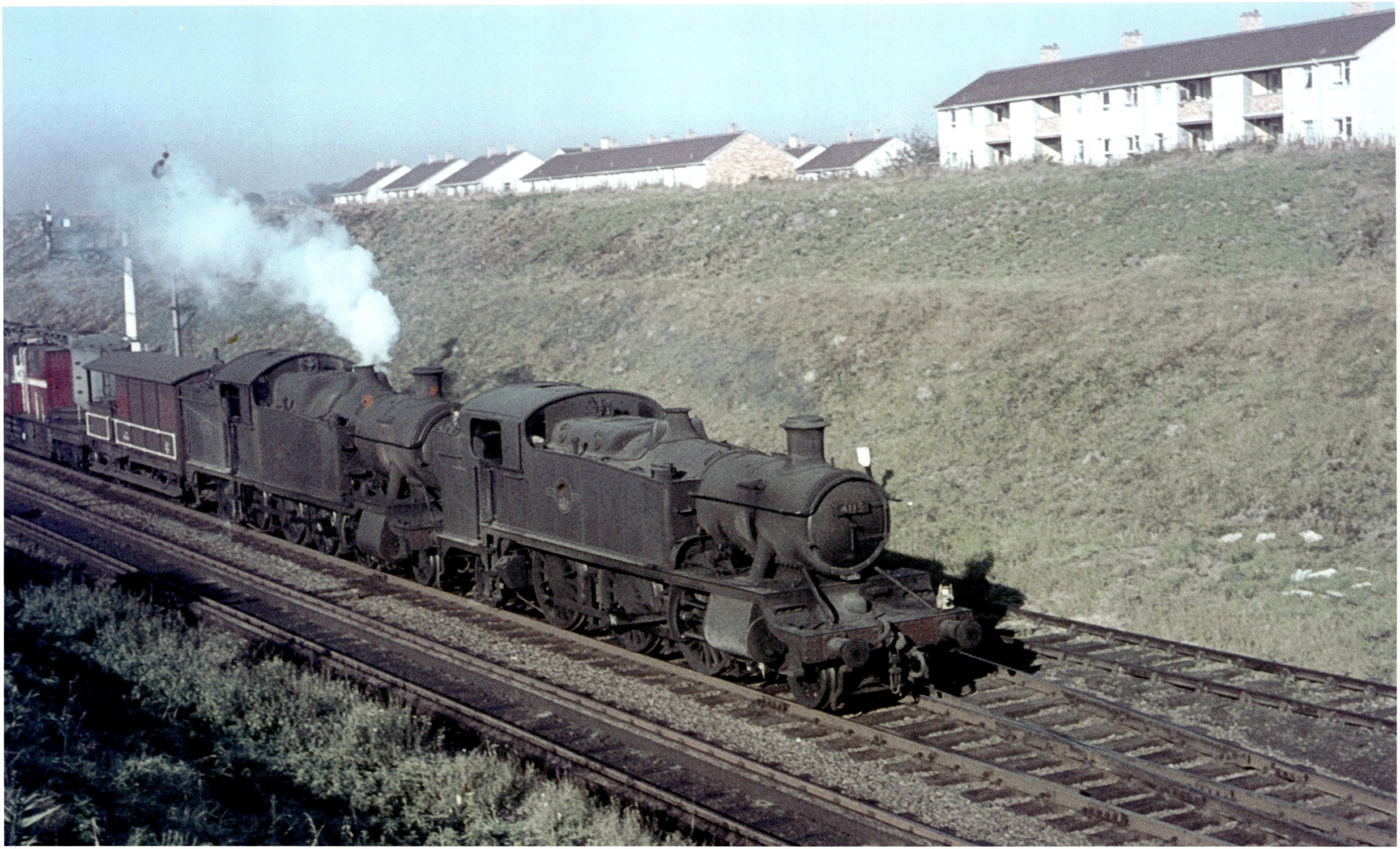

Put on the front to assist the powerful 2-8-2T 7252 which were Collett rebuilds of the Churchward 2-8-0Ts in the 4200 series, was Prairie 4115. The pairing are just getting underway at Caldicot on 18 October 1964. ***Dave Down***

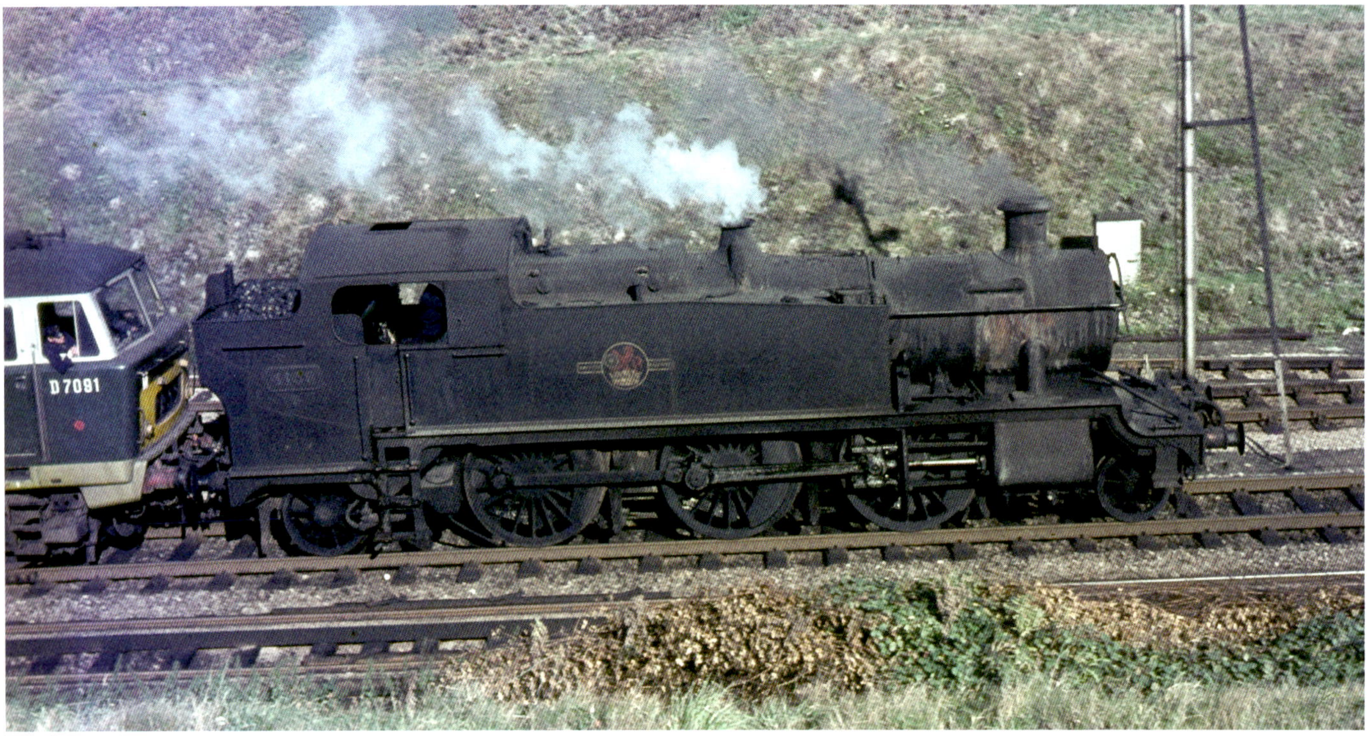

Even the shiney new diesels such as Hymek D7091 would be rostered for a steam pilot if their load justified it, as here with Prairie 4165 heading for the western portal of the tunnel at Caldicot on 17 October 1964. ***Dave Down***

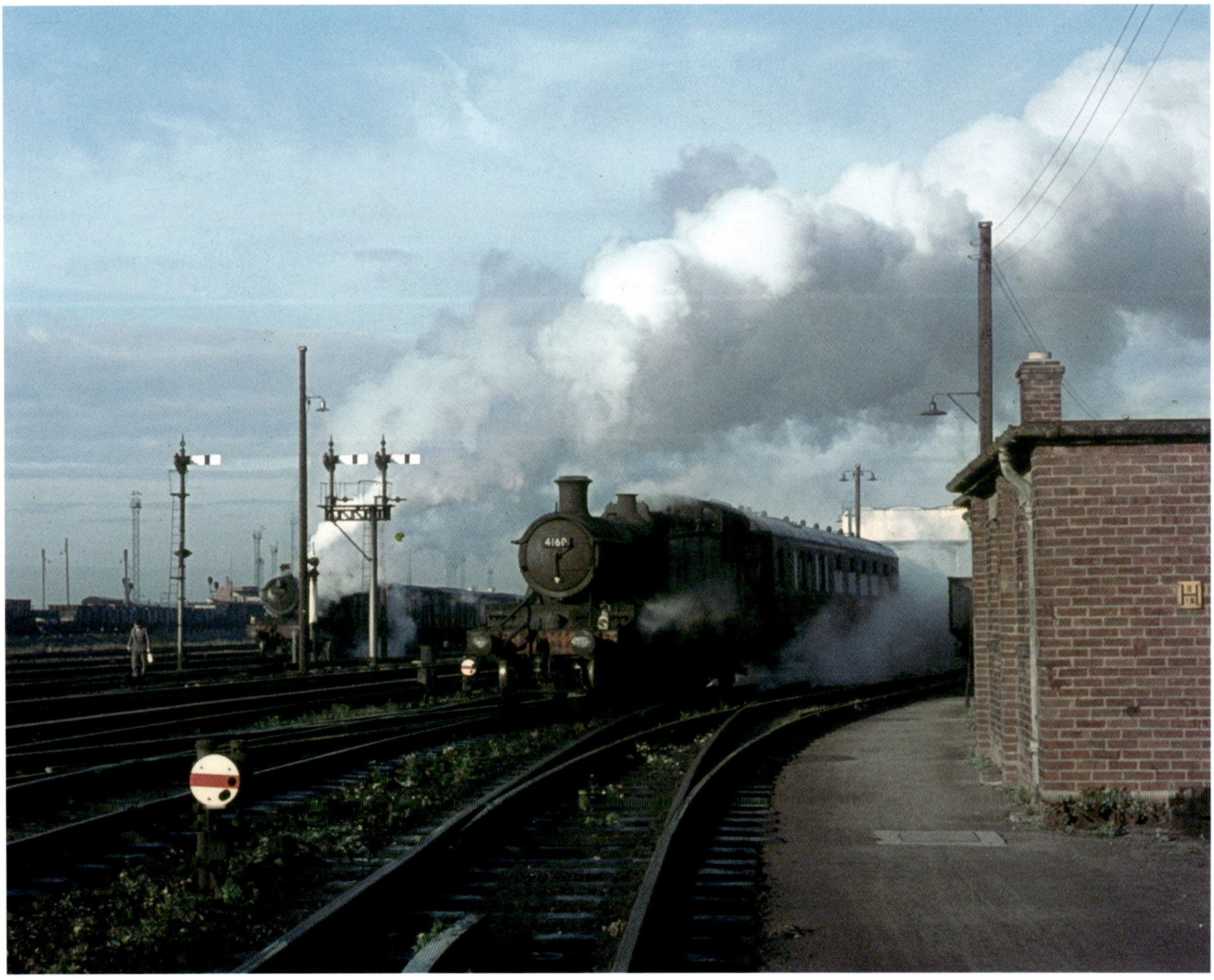

In the days before the now familiar Severn road crossings the railway offered a service from Severn Tunnel Junction by rail as a car ferry. Shuffling the stock for this once useful service on 10 October 1964 was Prairie 4160. ***Dave Down***

Gone With Regret

The former Somerset & Dorset route from Bath to Bournemouth holds a great affection with so many enthusiasts. With a number of trains being double headed such as this Standard 5MT pairing led by 73052 near Midford in 1962. ***Chris Forrest***

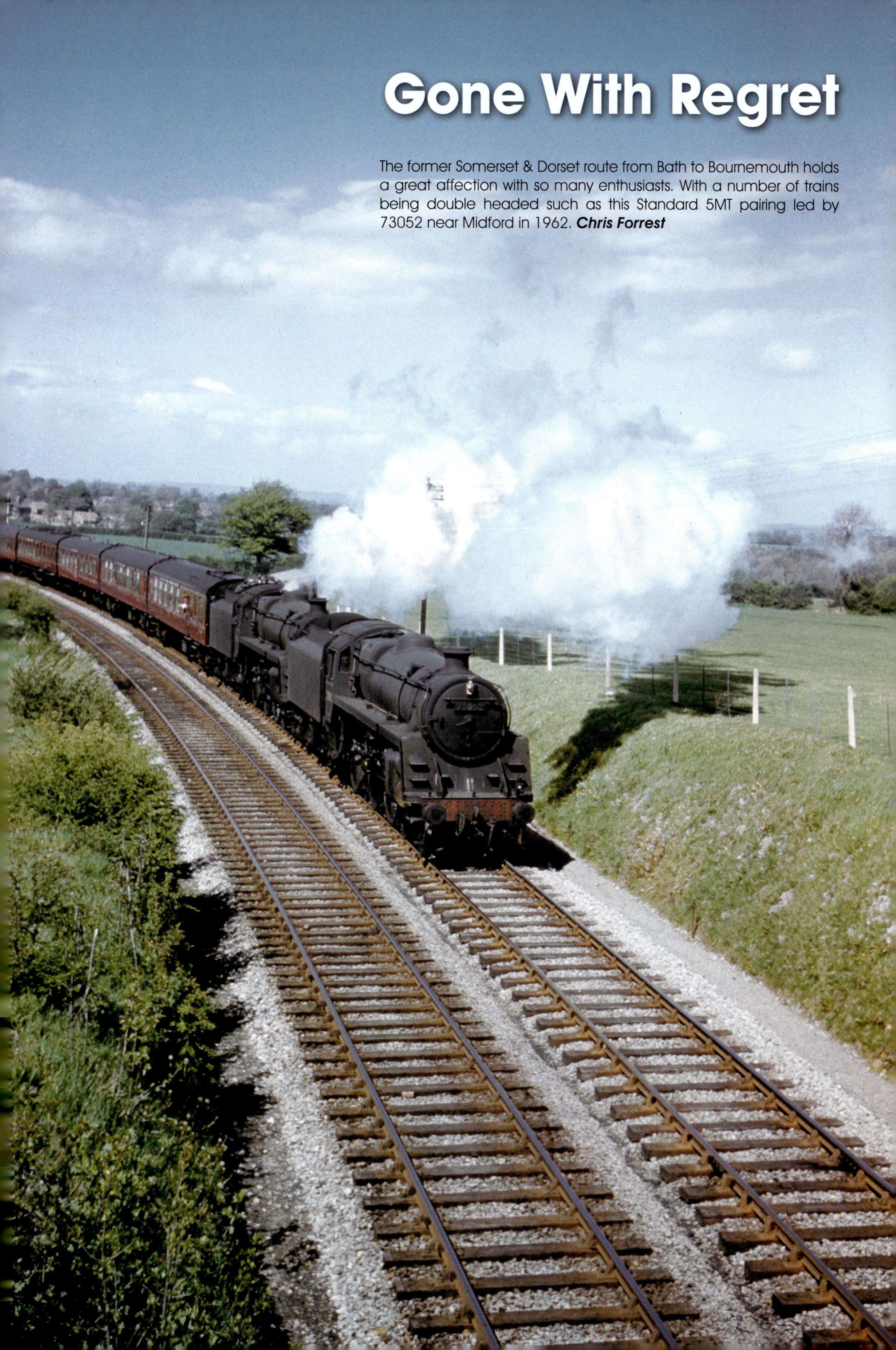

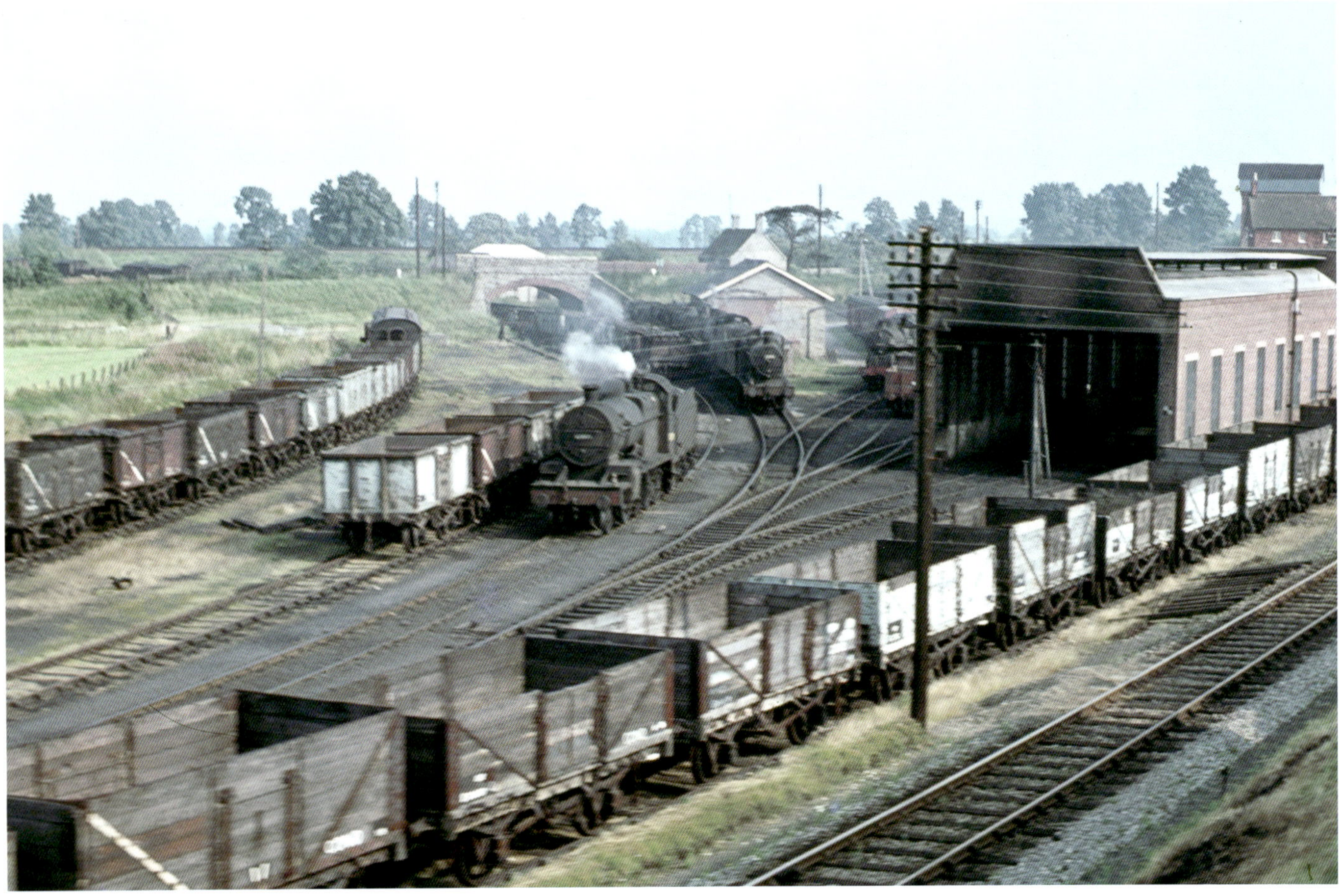

The Junction with the Southern Region for the route was at Templecombe where aside from some interesting train manoeuvres which were required due to the unusual track layout, spotters could also enjoy the sights of the engine shed here coded as 82G since it came into the Western Region's boundaries after the 1958 changes. This was the view from the train in 1962. ***Strathwood Library Collection***

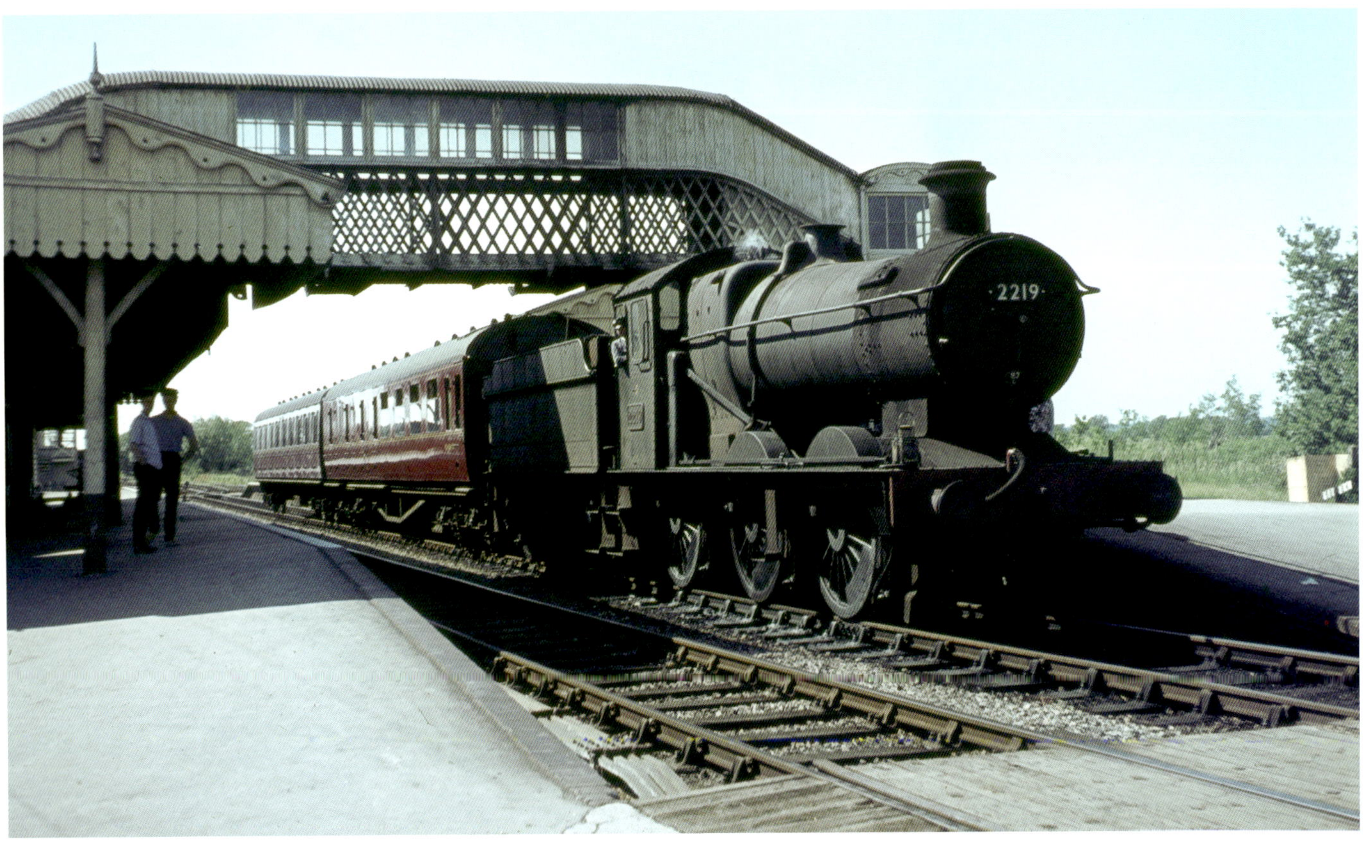

The relaxed and friendly nature of the line brought many to enjoy its charms such as here at Glastonbury and Street where an Evercreech Junction local pauses a while on 15 June 1963 with Collett 0-6-0 2219 in charge today. ***Peter Simmonds***

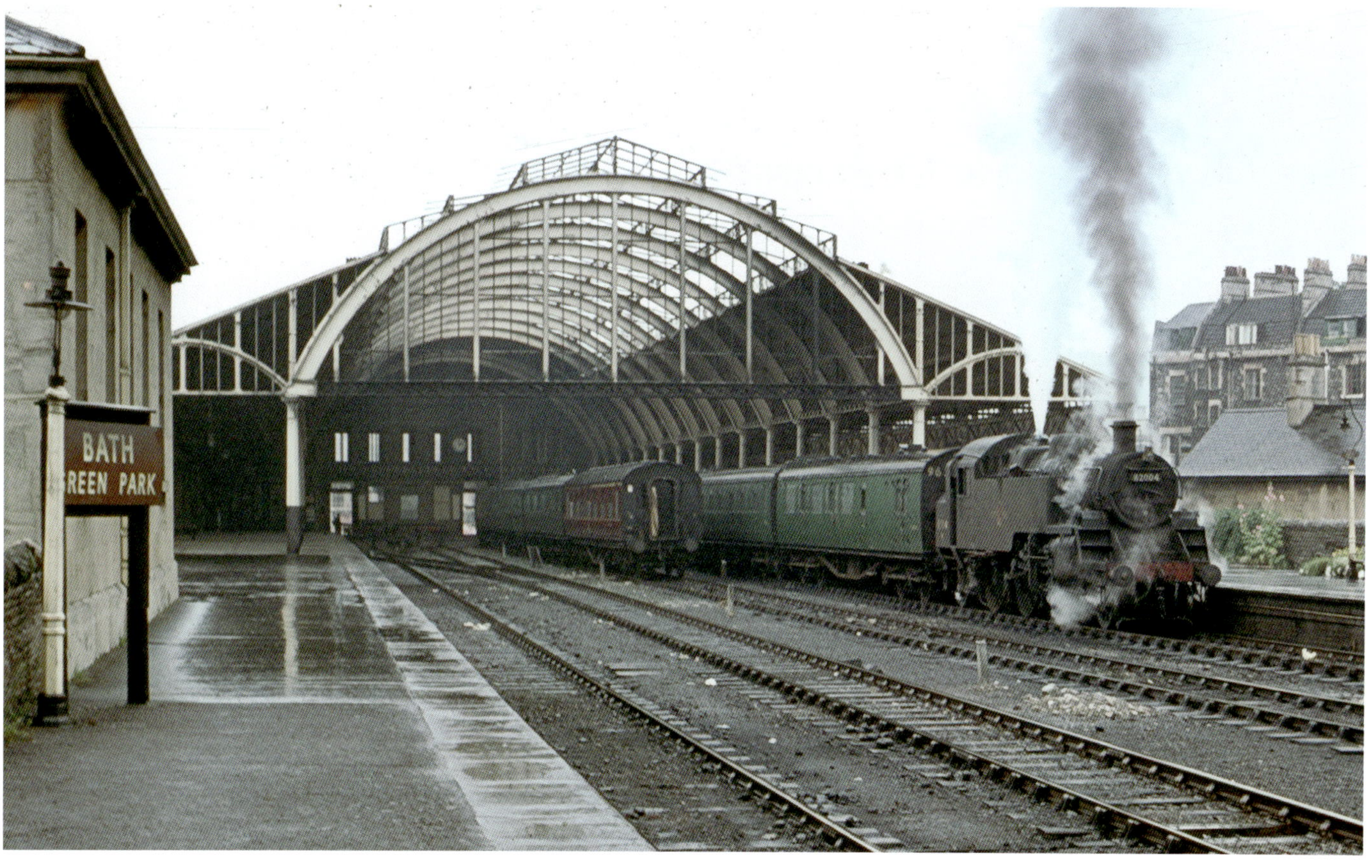

Contrasts on the route with a lonely view in the rain during May 1963 at the northern terminus with Standard 3MT 82004 almost ready for departure south with a stopping service. ***Strathwood Library Collection***

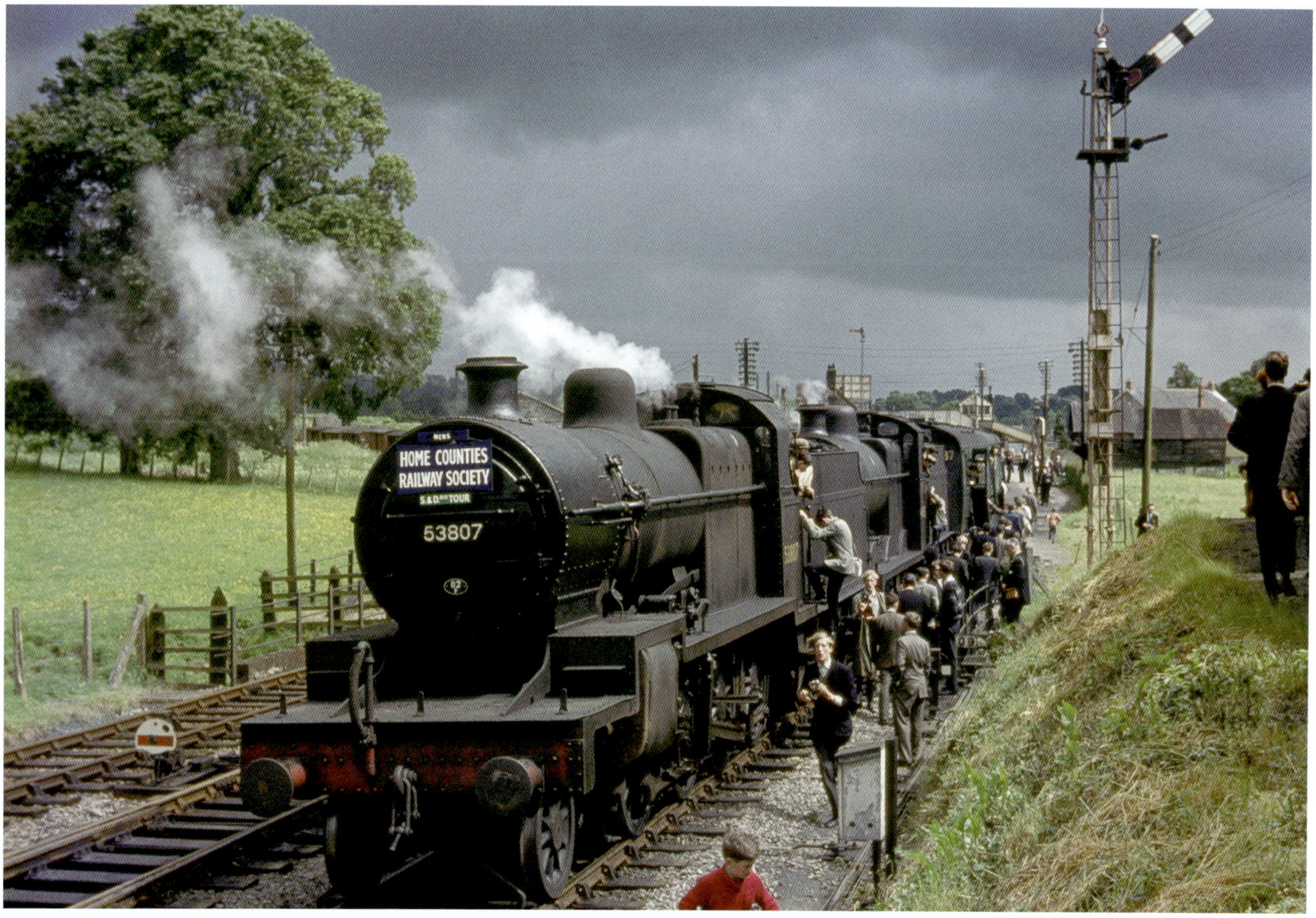

Whilst in the sunshine just before a thunderstorm on 7 June 1964 enthusiasts spill out trackside at Evercreech Junction with one of the line's famous 7Fs 53807 with Fowler 4F 44558 coupled inside during a photostop. ***Strathwood Library Collection***

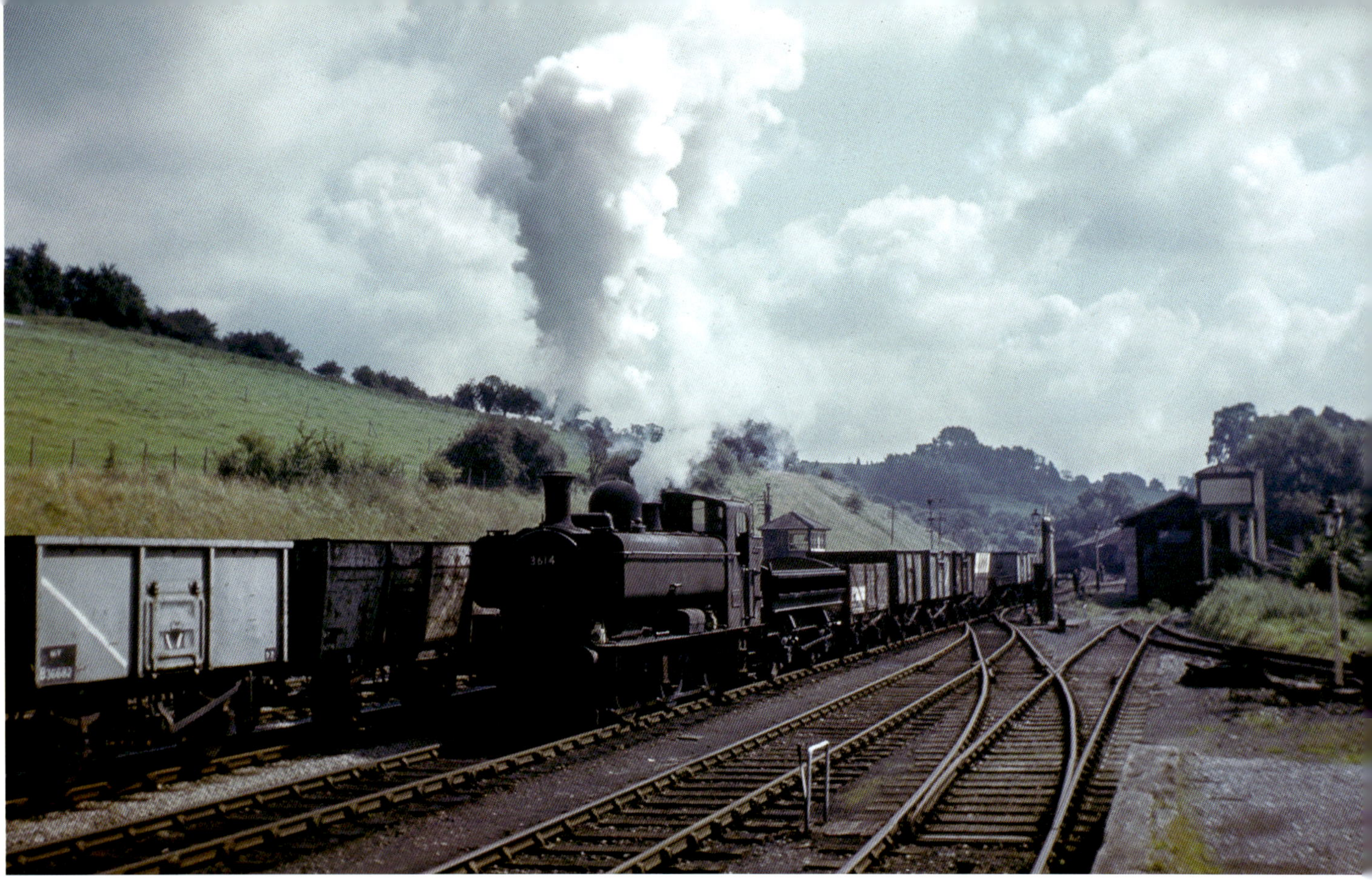

The now almost forgotten Radstock coalfield brought a lot of traffic to the route, this was the scene at Radstock in 1961 with Pannier 3614 engaged in a little shunting. ***Gerald Peacock***

A junction and connection once existed at Highbridge between the Burnham on Sea branch and the Bristol to Taunton mainline. Waiting patiently in the expansive and now sleepy station at Highbridge on 10 June 1964 was Collett 0-6-0 3210 in the hope of some passengers off a connecting service perhaps? ***Dave Down***

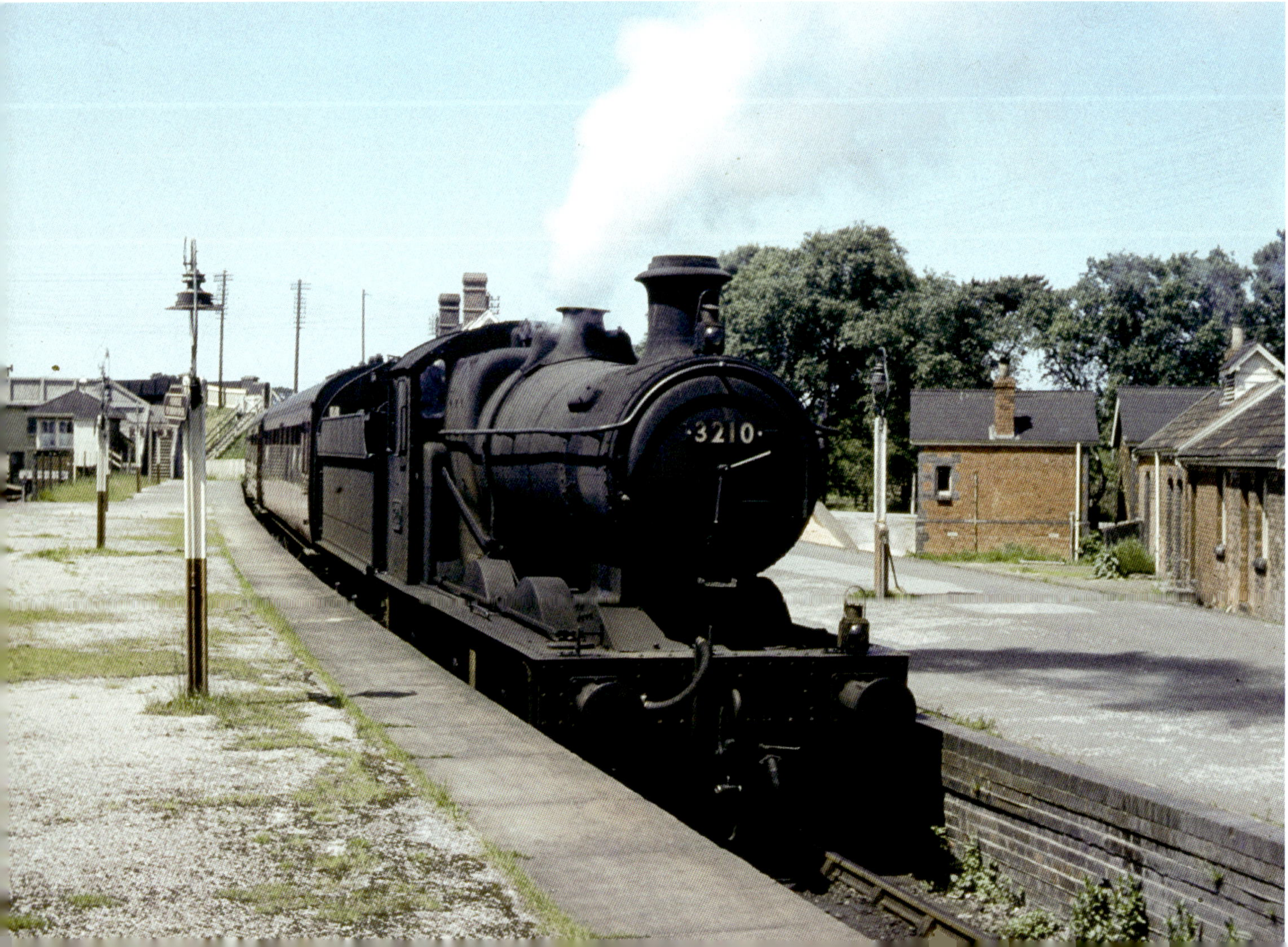

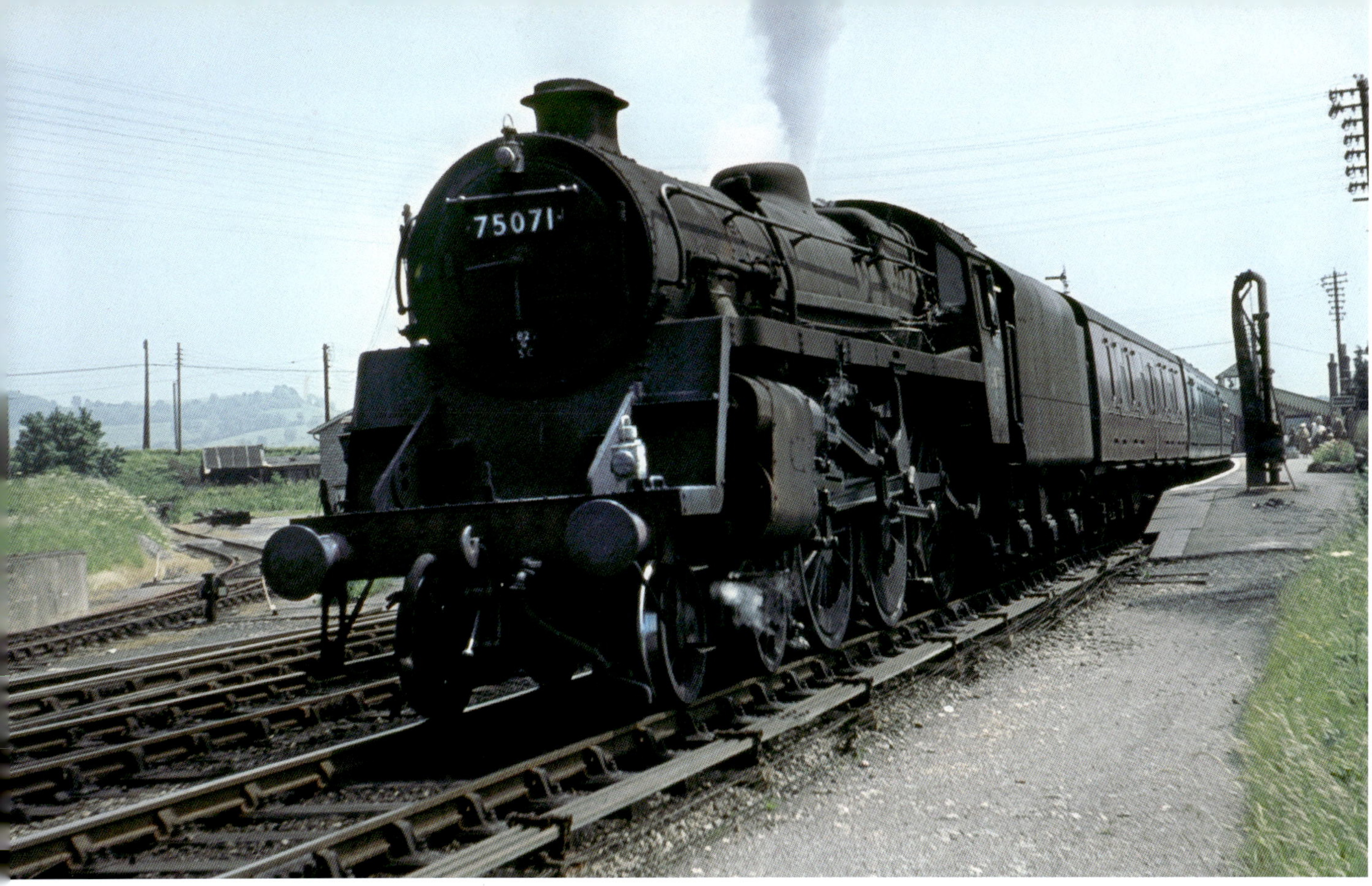

A chance to take a position trackside in those carefree days to record Standard 4MT 75071 at Evercreech Junction on 15 June 1963 with a Bath service. ***Peter Simmonds***

With the closure imminent, increased numbers of enthusiasts made their way to ride the line whilst they could, on a cold and sunny February day in 1966 the level crossing gates have been closed to the road behind our cameraman in preparation for Standard 4MT 80043 to depart from Radstock. ***Edward Dorricott***

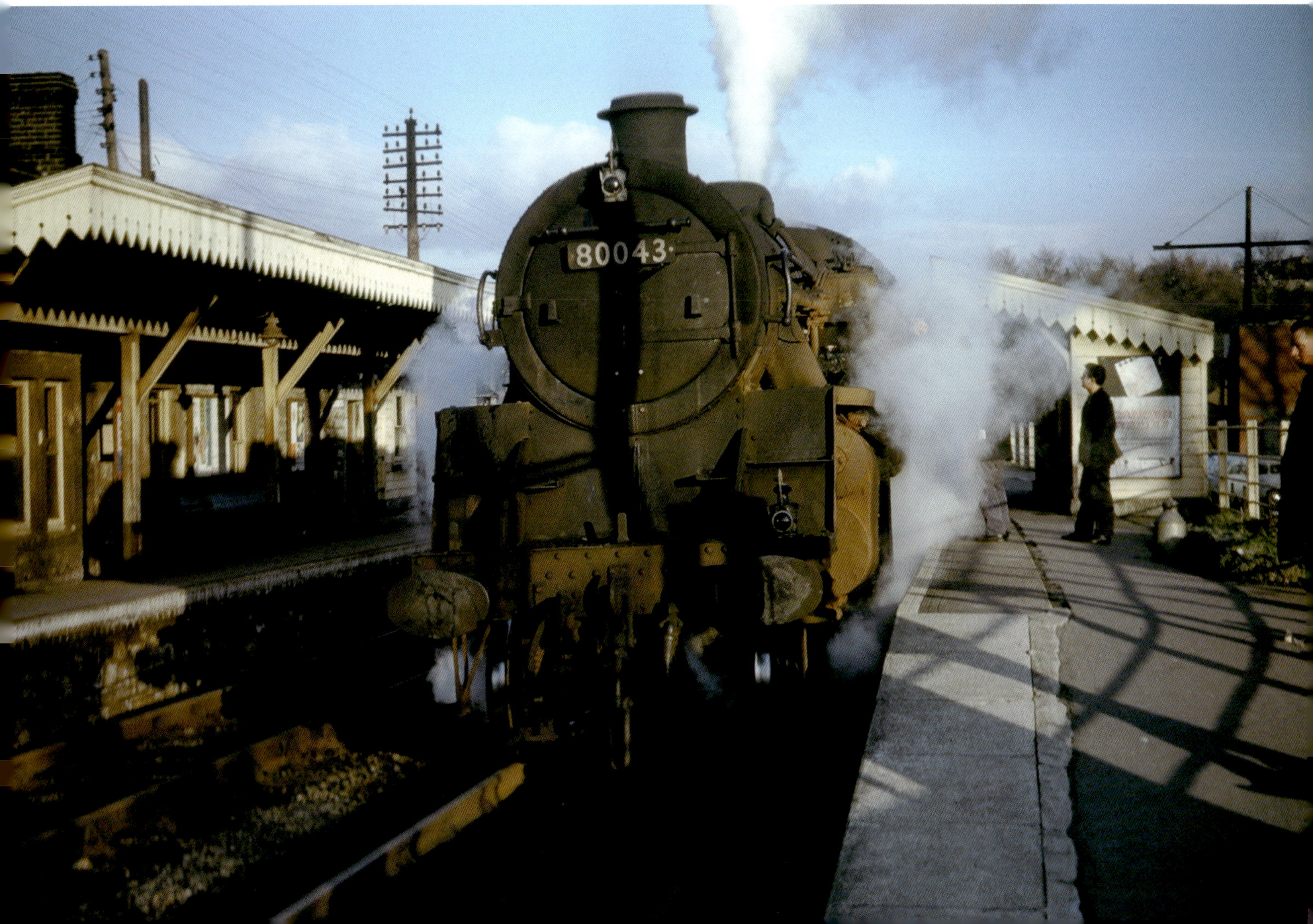

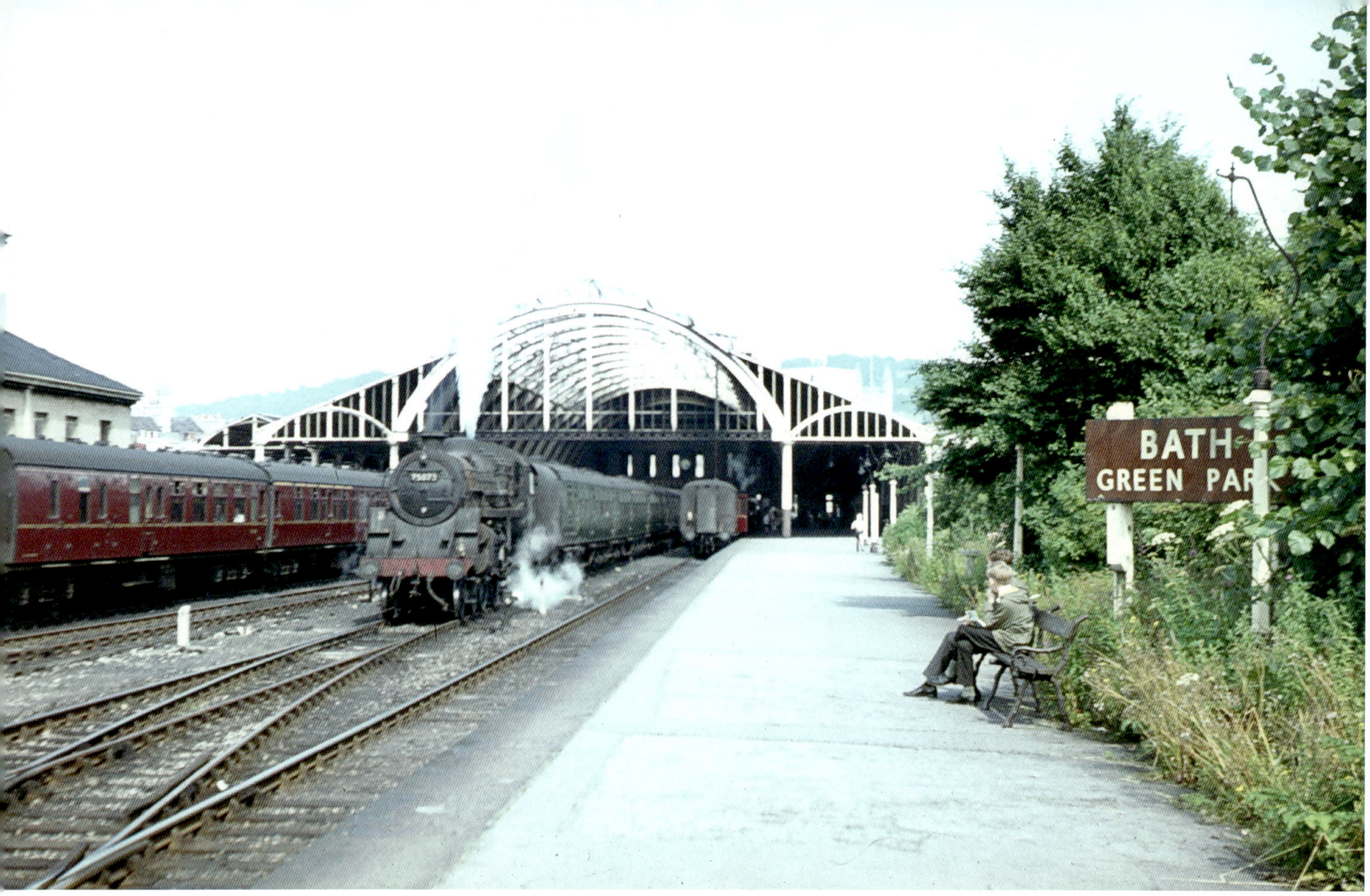

All seems undisturbed at Bath Green Park during that last summer in June 1965, in spite of the screaming of Standard 4MT 75073's safety valves singing out across the city. ***Strathwood Library Collection***

Our Standard 4MT is released from it's stock and makes a path out of Green Park station in February 1966. Do you remember the days when school boys wore caps and carried their books in leather satchels, long before the days of trainers and sports bags? ***Edward Dorricott***

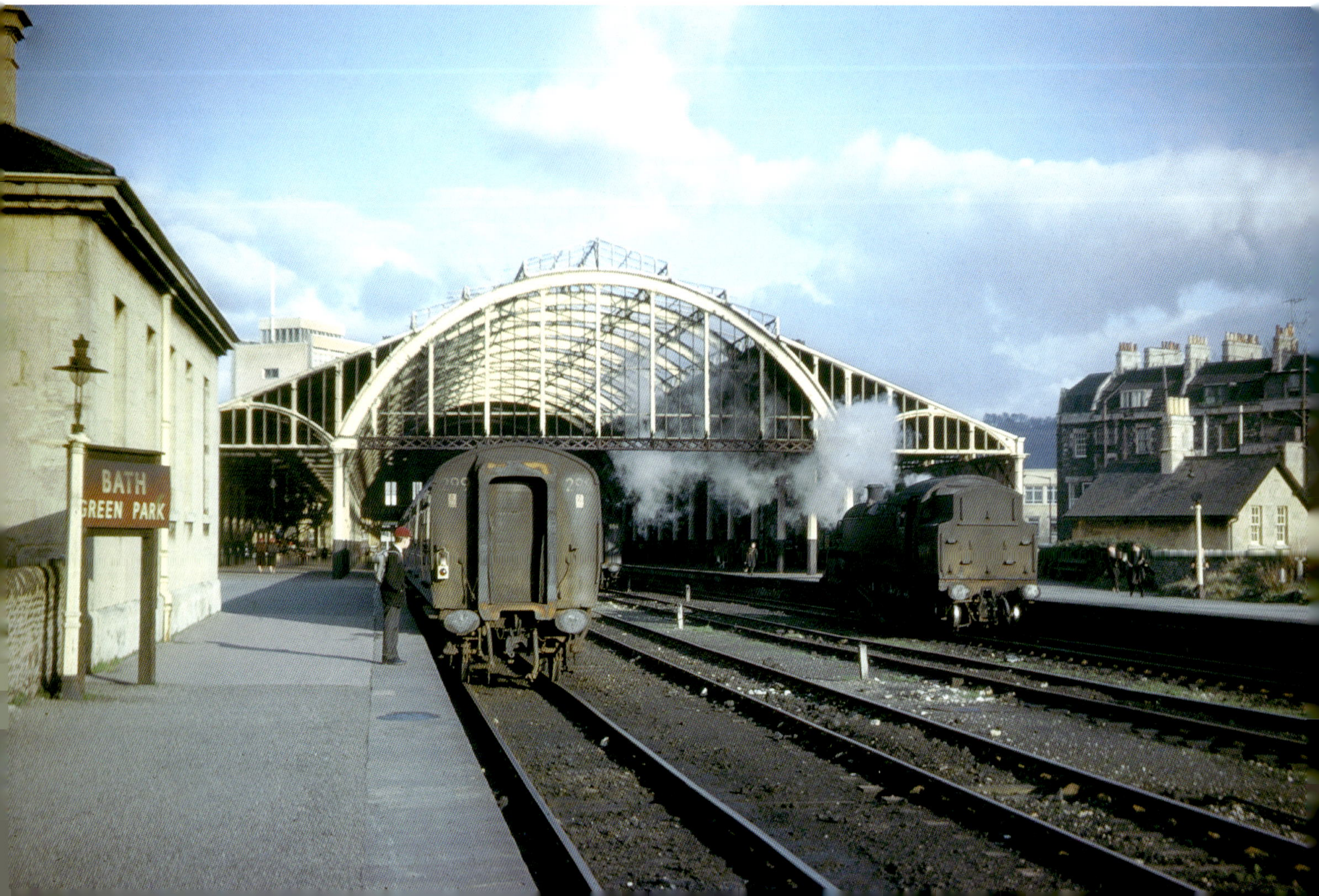

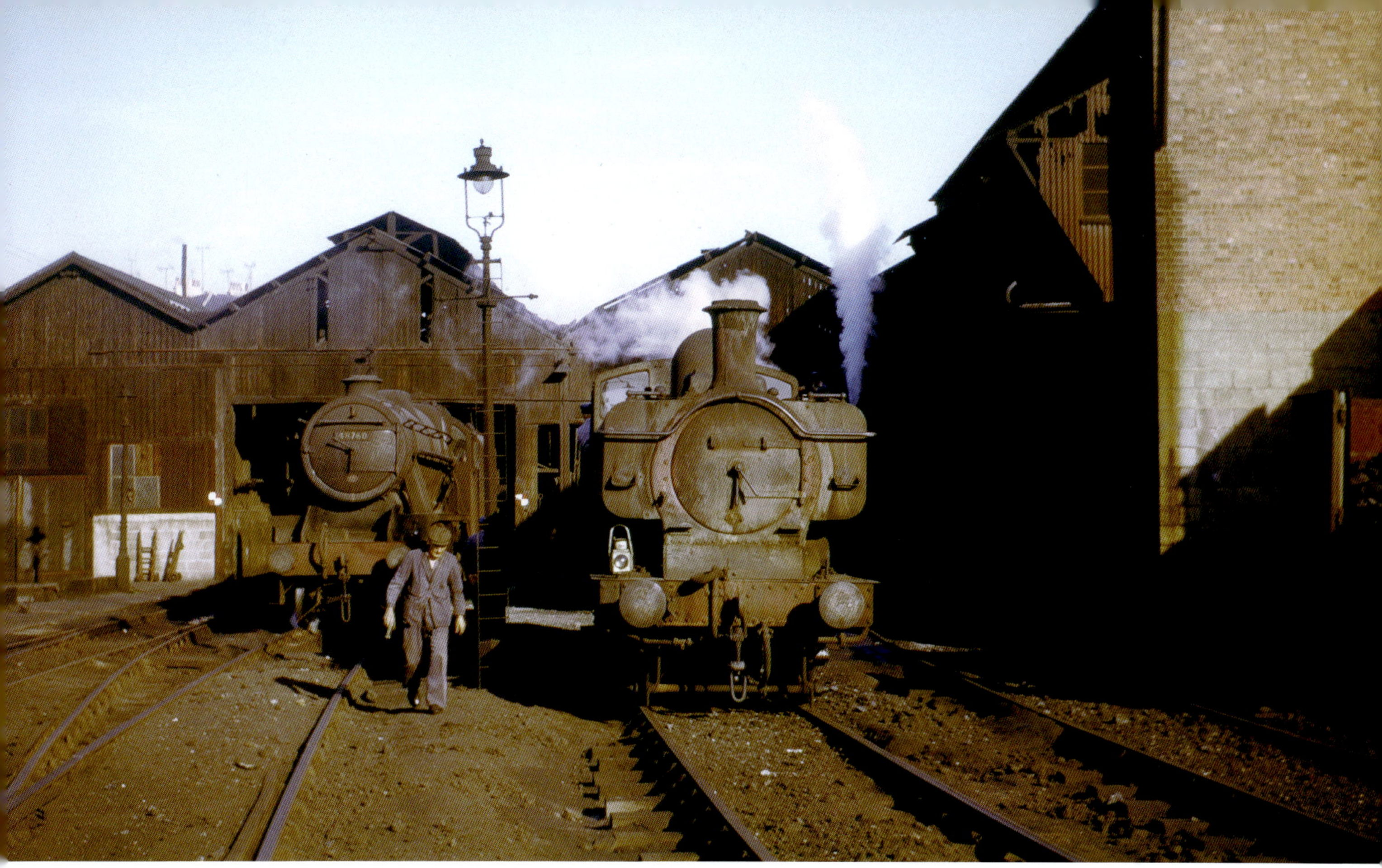

Another engine shed to visit, this time 82F Bath Green Park with Stanier 8F 48760 and that unfortunate Pannier 3681 we first saw at the Bath Road Open Day on 23 October 1965, this was the same engine in traffic still on 21 September the month before. ***Strathwood Library Collection***

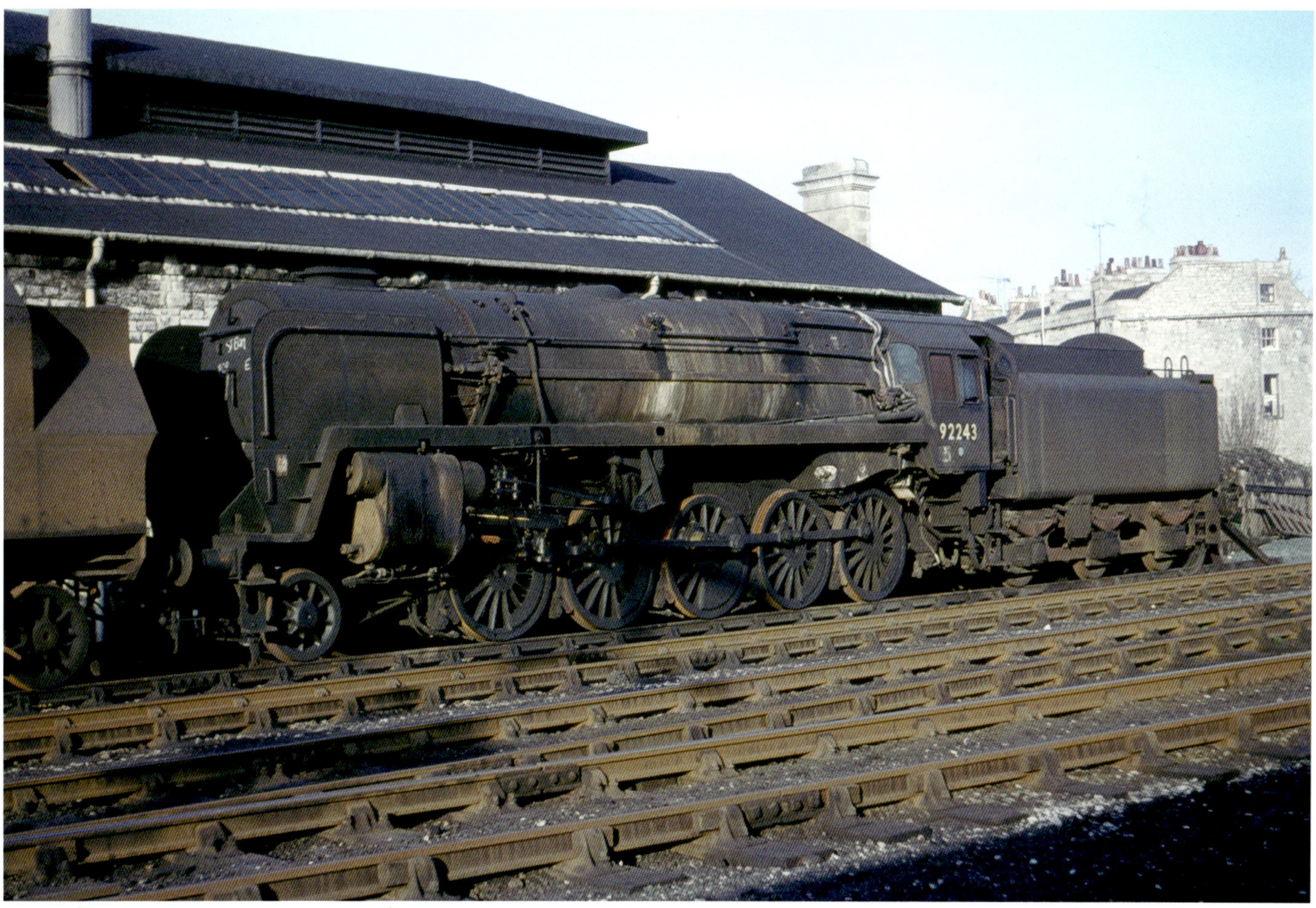

This was the scene on 5 March 1966 the day before the complete closure of the route at Bath Green Park shed with Standard 9F 92243 still here after being withdrawn the December before. The depot would close officially on 7 March 1966 with the remaining engines being removed in the following few weeks, leaving the site for clearance. ***Strathwood Library Collection***

The End of Cotswold Steam

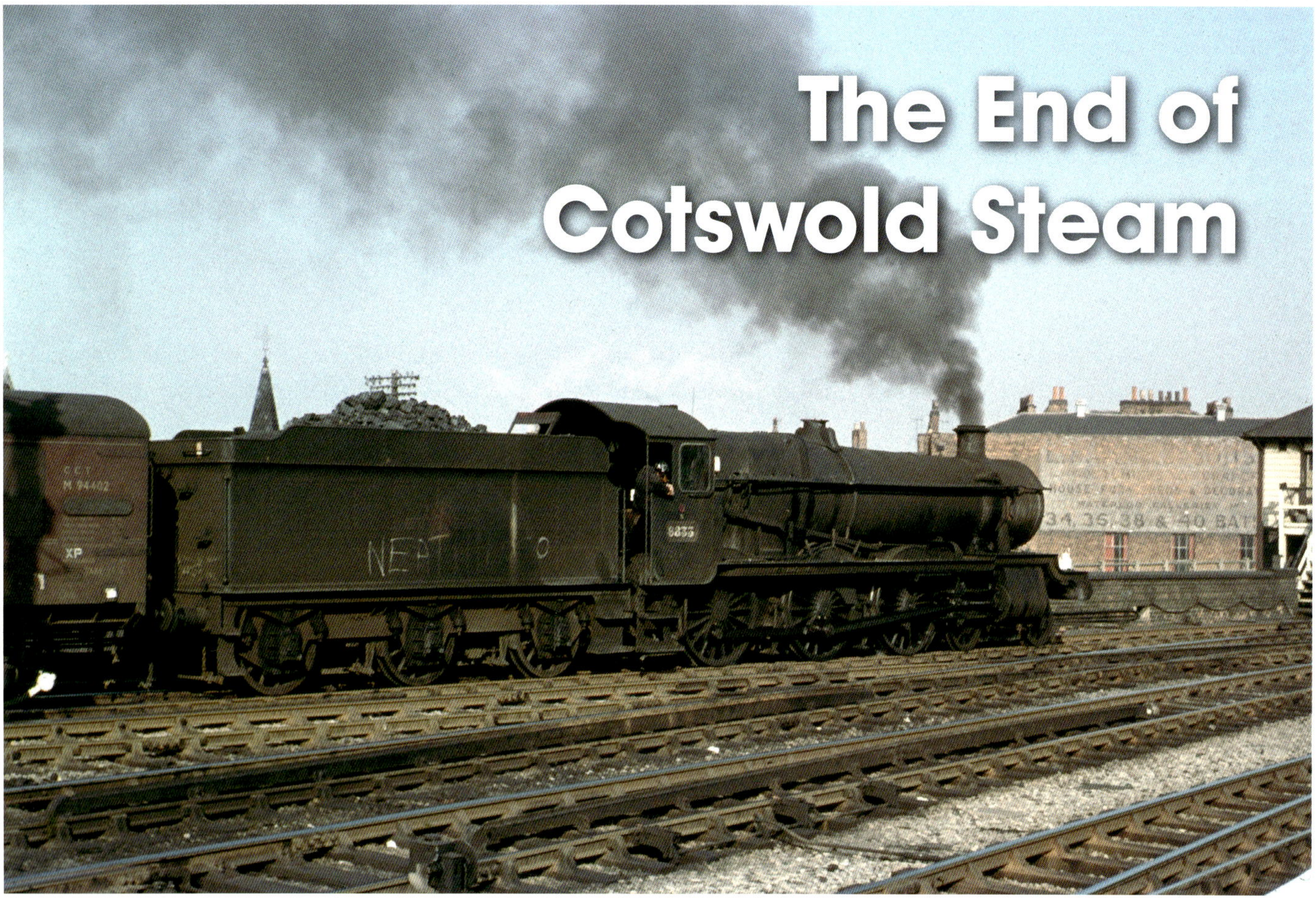

As seen elsewhere the last year of Western Region steam resulted in pitiful sights such as here at Leamington Spa with 6833 Calcot Grange getting away with a parcels service. ***Tim Meredith***

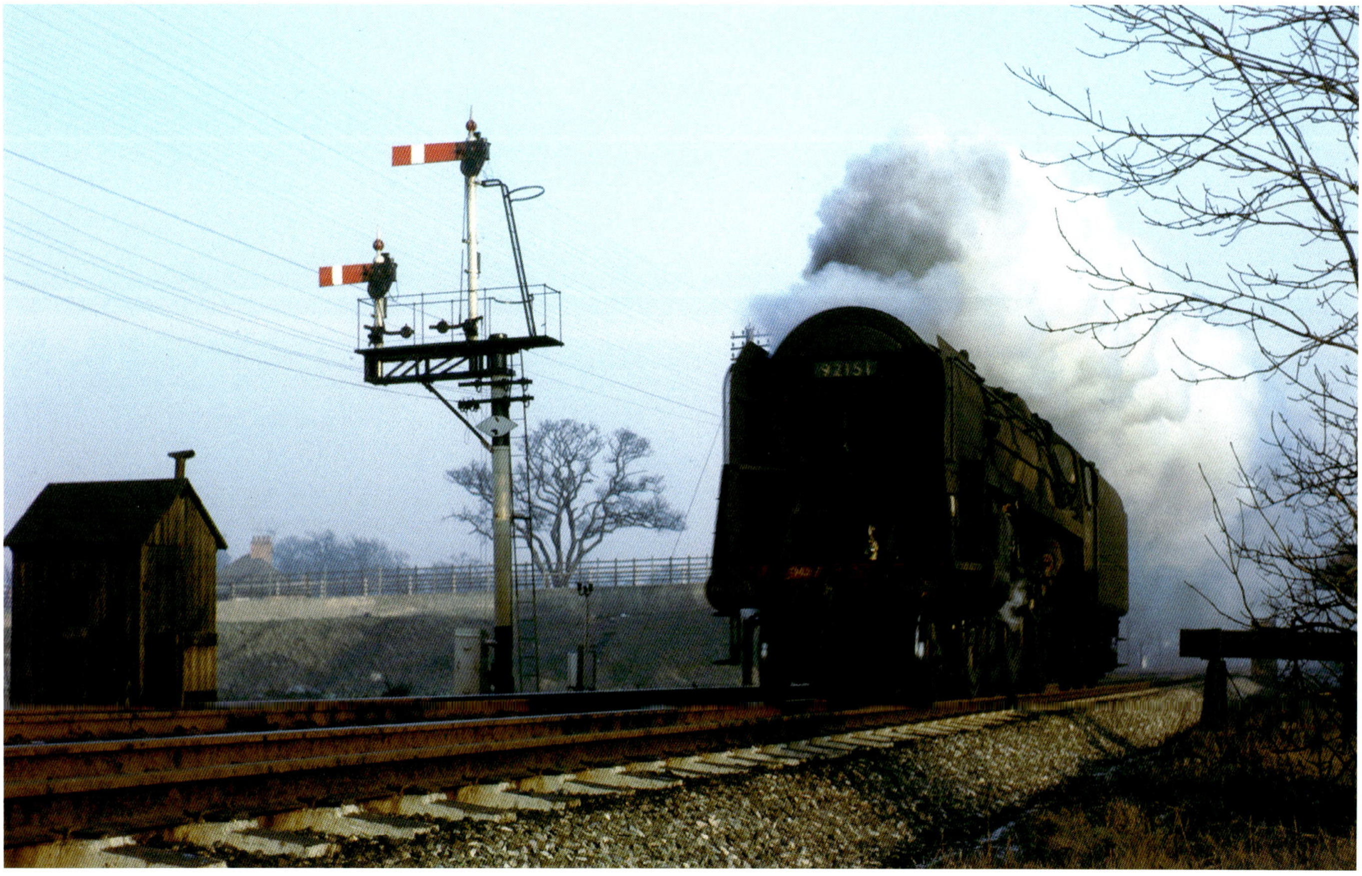

Making great haste light engine past a fogman's hut protecting the bracket signals opposite was Standard 9F 92151 near Leamington in January 1964. ***Tim Meredith***

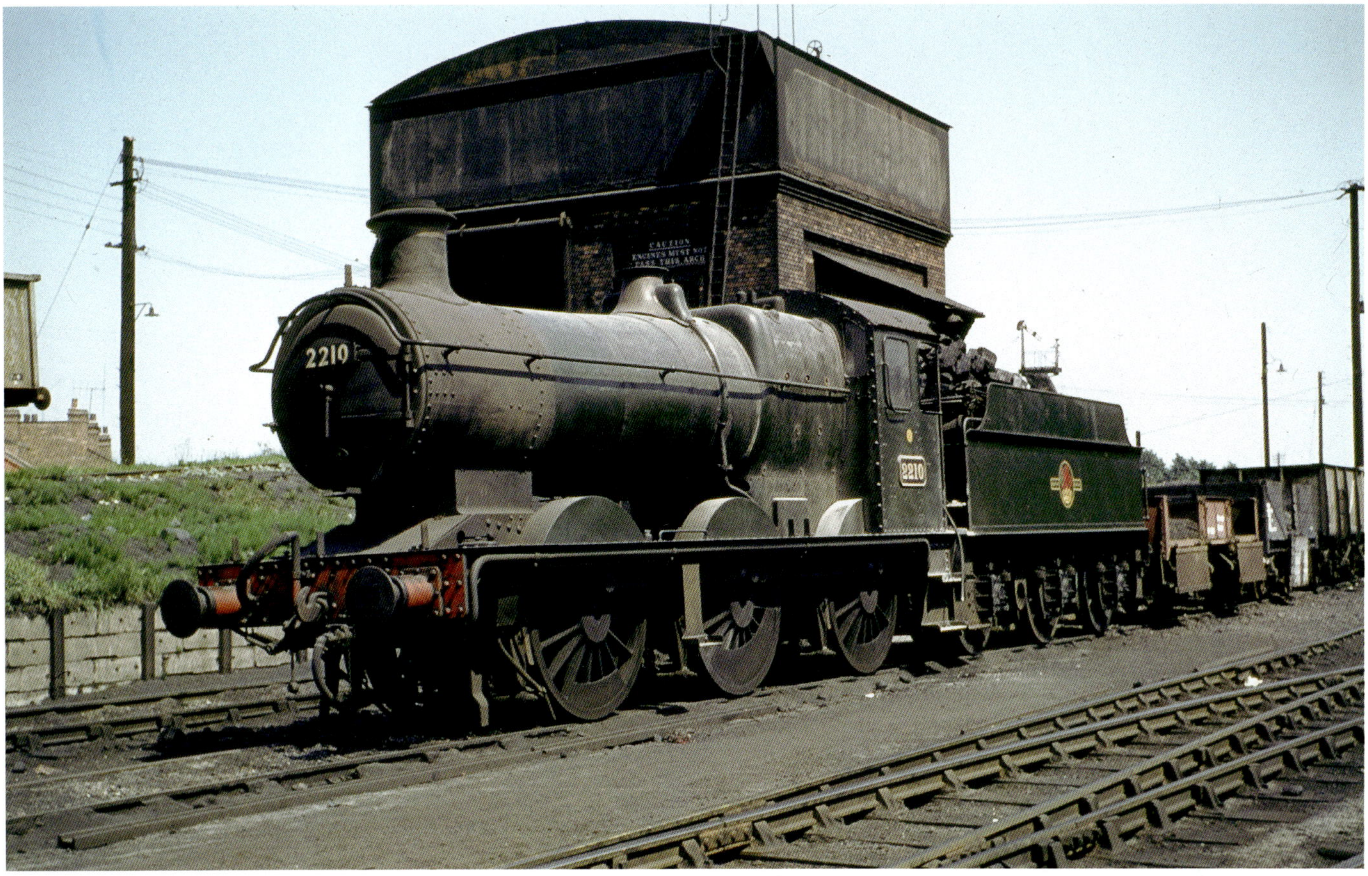

Unlined green livery has been bestowed upon Collett 0-6-0 2210 seen at Leamington shed in 1963, this was the year the code changed from 84D to 2L pushing it within the London Midland Region. ***Tim Meredith***

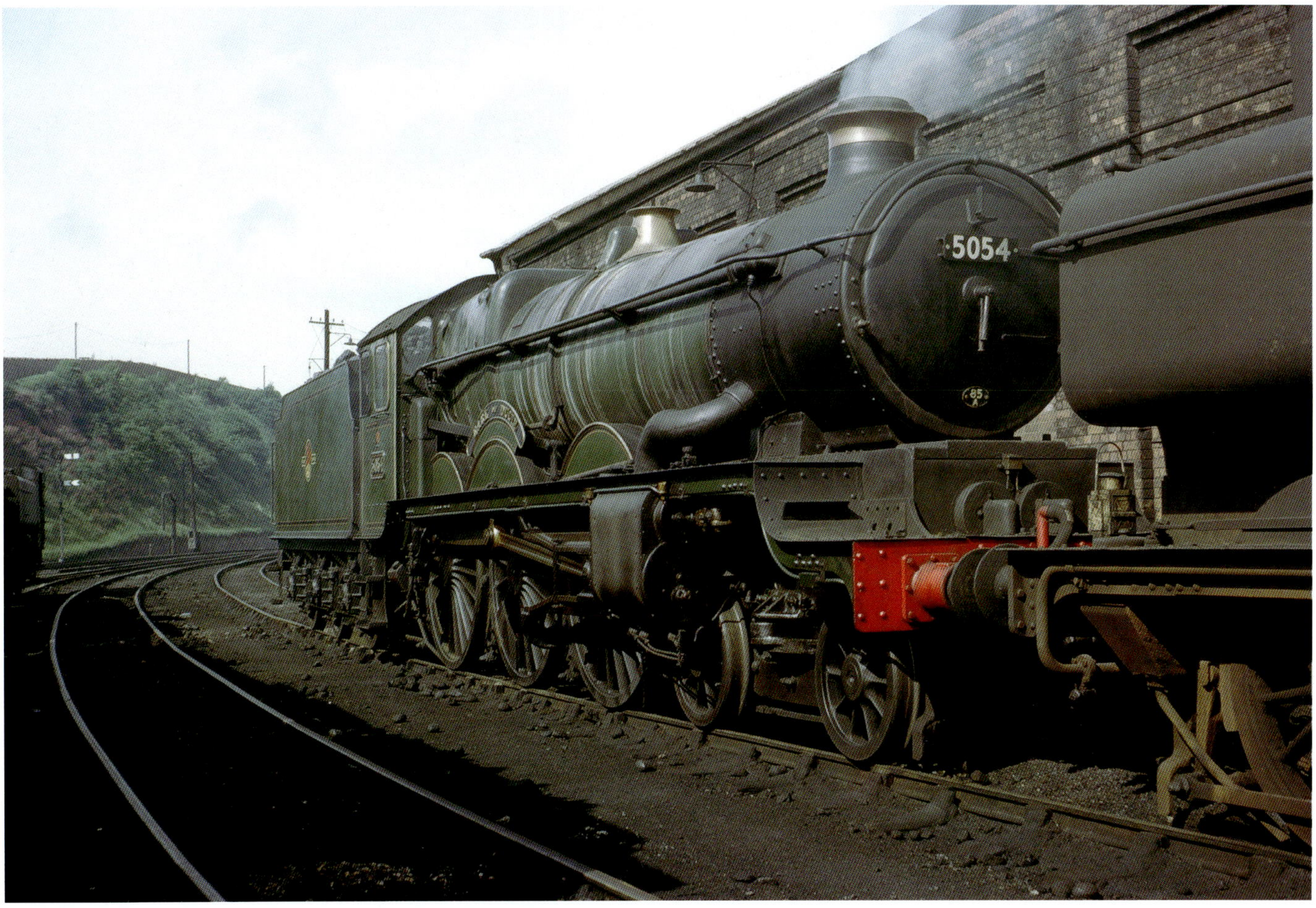

In previous years Worcester shed had kept their Castles in fine fettle for top link work, the last vestiges of this can be seen on 5054 Earl of Ducie on 7 June 1964. ***Win Wall/Strathwood Library Collection***

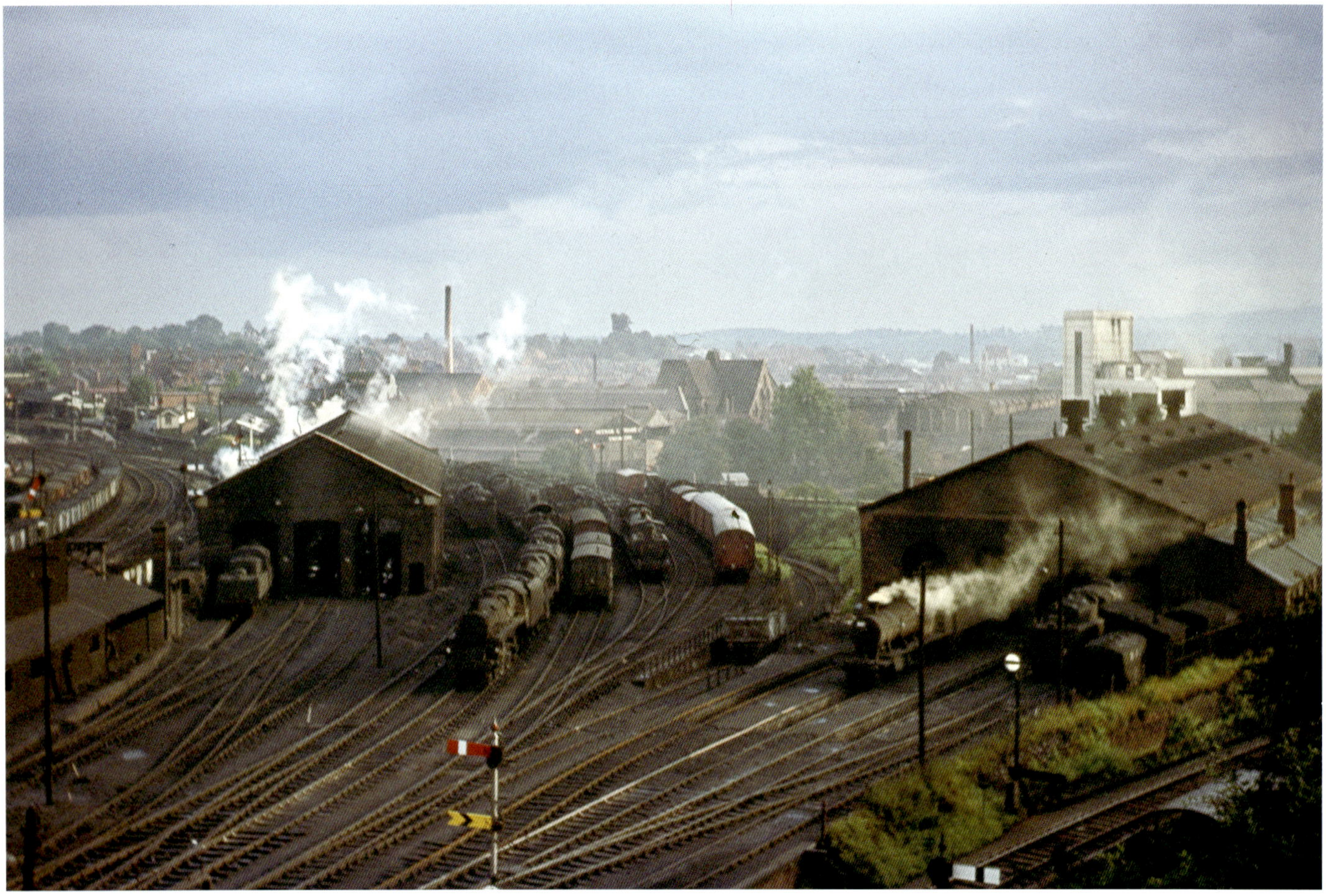

The shed facilities at Worcester were penned in the triangle of lines connecting Shrub Hill, Foregate Street and Droitwich. It would be closed to steam in December 1965, this view was taken two years beforehand. ***John Newman***

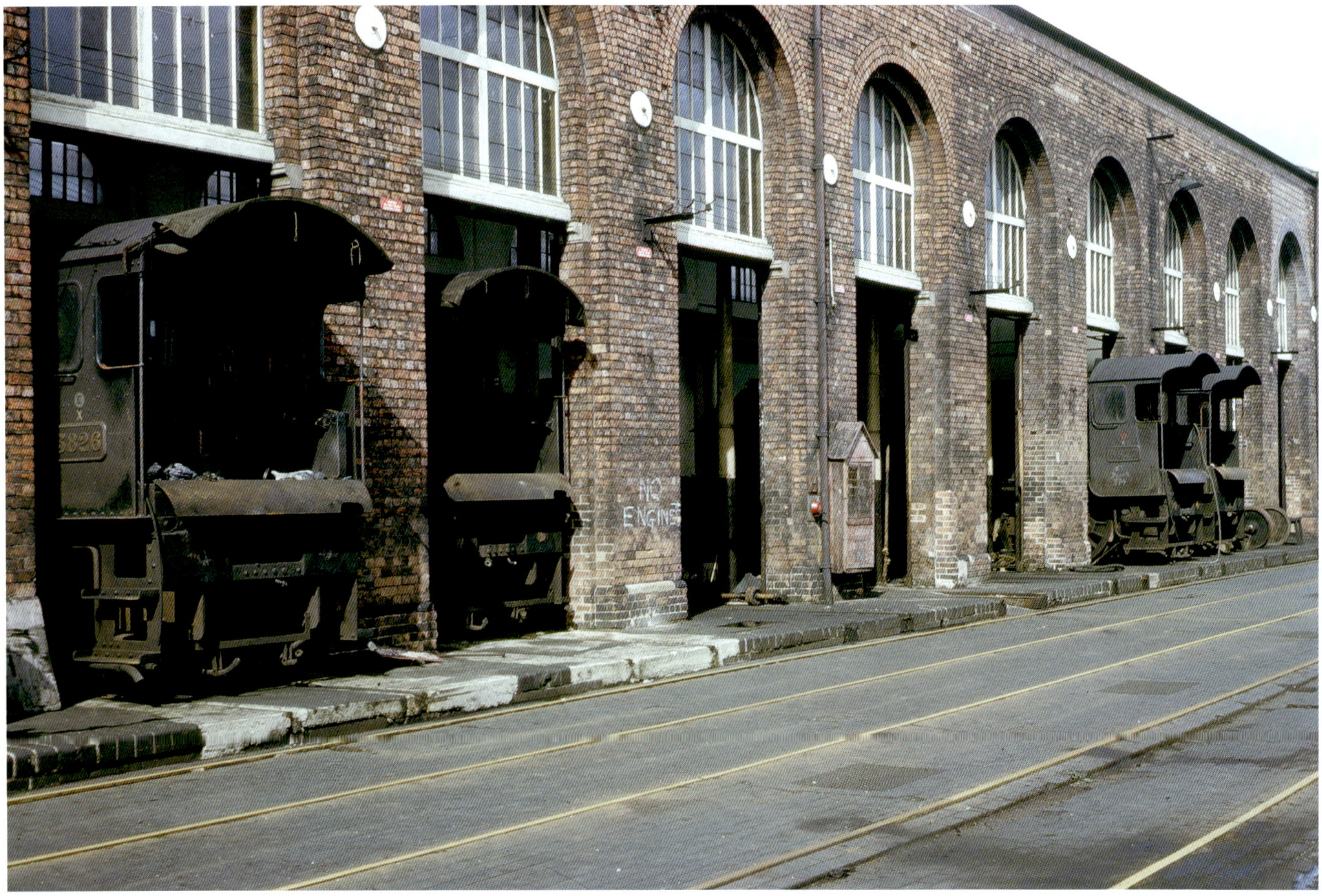

Locomotives were still being repaired in the locomotive works in Worcester on 7 June 1964 as witnessed by several Granges and Churchward 2-8-0s . The works was located on the opposite side of the line to the engine sheds. ***Win Wall/Strathwood Library Collection***

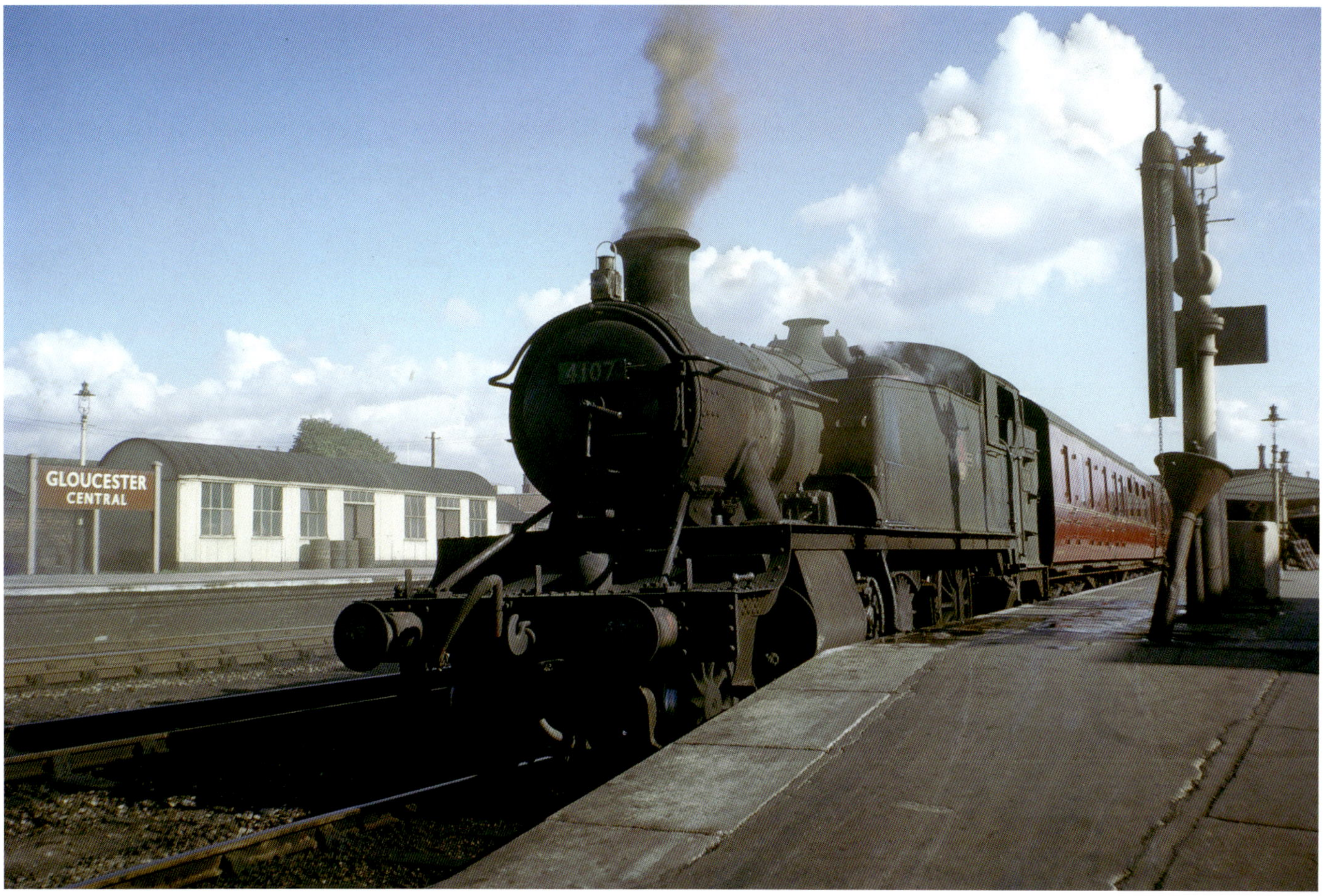

Steam was still to yield to DMUs from Gloucester to Hereford with local services on 15 September 1964. Where we find 1935 built Prairie 4107 having taken water from the column at the platform end awaitís the signal from the guard. ***Chris Forrest***

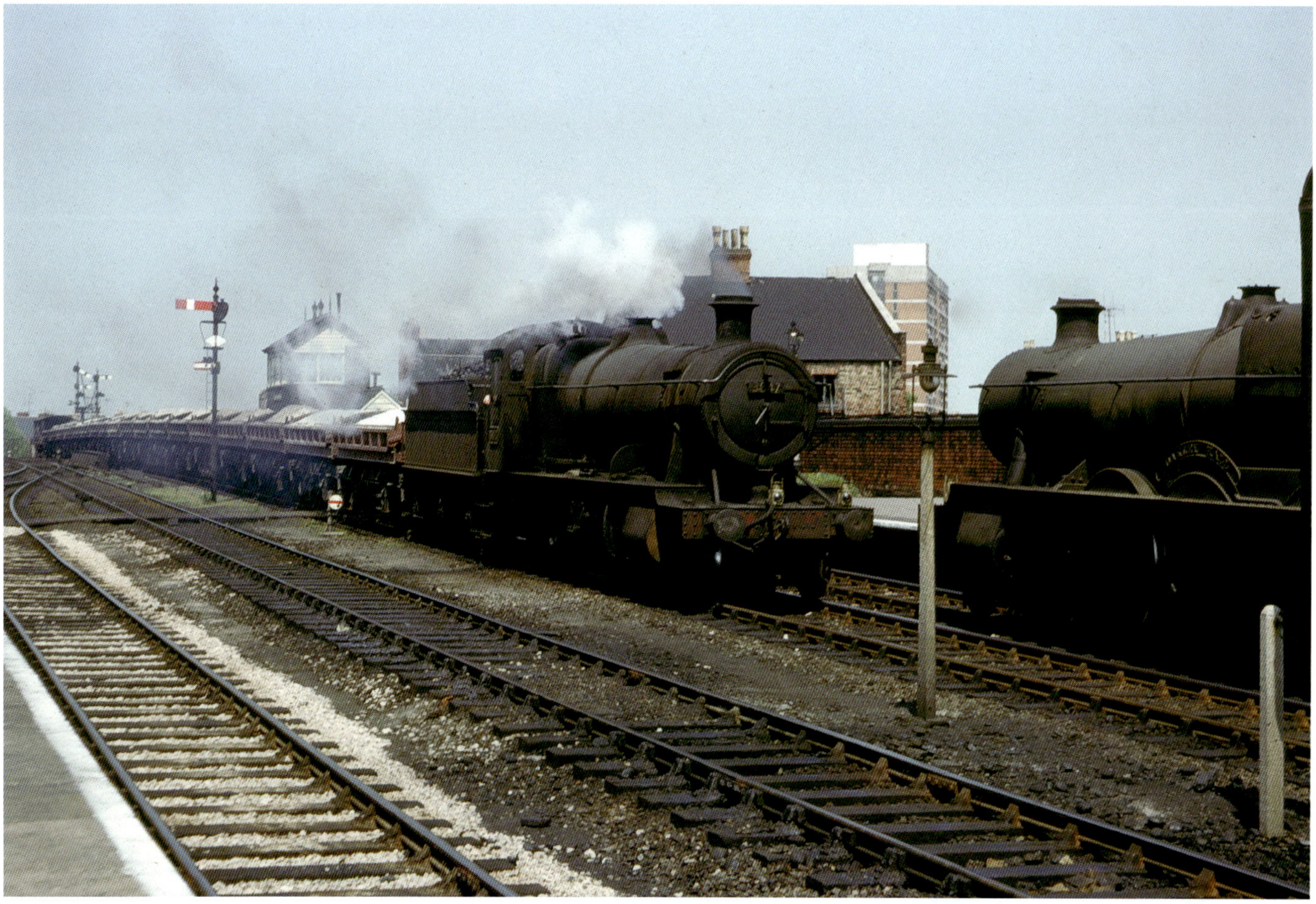

Drawing its heavy train up the incline into Gloucester on 1 June 1963 was 3847 one of the Collett improved 2-8-0s originally designed by Churchward. Whilst on one of the platform roads stands 5936 Oakley Hall. ***Frank Hornby***

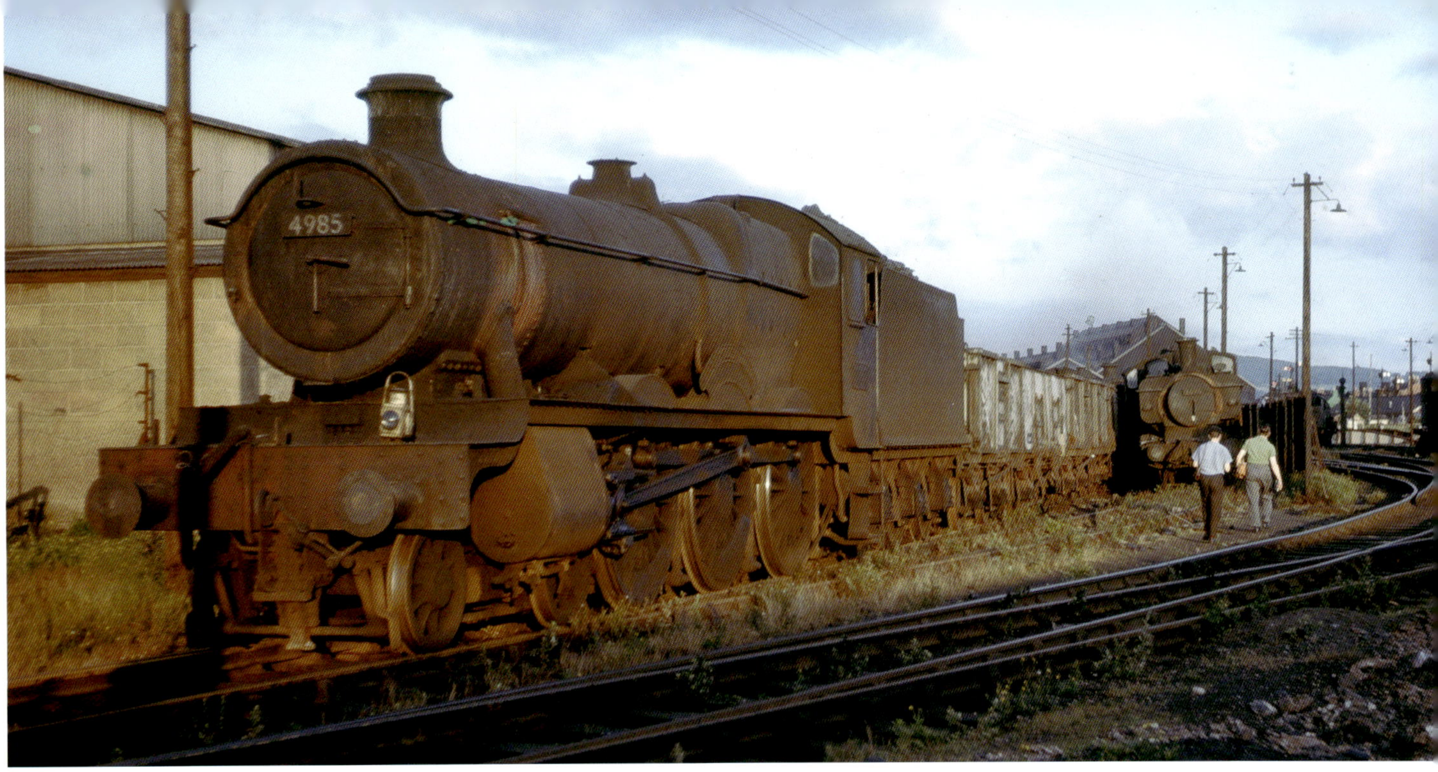

The unkempt nature of the region is recorded again in a dusk visit to Gloucester Horton Road shed on 7 June 1964 six months before steam ended here where a shabby 4985 Allesley Hall was to be seen.

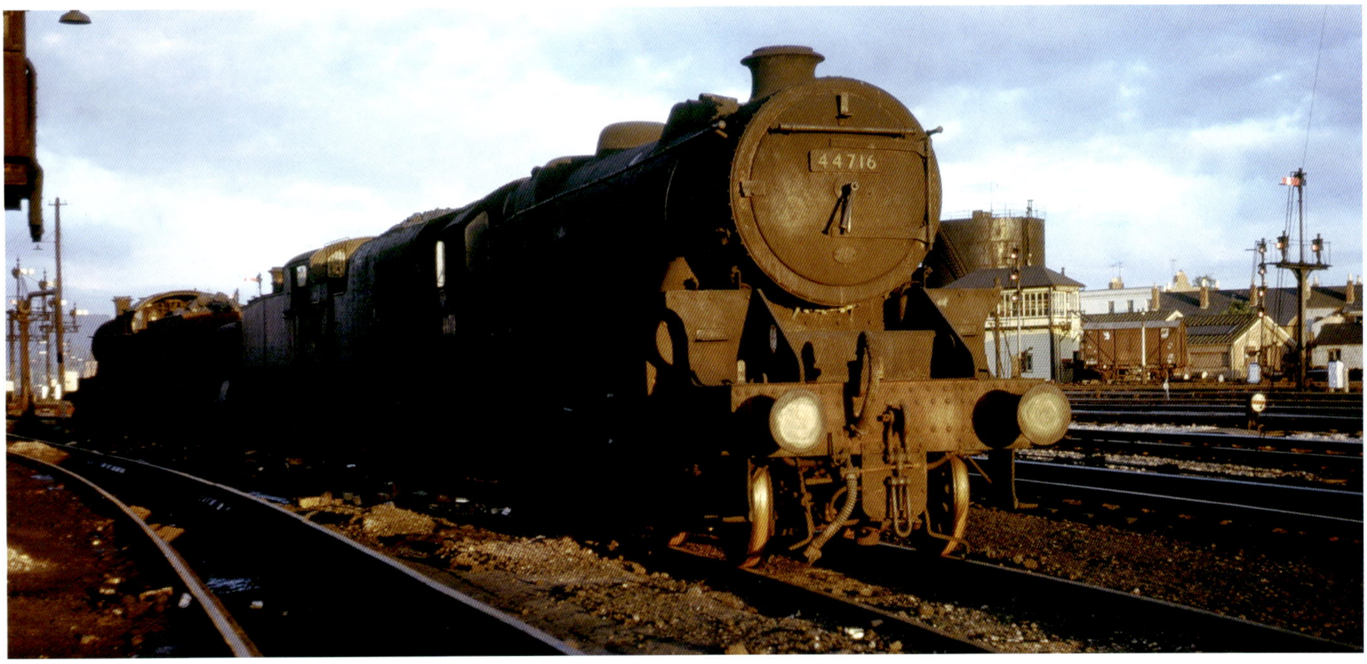

As can be seen it was a worthwhile stop off for the spotters as the sun went down, with Black Fives, Prairies and Panniers all on shed. ***All: Win Wall/Strathwood Library Collection***

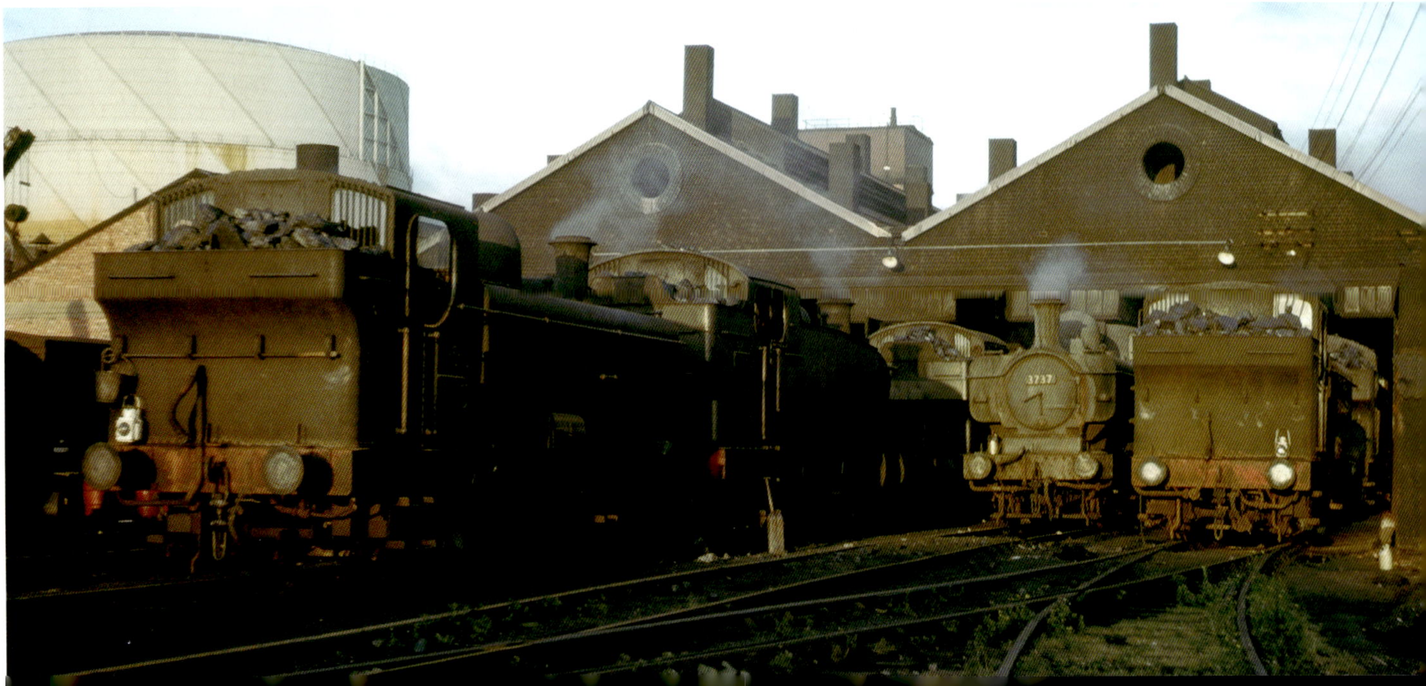

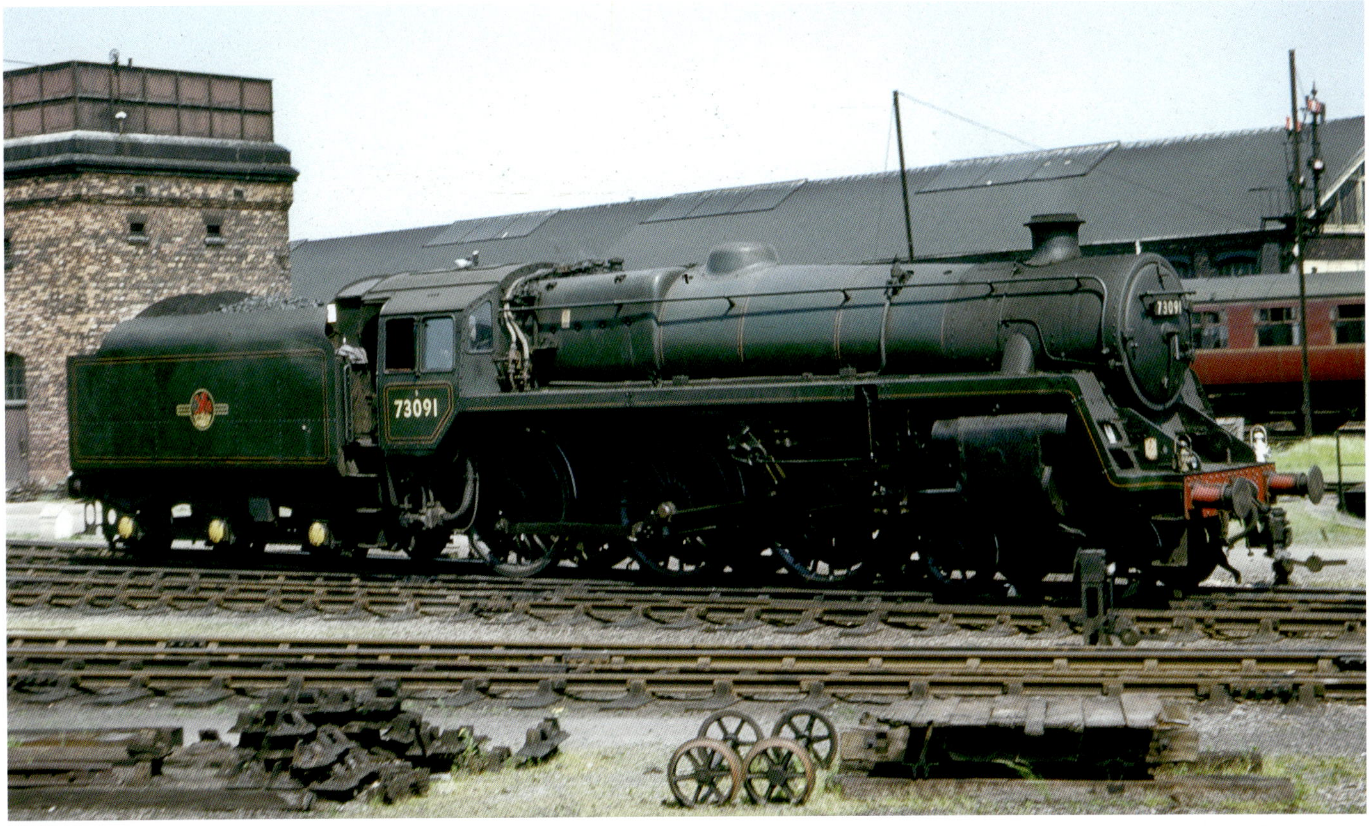

It must be said that the Western Region certainly improved the appearances of Standard 5MTs such as 73091 seen here at Gloucester on 1 June 1963, as long as they were kept clean of course. ***Frank Hornby***

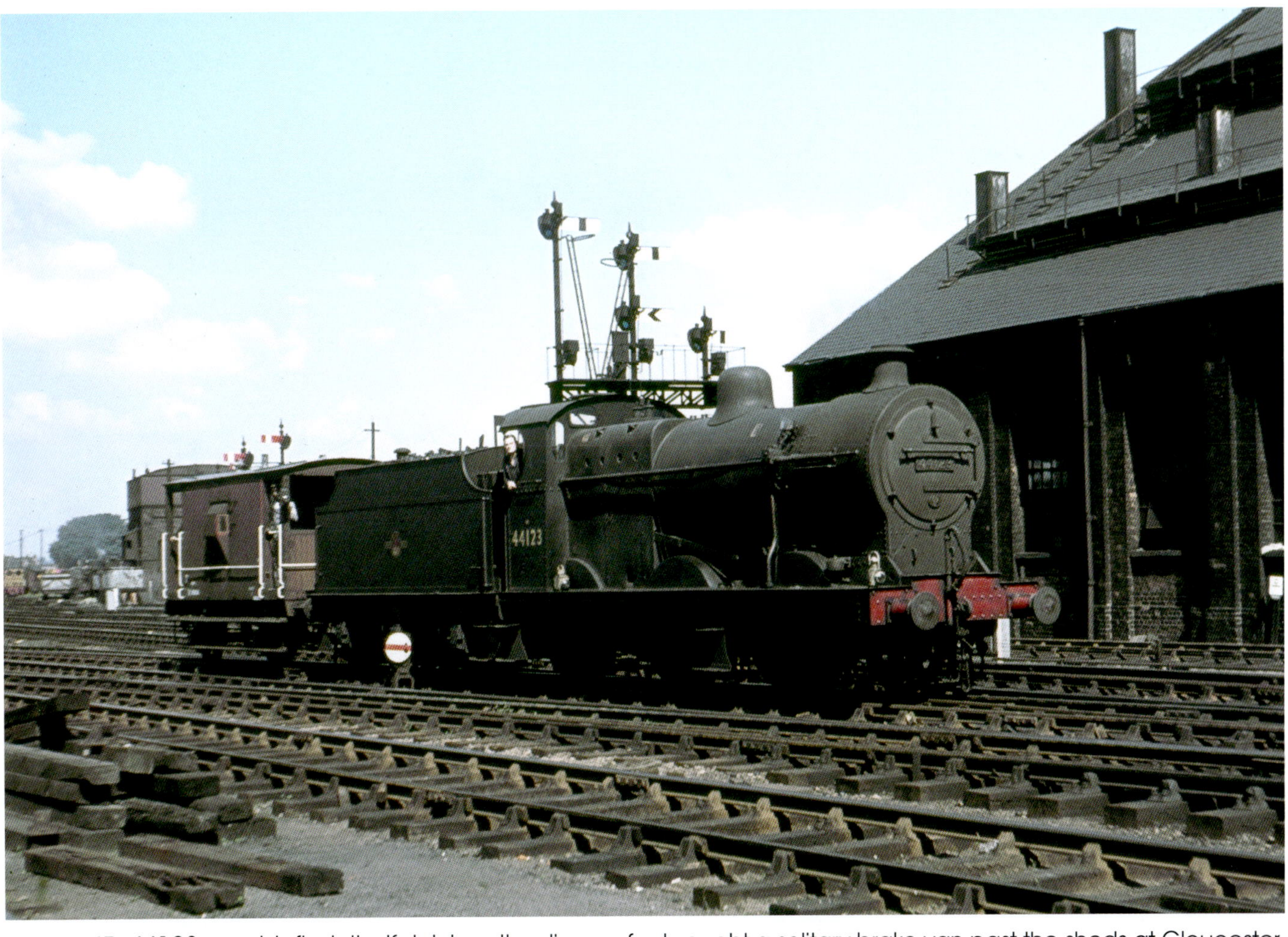

Fowler 4F 44123 would find itself joining the lines of locomotives at Barry after being withdrawn, but on 27 July 1963 it had just under two more years service to give, as it brought a solitary brake van past the sheds at Gloucester. ***Peter Simmonds***

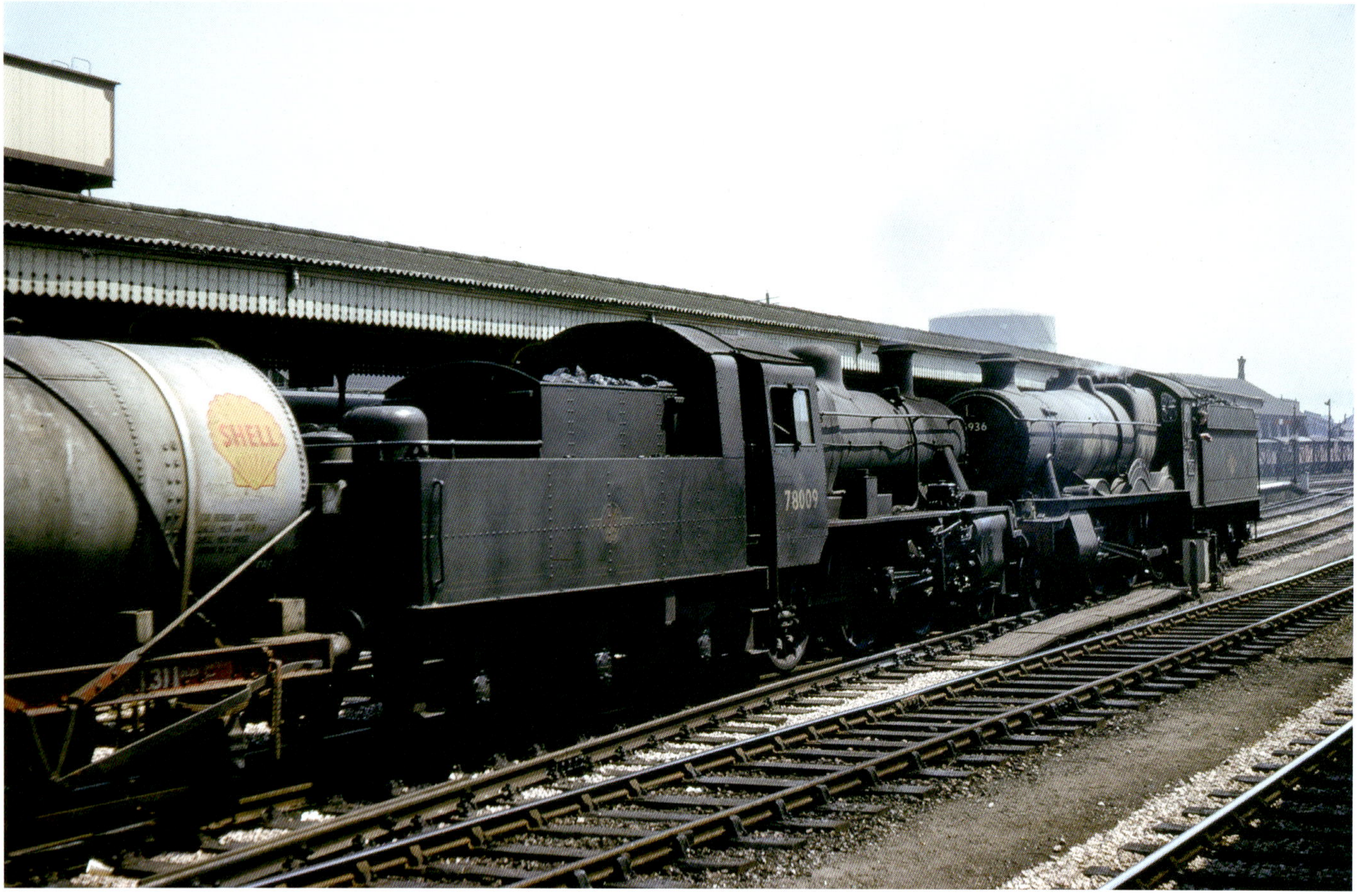

An interesting combination at Gloucester on 1 June 1963 as 5936 Oakley Hall which we have already glimpsed on a previous page has interestingly been put onto the front of Standard 2MT 78009 chimney to chimney at the head of it's freight. ***Frank Hornby***

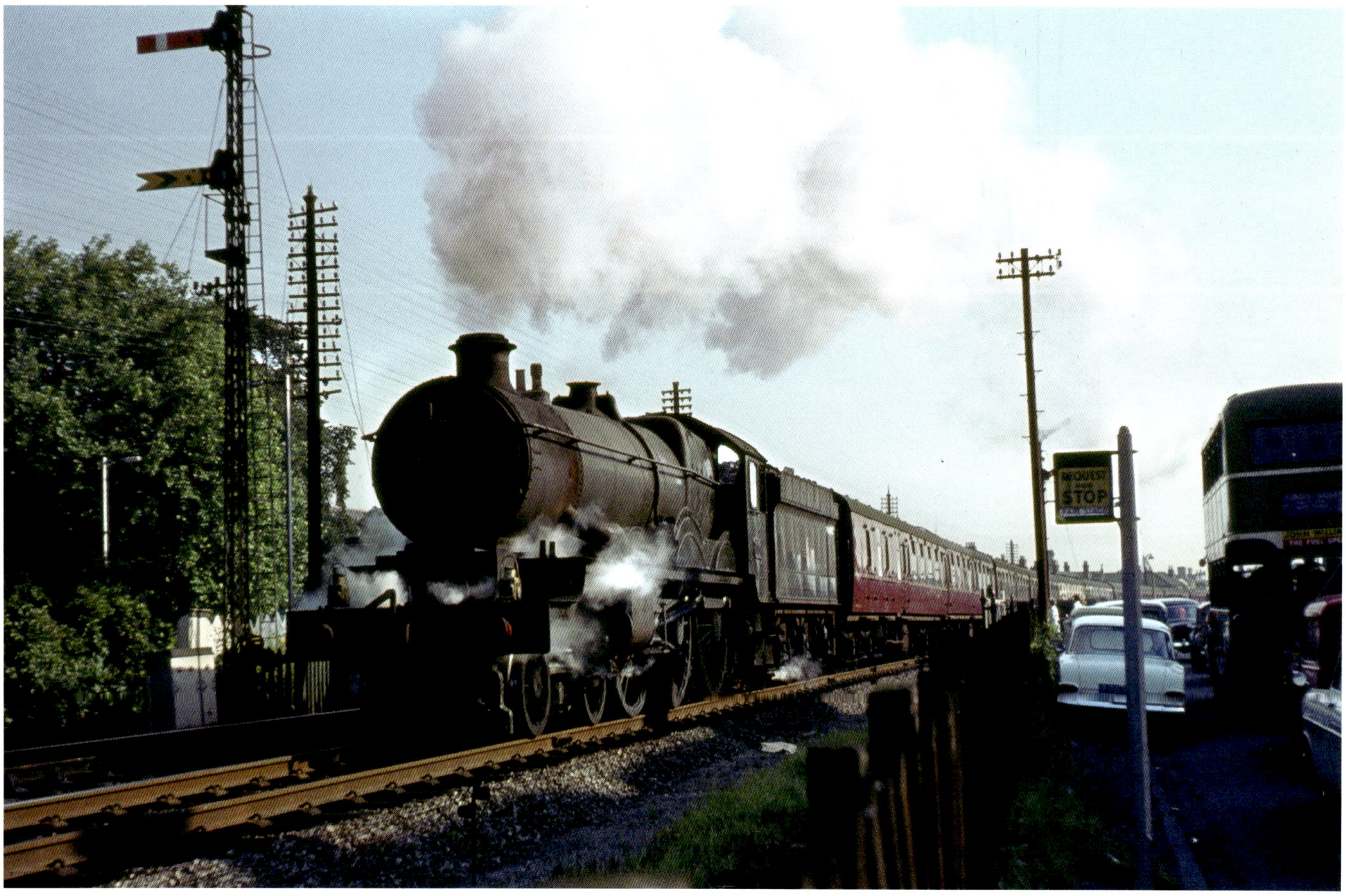

There appears to be some road traffic congestion around Gloucester and the level crossings on 27 July 1963, but these will not delay 5050 Earl of St.Germans making a storming southbound departure. ***Peter Simmonds***

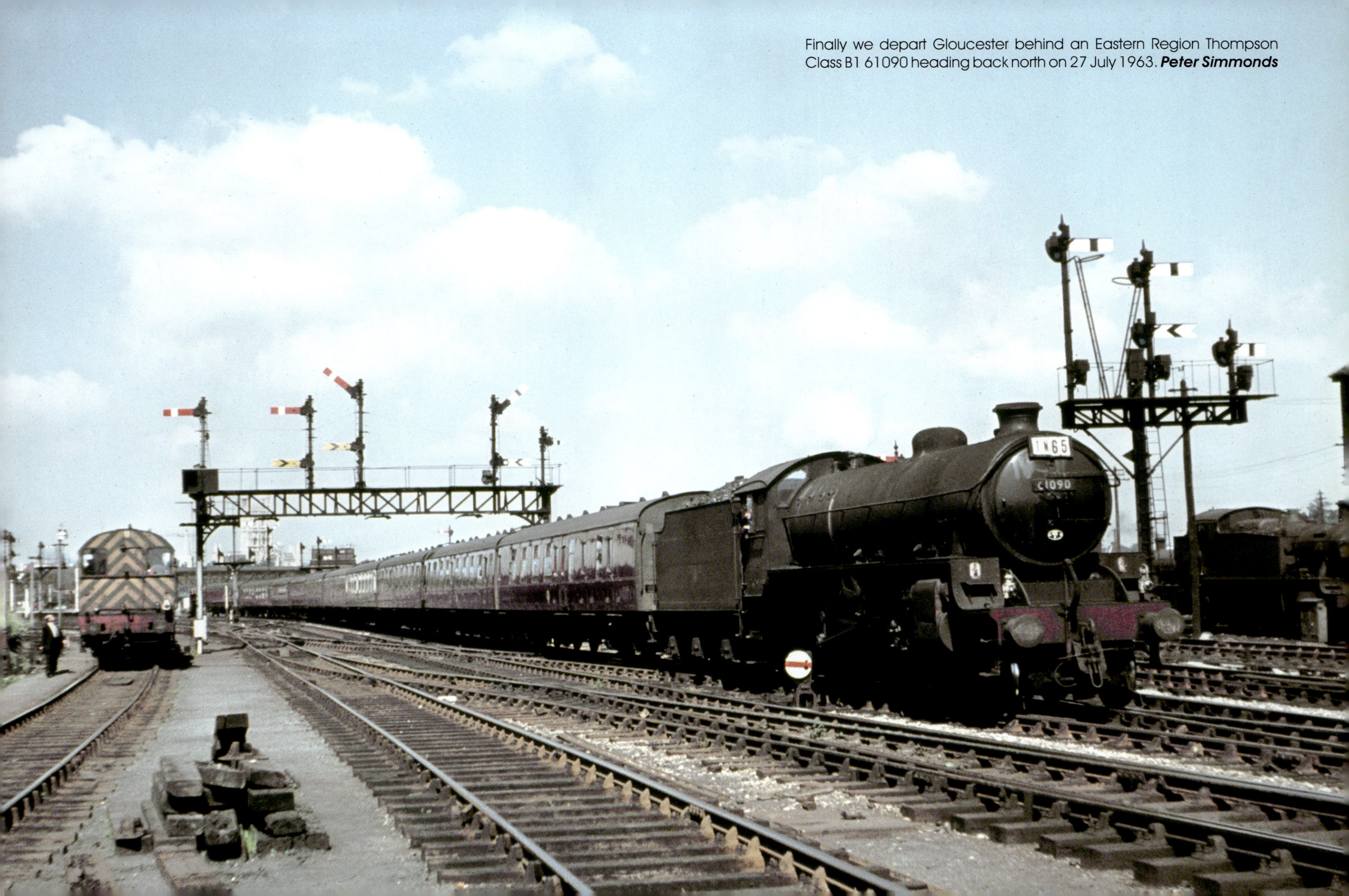

Finally we depart Gloucester behind an Eastern Region Thompson Class B1 61090 heading back north on 27 July 1963. ***Peter Simmonds***

Help To Preserve Our Railway Heritage

Strathwood not only publish books on our railway heritage but have also set up the Railway Photographic Preservation Association as a Charitable Trust to house an archive of images comprising over 200,000 photographic negatives and slides.

The archive was established to not only preserve the collections of over one hundred photographers both living and deceased, but to also make their work available to a younger audience for the future. To achieve this aim, we have begun an energetic programme to publish a considerable number of books. Allied to this we are making as many as possible of the photographs and slides we hold, available as copies to interested enthusiasts, individuals, societies and other publishers.

Many photographers have chosen Strathwood to care for their collections and to publish the best examples of their work for posterity.

If you have negatives or colour slides of transport subjects then we would like to hear from you. We purchase, accept on loan, or welcome donations of material to the archive. Photographers always receive recognition for their work when it is used by publishers (A N Other/Strathwood Library). To answer why so many images are just credited as Strathwood Library Collection in this volume, the reason is we do not know who the original photographer was. This is usually because their collection gets split up via auctions or collectors upon their death with no record of the late photographer for us to credit. Please do not let this happen to your collection. Make contact with us today to discuss what can be done to ensure you work is fully credited and recognised for both today and the future.

Please call us today if you would like to see your work in print, perhaps in a similar fashion to this publication. We also undertake publications to benefit charities and societies on behalf of our contributors. In addition we can store, and catalogue collections on behalf of clubs and societies by way of loan, thereby releasing such groups to concentrate on other aspects of their activities.

Strathwood Ltd,
Glenavon House,
Kinchurdy Road,
Boat of Garten,
Inverness-shire,
PH24 3BP.

Telephone 01479 831139

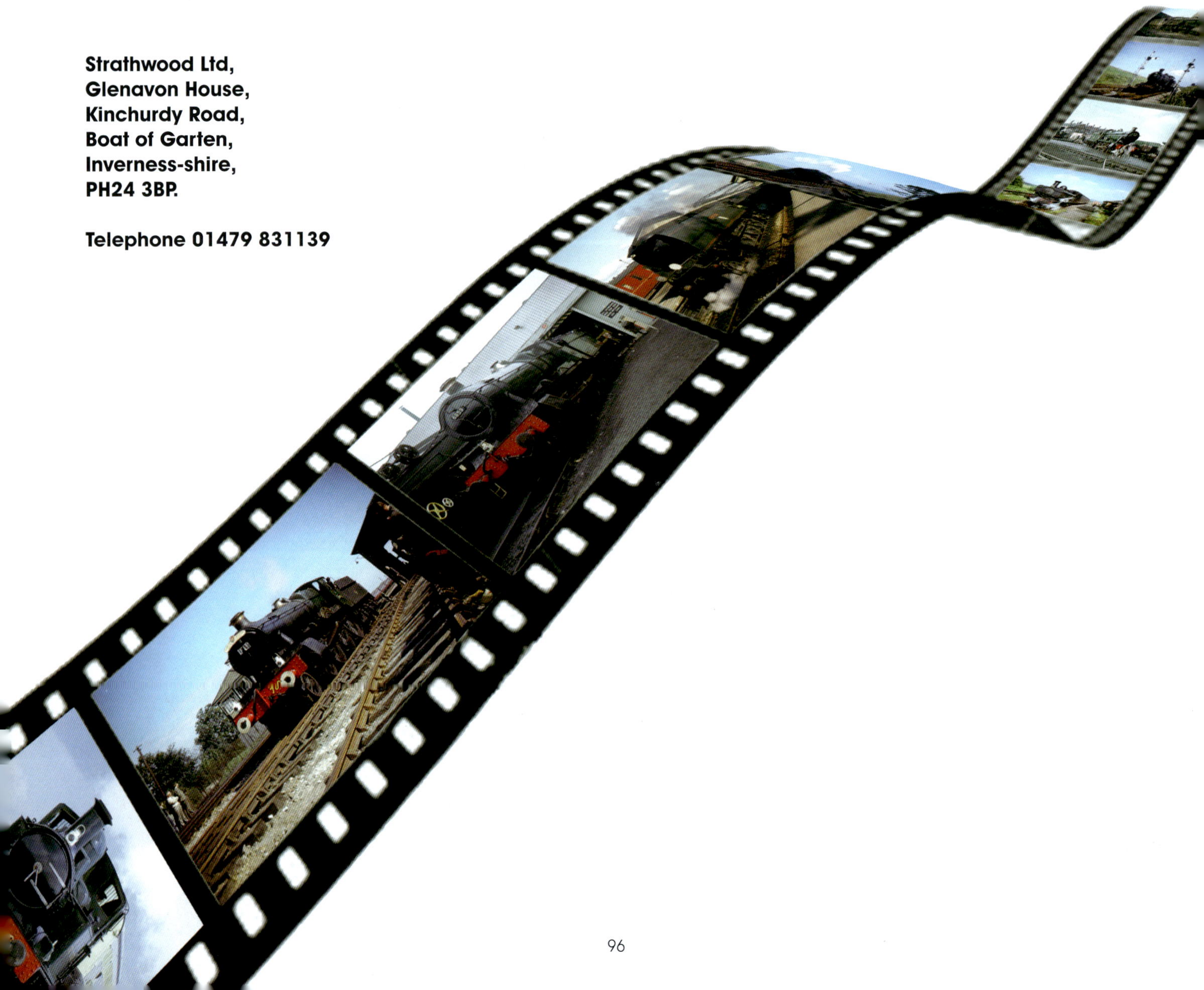

PARANOID SHEEP
(What if)

PARANOID SHEEP
(What if)

BY

LORD
M. A. FRICKER

Strategic Book Publishing and Rights Co.

Strategic Book Publishing & Rights Co., LLC
USA | Singapore
www.sbpra.com

For information about special discounts for bulk purchases, please contact Strategic Book Publishing and Rights Co. Special Sales, at bookorder@sbpra.net.

ISBN: 978-1-68181-223-6

This is dedicated to
all the sheeple out there who aren't feeling themselves lately, or feel slightly vulnerable or alone in the world. It is also dedicated to those sheeple who are now starting to question their faith and to wonder if there is more to life.

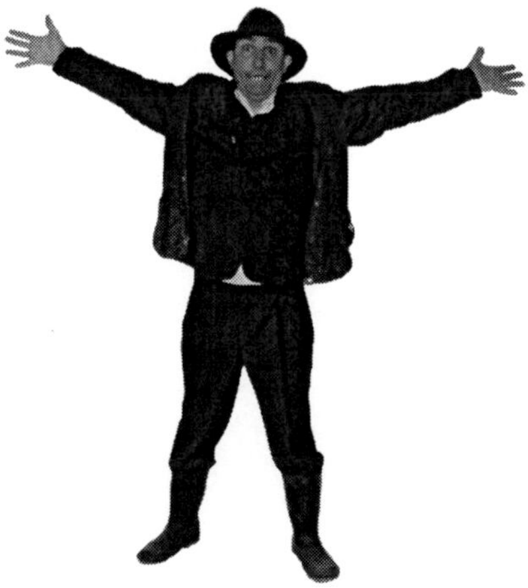

I'm only wondering what you're thinking.

It's time to open your mind and look at the world with a different perspective. 'The human mind is very complex' but you should listen to that voice in your head it may be trying to tell you something.

MAF

CONTENTS

A WARNING FROM THE AUTHOR:

Read carefully before you continue.
(This book contains a lot of explicit sexual swear words)

I would like to take this opportunity to apologize in advance if any of the content in this book offends you or scares you in any way. It wasn't meant to. It just seems to me that there could be a lot more to life than we think there is that's all. I want to explore this. I have added some subjects that have interested me over the years and make me personally think What If? What if all is not as it seems? This book is based on actual facts but mainly written for entertainment purposes only and not intended to upset anybody or influence your own way of thinking. I am not trying to criticize your own beliefs, it is simply my own personal thoughts and opinions that make me wonder if we are being told the full truth. You can take what I say how you wish, that's entirely up to you. Hopefully the subjects I am about to cover in this book will at the very least make you think with more of an open mind. Other than that I hope peace, love and contentment find you wherever your life takes you.

M A FRICKER
MAF

GENERAL INFORMATION

Just to let you know that this book is the sequel to my other one called Programmed Sheep which was basically me having a bloody good rant on behalf of the unappreciated working sheeple of the world. I was at the time very stressed indeed. If you haven't already read Programmed Sheep then I strongly advise you to do so before you start on this one otherwise you will probably get a little confused when I refer to you as being a sheep. If you decide to continue reading this book regardless... then that's entirely up to you. At least you are trying to be a free thinker if nothing else. Which is good; I'm not knocking it at all. It's very good as far as I am concerned. Anyway sod that let me start with the introduction.

INTRODUCTION

The word Paranoid is a word relating to the characteristics of, or affected with the Greek word παράνοια" meaning "madness" or it means to be suspicious, worried, nervous, fearful apprehensive, obsessively disturbed, unstable, manic, neurotic, mentally ill, psychotic, deluded, paranoiac or suffer with paranoid delusions, as put by good old Wikipedia

Now I guess you will think after reading this book that I'm a bit paranoid or at the very least that I'm mad, but I just think you sheep are misinformed. You have all been influenced to think the way you do. I reckon it's time for you sheeple to open your minds to an alternative way of thinking. You should question everything. If you were to do that you would be amazed as to what you would find, as I have.

For a very long time now I have had what I thought were recurring nightmares of being abducted by Aliens. That's right Aliens. But maybe they are not dreams at all, and this is really happening. I can tell you it's more frightening when you start to think you're not dreaming. I've woken up many times in my bed with unexplained scars on my body or bruising or even a rash. If that's not bad enough, I keep having this male voice in my head. However, this isn't anything new because I've had this voice since I was a child.

When I was very young I always thought it was my guardian angel talking to me, protecting me when I needed protecting and warning me of oncoming dangers. Well... that's what my mother used to tell me the voice was anyway. My mother once told me that a lot of children have imaginary friends when they are very young so I should look at the voice as being that, a friend or a guardian angel. She said not to worry about it because he'd go away when I get older and didn't need him anymore. So that's what I did. I stopped worrying about it and over time this voice and I became best of friends

The thing is, although my mother was right about it going away, she failed to tell me it would come back. That's right he came back and is still in my head even today. I just keep quiet about it now. I don't want sheeple thinking I'm mad do I? Besides, it's probably just my own thoughts or my own subconscious speaking to me anyway isn't it? I don't really believe in angels. Then again, I say all this but you can never be too sure can you? I'm not so sure, if I was being honest, because the thing is sheeple this voice introduced himself to me, which is new. I never had a name for this voice before; it was just a male voice to me. He introduced himself as 'Alf'. I was quite taken aback by it when he did that, I mean, what could I say? So at the time I just simply said 'Hello Alf' just to be polite. But then he said 'hello' back and began to tell me about himself.

He told me through telepathy that he was a Nordic Alien. He said it was time for me to know this now I'm older. He also said that I was chosen from birth to be a White Flame Warrior for the Nordic Alien race.

'Come again,' I said, 'A White Flame Warrior?'

'Yes,' he said, 'A White Flame Warrior.'

He then told me I was chosen from birth to be a messenger to the humans of Planet Earth. I know all this sounds bonkers doesn't it? So I just ignored him. But the more I ignored him the louder his voice became in my head.

I said, 'Look Pal, I'm not being funny but I'm a grown Ram now and you shouldn't be in my head anymore. So go away will you, please? Besides you're giving me a fricking headache shouting.'

'Sorry,' he said.

'That's okay you're forgiven' I said.

Then he spoke to me, quietly. 'Michael,' he said, 'please understand, the humans of Planet Earth need you. We Nordics need you.'

So with that I said, 'In that case how can I help?'

'We want you to be a White Flame Warrior,' he replied, 'and a White Flame Warrior comes with special powers.'

'Special powers?' I asked.

'Yes, special powers,' he said.

Special powers; how about that then reader? So I thought about it for a second or two and, as I thought of how good it would be to have special powers, he continued to tell me how special I was to be chosen in the first place by the Nordics. To be fair, it all did start to sound kind of cool being this 'White Flame Warrior' and I quite liked the idea of having special powers and all.

'How cool would that be?' I asked Alf. 'What does being a White Flame Warrior entail then?'

He said, 'Just type in White Flame Warrior on the internet and see for yourself.' Then he said, 'Remember to read the code.'

'I will,' I said. So I typed 'White Flame Warrior' into my computer, and was surprised to find out that there are loads of White Flame Warriors out there in the world. I proceeded to read this White Flame Warrior code that Alf was talking about. It said what was expected of me if I do decide to become one. It also gave a link to a YouTube video telling you all about what one is. I watched it with great interest. When it eventually finished I thought, *do you know, I like the look of that, that's right up my street that is.*

So I told Alf I'd do it. I'll be a White Flame Warrior for him and the Nordic aliens. He was well happy. So now I am a fully-fledged White Flame Warrior of the Nordic alliance. Brilliant isn't it?

However, since signing up I can tell you now my life has become weird, weirder than it already was before. At the time I was not really sure what Alf wanted from me to be honest, so I thought the best way to find out is ask, so I did.

'Alf,' I said, 'what is it you want me to do then?'

He replied simply, 'To spread the word of something big that's going to happen to the sheeple of Planet Earth if they don't buck up their ideas.'

'What's that then?' I asked.

He said, 'You will find out in due course.' He also told me that by being a White Flame Warrior you are always in danger of death and should stay vigilant at all times.

'Come again?' I said. 'You mean I could get killed?'

He said, 'Yes possibly.'

'Hang on a minute,' I said. 'I don't want to be a White Flame Warrior anymore. You can fuck off if it means I'm putting my life in danger.'

But he told me I didn't have much say in the matter anymore. He said I've already agreed to do it now.

'Well fuck you,' I said,' I have changed my fricking mind.'

'Tough,' he said, 'you can't change your mind; you have already given a verbal contract. Not only that, I've told the Nordic Elders you have agreed and if you go back on your word now I'm going to look a right idiot, and I'm not going to look like an idiot because of you.'

'I couldn't give a toss,' I said.

'Let me put it this way,' he said. 'If you make me look an idiot I will personally make your life a living hell.'

'Like what can you do to me?' I said,' you're just a fricking voice in my head so you can kiss my arse. What can you do to me hey? Tell me that?'

'For a start,' he said, 'I will stop protecting you as I've done all your life. Look Michael, I don't want us to fall out, we go back many years. Listen to me if you do this you will be greatly rewarded, I promise.'

'I couldn't give a flying fuck,' I said, 'I'm not doing it, I could get killed you said.' But then I had second thoughts.... 'What do you mean rewarded?'

'You will be given great gifts,' he said. 'For a start being a White Flame Warrior will give you a super power.'

I thought about it for a moment and to be fair I couldn't really say no to Alf could I? I mean he was a great comfort to me when I was down in the dumps as a young lamb. He was always there for me when I needed him most. For instance, he would warn me about things before they happened. When I was at school and the school bully was going to punch me in the face or stomach he would warn me beforehand so that I was ready for him. I knew whether to duck or tense my stomach muscles so the punch didn't hurt as much, or he would miss me completely and I could run away.

What about that time I was about to cross a road in front of an approaching bus? I hadn't heard it because I was miles away in my own world. Alf yelled at me 'STOP!' He saved my life that day. Yes, I could always rely on Alf. In fact I'd probably be dead if it wasn't for him. So as you see in a way it's my time to give him some payback, if I can that is.

'What super power are we talking about then Alf?' I asked.

'Special ones' he said.

'Okay how special,' I asked.

He said, 'You will be able to see into the future.'

I thought brilliant, being this White Flame Warrior sounds like fun after all. I quite like the idea of being able to see into the future. But as always all didn't turn out as it seemed. Later on I was to find out I'd been hoodwinked by Alf and I'll tell you why shall I?

This fricking super power consisted of me being able to see into the future like he said. But... what Alf failed to tell me is I would only be able to see bad things. I mean what good is that? They don't allow me to predict the lottery numbers or anything good like that. That would have been a brilliant super power to have. I would have been quite happy if I had x-ray vision or even if I was able to become invisible whenever I wanted to. That would have been fine by me. But oh no, my fricking super power is shit, it just allows me to see bad events coming.

I know I'm moaning a little and I guess it's better to have shit super powers than having no super powers at all. To be fair being able to see into the future is kind of cool in its own little way isn't it, be it good or bad? I mean, before I had this super power I used to rely on the voice of Alf to warn me about anything bad. Now because of my own super power I see them unfolding for myself. It does have its benefits as I usually know if there is going to be a hold up on the roads because of a crash or something. It gives me the chance to take an alternate route and not get stuck in traffic jams. If there is one thing I hate is traffic jams.

My super power is foresight; I can now see trouble coming before it happens. I can see when it is going to happen to individuals too. When I started to have this power, I would foresee something was going to happen to someone and I used to try and warn them about it. However, most of the time they just told me to fuck off or laughed at me. I don't know, some sheeple just don't want to be saved do they? So I don't even bother trying to tell anybody anything now. Fuck 'em....I just wait and watch it unfold and when it does I laugh to myself and say serves you right.

Anyway, just lately, I have foreseen a lot of major events starting to unfold around the world. I think we should all be concerned about this because it will affect all of us. Some bad things are most definitely unfolding and our long-term futures look quite bleak.

Alf told me that I must warn the sheeple of something really bad about to happen. Unless we change its course most of the population of Planet Earth is fucked. But I just didn't have a clue how I could warn the sheeple about what Alf and I could see unfolding or how to get any of you to take us seriously. Then Alf suggested we write a book. This is that book. So if you're reading this you may just have a chance to be saved. If you want to be saved that is. At the very least you can be prepared and ready for what we are going to warn you about.

Before we do this let me make it perfectly clear from the start. I don't pretend to be a brilliant writer but Alf told me he would help me write this book and try and increase my intellect as we progress.

Is he trying to tell me I'm thick?

I could just tell you straight out what it is I am supposed to warn you about, but anything I say wouldn't be taken seriously. So, like Alf said, I need to give you the reader some facts first to back up my claims. This foresight or prophecy that I have for you is massive. On a scale of one to ten it is big.

The last time I had a foresight like this was when I foresaw masses of sheeple getting killed by falling buildings. That was back in 2001 on September 11th. That's right... the Twin Towers tragedy. I saw that coming. It was a catastrophic event, but on a scale of one to ten that was only about a four. It wasn't until 9/11 happened I realized that was what I saw in my head months before. I had no chance to do anything about that. I still don't think I could've done much about it now. Maybe I could have put a warning on the internet but if I had done that I guess nobody would have taken any notice anyway.

But I am having these warnings again, these visions if you like, and now know I am supposed to warn everyone about them. There are major events unfolding; only I have one big fricking problem. I can't always remember what it is because no sooner do I have a vision, a premonition if you like, I am somehow mind-wiped to forget all about it. It's not until it has actually happened I remember it again, by which time it's too late.

You probably think what's the point of the super power of foresight of danger if you can't warn anybody about them? Remember my alien abduction dreams I told you about? Well, I keep having them and according to Alf he says it is the Grey Aliens who are responsible for my mind wipe. He might be on to something. Every time I have a weird abduction dream, when I wake up again I've forgotten what I was supposed to warn you about, which is no use to anybody is it?

Alf has now told me that the abductors preventing me telling the sheeple in time are enemies of Earth. I said if that's the case then what's the point of being told about or seeing any of the bad things if I am unable to tell anyone about them in time? He said that's why you need to write this book. On one hand I have a foresight in my head that I need to warn everyone about. On the other hand I have a weird dream of being abducted by Aliens who are making me forget all about them.

So you can imagine it has been really hard for me to write this book because of the constant mind-wiping I am undergoing. I feel like 'sheepy in the middle'. I am between two rival Aliens or something that is doing my head in big time. Am I completely off my rocker? Is this all just in my head? But what if it's true?

I just worry you won't be warned in time. It's no good me warning you about things if I don't have the facts to back my claims up. So Alf suggested I surf the web to gather the evidence, which is what I have been doing for the last couple of years.

RESEARCH

When I researched topics for this book I found it a real mission and got really frustrated at times. Alf bombarded me with website blogs he insisted I read. It would be fair to say I do have a real life Dr Jekyll and Mr Hyde relationship with Alf. Our personalities clash and at times I just wanted to throw my fricking computer up the wall. But Alf kept me calm in his own little way. I also found lying down in a darkened room helped. I often got very tired reading all the many articles and most of what I did read I personally thought was a load of bollocks and even boring.

Some sheeple do talk a lot of shit. When it was half interesting a lot of it was way above my reading capability. The main reason I found it hard to understand was because of all the big words used by the clever sheep. I didn't understand most of what they said because of hard to pronounce words such as 'Acetylseryltyrosylserylisoleucylth'. For those of you who are interested it means Tobacco Mosaic virus which is a dahlemensestrain, whatever the frick that is? You will find this massive word. 'Acetylseryltyrosylserylisoleucylth' used in the American Chemical Society under Chemical Abstracts. But the word 'Dahlemense'? If you ever find out what this means let me know. You get my point.

So you can understand why I got so frustrated when I found myself having to look up big words like this in a thesaurus. This all took time. It used to annoy me to find out that the big word I didn't understand in an article meant something so simple. Do you know I have never understood why the frick clever sheep have to use big words for everything? There's no need for it. Just say the simple meaning and stop showing off! Some of the subjects I had to read twice before it sunk in because they were far too complex for me to understand. Alf helped me through it and even somehow made me get cleverer, as you will see. In the end we ended up with this book.

So it would be fair to say we both wrote this book, me and Alf. It seems to have worked out okay. So 'We' promise you the reader you won't have any problems understanding any big words in this book. We both agreed to keep it as simple as possible. Hope you enjoy it but most of all get the message.

This book is non-fiction. For those of you who don't know that means based on facts. I have also used my poetic licence to exaggerate a bit on some of these facts to make it a bit more humorous, unlike the shit I had to read. Although what I talk about in this book may be laughable to some, it will still make you sit up and think about your life a bit more than you do. I will also try and bring to your attention that life may not be all as it seems. I want to explain to you why I

think we are in real danger of extinction. It's because you are acting like sheep.

'It's no wonder truth is stranger than fiction, fiction has to make sense.' Mark Twain

Here is a word from Alf (That's the voice in my head)

Hello, my name is Alf, and it is my hope that from this book you will see the world in a different perspective. That you will realize what's really going on behind the scenes. You're allowing your planet to be destroyed at an alarming rate by your ignorance and the influence of what you are brainwashed to think. I want you to realize your potential as a human being to make things different. At the same time I want you all to be more spiritual than you are. You all have the power to change the world. You just don't know it yet. There is an Evil Enemy that will try and stop you humans evolving to your full potential. This needs to be addressed. Me As well as what he said I want you also to realize you're lied to by government. You are kept in the dark about a lot of stuff. You can make your lives better if you get up off your asses and stop acting like the fricking sheep. Stop believing all the sheep shit and bollocks you're told. I warn you now... keep this up and you will all be following each other head to tail to the slaughter house. Mark my words on that.

Are you ready Michael? 'Yes I fricking am Alf. Let's try and save the Sheeple of Planet Earth.'

PROLOGUE

Back in December 2012 loads of sheep fled to a place called Pic de Bugarach, a French mountain where it was believed that the top would open up and Aliens emerge with spaceships to save everyone from the end of the world… this was all linked to the Mayan prophecy. Christ knows where they got that idea from. What made them think that the Aliens want to save any of us anyway?

I Do

'Apart from you Alf.'

I must admit reader I also thought something massive was about to happen on 21st December 2012 too. A lot of stuff went on building up to this date and it certainly looked like the end of the world was coming, what with the Twin Towers. I see now that I misunderstood the Mayan prophecy because I listened to others and believed in what I was told rather than look into it myself. I must say I'm kind of glad I did too because I feel much calmer and less fearful than I was. I'm glad the world didn't come to the violent end as was believed by so many sheeple, myself included, and giving us the chance to make sure it never happens.

When I read about the Mayan prophecy I pleaded to sheeple, mainly at work, to listen to me. I even offered to show them some of my research.

I said to them, 'Look at the evidence. It proves this could be the end of mankind in December 2012.' I told them, 'Look, I can give you the websites and links so that you can check it out for yourselves.'

Nobody was interested, but I believed doomsday was coming. I even told them I was making preparations for it; told them they should do the same. As it happens I still have a load of tinned beans and bags of rice left. Okay, it's 2015 now and I may have misinterpreted this prophecy but it goes to show how important it is to get your facts right. From that experience I now know that is important.

Okay, so we may have all survived 2012, but make no bones about it I still believe doomsday is coming. I mean we are already seeing loads of shit unfold as the years come and go aren't we? Sheeple dying in their droves. I tell you there is a cull happening as you read this. I believe this to be a Fact. Granted it's a slow one at the moment but, mark my words, it is happening without a doubt and will continue to happen, you can be sure of that. That is at least until the quota is reached, which is a lot.

Yes, my sheepy little friend, there are many ways to cull the population. Ebola is a cull. Aids was, and still is, a cull. Cancer is also a cull. I think they have had a cure for that for years. Poverty too is a cull. And let's not forget the old favourite War. Now War is most definitely a cull. I think this culling will pick up pace as the years go on. You'll get little warning signs though before it does so. If you want any chance of survival you should take heed as you see it happening. You could be next. Not only that you can bet your arse you will continue to see mini disasters happen all around the world. I personally think these are little rehearsals to the big event yet to come.

I am sure we will see more major events unfold around the world and more frequently. I'm talking events on a biblical scale and all, like all those so-called 'natural' disasters. I think that these will increase; some will shake the foundations of the planet like never before. What about the odd terror attack? You'll see more of them. Each time one or the other happens a few more of us will be culled. I think most are controlled culls.

But I think the big event is yet to come. What that will be I'll tell you later. Mark my words this big event is building up as I speak. Sooner or later you will see it unfold for yourself. I think it will all become apparent to us all within the next seventy years or so to my own reckoning. You think I jest. When I'm proved right let's see who's laughing then. Yes siree, the sheeple of the world are all about to witness things that have never ever been witnessed before, at least not for a very long time. Sheeple I'm afraid there will without a doubt be more tsunamis, volcanoes, big earthquakes and even some unexplained events happening right across the globe. You mark my words. Each time one of these events happens I fear masses of us sheep will be culled as a result. No, I'm afraid my sheepy little friends no Aliens are going to save you from the big event, far from it.

You will need to save yourself.

'Thank you Alf.'

Like Alf has said you will need to save yourself. Hark at me all doom and gloom and we have only just started the book. But it doesn't have to be all bad and besides I don't want to be called a scaremonger. All I am doing is relaying the facts as I see them and I know I will need facts to convince you reading this. I mean I looked like a right idiot last time, what with the Mayan prophecy. Sheeple were right to ridicule me and I may have worried some sheep needlessly by what I said... by the way sorry for that. So I want to make amends to all the sheeple I told were doomed back in 2012. I won't be wrong again. Next time when I tell you the end of the world is coming it'll be based on concrete facts.

I must stress at this point I don't think the end of the world is set to a concrete date. I now believe it is up to us if it comes or not. By the way when I say end of the world I don't mean the planet, I mean life on it, mostly us humans. No, the planet will last a long, long, long time after we have all gone. But with a bit of faith, and good luck, hopefully we humans still have many years to look forward to.

I believe we can change our futures if we really want to. All we need to do is change our ways. We must if we want to survive and thrive for the next thousand years or so. What we need to do is wake up to what unfolds around us. This is a beautiful planet and we should protect it and all life on it. We need to be ready to defend life so when the next threat does raise its ugly head we will see it coming and be ready to stop it. Yes, I believe together we can prevent Armageddon if we really want to.

Well for a while longer anyway Michael. You humans will eventually need to leave Earth someday.

Looking back now to 2012 I think that date may be just the beginning of the end. The Mayans, The Incas, The Egyptians, The Sumerians, The Native Indians of America all knew the year 2012 was significant. The Mayans were just one of many ancient civilizations who tried to tell us something or even warn us something was about to happen. Prepare us even, but for what?

ANTI-CLIMAX

To find out 2012 wasn't the end of the world was a bit of an anti-climax for us doomsday preppers. We expected December 21st to be the imminent end of mankind. Looking back, maybe we were all gullible silly sheep even to think this was going to happen on that date. A lot of us sheep fell for it hook, line and sinker. Even those of you who didn't think the end of the world was nigh, you still weren't one hundred per cent sure were you? This isn't your fault, sometimes we are just too fricking gullible for our own good. We seem to swallow all the crap we have been fed. Nobody knows what to believe anymore because we keep finding out it is bollocks.

I kind of think we are all subconsciously willing doomsday to happen, which is very sad when you think about it. Maybe we see it as an escape from the imprisonment of life. Work, Bills, Debt and what have you. Most of the working class of the world are so pissed off and fed up at the moment we wish it would all come to a fricking end. I think some of us have pressed the self-destruct button in our own minds and that's why we act as if we don't give a shit anymore and live like there's no tomorrow. We drink ourselves silly, over-eat and spend money we don't have and, yeah, we put up with the crap the government dishes out far too much in my opinion.

But not caring what they are up to is stupid because most of the shit in the world is because of them, as far as I am concerned. We feel we have no control over our lives anymore so why bother caring? Our lives are being dictated to us by our leaders, who don't care about us anyway. That's how we all feel. We have no control and no say so we feel no hope.

What you don't realize is you have a lot of power to change you're world for the better. You just don't think you have because you have been brainwashed to think you haven't.

Me and Alf will try and make you understand who you really are, what you are capable of, where you really originated from and, more important, where you're going. We will also try and explain to you why your life is as it is and what your purpose is on this planet. I will make you ask a lot of questions and here are a couple to start you off... Does God exist? If so, what if God was an Evil Alien? Funny questions to ask you may think but for me they are the biggest questions to ask because that could answer so many others.

If God was an Alien then that would explain, at least to me, why so many bad things happen in the world. We wonder why God allows them to happen. That's why I think we have a right to question his existence. To be fair he doesn't seem to do anything about all the crap going on and doesn't behave the way we think he should. God doesn't seem to meet our expectations does he? That's why the sheeple lose faith. If God represents love why does he then let the innocent suffer and babies die? Why allow the wars and misery and let evil sheeple get away with the monstrosities they do? Why? What? Who? Where is God? Is there a God at all? Is he an Evil Alien?

This is my mission to find out; my purpose; my message, my conclusion to the meaning of life.

Now I think I know who I am, do you?

PARANOID SHEEP (What If)

Many a true word is hidden in humour.

MAF

CHAPTER ONE

WHAT IF YOU HAD A PURPOSE?

SPECIAL

> **Remember you're special. Don't ever let anybody tell you different' MAF**

When I was just a little lamb I always felt I was special because my mum used to tell me that I was all the time. Other lambs just thought I was a goofy little weird bastard and picked on me constantly. Some sheeple can be very cruel and sometimes force you out of the flock, making you feel isolated and alone in the world. You become vulnerable and start to lack confidence in yourself. Eventually you start to get a little paranoid about almost everything; like the way you look and how other sheeple perceive you as a person. If you're not careful you can start to dislike yourself, which is a shame, because we are all special in our own little way. I think it's a shame a lot of sheeple don't realize just how special they are. I think my isolation from the rest of the human race allowed me more chance to be myself instead of a sheep, a follower, like most sheeple are. I know I am still a bit of a sheep but not as bad as most of the planet's population, and thank God for that.

I remember when I was just a little lamb I didn't seem to fit in with the others. I didn't have many friends and I was never involved in anything like football teams; nobody would ever pick me to be in their team. The only time I was involved in anything was when they wanted somebody to take the piss out of; which isn't nice. I put up with it because at the time I just wanted to be liked. I would act daft just to make them laugh and like me for a while. But this just fed their eagerness to take the piss out of me even more. I soon got a reputation as the village idiot but I suppose at least it gave me some friends. Before this I had to stand alone and be happy with my own company.

I remember I used to imagine I had an invisible friend and we would go on adventures together. I guess this is what gave me the good imagination that's been with me most of my life, as well as my invisible friend. I think when you're alone you naturally find something to help you cope and your inner strength kicks in. You have to do this to survive life no matter what age, even if it may seem a bit barmy to some. I say sod what sheeple think of you, at least my invisible friend was there for me. Sounds mad I know but I think being slightly mad helps you survive life. Look at me, I survived didn't I and I am as mad as a March hare? I'm middle aged and I still have an invisible friend. He has never abandoned me and has helped me learn about life.

MICKY FRICK'S TIP

THE NUMBER ONE RULE IS; LIVE YOUR LIFE FOR TODAY, DON'T LIVE IT IN THE PAST.

I like to forget what was and concentrate on the now. I am happy living in the moment. A lot of sheeple have hurt my feeling in years gone by. I've been called names, bullied and treated like an idiot. At the time all I was trying to do is make sheeple laugh and to simply like me. I have had many moments of loneliness too, but my mum always showed me the love that got me through the hard times.

One particularly good memory I have of my mum doing just that was on my tenth birthday. It was many, many years ago now, but I still remember it as if it were yesterday. It was when I found my inner strength more than any other time. I remember I felt extra special that day because I started to feel grown up after noticing pubic hair around my bollocks. I didn't have many birthday presents but my favourite was a new Aran jumper my mum had knitted for my special day. I loved it more than anything in the world because it fitted me perfectly, unlike most of the clothes I was forced to wear. I really loved that jumper, it was tailor made just for me and lovingly knitted for me by my wonderful mum.

I also had a new padded hat in blue, my favourite colour. I had a new padded hat every birthday; it was a tradition in our house. Even now I always have something on my head whenever I go out otherwise I feel vulnerable; funny that isn't it? But it's true. I must always wear something on my head. I think it is because I was told that a hat would protect me. I always wondered what it protected me from; not from bullies that's for sure. Nevertheless, this new blue one was different from the rest, different because it was magic. I remember my mum taking off my old brown hat and placing the new one on my head.

'This is a very special hat for a very special person because this one is a magic hat,' she said.

I asked why it was magic.

She told me, 'It just is. You'll find out one day just how magic it is because this hat will give you courage like a lion. Look after it because it'll probably be the last padded hat you'll ever have to wear'.

I will always remember that hat because, unlike all the others, this one had a propeller on top that spun in the wind as I ran about playing. I now know it was called a Beany hat.

The first propeller hat, or better known as the beany, was popularized by a television program called 'Time for Beany'. Beany was a puppet character who was a space hero. The Beany hat was first made out of pieces of plastic, bits of coat-hanger wire, some beads, a propeller from a model aeroplane, and staples to hold it together. It was also worn by George Young of Detroit at a world convention, where it was an enormous hit.

Yes, I was very happy playing outside wearing my new jumper and magic Beany hat. Then bullies started to pick on me as they always did. That's one thing I have learnt throughout my life is that just as you're having a nice time somebody will come along and try and ruin it for you. This time it was because of these bullies. If it wasn't having the piss taken out of my goofy teeth it would be something else. They made my lamb-hood fricking miserable. Not a great memory my lamb-hood, it was mostly crap to be fair, but that was then. I don't get bullied anymore because being bullied as often as I was eventually hardens you up. I became a bit more thick-skinned than most sheeple. I have since learnt if you enhance this strength eventually you will have the courage to have a bloody good go back at 'em, which I did. I think it was thanks to my magic hat that I did though.

What I will say to you is if you're a victim of bullying, if you do get the guts to take on a bully my tip is simple, make fricking sure it counts. What I mean by this is be as nasty as you can muster, throw everything at the git, just try not to kill the bastard. I must stress at this point it does take real guts to stick up against bullies but if you do find those guts make it fricking count. I can tell you from experience it can be very gratifying indeed, the advantage you have is the element of surprise. When you do blow it's totally unexpected by them. Remember they saw you as weak.

MICKY FRICK'S TIP

NEVER KEEP THE FACT YOU'RE BEING BULLIED TO YOURSELF; ALWAYS TELL SOMEBODY ELSE

As I grew up I learned you must never keep the fact you're being bullied to yourself, always tell somebody else. This is most important because then you're never on your own and, when you do blow, they will know why you did. I was amazed to discover ninety-nine point nine per cent of sheeple surveyed don't like bullies. So when you think about it you have a fricking big army to stick up for you against the tossers who get off by making your life miserable. Tell you what; I'm going to share with you now a little story of how I found the courage to take on bullies thanks to my magic hat. Well, it was magic to me at the time and that's all that matters.

PAYBACK

So it was my tenth birthday and I was quite happy to mind my own business and play with my imaginary friend, until the bullies decided to pick on me yet again. This time they took the piss out of my new jumper and new magic hat. They called me all sorts of names. Now I can take name calling but when they started to tug and pull at my new jumper, pulling it all out of shape, you can imagine I was very upset about it. I liked my new jumper very much as you well know and I wanted them to stop what they were doing or there would be trouble. What they didn't know was I had my magic hat to protect me. It all started with me running into the kitchen. I was rather upset that the bastards had pulled my jumper all out of shape and this made me cry. My mother was making a pie at the time and I ran into her arms weeping and looking the worse for wear.

'What's up my love are the big lambs bullying you again?'

'Yes,' I nodded, wiping the tears from my eyes.

'Come here' she said', and she gave me a big hug like only mothers can do, spun my propeller and asked why I hadn't used the super powers of my magic hat.

I shrugged my shoulders. 'I dunno,' I said

'What are they saying about you today my love?'

'They keep calling me names and pulling on my new jumper. They have ruined it look,' I whimpered.

'The rotten sods,' she said, checking me over. 'Never mind, you know they are only picking on you because you're special, you know that don't you?'

'I don't feel very special,' I replied

'Well you are.... I've told you before you're very special,' she said. 'Anyway haven't I always told you that sticks and stones may break your bones but names will never hurt you? Besides I can always knit you a new jumper if this one gets ruined can't I?'

I nodded.

'Come on then, let's see that big smile of yours again, after all it is your birthday and you must never let anybody ever ruin your birthday.'

I smiled and shook my head.

'That's more like it'.

She then kissed me on the top of my head as she always did and finished off by saying something that must have triggered what I did next.

'Your magic hat will protect you.'

Those few words I will never forget. Because I had had enough of being bullied I needed something to give me confidence to stick up for myself, so I thought today is going to be that day. It's time to put an end to all this bullying once and for all. I'm going to use the power of the magic hat to protect me. I'll always remember that rhyme my mum used to say to me every time I was upset at being bullied. So armed with my magic hat this time I skipped outside again, and as I did I kept on reciting that rhyme to build up my confidence for what I was about to do.

'Sticks and stones may break your bones but names will never hurt me... sticks and stones may break your bones but names will never hurt me' I repeated several times as I went outside.

I noticed straight away that the big lambs were still there waiting for me. I was a bit frightened but then the voice in my head was there for me again.

Time to stand up for yourself.

Suddenly I wasn't frightened anymore. I spotted my dad's spade on the lawn so I picked it up. I remember it was quite heavy but I found the strength from somewhere and dragged it behind me, calmly walking straight up to the biggest bully in the gang

'What you going to do with that dick head?' he said, as he slapped me across the head. My magic hat fell to the ground.

My confidence dipped for a while because I no longer wore my magic hat, but the voice of my imaginary friend said, *'You don't need your magic hat, Michael, you are special without* it.'

Suddenly I wasn't scared anymore and I said to the bully, 'I'll show you.'

And with that, and using all the strength I could muster, I picked the spade up over my head and with one last burst of energy swung it at the bastard's head. He spun around like a spinning top then fell to the floor. The blow had knocked him clean out. I thought I had killed the fucker but I didn't care at the time. To be honest he was a right wanker. His mates, obviously stunned at what they had just witnessed, ran off rather upset leaving their mate on the grass out cold, bleeding from the head wound I just gave him. I stood over him and felt fricking great seeing him lying there. *Fuck him*, I thought, *I don't care if he is dead*, although my heart was racing, I felt like I was superman. I just knocked out the biggest bully in school in front of witnesses Ha Ha. But I didn't stop at that. I got my willy out and I pissed the blood off the bastard's bleeding head. I thought it was so funny.

Do you know I have never been bullied since? 'Thank you voice in my head,' I said and then I bent over, picked up my magic hat, placed it back on my head and calmly walked away.

I was quite pleased with myself as you can imagine. Thinking back now, I think it was the voice in my head more than the power of that magic hat that gave me the confidence to do what I did.

Ever since that day I have been treated very differently by sheeple, my reputation of being unpredictable is my greatest weapon against all the wankers I have ever met. I was very happy indeed with my new confidence; together with my magic Beany hat I felt like I was invincible. I even remember jumping off my dad's shed once because I thought the propeller on my hat might help me to fly. It didn't. I just landed on my arse on a pile of manure my dad had left to put on his allotment. That was one of the times that I should've listened to the voice in my head. I remember just before I leapt he did say, '*Don't jump.*' I should've listened. I was covered in shit and stank to high heaven.

A few days after my tenth birthday that wanker came out of hospital. He had to have ten stitches in his head. I spotted him at school one day with his head bandaged up. I was expecting him to want revenge but when he saw me he cowered and walked the other way. From then on he and his mates avoided me like the plague; good job they did too because I was now oozing with confidence. I really did feel like I had super powers thanks to my magic Beany hat and the voice in my head.

Since then I don't give a toss about what sheeple think of me because I now know I am pretty special and, as my mum said, the voice had gone. It was thirty-five years later when I realized just how special I was. This time it was my forty-fifth birthday. Now that's a different story altogether as the voice came back. I could never have guessed in a million years just how special and important I was to become. This is when I became a warrior for the sheeple and hopefully your saviour.

MICKY FRICK'S TIP

I TELL MYSELF I AM SPECIAL EVERY DAY; YOU SHOULD DO THE SAME

IT'S WRITTEN IN THE STARS

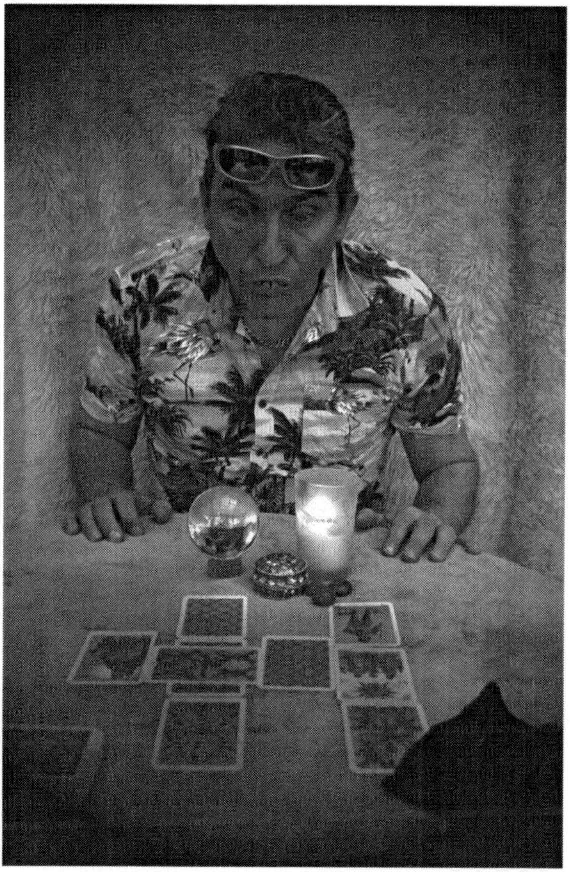

It started in May 2012, seven months before my first book Programmed Sheep was released. This was the year something happened that changed my life forever. It happened right out of the blue while I was on a well-deserved holiday in Tenerife in the Canary Islands with my best mate Andy. You see, my lovely wife has always allowed me to have a week's holiday with my mates once a year, which is really good of her I think.

MICKY FRICK'S TIP

ALL PARTNERS SHOULD LET THEIR OTHER HALF HAVE AT LEAST ONE WEEK AWAY FROM THEM WITH THEIR MATES ONCE A YEAR

I reckon all partners should let their other half have at least one week away with their mates once a year. I think it does a relationship good and I should know, I've been with my wife now for over thirty years. So, anyway, every year I take advantage of this gift from my wife and go off somewhere with my mates. Well I say mates, I mean mate. I don't have many mates. This particular year me, and my best mate Andy, went off to Tenerife to grab a bit of sun and get pissed a lot, as you do.

Now, before I go on, let me tell you a little bit about my mate Andy. Well, where do I start? He is simply the nicest sheep in the world and will do almost anything for anybody, nothing is too much trouble. He is a genuine proper good Ram and he can put his hand to anything you need made or fixed. He's a very Handy Andy. He likes a beer and the odd bet on the horses from time to time and that's about it. He really is a simple chap all in all. His needs are few. A good woman would make his life complete. So any Ewes out there who want a good Ram let me know and I'll give you his number... So that's about it really. That's my mate Andy. A top Ram on every level.

Anyway back to my story. Now betting on the horses was exactly what Andy was doing when I had my life-changing experience in Tenerife. He had buggered off somewhere to place a bet at the local bookies in the town centre and I stayed behind. I'm not much of a gambling Ram myself. I sat having a quiet cool beer on my own waiting for him to return. I remember I was at a little bar next to the beach looking out to sea and enjoying the day in the warm sunshine. The sea breeze was stroking my face, the weather was lovely and hot and sunny, and it was nice having the sun warming my pale skin.

As I slowly cooked in the baking sun 'chill-axing' in my own thoughts, supping on my cool beer and watching all the sheeple go by, I felt genuinely good about life at the time. I felt truly thankful and at peace with the world around me, which to be honest is a rare feeling for me as most of the time I'm quite uptight. But for now I found myself smiling... after all it was my forty-fifth birthday so I was in a good mood anyway.

So there I was simply marvelling about how good my life had turned out; I even had some deep meaningful thoughts too about life and that. I thought how wonderful this planet is and how amazing that we are here at all. It made me feel good and very special. I thought it was about time I stopped being so negative about everything all the time. Life isn't that bad when you sit down and think about it. I was starting to feel quite contented with my lot. I was finding inner peace in my world and I was quite happy about it. And then it happened; some split arse came along to ruin it all.

'Excuse me.'

I looked up, shielding my eyes from the sunlight. There stood a Ewe in a long white dress wearing loads of charms and beads and bracelets. I could barely see the outline of her body with the blaring sun behind her but I did notice she wore red knickers because the sunshine behind her made them stand out. Not only that, the sun made her look kind of angelic and her dress was almost transparent. To my delight she didn't seem to have a bra on either and I could see the outline of her nipples and everything. *Marvellous*, I thought, *life doesn't get much better than this*. Okay… she did have little boobies like fried eggs but she was very pretty all the same, so it didn't really matter. You find that don't you? Sometimes if a Ewe is pretty she has little boobies but if she is an ugly trog they compensate their ugliness by having great big boobies don't they? I suppose that's to keep your eyes from looking at their ugly face. But sometimes if you're really, really lucky, they'll have both a pretty face and big tits.

Anyway that's beside the point isn't it?… So there she stood before me with her long jet-black hair that went right down to her arse; lovely arse too may I add…

'Sorry to bother you,' she said, in a nice Spanish accent. 'This may seem a bit weird but I feel I must tell you something.'

'Sorry, you what?' I replied, still mesmerized by her hourglass figure and red panties and them nipples of hers pointing at me.

'I'm a tarot card reader,' she said. 'I don't normally approach people but I saw you sitting there alone and something in my head told me to come over to talk to you. This is so weird,' she added, 'but I feel I must tell you something rather important. I have a message for you from the stars.'

My first thought was *she's full of shit, she just wants my money or she is a prostitute. Either way I'm not interested, probably a Spanish 'Gippo' for all I know.*

But I gave her the benefit of the doubt considering she was so pretty and I asked, 'What is it you need to tell me then love? Go on I'm listening.'

I acted half-interested in what she was about to tell me but, between me and you, I wasn't interested at all. I just wanted to lust over her sexy body a while longer.

'I don't know what it is yet…' she said. 'I think I need to read your cards first to tell you what you need to know.'

I politely responded with a friendly smile. 'I'm sorry my love but I'm not really interested in that tarot card reading bollocks. I don't believe in that kind of hocus pocus clap trap sheep shit. You know what I mean?'

As I said this her face dropped. She looked so disappointed bless her. Me being a soft touch, when faced by pretty Ewes with puppy brown eyes and a nice arse and not wearing a bra and red knickers on, thought, *bah fuck it I'm on holiday and it's my birthday. Besides it'll be interesting to hear what the pretty Ewe has to say.*

'Okay' I said. 'How much is it going to cost me for this reading then? I don't mind having it done as long as it isn't too expensive.' I thought *she isn't ripping me off. I don't care how pretty she is.* Anyway she seemed overjoyed that I'd agreed to have my cards read and she gave me a great big smile.

She then said, 'I'm not going to charge you anything; it's on me.'

'Oh, that's nice of you,' I said, with a bigger grin on my face. 'All right then, you can do it if it won't cost me anything'.

I thought at the time she was flirting with me…for a brief moment. I suppose it was just wishful thinking on my part because I'm not that good looking to be chatted up by pretty Ewes. But one can live in hope. Then, I had a second thought, *hang on here,* I thought, *she has probably got the clap and is simply sexually frustrated. She's chatting me up because no other Ram will touch her with a bargepole. That makes perfect sense otherwise why flirt with a goofy old git like me?* Well you never know these days do you, chlamydia is rife these days isn't it? You need to watch out if you come across a Ewe that is a bit forward, there's always a catch or a 'rash on her snatch', mark my words....Well that's my thinking anyway, not as if I would know I just read about it somewhere.

So be warned you horny Rams out there don't go anywhere near a dirty Ewe. Remember there's no such thing as a free ride, that's all I'm saying. When you think about it that goes for most things, nothing is free is it? If anybody says it's free, you can bet your bottom dollar it's going to cost you in the long run in one way or another. It's always the case from my experience anyway.

Nevertheless, on this particular occasion I ignored my own instincts because I was quite attracted to the Ewe at the time and full of lustful thoughts myself. It must have been the warm weather making me feel very horny. I was thinking *you never know, my mate Andy may have fixed me up with a local prostitute as a birthday treat.* One can live in hope… and at the time I was really hoping so because the only way I was ever going to get a pretty Ewe like her to show any interest in me was if she got paid for it. Mind you, I did read somewhere once that some Ewes are attracted to ugly Rams like me and what's wrong with that? Some Rams are attracted to ugly Ewes. How many times have you seen an ugly Ewe with big tits and a handsome Ram? So I thought if that is the case maybe some Ewes think if the Ram's ugly, as I am, then he must have a big cock. This pretty Ewe just likes big cocks so she's chatting me up. Hang on… that rules me out an' all. Fuck it; got to be a tart. On the other hand, maybe she is just a nice Ewe who wants to tell me my fortune.

I said, 'Are you a prostitute?'

She smiled at me so I smiled back and my hopes lifted for a second. I thought *she is a prostitute…Thank you Andy; this is a nice surprise for my birthday. Thank you very much buddy.* Then a second thought popped into my head, *hang on here, Andy wouldn't do that as he's a nice Ram with morals. Damn it.* So I pondered a second or two longer as I looked her up and down and thought *come on use your head. Don't be fooled by a pretty Ewe's charms there's more to this than meets the eye. She's not flirting with you at all, and she can't be a prostitute because she said it's not going to cost me anything. I know my mate Andy too well and he wouldn't fix me up* with *one in the first place.*

'Buyer Beware' alarm bells rang in my head at this point. Now I am usually right about these things. I never get any Ewes talking to me normally; it's a very rare event indeed. As much as I would like to think she did fancy me it was very unlikely because it simply never happens. Pretty Ewes never want to stand by me, never mind flirt with me, so what does she want? I had yet another thought pass through my mind, *maybe she's leading me into a trap.* I thought *hey up here, I know what's going on, she will take me somewhere quiet and there'll be two hefty Spanish Rams waiting to mug me.* I've read about that sort of thing happening, it's quite common.

Even so, and against all my common sense, I still couldn't help myself. She was so pretty see; I was like in a trance, a moth to the flame. She then beckoned me to follow her into the bar. Against all my instincts, mainly because I was mesmerized by her sexy body which made me feel really horny now, I stood up and nervously followed, led by my twitching cock. One thing I did have the sense to do was grab my half empty glass of beer. I held that tight in my fist just in case I needed to defend myself from any muggers. I thought, *if I get mugged I'll smash it into their faces then run off.* Anyway, so here I was curiously following the pretty Ewe inside this bar.

'Come follow,' she said, beckoning me with her finger 'we go somewhere quieter?'

I thought *get yourself ready mugging time is afoot….* It was dark inside the bar but I was still ready for any prospective mugger should they fancy their chances. I tried to keep myself vigilant at all times with my beer glass weapon in hand. As we walked further inside I was distracted by her long dress flowing in the breeze, it was lovely to watch to be honest. I was checking out her arse all the way, she had such a lovely arse, very pert like a little ripe peach. I then noticed she wore a G-string too, the little minx. I expected to be mugged any minute but I was still like a moth to a flame and followed her regardless.

Then I had another idea pop in my head. I thought that while she had her back to me I would discreetly tuck all my Euros in my trunks to hide them out of sight. If I did get mugged they would get fuck all from me as my money would be safely tucked under my bollocks. So I stuffed all my money just under my testicles while my eyes were still fixed on her lovely arse. I think she sensed me groping at her bum because she folded her hands behind her back to block my view. Then she just happened to glance over her shoulder and smiled at me but her face dropped when she saw I had my hand down my trunks. I was so embarrassed I removed my hand as quickly as I could and smiled back.

We continued to a quiet corner of the bar. I looked around to see if I could spot any Rams ready to pounce on me. I had my glass ready if they did but all seemed okay. In fact the bar was full of sheeple, Rams and Ewes of all ages; one couple even had two little lambs with them eating ice-cream. I felt much calmer at this point. The Ewe stood at a little table in the far corner of the room which had a lamp on it and two chairs. I thought, *she could be a genuine tarot card reader after all, silly me*. As I approached the table she sat down on one of the chairs. I went to sit down on the other but just before I did I paused for a moment and enquired again.

'Just to be clear', I said to her, 'you did say it's not going to cost me anything for this reading didn't you my love?'

She turned to me still smiling and, with a little laugh, said, 'That's right, free of charge.'

'Oh lovely, okay then,' I said. And with that I pulled the chair out and sat down. I picked up the menu on the table, it was blocking my view of the pretty Ewe, but as I did I also took a quick glance inside. I was starting to feel a little bit hungry because it was nearly lunch-time. I studied it for a moment and as I did so the money hidden in my trunks started to scrape on my knackers a bit. So without thinking I tried to rectify the problem. I didn't notice at first but the Ewe was watching me all the time, I fondled with the money in my trunks. I just looked up at her and blurted it out without thinking, 'I might have crab. Do you want crab? Are you hungry?'

'Not really,' she said, looking at me as I firked about in my trunks.

'Oh…sorry,' I was so embarrassed. 'No, no that's where I've hidden my money. No, I don't have crabs … you thought I said I had? … No, all clear down there I can assure you of that, it's just my money scratching on my… never mind. …I'm hungry I might order something to eat, do you want anything to eat?'

She shook her head. 'No I've eaten thank you and I don't like crabs….'

Then we both laughed and all the Rams in the bar watched us. I was delighted, to tell you the truth, that they all saw me with her, sitting around a little table with a lamp on it and having a laugh together. It was very romantic and a nice feeling, like being on a date, not that I've been on many. The best thing of all was I bet they all thought she was my sexy girlfriend. *Brilliant*, I thought, so I smiled proudly and pulled my chair closer to the table with a great big smug look on my face.

We began to have a little friendly chat for a few seconds and then she started doing her thingy with the cards. She took out a large pack of cards from a velvet bag and then asked me my name. I told her, 'Mick'. She closed her eyes with the pack of cards in her two hands and then blew on them, they must have been dusty or something. Then she said some weird words, fuck knows what they were, some 'mumbo jumbo', then asked me to randomly pick some cards from the pack which she held in her hands in front of me. She took them all from me and placed them one by one face down on the table. She then asked me to turn them face up, one by one, and each time I did she told me what each particular card meant. She then followed that by telling me loads of other stuff about me.

I must admit I was quite impressed. She seemed to know a lot about me, and my personality come to that, my likes, my dislikes. But I have got to admit at this point I was a little bit suspicious because as far as I was concerned she knew too bloody much about me, you know what I mean? I've only just met the Ewe. Anyway, putting that to one side, I let her carry on regardless doing her thingy and she continued to impress me even further the more we went on.

Eventually all the cards were face up in front of me. She sat right back in her chair and took a deep breath. I couldn't help but notice her nipples protruded through that thin white dress of hers like two cigar butts. It was like nothing I had ever seen before; they were fricking massive I can tell you, pointing at me almost like baby fingers. She then enhanced the view by pushing her bosoms right out at me. That's something that doesn't happen every day so I didn't knock it ... Yes, I was quite delighted at the whole reading to be fair. I was having a great birthday treat and to top it off all the cards I'd picked said something positive about me which was really nice… She was a very nice Ewe, drop dead fricking gorgeous if you ask me…

Anyway back to the story. Like I said the Ewe pointed at each card in turn, no... not with her nipples her fingers…. She explained to me what each of the pictures meant because some of them were quite weird looking to me, a bit freaky even. Some said 'Death' and another said 'Clone' but according to her they were all very good cards overall. Which is good isn't it?

She then said in that very nice sexy Spanish accent, 'Do you know these are the best cards I have ever read in all the years of me doing readings?'

That's what she said I kid you not.

'Are they really?' I asked. 'Why's that then petal?'

'Because they are magnificento.'

I've since learned that means perfect in Spanish… Anyway, she continued to explain what all my cards meant as a whole package. As far as I could understand they were all very good indeed. Perfecto in fact which means perfect. Just as she was about to finish something rather strange happened and a tear rolled down her cheek from one of her lovely brown eyes. She wiped it away and smiled.

'I'm sorry' she said.

'That's okay my love? Are you alright? What are you crying for?' I asked, concernedly.

'No, no I'm fine,' she said. 'It's okay, It's just you're reading…it is so amazing'.

She sniffed again, took a hanky out of her sleeve and wiped her nose. She then looked at me, shook her head then, for no reason I can fathom, went very quiet and sat there staring at me. I found that a bit freaky to be honest. She never said a word just stared at me and for quite a while an' all. She just sat there, hands under the table, and stared. At one point I thought she was playing with herself and that made me feel a bit uncomfortable, a sexy Ewe lusting over me like that. Whatever she was up to I was mesmerized by her beautiful, hypnotic, angelic, glassy eyes gazing back at me over the table. For all I know she was hypnotizing me at this point. Once I realized that this may be the case I quickly snapped out of the trance and diverted my eyes. For some reason I was instantly drawn to her pert nipples again. Well, I mean I was fascinated by them wasn't I? They were sticking right out now, I couldn't help myself. So while she stared at me I stared at her tits. Realizing I was dribbling, I quickly wiped my mouth and diverted my eyes up to the ceiling, twiddling my thumbs. I even started to whistle at one point. Then she broke the long uncomfortable silence by laughing.

'What's so funny?' I asked.

'You, you are a funny man, very funny and totally oblivious to how amazing you are.'

'Pardon me?' I said. I looked behind and then I looked back at her. I thought *hey up here, here we fricking go, there is definitely some flirting action going on here*. So without thinking I licked my finger and stroked my eyebrow and grinned back at her sexy like.

'Is that so,' I said, 'I have other ways to make you giggle…'

I know, I know, that was a bit forward wasn't it and totally out of character for me? However, that's how she got me all wound up and my mind was full of lust. However, it didn't seem to deter her at all, I got away with it without getting a slap. She leaned over the table and put her fingers on my lips. I could swear I smelled fish. I thought *she's playing with her banjo string under that table, the dirty little sheep*. However, I came to realize later she was just shuffling her tarot cards under that table. But with the fish smell you can see how I was mistaken. The reason her fingers smelled of fish, I reckon, was probably because she had eaten some prawns or something before she met me. I mean, she did say to me she wasn't hungry when I asked earlier if she wanted something to eat didn't she?

Anyway that's beside the point isn't it…? Where was I? Oh are, so there I was sitting at the table with this Ewe leaning over with her fishy fingers on my lips. I could see right down her top the way she stood over me; I could actually see her cigar butts nipples totally naked now. I thought she could take somebody's eye out with them if she wasn't careful. Then it happened…. I started to get a semi on, which was really embarrassing but it wasn't my fault was it? A lot was going on and when I'm not focused I have no control over what my willy does, it has a mind of its own sometimes, especially at swimming pools. So anyway, here I was starting to get a hard on in public, yet again. This is not so good. I knew I must think of something to take my mind away from naughty thoughts, so I started to think about politicians and the government; that always does the trick.

Then she distracted my line of thought by saying, 'Are you listening to me? You must listen to me this is very important.'

'Okay, yes I'm listening,' I said.

She then continued,

'You are a very special person indeed Michael. I don't think your life is ever going to be the same after what I tell you now,' she said. 'All my life I think has led me to meet up with you, so that I could give you what you need.'

I thought, *I know what I fricking need.* I was getting quite sexually aroused at this point and rather excited too. I thought, *aye up. I'm going to be seduced by this sexy Ewe in a minute and there's nothing I can do about it.* At least that's what my willy was hoping. I was shitting myself because I'm a married Ram for fuck's sake. I was only meant to be looking not fricking. Then I had a whiff of her perfume and got a right stiffy on...

'This is big,' she said.

'Excuse me,' I replied. 'What is?'

'This message I have got to give you, it is so big and wonderful.'

'Shhh! Keep your voice down everybody is looking at us,'

I looked around the room and gave a friendly smile at everyone staring at me. I pulled my chair even closer to the table to hide my embarrassment.

'I don't want to rush you love but come on hurry up with this message will ya?' I pleaded, as my cock throbbed under the table. It was starting to twitch a lot and I was feeling quite flustered by it all. If that's wasn't bad enough she leant even closer to me. *Oh fuck,* I thought, *I wish she wouldn't do that.* I felt sweat roll down from my brow, my heart started to beat really fast. I thought I would shoot my load any minute if she kept this up and that would be really embarrassing. I didn't know where to look as I tried to divert my eyes from hers. Again my head was drawn down to her cigar butts, but that wasn't the best idea under the circumstances, not when you've got a stiffy on like I had.

Then to my surprise I noticed she had a tattoo on her left breast which distracted my line of thought for a moment. It was a tattoo of a lamb jumping a fence. *Well of all things,* I thought, *what an interesting tattoo that is*, and for a short moment it also took my mind off the bonk on I had. Then, just as I thought I had it all under control, she started again didn't she? She lifted my chin up with her fishy-smelling fingers, looked right into my eyes and smiled. She whispered my message in a sexy husky voice, almost in a trance.

THE MESSAGE

'Michael, your cards tell me there are two sides to your personality; it is as if you are two people. You are so very special but one side of you is angry while the other is spiritually divine. It seems everything you have ever done or experienced in your lifetime has led you to this moment in bringing both your personalities together as one. And now because both of you are becoming "as one" it will give you two perspectives on life. You will understand everything but nothing. You are so very, very, very special indeed to have this gift. I am honoured to be in your presence; you are a wise man but also very stupid.'

'Charming,' I said. 'What do you mean stupid?'

'Misguided, sorry I meant misguided. My English not too good, I sorry.'

'Oh that's okay,' I replied and smiled. 'Your English is very good, carry on.'

'Thank you..... You know so much about life and people but you get distracted by a voice in your head. You should not believe all he tells you, he is a demon'.

'Ohhh okay.....'

'Michael, Michael, I am so delighted that I, Maria, was chosen by those up above to relay this wonderful message unto you, Oh Michael', she said, stroking my face, 'this is such a wonderful day for you. You are so very, very lucky but beware of false prophets and demons that may lead you astray'.

'Okay, that's very nice of you to warn me about demons and that, but can you please cut the crap now and tell me what this message is? I'm getting bored and missing the sun.'

I was a bit pissed off by now and very uptight. I was also sweating like a glassblower's behind, it was very hot. At this point she sat back in her chair, which was a relief for me. I think she saw I was feeling uncomfortable.

'Okay. I tell you,' she said. 'Your cards, Michael, tell me you are the one; your cards tell me you are him, you are a messenger. But be careful, you have a lot of people who will look up to you, be careful what you tell them. Also, you will be expected to take over from somebody who is in great danger as we speak. I don't know what this means.'

'That's nice, who's that then?'

'I don't know.....'. She closed her eyes and held her head for a second or two and then said, 'John, John, the person is named John. It is he who will come to you for help.....Does this make any sense to you?' she asked.

'Not a clue,' I said.

'The name John is very important, but I don't know why. You have been chosen. You are the chosen one, Michael, to take after John. The message I have to give you is this.'

I waited with bated breath

'You are "the chosen one".'

'Oh fuck off!' I said. '"Chosen one" my arse. You're full of shit.'

'You are......You have been sent here from up above, you are a child of the stars, you have been sent here to try and save the planet. You must help everyone with the divine wisdom combined in both of your spirits. This is what you were created to do. This is why you are here to save the world, to save all of us.'

'Fuck off now,' I said, but she didn't stop there, she went on and on and on telling me how very special and important I was.

'This is your destiny; can't you see how important you are? It is a very special message that I was chosen to give to you. You have the full understanding of Good and Evil, Happiness and Sadness, Male and Female,

'Okay.' I said. 'Thank you very much but I must go now'.

I went to stand up but she grabbed my shoulder and pushed me back down; good job she did I still had a bonk on.

'Listen to me,' she insisted. 'Can't you understand you have been chosen to heal the world, to teach the people the error of their ways, lead them to a salvation the whole world has been waiting for?'

'Okay, okay that's enough,' I said, 'that's enough now you mad cow,'

She was very persistent and grabbed and held my hand really tight and continued,

'You have the divine gift given to you from the heavens above. Don't waste it, you may even be the answer to everything that is, or was, or ever will be. You may even have the answer to the meaning of life that we all seek and wonder what it is.'

And so she went on and on... but after being told more bollocks about how wonderful I was I just zoned out. Then right out of the blue she leant over the table and kissed me smack on my lips. I can tell you that took me by surprise; I didn't expect that at all. *Brilliant*, I thought at the time... *A sexy Ewe has kissed me in front of witnesses.* But, as I feared, the chain reaction of all this was that I groaned and prematurely ejaculated in my trunks. *Oh fuck....* This stopped her in her tracks that's for sure. She thought I was having a heart attack.

'Are you okay?' she asked, 'shall I call for a doctor?'

'No, no I'm okay, I just have cramp.'

'Oh... well you need to get up and walk around,' she said.

'No, no, I'm okay thank you; it'll wear off in a minute.'

'No stand up, it will help'.

I thought, *I can't fricking stand up* but this bloody Ewe insisted that I did to walk off the cramp. But then I had a brainwave. *I know*, I thought, I noticed the beer glass still with beer in it so I purposely tipped it over myself.

'Clumsy me,' I said, 'look what I've gone and done now.' And with that I quickly stood up and grabbed a napkin off the table to hide my embarrassment. I left the table and as swiftly as I could I limped off to the toilets to clean myself up a bit.

'Wait here ...I'll be back in a minute,' I said.

Luckily when I got to the toilets they were empty. *Thank fuck for that* I thought. Once inside I proceeded to clean myself up. Firstly I took off my trunks and looked down at the mess. 'That's just fricking great, look at that, all the Euros are sticky now,' I said to myself. So I began to peel them from my sticky inner thighs. It was like stripping wallpaper. One snagged on a pube, not nice... I placed them all down one by one on the side. After I had removed them all successfully I then pulled my T-shirt down over my privates, hurried over to the sink and washed my trunks as quickly as I could under the tap, wrung them out and put them back on before anybody walked in. They were wet but at least clean, but my Euros were in a very sticky mess. I washed all of the notes in the sink, careful not to ruin any of them.

Once I'd done that I left the toilets to return to the Ewe, but as I approached the table to my surprise she had gone. Very strange, I wasn't that long… she seemed to have just vanished into thin air along with everybody else, the bar was empty. So I thought *oh well…* and made my way back to the bar outside because, to tell you the truth, after all that excitement I really needed a stiff drink. With the damp money in hand, I went to buy myself a shot of whiskey. The bartender looked at the wet money I handed to him.

'Oh sorry about that,' I said. 'I jumped in the pool and forgot I had my money in my trunks' pocket, that's why they are all wet.'

He bought that. It must be a common thing to happen. So anyway, as he poured me a shot I thought *fuck it* and called over to him.

'Never mind that buddy, I'll have the whole fricking bottle.' That pleased him. 'I'll have the crab lunch to go with it too,' I said. 'Fuck it, it's my birthday.' I thanked him as he handed me a bottle of scotch and a glass and I headed back outside to drink it as I waited for my food to arrive. The sun was still warm so I found a table and laid out the rest of my wet money to dry, which didn't take long.

My crab arrived and after I ate it (it was very nice may I add) I must have dozed off because the next thing I remember I was woken up by Andy, back from the bookies. He found me by all accounts fairly intoxicated. He then joined me and placed a white captain's hat on my head he'd found on the beach.

'Suits you,' he said. 'Aye, aye, Captain'.

We both then finished the bottle off watching the world go by. When that was gone Andy bought another one and we drunk that too. We both got smashed. I can remember rambling to him about how I was chosen and sent from up above to save the world, that I am a messenger from the stars. I know everything about everything and I must tell everybody.

He just said laughing, 'You know fuck all, Captain, like me.'

'I am a super hero I have you know Hick!'

'Yes, Captain FA I have no doubt'

I was by now very pissed and Andy agreed with everything I said.

I asked him, 'Andy, Andy, Andy....Do you think I should go and do it then?'

'Do what?'

'Save the world'

'Why not,' he said. 'It needs saving and if there is anyone who can do it it's you'

Nice Ram Andy.... So at that point I decided to call myself Captain FA for the rest of the holiday and we had a laugh. I was from now on going to be a super hero and save the world. I made that decision in Tenerife. After that decision was made we both got really, really drunk and finally staggered back to the hotel where I think I passed out.

I had a weird dream I was watched by lots of Aliens and then woke up with a banging headache.

Thinking back I must admit it was quite an odd experience to be fair and, yes, I was told some bollocks. 'Divine' my arse. But it was nice that she spent time with me because Ewes never usually speak to me normally. This one sang my praises for half an hour or so which was nice. She even gave me a kiss on the lips and, as an added bonus, gave me a bonk on to hoot. I've had worse birthdays. Yes, it's nice to be told how wonderful you are and that doesn't happen to me very often.

Do you know thinking about it she was a very nice Ewe indeed, totally bonkers but very nice all the same. She put me in a good mood for the rest of my holiday as I remember it. It was some time ago now but I still smile when I think of her and that lovely see-through dress and those lovely nipples. However, that was then and this is now so I will shut the fuck up and stop reminiscing I have a story to tell you and, if you remember, I did start all this shit by telling you that something happened to me that changed my life. So I shall tell you about that now.

POST HOLIDAY BLUES

Returning home from that lovely holiday in Tenerife it wasn't long before I got a bit depressed. At first I thought it was just holiday blues, or sun stroke or the thought of going back to work. Then I started to think it was more serious as I got really depressed as the weeks past. It's hard to explain now exactly how I felt but I was so very sad and was living my life in a trance-like state. I couldn't be bothered to do anything and almost overnight my personality changed significantly. It was as if I was turning into somebody else. My wife worried about me but just kept her distance because every time she tried to talk to me I would jump down her throat.

I didn't know what the frick was going on; I was getting deeper and deeper into this spiral of doom. I just couldn't get myself out of this rut. It was like something was happening to me I couldn't control. My wife was a bit concerned too and told me to go off sick from work and see a doctor. Now usually I would jump at the chance not to have to go to work but this time I didn't and for me that's way out of character. No, I carried on going to work as normal and I just did my job. I kept myself busy and tried to keep my mind active. You would think being at work all day by nightfall I would be knackered but I wasn't. I started having lots of sleepless nights where I would just watch TV or lie in my bed staring up at the ceiling all night, thinking about this and that. If I did fall asleep it was only from sheer boredom. But every time I did I would have a weird dream just like the one I had in Tenerife. I have them a lot and they seem so real and get more graphic.

THE DREAMS

Most of the dreams are about being abducted by Aliens. Funny thing is I only ever vaguely remember them when I wake up. Every time I have an Alien dream all I remember is being taken to a UFO by Aliens and led to a white room. It is always very bright and there is always this one Alien putting its face right up close to mine. It is at this point I always wake up. This is the weird bit......when I open my eyes I am still in the same white room; this Alien is still looking at me close up. Then it is as if they freeze me because I can't move. This Alien will be staring right into my eyes and I can't do anything about it. I want to push the thing away but I can't. Behind that Alien there will be more of them standing staring at me. I say Aliens because, although they look very similar to humans in many ways, their heads are bigger and their skin is a light greyish colour. I remember I always see small Aliens with big eyes that have big heads and next to them will be tall Aliens that are very human-looking. The only difference is they have grey skin and jet black eyes. I always see my reflection in the eyes of that fucker right close up to me.

Do you know, even though I know I am dreaming I still feel their touch and I also remember feeling needles stuck into me from time to time, very weird. If I was dreaming surely being pricked would wake me up? Every time I have this Alien abduction dream they do something to me like prod me with something or cover me in some funky stuff. One time I felt something under my skin, in my left lower arm as I remember. I felt a lump and when I rubbed it, it would sting and go hot. I got a pen and put dots all around it and it was triangular in shape. That was very worrying at the time but I think it's gone now. Hang on I'll check............ yes it's gone.

I remember having similar Alien abduction dreams like this when I was a lamb. I recall they always seemed so real back then too. I also remember I would always wake up next day in my own bed in my own bedroom, the same as I do now, but I would have these strange marks or bruising on my body that weren't there before. That's right I can remember it all now, it's all coming back to me...... I remember there was this one time I woke up with a ringing sound in my brain like a high-pitched whistle. This worried me at the time because I thought they had put something in my head but then it would go away...How come I remember all this now?

It is because you are writing your memories down

That is why I am deaf in my left ear I reckon... it's weird I remember all this now. I tell you what it's a bloody frightening experience, having dreams you feel are so real.

Since these recent dreams I am too frightened to go to sleep and am quite an insomniac. That's probably why I was so depressed after my holiday, I was overtired. Mind you, I have always been a bad sleeper even when I was young. My schooling suffered because of it. I was always tired at school and that's why I suppose I never got any qualifications. You see, I could never store information so I was shit at exams. No sooner was I told something I would forget it, like names; I can never remember sheeple's names.

The first abduction dream I ever had was when I was about five years of age. I can remember sitting on a cold metallic table surrounded by what I thought at the time were the seven dwarfs from Snow White. Well, that's what I thought back then, I was very young remember. I couldn't fathom out what was happening to me. I felt like I was in a cartoon or something; everything seemed so surreal. But I also remember I couldn't move a muscle as one of the dwarfs inspected my eyes, nose and ears. I thought I was dreaming back then too. But then, like all the other times right up to present day, I'd always feel like I had woken up. I open my eyes and I am still in the same white room either sitting or lying on a table or standing up, and each time I cannot move at all. But I can always feel them touching me which sometimes really hurts, enough to make me yell out or make my eyes water. Yes, dreaming you're abducted by Aliens is a bloody frightening experience I can tell you.

It is called by some a false awakening but you're not dreaming Michael

A false awakening is a vivid and convincing dream about awakening from sleep, while the dreamer in reality continues to sleep. After a false awakening, a subset of false awakenings, namely those in which one dreams that one has awoken from sleep that featured dreams, take on aspects of a double dream or a dream within a dream. Wikipedia, the free encyclopaedia

I have visions which first happened to me back in 2000. I kept having these headaches and flashing images in my mind of fires and wars, sheeple being herded together, coffins being burnt, that kind of thing. My heart would race and I would come out of these visions not knowing where I was. Straight away I always thought I must tell somebody about them but who to tell? They would play on my mind all day. I would go to bed, have one of those Alien abduction dreams again, and when I woke up next morning I'd forget what the vision was about. I just remember them being horrible and disturbing and that's it. It got that bad in the end it was a toss-up between sleeping, and having Alien abduction nightmares, or staying awake and having horrible visions of doom and gloom which seemed to happen every other day. But everybody needs sleep; I opted to take my chance on the nightmares. As you can imagine I was still a bit frightened to go to sleep so I would take sleeping tablets to help me drift off (herbal ones may I add) but just as I dropped off this fricking voice in my head said *wake up, wake up.*

That was me trying to stop you being brain-wiped

'I know that now but at the time you used to just really piss me off.'

It was for your own good

'Yeah but I felt like shit because of the lack of sleep.'

I tell you reader I was really unhealthy and mentally exhausted by it all. Then I lost all my appetite for food which in itself was really weird because I love my food normally. Eating is like a hobby of mine, but not anymore. I never felt hungry and food actually bored me, I just couldn't be bothered to cook or eat anything, not even a packet of nuts. It got to the point I just forgot to eat altogether because I was never hungry at all. I would forget to eat completely, how weird is that? How can anyone forget to eat? I was losing weight like nobody's business. I lost four stone almost overnight and became very docile as if I was on drugs or something. I'm usually a very lively frisky sheep but I was very lethargic. I went into a trance-like state and dribbled and then another vision popped into my head. You would think it was because of the lack of sleep and I was just hallucinating but they were visions, I know this now. Every time I had a vision I would then have an abduction dream to follow.

Then one day I stopped having visions altogether, which I was quite happy about, because they were so depressing and I always had a fricking headache when I had them. So I was glad they stopped. Then one morning I noticed that my skin had turned a greyish colour and my pupils were massive, almost taking over the whites of my eyes to a point you couldn't see any white at all.

Do you know, thinking back now I was in a right mess; my skin was grey, eyes black, okay they've gone back to normal now but it did make me feel strange whilst all this was happening. I didn't feel myself that's for sure. I felt I was losing my identity completely and it wasn't long before I was dangerously unhappy. I say dangerously unhappy because I felt suicidal. I really didn't like who I'd turned into and how I felt inside. Life seemed pointless and I thought if I was to kill myself nobody would even care. This deep-down depression went on for a while. It was as if my soul was dying inside of me.

Then right out of the blue I had another abduction dream and when I woke up I snapped out of this depression, just like that. I just opened my eyes and was lying in bed staring up to the ceiling. Then a voice in my head, which I know now as Alf, said to me as clear as day, *Welcome back. You're needed now get up.* Anyway hearing Alf's voice is what jump-started me back into life. Alf again came to my rescue as he always does. I tell you this, it is a good job he did because I was falling apart.

'Thank you Alf.'

You're very welcome.

'This was when you introduced yourself to me as Alf wasn't it?'

It was and I got you to join the White Flame Warriors.

At that very point in my life I made a conscious decision to make every effort to get myself out of this pit of depression I had fallen into. I would start to help Alf and the Nordic alliance to save the sheeple of planet Earth and be a messenger for the Nordic race.

FEELING ALIVE AGAIN

I remember it was Sunday morning. It was a lovely day, the sun was shining and I could hear birds singing outside. As I opened the curtains to look out the first thing I saw were Lambs playing. It was that moment I knew life was worth living and it was the Lambs I needed to save more than anything because they are the future. I jumped up out of bed, had a shower and a shave and went downstairs to my wife. She was in the kitchen reading a book and drinking a cup of tea. As I entered the room she was quite taken aback by the difference in me. My hair was clean and tidy and I was clean shaven which made her happy because she hates beards. I could see the delight in her eyes. I walked over to her and gave her a kiss and simply asked if she was hungry. She looked at me strangely and said, 'Yes.'

'What do you want?' I said.

She said, 'Do me one of your Michael Fricker Specials.'

So I began to cook up a full English breakfast for the both of us. Once I had finished cooking what can only be described as the greatest full English breakfast ever, bacon, eggs, sausage, black pudding, fried tomatoes, beans and hot buttered toast, we both sat down to the table to eat. I finished mine in no time at all. I sat back in the chair feeling quite satisfied with my fill and wiped my mouth with great satisfaction.

'I needed that,' I said

'I bet you did,' she said.... 'Are you feeling better now then?'

'Yes I'm okay thank you?'

'Good because you haven't been yourself for quite a while now. I was getting worried about you.'

'How do you mean, not myself?'

'You've changed since that holiday.'

'How do you mean changed, tell me what changes?'

'Well for one thing you're getting very absent-minded,' she said

'How do you mean absent-minded?' I asked. 'Is it our anniversary? Oh I'm sorry babe have I forgotten our anniversary? I..........'

She said, 'No, you haven't forgotten our anniversary,' then she raised her eyebrows and nodded her head beckoning me to look down.

'What?' I looked down and noticed I didn't have a stitch on. I was sitting butt naked at the table.

'What the...Why didn't you tell me I was naked?'

'I thought you knew besides you always walk around the house naked these days. I thought you were turning into a naturist or something.'

'What? You're saying I've done this before?'

'Yes most days you do it, I don't mind.'

'Oh dear!' I said, and I laughed at the thought of it.

'It was quite nice really, that's one change in you I don't mind.'

With that she took a suggestive big bite out of the sausage and laughed. She may have thought it was all funny but deep down I was concerned. I mean how can you not realize you're naked? It just goes to show how fucked up my mind was. My wife told me over breakfast of all the different changes she noticed in me and some of them were ridiculous, unbelievable some of them. I was soon aware of lots of different changes about me that were out of character. For a start my taste in music changed. I suddenly took a real liking to classical music; what the frick is that all about?

I was trying to introduce you to some culture.

'But classical music? Anyway, shut the fuck up I'm talking.'

You still listen to it, you must like classical music.

'Okay, some of it anyway, shut up …'.So okay, I now do in fact like classical music such as Bach and Mozart that's true. I even pretend sometimes I am a maestro. Whenever I have it on I even pretend I am conducting the orchestra, which makes my wife laugh.

That's because you used to be naked and used your willy as a baton.

'Ha ha very funny. I didn't do that did I?'

I'm saying nothing.

I also like hard rock music now, 'thrashing' I think they call it. My wife doesn't like that as much as classical so I don't play it until she goes out; then I'll have it on full blast. To be honest that all started to drown out the constant ringing that I began to have again back in 2012. Last time it sent me deaf in my left ear as I've already said. Anyway, now I am having it in my right ear. But that's beside the point.

As you know that ringing has nothing to do with me nor did it have anything to do with me before.

'I'm not so sure.... What if I go completely deaf? That's what I'm worried about.'

I am trying to prevent that.........Remember Michael I have never brought you pain or discomfort, only knowledge and protection. I will continue to use music to protect you

'How the frick can music protect me from the ringing Alf?' Sorry reader, I'll get back to the story in a minute...

Earth music is well known to soothe or relax humans. It can also help you humans switch off and drown out unwanted noise. Music also affects your emotions. We the Nordics have learnt humans tend to listen to music that reflects the mood they're in. When they are happy they will listen to upbeat music or if they are feeling sad they will listen to slower beat music. When they are angry they will listen to rock music and singers that reflect their anger. Music can also change your mood. What you are having is music therapy; you are having a mix of all these emotions all at once. That's why one day you will be either acting like Sir Simon Rattle listening to Mozart, then the next day head banging and playing air guitar to bands like Rammstein and Metallica. Then another day you would be listening to Disney songs like what is it.......... My Little Mermaid and Frozen?

'Okay fuck off now. Don't want the reader thinking I'm a sissy. Anyway, from what you've said it is you making me want to listen to all these different types of music?'

Yes. It is part of your music therapy.

' "Music therapy" my arse. What the......?'

Anyway fuck him, back to the story. I don't know about you reading this but I think it's all weird. I mean, what is it all about hey? Music therapy my arse....The comparisons of all those types of music are worlds apart for a start. I mean, how can anybody like any of that shit?

It is good to have diversity in music, it broadens the mind

'Before you came into my head Alf I didn't like either types of music, never have done. Normally my wife and I listen to only eighties music like Boy George, Madness, and Michael Jackson, proper music. Can't you use eighties music as part of my music therapy?'

No that is the whole point. If you only listen to music you are comfortable with then your mind is too relaxed and you are more vulnerable to influence or brainwashing. You should always change your music. Keep your mind wide awake and play music you're unfamiliar with. Now, when are you going to tell them about your super power?

'I'll talk about that in a minute Alf, but first I think the reader needs to understand why I have your voice in my head.'

Whatever, just hurry up.

Sorry about this reader but I am trying to write this book as the thoughts come into my head and sometimes Alf puts his two penn'orth in, as you can see.

We are writing this book together are we not?

'Yes, yes, okay but the reader might get confused.'

Oh whatever, carry on...

As you see, my fellow sheep, some weird shit is in my head at the moment and I guess to you, reading this, I sound like a right head case. I do have a warning message that this voice (Alf) and I want to tell you. But, before that, let me tell you about Alf.

CHAPTER TWO

WHAT IF ALL IS NOT AS IT SEEMS?

ALF (The voice in my head)

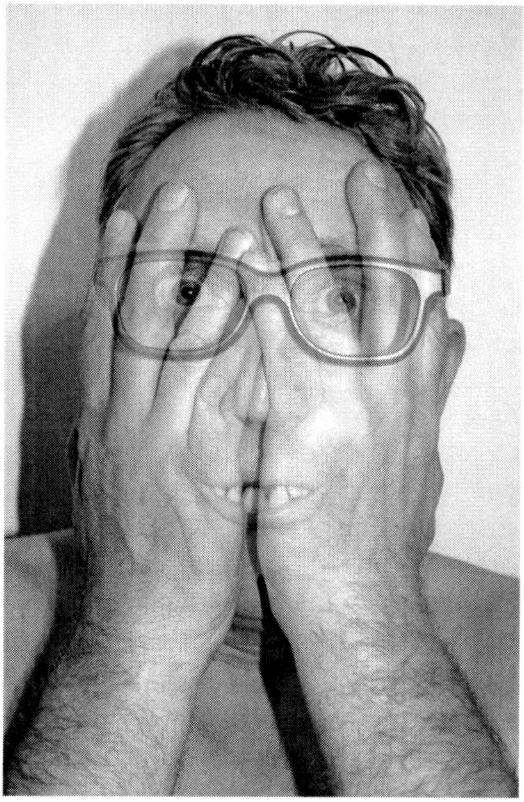

As I have already stated, I was only a little lamb when I started to hear a voice in my head and I wasn't much bothered about it back then. It was like having a friend; and I didn't have many, but this invisible friend of mine always got me out of trouble. On my tenth birthday, or shortly after my birthday, the voice went away.

But now it's back. When it came back I was a lot older, a lot, lot older, so really that's quite worrying to me because I thought that's a definite sign I'm losing my mind. I was forty-two years of age for frick's sake; what's this fricking voice doing back in my head? It gets worse because instead of ignoring it I tried to communicate with it. Okay, at first I couldn't make any sense of what this new voice was saying to me I just heard loads of different languages, sometimes French, German (well I think it was German), Russian, Urdu which was amusing I must admit. I even think I was spoken to in Latin at one point. And all these were spoken to me at the same time.

Crikey, you would've thought I was surrounded by foreign tourists. Then, after a while only one voice came through and that was in English. But I still couldn't understand a fricking word he was saying because he was speaking very posh like he had a plum in his gob; he sounded like one of them toffee-nosed politicians.

Charming I must say, I was speaking the Queen's English.

'Fuck off.'

You should've known that when I hear a toffee-nosed politician talk I just zone out from the fucker completely. I have no interest in anything they ever say because to be fair they usually talk a load of bollocks anyway, but that's beside the point. Even so, I did get the feeling you were trying really hard to communicate with me so I was patient with you. Then one day I answered you didn't I? I said to this posh-talking voice in my head, 'Look, you'd best take that plum out of your fricking gob if you're talking to me or I ain't listening to ya.'

Yes I remember that...so common.

Then almost as soon as I'd spoken to the voice that I now know as Alf, he started to talk back to me in my own dialect and, bingo, I could understand every fricking word he said to me. He said to me 'Can ya understand me now cocker?'

'That's better, I said. 'Yes, I can'

I was taking the mickey.

'Even so, at least we had some sort of communication going now. Anyway, that's when you introduced yourself to me as "Alf". I said, "Hello Alf." You said "hello" back and then you began to tell me about the Nordics and you wanted me to be a White Flame Warrior. After I agreed you then gave me the power to see into the future............'

Yes, yes we've covered this already.

'Shut ya cake-hole you, I'm telling the story.'

Tut! Hurry up then.

I then took a step back to think about it... I started to think I had developed psychic powers with Alf talking to me; I thought I could talk to the dead like that Derrick Acora Ram off the telly or that Lynne Caddick Ewe. For a short time I thought I was the new voice of the spirit world. I thought, *brilliant I'm following in my Great Uncle Ted Fricker's footsteps*. He had the power to heal sheeple you know, well, he was famous for it. Anyway that's beside the point. I thought, *look at me, I can talk to dead sheeple*.

So I was quite excited about this new talent and told my wife about it. But she wasn't that impressed, she just called me weird. I think I freaked her out telling her I can talk to the dead so decided to keep it to myself from then on. But I found out later I wasn't talking to dead sheeple after all, which disappointed me at the time. Anyway, I suppose when you think about it, it makes sense really. Nobody can talk to the dead. Like my Nan once said, 'When you're dead you're dead'. And she should know because she's dead.

Now believe in what you want that's your prerogative but I believe once you're dead, you're dead. That's what my grandmother used to say and I believe her. She told me once, 'Look Michael, if

I find out that there is life after death when I snuff it I'll come and tell you.' I'm still waiting. No, I now know I'm not talking to the deceased or my nan would've come back and told me I was. No, I'm talking to a Nordic Alien. I'm not stupid.

I remember being in the bathroom once. I was sitting there asking if anybody was there like a mini séance. 'Knock once for yes, twice for no. Speak, spirit, speak. Let me know you're there.'

I heard this voice in my head say, 'You must stop what you are doing.'

I never understood what the voice was on about at the time because I wasn't doing anything apart from sitting on the toilet having a shit and you can't stop shitting once you start.

You're so uncouth.

'You said "stop what you're doing" didn't you Alf? So when you asked me to stop whatever I was doing, I thought what? Shitting? How can I stop shitting? So I said back to ya, "What do you want me to stop shitting for? I can't stop shitting once I've started can I?" '

That wasn't what I meant. Tut. Look does this matter.

'Well, I thought it was. At the time I thought what a stupid thing to ask anybody to do. So I said to you, "Who the fuck do you think you are telling me what I can and can't do? Get out of my head you cheeky bastard and give me some privacy. I'm busy."'

Must we go through all this?

'Shut your face.'

I tell you what reader, I do get pissed off if anyone tells me what I can and can't do, and I wasn't having any of it from this fricking voice in my brain either. Stop shitting indeed. *Who the fuck does this voice think he is?* I thought.

Okay that's enough now......

'Kiss my arse you,' I said. 'Fuck you.' I said and carried on with my business at hand.

Then the voice unexpectedly replied 'Sorry.'

Anything to shut you up... give me strength... Sorry about this reader.

'I should think so an' all,' I said. Good job you did apologize an' all, or we would've fallen out there and then. Anyway we didn't, did we? Over time we eventually reached an agreement didn't we? One we could both agree on. I told Alf to stop telling me what to do and we might just get on.

Okay can we stop there now? You have told the reader how we met; we really need to move on.

'Okay ....and anyway that's how we first started to communicate with each other wasn't it?'

It was, now can we......?

He would say something to me and I would ask did you mean 'blardy blar'... And the voice, Alf's voice, would then say either 'okay' or 'yes'. So I thought, *brilliant at least it knows where it stands with me*. It wasn't long before we became sort of friends.

'I found myself having a proper conversation with you in the end. I must agree, Alf, some of our conversations were quite interesting.'

Thank you... look can we move on we have a lot to cover.

'We had the odd disagreement form time to time didn't we?'

We did. Look Michael, all this is irrelevant can we please move on....?

'I even found myself arguing with you at times, which was embarrassing, especially in a public place. Everybody must've thought I was a right nutter. So what I do now, when I talk to you in my head, is pretend I am on a hands-free mobile phone don't I? That works a treat, most of the time anyway, but I still think the sheeple out there stare at me when I talk to myself. Which isn't very nice having sheeple nosing in on my private conversations. Nosy bastards anyway fuck 'em.'

Sorry reader I may as well let him finish.........

I know, I know. Talking to a voice in my head may seem a bit weird to you the reader but nothing is normal in my life these days. It's never been the same since that holiday in Tenerife. For a long time I couldn't put my finger on what the frick was going on, what with having voices in my head, changes in my personality and what have ya. And to think I had turned into a psychic? Then I thought maybe I am just really stressed, overtired, frick knows. Whatever the case something really weird was happing to me, I wasn't myself at all. I even thought at one point that maybe that fortune-teller in Tenerife was right and I was a messenger sent here to save the sheeple, but save them from what? Everything to me seemed weird, the world seemed weird, this voice in my head; it was all fricking weird. Sometimes I felt like I was somebody else because I didn't recognize anything that I did; nothing seemed normal for me anymore.

What he didn't realize was his life was about to get a bit more complicated. There was more going on that he was yet to discover and it was up to me to point this out to him and push him in the right direction; to see it for himself so he could warn you. So I introduced him to the Worldwide Web or the 'inter-web' as Michael likes to call it.

Reading conspiracies can make you paranoid but finding out some are backed up by concrete evidence should make everyone really concerned. MAF

Because of Alf I now have an ongoing interest in conspiracies. I share some of my finds with other sheep but it is hard to grab their attention. I have been called paranoid, laughed at, even been the victim of piss-take. A lot of sheeple treat me like I'm an idiot. Yes reader, I have undergone insults on many occasions especially when I told them of my visions. I'm only trying to help. It can be hurtful at times but I'm thick-skinned.

Tell them about the visions.

'Visions?'

Yes visions ... tell them what a vision is first ..... No, better still don't bother, I will. A vision, reader, is a prophecy and are literary devices used to present a possible time-line of future events.

THE VISIONS

Alf told me I must tell the sheeple of my visions, to warn them about unfolding events that I see, but I must admit sometimes I wonder why I bother. Do you know, I did once, I told a work colleague about a vision I had. I wish I hadn't but I just blurted it out.

Tell the reader about it.

'Okay I will Alf.'

I had a vision back in 2001 and I said to one of my colleagues, 'I think something terrible is about to happen.'

'What the fuck are you on about?' was my colleague's first response.

'No forget it,' I said

'No go on Mystic Mick,' he said, 'tell us about your vision?'

At this point other sheeple started to gather round.

'What's going on?' somebody asked

'Mystic Mick here has had a vision. He thinks something bad is about to happen, Go on Michael, tell us about the terrible thing that is going to happen that you saw in your vision,' he mocked. I could've nutted the fucker but I didn't.

The group laughed.

'Go on tell us...this should be good.'

'No, no, forget it,' I said, wishing I could turn back the clock as I started to blush with embarrassment.

'Go on Michael tell us. No seriously I'm intrigued, so is everybody else here,' a woman said.

'Yes, go on tell us Mick,' somebody else piped up.

So, against my better judgement, I began to tell them all of this vision I had a few days before.

Looking back now I wish I'd kept my mouth shut because ever since I've been looked upon as a freak.

'Okay,' I said, 'I'll tell you......' I paused a moment then told them what I saw. I said, 'I can't put my finger on exactly what is going to happen but I fear whatever it is will be catastrophic.'

'What did you see?'

So I told them I saw a plane crashing into a mountain and the mountain collapsing.

'Is that it? Can't you be more specific? What type of vision is that? When? Where?'

'It is going to happen this September'

'Where?' somebody asked

'Amsterdam. Amsterdam,' I replied, this was in August 2001.

'Oh, so you reckon a plane is going to crash in Amsterdam in September? There aren't any mountains in Amsterdam,' said the prick.

I said, 'Yes, the new part. I saw the words New Amsterdam in my vision.'

On September 11th 2001 we all know what happened. As the events started to unfold I came back and said to them, 'I knew it, I knew something was going to happen. I told you last month something big was going to happen and you wouldn't listen to me would ya? This is only the warm up; this is the beginning of the slow cull.' I said.

'What the fuck are you on about now Fricker? You were wrong.... you said something was going to happen in Amsterdam not New York?'

In my defence I said, 'Okay, I was wrong on some of the details and about the place but I was right about the planes' But because I got the place wrong I now looked like a right fool. Next time I'll keep stum I think.... until I get the facts right at least and I'll be careful not to just blurt it out either.

Yes, you do that a lot, your mouth gets into motion before your brain is into gear. Just for interest sake did you know New York was once called New Amsterdam?

'Was it?'

CONSPIRACY OR FACT?

I have been somewhat intrigued by conspiracy theories ever since Alf came back into my head. It was him who told me to check out the inter-web in the first place. I wasn't that bothered at first, but I did and now I'm hooked; even more so since I stumbled on a blog written by a Ram named Jon Doe. It's this Jon Doe Ram who started my lust for seeking out facts rather than just reading theories all the time. Then it dawned on me one day. This could well be the John that was mentioned to me in Tenerife. Maybe, I'll tell you about him later.

MICKY FRICK'S TIP

YOU MUST ALWAYS REMEMBER THERE ARE TWO TYPES OF CONSPIRACY, THE CONSPIRACY THEORY AND THE CONSPIRACY FACT. KNOW THE DIFFERENCE BECAUSE ANYBODY CAN COME UP WITH A CONSPIRACY THEORY.

I soon learned that there are two types of conspiracy; you have the conspiracy theory and the conspiracy fact. It's the fact ones I am particularly interested in because they're the ones I base this book on. I'll tell you what else an' all… some of them will make the wool on the back of your necks stand up on end, as they did me the first time I came across them. It's a shocker to realize what you are reading is backed up with facts and not just theories. I think these facts should concern all of us because if they are as true as they seem to be we are in fricking big trouble.

I'm going to share some of these conspiracy facts with you throughout the next few chapters, so get yourself ready. Some of you sheep will say you shouldn't believe all the conspiracy theories you read. Well normally I don't; okay, I do. But now I've found out a lot are backed up by other sources out there making them become a concrete fact. As always when I tell you about them you can make your own mind up if you want to believe them or not. But for me, I can now confidently stand in front of you all and wholeheartedly say I definitely think there's more than meets the eye out there and that's a fact.

As well as conspiracy facts, I also like to read prophecies, mythology and legends, that kind of thing. I also love to read about the Mayans and the Egyptians, ancient civilizations of bygone years. I have read a load of stuff on ancient civilizations, like the Aztecs and Sumerians. I am also quite interested in the beliefs and the ancient rituals of pagans and native Red Indian voodoo and such like. I genuinely do have a keen interest in why sheeple are religious in the first place. I find religion fascinating. So I would like to understand more as to where these religions and beliefs stemmed from.

However, my favourite of all subjects, as you have probably guessed by now, is Ufology; this has been my favourite subject since I realized I am regularly abducted by Aliens. I think all the dreams about being abducted by Aliens may not be dreams at all. In fact I am starting to think I am serially abducted. Why am I so special? I'm not that interesting, at least I don't think I am, but what is interesting is I can remember things I never used to. I can even remember the moment I was born; I never could before. Now that's weird isn't it? Yes, my fellow sheep, a lot of weird things have happened to me of late and one of them is that these abduction dreams and visions seem to be getting more and more frequent.

I'm going to share something with you now, a story I haven't told anybody before. Well.... I'm still not one hundred per cent sure if it wasn't just a dream, but at the time it seemed very real to me indeed when I had it, and that's all that counts. So I will tell you about it anyway. This experience I had was interesting because it was a lot more intense than any other times before. This time it was very real and I was wide awake, or at least I thought I was. Okay, I was a bit pissed too. The reason I was a bit drunk was because I'd just come back from a stag do but, saying that, I was still fully aware of everything happening around me. Unlike all the other times I have been abducted, when morning came I usually forgot most of what happened, this time it was different; I remember most of it which I will share with you now.

ABDUCTED AND ABUSED

I've been sexually abused by Aliens. It's true. I lay in my bedroom after a good night on the piss; the room was spinning a bit, then I was abducted by Aliens. I remember I wore my 'jimjams' because it was a bit cold, as I recall. Anyway, they walked into my bedroom as they always do. Just as I was dropping off to sleep the wankers woke me up. As I saw them I thought *oh fuck, here we go again.* I said to the Aliens, 'Come on now, I am really not in the mood tonight. I've already had a rough night on the beer. Leave me alone.'

I just wanted to go back to sleep but I was wasting my breath. It's no good moaning about it, when they come for you you don't have any choice in the matter. They just abduct you and if you struggle they zap ya with something like a cattle prod so you can't move. So from experience I've found you might as well just go along with them. So that's what I did and as always they led me out of the bedroom to their craft.

Once inside they stripped me naked. They seem to prefer me naked for some reason but it was warm in the craft so I didn't mind. Besides, after just being woken up I had a semi hard on. You see I don't suffer with drinker's droop. So I wasn't embarrassed about having a little crunched up willy, as like the other abductions. Do you know, one time I remember when they abducted me one of the little Aliens pointed at my willy and sniggered. But this time I had a bit of blood in it; I think I needed a piss. So of course they soon spotted that I had this semi hard on and straight away one of the Aliens started to tickle my bollocks which was, well, kind of nice to be fair and I did get a little harder. Then another Alien slapped my cock and it soon started to go soft again. Fricking hurt, no need for that is there? So I had a go at 'em and then I was hit by their cattle prod. I couldn't move, bastards.

So anyway that's beside the point. After I was back to little ole me again they led me over to the same old metallic bench as all the other times, but this time they turned me over onto my stomach. They started probing me up the arse with something smooth, cold and hard. I remember I wasn't able to move at this point so I had to grit my teeth and just put up with whatever they were doing to me; for a short while anyway. Once they finished butt fricking me with this metal probe I was flipped onto my back and for some unknown reason I was hard again; it stood up as hard as you like. What the frick....? This suggests I enjoyed being butt fucked but I'm not gay......

Anyway, as I worried that I might be turning homosexual, I saw this Grey Alien walk over to me. It was a little fatter than the rest, as I recall, and a lot taller and stocky built. In fact, thinking about it now, it was almost human looking. It stopped and just stared right into my eyes like it was glaring into my soul, a very weird feeling indeed. But as it did, I heard words in my mind saying, *You're mine.*

What the fuck does that mean, 'you're mine?' I thought. In fact, as I recall it now, I even think it climbed on top of me and shagged me but I think I passed out at this point. When I came round I was back in my own bed again. Yes, I know you're thinking it could've just been a dream, but the funny thing is when I woke up next morning I had a sore arse and my cock was very tender with a rash around my bollocks and I felt quite sick all day, coughing up green gunk.

That's when I started to think I had been raped by these Aliens which was a very weird dream if it was a dream. I've been violated!...Hang on a cotton-picking minute... I just had a horrible thought cross my mind, about the night before. As I said, I went to a stag party didn't I? Well I did and I remember the theme was pyjamas; we all wore pyjamas and I did get very drunk with the other Rams. I also remembered talking to a short fat Ram wearing a grey nightgown. I think it was a Ram anyway; I was extremely intoxicated so I couldn't tell if it was a Ewe or Ram. If it was a Ewe, I tell you what she was butt ugly, and I mean proper ugly, she looked like a 'hippo croc frog'....

Fricking hell, hang on a minute here; before we go any further with this let me have a think about this for a second.......... Oh fuck....What I'm saying .... I'm thinking now what if it wasn't abduction after all? You don't think....and I hope not.... I'd remember that surely...? I'm wondering now if I was date raped by an ugly pot-bellied midget with sunglasses wearing a grey nightgown at the party, rather than abducted by Aliens. Fricking hell, I'm so confused, I don't even know why I am sharing this story with you...... My mind's gone blank. Fricking hell, I hope I was abducted now because it sounds much better on all accounts than what's going through my mind right this minute. Fricking hell what if it was a Ram? Oh my Fricking God ...

Look, I'm sticking with the abduction story. I haven't been bummed by anyone okay? I know what you're thinking and you're wrong - my arse has 'exit' not 'entrance' on it. Anyway, I don't know why I even started sharing this stupid story with you in the first place...... forget everything I have just said, okay?

Thank heavens for that.

I've just had a brain fart.......Do you think the Greys are responsible for genetically modifying the puffs of the world because there seems to be a lot of them now?

What is your point to all this?

It was supposed to be leading to a point but I've forgotten what it was now. I wanted to make a point about Alien abductions but it's all gone pear shaped. I'm still thinking about that stag do. Oh forget it, I'll leave it there. I think I've said too much already. OK here is a point...

MICKY FRICK'S TIP

DON'T DRINK TOO MUCH

Don't drink too much, there you go that's it.....I know I won't ever drink so much alcohol in future or, if I do have a beer, I will be very careful how much I do consume. Thinking what I'm thinking now, I'm not even sure if I was abducted at all, maybe all this abduction malarkey is linked to alcohol consumption; I have been dreaming everything because I have always been pissed…Okay okay, so my lesson is learnt. From now on I will never go into nightclubs called the Pink Feather when drunk...... I should've known better when I saw the doormen wearing skirts and frilly shower caps and sunglasses. Oh fuck, it's all coming back now...

Anyway forget it. Oh, oh hang on...... I got it, the point that is... the point I was trying to make was this; I am not the only sheep to be abducted. It seems there are many cases of reported abductions all over the world that all describe the same thing happening to them that happened to me...well kind of. These sheeple, when put under hypnosis, all share very similar stories about what happened to them which I thought was very interesting.

Very interesting but can we move on?

'Yes okay in a minute Alf...'

Do you know it is also believed by some that it doesn't have to be physical abduction either, No, some believe Aliens can get into our heads and communicate to us through telepathy. When I read this I found it all very interesting indeed because, if Aliens are manipulating our minds, this at least explains the voices in my head.

Look we really need to move on now.....

I'll tell you something else that's interesting... well I think it is. Do you know since I have been abducted I can predict the future? That's right.... I can predict the future.

I gave you those powers, remember? You have already told the reader about this.

'When?'

Just now

'I haven't.'

Yes you have... Oh forget it, you've been mind-wiped again, carry on. Sorry reader, he's been mind- wiped again.

Anyway, it seems I can do this all the time now, see into the future. I can do it just before I have a dream about being abducted but I'm still not sure if all this is in my head yet....... Do you know, I predicted the tsunami in Japan back in 2013 and then the Earthquake in a place called Loon?

You're a loon.

'What?'

Nothing.

I think Loon is in the Philippines. Anyway it happened in October 2013 and I think it was the Philippines, I forget now. Anyway, this got me thinking maybe I am here to save the world.

Give me strength .....Don't think I can take much more of this.

'What?'

Never mind, why don't you go and have a lie down in a dark room again for a bit Michael? Come back later when you have had a rest.

'Oh, okay.'

Whilst he is doing this reader I am going to try and input some intelligence in his brain.

(Some considerable time later)

Oh, you're back so soon...feeling better now?

'Yes thank you, what shall I talk about today?'

I don't know; tell them your theory about the beginning of the universe.

'Okay, shall I?'

Yes please, do give me a break. It'll also give the reader an idea who I am working with. Trust me you'll love this reader but, bear with him, the book will get more interesting as it continues, I promise.

'What? Are you talking to the reader, for you're my thoughts.'

Sorry.

'I should think so. Okay where was I?'

The universe...tut.

'Oh are.'

Now a lot of scientists, astronomers and religious sheep go on about creation; they all give you different ideas of how they believe life all started; the beginning of time. On one hand you have the religious sheep saying it was God's intervention, and then on the other you have scientists and astronomers who think it was a natural phenomenon billions of years ago; a chain of natural events and a little luck thrown in as to why everything exists as it does today. Some sheep go along with Albert Einstein's E=Mc2, you know, the 'Big Bang' theory. Just for interest's sake, did you know Albert came up with that equation E=Mc2 way before the Big Bang theory was ever talked about?

Now don't worry, I'm not going to pretend I know anything about quantum physics because I don't. If you want to know more about E=Mc2 look it up yourself, I'm not a fricking science teacher. Anyway, that's beside the point. The thing is everybody is entitled to their own ideas as to how they think creation started and why we ended up with planet Earth that we all call our home.

'I want to take a minute if I may to talk about Earth.'

Go on then.

EARTH

Exactly how old Earth is is unsure. But if you think of Earth being a week old, humans have only been here about five seconds. That's what they say anyway. But do you realize we humans are the worst species Earth has ever had to put up with? Don't take my word for it read what Martin Jenkins, senior adviser for world conservation Monitoring Center in Cambridge, said and I quote

> ***'It seems things are getting worse faster than possibly ever before here on Earth. Never has one single species (Humans) had such an overwhelming influence'.***

Basically he said we humans put great strain on Earth. It was doing okay until we arrived. We should show some respect as it's a nice place. We are very lucky to live here, it's an amazing planet. Earth revolves, so we are told, at nine hundred miles an hour. The Sun is the source of all its power and all the stars you see at night (if you're lucky it's not lost by light pollution) move at a million miles a day. There are hundreds of millions of stars in the universe. It is the only known planet to have life on it but, to be fair, this is unrealistic when you think how vast this expanding universe is.

But just for the moment let's pretend we are alone in the cosmos. Let's pretend Earth is the only living planet in the whole of the universe and a lot of sheeple still think this is the case. So okay then, let's say we are. If this is the case then surely you would think us humans would concentrate all our efforts in safekeeping and looking after it? But we don't. Now, if I was say the landlord of Earth I would make plans to evict the lot of us because most humans are just too fricking destructive and don't know how to look after the place, As well as that we don't respect other life that shares this Earth with us. We are noisy, dirty, we have bad attitudes, we are aggressive and, I think, really selfish. We are no better than those scutters you moan about who claim benefits, smoke fags, drink beer in the street; those ones who empty ashtrays in car parks; those scutters who leave their crap everywhere. It's quite sad but most of the human race is no better. I thought about this for some time and I don't think it's our fault though. I'll tell you why.

Please do.

It's because I think it is inbuilt in our minds to be self-destructive.

What do you mean?

I think we, from the start of our existence, were only given a short term tenancy agreement by the landlord, who I think could be Alien, and it's just about to run out. By the looks of things it's a bloody good job an' all. I say we need evicting.

Interesting analogy I'll give you that.

That's what I think anyway.

You are right about one thing. You humans do share Earth, you don't own it, and I like the 'Alien landlord' bit.

Most seem to think Earth is ours. Well it's not. It's about time we woke up to the fact. We share this planet with billions and billions of other life forms and like them we are merely lodgers upon it. You don't see animals leaving crap everywhere and they usually stay in one area, not like us. Most animals know their place but we think we are oh so much better than them. Okay, we may be smarter than most other creatures in some ways but, instead of using our brains for the good of all, we fuck everything up. We are very, very, very lucky to have Earth and we should look after it.

Well said.

We are told Earth sits in the middle of one of millions of other galaxies in the vastness of space that we call the universe which supposedly expands at twelve million miles a minute (speed of light). The universe, we are told, is the keeper of everything that exists. I know reader you're saying 'so what?' as you read this but I don't really give a toss of the 'whys' and the 'hows'. The universe was created but I do care about looking after it and all life upon it. The point I'm making is this, at the moment it seems us Earthlings are too set on trying to find life on other planets and I have to ask WHY? Because I think it is a total waste of fricking time to be honest. I don't know why they don't just spend all that money and time on looking after Earth.

You would be better off trying to protect it that's for sure.

'From what?'

You know those landlords you were on about?

'Yes?'

They are coming to evict you.

'Who are?'

The Anunnaki

'Who the fuck are the Anunnaki?'

I'll tell you later but they are on their way.

'The Anunnaki are our landlords?'

Yes.

'You talk as if they are Aliens.'

They are.

See reader, the Alien landlord of Earth is coming to evict us and I fear if we don't tidy the place up a bit by the time they do get here – well, we will most surely be evicted. We are a classic case of bad tenants.

Earth is like our rented home; we should look after it and be good tenants or we will be evicted. MAF

Maybe that's what it's all about. We already have our date of eviction and the bailiffs, these Anunnaki lot whoever they are, will be moving us on soon; they will kick us off Earth. Our tenancy agreement between us and the Aliens has expired and it's not going to be renewed, by all accounts. Maybe last time these Aliens came here we humans had our final warning, a last chance to tidy the place up a bit, and we've blown it. Life for us sheep on Earth won't continue much longer I fear. This is the end I'm afraid.

No, you do have a chance to have your 'tenancy agreement' renewed.

'So we still have a slim chance to get a new contract from them then? That'll be nice.'

But reader, I bet only if we can prove to our landlords, whoever or whatever they are, that we will tidy the place up a bit and try harder to be good tenants in the future. Then maybe the Aliens will let us stay a little longer until we find somewhere else to go at least....... Hang on, that's why they are so set on trying to find another Earth-like planet? The government know we are to be evicted and are trying to find us a new home. Mind you, I wouldn't be surprised if they have already built bases on the moon or hideaways under the ground; only for the rich I bet.

'So, Alf, all we have to do is to convince whoever our landlords, these Anunnaki Aliens, are that we can change.'

No it's not as easy as that.

'Why not....? All we need to do is our best to look after Earth and we should be alright.'

Not exactly.

We all live here at Number Three, Sun Rings, Solar System Street, The Galaxy, WW0 4LD. It's a shame we have no respect for it. I mean every bird, flower and creepy crawly we share the place with is threatened by us humans at the moment. So we must show the Landlords we understand that we must share the Earth; that all life on it has a right to be here as much as we do. They should be okay with that. It's a nice place Earth and a lot better than the Moon or Mars because, to be fair, they look dead.

You're rambling on....Are you trying to make a point here or what?

'My point? My point is Alf that although I would like to think we could become better tenants I have my doubts.'

You do?

'Yes. We will never change. That's why deep, deep down I think we are screwed. I mean, this could be the natural way of things. Maybe we humans weren't meant to be here forever anyway? In fact maybe our time is naturally running out. So whether it's Aliens, an asteroid or a Third World War or even a pandemic that finishes us all off, whatever the case it doesn't seem to matter one way or another; we are doomed whether we like it or not. Because we can't change; you can take the scum out of the house but you can't take scummy behaviour out of the sheeple.'

The problem with the world is as one good person dies they are replaced by a scumbag. MAF

But what if I was to tell you you can do something to prolong your existence or, as you would put it, your tenancy?

'How? And even if this could happen, why? I mean we humans are one big dysfunctional family.'

Now reader, I read a report based on scientific data from across the world the other day that revealed that we humans destroyed more than a third of our natural world over the past three decades. Not only that, scientists who examined data for over 350 kinds of mammals such as birds, reptiles and what have you found that many species have more than halved because of one reason, humans. A Ram named Martin Jenkins, senior adviser for World Conservation Monitoring Centre, Cambridge said, 'Things are worse than ever before'.

'You know why, don't you?'

Why?

'Because the world is full of scumbags.'

Scumbags?

'Yes, Alf, scumbags. I'm talking about humans who couldn't give a flying fuck about the world or anybody and definitely no wildlife come to that; you know the type I mean?'

No, sorry I don't.

'Scumbags. The ones that make a mess everywhere; empty their ashtrays in car parks and throw litter on the floor instead of finding a bin. The ones that drink cans of beer in the street and merrily go along being 'scumbaggy.' They bend trees, write abusive graffiti on walls, piss up shop doors and fly tip. They just generally spoil it all for everyone else with total disregard for others, never mind the planet.'

Oh yes, there are a lot of despicable humans in the world.

'They shouldn't be tolerated - enough is enough. I think the good decent sheeple of this world should flock together and hunt these types down, flog 'em in the street. Beat the shit out of them; that's what we should do. No, I have a better idea, put them to sleep by shooting the scutters on sight with a tranquillizer dart, then castrate them so they can't breed and hang the bollocks to a wall with a fuck off sign saying, BE A SCUMBAG AND THIS WILL HAPPEN TO YOU.'

That's barbaric.

'I haven't finished yet....what about once we catch the scutters we not only kick the shit out of them, we tie their feet together with rope and then we drag them to the local sewerage works and lower them slowly into a cesspit, head first. We keep them under for say three minutes or so until they promise to be good and clean up their act. As compassionate a sheep as I am.'

Really??

'I am, and I'm all for giving them a second chance.'

Sounds like it, I must say. Why not just educate them instead?

'You can't educate scumbags like that; it would be like trying to teach a dog never to bark.'

No, I say dunk 'em in shit for a while, that'll teach 'em. And for repeat offenders, well, if they blow their second chance that's it, fuck 'em - we hold them under a while longer, for a few minutes or more and if they drown, fuck 'em, at least it would be one less dirty bastard off the street.

That's terrible Michael.

'Okay it may sound harsh to you, Alf, but what else can you do with scumbags?'

Not everybody is a scumbag; some humans are very caring souls.

'No. No okay you're right Alf, to be fair most sheeple are decent. You're right and I agree it's wrong of me to tarnish everybody with the same brush. I just get so angry.'

You're telling me. My hope is I can help you to stop being so angry. I'm trying to help you to spread the love. But you are right on one thing, humans do need to learn to love their planet more than they do.

'True. You know Alf, when I think about it I can kind of understand where you are coming from?'

Good. The world is not perfect, and there are a lot of bad humans in the world, but you must realize you have the power to turn things around. And that starts with every individual.

'What a crock of shit... Sometimes Alf you need to be hard on scum and most of the readers of this book would agree with me on that. There are sheeple out there who are past saving, they are bad to the bone and as far as I am concerned we should come down on them hard. Fricking hell, Alf, you're starting to sound like one of them do-gooders... Human rights, political correct brigade.'

Okay if you say so .....Can we move on now? You were going to talk about Earth.

'Yes I was.'

Well, carry on then.

Our planet, reader, is the perfect distance from the Sun and we also have liquid water on it, which is very rare. That is why Earth thrives; all because of water. Water (H2O) is the prime ingredient to all life and Earth has more than enough of it. Did you know reader, our fresh water supplies are becoming scarce and polluted? Did you know one litre of oil can contaminate eight hundred thousand litres of water? 'We dump approximately three thousand one hundred and seventy-seven million litres of oil into the world's rivers and oceans every year.'

www.sciences360.com › Earth Science › Earth Science – Other

Fish are the first to be affected by pollution even at a small degree. No wonder there are so many weird looking fish down there. Don't take my word for it, take a look for yourself.

www.iflscience.com/watch-25-most-terrifying-looking-sea-creatures

If you're not careful, and you humans keep contaminating your water supplies, you will soon be bringing your children into the world with two heads.

'Then we will have even more two-faced bastards in the world!'

You are very lucky to live on Earth, it has everything and that is why your planet is so desirable to other Alien species thrown out of the cosmos.

You would have to agree with Alf though reader, that if you take away all the shit it's a very nice planet is our Earth, in fact a wonderful planet. Not only that it is blessed with an abundance of all kinds of life forms other than just us, but the greatest of all the life forms here on Earth is us the intelligent human. 'Now wouldn't you agree Alf?'

It is...It's just a shame most humans don't fully realize it yet. But all is not lost for you yet, you do have the power

to change the way things are; whether you will is another question.

He's right on that point

I know I'm right. I'm always right. Now, are you going to tell us your theory on the Frixta galaxy now?

'Yes, yes okay, I'm getting to that.'

So, according to space science, it is believed that the universe was a natural phenomenon and that during the immense nothingness and pitch darkness of space over quadrillions of years, it is then believed that a mass of pure energy was forming. How? When? Why? Nobody knows for sure but, for me, I don't really give a toss how it all started to be honest. It is said that when it was no bigger than a peanut this intense mass of energy got so great in density it eventually exploded and started the chain of events that led to everything that exists today. That is according to the Big Bang theory. So, if this theory is true, it seems to me that at the very start of time everything that exists today began by simple chance, and not by God.

Not everything is by chance.

I don't think there was any holy intervention at all that started the ball rolling, as believed by so many religious sheeple; it just happened by chance. The beginning of the universe I mean. It was just luck at the end of the day.

Was it? Oh okay, you're entitled to your opinion, carry on.

So this big explosion eventually formed the very first galaxies, okay? I bet the first ever galaxy was never given a name either, or claimed. In that case I am officially claiming it now and I will give this first galaxy a name. I will name and claim it as mine to be called 'The Frixta Galaxy' Got a ring to it hasn't it? Now I want this to be put in all the science books around the globe from now on, okay? Before I continue, just for those of you who don't know already, a galaxy is a collection of stars and planets that rotate together around a large black hole; they are all mine too.

Hark at you...... Did you also know there are over one hundred trillion galaxies in the known universe and all are different?

'No, and to be honest I couldn't really give a toss, Alf. But whatever the case 'The Frixta Galaxy' was the first one and that's mine.'

Whatever.

'Anyway, stop butting in Alf, for fuck's sake, I keep losing my flow.'

Sorry. Go ahead, your Lordship, the stage is yours, as they say.

'Thank you.'

THE BIG BANG

Let me start at the very beginning of time itself so we can understand what the fuck went wrong.

You have all heard, I guess, of the 'The Big Bang Theory.' If you haven't it is a scientific theory of what is believed to have been the start of the creation, the birth of the universe if you like, that supposedly happened fifteen thousand million years ago… Firstly, how can they ever know that for sure; they are just guessing? I want facts in my book please. Secondly, who really gives a fuck when it happened anyway? It's hardly going to change mine or your life is it? Who really cares? Tell you what I will now give you my own version of The Big Bang Theory as I see it at least. Which as you know was the birth of my Frixta Galaxy - the first one. My galaxy was the one that led to all life as we know it today. In a way I am lord of the universe.

Tut, don't look at me reader.

'Shut the fuck up, Alf.'

It is said that just after the Big Bang explosion loads of subatomic particles flew about randomly in every direction. Eventually they formed into what we now know as matter. From this matter they then had to fight off the antimatter; physics tells us that if antimatter and matter meet they cancel each other out.

Ohhh, somebody has been doing some research... I'm impressed.

'Yes I have Alf and it got me thinking.'

Oh dear, we're in trouble now.

Now reader, it's not as if I know much about physics you understand, I did have to look all this up. The reason I am interested in matter and antimatter is because, when I thought about it, in a way it represents positive and negative. Good and bad. Right and wrong... Well it does to me. So I want to use that analogy to make my point about the power of positivity.

Don't ask me reader I haven't a clue where he is going with this either?

'Shut the fuck up for a minute, Alf, let me talk.......I'm on a flow.'

Sorry.

So any way up....I want you to look at 'matter' as being 'Good or Positive' and 'antimatter' as being 'Evil or Negative'. Good v Evil; Positive v Negative, you get the idea. Now I noticed this but did you ever think the reason you are here today, in fact the only reason you are here today, is because positivity, the positive matter, eventually overpowered the negative antimatter? If the bad antimatter would've won, then life would probably have never happened at all. So the fact space was just a mass of nothingness for possibly quadrillions of years told me that the negative or the bad antimatter must have won every other fight for life, except the last one. Matter was victorious so Good can overcome Evil. Do you get my point? Are you following me so far?'

Kind of...

'Good, and luckily it did too.' For me that indicated there was still more good in the world and in the universe than bad. With the law of physics Good will or should always overcome Evil. But, with all the crap going on around the world today, it seems to me that Evil is getting stronger because of the frequency signals from our brains.

What are you on about Michael?

'Frequency, you know brainwaves.'

Oh right...

What I say is at the moment we humans submit too many negative thoughts, negative brainwaves, which feed a dark entity or something. We need to start thinking more positively about things to prevent it from growing even stronger, if we want the universe to continue and not implode.

Okay.......

We can use this to start to save all life on Earth.

No you won't.

'Won't what?'

Save all the life on the Earth.

'Why not?'

Because ....anyway what is your point to all this?

'My point is we need to believe in our own power to make the change.'

And what's that??

'Think positive. We need to all start to think positive.'

MICKY FRICK'S TIP

ALWAYS THINK POSITIVE

Nice theory but you're still wrong.

'Why am I wrong? Good always can beat all that is bad.'

But don't think antimatter isn't still putting up a fight though, it is. Antimatter is still present, we all have it inside us, but luckily matter is also present in us too. There is a constant fight between good and evil in our own bodies and minds, there has been since the beginning of time. Every living thing in fact has got a bit of both in its genetic make-up and, depending how much of one or the other takes control of you, determines whether you are a good person or a bad person genetically. Adolph Hitler had more evil antimatter in his genes than good. Mother Teresa had more good positive matter in her than bad.

There is more to it than that Michael. As you will soon find out thinking positive is not going to change a thing this time.

'Why not?' Tell you what let me tell you a story of the beginning of time and what I think really happened.

Go on then this should be entertaining.

THE STORY OF THE FRIXTA GALAXY

The Frixta Galaxy most surely had one star, a lot like our sun, and it probably had a few planets and moons rotating around it too, just like the Milky Way. I guess most of it did contain liquid water, the main ingredient to all life as we know it, and therefore some of these planets teemed with all sorts of life forms of every description. There must have been intelligent life I reckon, as well as primitive life-forms. Yes, there were all sorts of life from animals to insect plants and even extra-terrestrial life, what we think of as Alien life forms. They may have looked very similar to you and me and may even have walked about on two legs just like us humans. They may have been at different stages of evolution but I bet some of these Aliens were hugely intelligent and some not so intelligent. I also believe some of these Aliens may have had technology that was far more superior than we could ever imagine today. Because of the superior intelligence of these Aliens my guess is they were very peaceful and placid. They wouldn't want for much and they would know that wars and falling out with one another doesn't achieve anything. That is something I reckon we humans need to work out.

Oh very good Michael

Anyway.... so these Aliens were all living on their own planets as happy neighbours to one another, all minding their own business getting on with their own lives. They lived in perfect harmony with nature and I guess cared for it too. I would imagine there were lush green fields, mountains and even massive lakes and oceans on most of the planets, much like Earth has today. Each planet, I'm guessing, had its own little character; some had advanced Aliens living on them, they may have built cities and towns, or had their own little communities. They worked together for the good of all like Mormons do here on Earth - shame they are religious....

I'm also guessing there were Aliens of all shades and colours depending on the chemistry make-up of the planet they occupied, like green Aliens or yellow Aliens, grey Aliens, some were possibly white. You may have had black or blue coloured Aliens as well, who knows. But there wouldn't be any racism, like here on Earth, and they all lived lives not bothering one another, all doing their own thing; all merrily rotating around the same star and enjoying the benefits of all that life had to offer, They had daytime and night-time, seasons, the lot. Everything was just perfect in my Galaxy, the Frixta Galaxy, because positivity was the victor over everything negative. Do you know, when I sit here I sometimes close my eyes and imagine what life must have been like on one of those planets rotating around one of the first suns in the Frixta Galaxy?

Oh now he's off.

I see blue birds flying and singing in an almost clear cloudless sky. I see flowers buzzing with honeybees that catch my wondering eye. I can see waterfalls, lakes, fresh water rivers, ponds full of fish and frogs and there goes one magnificent dragonfly. I see the waves crashing down on the rocks resting on a pearl white sandy beach just in front of me and dolphins leaping in the air from an almost perfect turquoise sea. I see snow-capped mountains surrounded in mist and just there, behind me, forests gently flowing back and forth in a gentle breeze. I see kittens playing on lush green grass and climbing laden fruit trees, and the Aliens are singing and laughing. All are happy and gay and so wonderfully free. I now see one little Alien child playing with a puppy that's wagging his tail, ah; this is heaven to me…

'That was almost a poem wasn't it?'

Yes very nice.

'Now this is where I think it all went tits up.'

Here we go.

Sadly it started to go badly wrong when the negative matter got stronger, all because of one negative thought from one solitary Alien.

Really?

Yes, I reckon everything wrong today on our planet Earth was because of one unfolding event that happened millions of years ago on one of those heavenly planets that I have just described. This is how it all happened....... I think one day a 'know it all' smart arse Alien invented what we know today as government; an idea never heard of by any Alien species before. This was because they never needed a government before. Until this tosser had a brain fart. Before then everybody was doing okay, thank you very much. So, anyway, this Alien, let's just say he was a blue one, came up with this idea as he sat by a river playing with his little dick. That's right he was having a wank. Whilst he was wanking he realized the control he had over his cock. When he eventually shot his load he noticed, by having a stranglehold on his cock, he could manipulate it to do whatever he wanted, which was to ejaculate. He realized if it didn't conform straight away all he had to do was grip it harder and shake it more vigorously to make it conform to his will and force it to do what he wanted. He realized he had complete control over his John Thomas.

He then wondered if he could do the same to the occupants of the planet. That, my friends, was the first negative thought that started the downfall of all that was, or could have been, good. He wondered if he could manipulate the masses like he could his knob; if he could become a leader of the land everybody would do as he told them to do, giving him immense power. But the problem was how to go about it? How could he get a stranglehold on the masses? This was his second negative thought. This blue Alien was the first ever wanker. Then he had another brain fart, he thought it would be a good idea to organize everything (third negative thought). He thought he would form a governing body to control and manage all the land's assets (fourth negative thought) and he would run it.

That's how the universe was doomed from the start. That's why we have so many wankers in government today.

Is that right........I kind of knew this would be a dig at politicians.

He thought if he could stock load some of these resources of the planet he could probably use them as a trading tool later on with other planets. If he could encourage the other planets to do the same they could all trade with one another which, if they had a good trading relationship, would eventually bring all the worlds together as one big happy coalition family. They could share each other's technology and what have you, which in his negative mind was a brilliant idea. It was a shit idea but, unfortunately, it also sounded a good idea to all the other gullible blue Aliens living on his planet.

So from an Alien public school that I guess he attended, over many years he finally became a governor, the very first politician. But as negative thinking increased nothing happened smoothly, so he learned how to lie and cheat to get all the others on his side. You can see how the negativity grows can't you? So it continued and this little twat soon mastered the art of bullshit so he could then use it to get anything he wanted. If they refused to give him what he wanted he would buy their support by giving them a bit of the stock on the quiet or, failing that, blackmailing them to do as he asked, a technique he invented called 'mind-twister'. Later this term was shortened to 'minister', He was known for a long time thereafter as the prime minister to all his other fellow blue Aliens.

So anyway one day this blue Alien knocked on doors to campaign his stupid ideas to other blue Aliens. Eventually he went on trips to different planets to sell his vision to the yellow, the red and the green Aliens too, all of whom remember were doing ok, thank you very much. But they blindly signed up to this little fucker's vision. As a mind twister (prime minister) he won loads of support, mainly from the males because they are, and always have been, stupid. He had a party to celebrate and they flew blue flags and had blue balloons. He then formed the first ever parliament and he got other Aliens to join his blue party.

His idea spread like wildfire to other planets until one day it all went tits up. Negativity had set in good by now. Because other planets didn't want him to have his own party they all started to form their own parties and wanted to govern their own stock. So many governments were invented across the Galaxy and Alien politicians of every colour popped up everywhere. But, because of differences of opinion and culture and colours, one by one each planet started to fall out with the other. This little fucker started a war of words and overnight it spread to full blown hate. Before long arguing was invented and instead of rowing in the streets upsetting the children they decided to make one meeting point to shout at each other. They built an arguing house called a parliament building - an enclosed place to resolve disagreements.

Soon it got really crazy and the blue Aliens began to hate the red Aliens, the yellow Aliens detested the white Aliens, the white Aliens hated the green Aliens and so it went on and on. The grey Aliens hated every fucker and didn't get involved, so anyway racism was born. All the Alien races started fighting amongst themselves. The world's governments bickered about everything, all accusing one another of lies and underhanded deals and backhanders which, of course, were ripe in government then, as it is today. Eventually it affected the normal everyday Alien as food and water ran low because the fricking governments had stockpiled it for trading purposes and left none for the citizens.

So one after another every poxy government decision spoilt everything they used to have. Life soon became shit and, when the everyday normal Alien spoke up, they were ignored. So they began to resent this little twat's government idea and to regret ever signing up in the first place, realizing now it was a bad fricking idea after all. So they started to protest by the only way they knew how, by refusing to work, and before long everybody fell out.

So to try and keep the peace one race of Aliens invented the police force who worked for the government as volunteers. Other planets followed suit. Following the police were rules and these rules soon became the law of the land. Aliens were forced to abide by the law or face castration or imprisonment. But this only bred more resentment 'law breakers', anarchists, freedom fighters, and so unions were invented, and government didn't like unions at all. When finally the police weren't able to enforce the laws to the union members, the unruly lot who refused to work, the government decided to form a highly trained task force called the army with weapons to try and bring order back to the land and, most of all, to get the Aliens back to work. Of course, the working Aliens stood firm and so the government brought in marshal law.

It wasn't long before every planet followed this idea too, the army patrolled the streets and was ordered by government to look for anybody not born on that planet and arrest them, which was easy because of their colour. Once caught they were extradited back to their own worlds and it wasn't long before their borders were closed off completely to any foreigners. Of course some crept through the net by painting themselves the same colour as the natives or agreeing to work for fuck all. So some thick bastard yellow Aliens were allowed to stay and were given short-term working visas. Some were trained up as marines and if they saw that one of them had half a brain they were trained as spies, so espionage was invented. Secret societies were formed - it all went crazy.

Then… it all went quiet for a while, until one day a spy was caught and filmed being tortured to death and shown on their version of Sky TV all around the world. This became a popular TV show called *How To Kill Your Big Brother.* But it wasn't long before even that got boring so slowly, day by day, each planet started to get bloodthirsty for war and a little paranoid of each other. They thought what if one of their rival planets wanted to invade theirs and what if they had better weapons than them? So they started to make more sophisticated weapons and trained more solders to add to their ever-growing armies, all highly trained and ready to defend their planet if needs be.

Unfortunately their suspicions eventually came true because one day a planet did invade another. So the first ever war broke out, planets joined alliances. Except the grey Aliens - they hated every fucker remember… It wasn't long before a full blown galactic war kicked off. Aliens died in their masses. The female Aliens were appalled by all the killing of their menfolk in this new game of war they were playing. They were totally disgusted at the destruction of the planet's wildlife and plant life from falling bombs and the building of defences. So all the world's female Aliens got together secretly and formed the *Save The Planets Foundation.* They agreed that they would refuse to have sex with the males until they stopped fighting and tidied up all this mess. They called themselves The NAGS which stood for the *No Aggression Girls Society*. So homosexuality was invented and all the NAGS turned lesbian.

Therefore, the population started to decline rapidly. There were broken marriages and the Alien children soon got lost and confused. Not only did they see same sex Aliens kissing, they were missing their absent fathers too, who were probably either dead or somewhere with an Alien cock up their arse. So with no parental guidance they were angry and soon turned into feral kids. They started experimenting with drugs, smoking shit, eating magic mushrooms and drinking lots of alcohol. Their minds got all fucked up and you had bad mouthed, unruly little bastards everywhere. It was chaotic - something had to be done.

Whilst all this manifested itself, the prime minister (that little twat blue Alien who started all this shit) went into hiding. The little fucker who came up with the idea of politics in the first place was forced into hiding by his very own Alien race and so he lived in a cave for years. But remember he was a genius and so, while all the worlds were fighting amongst themselves he, the wanker, invented a super atomic bomb in his feeble attempt to win back some respect. It was a bomb more powerful than anything any Alien has ever seen in any of the worlds, clever little twat he was. All he needed to do now was to show it to his government.

So he crawled out of his hole and proudly showed off his weapon. Being a Jedi of sheep shit they fell for this smooth-talking bastard yet again. It was decided by parliament to forgive him and imminently tell the other worlds of their new super weapon. So it was broadcast galaxy wide as the 'Planet Destroyer.' It worked a charm. It frightened all of the worlds to surrender, all except the red Aliens who still hated the blue Alien race; they stood firm, the thick bastards, and called their bluff. The blue Aliens set up their weapon and aimed directly at the red Aliens' planet and gave them an ultimatum - comply or die. The grey Aliens, who were mainly female, watched all this and thought 'fuck this for a game of soldiers we're off' and their grey government, run by the first female minister called Magi, evacuated the planet completely... They could see how this was going to end, so they swiftly jumped into their massive pink Alien crafts and abandoned their planet. They left all the males fighting and fucked off into the unknown at warp speed down a wormhole. Where did the grey Aliens end up? Earth, of course; I'll get back to them later.

Anyway time was up for the red Aliens, so the bomb was deployed and fired on their planet. It broke through their atmosphere and flew over the lovely turquoise sea. All the dolphins popped their heads out of the water to observe what was happening and their happy playful behaviour soon changed and they swiftly turned tail, in a feeble attempt to swim in the opposite direction. They saw this fuck off bomb coming their way; a bomb remember that was more powerful than any Alien expected. When it exploded, the force not only blew the red planet to tiny atoms but the shock wave destroyed all the other planets in that galaxy too. The force obliterated them all into oblivion. So the female grey Aliens were right to flee their world or they would have faced the same fate.

This shock wave continued for millions if not billions of years which brings us up to the modern day Big Bang theory. Antimatter fought with matter yet again but this time it mixed with DNA and eventually formed a new universe and loads of other galaxies, one being ours. Unfortunately for us, some of that male blue Alien's DNA survived and got into our galaxy, finally settling here on our young Earth. And over thousands of years of evolution that DNA eventually mixed with some early life forms that became us humans. That's why today some Earthlings decide to become politicians (antimatter and a mixture of blue Alien DNA). That is why politicians are a different breed to most of us.

Sorry to interrupt this fascinating concept Michael but before you continue you should explain to the reader what DNA is. Not everybody knows what DNA is...let me input that information into your brain.

'Oh.....okay.'

There done... now you know about DNA.

'Oh do I? Okay, I'll explain to the reader what DNA is.'

Good and then we might get back on track.

DNA CODE (Are we all DNA programmed?)

We all have what they call a DNA code

DNA is deoxyribonucleic acid, a substance found in cells of all living things. It determines the structure of every cell and is responsible for characteristics being passed on from one parent to their children. Every living thing has a DNA code. DNA is the basic blueprint of all life and that being the case it must control all life as we know it. It's a bit too complicated even for me to understand fully, but it kind of works like a computer, it learns and absorbs information and then adapts to the information it receives. And it can be programmed, even manipulated. DNA is what makes up our genes... fricking hell how do I know all this?

I imputed it into your brain

'Brilliant....'

Shall I carry on?

'Please do Alf.'

DNA works like a computer. It learns and absorbs information and then adapts to the information it receives. And it can also be programmed too, just like I have done to you Michael...

'Tell them what a gene is ALF, not everybody knows what a gene is either I bet?'

Oh, are you going to let me have a word in? I'm honoured. Well reader........A gene is the basic physical and functional unit of heredity; the genetic make-up of all living things.

'What does heredity mean Alf?'

Heredity - this means the passing of characteristics to the offspring of either its parents or ancestor.

It is these 'genes' which are made up of DNA, act as instructions if you like to make molecules called proteins. In humans genes vary in size from a few hundred DNA bases to more than two million bases.

'I read they estimated that humans have between twenty thousand and twenty-five thousand genes. But there are two hundred and twenty-three genes in the human DNA code that are not found in any other living organisms studied on Earth.'

Where did you dig that up?

'Off the inter-web of course; The Human Genome Project.'

www.genome.gov/10001772.

Oh very good Michael, what else did you find?

'It also said us sheeple did not inherit these genes from any other form of life on this planet.'

That's very true. Anyway, you can carry on with your story now if you like.

'I've lost my fricking flow now you keep interrupting, and stop keep putting stuff in my head, I feel dizzy now. Where was I?'

As I recall you were on about something called The No Aggression Girls Society. And a pink Spaceship and something about blue Aliens' DNA ending up on earth and that's why earth has politicians; and some other insane theories.

'Oh are, I remember now. So the blue Alien is why we have politicians here on Earth, wankers the lot of them.'

So anyway reader, it seems to me our only hope is divine intervention, or maybe the female grey Aliens will save us. Therefore, I conclude my story simply with this. We Earthlings were doomed from the start of creation because some fricking accent male blue Alien on a faraway planet millions of years ago had an idea whilst he was having a wank (which is where the term men's brains are in their dicks came from). His idea was to form a government; stupid idea. He was the first ever politician and life for us all on Earth has been one cock-up after another. It all went tits up because this wanker didn't know what the fuck he was doing or talking about, but he sold it really well to other gullible male Aliens of his planet and others. That trait is in all politicians today.

Therefore the universe and everything as we know of today is nothing less than the debris from that bomb that gathered over millions of Earth years ago to form the planets and stars and moons we know today. Because of an Alien's invention of a first atom bomb, remnants of his DNA through antimatter had contaminated our planet. Over many years it got into our food chain which in turn has made some human male species become politicians. The so-called 'Big Bang' was a political Aliens fuck up as it always is. From a fuck up came everything and one day everything will end up as fucked up again. So there's no point worrying about shit because there's nothing you can do to stop it as long as we have politicians. There isn't a scientist on the planet that can prove me wrong. Nevertheless, you can go with the other Big Bang Theory of Einstein if you want, that's up to you.

You really don't like politicians do you?

'No.'

Well, you will find out it's not all their fault.

'Fuck off. It's always their fault.'

No it's not, they are just sheep too.

'Whatever'. Anyway I want to talk now about Old Albert because, as clever as he was; he was a fricking stupid sheep in some ways.

Old Albert?

OLD ALBERT

Here on Earth it was Professor Albert Einstein who came up with the Big Bang Theory. He did so around about the same time he came up with the Theory of Relativity. Everybody knows good old Albert but I just want to explain to you that even clever sheep can fuck up from time to time, usually because of mind manipulation or naivety. Yes, mind manipulation even works on geniuses. Even Albert Einstein was susceptible to it so don't think it's because you're thick that you're being shit on, politicians have great methods to control the sheep.

The invention of the atomic bomb here on Earth stemmed because of Einstein's ideas on mass to energy conversion with the famous equation E=Mc2. Of course you already knew that. Now I know he didn't invent the atomic bomb, neither did he discover fission that led to this massive fuck off bomb being built, but he did start the ball rolling. Albert was undeniably a clever Ram yet he still was, in my opinion, a sheep and easily manipulated by the farmers of the time.

(When I refer to farmers I mean government leaders, the ones who run Earth's Farm)

Old Albert probably started to trust fricking politicians without realizing he did it, and yet you would have thought Einstein, being as clever as he was, would have surely cottoned on to the wankers straight away, but he didn't. Why? His mind was manipulated just like most of the sheep of this planet; his line of thought was being controlled.

Now I don't know much about science and/or this Einstein Ram to be fair. But what I have read about him he has earned a little respect from me, and that's very good coming from me.

This is only because he did, after all, do some great things in his lifetime. He was 'almost' a free-thinking individual, unlike most who are just programmed sheep. His marvellous brain benefited a lot of sheep before it was pickled and put in a jar. Even though he fucked up on that occasion regarding the nuke, in my opinion it was probably only because he was too clever for his own good. What I mean by that is over the many years of my life I have met a lot of sheep of all backgrounds. And I have learnt in all my experiences, after talking to the so called 'clever sheep' of the world, that they all, and I mean all, lack basic common sense. So in effect the whole world is run by sheep with no common sense at all.

Mr Einstein was the same. Although he did come across to me as a generally nice Ram he wasn't street wise. This I guess was because he buried his head in books like a nerd. So he must have often been isolated from the 'real world'. So I guess all the time he did his science thingy and came up with equations and shit his genuine aim (and I truly believe this) was to benefit the world. You can guarantee in the background there was some twatty politician or some other slimy bastard picking his brains or using his intelligent mind to plot shit for their own fricking agenda. They most probably wanted to feed their lust for money, power and greed which is very often the case.

So it wasn't entirely Einstein's fault, he was probably fed sheep shit and lies like the rest of us.

Albert Einstein did apologize later on for his fuck up regarding the nuke. That's all well and good but it's no good closing the gate when the horse has already bolted, as the saying goes. If he had kept his idea locked away in his head at the beginning there wouldn't have been ninety thousand to one hundred and sixty-six thousand sheep in Hiroshima and sixty to eighty thousand in Nagasaki dead today when those Farmers Harry S. Truman, Joseph Stalin, and Winston Churchill ordered two of the things to be dropped on the heads of thousands of Japanese sheep.

So in my opinion, Albert should have used his massive so-called brain and thought about what he was doing before he told the world what he had discovered. He should have used his massive brain and mathematically worked out the consequence of his actions, because every action has a reaction. Anyway, it's too late now isn't it? I'm not going to start talking bad of the dead. So rest in peace, old Albert, I forgive you. Not sure if the Japanese ever will….

Professor Albert Einstein was a great human, Michael, don't be too easy to judge.

Just had a thought… 'Old Albert' that's a nickname for a Dick isn't it? Anyway up…just goes to show the dangers of trusting farmers, dunt it? ('Dunt' is my new made up word means 'doesn't it just.' You can add that to the Oxford dictionary too). So for all you so-called clever dicks out there, for fuck's sake listen to me and listen to me good…

MICKY FRICK'S TIP

DON'T LET YOURSELF BE A PUPPET FOR THE GOVERNMENT; USE YOUR HEADS

In November 1954, five months before his death, Einstein summarized his feelings about his role in the creation of the atomic bomb: "I made one great mistake in my life... when I signed the letter to President Roosevelt recommending that atom bombs be made; but there was some justification - the danger that the Germans would make them." Albert Einstein taken from (www.doug-long.com)

That's right, blame the fricking Germans…most German sheep are very nice. Yes, Albert, you should have shut the frick up…All being said though... for what I have read about old Albert, and it's not a lot, he did come up with some good stuff. I kind of like some of his quotes too - I particularly like this one

In order to form an immaculate member of a flock of sheep one must, above all, be a sheep. Albert Einstein

Very true my old 'togger'… look, as clever as he may well have been, in his day he still was a fricking sheep like the rest of you. He didn't know everything. You can never know everything. For one thing he didn't know he shouldn't ever trust politicians. As a matter of fact nobody should trust politicians

You are right about that.

MICKY FRICK'S TIP

NEVER TRUST A POLITICIAN BECAUSE THEY ARE ALL WANKERS

Yes......it's just a shame my book wasn't around when Old Albert was alive, it would have made him aware of this fact. I could have given him a heads up on the bastards. Then he would have probably done things differently. Like, for instance, kept his frigging gob shut for one on some of his ingenious discoveries, those ones that led to the creation of that fuck off atom bomb that ended up killing and maiming a lot of innocent sheep. Talking about intelligence, I now want to talk about 'The Missing Link' and primitive Ram brain development.

Oh go on then.... this should be interesting...

CHAPTER THREE

WHAT IF WE ARE RELATED TO ALIENS?

Interesting...

THE MISSING LINK ACCORDING TO ME.

You have probably heard of the term 'The missing link'. It is used by scientists when they talk about the evolution of Ram. Well, apparently they found out that some time in our evolution process we leapt from being a thick ape to a clever ape. According to them that know about this sort of thing, they also say that it took thousands of years of evolution for us to move from pond life to an ape-like creature; yet as an ape in a small period of time, we leapt from breaking nuts with our heads and living in caves sitting scratching our bollocks all day and grunting to each other, to making mud huts equipped with fires. We also made tools to work with; we painted pictures, did sculptures and even wrote. We put together musical rhythms and cultivated and grew our own food. And we started to bury our dead instead of just leaving them to rot where they dropped.

Not only that, there is now evidence to suggest primitive Ram also started to worship Gods and had lots of religious rituals and stuff. Scientists from all over the world are baffled; they all think it is amazing how quick our evolution accelerated as if it was overnight. How did this happen? Our evolution seemed to jump from thick monkey doing fuck all and scratching our arses a bit, like most of the unemployed population of today, to an almost sophisticated species as if overnight. Amazing isn't it....? This is what they call the missing link.

Nobody can understand how it happened. Some even say it took less than a hundred years for these changes to take place. Our evolution has been a mystery for many scientists for many years and they still question it today. I thought this was quite an interesting subject and I have thought about it for a long time. The reason, I think, is a simple one.

Here we go.....what's that then?

'Alien intervention.'

Alien intervention okay....I thought you were going to say something stupid like magic.

'No, it was Alien intervention, and this is what I think really happened.'

Oh no, here we go. We have got to put up with another one of his mad theories.

I reckon sometime, when we were Homo Heidelbergensis, a primitive ape-like Ram six hundred thousand years ago, I reckon Aliens came to Earth.. I don't think any of us would have evolved any further if they hadn't. So where did they come from these Aliens? I hear you ask. Who were they? Well I'll tell you......They are the red Aliens from the Frixta Galaxy I spoke about earlier.

Oh dear, not again, I'm going to have to zap some intelligence into his brain again in a minute....

They must have found refuge on Mars and became 'Martians'. Yes, that's right, I think the red Aliens found their way to planet Mars, that's why it's red... makes sense.......

To you maybe...

I guess they lived there for quite a while and after they fucked that planet up they then came to Earth. It all makes sense when you think about it, You see, the way I see it, at the time of the Homo Heidelbergensis (and take note what I say because this has been kind of proven from some evidence gathered from Mars expatiations) Planet Mars could have well been a planet much like our own Earth millions of years ago. But, for whatever reason that nobody really knows yet for sure, Mars died. Mars became lifeless. All that is left today on Mars is a lot of red dust and the scars which suggested it may at some point have had oceans, rivers and lakes, much like Earth. There are even some photos from Mars that look very much like what could be depicted as ancient cities. They do have some evidence to show that too. Yes... Mars at some point did have liquid water; that's a fact which, you also know, is the prime ingredient needed for all life to exist. If this is the case then it's not unreasonable to think that Mars did have life on it as I suggest, at some point in the past. Not only that, possibly intelligent life too.

From what I have read and understood about Mars it all makes perfect sense to me that when the planet was starting to die the occupants naturally sought somewhere else to live - Earth. Now I reckon Earth to the Martians must have been the obvious choice. I mean, Mars is only a hop, skip and a jump away from Earth isn't it? In fact I wouldn't be surprised if the Martians already came to Earth for a holiday from time to time and why not? It's a nice place is Earth. It should be called 'Costa Earth' because it costs a fricking fortune to live here.

No, it's not unreasonable to think they did holiday here. I mean we humans are already talking about holidays to the moon in the near future so I guess the Martians once thought the same regarding the Earth once, and eventually they did. We will probably have holidays to Mars one day. Mind you saying that, why bother? There's frick all there now, not even a seaside.

So, anyway... I still wouldn't be surprised if when Mars was a thriving planet millions of years ago the Martians went on what we call a holiday to Earth. They probably had a lovely time here too (we do have a seaside) and the different climate would have done them good. There's loads to do here, like watching the wildlife and that. I bet it was great fun here on Earth once, a bit like us going to a zoo or a safari. Yes, Earth would have been an ideal destination to emigrate to I reckon, it was a nice warm planet back then. In fact it wouldn't have been much different to a Brit emigrating to say Spain, like some British sheep already do. I bet Earth had everything the Martians needed to settle in and make it their new home; they just needed to kill off a few of the dinosaurs first because they would have eaten them.

I do think the Martians occupied Mars in the time of the dinosaurs.

Really?

Yes. The thing is see; I don't think Mars died that long ago. It must have taken a few years for a planet to die completely and so I guess there were many, many, many generations of Martians were born, lived full lives and even died on their own planet before it started to get really bad on there. I guess they must have tried all sorts of ways to reverse the inevitable, like cutting back on the population and cutting down on the emissions from burning solid fuel, for instance. They probably even banned the use of chemicals, you know that sort of thing.

Yes, my guess is Martians tried really hard to save their planet but obviously sadly they failed. Mars died probably because of a number of factors such as pollution and over-population. Over-population adds to pollution because of the consumption of the billions of Martians. I bet the Mars ozone layer got a right battering and started rapidly to deplete as ours is, or was as they do say it's getting better now. I think they are full of shit. Talking about shit, here's an interesting fact I'm throwing in for good measure; did you know termites fart more than any other creature that inhabits the planet?

Really...... tut.

And cows are responsible for eighteen per cent of the greenhouse gases that cause global warming - more than all the cars, planes, or any form of transport on the planet. Anyway where was I?

Ozone layer........

'Oh are, yes that's right....' So Mars's ozone eventually disappeared altogether. When this happened, all the water that was left floated off into space. But before this the air on Mars got very dry and hot, even toxic, then all the vegetation withered and died. First rivers dried up long before the seas disappeared into space, so all other Alien creatures and many Martians who occupied the planet perished long, long before the planet was dead. When all hope was lost they then made preparations to leave Mars altogether and migrate here to Earth. They knew years in advance Mars was fucked. But at the time this was all going down, Earth was flourishing and full of life including, like I said, dinosaurs. I wouldn't be surprised if the Martians came to Earth big game hunting once, when Mars was thriving that is. They possibly came to Earth to hunt dinosaur; it all make sense when you think about it.

Does it really? In your mind maybe...

Yes, all this was when Earth was a planet of giants. They knew Earth had millions of dinosaurs and they knew they must fuck them off before they moved in. We all know that millions of years ago Earth was a dangerous hostile planet full of wild beasts and giant dangerous animals so they needed to be culled before the mass evacuation from Mars started. I think the Martians sent a super bomb to do the job. They wanted to wipe out the dinosaurs before they moved in so they got this technology from that wanker the blue Alien, I bet. That's why a lot of dinosaur bones found over the years have been found to be radioactive FACT.

www.2012Inyinfo.com/.../mostdinosaur-bones-discovered-are-radioactive-tr

That's right, they are radioactive. They are painted in lead paint in museums to protect visitors from radioactive poisoning. The reason they are radioactive is because they were nuked by a super Alien bomb much like what we have today, only a hundred times more powerful, I'm guessing. Once the deed was done and all the dinosaurs were wiped out, extinct, the Martians just waited for a few more hundred years until the radiation levels dropped here on Earth; for the atmosphere to right itself and then they began the mass evacuation from Mars. I know, I know, you were made to believe it was an asteroid that hit Earth and wiped out the dinosaurs. Well, that's bollocks; it was a Martians' bomb. The reason some creatures survived was because of sheer luck. But the fallout from this Alien bomb over time created a lot of the weird-looking creatures that we have today.

Really...?

It's true some mutations happened because of radioactive fallout. In fact a lot of the mythical creatures you read about such as the Pixies, Fairies, Dragons, Mermaids, Ogopogo, Cyclopes, Grendel, The Abominable Snowman, the list goes on and on; they were all because of radiation. Even Trolls existed once and they looked like they did because of radiation poisoning, I reckon. Even today there are still many weird-looking animals, insects and fish about; you may come across them one day. This is all because of the Alien bomb sent by the Martians about sixty-six million thirty-eight thousand years ago - give or take a year or two.

Even the weird-looking humans you see are because of the radiation poisoning that infected their DNA at the start of their evolution, possibly from drinking infected water. What a lot of sheep don't know is that the Homo Heidelbergensis also walked the Earth at the same time as the dinosaurs. For those of you who don't know, the Homo Heidelbergensis were our early ancestors and there is much proof that early Ram walked with dinosaurs.

www.yourriginsmatter.com/conversations/...dinosaurs..man/30

They also found fossilized human footprints next to dinosaurs. You didn't know that did you? This is because they don't want you to know the truth.

www.bible.ca/tracks/taylor-trail.htm

Interesting don't you think? So anyway, let me get back to the time the Martians came to Earth. Where was I? Oh are, so Mars was eventually evacuated, it was no longer inhabitable and so the Martians all came to seek asylum here on Earth.

THE MASS EVACUATION OF MARS

My guess is they touched down probably near China because the dominant colour even today is red, their flag is red and the lucky colours to the Chinese are red, yellow and green. My guess is the skin of the Martians was red but due to our climate it faded and went yellow over time. Not only that, the Chinese sheeple are the longest living civilisation; their history goes back thousands and thousands of years. Anyway that's beside the point. All I'm saying is I would guess the Martians must have come over in their droves, in fact you may not know this but the Martians were the first ever asylum seekers. So you see nothing changes, asylum seekers have been taking over for thousands of years.

Anyway, when they moved in and, like all asylum seekers do, eventually took over the place, they brought with them all their families and friends, and it didn't take them long to settle in. The dinosaurs had long gone, pushed out of the way and forgotten about. All that walked the Earth now were a few of the native Earth creatures such as the Homo Heidelbergensis and, as I have already mentioned, there were pixies, fairies, giants, trolls and dragons walking the Earth at this time too.

Hmmm! I'm saying nothing

'Say what?'

Nothing you carry on...

So anyway, the Chinese Martians, I guess, dominated Earth for about ten thousand years or so undisturbed, living peacefully with all the other life forms here on Earth. It was turning out good for them and everything else, There was an abundance of food, water, everything. It couldn't be better, they had everything they needed to live a full happy life and, may I add, all for free. The Martians then built massive cities. One of these was called Atlantis - you may have heard of Atlantis.

We will touch on Atlantis later.

'Oh right'... Anyway they built Atlantis when expanded their empire and eventually that stretched from one end of the planet to the other. It had to be that big to accommodate all the Martians who were breeding like rabbits. Don't the Chinese ever learn? That's why Mars got destroyed the first time. Horny buggers the Martians, it's just a shame they didn't invent condoms on Mars and maybe it could have all been avoided. Anyway, it was a shag fest here on Earth now.

Whilst all this was going on the Martians and mystical beasts lived in perfect harmony for many, many years. The Martians even started to have Homo Heidelbergensis as pets.

Say what?

Pets; they then educated them and taught them to do tricks which, although very entertaining for the Martians at the time, also paved the way for primitive humans to be able to store information and remember; we had the ability to learn rapidly and develop new skills, hence the missing link. So, I conclude that over the course of time the thick Ape, the Homo Heidelbergensis, turned into the early human species we are today (Homo sapiens). We are still a bit thick but not as thick as we were six hundred thousand years ago, thanks to the Martians that is. There you have it, the mystery of the missing link solved.

Interesting how your mind works Michael and you're right about the Alien intervention, but it wasn't because of Aliens from Mars.

'Eh?'

What if I was to tell you human DNA is part Alien, and all humans do have Alien DNA strands in their genetic make-up; that much is true.

'Oh....so I'm right saying we only survived and thrived thanks to Aliens?'

Yes that's right.

'And some Aliens made us smarter because of Alien DNA?'

Yes that's right too.

'And Homo sapiens were pets and were taught tricks to entertain the Aliens. I bet every Alien had a pet Homo?'

No that's where you're wrong

'Oh....'

No, they didn't have early humans as pets.

'Why not? Early Homos would have made good pets..... I would have liked one. I would have called him...Mongo.'

No they didn't have Homo sapiens as pets.

'Shame, they missed out on an opportunity didn't they?'

MICKY FRICK'S TIP

GRAB ANY OPPORTUNITIES THAT ARISE

Tut!

'Do you know, Alf, I read somewhere there were some Homo Heidelbergensis who didn't get to be Homo sapiens, is that true?

That's right the Homo neanderthalensis (Neanderthals) wandered around Europe before they all starved to death some time later, letting the Homo sapiens thrive and take over.

'I'm not sure about that, not all of them starved to death.'

They did, how do you mean...?

'I don't think so because I still see some of them wondering around even today.'

What are you on about Michael?

'I'm saying if you look for them you can always find Neanderthals because they all seem to wear hoodies and have their trousers down their arse.'

Ha! Ha! Very funny.

'Good that isn't it? I wonder if any of their names are Mongo?'

Look Michael we have a serious message to put to the reader so can we get back to the subject at hand? By the way...you are right with the date six hundred thousand years ago and human evolution was, as you said, helped by Aliens' intervention, but not Aliens from Mars.

'Oh right...Who then?'

The Anunnaki.

'Oh yes... you never told us who these Anunnaki are.'

Well, humans only succeeded as species because of a little help from this Alien race called the Anunnaki, and okay we Nordics helped you a little too.

'So who are the Anunnaki Alf?'

The Anunnaki are an Alien race that visited Earth about six hundred thousand years ago when you humans were just evolving into Homo Heidelbergensis (an upright walking ape). They landed in what you now call Africa, not China that came later. The Anunnaki only helped early man to evolve for their own reasons and no, it wasn't so they could have them as pets. They chose a bunch of African Homo Heidelbergensis, genetically enhanced their brains and, yes, eventually they became Homo sapiens as you said. The Homo sapiens were then bred and trained for one purpose and one purpose only, and that was to work for them, to be their slaves.

> ***For a long, long time the Earth has been a planet run by these slavers and now the Anunnaki, already here on Earth, are preparing for the arrival of thousands more Anunnaki Aliens to join them. That's right, you heard me, and some of these Aliens are already here. You may laugh but it's not so ironic to think that this could actually be the case.***
>
> ***Dr Steven Greer - Dr M. Jacobs PhD abductee investigator, Dr Karla Turner, PhD***

'They don't seem very friendly these Anunnaki lot.'

No not a very nice race of Alien at all. It was around one hundred and fifty thousand to one hundred and ninety thousand years ago the Anunnaki last came to Earth. They saw the Homo sapiens as a potentially useful creature and began to do even more experiments with them. They set us tests to test our brains to the max and make us understand certain instructions; training us to do not tricks but tasks. They eventually made us work for them, taught us skills like carpentry and farming and building. They found Homo sapiens' strength was a great asset. They were easily educated and obedient.

To manage the Homo sapiens the Anunnaki created a hybrid creature known to you as the Greys. The Greys are a small, scrawny and weak species so to have strong obedient slave humanoids was a brilliant advantage for them. And so over many years these Greys trained and took over Earth under the instruction of the Anunnaki leader their creators and enslaved the Homo sapiens to work for them. But as well as that, and not a lot of you humans know this, but not only were Homo sapiens used as slaves by the Grey Aliens they were also extremely attracted to the Homo sapien females.

'Then why am I an Alien sex toy? I'm a Ram.' I'll tell you the reader about that abduction later.

Well that's still a mystery to me because usually they are more attracted to the female sex but I guess they will sexually abuse either sex.

'Horny little buggers aren't they?'

The Anunnaki Grey has an uncontrollable urge for sex that's true

'You mean they will fuck anything, even a frog if they can stop it hopping?'

Not exactly what I meant but I get your point... Anyway the Greys started regularly having sex with a few of the Earth females resulting in getting some of them pregnant.

'So all the Greys Aliens aren't female?'

No, most grey Aliens don't have any genitalia at all. It is only the Big Nose Grey that has sexual organs and this is only because they were genetically modified to have them. Over the years some female humans gave birth to big nose Grey children, they are what we call hybrids of the Greys but they usually stay with the Greys and rarely come to Earth at all.

'That's who shagged me last time I was abducted.'

Possibly... look I don't know. But other than that a lot of you humans unfortunately do have Anunnaki Alien DNA in you. This is because the Anunnaki used their own DNA to create the Grey and they are the ones who are here on Earth and running things here today.

'Interesting I'll look that up.'

You do that then I won't have to zap you

'Say what?'

Nothing.

WE ALL HAVE ALIEN DNA

I have looked it up and it's true we all have Alien strands in our DNA. It's been baffling the greatest scientific minds of the world for a very long time. They can't understand why we do all have this Alien DNA. I'm talking about a DNA strand that is not from this planet and we all have it inside us, it is part of our genetic code.

Told you so

According to a team of researchers working at the Human Genome Project, this appears to be the case. The team believes that more than ninety-five per cent of the non-coding sequences (also called junk DNA) found in human DNA is actually the genetic codes of Alien life forms. (Research was done in 2013).

beforeitsnews.com/r2/?url=http://nutshellurl.com/AlienDNAHuman

What's also interesting is not one other mammal that originated from this planet, as they know it, has this Alien DNA strand. Not one. It's just us 'Hu-sheep'. Did you also know that some fungi and some mushrooms on this planet are thought to be of Alien origin and did not originate from Earth? So be warned if you eat that Quorn stuff you could well be eating an Alien organism. Come to think about it maybe that's what's given humans the Alien DNA.

No it wasn't from eating fungi.

There are many theories why we do have this Alien strand but no scientist can agree on where it came from for sure. However, there are many theories floating around. I have an idea where it comes from though, and I'll share that with you later on, but for now remember our top minds and the cleverest sheeple of this planet just don't know; it is an ongoing argument. However, they do all agree, and this is a concrete fact, that this Alien DNA strand that we all have inside us is not from Earth.

rense.com/general74/d3af.htm

www.news.com.au/.../science/...scientific...Aliens/story-fn5fsgyc-1226617200225

EVOLUTION

Humans are generally diverse and clever, are they not? They are curious and usually able to adapt and learn new things which have helped us thrive as we have for many generations. Okay we all know a dumb fuck but generally humans are quite bright; that's why we have as a species dominated the planet for thousands of years. For us our evolution process works like this, in simple terms that is, sperm to egg, from infancy through to childhood, adolescence, maturity, menopause, ageing and death. All the time we grow older we keep learning new stuff, or rather being programmed. We are also tricked into believing in something that doesn't really exist. So when we talk of seeing ghosts for instance we could I suppose, and a lot of people do believe, that we are seeing the apparition of somebody who once lived but is now dead; a spirit of some kind hence the term a ghost. Maybe we are, maybe we are not.

www.laitman.com/2010/01/why-do-we...

It could just be a figure of our imagination seeing a ghost, like seeing angels for instance or an Alien like Alf. ... 'Hang on.... Come to think about it Alf, I've never seen you. I don't know what you look like?'

Yes you do. You have seen me, you have just forgotten.

'When?'

When you were a child.

'What do you look like? Show yourself to me.'

What now?

'Yes.'

Not now, but I will come and visit you again one day.

'Why not now?'

It's not the time... look Michael we need to finish this book; once it's finished and published I will visit you.

'Okay and don't scare the crap out of me when you do.'

No, I won't scare you. Look can we please carry on now?

'I don't want you to visit me at night either. I'll think you're a ghost or, worse, an intruder and I'm liable to beat the crap out of you.'

Okay, okay not at night.

'I mean don't creep up on me or anything...'

Okay I won't... can we continue now?

'Okay.'

So anyway reader back to Evolution. Now it's hard to comprehend that we started life as a sea bacteria. We must have originated in the sea because scientists tell us most of the world was once covered in water. Anyway from these bacteria we evolved into a water living organism, some kind of fish maybe, and from a fish we ventured onto land. As the sea receded we learnt to walk and we weren't on our own either. I think lots of other species followed suit. That's why we have the variety of different land animals as we do. We know that birds are cousins of the dinosaurs; well at least that's what they say. They also say they walked the Earth way, way before we even came on the scene.

No that is untrue.

'What's that Alf?'

Humans did coexist in the same era as dinosaurs.

'No.....'

It's true. There is evidence on the internet to prove this. Just type in the question: 'Did giants exist?' on an internet search.

'I will that's very interesting Alf....'

We have already touched on this Michael... you must have been mind-wiped again... look check out these YouTube vids.

Fricking hell reader, he's right they did. Watch these two videos on YouTube:

www.youtube.com/watch?v=LxNq5_keJU0

www.youtube.com/watch?v=6jx3vVSSfEs

Fricking hell, reader he's right. There is a lot of evidence to prove giants once walked the Earth reader. How amazing is that?

The giants were not of human origin, they were not of this world. But they did take human woman and impregnated them and later those women birthed half-breeds. When they had enough half-breeds they then left them with special mechanisms to control the populace and, using the division of languages, they also created religion. They moved on to create a monetary system. Money was put into place as a mechanism to control the populace of Earth and it has worked brilliantly.

Giants are also mentioned in the Bible too. In the Old Testament Genesis 6:4, and you can check it out yourself reader, it says, ***'There were giants in the Earth in those days, and also after that, when the sons of God came in unto the daughters of men and they bear children to them, the same became mighty men which were of old, men of renown'.*** Fuck knows what that all means but it does say giants were on Earth. But... I'm thinking how did they have sex and impregnate the Ewes; did all giants have little dicks?

Really Michael, do you have to?

'I think it's a valid question to ask. And did you know, apparently the female of the species no longer needs a male.'

Where did that come from...?

'Read it on the inter-web.'

Oh of course you did..... And you are right most babies born into the world today are in fact female.

'Thinking about it, and what I have researched, it is also my observation that there aren't many women philosophers; never has been. If woman ruled the world I think things would be run differently. My guess is they would probably bump off all us Rams, that is unless you were good looking of course, or muscular like them Chippendales, and obedient and good at DIY and had a big dick.'

Does it really matter?

'Well I think it does or how can we believe any of it ... is that why women like big....'

Okay, okay, can we move on now?

'And if the Ewe was giving birth to baby giants, fricking hell, they must have had a massive …'

Okay now that's enough talk about evolution.

'Okay......But one thing's for sure, if the Earth was ruled by Ewes it would look a prettier place I reckon. We have a lot to learn from the fairer sex I think. Maybe if we all got in touch with our feminine side there wouldn't be so many wars for a start.'

Probably right there.

Evolution, can you just talk about the subject matter please?

'Okay keep your hair on... have you got hair?'

Michael...

'Okay Evolution.'

Evolution, reader, happens over thousands of years and is happening right now. I think for us humans it is probably happening at a more accelerated rate than ever before, what with the technology that we have today. I mean did you know we are even now at a very close stage where we will be able to alter the DNA structure of anything?

It's because of DNA life does not ever die, it only evolves. Each living thing on this planet also evolves, so that means it has a purpose of being here. It's interesting that some of you humans still hold to the theory that all life forms came from one cell. As that cell continued to multiply that same cell, which is a copy of the master one, suddenly became a `brain cell', a `liver cell', or a `kidney cell'. One even became a dinosaur. How did that happen if it is a copy of the same cell?

They also say each of our DNA codes is unique. Look at the Chinese sheeple, The Native Americans, The Black Race, and all the other different races around the world. Where do they come from? I'll tell you, the Frixta Galaxy

Yes okay Michael, whatever. What if I was to tell you that you were genetically modified to be who you are?

'What you mean?'

What I mean is some of your DNA was reconstructed by Aliens.

'What by them Giants with the big......'

NO. But you are descendants of a more intelligent Alien life form. Did you also know most of you humans are related or, should I say, have been interbreeding?

'Interbreeding, how do you mean?'

If you traced back your genes with other humans you would find you are all related in some way.

'That's interesting Alf.'

CHAPTER FOUR

WHAT IF ALIENS ARE REAL?

LET'S TALK ABOUT ALIENS

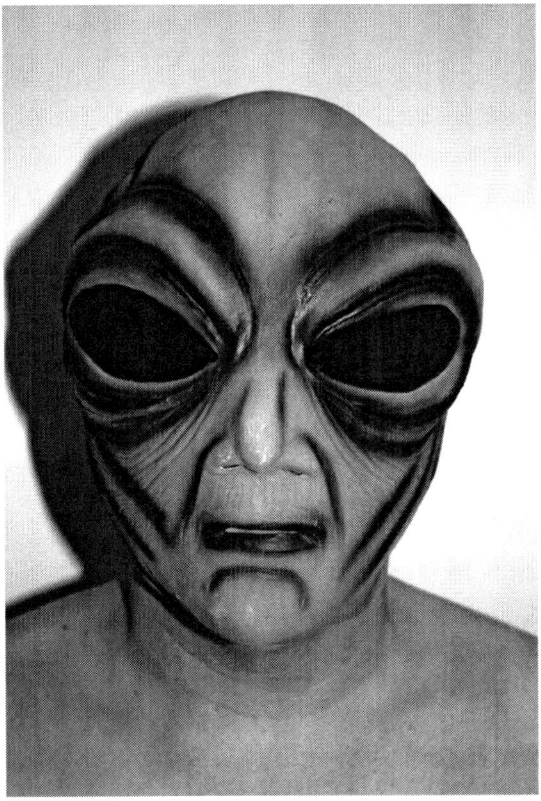

There are a lot of accounts describing what Aliens actually look like. Some sheeple believe that there are four types of Alien, all of which are said to come from the star constellation of Orion. These are the Large Grey (or Big Nose). The Big-Nosed Greys are usually tall, about seven to eight feet, and physically are very similar to other Greys with the exception of large noses and genitalia. They are said to have some vestigial reproductive capabilities; this is the one I think shagged me when I was abducted.

The Little Grey, that's the one everybody has heard of, is the one you most associate as the little fuckers with a big head, big black slanted eyes, and a small slit-like mouth, two holes for a nose and no ears. They are about four foot in height, have little legs and arms and four long fingers on each hand. They are light grey in colour and walk around naked with no genitals at all; I know I've looked.

Now I know a lot of you believe that the Grey was an Alien that was invented and created for a movie called *Close Encounters of the Third Kind.* Well you're not wrong, in one sense it was but this is not an idea that was picked out of the air. The creators of the Grey Alien were helped by research from old accounts dating back thousands of years found in ancient paintings and carvings from all around the world. The creators of the Grey Alien, that you know only too well, is based on old accounts and records of real evidence which was documented by early man, so it wasn't just made up. So the Grey Alien you see in the movie is not that far from the truth of what these Aliens really look like. In fact it's very close indeed to the real thing.

Then you have what is called The Orange. The Orange Alien is a hybrid race with partial reptilian-like features, yet possessing human-like reproductive organs and even certain artificial or cybernetic features, meaning they can change their appearance. It is believed that the Orange consists of Hu-brids (meaning crossed with humans) and Re-brids (crossed with reptiles). A Ram named David Icke believes the Royal family are reptilian hybrids. I wonder if they are descendants of the dinosaurs. Because there are one or two who look like lizards.

Tut!

As well as that it is also believed by many that there are loads of other types of Alien right across the cosmos who visit Earth from time to time. Some races of Alien are even extinct... I'm thinking if they are extinct how the frick do they know they ever existed in the first place? Anyway as there are so many Aliens you're probably thinking now why don't they introduce themselves?

I'm going to let you into a secret. You have already seen a real life Alien, they walk amongst you humans every day, and you just haven't noticed them because they look very similar to humans. The reason they hide is because you humans couldn't handle it. The other reason is because it is part of the plan of having the element of surprise when they do show up.

Alf is a Nordic. I haven't seen Alf but I have read that Nordics are very human like with blond hair and are said to be quite friendly. Anyone who ever does see one would believe they were looking at an angel because of their beautiful looks. It was a Nordic who told the shepherds of the birth of Jesus; well some believe it was.

Yes I am a Nordic and we Nordics have been described as benevolent or even magical beings who want to observe and communicate with you humans. This is very true.

Also it says in Wikipedia that Nordics are concerned about the Earth's environment and prospects for world peace and may transmit messages telepathically. 'Is this true Alf?'

Erm....Yes hello! I'm in your head.

'Oh are... Ha Ha.'

ALIEN INVASION IS COMING...I THINK.

I thought about something Alf said when he said 'it is part of the plan of having the element of surprise when they do show up'.

This got me thinking and wondering why they would want to use the element of surprise. What do these Aliens want from us? Most of all why do they keep abducting humans like me? Then it hit me - anthropology. What the frick does anthropology mean? I hear you ask. Well I'll tell you....anthropology is the study of humans. Why do they want to study us? Because they want to know our strengths and weaknesses before they invade.

'That's it isn't it Alf? We are going to be invaded by Aliens.

I have already..... Never mind, carry on.

It seems to me our only hope is the Nordics, well that's what I tend to think these days since I got to know Alf that is. Well, at least I hope so. I used to ask lots of questions like: What are they doing here? Do they mean us harm? As professor Steven Hawking stated it's not as if they would be friendly is it? He has a very good point I think. I've seen a lot of Alien movies and in most, if not all of them, the Aliens are set on taking over the world. I sometimes wonder if some of these films are kind of subliminal warnings. Somebody is trying to prepare us all for an Alien invasion. I mean, apart from ET, all the Aliens in the films I've ever seen want to kill us and take over the world. This got me thinking of a real life scenario; if this was to ever happen, and I have done many scenarios in my head...

I bet you have

..And I came to the conclusion if we were invaded by Aliens we would lose. That's right we would be screwed against any Alien invasion. Why? Because, if they have the technology to get here in the first place from the far reaches of space, what makes us sheep think we have the technology anywhere close to theirs to fight the fuckers if they were hostile? I think we must be aware they could attack us at any time. There is a real threat of an Alien Invasion, so much so that the government have put a contingency plan in place just in case they do. What's that tell you?

Well, don't worry about the element of surprise. You will know an Alien invasion is imminent if the government right out of the blue do a public announcement telling us all that a terrorist group has entered the country with a Nuke. You will probably be told they plan to detonate this bomb in a major city. If this ever happens make peace with your maker. I say all this but I have my suspicions the government are working with the Enemy.

I am a true believer in Aliens now and it amazes me sometimes why so many sheeple don't believe in them? If you're one of those non-believers well you should start to think about the 'what ifs'. I tell you now they are real or why would the government go to so much trouble and expense in hiding the fact? That's unless they are working with them. The reason we haven't been taken over just yet is because they don't need to; they just want us to be their slaves. Check out:

www.thewatcherfiles.com/cooper/operation_majority.htm

Just because it sounds a little far-fetched at the moment it doesn't mean they don't exist. When you do look you will start to see them and then you will believe. This book is to get you ready for that day. If you never see one you're not looking hard enough. They are there, I promise you. Unfortunately we are too primitive in our mental development to accept anything different. But to see is to believe.

'If you put the ETs in the middle, you begin to see the pieces of the puzzle. It is a fact and absolute fact. They do exist." William (Bill) Cooper

(FACT) Milton William Cooper was a member of the Intelligence Briefing Team of the Commander in Chief of the Pacific Fleet as a Petty Officer in the United States Navy and the author of a very controversial book called *Behold a Pale Horse*. He was one of the first sheeple to expose the government for the Alien cover up. When he did they didn't like it so he was killed by the Authorities on 5th November 2001.

And I looked, and behold, a pale horse! And its rider's name was Death
The Bible Revelation 6-8

Reader, have you ever seen a UFO? I want to talk about UFOs now.

Go on then

THE UFO PHENOMENA

A UFO is an Unidentified Flying Object, so if you didn't know what one was you do now. However, it doesn't mean every UFO you see is an Alien spaceship with Aliens on board flying the thing. But there is a very good chance the UFO you saw originated from Alien technology; at least this is what I believe is the case. I like most sheeple once thought it was all bollocks about Aliens and UFOs.

When I used to read or hear that some sheep had seen a UFO I would look at them as if they were some sort of crackpot. Surely it was just a shooting star they saw? But now, since I think I was abducted by the little bastards and was not just dreaming it, I have a keen interest in these phenomena. I like to read all I can about UFO sightings and any other Alien-related topics that are reported on the inter-web or elsewhere. Do you know I was amazed to find out that there is a huge amount of evidence to prove UFOs are for real? Alien spaceships are for real.

I and loads of other sheep have had a close encounter of the fourth kind; there is loads of evidence to back up claims that Aliens abduct sheeple. If you take the time to look for yourself you will see as it is widely available on the Inter-web for every sheep to find. So perhaps you should take all this Alien malarkey a bit more seriously and learn to accept that there is more going on than we are led to believe. So listen up you non-believers, listen to me... I'm telling you now they do exist and that's a FACT.

The first step to being liberated from your chastity and enslavement is to accept Aliens do exist. Then and only then do have a chance to be free again.

I remember reading somewhere that the reason we have advanced in technology as rapidly as we have is because we made friends with the Greys and they have shared their advanced technology with us ever since. President Eisenhower apparently met with these Greys, shook hands and made a formal treaty between them and the United States in 1954. In return for this Alien technology, which helped us in our own technological development, Eisenhower gave the Greys permission to abduct humans. He told them they could freely abduct humans on a limited and periodic basis for the purpose of medical examination and understanding of our species. This was as long as those abducted were not be harmed and were returned to the point of their abduction afterwards. So that they were not mentally scarred from the experience they had endured, any memory of the event should be erased. What the frick gave him the right to do that? The government don't give a shit about you as I keep trying to tell you all. What the frick was he thinking?

www.arcturi.com/GreyArchives/USAndGrey's.html

www.dailymail.co.uk/news/article-2100947/Eisenhower-secret-meetings-Aliens-pentagon-consu...

www.thewatcherfiles.com/Alien-treaty.htm

'Because the power and influence of the U.S. Government they decided to make an official contact in the year 1952. Obviously, facts of such an incident have not been disclosed to the public and may never be. Making a deal with the U.S. Government, the Grey Aliens exchanged technology that they once shared with the German Government (Nazi) near the end of WWII. Through this shared technology, the United States was able to make several advancements in micro-

> ***biology, Nano technology, Aerodynamics, Space flight, and much more. With the exchange of this technology they allowed the Grey Aliens the ability to continue their experimentations'***
> ***RCTURI.COM***

This basically meant the freedom to do experiments on us sheeple, hence why some sheeple have been abducted. It is thanks to your very own government this is going on. The rate of abduction climbed dramatically at one time, but it's calmed down a bit now. Even so the government are bastards in my opinion for allowing this to happen.

There are thousands of sheeple all around the world who say they have seen a UFO. You might have seen one, or at least thought you had, or you might just know somebody who says they have. If so many sheeple reported seeing one that means there are a lot about. Our governments for a very long time fobbed these reports off. If you reported seeing a UFO back in the fifties you were probably laughed out of the building, then watched or threatened to keep quiet. But I can tell you now the government are not only too aware of their existence they work closely with the Aliens today. Before they did become mutual friends so-to-speak they took every UFO report that came their way very seriously indeed. Behind closed doors they investigated every single one with immense interest. You may have heard of The Blue Book Project which started in 1952, seven years after the Second World War as it happens.

The Blue Book Project was set up to investigate specifically the UFO phenomena and it had two goals in mind (one) to determine if UFOs were a threat to national security and (two) to scientifically analyse UFO-related data. So see, there you go, even government wanted to understand more about UFOs because they have always known they were for real. But where they came from and what they wanted was a mystery. Yes, the government have known about UFOs for a very long time and every claim brought to them was taken very seriously indeed. Otherwise, why bother setting up the Blue Book Project?

Where did you get this information from?

In Wikipedia and other sources I also found out The Blue Book Project ended in December 1969. During its investigations they are said to have collected over twelve thousand six hundred and eighteen UFO reports. They concluded that most of them were, as first suspected, just misidentifications of natural phenomena such as cloud formations, stars, etc. or secret military aircraft. Only a small percentage of UFO reports were classified as unexplained (a proper Unknown Flying Object). Even after stringent analysis they could not come up with a conclusion to what they saw.

The only reason some of these UFO reports are available now is because of the Freedom of Information Act 1996. You may or may not know that this Act has always been there, just not many sheeple knew about it until 1996. Under this Act every sheep has the freedom to read all reports about UFOs investigated since 1952. You can even find information of reports before that. It's not a new thing, UFO sightings go back hundreds of years. Christopher Columbus made a report of strange lights when he sailed around the world. But all the sightings from 1952 were added to the Blue Book Project.

Yes, but did you also know even with the Freedom of Information Act all names and other personal information of every witness was redacted; that some of the evidence was edited by the redactor. This is when they add elements of their own to hide the truth. So, even though you think you are reading actual reports into the evidence of UFOs, you're not getting it all because a lot of it is still hidden from the public.

'Why?'

I'll tell you why, because they feel it would be a threat to national security that's why. They know if you humans knew all the truth it could cause widespread panic.

'True, you're right, Alf. A lot of sheeple would find the truth very hard to handle I reckon. Even though The Blue Book

Project is finished you can bet your arse that the investigation into UFOs continues, but the evidence they gather this time will never be made public again.'

That's true also and there is a reason why. I will explain later.

Things have moved on since the first reports into UFOs and I reckon the government use what they have learned from these Aliens against us sheep. They have been fully aware of their existence for many years but what they tried to do all this time is understand their technology and what they could do with it. I guess they also wanted to know what they were dealing with in case the Aliens turned hostile.

I will explain what is going on later but for now why don't you talk about Alien technology?

'Alien technology, okay, but what do I know about Alien technology?

Hang on I'll zap you.

ALIEN TECHNOLOGY

It seems every UFO spotted is not always an Alien spaceship, with Aliens on board flying them, but there is a very good chance the science behind them originates from Alien technology. What I mean by this is that some UFOs seen by sheeple fifty to sixty years ago that were entered into the Blue Book files were in fact home-developed secret military aircraft. I can tell you there are a lot of them out there. Most have such advanced technology incorporated into them it would blow your mind. I can assure you, from what I have read, they have military aircraft out there that far outclassed the well-known stealth bomber, for instance. The stealth bomber was actually invented in 1902; it sat for years as a drawing and only came to be constructed after years of research into the said Alien technology. All this stemmed from the recovery of debris from a UFO that crashed in a small town called Aurora in Texas in 1897. Records say that on April 19th 1897 a slow moving UFO crashed into a windmill and burst into pieces. As the debris was searched a small Alien body was discovered

www.rense.com/general3/aurora.htm

Many witnesses backed this up and they even gave the Alien a Christian burial when he died. I believe this was the first real proof that Aliens exist and as you can imagine it was instantly covered up, only revealed to the public in the last ten years or so.

The world since this very significant event hasn't been the same and, although reports of UFOs go back hundreds of years, this was the first time in the 'modern world' that they had their hands on Alien technology, the debris from the crash. A lot of it was pushed down a well but a lot of it disappeared.

You have been busy.

What we did with this new technology was another thing. We could have used it in a positive way but it seems we didn't. It took many years after this historic event before we got to grips with what we found. When we did discover the capabilities of this technology, what happened next changed the world we thought we knew forever. One of those significant events to kick start the new technological world was when somebody realized it was possible for a craft to fly, carrying a person.

> ***The Wright brothers began their experimentation in flight in 1896 at their bicycle shop in Dayton, Ohio. They selected the beach at Kitty Hawk as their proving ground because of the constant wind that added lift to their craft. In 1902 they came to the beach with their glider and made more than seven hundred successful flights. www.eyewitnesstohistory.com/wright.htm***

Take note of the date 1896. This was the year before the Aurora incident. I bet the Wright brothers got their first idea of flying from being abducted by Aliens or from seeing a UFO in the sky; at least this is what I think. We will probably never know for sure but it's a theory nevertheless.

Okay, I understand that there are a lot of sheeple out there who still don't believe in Aliens and that's up to you. It's hard to believe in something you haven't seen or experienced yourself. There is always a big question mark when you talk about Aliens and their existence; that's understandable, but this is for real my fellow sheep, take it from me. If you wish to bury your head in the sand you do that by all means, you are free to believe in whatever you want that's your prerogative. All I ask is you keep an open mind and check out the evidence widely available via the Inter-web before you become judgemental. I really think you should take the time to check some of the evidence; I've not made all this up, you know.

He's right you should.

A Ram named Ben Rich, general manager of Skunk Works (Skunk Works was responsible for a number of famous aircraft designs including the Stealth Bomber) admitted on his deathbed in January 1995 that Aliens were real and that the American military travelled among the stars with them. His statement helped give credibility to reports that the US military had flying means that mimicked the Alien UFOs that some sheeple had seen, thinking they were Alien spacecraft. Not all you see in the sky is flown by Aliens. It's all to do with reverse technology.

Alien-are-real-ufo.blogspot.com/.../fathers-of-stealth-technology-admit-are.html

I have read into this in great depth and it seems that the Stealth Bomber only came about as a result of reverse technology from a UFO crashing here on Earth. We all know about the one that came down on rancher Mack Brazel's property near Roswell in New Mexico in 1947. I bet you didn't know about the Alien craft recovered after it crashed in Russia the year after. It was kept in a secret location called Kapustin Yar, a secret base of the former Soviet Union similar to the American Area 51. Known as the Russian Roswell, in 1948 the Russian military recovered a flying saucer that crashed and it was also alleged they too found Alien bodies just like Roswell.

zighydevourer.wordpress.com/.../1947-ufo-kapustin-yar-the-russian-area-51/

By the way, talking about Area 51, did you know this isn't the only secret base on the planet that could be housing Aliens? No, there are loads. Aliens are living all over the globe in fact. See secret bases:

www.gizmodo.com/.../15-super-secret-bases-that-everybody-seems-to-know-about/

So you see UFOs crash on Earth all the time, just most of them aren't reported. I bet you didn't know that a UFO crashed here on Earth ten years before Roswell? That's right, it happened in Germany 1937. As Nazi Germany rose from the ashes of the old German Republic and became the world's first super power an Alien craft, a flying saucer, lost control and crashed onto the countryside of Germany. This was two years before World War Two kicked off, which I thought was interesting.

It might be just a coincidence but I noticed that every time one crashed we were in the midst of war, or war followed soon after. Was this the Alien's agenda to start wars and get us to kill each other? This German UFO was covered-up by both the US and USSR for more than seventy years. I bet you also didn't know that Adolph Hitler himself tried to do some reverse technology of his own. After that UFO crash of 1937 he tried to manufacture his own flying discs to aid his war effort. Thankfully he wasn't successful because I think if he had mastered the technology back then we would have been fucked. The War would have turned out very differently indeed.

Let me make it clear, all your major governments from the USSR, USA, UK, China and India know of Alien Flying Objects' (AFOs) and have done for years. At first it scared the crap out of them but you may have noticed we haven't been invaded by Aliens flying them or had a World War for a very long time. So have the governments of the world all made friends with each other or are the Aliens pulling the strings now?

'Well are they Alf?'

More than you may think.

'Look I know Aliens are for real so what are they up to Alf?'

I reckon at first, when the governments of the world didn't know what was flying in the skies above them, they thought it was some sort of new technological development. I guess they all wanted to find out more about what they had seen. I bet loads of investigations kicked off back in the day, such as the said Blue Book Project of 1952, not specifically to research Alien crafts but secret military aircraft of rival countries. At first each must have thought the other had developed some form of advanced fighter plane; until they found out different. Before they realized it was extra-terrestrial technology they were dealing with, before any of these UFO crashes took place, I think they felt quite vulnerable, especially Russia and America who have always been rivals. So both of these super powers must have felt very threatened by one another, each one thinking the other had advanced military technology that they didn't have. I believe now that this was one of the major causes of the tensions that added to the Cold War of 1947 to 1991.

A lot of humans don't know this but the reason the Cold War eventually did come to an end was because of an incident that happened in a place called Shaitan Mazar in Russia on August 28th 1991.

'What happened on August 28th 1991?'

Look it up.

'I will Alf.'

RUSSIAN ALIENS: AUGUST 28TH 1991

It is documented that an extremely large UFO approximately six hundred meters long and one hundred and ten meters in diameter appeared over the Caspian Sea, showing on all radar screens of tracking stations of the Mangyshlak peninsula. The radar showed a UFO moving at the speed of six thousand three hundred miles per hour, at an altitude of twenty-one thousand

feet. Two MIG 29 fighters were diverted from a routine mission and two others were scrambled from the peninsula to interact with this UFO. When they reached visual range of it they were shocked to see a gigantic, elongated metallic grey object. They reported it in and were ordered to force it to land and if it doesn't comply to shoot it down. It didn't comply so as the pilots squeezed their triggers to shoot it down there was no response from their controls, none of the electrical systems of their jets worked, the cockpit controls were all but dead, and then to make matters worse the engines began to fail and sputter. With this the UFO began to pull away at speed from the MIGs and approximately forty-five minutes later the UFO simply vanished from all radar screens. www.ufocasebook.com?Russia.html

It was at this point I think the Russian Government knew this had nothing to do with the United States who may have developed superior technology. They must have realized that there was a greater threat from an Alien Invasion. Do you know I think they were right? Just because we haven't been invaded yet, doesn't mean it won't happen one day in the future. I say this but to be fair I think the governments of the world are, as we speak, preparing for the probability of such an invasion. I wouldn't be surprised if they were working with what they know already to try and advance in technology so that they can defend against such an invasion. That is why they are eager to catch UFOs or get their hands on Aliens so they can learn as much as they can from them as possible. That is exactly what the Aliens do to us when they abduct sheeple like me and fly UFOs near our military bases. They test our defences and learn all about us.

I think to the Russians this was a lot more to worry about than the Americans dropping a nuke on them. Since then I think that both the Americans and the Russians have shared their evidence of UFOs with one another and have started working together in joint efforts to protect our planet against whatever threatens it.

Now years later the whole world is jointly united in protecting Earth from space threats, whatever they may be.

Well they did once but not anymore.

'Why, Alf?'

Because the Russians now know the Americans are working with the Aliens.

'Say what??'

www.sott.net/.../263190-FEMA-Russian-Emergencies-Ministry-to-join-forces-against-space-threat

www.spacemart.com/.../Russia_US_to_join_forces_against_space_threats_999.html

Don't you think it is ironic how loads of sheeple who said they had seen a UFO were once told they were seeing things or mistaken? They were told that there was always a perfectly logical explanation to what they thought they saw, other than a UFO. But when the government started seeing UFOs themselves they were threatened to keep quiet about what they saw. Sightings of UFOs over the years are more frequently reported and no, it's not because the sheeple are making it up, like some think. I bet a lot do think that but not the majority, they are reporting what they saw. Sheep are starting to notice them more and more because I think they are increasing in quantity. It is also thanks to the modern Alien technology we have today such as the cell phone. That's right your cell phone. You may not know this but cell phones are thanks to Alien technology.

We live in a world of smart phones and stupid sheeple. MAF

Your digital camera and your laptop are also thanks to Alien technology. Although the first ever computers were invented by Rams, with Alien technology they got more advanced and compact.

Some good has come from scientific projects, I'm not disputing that, but you humans had a chance to use this gift of

technology and science for the good of all life on Earth, yet I begin to think you have basically abused it.

Thanks to this Alien technology a lot, and I mean a lot, of sheeple are able to catch footage of them in the skies and the seas; that's right seas. Some UFOs have even been spotted entering and exiting the sea or lakes and these are called USOs (Unidentified Submerged Objects). When they do catch something weird like a UFO or a USO on their phone or a camera they are swiftly downloaded onto YouTube for the whole world to see. But don't think for a moment the government aren't keeping a keen eye on what is downloaded onto websites such as YouTube because they are. If it is unmistakably an Alien craft they will remove it off the net straight away, because they don't want you to know the truth, but thankfully some get through the net. A lot of the very good video footage of UFOs and USOs was taken off line to hide the truth by government officials under the Official Secrets Act or National Security Agency.

Their aim is to make it look like a hoax because they don't want you humans to know the truth of their existence. Not just yet anyway.

www.ufoevidence.org/Government.htm

www.rense.com/politics6/secdocs.htm

When you think how good the technology is on your camera phones and the advanced umpteen surveillance cameras that we have now all over the planet, you can be pretty damn sure that somebody somewhere caught something unexplained. What they think they saw has been caught on some sort of device so that you know it was for real and not a figment of your own imagination. The government would like you to think it was just a figment of your imagination but because of Alien technology you can get the concrete evidence to prove what you saw was for real. These days usually there are many other sheeple who saw what you saw too, which will back you up.

So, no matter what type of cover up the government tries to put in place, sooner or later they will have no option but to come clean and tell us what they know. But I think they postpone it because they want to manipulate the truth for their own ends. As far as I am concerned the government can no longer ignore when there are reports of UFOs or USOs because of the clear indisputable evidence that is at hand. The factual evidence prevents them from just fobbing it off all the time like they used to, saying it was just a weather phenomenon, shooting star, satellite; the sheeple no longer buy it.

So I tell you now, you can be pretty damn sure if it looks like an Alien spaceship it probably is one. Did you know that there are military personnel, police officers and judges all reporting sightings of UFOs all the time? These are well-respected peers of our community. So remember, every flying craft you see passing over your head isn't always a plane. Every cloud isn't just a cloud. Every light you see in a night sky floating by isn't a satellite or shooting star. Every object spotted in the sea oceans and lakes is not a boat. It is most probably an Alien spacecraft or at the very least a military aircraft built from Alien technology.

We Nordics have bases under the sea and lakes all around the world but you will never find them. It might be one of our crafts you see.

See, my sheepy little friends, Aliens are here and at the moment I don't think they are hostile.

Not at the moment.

But whatever they are they are most definitely very real. If all this worries you then good, you should worry. It might make you wake up and take note of what's happening on your planet. If this goes against your religious beliefs, tough. I think religion was invented because of Alien existence anyway.

We will be talking about religion later

The evidence is vast you just need to seek it out. Have a break now and check out *Aliens Caught on Camera* YouTube

UFOs ARE REAL

It is thanks to the advancement in technology given to us by Aliens that we now have the ability to do this. Thanks to video surveillance, digital cameras and cell phone technology we can gather these facts for ourselves and, because we can, I wouldn't be surprised if the government are now shitting themselves that we will someday work it all out. There may come a point when the government will have to come clean with us about Aliens and the consequences of telling us we might be invaded by them could be devastating, but it will also unite the sheeple right across the world.

Fear is a powerful weapon and because of this fear I believe the government may one day stage an Alien invasion or, at the very least, tell us they made contact and are unsure if they are friendly. This would give the world governments power to implement new rules to control the sheeple. The sheeple would be more than willing to accept anything thrown at them as long as they thought they were protected from a possible Alien invasion.

MICKY FRICK'S TIP

ALWAYS TAKE THE TIME TO LOOK UP TO THE NIGHT SKY; YOU MAY SPOT SOMETHING OUT OF THIS WORLD

I, like you, am keen to know the truth. There are too many sheeple out there similar to me who sound like nutters when they say they believe in Aliens. So, as you can imagine, I was interested to find out all I could about UFOs and Aliens and have been on the Inter-web a lot to do just that. I can tell you categorically, with my hand on heart.... Aliens exist without a shadow of a doubt. Just check out all the footage you can find on YouTube; not all you see is fake. So once I knew for sure they were for real I then wanted to know why they were here. What is it they want? Why have they not yet made formal contact with the world? Or if they have, which I believe they have, why are we not told? What's their agenda - that goes for government and Alien? I'm not sure yet but I think Alf will possibly enlighten us later on, and I for one am intrigued with these Anunnaki.

All in good time Michael... but I must commend you on the research you have done. You have been a busy human haven't you? You even sound more intelligent.

'I know I do, don't I? Fuck knows how that happened?'

I have no idea...... possibly thanks to me, your friend.

'I would like to know who is friend and who is foe because at the moment I'm not sure...'

I'm your friend that's all you need know for now. It's the Anunnaki who are not so friendly. We need to talk about them more.

'Okay we can later.'

As you can imagine reader I became really interested in Alien conspiracies, even more so after I read a blog in 2012. It was one that I stumbled across by chance whilst taking a break from my research for this book. As I randomly searched the Inter-web for some porn, I saw a title pop up on my computer monitor called Mind Fuck.

'Do you remember Alf?'

Yes I remember it well........This is when I was worried we Nordics had picked the wrong messenger.

Let me tell you a story.

Here we go again.... sorry reader; I'll zap him again in a minute.

CHAPTER FIVE

WHAT IF WE HAVE ALL BEEN LIVING A LIE?

MIND FUCK

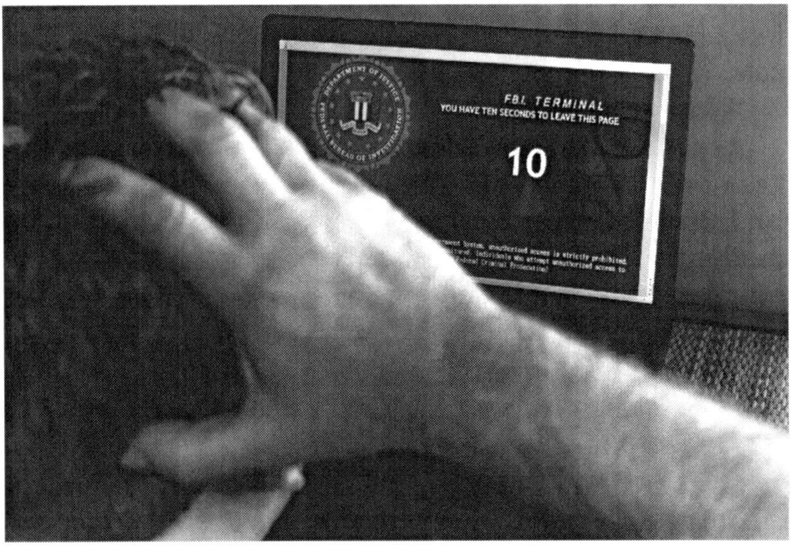

Now I'm not a pervert.

That's debatable......

I'm not a pervert but like most Rams I like to watch porn from time to time. I particularly like to see a Ewe giving head. I've always wondered what that must feel like to have your cock sucked by a Ewe. So I thought I'd have a look at this page called

Mind Fuck; it sounded interesting. As I always do when I watch a bit of porn, I stripped off naked, got some hand cream at the ready and, of course, a can of beer, as you do, and then clicked to open the page. I remember it was a Friday night, the start of the weekend, which was more than welcome after the shit week I'd just had at work. My wife had gone to bed with a headache. Unsurprisingly she knew I felt a bit horny. Do you know it's funny that she always seems to have a headache when I feel a bit horny?

Anyway, being frustrated as I was, you can understand I just wanted a quick release before I went to bed, you know what I mean? There I was with my cock in hand ready to go but to my disappointment 'Mind Fuck' wasn't what I expected. In fact it wasn't anything to do with blow jobs at all. It was a blog written by some guy calling himself Jon Doe. I was just about to click off thinking it was about some puff sucking another Ram's dick or something gay, and I'm not into that, when I saw the heading at the top of the page. It said, 'What you are about to read will blow your mind, because everything you think you know is all lies.'

It sounded intriguing so I read on and, before I knew it, my cock had gone soft and I was engrossed in the blog. It kept me captivated for two hours or more. This Jon Doe Ram was so right, what I did read blew my mind. In fact I was dumbfounded and stunned, right up to the moment my computer suddenly turned off by itself.

Now before I tell you about that and what I read, be warned, it really is a mind fuck; it fucks with your mind big time. I'll tell you something else an' all, after long hours of researching what I'd read, with Alf's help of course, it posed yet another question. What if? What if all I read by this Jon Doe was true?

It would be fair to say this is possibly the point when I got really paranoid. Of course I now know that I wasn't just being paranoid for silly reasons, it seemed that I, like you, was misinformed about what was really going on that we don't see. I soon realized that all my life I had been kept in the dark like a mushroom and fed shit.

Let me start by telling you a bit of what I know about Jon Doe before I tell you what he had to say. I'll leave the best bit of what he said for later on but, I warn you again, what I am about to tell you will blow your mind and, what makes it even better still is, this is a true story.

So then...... who was Jon Doe? I say 'was' because I he's dead now.

JON DOE

Jon Doe apparently used to work for the CIA. In his blog he said that he was now retired after many years' service. He explained that before joining the CIA he was in the Armed Forces and at the top of his game in his particular field. He said how much he loved his job, fool. But, to cut a long story short, his life was about to change dramatically.

One day out of the blue he was approached and asked if he would like to join the CIA. Being a young ambitious Ram at the time, without hesitation he said that he would. He was then told that in the meantime he should continue with his regular duties and they would be back in contact with him at a later date.

Some weeks passed then Jon was contacted again. He was given a message to meet a Ram and for the purpose of the blog he stated he changed the Ram's name to Mr Smith. He was asked to meet Mr Smith at a secret location of which he was given directions, asked to memorize them and destroy the note. He did this by putting it in his mouth, chewing it and swallowing it. Once he arrived at this destination he was met by two black cars. As he approached the cars, six Rams dressed in black suits got out of them; one of the Rams walked up to him and introduced himself as Mr Smith. They shook hands and then he was introduced to another Ram who Jon called Mr Jones. It was very 'cloak and dagger' as he recalled.

Jon Doe was then told that he would be working under Mr Jones from now on. Mr Smith then shook his hands, said simply, 'Welcome to the CIA' and got back into the car. Jon was led into the back of the other car and given a plastic ID card with a picture of himself and a new name. He was told he must use the name given to him on the card whilst working for the CIA to protect his true identity. He was told the card gave him access to all US military bases and restricted areas throughout the world.

He was then reminded that he was now a full member of the CIA and this meant he must follow the rules. Rule number one was not to discuss anything he witnessed or working on as from that day forward to anybody; not even to his closest family members or his wife. That was, of course, if he ever chose to marry in the future, as he was single at the time. Every aspect of his job was classed as top secret and he was warned there would be dire consequences if he didn't follow the rules, not only for him but anybody they suspected he has spoken to.

Jon did marry later on in his life. In joining the CIA many years ago he said he had no idea what he had actually signed up for and no idea that his life would be turned upside down from that point forward. He said what he worked on and witnessed was no less than mind-blowing. He stated in his blog that he was an old Ram now and had recently been diagnosed with a terminal illness with only months if not weeks to live.

He said had been holding onto secrets all his life which had been really hard. He explained was not easy living a life as a lie. His wife, his friends, his family, acquaintances, all the sheeple he ever knew or met or loved, never had any idea what he really used to do for a living, and he added they still don't. Jon Doe said he had kept his oath that he gave to the CIA. But since he was diagnosed with this life-threatening illness, and after long hours of consideration, had decided to take this load off his back once and for all and come clean. Knowing so much had been such a tremendous burden to him and the only reason he was breaking his oath now was because he thought the world really needed to know what was going on.

I guess Jon Doe is probably no longer with us, and may he rest in peace, but what I read will stay with me personally forever. I remember reading a sentence he wrote which went along the lines of, and forgive me I am only para quoting, I can't remember it word for word, it went something like this...

'I can assure you all that what I am about to disclose to you has never been revealed before.'

He also said, 'I don't want to go to my grave without the sheeple knowing the truth, the real truth, when they could change the outcome of their fate. I see this blog as a way to come clean on what I know and by not sharing what I know with you is fundamentally wrong. I have lived with the guilt of knowing things that could have saved so many lives, and could still save so many lives even today, it's not too late.'

He continued, 'This was probably going to be my final chance to communicate to the world before I die so there is nothing more for me to fear but so much for the human race to be fearful of.'

PARANOID

This was the moment I thought what have I stumbled on here?

Then he followed that statement with, 'Before you continue please be warned you may put yourself in extreme danger to learn what I have had to keep secret for so many years. Let's just say there are some things they just don't want the people to know, so you may want to consider whether or not if it is in your own interests to continue reading this blog any further, as sometimes not knowing everything is the best call and a luxury that I never had.'

I thought, *oh my, this is interesting*. I should have logged off at that point and looking back I wish I had. But I didn't. I was curious and so I decided to read on against all better judgement. He then disclosed in detail the things that he had been involved in whilst working for the CIA. I can tell you they were fascinating to say the least.

His blog was only online for about two hours before it was swiftly taken off line. I know this because I was reading it at the time when it did just that. I shit myself to be honest because of the way it happened. Even so I feel I must tell you what I did manage to read, if nothing else, as respect to the now deceased Mr Doe. That is, of course, if you want to know, because what I read still haunts me today.

If all that he spoke of is as true as he makes out (and I am now starting to believe it more than ever since I have done my own investigations) it is without a doubt quite worrying to say the least. He wrote about what went on at places like Area 51, for instance. The government's vision of 'World Domination' is without a doubt a frightening read in itself, but the best bit for me was when he said that the government have known about Aliens for years. I thought, knew it! – As you see, this is the subject I cover most in this book.

Jon's blog sounded quite unbelievable and a little far-fetched at first, but as I read on I got more and more immensely interested in the Alien phenomenon. At first it would be fair to say I found it more entertaining than worrying and I didn't take any of it too seriously. This was until I started to look into the Alien phenomenon in more depth and, as you delve deeper, you find out that there are many different Alien species out there. I have only mentioned five.

So anyway, I read this blog with great interest for two hours before something really weird happened and my computer screen went blank. It happened just as I was about to read the bit about the Anunnaki Aliens, 'which was really interesting because you Alf have been on about these too haven't you?'

Yes I have

'There was something else Jon said and that was God being an Alien??'

I know, I know you are itching to know more about the fricking Anunnaki. I promise I'll come to them in due course. Let me just tell you my little story first okay?

Hurry up then

Okay... Anyway, I remember it was about 4am when my screen went blank. I thought at the time my computer had crashed. I swore at it a lot and banged on the monitor but then the unexpected happened; a federal warning popped up in front of me on my monitor saying in block capitals;

'THIS IS A FEDERAL WARNING LEAVE THIS PAGE IMMEDIATELY' and a countdown started ten…nine…eight… seven….six….five….four….three…

Fricking hell, I thought. I instantly logged off my Inter-web, shut down my computer and jumped out of my chair. I stared at the blank monitor in bewilderment. *Oh Fricking hell*, I thought... *I never expected that.*

This was the moment in my life when the world got weird.

'You made me read that,' I said to Alf.

He said, 'yes.'

'That's it no more secrets. Come on if you know what the frick is going on you need to tell me right here and now.'

But he kept silent.

'Speak up you bastard, tell me what you know.'

But Alf was saying nothing.

My wife was fast asleep in bed. I didn't want to disturb her so I dragged myself to the bathroom mirror, shut and locked the bathroom door and turned the shower on to disguise the conversation me and Alf were about to have. The mirror soon steamed up so I wiped it and saw my reflection looking back at me. I looked bewildered. It didn't look like me; it was as if I was looking at a complete stranger. I guess I was tired

'Then we had a bit of a deep discussion, didn't we Alf?'

I don't know about discussion, you did all the talking.

I said, 'Look you and me are now in big shit. We need to work together on this because you saw for yourself there is a very good chance the government will come to get us; when they get here they will arrest us and take us away. So, come on, what do you know?'

I was genuinely concerned but Alf didn't seem to give a shit. For once his voice in my head had nothing to say. I thought I was in extreme danger. I hatched an escape plan in my mind as I interrogated myself to get Alf to talk. I was really edgy because I expected the fricking police (sheep dogs) to burst through my door at any given minute, wielding guns about, tear gas, the lot in full SAS style, all because of what I had just read. After all Jon Doe did warn me it could happen?

It was fair to say I was shitting myself and Alf wasn't letting on to anything. I thought maybe he doesn't know anything? Maybe he is the victim as I am? I needed to calm down so I jumped into the shower and had a wank. I then spent the rest of what was left of the night pacing the house trying to work all this out, with no help from Alf.

Anyway, time ticked by and the house wasn't raided so I did calm down. Then my wife woke up. I remember it was a Saturday morning about nine o'clock. I was by now sitting in the kitchen biting my nails.

She saw me and asked, 'Haven't you been to bed? You look like shit?'

'Good morning to you an' all. No I haven't, as it happens, not after what I experienced last night.'

'Why what happened last night?'

I started to tell her about what I had read and about the federal warning and that. At first she didn't take much notice of me. She just laughed it off, called me an idiot and put the kettle on suggesting it was just somebody messing about. I knew different and now I needed to protect her as I might have put her in danger. She didn't take anything I told her seriously, just kept taking the piss. I insisted she took me seriously. The fear and apprehensiveness in my face and the sweat rolling down my forehead, together with my bloodshot eyes and pale complexion; followed by me neurotically running around stopping her opening the curtains and blinds, finally warranted some concern from her. She took the time to hear me out.

So as we sat down and drank a cup of coffee in which I had stirred in about seven spoons of sugar….

'Where were you? Hey... where were you Alf?'

I was keeping my distance, you were acting crazy.

'Well I was in shock, wasn't I?'

So, anyway, I told her everything. Mind you, not everything. I wanted to protect her like Jon Doe did his family. The way I saw it the less she knew the better, you know what I mean? Mind you what I did tell her she didn't believe, she just kept laughing at me throughout. So I guess it did me no good conversing with her in the first place; she had already made her mind up I was bonkers.

You were acting a bit neurotic Michael.

She threatened to have me committed if I didn't calm down and then insisted I go to bed and have some sleep and forget all about it. So, a little calmer now, I took her advice, I put myself to bed but I couldn't sleep could I? I just couldn't let the experience I just had go from my mind. My head was all over the place; the more I thought about it the more I got worried about it, all the time. I tried to close my mind off and think of other things but that federal warning kept popping back into my brain.

Eventually I must have dropped off because when I woke up again it was Sunday morning. I had slept for fifteen fricking hours, 'kin hell fifteen. I think she drugged my coffee when I wasn't looking or something. Mind you, the long sleep did do me some good because I woke a little calmer still. In a less neurotic manner I tried to tell my wife again about the blog but she just told me to shut up. We had a full blown row in the end, which wasn't my plan at all, and not the greatest way to spend a Sunday. We didn't speak much all afternoon come to that, the atmosphere in the house was quite tense until nightfall.

I tried making things right by smiling at her from across the room every time she looked up at me. But I could see she was still in a vile mood because she had a face like a baboon's arse. She went upstairs to bed and I slept downstairs on the settee that night with the dog, which wasn't a pleasant experience because he kept farting all the time. I tell you, I'm taking him off that Pedigree Chum. I did fall asleep eventually whilst watching a DVD on gardening. I do like gardening but got bored with it and dropped off leaving the TV on, which wasn't clever. The news was on when I woke up; fuck knows what subliminal messages I've been subjected to all night whilst I was a sleep...

Anyway it was soon Monday morning, about four o'clock I think. I woke up cold with the dog licking my face and so, after a good tonguing from him, I sat up. As I attempted to get off the settee I found my leg had gone all numb and, as I stood, I hit the floor with a thump knocking the coffee table over. To make matters worse as I lay on the floor the dog lifted his leg up and pissed on my head. The dirty little..... But it distracted my mind for a while. Then I thought, *oh fuck, I forgot the government are after me int they*?

I then tried to get up off the floor but the pins and needles sensation kicked in and I hopped around the room like a marching German soldier, just as my wife walked into the room.

'What's going on?' What's all the noise?'

'I fell over. My leg has gone numb int it?'

'Like your brain, what's that awful smell?'

'Piss. Doofy has just pissed on my head'

She smiled, which I didn't expect. 'Good boy' she said, and then she gave the dog a big fuss. It wasn't long before I started to feel my leg again without it feeling like an electric shock every time I put my foot to the floor.

'Go and have a wash, you stink,' said my wife lovingly… not. 'I'll clean this mess up for you.'

She was still a bit pissed off with me from the day before. I thought it best to get out of her way for a minute or so and have another shower.

'Okay,' I said, 'once the pins and needles wear off.'

When eventually they did I ventured towards the stairs to head for the bathroom. As I set foot on the first step my wife shouted to me.

'Whilst you're up there you can shave that fungus off your face an' all. Smelling like a tramp is one thing, looking like one is another.'

To be fair two days had almost passed since I read that blog and I hadn't had a shave at all, and beards are one of my wife's pet hates; she has never liked them. So to please her and possibly win back some brownie points I shouted down to her, as I proceeded upwards, that I would shave it off. But when I got to the bathroom and looked into the mirror I thought *what a great disguise a beard is*. So I had second thoughts and decided to leave it. I just had a good shower, got dry, combed my hair, brushed my teeth and went back downstairs again, smelling a lot better at least,

My wife sat at the kitchen table reading a magazine, flicking the pages over with one hand and a piece of toast in the other. She took a large bite from the toast and happily munched away. The aroma of toast filled the air and was a very nice smell; it made me want some myself. I walked over to the bread bin, opened it up and reached for the loaf inside. I was pleased to see it was extra thick bread as I like extra thick bread. I took two slices out of the wrapping and proceeded to the toaster. We have one of them electric ones that you drop your bread in and just push down the lever to cook it. On my way across the kitchen I made sure to hold the bread slices up in front of my face. I wanted to hide from her the fact I hadn't shaved.

She casually looked up at me and said, 'I'll have another one of them please?'

I had my back to her at this point but I cocked my head to acknowledge her and said, 'Okay my love, no problem.' I walked sideways like a crab towards the bread bin again, just in case she looked my way.

'I thought you were going to have a shave,' she said.

I rubbed my chin and nervously replied, 'I, I, I thought I might leave it for a while since I'm off work.'

'What do you mean off work?'

'I was thinking of phoning in sick.'

I glanced sheepishly over my shoulder smiling, waiting to see her response.

'What you mean phone in sick?'

I strolled back over to the toaster, dropped in the piece of bread and pushed down the lever.

'I thought...well I thought I would phone in sick today.'

'Why? There's nothing wrong with you.'

'Well…I, I, I've been feeling a bit peculiar just lately and I'm very tired, I think I might be coming down with flu, or something; thought I may need some time off.'

She frowned at me, closed her magazine and bit into the toast. I say bit into it more like snapped at it and almost grunted as she chewed.

'Tell you what,' she said, munching away and grunting, 'I'll phone in sick too shall I? Fuck work shall we? Let's both go off together; that'll be nice won't it?'

She bit into the toast and I could see she was annoyed with me yet again. I turned and smiled at her and in a more concerning tone I said to her, 'Oh …... yes why not. You should phone in sick my love if you want to. You look a bit rough yourself.'

At this point I thought *what a great fricking idea if she was to go sick as well as me*. We could both keep a low profile for a while until the dust settled. With both of us sick we could keep out of sight.

'What, you're saying I look rough now are you?'

'No, no not rough as in rough.... you know my love tired....'

'Tired and rough,' she yelled. 'I'm fucking tired because some imbecile woke me up.'

'Who?'

'YOU!'

'Shhhhhhhh you'll wake the neighbours,' I said.

She just threw the magazine at my head.

'See, see, the more I think about it the more I think it is a great idea you should phone in sick too. To be honest you do seem a little bit stressed just lately, you might..............'

'Stressed? Stressed? It's you who's making me pissing stressed,' she snapped, spitting toast as she spoke.

'See there you go, you can see you're stressed. Tell the doctor you're stressed. The doctor will give you a note for stress and I'll tell work I have a bad back or something.'

'HUH! God give me strength.'

The toast I put in earlier popped up. I grabbed the slices, reached for the knife and butter and spread it all over evenly. It melted into the hot toast almost straight away and I passed her one slice.

'This'll make you feel better. Here you are my love.'

She snatched it out of my hand

'Ta,' she said. 'You know why you are tired don't you? It's because you were up all Friday night reading that crap about Play Doe.'

'Jon Doe, and it's not crap either.'

I bit into the toast, butter dripped on my stubble as she watched.

'That's disgusting! Have a shave for fuck's sake. You know I don't like beards.'

'Well, I think it makes me look rugged and manly like.'

I stuck my chest out, gritted my teeth and growled like a bear. 'It's a good look for me.'

She shook her head but it did raise a smile from her. 'Yea it is, if you think the look of a hairy arse is a good look for you?' She gave me a sarcastic grin back.

'Ha, ha, very funny; see you're feeling better already?' I replied, somewhat relieved she was making jokes. I walked to her and leaned over to give her a kiss but she blocked me instantly with her toast in hand.

'Don't think you're coming anywhere near me with that fungus growing all over your face, bum head.'

Feeling rather rejected, but kind of understanding her response because I guess she was probably still pissed at me, I just backed off. I thought, *best not push my luck, a smile will do for now*. Then the other toast popped up out of the toaster so I walked over to retrieve it.

What my wife didn't understand was the reason I hadn't shaved was an attempt to try and disguise my appearance. I needed it to grow for a few more days at least before I ventured outside. I was sure by now that I was being hunted by everybody. I needed a good disguise and the beard was it. I mean Scotland Yard, the CIA, FBI and even NCIS were looking for me by now I reckoned ...Well I say NCIS, my Dad was once in the navy so you never know do ya? NCIS might get involved. Do they actually exist? Doesn't matter......

So anyway up, I thought I was probably on the most wanted list all around the world and very soon would have a bounty on my head. So I thought I needed to disappear somehow or at least blend into the background so to speak. If I grew a beard and let my hair grow a bit longer it wouldn't look like any photos they had of me. This was something I realized after looking at some family photos. I had never had a beard before so I thought it was a great idea for a disguise. So my plan was to grow a beard, not just a goatee but a full blown one, the scruffier the better. *Brilliant idea*, I thought, *because the worst scenario is they'll think I'm my brother if they see me walking from the house looking like a scruff; they'll think I'm him because he is always an unshaven, scruffy git and I look* a *bit like him with stubble.* It was no good me trying to look like my other brother because he has a moustache and that's not a good enough disguise. I thought, *I would just look like Freddy Mercury and everybody knows he's dead.*

At first the main reason for the disguise was so I could walk to the doctors and back without being spotted, especially after my self cert ran out on Friday. When it did I had no intention of returning to work the week after either. I would, at some point, need a sick note from the doctor to hand in at work to cover me for a couple more weeks.

So for the rest of the week I sat down and statistically worked it all out on a piece of paper in fine detail. Eventually I came up with a brilliant plan, at least one I was happy with, and if it all went to plan it would buy me some time. All I needed to do was get a sick note from the doctor for a few weeks then build a hideaway in the woods, somewhere remote. It could dig an underground base and stock it out with food and water. Time was of the essence; remember I thought I was a hunted man at the time.

The plan I made went something along these lines.

First thing was I would get my wife to phone work for me and tell them I wouldn't be in for the rest of the week. A bit of a setback was my wife decided to go to work in the end which I rather she hadn't, but there's no talking to her. So my plan was this, get her to phone in sick for me, then on Wednesday she could make me an appointment to see my doctor for the Friday. She would do this from her place of work because they would be tapping my phone now, that's for sure. I'd tell her to make my appointment for about eleven o'clock on Friday morning. I would leave the house at about ten on Friday when everybody was at work and rush hour was over, so the roads were less busy. That way I'd be able to spot any suspicious cars going up and down the street or any black vans with darkened windows parked up or any suspicious sheeple walking about, that kind of thing. I also needed to plan as many escape routes along the way as I could think of. Since I know the area well this shouldn't be too hard. That way if I needed to lose anybody tailing me I could make a swift getaway down one of the back alleys, my bolt holes if you like.

As well as my beard as a disguise I also thought about my appearance overall. What to wear? I had to think what I could wear that was good enough so that, if anybody who bumped into knew me, even they wouldn't recognize me. I bet the CIA without a doubt was watching all my friends and family members to get at me. So my best disguise I came up with was to pretend to be an Irish Ram. Besides it's the only accent I can do other than cockney and that would stand out too much because I live over a hundred miles from London; you don't normally see many Londoners around here. But there are a few Irish sheeple scattered about. It's a shame I can't talk Bengali or Polish, but I can't.

As I worked out my plan, supping on a cup of coffee, I had a second thought pop into my brain about looking like my brother. Because when I thought about it, he has loads of friends and what if one of his friends stops me thinking I'm him, then sees I'm not him and, bang, my cover would be blown. *That's a bloody good point*, I thought….. No I had to be a sheep nobody would know or recognise at all. It took me some time but I soon had it all worked out in my head what I needed to do. To be fair it was a brilliant plan, if I say so myself, I felt confident that it would all work out just great.

So Friday came and it was time to go to the doctors as planned. Up until now the plan had been faultless and so I was ready. I had five days' growth on the old beard and I was looking good, well scruffy good that is.

At one point it looked like my plan was going to fall apart… when my wife piped up, 'I'll come with you.'

'WHAT!'

'I'll come with you.'

'What you mean you'll come with me? Haven't you got to go to work?' I asked thinking, *shit; this has put a spanner in the works.*

'No,' she said. 'I told you I've got today off. You never listen to me; that's your problem.'

'Shit, shit, shit,' I muttered to myself under my breath.

I forgot she had this fricking Friday off, damn it, now she could blow my cover. If she walks out this house with me it could put us both in great danger…what am I going to do now? She can't come.

'Why do you want to come?' I asked, 'I'm only going to the doctors.'

'Yeah and I thought I'd do a bit of shopping whilst you're at the doctors. You don't have a problem with that do you? Anyway we need bread and milk.'

Damn it! This wasn't part of my plan at all, I thought, *I forgot she had the day off, fuck, fuck, fuck...I wanted to go alone. That's it I'm going to be exposed now, shit.* But I couldn't avoid it, she was coming. I got increasingly nervous. I had to think of something quick to prevent disaster.

Then I thought... *Got it... I'll pretend I don't know her.* My wife stood by the door looking inside her bag.

'Are you ready?' she asked as she put her handbag on her shoulder, holding a set of keys.

'Yes, give me a minute my love,' I said as I finished tying my shoelaces. At this point I proceeded outside. *This is it*, I thought. *It's time to put my plan into action. I need to put all my acting skills into action. Firstly get into character.*

I stood up, looked into the mirror and quickly tested my Irish accent. 'To be true to be true, I'll have a Guinness tank ye kindly.' Brilliant, I thought, *I've got that cracked*, now *for the limp*. I decided it would be good to add to the character if I gave myself a limp, frick knows why but somehow it made me feel like I was properly acting. So I limped out of the house.

My wife saw me limping and said, 'What you done? Hurt your leg?'

'Shhhhh. No just cramp again I tink.'

'You should have that checked out too whilst you're at the doctors, you've suffered a lot with cramp just lately, you might have a blood clot or something'

'Thanks....I'm okay it comes and goes. Anyway come on let's go, I'm going to be late for my appointment.'

It's true I did walk with a limp prior to this acting thingy-ma-jig. The reason is I think I subconsciously look for sympathy. I do that from time to time; it never works but I still do it. I think stress brings on a limp. Anyway fuck that. So my wife and I left the house. I pulled the hood of my coat over my face as we stepped out into the drive; luckily it was drizzling a bit so wearing a hood was perfectly acceptable considering the weather. The wife said nothing. It was only a short walk to the doctors and the local shops but because of my pretend 'bad leg' my wife suggested we use the car. I snapped at the suggestion right away

'NO! We don't need to go in the car, I'm okay,' I said.

'Are you sure?' she said. 'What about your bad leg?'

'It's okay, besides walking gives me chance to walk it off. It will do it good. Come on let's go, it's going to piss down in a minute.'

'If we go in the car we won't get wet,' she muttered.

I thought, *fricking hell I can't use the car it could have a tracking devise fitted to it by now or, worse, be wired to blow up as soon as you turn the ignition key, I've seen that happen in movies......* So I insisted to my wife we walk, or rather I demanded. So I limped and she walked to town. As we went down the road I straight away noticed two Rams walking towards us. They came as if from nowhere and they were in black suits which made me really nervous. *Fricking hell,* I thought, *it didn't take them long to find me did it? The frickin CIA 'Rams in black' have found me already. Fuck it I'm dead........we are going to die unless they don't realize who I am.*

So I put my acting skills to work and started to act proper Irish which I reckon was very good to be fair. I thought pretending I was Irish was an ingenious idea on my part; it was time to see if I could really pull it off.

I was still somewhat nervous the closer these two Rams got so I thought *how can I enhance my Irishness*? *Got it, I'll river dance.* So I started to river dance as they approached and made up a little Irish tune on the spot to go with it. Because I know Irish sheeple like to sing as well as dance; you will find that if you ever go to Dublin as it's a well-known fact.....anyway my ditty went something like this,

'Diddley diddley diddley dee
Diddley diddley diddley dee
Diddley diddley diddley dee
Diddley diddley diddley dee'

As the Rams got even closer I continued to dance my heart out and sing my merry little tune. It is quite hard to do both I can tell you. My wife was so far in front that if it all kicked off she wouldn't be able to assist me in any way. If the CIA apprehended me I was fucked. She wasn't even in arms reach to hit them with her handbag. I was on my own now.

So, as the two Rams got even closer to me, to emphasize being proper Irish and in a broad Irish accent, the best I could muster, I said to the Rams as they approached, 'Could ye be as so kind as to spare me a few coins for me river dancing?'

I kicked my legs up really high, nearly pulling my back out to tell you the truth and with that I also continued to sing my tune.

'Diddley diddley diddley dee
Diddley diddley diddley dee
Diddley diddley diddley dee
Diddley diddley diddley dee'

My arms were stiff and straight by my side. I was just like that Michael Flatley Ram. They both laughed as they watched me dance. I think I farted at this point, I was that nervous. One of them reached into his pocket and I thought *here we go, he's going for his gun or knife I'm dead*. But it wasn't, it was just a coin.

'Ere you are mate,' and he handed me a pound coin and carried on walking. 'Love the dancing mate' and they both continued to laugh as they walked on by.

I replied, 'Ah tank you kindly. Top o' the mornin' to ya both! If you ever need your drive tarmacked look me up.....?'

I continued to river dance my way up to my wife who had marched way ahead of me. I found it hard to keep up I was knackered by now..... I kept looking over my shoulder just to make sure them two Rams kept walking in the other direction. I didn't want them to turn around and come back.

'Hold ye up there wummin!' I shouted, 'Why do yer keep a-marchin away from me?'

Still in an Irish accent; one thing I have learned is you must always keep in character. I learned from years of amateur dramatics.

'Hang on there, me wi lass!! Wummin, lass??' isn't that Scottish slang? Bah... fuck it, who cares... so what if it is? I could be an Irish Scotsman, I mean it's not unknown to have Irish sheeple in Scotland is it? Besides loads of Irish immigrants settled in Scotland back in 1841, I read somewhere, more than anywhere else in Europe as it happens. They'll just think I'm a descendent of one of them won't they? 'Wi I Mac noo by gum to be true, to be true!' Okay maybe I need more practice with accents.

Just get on with your story Michael so we can move on, I feel a zap coming on.

So my wife turned to me and said, 'Do you know you're a fricking embarrassment Paddy? What was that all about back there you fricking idiot?' Not amused with me at all. 'What the fuck is wrong with you? Why the fuck are you suddenly acting like a frigging leprechaun? What's that all about you stupid fool? What's wrong with you, I'm going to have you committed if you don't stop it now?'

I tried to explain to my wife as we walked, or rather limped, on. I told her that I thought the government was after me but she just wasn't having any of it.

'Oh fuck off nutter,' she said, 'you should ask the doctor to look at your head when you see him, you'll be telling me you think the men in black after you next are Aliens?'

'They might be ....' I said.

'Oh fuck off ... it's the men in the white coats you should be worried about,' she said.

'I don't think you are taking this seriously enough love. Can't you see we could both be in real danger because of what I now know? The government are after me and they will want to silence me. And you possibly.'

'Oh fuck off I wish they would silence you....., anyway if the government are after you as you seem to think they are I best not get too close to you...... Now you have a target on your back. I mean if the marksmen from the FBI, CIA, Special Branch want to shoot you they might just miss you and hit me instead...I'm not catching a bullet for you that's for damn sure.'

'That's not funny... anyway they may want to blow me up, not shoot me. They are not bothered what method is used just as long as I'm dead. I'm an enemy of the state I am.'

At that point a Muslim Ewe in full attire pushing a pushchair came around the corner, I thought, *oh fuck.* But thankfully she walked on by. As you can see I was on edge. I was a nervous wreck. I thought, as we made our way to town, that it was a bloody good point about the target on my back; my wife could be on to something there. So I stepped back two paces or more to make distance between me and her. I don't want her to get killed because of me because I do love her even if she doesn't love me.

She just marched ahead so I shouted, 'I'll catch you up my love I think I have cramp again. You carry on my love, don't worry about me.'

She raised her arm, gave me the finger and continued marching. Do you know, I think she used that bit about the marksman as an excuse to get away from me? I can't blame her really. The more I thought about it I don't think an FBI or CIA sniper would miss would they? That thought alone made me even more nervous than I already was and I think I farted again. I was way behind my wife now and I watched as she disappeared over the brow of the hill. Alone I began to look up at the rooftops of houses and buildings I passed, just to be sure I wasn't an easy target for any sniper up there. And I thought it would be a good idea to walk and run alternatively, walk, run, walk then run again. I also mixed this by doing both in a zigzag motion. *Keep moving*, I told myself, *keep moving.* I bent my knees and hid behind every lamp post and every tree I passed because I knew a moving target was harder to hit. I saw that in a movie once too.

Eventually I got to the doctors surgery. My doctor is an Asian Ram with a twitch who winks as he talks to you. I once thought he was a puff and that he fancied me because he kept winking at me all the time, until I was told by some Ram he had a tick, a nervous twitch... I don't know about nervous, I tell you it can be very off-putting being winked at, especially when I once had a rectal examination when I had piles. He winked at me and then walked behind me and shoved his finger right up my arse. Hope it was his finger..... So anyway, he took one look at me, winked and I winked back... Frick knows why I did that...

Anyway, bless him he gave me a month off with stress and a prescription to go with it. I thought, *brilliant at least I don't have to go to work for four weeks*. I thought my plan was a success so far, I could keep a low profile for a month that I wanted. *Great*, I thought, *it'll give me time to move on to plan B and build that hideaway in the woods*.

But for now my only thought was I had to back track home without being shot by an FBI sniper. So I got my prescription from the pharmacy next door and decided I wasn't going to frick about this time, I would go straight home. I left the wife happily shopping and headed home. I thought I'd run all the way but that didn't last long because I'm a bit unfit. So after just a short burst I reverted back to walking again, or should I say limping. This was a real limp this time as I twisted my ankle fricking running. With a combination of zig zagging and limping, running and walking I got home as quickly as I could. I bet I looked pissed to those who saw me but I didn't care, it just added to my disguise; I mean I find most Irish sheeple are usually pissed anyway.

As soon as I got home I locked and bolted the door behind me. I was in a right fricking state by this time I can tell ya. I was sweating like a glass blower's behind, my heart was racing and I even started to tremble; a little adrenaline I suppose or

I was having a panic attack. So I made myself a sweet cup of tea, took one of them pills the doctor prescribed for me and sat down on the sofa thinking I was never going outside again. Fuck that. I then fell asleep as I was fricking exhausted; all the excitement of the day had worn me out good and proper. But I was quietly satisfied my mission was accomplished. I remember I did have another of them weird dreams but I'd be fucked if I could remember it now, but my arse wasn't sore and I didn't have a rash so that was good.

Two weeks into my sick note and I had not ventured out of the house at all. My wife started to get a bit pissed off having me under her feet but I think she was getting concerned. She tried many ways to get me to venture out the house but I just couldn't do it. I lived like a hermit. I was too frightened to even put plan B into motion and build that hideaway in the woods. It got that bad I wouldn't even get out of bed some mornings and I was even frightened to have a wash. I told her I didn't want any visitors although I did have the odd card off well-wishers. I lost my appetite too. It would be fair to say my mind was beginning to get fucked up. I couldn't get that Jon Doe blog out of my head and I kept thinking about all the different things he talked about.

My wife was really good and patient with me and I could see she was increasingly concerned. Then one day she came into the bedroom and sat on the end of the bed.

'Mick,' she said. 'What's happening to you? I'm worried now. Look at you, you look a right mess. You haven't eaten anything in days, you won't answer your phone and you won't see anybody. If you don't tell me what's wrong with you I'm going to get a doctor in to see you.'

''No, no don't do that, I'll work it out,' I said.

'Work what out? Come on tell me what's up?'

So I eventually told my wife why I was so uptight. My wife bless her took the time to hear me out for a little while, at least up until the point I told her that I thought we could be in real danger; that the government might be after me because of the

Jon Doe blog I'd read. He said Aliens were coming to take over the world.....

'Oh fuck off,' she said. 'That's it I'm getting a doctor, you're going mad.'

I grabbed her, my eyes opened wide, and I said, 'I'm not fricking about here, I think what I read on Jon Doe's blog has put us all in danger.'

But at this point she pushed me away. She wasn't having any of it. She didn't want to listen to me anymore and she didn't want to believe anything I told her.

As she stormed out of the bedroom, she said, 'If you don't sort yourself out soon I'm leaving you.'

Which was a kick in the bollocks. I ended any attempt to discuss the topic with her. It seemed I was going to have to deal with all this by myself. I didn't want my wife to leave me did I? Besides, I thought it was best she knew nothing anyway.

At that point I decided to shut up about the subject altogether and I told her I was just stressed. Well I was stressed to be fair, I wasn't lying to her. I expected a knock on the door at any given minute, with Rams in black coming in to arrest me and take me away. I remember I used to hide in the loo, the wardrobe or under the bed until I recognized the voice of any visitors that came to the house.

I remember my daughter came to visit me one day. She brought me some flowers and a get well soon card and, whilst she was talking to her Mum, I went into the kitchen to put the flowers into a vase. Well, to be honest, I was more interested in inspecting the flowers for bugs. I didn't mean creepy crawlies either. I meant listening devices or hidden cameras; I was taking no chances. Then when I was fairly satisfied all was okay I put them into a vase, flowers first. The reason I did this was because I saw it done in a spy movie once. If you submerge a spying listening device in water it fucks them up. So that's just what I did, I submerged the flower heads in the water leaving the stalks sticking out... well they could contain microphones or cameras couldn't they? I planned to turn them the right way up but before I had chance my wife and daughter walked into the kitchen and saw what I had done. They both went quiet and looked at each other. I thought, *oh shit now they both think I'm bonkers.*

My daughter then smiled and said that she liked my beard and that made me smile because my wife hated it. She had been nagging me to shave it off ever since I started growing the thing, so with my daughter saying she liked it, and saying it suited me, was nice to hear for a change. I have got to be honest with you, I am not a big fan of beards myself, but needs must. It took time to get used to having one. I remember, as it got longer, I kept getting food stuck in it whenever I did eat anything which was quite disgusting. And it itched like buggery until it got to be some length but, like I say, needs must.

Time passed since I'd read Jon Doe's blog and I calmed down a bit. It may have been the tablets kicking in I don't know, but I even started to let my wife open the curtains again during the day. Our conversations were more civilized. I even cooked her a nice dinner once or twice and helped clean the house up. My anxiety had eased off a lot as the days passed and I started to forget I was a wanted Ram. The anti-depressants really helped and I started to feel happy and relaxed again.

It wasn't long before I was keen to get my life back on track and to some normality again. I tried to get that happy feeling I had in Tenerife because part of my self-therapy exercise was to think of times I was happy, and I was really happy there. I continued this therapy and tried to face my fears with a more positive attitude. Sometimes I would sit in front of my computer and just stare at it. At first I had flashbacks of that day when that message popped up on the screen in front of me. But nevertheless I forced myself to do this every day for at least an hour. I still didn't sleep too well and had nightmares of being abducted, my eyes looked like two piss holes in the snow and my beard grew to about a foot long; it was a proper full on beard now. I lost about two stone in weight, with all the worry I reckon, and I started to smell. It must have been bad because the dog wouldn't come anywhere near me.

NOW I STINK

One morning I realized that I had started to hum a bit more, you know really stink. It dawned on me I might smell a bit when my dog sniffed me and was then sick on the floor. I lifted my arm up and sniffed. Okay, I needed to freshen up a bit, but there was a reason why I stank. It was something I read in Jon Doe's blog, about fluoride.

I remember he talked about why they put it in water; he said it was used to dumb down the sheeple. A chemist named Charles Perkins once wrote a letter to the Lee Foundation for Nutritional Research in 1954 condemning the use of fluoride in the water supply. If you don't know who he was I'll tell you. He exposed the German plans of mass water medication.

Did you know it is also believed fluoride was used in concentration camps to keep the prisoners docile and easier to control? But this is a controversial claim and there aren't enough facts to back it up. Anyway, it was revealed to Mr Perkins by a prominent German chemist, who had spent years studying the effects of ingesting fluoridated water, who said fluoride was primarily to make the population docile and ineffective. This has been proven as a fact; that is exactly what fluoride can do.

Now I bet you probably haven't taken the time to look into fluoride but I have. I can tell you that, as well as making you submissive and docile, it can also potentially kill you. It's true. Fluoride is quite toxic and is known to cause illnesses and countless medical conditions. Now I know most sheeple believe fluoride is important to maintain good healthy teeth. Having it in toothpaste prevents you having tooth decay and many toothpaste companies claim it is safe. But I tell you there is no end of evidence, from researchers across the globe, who say it's not safe at all. Fluoride is bad for you and that's a fact. Here is the evidence to back up what I say:

www.nteu208.org/issues/Fluride/Nteu208-fluoride.htm

Anyway, after reading Jon Doe's blog and then researching it myself I can categorically tell you fluoride is bad for your health. It is an unneeded chemical added to your water to make you docile and easy to control. Fluoride also has the ability to interfere with the functions of the brain, FACT. It has been proven that too much fluoride exposure can reduce your IQ. It is at least a contributing factor in many health problems like liver failure and kidney failure. I bet you didn't know fluoride can also destroy the male reproductive system? I believe it is used now at an increased dosage to aid the slowing down of the Earth's population. Fluoride also causes symptoms of arthritis and is a contributing factor to most cancers such as bone cancer, FACT. Don't take my word for it, check it out for yourself:

fluoridealert .org

I say this with all the earnestness and sincerity of a scientist who has spent nearly 20 years' research into the chemistry, biochemistry, physiology and pathology of fluorine--any person who drinks artificially fluorinated water for a period of one year or more will never again be the same person mentally or physically. Charles E. Perkins, 2 October 1954

FLUORIDE IS POISONING US (FACT)

As I say fluoride destroys the male reproductive system because it damages sperm and increases the rate of infertility in a number of species. Fricking hell, the way things are going they will have to clone sheeple because the ability to breed naturally will be taken away from us all soon. Mind you, the way things are looking you'll probably die of food poisoning first.

As I said earlier, I read that fluoride can reduce your IQ levels too and even give you brain damage. They say this happens when it accumulates in the brain. It can alter your mental behavior too and impact on learning and behavior difficulties in children. At least that hasn't affected me yet.

I'm not so sure....

Did you know fluoride is linked to Alzheimer's disease? It also has negative impacts on your thyroid glands and causes symptoms of arthritis and loads of other kinds of bone damage. The list goes on and on.

My advice is drink only spring water or just recycle and purify your own piss. Drink that and you'll probably be better off.

Oh really Michael stop it now... you're heading for a zapping.

Fluoride is a toxic industrial waste product that is a poison to your body and in no way a "nutrient," offering no benefits at all to the human body. The fluoride added to water supplies can be contaminated with lead, arsenic, radio nucleotides, aluminium and other industrial contaminants. By Dr Mercola – Mercola.com

I also learned it can be absorbed through the skin. That's why I stank because I wouldn't have a bath. But as much as I tried to resist bathing it came to a point where my body odour was unbearable.

So one rainy Sunday morning, one week before my sick note ran out, I decided to have a shower but not using the house water. Oh no... I stripped off naked and went outside in the garden equipped with my shower gel, shaving foam and a razor. I washed my body all over in the rain. I was taking no chances. I also shaved my beard completely off. When I was all clean I realized I had forgotten my towel so I ran into the house and upstairs to grab one. I was fricking freezing, my willy had shrivelled up and everything. As I dried off my wife walked into the bathroom and to her delight saw that my beard was gone and I was clean and smelled fresh.

She smiled and said, 'Are you feeling better now then?'

I nodded and said, 'Yes thank you very much.'

She gave me a peck on the cheek and then unexpectedly snatched the towel from my naked wet body. We had a shag for the first time in many weeks and it was very nice indeed may I add; my shrivelled up willy soon perked up.

That's too much information.

'Oh is it, sorry?'

So with my sick note running out, at the end of the week I decided to sign off the sick and on Monday went back to work. It was difficult at first but life was almost back to normal by Christmas. By the first signs of spring I felt all was good in the world again. The business with that blog was like a distant memory and I had weaned myself off the pills.

But then I had a relapse. I remember it happened one bright sunny afternoon in March when I did something I wished I hadn't and regretted to this day. I turned the bloody computer back on didn't I? I remember I just plonked myself down in front of it and sat quietly for a couple of minutes. I thought about the blog, the federal warning and all that. I even remember I laughed at myself thinking what a stupid fool I'd been.

Then I did it….. I removed the sheet that covered it, plugged it in and fired it up. I must admit I was still a little apprehensive turning the thing on again but, with gritted teeth, I did. I waited for a moment for it to boot up. When it was up and running, without thinking, I logged straight back online. In the back of my mind I still expected some Ram in a black suit and sunglasses to appear on my screen and tell me they were coming to get me. But it was ok no one was there, just a warning popped up, not a federal one, telling me my antivirus had expired and did I want to renew it. So I clicked *ask me later*. I thought it should be ok for now.

The first thing I checked was my umpteen emails. I'd missed nothing there, just the same shit - somebody selling stuff, the odd e-mail from friends and family that were way out of date. I then had a look at my Facebook and Twitter. The longer I used the computer, the more I started to think again how silly I had been all those weeks ago, thinking I was in danger and the Government was after me.

I then took a deep breath and looked into my history folder to go back to that blog by Jon Doe. I said to myself *let's see if it still there*. But it wasn't there at all, it was gone, in fact, my whole history folder was completely empty, which was very strange. So I typed 'MIND FUCK' into Google search and waited with baited breath for a few seconds. Then it came up. There were loads of pages linked to the words Mind Fuck but not the one I was looking for. So I then typed 'Mind Fuck Jon Doe', but again nothing. I tried to find anything associated with this Ram Jon Doe but I found nothing. All I came across was loads of unrelated stuff.

This made me suspicious again. I tried different search engines but still nothing. I was baffled how all the histories of all my visited websites, everywhere I had visited, was all gone from my system, they had completely vanished into thin air. How could that happen? Every time I tried a new search it came up blank or 'search unknown', why had it all just simply disappeared? I tried YouTube and various other sites. I was on the computer for over two hours searching but came up with nothing.

I started to doubt my own sanity at this point. *This is very strange indeed*, I thought, *did any of it ever happen at all? Did I dream it all? Fricking hell, what's going on, where is Jon Doe? I think I am losing my fricking mind.* Then I thought, *hang on calm down, my computer's maintenance must have kicked in and deleted my past histories*. So I checked the last time my system was cleaned but it told me it was over two years ago. I still had loads of cookies and shit there. I tried using them but no good. *Fricking hell my computer could have been hacked; can they hack your computer when it's turned off? I didn't think they could do that. But hang on we are talking CIA, FBI here, who knows what they can do?*

At this point my wife walked into the room. 'You're not on that thing again are you? I thought you were never going to use it again; you promised me.'

'It's all gone,' I replied.

'What's gone?'

'Everything, the blog, everything even my history folder it's all been wiped clean.'

'Doesn't matter, does it?'

'Yes it does because that can't happen if the computer is switched off. It wasn't even plugged in the wall.'

'Anyway your dinner's done. Are you coming down to eat it or what?'

'Yeah okay, I'll be down in a minute.'

At that she left the room. I sat looking at the monitor shaking my head. I was completely baffled as to where all my history files had gone; beats me even to this today. So I shut down the computer and went downstairs to eat. As I walked slowly down the stairs I thought, *Fricking hell, what if all I'd read was actually true and this Jon Doe bloke was for real after all. He tried to warn the world and now he's fricking dead the government have taken anything and everything associated with him offline. They even somehow tapped into my computer and wiped off all the evidence. How could they do that when it's not even plugged in the wall?*

So here I was worrying again and at the same time a bit disappointed that I never found out if it was all just a hoax. I was left in limbo. Deep down I hoped it was a hoax, just a clever hoax done by some spotty student and his buddies with nothing better to do with their life but scare the crap out of simple sheep like me. But I couldn't find anything anywhere, diddly squat, it had all gone… the blog was gone, my history was gone, all vanished into oblivion. Anything associated with Jon Doe had disappeared off the face of the Earth it seemed and that's why you will never find Jon Doe on the World Wide Web today, I guarantee it.

So here I was once again confused, disheartened and worried, sitting eating my supper my wife had lovingly cooked for me. We had my favourite dish of steak, chips and mushrooms, but I kind of lost my appetite and picked at the food, my mind in deep thought.

My wife asked if I was alright.

I said, 'Yes ok, just tired.' But I wasn't tired I was starting to worry again wasn't I? I thought, *I need to calm down before I make myself ill again. I need to relax and forget about it.* Eventually the day came to a close and my wife and I went off to bed.

That night I had one of those dreams about being abducted by Aliens again, only this time they kept me captive in a room. However, like all the other times I felt like I had woken up and was wide awake in this alien craft with these Aliens looking at me.

This time one stepped forward and as if it was in my head said, 'Don't involve yourself in matters that don't concern you; you don't understand. Forget about Jon Doe. Forget about everything.'

Then I don't know what happened but I was woken up to the voice of Alf saying, '*Michael, Michael, wake up, wake up Michael*!'

Okay have you finished your little story? Can we move on?

'Yes okay.'

Thank heavens for that.

CHAPTER SIX

WHAT IF WE KEEP IGNORING THE WARNINGS?

JON DOE'S WARNING TO THE WORLD

Did you know that five mass extinctions on this planet have been documented?

No, I didn't know that Alf. I did know a species has to disappear for fifty years before it can be declared officially extinct though. There is a lot I have learned over the last few months I can tell you, especially since I started to investigate the things that Jon Doe spoke of in his blog. I found a lot of what he did talk about had a fair bit of factual evidence widely available on the World Wide Web to back him up which I thought was very interesting indeed. It also made me think maybe Jon Doe was on to something big. He talked about many subjects in his blog like government corruption; they are all at it, it seems. He even gave a link to an article that I jotted down and when I checked it out:

www.globalissues.org/article/590/corruption

It seems wherever there is big money involved there is always corruption. If you readers are interested to read what dodgy deals there are check out the link above. Jon Doe also talked a lot about the banking system, which was a bit too complicated for me to understand. From what I could gather he said banks were holding the world to ransom. He said that a Ram named Thomas Jefferson, whoever the frick he was, definitely got it right two hundred years ago when he warned that banks were more dangerous than standing armies. He said if banks were allowed to control currency they would 'deprive the sheeple of all property until their lambs wake up homeless'.

Well it seems to me the governments and the banks work hand in hand; they are both corrupt. I've said it before and I'll say it again, the reason why the world is in this fricking recession is because the rich bastards are hogging all the money for themselves. They are greedy bastards the lot of 'em...

I don't know how they can sleep at night knowing sheeple are dying because of abject poverty; sheeple young and old are dying because of starvation and there is no need for it because they could put an end to it all if they really wanted. But they won't do that will they? Oh no. SHARE YOUR WEALTH YOU BASTARDS!! Anyway don't start me on that subject – I covered that in my other book.

HEADING FOR EXTINCTION

Jon Doe also talked about climate change which I am personally interested in. It is a popular subject for most sheep. We all love to talk about the weather don't we? Or should I say moan about the weather, especially here in Britain. I think it gives us sheep something to do whilst we stand in a fricking queue... Anyway that's beside the point so I shall move on shall I...?.

So anyway, this Jon Doe Ram said, 'We can already see the effects of global warming, and its velocity is increasing at an alarming rate; volcanoes, earthquakes, tsunamis just to name a few.' He said all these are killing sheeple right across the world on a regular basis it seems.

He also said, 'I think no matter what we try to do to avert this crisis it is probably a pointless exercise.'

He reckoned it was already too late to stop the impact of global warming on this planet and by the end of its cycle, he said, most life on this planet would be on the brink of extinction. Anyway up, here are some Facts:

Did you know the UK birdsong population has declined by ninety-two per cent? The black rhinos' numbers have fallen from sixty-five thousand to around three thousand one hundred. The African elephant population has fallen from around one point two million to just under a half a million and the population of tigers has fallen by ninety-five per cent during the past century. All these and many other species of bird, fish, dog, cat, reptile, insect and plant under threat would run to about five hundred pages if listed.

But now it seems we humans are also headed for extinction. He said the weather would get a lot worse and that weather events would become more violent and frequent. This was because it was being aided by governments of the world to prevent all-out human extinction by culling some of us. What he meant about that I will cover in a minute; it's all to do with Alien technology and a weather weapon.

Earthquakes would be here and there and that they would increase in frequency and intensity before the return. Jesus said that, apparently.

The return of what? Who?

Let's talk more about the weather for a minute…

In Britain the weather in 2012 was the wettest I had ever known; in fact it was said to be the second wettest since records began. Yet all around the world the weather has also been somewhat weird. There have been earthquakes, volcanoes and tsunamis all over the planet. It is understandable why to some it looks very much like the end of days. The religious nuts love it because they think it's the wrath of God kicking off. They don't give a toss because they believe they will be saved.

Well, that's all well and good to think that but you're wrong. The weather is being manipulated. I read an article on the inter-web where a very clever Ram named Professor Michel Chossudovsky on the Global Research website talked about the HAARP programme. The HAARP is a weapon of mass destruction capable of destabilising agricultural and ecological systems globally.

Does this have something to do with what's going on? Jon Doe thought so. He said, and I paraphrase, that the debate on global climate change rarely acknowledged that the world's weather could be modified as part of a new generation of sophisticated electromagnetic weapons. He said both the United States and Russia had developed the capability to manipulate the climate for military use.

THE HAARP PROGRAMME

Established in 1992, HAARP, based in Gokona, Alaska, is an array of high-powered antennas that transmit, through high-frequency radio waves, massive amounts of energy into the ionosphere (the upper layer of the atmosphere). Their construction was funded by the US Air Force, the US Navy and the Defence Advanced Research Projects Agency (DARPA). Operated jointly by the Air Force Research Laboratory and the Office of Naval Research, HAARP constitutes a system of powerful antennas capable of creating 'controlled local modifications of the ionosphere' Michel Chossudovsky

Where did all this technology come from? I'll tell you, from Aliens.

THE EVILNESS OF ALIEN TECHNOLOGY

I fear the day when the technology overlaps with our humanity. The world will only have a generation of idiots. Albert Einstein:

I personally think technology is an evil thing and if we aren't careful in years to come we will probably be slaves to it. Maybe the robots we invent from this Alien technology will turn on us? That is, of course, if we last that long.

www.ancient-code.com/ancient-technology

The way we have progressed so quickly in technology over the last few years worries me. I'm a little suspicious that some Aliens have a hidden agenda to take over the world, and that we are helping them do it. I think we have blindly welcomed a new Alien army with open arms. I think this army is a thinking mechanical army that could eventually contribute to our total demise. Instead of using this knowledge we obtained for the good of the planet we have inevitably invented our own killing machines. That is exactly what they wanted us to do.

Soon, if we aren't careful, robots or super intelligent computers will run everything on this planet and so the human slave will no longer be needed. I think a life similar to the movie *I-Robot'* may not be far from the truth. The more we progress in this Alien technological age the more vulnerable we become.

That's true; you humans are already too reliant on technology and machines.

Imagine if they all just one day decided to stop or, worse, turn on us.

You may not be too far from the truth there either.

I know Alf.... The computers we have today get smarter all the time. Phone technology is more advanced day by day, week by week. We are being invaded and taken over by this Alien technology. These machines control our lives already and it's getting worse as the years go by, as we get more reliant on them.

I reckon it is because of technology that there is so much unemployment in the world. The basic fact is sheeple (humans) are slowly becoming obsolete and unnecessary. The evidence is all around us. Computers already have minds of their own don't they? Humans no longer have to think. Yes, Albert, you were right; we are already the idiots you warned us about. Maybe this is how our species will come to its demise, because of this Alien technology. President Eisenhower made a deal with the devil.

Or an evil God.

'Huh? What you on about Alf?'

Technology and religion are the same. Both came from an evil Alien race. It is both of these things that will add to the demise of the human race if they are not stopped. You humans don't know anything, about yourselves or your importance to the universe as a whole. You are blinded by this need to have a belief in something other than just believing in oneself and you also have this need for modern technology. It is these that make your great minds lazy. With a lazy mind you become vulnerable.

'What the fuck are you on about Alf?'

What I am saying is both religion and technology are aimed at controlling you. They keep you all enslaved to an Earth Prison. You are prisoners on your own planet and you will stay prisoners until you open your minds and see what is happening around you.

'So you're saying we are all in prison?'

Yes, an open air minimal security prison, but a prison nevertheless. Not only that you are all stupidly helping the Anunnaki with their plan to take over the world. Your humanity is at a threat unless you all escape.

'And how do we do that then, Alf?'

Open your minds. Open your eyes. If you started caring about each other that would be good. Speak out at the unfairness you see or the injustice you witness. Don't just moan about it, do something about it. Stand together and right the wrongs. Not only that, slow down the use of technology, it takes way your ability to think. You must do this or one day it will take over your planet completely. Then you humans will be no better than robots, which means basically the evolution of your great minds will come to a stop. You will get to a point where nothing will be or seem to be real anymore.

'What do you mean?'

What I mean is you humans, if you're not careful, will turn your world into a virtual reality one.

Virtual reality?

Yes, nothing will feel real anymore.

You might have a point there Alf. We already have artificial flowers, grass and flavourings; artificial intelligence even.

See there you go..... Also you humans are too reliant on religion and technology and have imprisoned yourselves, enslaved yourselves to a make-believe world of lies and deception. It is this Anunnaki religion and their technology that takes over your ability to think; to use your brains to their full potential.

'The religious sheeple of the world ain't going to buy that comment Alf, fricking hell; you're basically telling them that their faith is codswallop.'

I'm sorry but that's exactly what I'm saying.....Well at least exaggerated massively to control your natural thought. Religion has been used to divert your minds from spirituality; your own divine wisdom. It only creates and feeds hate amongst humans, and although disguised by love it isn't love at all. It is a false love. Love doesn't kill people.

Religion was designed to turn humans against one another and that's the truth, whether you like it or not. Only religion can justify killing another divine human soul, as you all are. No true God that represented love would ever condone war and killing of any kind.

The problem is a lot of humans are genuinely good souls and you will come across them every day of your life. The world is full of good souls and they would possibly tell you if you asked them that they believe in God. But the truth is humans are misled by religion. It isn't religion that makes you a good person? It's not because of any belief or faith why you are a kind soul.

You humans seem to need something to believe in to justify being good. No need, just believe in yourself and each other. Be naturally nice and caring. You don't need to have a faith to do that.

'Makes sense to me.'

Ask yourself this Michael. Why haven't humans used all this technology to protect, improve or safeguard their planet's needs? Why do they concentrate more in how to destroy it? No, I'll rephrase that, destroy themselves? How many humans have died because of religion or because of technology? I'm telling you religion breeds hate and technology gives birth to unsocial behaviour, selfishness and greed, leading to hate. In the long term it will be this selfishness and greed and hate that will be the downfall of human race.

> ***'Like an unchecked cancer, hate corrodes the personality and eats away its vital unity. Hate destroys a man's sense of values and his objectivity. It causes him to describe the beautiful as ugly and the ugly as beautiful, and to confuse the true with the false and the false with the true.' Martin Luther King***

It is this negativity of hate towards one another that is bred into you, but this only feeds resentment, jealousy and greed. You humans have no need to be so hateful, or jealous, or greedy.

'Guess not.'

So why blame your fellow humans for what you don't have or be jealous of what they have and you don't? Being hateful helps no one it only destroys your natural good souls and turns you all against each other. All this hate and resentment is because of the incompetence of the politicians. The media don't help matters when they feed us stories about all the shit that's going on all over the world, making us all miserable and angry. Then they show us some fucker living the life of Riley when everybody else is working their balls off to scrape a living. I know this frustrates the hell out of me because I can't do anything about it.

Yes you can.

'How?'

You need to enlighten the humans and make them understand they can. It doesn't have to be that way.

'I think that would be a waste of time even if I knew how. No Alf, I think we are doomed; the sheep will never listen to me.'

You are not doomed just yet or there wouldn't be any point talking to you.

'So then Alf, how am I going to make them understand?'

You're doing it now...give the reader one of your famous tips.
'Okay....'

MICKY FRICK'S TIP

STOP BUYING THE LATEST GADGETS; THE ONES YOU ALREADY HAVE ARE GOOD ENOUGH. YOU'RE JUST FUNDING RESEARCH ON WEAPONS OF YOUR OWN MASS DESTRUCTION

Well, at least slow down.

That'll do, but now we need to move on and tell the reader about the coming invasion.

'An Alien invasion?'

Yes, now I need to zap you.

AN ALIEN INVASION IS ON THE CARDS

We Nordics have noticed that your governments of the world have now cottoned on to what the Greys are really up to and are seriously and desperately trying to find ways to protect Earth from this Alien invasion. Check out:

www.exopaedia.org/staar+project

This website is about a low frequency pulsed sound generating weapon. Codenamed Zeus Project it is said that this weapon would be effective against any Alien craft. But then you have The STAAR Project allegedly launched in 1958 as a response to the possible threat of an Alien (as in extra-terrestrial) invasion. STAAR stands for Strategic Tactical Advanced Alien Response. An extremely secret and extremely advanced elite strike force was created to deal with the possible threat of an Alien invasion. It's not much of a secret now because I've just told you about it.

Be rest assured, Michael, the Americans at least are taking a possible Alien invasion very seriously indeed.

'I still don't believe you can trust government. Have you thought, Alf, that it may be just a red herring?'

What you mean?

I think the government are trying to look like they protect Earth from an Alien invasion so we don't question why they spend billions of taxpayers' dollars on the development of super weapons, when really they are developing them so they can turn them on us.

Now you are becoming paranoid. As we see it, at the moment the government have learned that the Greys can't be trusted. They are desperately trying to use the technology they obtained from the Greys to protect Earth from what they believe is going to be a full blown Alien invasion in the coming years.

'Really Alf, do you really think so?' Mind you if we don't expose the Hybrids in government who work for the Greys......... the sheep trust government too much. Trust me reader they are two-faced, lying bastards, the lot of them.

An invasion is coming Michael.

'Fuck off......'

Check out www.bloomberg.com

I hoped you were wrong Alf but apparently not; it seems this invasion has already begun. The Americans have joined forces with India, China and Brazil to develop weapons to defend Earth from the probability of an Alien invasion. They are all actively preparing defences for such an event. You're right Alf. They have this new super gun that can launch a projectile five thousand eight hundred miles per hour that and can penetrate anything up to one hundred and twenty miles away. The Star Wars Project is again active.

However, Russia is suspicious that the Americans are still working with the Aliens, so much so that back in 2013 the Russian president told President Barack Obama to come clean and tell the world about the Aliens, or they would. If the government did ever confess to knowing all about Aliens what will that do to religion? What will that do to a lot of sheeple who believe in God? Are they all going to pray to God to help us?

They can do what they want but unfortunately God won't help them. You humans are on your own when they get here.

'What's that? Are there Aliens on their way?'

I'm afraid so.

'When...?'

Soon enough... I fear Earth won't be ready to defend themselves either if they don't work out their own differences down here. Hopefully we Nordics will recruit more White Flame Warriors like you to educate the world before this happens. But it is getting more and more difficult to get through to you humans.

'I can tell you why I think that is Alf.... Did you know the Americans have developed another new weapon? I read about this just the other day.'

What's that one?

They are radio waves that destroy human DNA. I tell you the Americans are working with the Greys and you can't trust the little bastards. I've seen the proof on the inter-web. According to Dr Boian Alexandrov at the Centre for Nonlinearly Studies there is such a wave called terahertz (THz), which are found to destroy human DNA. The waves literally unzip a thing called the helix strand. Also exposed is a plan to put these DNA killing chips broadcasting THz waves into mobile phones for use as an imaging system for all new phones. But it is said that doing so could be potentially deadly to humans. This isn't conspiracy. It's a Fact. This technology exists and is already implemented in a lot of places. It is feared by many that this technology could eventually kill millions of sheeple; there are lots of scientists and top doctors all over the world warning about this THz wave.

www.sciencedaily.com

Doesn't surprise me but what has that got to do with me?

It could be that these THz waves are blocking the Nordics communicating with us telegraphically.

That's possible.

'See....told you Alf, the American Government still works on behalf of the Aliens. Listen to me for a change, Alf you can't trust government.'

MICKY FRICK'S TIP

IF YOU BUY A CELL PHONE ASK IF IT HAS AN IMAGING SYSTEM RUN WITH TERAHERTZ (THZ). IF IT HAS DON'T BUY IT. IF THEY DON'T KNOW FIND OUT FIRST OR SIMPLY DON'T BUY ANY PHONES MADE AFTER 2012; THAT'S YOUR SAFEST BET.

'See Alf, there's something dodgy going on, or why would they even invent a weapon that attacks the brain and kills human DNA? They are helping the Aliens take over the world. You Nordics are trying to save the planet are you not?'

Yes...

'Can't you see Alf? It is because they know you Nordics communicate to us through superconscious telepathy. This may be the reason the government are intent on developing weapons that use high frequency radio signals to block you talking to us. It seems quite obvious to me that the reason the sheeple ain't getting the warnings from you is because they're being blocked.'

You have a point.

You know reader that voice you have in your head may well be Nordics talking to you? You should listen to them. But the government, the fricking low life picking government, have found a way to block them communicating with us. Don't use your cell phone; bin it. Throw it in the trash. We got along just fine without them before. I tell you reader they were invented to make us anti-social. We are turning into brainwashed mongs because of mobile phones.

Yes but........

They use mobile phones (cell phones) to 'mongify' us. Not only that, but also to tag us. Mobile phones take away our privacy and freedom. They know where we are and what we talk about. That also explains why Alf disappears from my brain.

'Can't you see they are trying to block you from getting into my head? What do you think about that Alf? Am I right or am I right? Alf......... are you there Alf? Oh fuck.... they are doing it now. ALF ARE YOU THERE!'

No he's gone... Shit looks like I'm on my own for a bit. 'ALF!' Sod it. I best turn my phone off now and hopefully I can get him back.

Look reader mobile phones (cell phones) mess with your brain. Turn the thing off now.

In Alf's absence I'll continue to do some more of my own research about these Anunnaki Aliens until he gets back; also I want to talk about freedom or the lack of it. But before I do I would like to know how these fricking Greys got to know how to manipulate us like they do? How did the Greys get to take control of us?

Do you know I thought about this and I think I have sussed it? The answer is anthropology. They have learned our weaknesses for years and found out how to manipulate our minds. Yes reader, I truly believe that some of the government leaders are guided and directed by Grey Aliens. The Greys control our leadership structure too. It is also them who take away our freedom.

So now it's up to us workers to get it back and save the planet. The government are no longer our leaders they just work for Aliens. I guess we should forgive them for they know not what they do....... I recall somebody else saying that... who was it? Never mind.

The government, the fricking government, have been mind-wiped like a lot of other sheeple around the planet. That is why they are so stupid. To think all this time I blamed them for all the shit going down, but now I find out I was wrong. Well, not completely wrong. They are still wankers in my eyes but most of the shit is because of the Grey Aliens pulling the strings down here on Earth. For years they have been using the Illuminate to control government who control us; it all makes sense really.

We've already been invaded sheeple. Lucky for you I'm not fully brainwashed yet and I understand why the Nordics have chosen me to relay this information to you.

It's because I am special, really special. I am the chosen one.

Okay calm down...

'Well I am.'

Whatever...

'Oh you're back....'

I am... Unfortunately I am the bringer of bad news.

'Why?'

It very much looks like you humans are up the creek without a paddle, so to speak.

'Why?'

Because if they have developed the technology to block our communications to you humans, as it seems you're right, we are powerless to stop the Anunnaki taking full control.

'Well it could be a lot fricking wosserer.'

Say what?

'My own made up word, it means worse than worse. Stick that in the Oxford Dictionary you clever dicks... What I'm saying is... it's lucky for the sheeple they still have me. I will give the sheeple the tools to win back their freedom and beat back the aliens with or without Nordic help.'

Like I said you're up the creek. Look can we move on.

'Hang fire Alf, I was just about to talk to the reader about freedom or, like I said, the lack of it.'

Before you do that, I want your readers to have a look at this web page:

www.crawford2000.co.uk/ufo-planetx-nibiru-marduk.htm

'Oh okay, why?'

Because you said the government weren't running things and you're right. I think this is a good website to explain just that. I believe it is important to understand what's really going on. This website may help.

'Hang fire Alf I'm going to have a look.......'

(Several minutes later)

'That's a lot of reading Alf but very interesting. I bet a lot of sheeple reading this book won't check it out though. But they should, it was very interesting indeed.'

Yes there is a lot to read but if the reader takes the time to do so they will see the government have no control over themselves, never mind of what goes on here on Earth; they have limited freedom too.

They are also cowards. That's why they hide and don't want us to think there is such a thing as Aliens; it is the best cloaking device there is. They do this so we will be taken by surprise when they eventually show up and completely take over our planet. By then it'll be too late because we won't see them coming, or expect it.

Reader, because of most sheeple's ignorance they won't be able to defend themselves when this invasion happens. The denial to accept Aliens exist is part of your weakness. It is the Grey Aliens that mess with everybody's heads as they control the way you think and behave.

Thanks to Eisenhower, the prick, they now know how to manipulate our thoughts and behaviour to get what they want from us. But you should ask yourself, what is it that you want? I already know what you want, you needn't answer; you want freedom. Every sheep just wants to be free don't they? Free from debt, free from going to work. I know I fricking do.

Most of the sheep of the world living in a concrete jungle want freedom that's for sure. No matter where we look there are umpteen devices to control our lives. Think of traffic lights, traffic islands, no parking signs, neon advertising boards the list goes on and on. It seems the only places we are welcome are the ones where they want us to spend our money. Loyal obedient sheep like us are herded to these very places, day in and day out. We are subjected to more and more bullshit and bollocks every day of our lives and all they want is our money, we are not free at all. We don't live in a free world. We don't have free speech. We are only free to do what they want us to do.

Who is 'they'?

'Government!'

I know where this is going.....

'It's the government who have taken away our freedom.'

You humans weren't supposed to be free on Earth, ever. That was not the plan at all. You're slaves, and you have always been slaves.

'We don't have any rights at all, do we Alf?'

Only the ones they choose to give you

Some sheeple think they do, but they don't unless it suits; they don't have anything to call their own not even their thoughts and even they are manipulated by the government. I don't know. The government fuck with our lives and the Aliens mess with our heads. Nothing is real anymore; we all live in a virtual world that we have to pay for.

Here we go again I sense a rant coming on.

I'm not ranting, I just think the Sheeple need it drummed into their thick skulls that nothing is as they see it; we all live in this virtual or artificial world and have to pay for the privilege. What about our so called freedom hey? Ask yourself this question, what is actually free? The answer is nothing. They make you think you have freedom but you don't have any, not really. You are free to work and that's about it. You definitely don't have an opinion or any power to change policy either.

I tell you now sheeple, democracy doesn't exist, it's all bollocks. Voting is all bollocks. It can be rigged and it usually is. Americans think they have a choice on Election Day when really they are, and always have been, in a coalition dictatorship. The One World Government is well on its path; the plans are in place and all they need to do now is get you lot to fall in love with the idea, or get some clever speaker to sell the idea. They lie about everything – Aliens, God, the lot; it's all a lie.

I thought it was a while since you did some government bashing…tut.

Let me quote something I read in that website:

> ***No matter what your belief is, on a religious or on a spiritual basis, the same issue is `freedom'. Do you surrender your freedoms? The same issue that you all have to deal with is, `freedom', `self-responsibility', and `self-rule'. That is the bottom line issue, no matter what. You are all going to need to stand together if you want that. Or are you going to wait for Jesus to come and save you all? Sorry to say this but he's not coming. www.crawford2000.co.uk/ufo-planetx-nibiru-marduk2.htm***

So let me the chosen one help you get back that freedom, with Alf's help of course, at least as long as I can keep Alf in my head.

Yes Michael and you may need to get a move on. Once I am out of your head that's it, you'll be on your own. Have you finished your little rant?

'What rant?'

Never mind…shall we talk a bit about war?

'Yes if you want.'

IN GOD'S NAME LET'S ALL KILL EACH OTHER HEY?

Have you ever thought sheeple why we have wars? It's because of our leaders isn't it?'

True, it always is.

However, you will never see a general, president, or any prime ministers or royal members on the front line, will ya?

No.

You will never see any of them fighting side by side with the troops. Okay, they might be in the vicinity but they are not shot at because they never let themselves get in harm's way

What's your point?

I think sheep who join the armed forces are stupid.

Stupid?

Yes stupid, they are just brainwashed to kill each other. I mean who in their right fricking minds would want to do a job that might entail killing your fellow human? I think the sheep need to start to realize this isn't normal behaviour; it's quite insane really.

They always were brainwashed to kill, Michael... they believe they are fighting for either God or Country, only most of the time it is only so that some human, a king, queen or president, can expand their 'empire' for their own glory.

I know, it's stupid......I watched the news the other day, which is against the grain for me, and I saw a solder on the TV do the sign of the cross and kiss a crucifix around his neck. He then said a little prayer to himself. But then he pointed his gun and shot some fucker. What's all that about?

What do you mean...?

Wasn't it God who said, "Thou shalt not kill"?

It is one of the Ten Commandments, yes.

And I am right to say that this commandment is right there at the top of the "don't do list" for religious sheeple to guarantee a seat in heaven?

Yes

So what makes sheeple think praying is going to help them? After they have blown some fucker's head off with a gun, or slit some fucker's throat, under the laws of God they are doomed to damnation for eternity. See, fricking stupid, if you ask me they have just broken the biggest number one rule in all religious faiths. So if you're a religious soldier reading this, sorry but you're going down, that is if you believe God exists. Think about it, under your own faith it states you will rot in eternal hell for taking somebody's life...

I don't get why so-called religious sheeple join the army. They are not heroes, they are fricking contract killers. Mind you

I shouldn't worry too much because there isn't a God and if there is he is an Evil Alien. Remember sheeple the only hell you'll ever see is the one you create yourselves here on Earth. Can't you see you kill each other in the name of whoever has ordered you to do so?

God, a loving God, would not condone killing in any form unless it was to end somebody's life with their consent, because they were suffering and asked you to help them end their life.

If I achieve anything in this book I hope I make you sheep see that you can be a free thinker and in control of your own minds and lives. You don't need to be led by anybody. Be a free spirit and understand there is never any good that comes from War. That's a Fact.

Well said Michael.

MICKY FRICK'S TIP

ALWAYS REMEMBER WAR IS JUST ANOTHER METHOD OF CULLING YOUR FELLOW HUMANS

Maybe you are a Catholic or a Christian reading this? I only guess you are one or the other because my book is currently only in English. So let's talk about Jesus shall we?

Jesus is in fact an Avatar of the Light who incarnated here to remind and to re-awaken the true Divine human origin.

'Shut the fuck up Alf.'

Sorry

Look, whoever he was, I truly believe Jesus tried to teach the sheeple to believe in themselves. He told his flock they had a choice in life. But now I think the freedom to choose has been taken away from us through brainwashing. I think we need to get it back. I understand Jesus was a very wise even nice Ram but unfortunately he failed in his mission to save the sheeple. In my opinion his downfall came because he trusted too many of the wrong sheep.

That's true...

'It is?'

Yes ...well sort of.

I also think Jesus's biggest downfall other than that he was betrayed (stabbed in the back) was that he was also a bit naïve. He had too much faith in his followers' ability to actually grasp what he tried to teach them.

Jesus knew exactly why he was here; we told him like we told you. What are you getting at?

'I'm saying that because of the low intellect of the sheeple of the time they just didn't get it....'

Get what?

'His message; understood his teachings.'

Some did....

'Yeah but not enough it seems.' Hopefully the modern sheeple of today are a lot more intelligent than they were back then. That they now understand what he tried to teach them and what I am trying to teach them. I guess have taken over from where Jesus left off.

No you haven't......

'I have...'

No you haven't......

'Well kind of...'

No Michael you haven't......

'Okay fricking hell okay, I haven't, well I have....'

Look you religious sheep reading might think I'm evil, maybe even Satan's love child, Well I don't have six, six, six on my body anywhere. I know I've looked, so don't panic. I'm not evil at all. I just think I'm like him in a little way.... I mean I am just trying to explain to you thick sheep what I think Jesus tried to teach. That's why I am the chosen one.

Look Michael, you're not a teacher you're a messenger. Jesus was a teacher, you're a messenger. You won't teach the humans anything, all you can do is pass on a message. That is your only purpose and I wish you would hurry up because time is running out.

Let me just say, I think the Bible was tampered with, or at least misinterpreted, to hide what Jesus tried to say.

You're right there Michael.

'I know I am.'

The Old and New Testaments were manipulated by the Anunnaki. The book of Exodus was definitely written by Aliens and Moses met an Alien believing him to be God.

www.ancient-code.com/prophets-prophecies-and-Aliens

Even today, because of Moses's belief that he met God, most Christians are Alien followers without even knowing it. In the book of Genesis 1:1 it says, 'In the beginning God created the heaven and the Earth.'

What a load of bollocks that is. We know it was a natural phenomenon, but I guess if that Alien wanted to convince Moses he was the true God almighty, without a doubt, he would have told him he created the world, and the universe come to that.

I suppose.

'Do you know, Alf, the more I look into the Holy Bible the more I find holes in it?' I dislike it. It seems to be nothing but threats and orders, contradictions and bullshit. On every page some fucker tells us how we should all live. In my opinion whoever wrote the Bible wasn't interested in spreading the word of love, just giving orders. I think most of the Bible, if not all of it, was written or at least manipulated with evil intent.

I guess if you want to be a world leader you need a set of rules for the populace to follow and, most of all, to make them fear you. So the Bible is a kind of order book rather than a holy book; a book of orders and threats to make the populace obedient to its rules.

It is also a belief which is unable to be changed.

'Eh?'

All religious books are set in stone. What I mean by this is they don't give humans room to expand their thoughts. They think because it is written in a holy book they must live their lives by it. Then it becomes a religion, a way of life for many humans based on a faith that someone else tells you to have. Remember it was humans who wrote the holy books but if you humans were to open your minds more, and be more spiritual, all reality becomes different. The Bible is a tool to control and keep humans in one reality.

And to get everybody who reads it to live in fear. In the beginning God created the heaven and the Earth that's what it says in the Bible. But that's not true because science proves that isn't the case at all. See, the Bible is full of shit. No wonder, as the human race evolves mentally, they see the Bible as total bollocks. It's no wonder the sheeple now think, *sod religion, there is no God to worry about.*

That is why society is breaking down. Most sheeple have no morals these days and think, *fuck it, I am going to do what I want to do even if it upsets somebody else*. The problem, as I see it, is that sheeple are not doing what they want to do, they just think they are. Humans, I think, do need certain rules to keep order or it will all go tits up, as it now seems to be.

'So Alf, how can sheeple have freedom and rules to keep order if not through religion?'

There is only one rule all should abide to and that is the rule of Love. All the Nordics want is you humans to be free but to also stay caring, loving, and helpful. Be nice to each other and animals and every other living organism on Planet Earth. Just seek knowledge.

'Yeah in an ideal world Alf; that's never going to happen though is it?'

It is only the Anunnaki influence that stops you achieving this.

Before I tell you the reader all I know about the Anunnaki and the Illuminati, I just want you to understand that the Greys are not the Anunnaki. Let's be clear about that, they only work on their behalf until the Anunnaki return once again, in around 2076.

No. You're wrong Michael

'What you mean I'm wrong? If that's not the date why did I come to that date? I mean it just popped into my head? I thought you put it there.'

I'm not going into that now. But what I will say is that by this date all you humans will know for sure that Aliens exist. Look, forget all that for now, carry on and tell the reader a bit about the Anunnaki Grey.

'Right okay......'

THE ANUNNAKI GREY

In Jon Doe's blog I remember he said something about the Anunnaki creating the Greys. The Greys are not in a sense a living being. Although the Greys are way more advanced than anything we understand, and may appear as a life-form to us, they are basically robots, they have no feelings or emotions. They just do as they are instructed to do by the Anunnaki Race.

Now you're being a messenger; carry on.

Earlier you may recall I told you how I was about to read what Joe Doe said about a race called the Anunnaki when my computer mysteriously went blank and a federal warning popped up. Well I can tell you, I never did get chance to read all he had to say about the Anunnaki. But I was nevertheless intrigued by what I did get to read, especially when he said something about God being an Alien. So I took it upon myself to look up these Anunnaki on the inter-web to see what I could find out about them. Do you know, I was amazed how much there is out there. From what I have read they don't come across as a very nice Alien race at all, in fact they are nasty bastards.

Now before I continue on the subject of the Anunnaki I must stress I am no expert on them. If I have got some of my facts wrong in places I do apologize. I am just saying it as I see it, that's all. Besides, I found in my own research that there were too many conflicting versions about the Anunnaki scattered about on the inter-web. Because of this, I am still not sure if I've got my facts right now.

There's a very good chance you probably know more about the Anunnaki Alien than me. If you do then you will also know that they are based on myths and legends like Giants, Trolls, Pixies, Fairies, Dragons etcetera etcetera. So what if they are just myths and legends? Most religions are based on myths and legends too. If you don't believe the Anunnaki ever existed, how can you believe in God and follow a religion. They too are all just based on myths and legends? Did you know reader if you were to look into it you would find the same amount of evidence to say that God exists as there is about the Anunnaki and Anu existing; what if both are the same? It's just a thought.

There is no real concrete evidence to prove, without a shadow of a doubt, any of them exist or existed at all. However, these stories had to come from somewhere. There are a lot of facts and evidence that I personally came across that suggest there is a very good chance they did and still do exist. I could write a book all about the Anunnaki alone but I'm not going to because I think that's already been done. Besides, I can't be bothered to be honest. I may talk about them a lot in this book though because they fascinate me.

You don't have time either.

'Okay Alf shut the frick up for a minute will you please?'

Sorry.

'Thank you.' Look reader, from what I have already read on the Anunnaki, I have come to my own conclusions about what they are all about. There is loads of evidence to say they definitely exist. To me that is quite worrying but also fascinating. I wish they had taught us about them in school instead of all the other boring shit like Henry V111. I think I know now why they didn't. It would scare the shit out of ya and throws everything you think you knew about the world to the wind. Did you know it is even believed, and proved in many cases, that some of us descend from them? This is amazing news. Why isn't this taught in schools? I'll tell you why I think this is. The truth is just too much for sheeple to handle.

The Anunnaki.......

The story of the Anunnaki goes something like this. Around three hundred thousand years ago this superior Alien race called the Anunnaki decided to create a race of workers. They genetically manipulated the primates on this planet and used the Greys to do just that. The result was Homo sapiens, that's you and me, and we became their slaves. The Greys then created leaders, kings and queens, to enforce loyalty and obedience amongst the slaves. They formed armies from the most loyal to enforce their power over the sheeple as the population grew. War was found to be a great way to get you to do as you're told and, not only that, a bloody good way to control you and over-population.

Their intention today is to affect complete and total control over every human being on the planet and to dramatically reduce the world's population by two thirds.

'Shut up Alf.'

Sorry carry on, just thought I would add that.

'We can talk about that later, stop butting in.'

Sorry.

'Thank you.'

So anyway....As I was saying the sheeple began to accept being ruled and War wasn't seen as needed as much. Humans started to turn into the sheep you are today. The leadership of the planet was then handed over to the Illuminati that have bloodlines going back thousands of years. Jon Doe said the Illuminati are now the overseers of Earth. They have run things down here on Earth for a very long time, ever since they took over and manipulated all religion centuries ago. This includes every faith you can name. Some believe even the Vatican, an arch enemy of the Illuminati, is now ruled by the Illuminati.

It is then written that the Anunnaki Aliens left Earth some four thousand years ago to explore the universe. Once the Anunnaki was satisfied Earth was in good hands, they apparently just buggered off and left us to it, under the watchful eye of what I like to call 'The Earth's landlords' the Greys.

THE EARTH'S LANDLORDS

The Illuminati are our current puppet masters who manage, manipulate and control the world and all its governments today. So, unfortunately, we can't solely blame the government for everything anymore. But it's the Grey little bastards running the Illuminati.

Talk more about the Illuminati Michael.

'Okay I will.....' They are an evil bunch of bastards and worship Satan.

Say what?

I read that the name Illuminati comes from devil worshipping. The name of Lucifer (that's the devil) was a fallen angel also known as the bringer of light; it was him who gave the name Illuminati meaning the enlightened ones.

Oh really. What have you been reading?

www.thetruthseeker.co.uk

From what I understand, the Illuminati are made up of a group of elite families; trustees appointed by the Grey Alien race to manage everything that happens on this planet. They are secret societies that everybody's heard of and yet they don't really know what they are all about. These include Skull and Bones, Freemasons, Rosicrucians, Opus Dei, The Priory of Sion, The Bilderberg Group, The Knights Templar, Hermetic Order of The Golden Dawn, Ordo Templis Orientis. All of these work alongside the Illuminati.

Tell them what they do?

Well, it's simple really; they manage the planet as I have already said. That means manage everything that is on this planet including you sheep. Everything is controlled by the Illuminati.

Tell them how many members there are?

Well…It is believed that there are possibly six managers overall. These managers each have a specific job to do and also have teams to help them carry out that job. For instance, one manager looks after the military aspects of running the planet; in his team he has the army generals and his job is to control the wars of the world.

You have somebody who takes care of the diplomatic issues and his job is to take care of relationships between nations and sell ideas, that sort of thing. His team are all the presidents and prime ministers of the world.

Then you have the intelligence section where the manager's job is to collect data and statistics on everything and everyone and store them on a super computer. His team would be the FBI, CIA, MI6, etcetera.

Another manager has a team of bankers to take care of the economic issues. His job is to control the money and trade. He is over all bank managers and in charge of every World Bank.

Then you have somebody who looks after the scientific stuff and his job is to invent and improve technology with the guidance of the Greys. He may be the one who reports back to the main man and gives him all the different methods on how to cull us sheep using chemicals and controlled viruses like Aids and biological methods. Yes that's right, culling. I haven't yet covered culling fully but I believe that there is a plan to cull most of the sheeple of this planet. I will come to that later.

Then finally you have the one that looks after the political issues; this is the one that feeds you the sheeple sheep shit and propaganda. They do this by brain-washing the flock and then program your mind to accept rules to make you conform to all the other five. You may have heard of the pyramid of power, well the Illuminati are at the top and you sheep are right at the very bottom – like insignificant peasants.

HALFWAY TO ENLIGHTENMENT

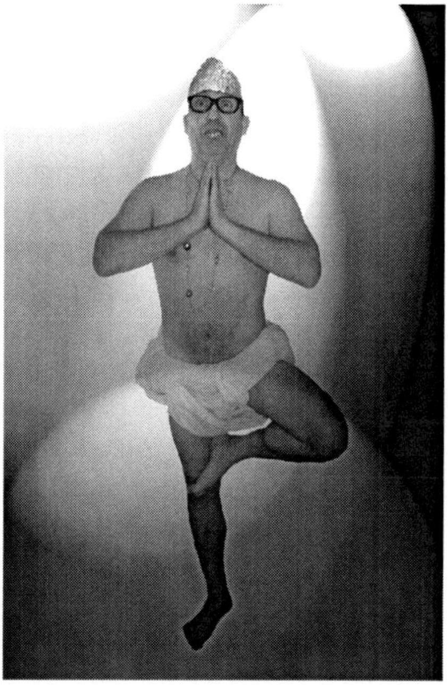

Congratulations reader you are now halfway through the book. This is when it gets really interesting.

After I looked into some of the things Jon Doe talked about it did make me a little paranoid, but most of all it got me to ask many questions about life such as, what's it all about?

I have had an interest in conspiracy theories for some time, ever since I read Jon Doe's blog. This made me ask, what's it all about?' We are all, if we were honest, a little paranoid. This is because we live in an increasingly paranoid and fearful society, and for good reasons too I reckon. But it is important to point out that in most cases a lot of what you see, hear or read is made up and not true. I found you have to be careful what you believe in.

There is a lot of stuff out there that was put together by a student, or by some sheep with mental issues. More often than not you will find it's been put there by a religious nutcase. Also widely available on the inter-web are what I like to call the Purposely Put Conspiracies, or PP conspiracies for short. I think they are put there by government in an attempt to disguise or hide the real truth of what's going on in the world.

I will now tell you about some conspiracies I personally think are the real deal, a fact or based on facts. You can if you want check out all I put to you. It's really up to you at the end of the day to decide if you think I am simply another nutcase or not.

Okay get on with it then.

Look all I'm saying is if you want to be paranoid, at least do so for the right reasons … I have always thought it good to keep an open mind about things. Over many, many years, and I have said this before, I have learned there's a distinct difference between a conspiracy theory and conspiracy fact. So I will put to you some more really good conspiracy facts that, in my opinion, should warrant a little concern from all of us.

'There is no great genius without a mixture of madness'

Aristotle

CHAPTER SEVEN

WHAT IF I WAS TO TELL YOU YOU'RE BEING CONTROLLED?

CONTROLLING THE SHEEPLE

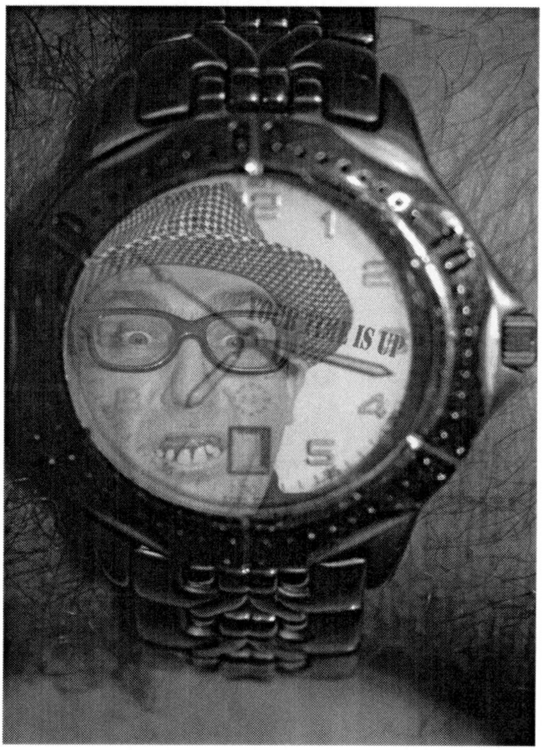

'Those who manipulate the unseen mechanism of society constitute an invisible government which is the true ruling power of our country. We are governed, our minds are moulded, our tastes formed, our ideas suggested, largely by men we have never heard of. This is a logical result of the way in which our democratic society is organized. Vast numbers of human beings must cooperate in this manner if they are to live together as a smoothly functioning society. In almost every act of our lives, whether in the sphere of politics or business, in our social conduct or our ethical thinking, we are dominated by the relatively small number of persons who understand the mental processes and social patterns of the masses. It is they who pull the wires that control the public mind.' - Edward Bernays 1929

You are controlled more than you realize; you may not think you are because you are classically conditioned to accept it. Most of the population has been programmed to accept being controlled. Left unchallenged you will all end up submissive to a New World Order.

'A New World Order, Alf?'

Yes, and if this New World Order does come in you will have lost your freedom forever.

'How are they going to get us to accept this New World Order, Alf?'

By intensifying classical conditioning to all of you, mainly your children; from a very early age your children will be conditioned to obey, no questions asked.

'How are they going to do this?'

It will be introduced in schools. By using schools they will prime the children to accept being a slave. Your children will grow up to accept a new system of work and obedience as a way of life, just as the Chinese have already done. The Chinese populace for a very long time haven't had much of a say in anything. A lot of their sheep work very hard for very low income and just accept it as the norm. This is because they have been trained to accept, obey and comply.

'How do they do it?'

It is impregnated into their minds from a very young age.

'What can we do about it? Not a lot I bet.'

Encouragingly, the humans of China seem to be trying to take back some control of their lives again. They are speaking out and protesting, just like the rest of the world. You humans have started to see the light; you all feel that there is another way, a better world for you all. This is because I think you humans have evolved mentally and spiritually. But this is still being suppressed by the powers that be... because they want to keep you all as slaves.

The miracle is not that we do this work, but that we are happy to do it

Mother Teresa.

A CULL IS HAPPENING RIGHT NOW

Over the next few years, reader, you will see unemployment soar and poverty increase. If you are lucky enough to still hold a job, you will notice more and more work being put on to you. This is already happening.

The world is changing very rapidly and you need to take control of your own lives or somebody else will, starting with a cull which will intensify very soon.

'Why a cull now, Alf?'

The reason things are accelerating as they are is because the Illuminati haven't got very long to get the house in order before their masters return. Many drastic measures are being taken to speed things up a bit and force this NWO in. But before this happens they need to cut back the flock somewhat.

Did you know reader, each year about ninety million extra sheeple are added to a world population that already exceeds five thousand million? This is the equivalent of adding the population of the United Kingdom, Germany and France to the world every year. That is an increase to the world population of one point seven per cent every year.

This is because humans are living longer than ever before and it is causing major problems for the Illuminati. But take heed they want to rectify this problem by a mass cull of the human race.

'That'll be easy for 'em, they can just work us to death.'

Sorry??

Did you know reader it's a fact, when sheeple who work well into old age eventually do retire it usually takes about five years or so before they drop dead. Already statistics show most sheeple will die by the time they reach the age of retirement, a known fact that work can shorten your life expectancy. That is why the retirement age is being lengthened all around the world. It is so we will never be able to retire. We will literately be worked to death. We will all die as workers. I reckon this is part of the culling plan.

MICKY FRICK'S TIP

IF YOU CAN RETIRE EARLY DO SO; DON'T WORK ALL YOUR LIFE

I suppose that's one way to do it, but it would take too long. No Michael, this cull will happen sooner than that if the Illuminati get their way.

'I blame modern technology for the over-population of the world.'

Why do you say that?

'Because I think the world started to get over-populated when the nuke was invented.'

Really? Explain.

'Did most of our technology and advancement weaponry that we have today come from the Greys?'

Yes it did, and most of it was given to you humans to aid your own destruction.

'Exactly, but it didn't happen that way did it?'

They gave us this technology in the hope we would use it to kill ourselves, and we actually did up to a point in Hiroshima and Nagasaki. But, seeing the destruction from this super weapon, now we humans are too frightened to go to war. We saw the immense power of what a nuclear bomb could do and it scared the crap out of us. That's why we keep them safely locked up and they are used as a deterrent, but nobody wants to risk a full-blown world war so the world is overcrowded.

Yes thankfully it has done the opposite and prevented wars, but what's your point?

'I'm saying because of the nuclear bomb or this autonomic bomb, whatever you want to call it, there has not been a worldwide war since 1945.'

But that's a good thing isn't it?

'Yes it is Alf, but...... well... on the downside because of the lack of wars the world has now got so over-populated it's out of control; we can't keep going on like this can we?'

So you're saying there should be a cull?

'Well, maybe a little one.'

There is no need for a cull, this is the point.

'I mean come on Alf, a little war here and there is needed to keep the population under control surely?'

No, you're so wrong. Listen, Michael, although war may seem a very effective way to cut the population, and has been for hundreds if not thousands of years, it's really not needed in the modern world. As I have already mentioned there is an abundance of all you humans need here on Earth; there is enough of everything for everyone. But you are all deprived because they want to control you. And because there are too many of you they also want two thirds of you dead.

'I bet I can guess how the bastards are going to do it too?'

How dare I ask?

'I'll tell you how....'

Firstly, they attack the poverty-stricken third world countries that already have high death rates. They'll do this by withdrawing funding and cutting back on much-needed charity hand-outs. Then they'll attempt to try and make the rest of the world poorer; poor enough so sheeple can't afford to buy healthy food to sustain the proper diet we need. Without a healthy diet no doubt we will take ill. What they will then do is make sure we don't have enough money to afford proper healthcare either, because it won't be free for long. Because of that lack of proper healthcare we will eventually and most possibly die from illness. The government......

Oh dear he's off.....

Already the UK Government are not funding the National Health Service like they used to; they tell us there isn't enough money. What a load of bollocks that is. Don't you think it's kinda funny how they always seem to have enough to go to war with the USA? But they tell us there is not enough money to give to the hospitals for the necessary essentials they need to give proper healthcare to ill and sick sheeple. There is only one outcome, without the funding somebody will inevitably die and the less the funding the more sheeple die.

Saying there isn't enough money is all a pack of lies. There is more than enough money available. Most of it sits in rich bastards' banks...Mark my words sheeple; you are being lied to...

As the years go by and because of these lies you will see more and more hospital wards closed and a lot of hospitals themselves will be closed. Funding towards medical research will be cut too and you will see this again and again. So much so that in the end you will not get any advancement in medical research at all, well at least not enough. I'm talking about research that may cure a lot of sheeple from illnesses such as cancer. Mind you I think they already have a cure for cancer, they just don't want to use it. Remember they are trying to deplete the surplus population not aid it.

Anyway don't just take my word for it the evidence is looking at you square on, so open your eyes. Can you not see what's going on? You're being slowly culled reader. They are forcing poverty onto all the Sheeple of the world. This is quite easy to do as all they have to do is lie to you and say they don't have the money. There is plenty of money out there; they are just not investing it in you.

Did you also know they use technology like the Haarp project, as I mentioned earlier, as a weather controller? It's a weapon capable of manipulating the weather. If they want they can use this weapon to destroy crops, enforce drought or floods and make food scarce. These are all good ways to cull the sheeple.

MICKY FRICK'S TIP

REMEMBER HEALTH IS YOUR WEALTH BUT BEING POOR WILL KILL YOU. THEY'LL MAKE SURE OF THAT

Have you finished?

'No I have more.....'

There are many methods to aid a human cull. One way is to make you accept it. They can do this by putting the idea and acceptance of it into your mind. I'm talking about a cull that uses mass mind control or persuasion... Check this out:

www.disclose.tv/...Mind Control weapon of mass persuasion-Disclose.tv

Did you know they can brainwash sheeple to kill each other or even themselves? Yes there are many ways to do a cull other than just a bolt-gun put to the head. Like, for instance, they can cause a riot... When sheeple get desperate we are naturally frustrated and angry which can lead to riots, fights and violence. Sheeple do and will get killed in all three and the idea to riot can be put into your mind. Governments, no matter what you may think, love riots because they are a great way to enforce curfews and bring in new laws to repress the sheeple. But you shouldn't fall for it.

Did you know it is now legal in some countries to shoot rioters dead? I know when I read this I thought *frickin hell that's bloody charming that is, next they'll be using rubber bullets and water cannons on striking workers*.... then I read they already do, the bastards.

Can't you see that slowly, bit by bit, they are taking away all your rights, your wealth, health and even your food, along with manipulating your thoughts, to kill your fellow sheep? All this will aid a cull programme. Already you can see that all around the world sheeple are desperate and revolting. This will spread and become more frequent if you don't cotton on to what is really going on. They are fricking with your minds:

www.motherboard.vice.com/.../a-complex-systems-model-predicted-the-revol

Using mind control weapons or weather weapons they will try any method they can muster to not only cull you but demoralize you. They want to beat you down into submission to enforce this New World Order upon us. The government are shady bastards who love winding us all up and they are good at it too. I hate the twats. And I know it is all an attempt to turn us against each other. They are trying to make us hate each other, because when we do we are weak and easy to control.

MICKY FRICK'S TIP

STAND UNITED NO MATTER WHAT. TOGETHER WE HAVE LOTS OF POWER TO CHANGE THE WORLD

We have a mixture of nationalities throughout the world and our skin colour has many shades. But we are all human brothers and sisters and if we stand together

against the greyness of world domination we can glow in the sky like a rainbow MAF

That's very sweet Michael

'Good isn't it?'

So take it from me, no matter what you think about the governments of the world you can be sure they will always encourage racism and hate. This is done by many methods such as the news, media outlets, TV and radio which the government control. All of these are regularly used as a propaganda tool to wind us up. When you hear of stories, such as a gang of black men killing a white guy, this feeds vigilantes. The government love territorial gangs and gang warfare because, by having them, sheeple always die. Not only that the government make a lot of money from gangs, what with the drugs and guns they share in. Yes, the government wankers.

Did you know they use the media to spread rumours which usually force small inner city wars to kick off in the hope we again kill each other? They want societies to crumble and violence to accelerate, so bit by bit they beat us down so they can introduce more laws and restrictions against us. And like sheep you all fall for it every time.

Sheeple themselves feed chaos and destruction and the dismantling of society. All this is helping the New World Order to come in. The human cull has started my friend and the plan for a New World Order has started. Be warned and mentally alert. You need to try and take back control of your minds.

And take heed of the voice in your head too, it might be one of us Nordics trying to guide you.

MICKY FRICK'S TIP

IF YOU THINK IT'S WRONG DON'T DO IT, SIMPLE.

SOCIETY GETS WHAT SOCIETY WANTS.

In the end, when the streets look like a bombsite and you're tired, hungry and your home town smells of death, you will come to a point when you want it all to stop. But you sheep will turn to the government to do something to stop all this chaos. By doing that you will find you will agree to anything they offer just to try and bring an end to all the shit going on in your neighbourhood... Then, my friend, the police state is born. They will take back full control of your lives but this time it'll be tenfold. Why? It's because you asked for it.

The world media purposely bombards humans with a barrage of reports of all the horrific and bloody atrocities going on around the world. When you see this, the cry from you goes up to ask or even demand that something is done about it. That is the reaction they want from you because this gives them the power to do anything; like invade other countries, implement new laws and enforce new restrictions upon you.

We could prevent all this by not falling into the trap, we really could. My guess is you will walk right into this trap. I hope I'm wrong because, good or bad, our future is really up to us and always has been. You must ask yourself *do I want a Good or Bad future*. At the end of the day it's your choice.

Humans are unfortunately an aggressive, violent, destructive race; they have a natural aggression against anything they don't understand and this is because you have been infected by alien DNA

Yes that's right, let's not forget about the Aliens. It's because of them we are in this mess and are losing our individuality and our free thinking ability. Our identity as true humans is being stolen from us. Not only that they have systematically destroyed our will to fight back or even want to fight back. We put up with the shit. The Aliens like it when we are all antisocial towards each other; they encourage racism, hate, jealousy and greed. Let's not forget it is they who run the world we all walk upon.

You humans could change your world you know, if you wanted to; if you were to unite against this directive.

Yes sheeple, you want to hurry up too. The way you're going you will soon lose the ability to do so if those THz radio waves take effect. Not only that it's Racism, Hate, Jealousy and Greed turning sheeple against sheeple. It destroys your unity and soul. All common morals go out of the window. Community spirit is depleting. You act like dumb animals. You act like zombie sheep. STOP IT NOW!

*www.theecologist.org/blogs_and.../**unity_what_does_it_mean**.html*

CHANGING WORLD

The world is changing at an alarming rate and I fear not for the better either. Do you know why? The Illuminati are winning which is why we are in this worldwide recession. It is them who provoke all the Wars, Social Unrest and Poverty. All the shit that goes on all around the world is down to them. Why? It's because you allow it to happen. As for the Aliens, they help them enforce discipline and order back on Planet Earth like they once had.

Like a flock of dumb sheep you will soon be tagged, herded, penned up, fleeced, worked and culled at their beck and call if you don't make a stand now. Do you know what's crazy is that you will even ask for it to happen. That's right, ask...no... demand it to happen because you're brainwashed to do so. I can see the future now...You will one day demand better discipline which will even include bringing back capital punishment. There will be public flogging, the birch on every street corner, if not the birch stocks. Because of all the youth unemployment and the wars around the world, I can see compulsory conscription of our young Rams and Ewes. Crime will get out of control so you will demand the government build more prisons.

That wish is already being met check out:
www.youtube.com/watch?v=0vOWh5G_Q70

You will back and support the police to enforce curfews in trouble-spot areas, which will eventually be all across the world. After midnight you will need a permit to leave your house or face imprisonment. You will ask them to add even more surveillance cameras on every street corner. You will even agree that it is necessary for every sheep to carry ID all the time day and night.

You will want some process put in place so they can keep a check on who is illegal in your country and who is not. This will happen because they will brainwash you to think it is needed. The way they will do this is tell you it is these illegal immigrants who take away all your jobs; it is because of them that crime has gone up one hundred per cent.

So, to rectify this growing problem, they will suggest that maybe they should have a microchip put in your hand so they can keep a check on who you are and where you are 24/7, like they do with dogs and cats. Because you are so stupid...no sorry, brainwashed, you will think it's a great fricking idea and gladly let them insert this microchip into your hand. Did you know they are already making preparations for that day?

www.tech.firstpost.com/.../2017-microchip-new-world-order

MICKY FRICKS TIP

DON'T LET THEM EVER PUT A CHIP IN YOUR BODY

As far as I am concerned it is barbaric to have this chip inserted into you. This is the same as letting them put a metal collar around your neck and putting you in shackles as they did to the black slaves in the seventeenth century.

Fricking hell sheeple, wake up. The next thing is you will demand the right to work and of course they will be only too happy to oblige you. Yes, my sheepy little flock, in the end they will have full control of all of us and cull the ones who moan or speak out; that's me fucked. I tell you they want to be able to decide what you can and can't do, when and where you can go, and even when you should die.

Does this worry you? It fricking should. Make no skull and bones about it sheeple; we were bred to be workers from day one. We are and always have been Anunnaki slaves. They just relaxed their restraint upon us. Now they are beginning to tighten the leash.

Well said Michael, a bit melodramatic but you are on the right track.

THINNING OUT THE FLOCK

As you can imagine it's a big task to try and control every sheep on this Earth Farm. At the moment there are just so many of us that it's really hard for them to control us. So they know the only way they can implement their ideas for this New World Order vision is through a mass cull. Thin out the flock. I'm sorry to say this has already begun. Don't believe me? Then just look around you.

I think most humans pay attention to what goes on in the world, at least we Nordics hope they are, because there is clearly a process of speeding up towards a One World Government. They are slowly eliminating individual rights, even their right to live, and this is happening right this minute.

'That's right Alf, I seeing this happen every day, every time I turn on the news.'

Do you know sheeple it's your own fault why the world is in such a shit state? It's mainly because you all too easily trust politicians. You are followers. Most sheeple live in their own fairy tale world. You sheeple of the modern world like America, the United Kingdom, China, Russia, Australia, are all too easily manipulated by clever talkers, modern technology (sorry Alien Technology), TV and newspapers. Not only that you are driven by the want of money. All this does is make you slaves to a system designed to control your life.

If you don't know about something you cannot protect yourself from it. MAF

Up until now I have learned one thing in life and this is unquestionably a Fact.

YOU'RE ALL SHEEP!

I am going to keep saying this until it sinks in and you accept it. I now want to talk to you about money because in my opinion this is the human race's biggest downfall.

THE INVENTION OF MONEY

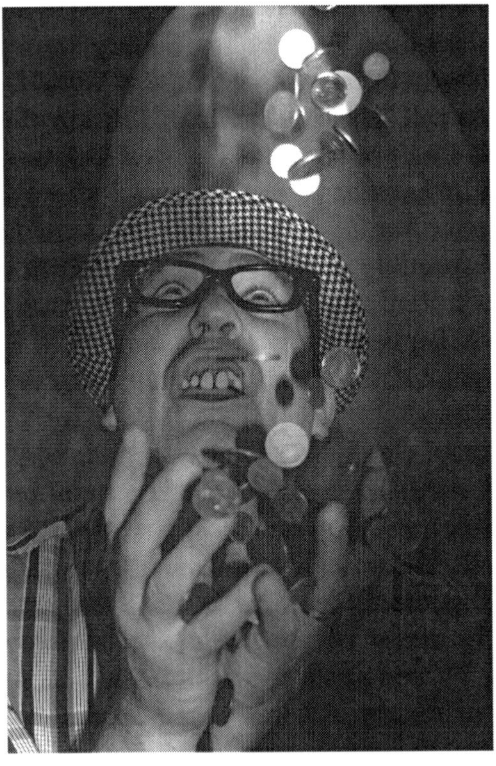

Money was invented to keep us sheep enslaved. It was no accident it was made out of metal either. Metal, back in the day, was quite rare, but also quite pretty to look at too, especially when it was polished up. Our primitive minds were attracted to a shiny piece of metal. It works even today, think of gold or silver. When something looks pretty and shiny it becomes precious and desirable. Every sheep wants something that looks nice, shiny and pretty, and a metal coin back then was one of them. I mean think of copper. Now copper looks very nice polished doesn't it? Gold looks even better.

It does.

Did you know the first ever coins were made from a substance called electrum? For those of you who don't know what electrum is, it is a naturally occurring alloy of gold and silver with traces of copper. It is often known as green gold, especially by the ancient Greeks. This 'green gold' looked very pretty polished up and when made into a coin it possibly had an animal picture stamped onto it. So not only did you have a pretty coin but one that had a cute little animal on it, like maybe a little bunny rabbit or something. As you can imagine early humans loved this.

So now you have the first part of the master plan by the Anunnaki in place; to get you primitive humans attracted to the look of a coin. They did this by making it look shiny, pretty and interesting with the little bunny rabbit on it. They knew very well we wouldn't be able to resist. This was because the Anunnaki was 'clevera' than us ('clevera' my own made up word. It means more intelligent).

Anyway, because of this beautiful object (the coin) the humans around then would have given anything to get their hands on one. Every sheep wanted a precious. At the beginning it was so they could show it off to their flock. Can you see how they would have got the human hooked?

I guess....

So anyway, the next part of the plan was to make you prepared to work to for one. Back in the day sheeple were still very primitive; their brains weren't fully developed like they are today, Okay... let's pull no punches ...Your ancestors were a bit thick. (Thick meaning not very intelligent)

Primitive Ram would have done any kind of trading deal with any Ram who had a coin. For instance if they had a pig they would swap it for a coin and both would then happily go their separate ways.

I guess this was how it happened in the beginning. It was commonplace for Rams to trade pigs, their Ewes, even lambs, just to own a pretty coin. But it didn't stop there, oh no, because Rams are naturally greedy. One precious wouldn't have been enough and they would want more pretty coins.

What you have got to remember is there weren't a lot of coins around back then, they were quite rare. To own one you would have made yourself a very popular Ram indeed in the field... So you can imagine to own two... well it wasn't heard of to own two pretty coins. I mean that would have put you right up on the credibility ladder.

But when you went off to purchase another coin you were surprised to find you now had to give two pigs for one coin. The price had gone up. Because of the power of the precious you still would have shook hands on the deal because like a magpie you wouldn't be able to resist it. You would have been too attracted to a shiny coin, more than you could handle. Without knowing it, you developed a lust for shiny nice coins of precious metal... A lust for money.

So the power of money grew and before you knew it you sold all your pigs, your Ewes, maybe even all your lambs and even your body to get as many pretty shiny coins you could get to show off to all your flock in the village. But then you realized you had nothing left to trade. *Oh shit,* you thought... *What am I going to do for food now?*

You forgot that you still needed to eat so this put you in a slight dilemma. You need food for you and your family, if you have any left that is... so now the tables have turned on you.

You're hungry. Your family are hungry and you need to get one of your pigs back. Then you hear about a Ram down the track who has five pigs for sale and you're so hungry you go straight away to buy a pig from him to feed yourself and family.

Winter is coming but the Ram down the road is a greedy fucker like you are, not for food but for money; for the pretty coin. He knows you want one of his pigs really badly. You have no choice but to buy a pig from him at any cost, so when you go to buy this pig you then find the price has gone up. He asks you for two pretty shiny coins for one pig. You think, *robbing bastard* but even so you have no choice but to agree the price. So you reluctantly pay the robbing bastard two coins for the pig.

Then before long this greedy bastard realizes that his pigs are worth a lot of pretty coins. Demand is high. He gets a lust for money and sells all his pigs to get lots of pretty shiny coins. Now he too is pig-less and has to go to market to buy some pigs to feed his family. But when he gets to market he finds the king or leader of the flock has bought every fricking pig in the land. And now, right...and now they are six shiny coins each. He himself now thinks, *bastard* as he would. But then he finds he only has four coins left. He realizes he doesn't have enough money to buy even one pig. *Oh fuck*, he thinks.

So the king says to him, 'No problem my old chum, work for me and I'll give you a coin a week. If you work for me for two weeks you will have enough money to buy one of my pigs.'

Having no choice he takes his offer and agrees to work for payment of one shiny coin a week so he can buy one of the king's pigs. But it doesn't stop there. Fricking hell no... Eventually this ram will eat that pig and so he will need to buy a new one. The king has got you by the bollocks and every other sheep in the land by the bollocks. By now he owns all the animals in the land, he owns everything in fact, so you find the price of pigs has gone up even more, considerably more, to seven coins each. Even the vegetables are expensive because he owns them too, everything is expensive so all the sheep in the land soon find they have to work every week just to earn enough coins to eat.

Bingo! Labour was born. You may think why didn't they just breed and grow their own food? That would have been good. But they weren't given the chance of breeding or growing their own food because they were too busy working for the king. See everyone fell for it and even today are still falling for it. The sheeple of the world are slaves to the nice shiny coin or pretty paper money that we have now. Ingenious, really, how they did it.

Erm.... interesting story Michael. I'm not sure if that is exactly how it happened, but nevertheless.

I'm telling ya...Our ancestors should have told them, 'Bollocks! Shove your shiny coin up your arse!'

But it's too late now isn't it? Yes, we have a lot to blame our ancestors for because it is their fault we have to work; those stupid, thick sheep. Hopefully future generations will be a little smarter and refuse to fricking work....... Oh they already do..... The youth of today don't want to work do they? They all want to be stars on X factor............ Well, good for them, I say, fuck it. Working is over-rated anyway.

Okay shall we move on now?

Why should they be forced to work for the pittance they are offered? In some cases the government bastards want them to work for free, for fricking free, they are taking the piss. I reckon we should all flock together and tell them 'bollocks' right now. 'Give us some more money you arseholes.' Work, I hate fricking work.

Okay Michael calm down....

The technique to get us to work is simple really. They make us want for stuff and then make us want to work to get it. The one thing you are most willing to work for, or should I say have no fricking choice to work for, is so you can buy food. And now we all even have to pay for the water we drink an' all. How the frick did they get us to do that? I mean, rainwater is free and abundant....... well it is here in the UK anyway. Maybe not so much in the desert, but you got my point.

One thing is for sure Michael. Because of the dependence on money you Humans are slaves. That is why it was invented.

MONEY IS GOD

> ***'The love for money is the root of all evil'. Originates in the Bible, Timothy 6:10***

In my opinion money is the worst invention ever. Why? It is because it controls your life. A lot of sheep are unhappy because of it and some even die because of it. This want for money is most sheeple's weakness.

Most of you sheep think money is the be all and end all of everything. This is not the case, or your fault, it is how you are programmed to think, as covered in great detail earlier in the book. You are made to believe that you need a lot of it to get the best out of your life, which is totally untrue. You are programmed to want for money and, not only that, most of you sheep are too money-focused in my opinion. You live your life with tunnel vision because of it. Nothing else matters to you but the want of financial wealth. Yet, whilst you're so into money, the world you walk, live and graze on is falling apart around your hooves. You are controlled by this lust for money and ignoring what life has to offer for free.

You ignore everything else going on around you and this is stupid. Let me tell you, money will not save the planet, only you can do that. First thing you need to do is change your mind set.

Think not of what you can buy, but what you have now and how you can look after it. MAF

Very well said Michael

'Thank you.'

To a lot of Sheeple money is God; it for damn sure controls your life, just like any religion does. It is good to understand that these Greys are the ones who make you believe you need and want money. They use the government to help them implement the idea into your heads. It is the only way to get you to work as a slave. They are intent on making you all want money because to make you want money you will be under their control. The next step is not to give you enough of it, so you will be willing to work even harder to get more of it. When you get it you will love having it so you want even more still.

They even try to get you in debt; when you don't have enough money you become desperate to get some so the loan was invented. They then keep you in debt for as long as they possibly can. As I covered quite extensively in my other book, Programmed Sheep, once they have you in debt they will brainwash you to want even more, hence the Lottery.

In many senses we, in this technologically advanced age, are all slaves to money. We all want the modern commodities out there. We are all controlled; we just haven't been branded and tagged yet by our masters. The Greys, like I said, are the ones who made us want and have to work. Some sheeple say they love work, but it's not work they love but the money they get from doing it.

MICKY FRICK'S TIP

REMEMBER THERE IS MORE TO LIFE THAN JUST MONEY

WORKERS ARE NOW BECOMING OBSELETE?

I know you work because you think you have to so you can pay the bills, your mortgage etc. But you also work, I guess, in order to better your life. You want the latest gadgets like and up-to-date cell phone, surround sound 3D TV, that posh car, a nice home, trendy fashionable clothes and a holiday. Am I right? Or am I right? Of course I'm right. You also hope by working hard in the future you might even have enough money saved so you can have a good long retirement.

You're not on your own, most sheeple have this dream that maybe someday they will be able to retire to the countryside somewhere and have plenty of money to do what they want to do; I'm the same. This is because we are programmed to think that way.

Well, I don't want to be the one to piss on your dreams, but I have seen the light. You may as well forget it my sheepy little friend. Why? I'll tell you fricking why, because soon there won't be any need for you as a worker anymore. There are plans to replace all of us. So you won't be able to earn any money at all. In fact you will be lucky to have a job by the end of the century if they get their way. You can laugh but this will be apparent to you very soon, mark my words.

Over the next few years you will see less and less jobs available. Why? Because of Alien technology, that's why. You will be replaced by robots or computers so there won't be a need for as many workers, or money come to that. Money has already lost its worth and there isn't much of it about on the streets these days. This is because the ones who have it, them rich fuckers out there, are keeping it in banks. Money is losing its value because of the rich sheep. The rich fuckers ain't spending it. The money they have is doing fuck all in banks. A lot of sheeple don't realize that if you don't spend money it's worth fuck all.

While I am on the subject of money, you will very soon notice that the wages you get now will deplete. You will hear on the news that your company has to give everybody a pay cut. Not only that, there will be less working hours for most of the working population available. The only available work that sheeple will get is part-time hours, to make you desperate again to obtain money.

Being made to become desperately poor when you have been used to having money will wind the sheeple up to riot. This will yet again aid the NWO. Thanks to the greed of the rich and advancements in the technology that the Aliens gave us, once this technology has peaked over the next century, there won't be any need for most of us.

Hence the cull; it's already happening now. There just aren't any well-paid jobs left anymore for us sheep' robots. Machines and computers are replacing the workforce and as a result soon they will do away with money completely as none of them will need paying.

Before this happens, you sheep will be encouraged to have a microchip put in your hand to replace money; it'll be called credits. You will work for credits that will be inputted into your chip. They will also use that chip to track you as it will have everything in this chip about you.

Remember all this advanced technology came from Aliens set on taking over the world. I don't wish to scare you... no scratch that, I do..... That chip they want to put inside you is also a robot chip; it is intelligent to the point it is almost alive like a tiny parasite. It will live under your skin, a highly sophisticated artificial living organism, and it will take over your body in the end. But they don't want you to know that because to think you have something inside you that is alive would freak anybody out. Anyway don't take it from me, why not check it out for yourself:

www.youtube.com/watch?v=ncXjBih6mcw

Or:

www.panoffolin.wordpress.com/.../the-shocking-truth-about-rfid-chip-implant

A human microchip implant is an identifying integrated circuit device known as the RFID transponder encased in silicate glass and implanted in the body of a human being. A sub dermal implant typically contains a unique ID number that can be linked to information contained in an external database, such as personal identification, medical history, medications, allergies and contact Wikipedia.

MICKY FRICK'S TIP

DON'T LET THEM EVER PUT A CHIP IN YOUR BODY

You said that already.

'I know but it's important.'

Fair enough.

WORKERS, WE'RE NOW BECOMING OBSELETE?

Michael is right, there is research going on to find ways to cut out the need for humans to work altogether. They want machines and robots to replace you as the worker. Sounds brilliant at first but when you think about it it's a scary thought because, for one, they will achieve this goal and, two, when they do get there, there will be no way for any of us to get a job; unless you are a robotic engineer or a computer programmer or have a high grade in quantum physics. Because of alien technology we are becoming obsolete.

*www.washingtonpost.com/.../some-predict-***computers***-will-produce-a-job*

You can see this for yourself as it has already started to happen. My advice to you is this. Don't let yourself be ruled by money. Stop it now, because one day that too will become obsolete especially, when you have that chip put in your hand.

There is a better life waiting for you all if you want it without the need for money at all.

'How do you mean Alf?'

Earth, believe it or not, was a free planet once. Everything on it was once free of charge; a free gift if you like for everybody.

'Was it?'

Yes it was.... What if I was to tell you that there is enough of everything on this planet for all of you humans to have an equal share, and it shouldn't cost you a thing to have it.

'You were saying this earlier. Then why can't we have it?'

Like you said, it was because of the invention of money. Money is an effective way to control the masses; that's why it was put in place. The Earth's bounty is abundant. Look around you, there is enough water to drink and keep fish, enough land to build hundreds of homes and grow as many varied crops and herbal medicine as you wish. You could breed millions of animals and yet still have humans living on the streets, dying through lack of proper health care, starving to death because of the lack of food. The Anunnaki invented money to take control of you humans.

'This is all happening and they keep blaming the lack of money.'

That's right, and there is no need for money at all.

'We sheeple are neglected on a daily basis by our farmers and they use money, or the lack of it, as an excuse.'

That's also right.

Look reader how you let your fellow sheep be treated? I mean if you saw neglected animals on your 3D television, like a rancher treating his cattle badly, most of us would be outraged. We would be disgusted at the way the animals were neglected. We would call for him to be locked up and banned from ever keeping any livestock again. But we allow it to happen to our fellow sheep. That's barmy.

Remember Earth survived for thousands of years before money was even invented - it must have done, or you wouldn't be here today.

Up until 1500 BC all money was in the form of goods such as cattle, lambs, goats or pigs. Sheeple used to trade with what they had for something that the other had. A lot of what you pay for today, such as water, heating, vegetables and fruit, used to be free once. Did you know the use of money was first thought up by a Greek philosopher named Aristotle in 3500 BC? Then in 1500 BC it was the Phoenicians who invented metal money (the coin). Did they get the idea from the Anunnaki?

Yes they did. Well done on your research Michael.

CHAPTER EIGHT

WHAT IF GOD IS AN ALIEN?

It seems the Phoenicians knew more about the origins of the Anunnaki than first thought and about their empowerment over early humans. In ancient texts they described how Aliens were once on Earth. They called them gods. According to them it was the gods who created the slave and they did it over several stages. It was just a matter of training the sheeple to work, or want to work, as I have already touched on. Later money was invented to control us completely.

That's very good Michael, somebody has done their homework.

'Thank you Alf and hang fire I have more....'

Go on then.

THERE ARE LINKS BETWEEN THE ANUNNAKI AND RELIGION

> ***'Religions and money were put in place by the Anunnaki as a mechanism to specifically divide the people and make them fall out with each other' Jon Doe***

The first thing to interest me about the Anunnaki was to find that they were mentioned by many different ancient cultures all around the world, even in the Holy Bible. There is also evidence to suggest that the Anunnaki authored much of the Old Testament and corrupted it for its own agenda.

In a lot of the Old Testament you will find references to sheeple being obedient to God such as in 2 Samuel 22:25 where it says, 'Strangers shall submit themselves unto me: as soon as they hear, they shall be obedient unto me'.

In Exodus 24:7 there is a passage telling the sheeple that they must "be obedient"

> **Religious ideology helps them make us think like they want you to think. If you follow a religion that's why you are referred to as a flock. It's because you're acting like a Sheep. MAF**

Now I don't know about you but I thought God was about love and caring for one another, not wanting obedience from anyone. But according to this Ram Samuel, and Moses in fact, both said God demanded obedience. So this beckons the question, is it true? Did the Anunnaki write most of the Bible as believed by so many sheeple? Reading about it, I find that the answer to that question is very possibly yes. I say this because when you flick through the Bible it is always on about doing as you're told and being fearful of God.

The God I was brought up to understand never came across as the bully written about by Samuel and a lot of other ones in the Bible. Obedient, what the frig is that all about? Well he/God can kiss my arse.... Also in the Old Testament the Anunnaki are referred to as 'heavenly visitors' called 'Anakim'.

It is said when they visited Earth they were looked upon as Gods by the sheeple of the land. I can understand why because the Anunnaki apparently were giants. They were big bastards. And from my experience all big sheep tend to be bullies. I tell you now.... If a big fricking Ram told me to be obedient to him I'd kick the fucker right in the nuts and tell him to kiss my arse... the cheeky bastard. I wouldn't care how fricking big he was one swift kick in the bollocks and he would soon be brought down to my level... Yes kneel to me you twat. Obedient my arse, who the frig do you think you are?

God, or no God, I'm obedient to no-one. Hark at me cursing God.... Look I know religion means a great deal to a lot of sheeple, I also believe most sheeple genuinely try to be kind, do a lot caring things and put themselves out to help others. There are a lot of good sheeple out there but I feel a lot of them cover themselves with their religious comfort blanket a little too much.

Just because they say they are religious, they think it gives them the right to be a prick. Some think no matter what they do they can pray and be forgiven... Well fuck off, I say... Don't be a prick in the first place then you wouldn't need forgiveness.

Why do humans have this need to believe in anything anyway, why not believe in themselves?

'Beats me Alf....'

Do you know reader what I find encouraging is a lot of the sheep these days have started to question their faith? I say it is encouraging because I think they should. We all look for something more. Now, before I am jumped on by all you religious sheep, I am not attacking your faith, far from it. I just don't think a lot of you fully understand what it is you believe.

What I do want to bring to your attention is this. I think most of the religious stuff you have either read or been told has been manipulated or re-written over and over again by humans with their own agenda. This is to control you by fear; or the fear of God. Maybe it has been written with sinister intent, or even by an Alien calling himself God.

That's right Aliens could have written the Bible. No one knows what to believe anymore. With all the shit going on in the world lately, this belief that God is good, God is just, doesn't seem to carry much weight anymore; not to me anyway. I'm sorry but, for me, the God most sheeple follow seems to be a hypocrite, a sadistic, cruel and vindictive God. What God of love allows bastards to get away with what they do? This is not as I perceived as being a good God.

So maybe the God you visualize in your own heads as a benevolent being doesn't exist at all. I know, to even think this it suddenly makes us feel vulnerable and alone. Religion, as I see it, is mainly to fuck with your brain and control you with fear. Fear is a powerful weapon. Nobody wants to think they will die and go to hell. Hell doesn't seem to be a very nice place.

I have come to the conclusion that the real truth about God is hidden from us. Why? It is because he is an Alien.

There is one thing all religions have in common. I am sure, no matter what your faith, you agree on the fundamental thing that there is one over-all God. But who is this one God? I want to throw a thought in the mix for you sheep to ponder over. What if all the religions out there all stemmed from this one over-all God who is an evil Alien? If there is only one God have you ever thought, in that case, why are there so many different religions out there?

I think I know why this is and I'll explain that later. But for now I think a lot of sheeple who follow a religion are possibly followers of an evil Alien without knowing it.

Under this cloak of religion which I think, like any other cult, is stupid and very dangerous, there are atrocities carried out. Think about all the vicars and priests you hear about who molest children, or those crooks who feed off other sheeple's devoted faith. I'm talking about the so-called religious speakers who get very rich conning good decent sheeple out of their money by preaching God's word, or trying to sell them a seat in Heaven. What about all the religious leaders who send our young men to war to die?

God is good is he? Bollocks. He is an evil Alien. If there is only one God then I think we are screwed. When you cut out the chaff, every religion is linked by this one over-all God who it seems is a fricking Alien. There is enough material out there that points to this being a fact. You may think I am a terrible sheep to say all this, and totally insane to think God is Alien. But who is to tell me different? Prove it.

MICKY FRICK'S TIP

YOU REALLY SHOULDN'T BELIEVE EVERYTHING

Most of what you read, are told or see is a lie as far as I am concerned. There are always too many versions of the same story, turning it into fiction rather than fact. When you think about it seriously most of you believe in a fairy tale written by another programmed sheep. Can't you see that is just slightly mad?

What interests me is these fairy tale religions cause us to fall out with each other and creates wars. Religion breeds hate and millions of sheeple have died over hundreds if not thousands of years because of it. Don't you think this is kind of weird? God is love. God is just. I fear God alright because he can get you killed.

In my observations I haven't met anyone yet who knows what or who God is or what he really represents. Some think they do but they will not accept or respect somebody else's beliefs. I just don't get that. You all believe in one loving, caring God don't you? To most of you God represents love, yet you seem to hate anybody who criticizes your own beliefs. A lot don't act on the love in religion, they find it easier to hate. Why? It's because that is its purpose.

"Darkness cannot drive out darkness; only light can do that. Hate cannot drive out hate; only love can do that". Martin Luther King.

What if God is an evil Alien?

Now I know you're tittering at what I have just said, but it's not a laughing matter. This is a very serious situation we all face.

So stop laughing and take note of what I say because this book, my sheepy little friend, may just save your life.

God is an Alien. Imagine all the religious sheeple's faces when they are told Aliens are for real and they are our creators. This would probably send the lot of them into fricking frenzy. I guess a lot would stay in denial even if the Alien stood in front of them. One thing for sure it would probably trigger mass hysteria, mass suicides, the lot. You would possibly get sheeple with different faiths falling out with one another on a huge scale, bigger than ever before; protests, riots, the world in panic.

What do you think would happen if all the Catholics, the Christians, Buddhists, the Jews and Muslims and every other religion on the planet suddenly found out their faiths were a load of bollocks? That God was in fact an Alien? Fricking hell it would be worldwide mayhem. Best they don't know eh?

I'm not sure if you're ready to find out yet. But ask yourself this. What if you personally found out that Aliens are for real and God is one? Not only that, that it is this Alien God who created you? How would you feel about knowing that? What if I told you it is a rock solid fact?

I think most of the world is not ready to accept this yet. I'm going to talk about it anyway; you need not accept it. But your future descendants will have to accept it someday. We need to get them ready for that day.

THE ALIENS ARE COMING!!

It has been written that they will return someday. Some even think they are already here. It is mentioned in many ancient texts of the Hopi Indians, all the Native American Indian tribes and the Mayans. It's written in Egyptian hieroglyphics, the Holy Bible and the Quran (Koran) as in every other religious manuscript across the planet. Even the Chinese religions such as Buddhism, Taoism and Confucianism; all of them, every single one, believe in one God and also believe he will return. Only the Chinese believe God will come back as female. Interesting... Well I don't know, maybe he's had a sex change.

Whatever, the fact is the same God is coming back. Now a lot of you believe in God I know, but God being an Alien has real credibility; so much so that the world is being made ready for this Alien God's arrival.

The Vatican knows God is an Alien. Most of the governments of the world know he is an Alien and that he is coming back to Earth.

'What's that Alf? The Vatican know about Aliens?'

The Vatican has known for a hundred years. The only ones who don't know at the moment are you sheep. I mean humans....

Well that's interesting isn't it reader?

Yes and later Michael I'll give you the facts to put in this book.

Now I understand you sheeple still need convincing that God is an Alien and I understand it is a lot for most of you to grasp. But just imagine an Alien ship one mile wide suddenly appearing in the sky above say London and landing in Hyde Park. Then an Alien stepped out and spoke fluently in multiple languages of every country of the world, so everyone could understand, and said, 'Hello Earthlings, I Am God'

Frick-kin-hell, just imagine that! What would the Earth's population do if they saw this on the television? It would be hard for a lot of sheeple to deal with that's for sure. It would not be part of their reality at all to find out we may well be descendants of Aliens. Imagine it sheeple, finding out God is actually an Alien. Fricking hell, most sheeple wouldn't handle it at all would they?

So I guess you can kind of understand why the government and the church would never admit that they know about these Aliens, and that God is one. I know a lot of religious sheeple would never question their faith nor accept that there could be an alternative reason to why we are all here. Their faith in God as they perceive it is rock solid to them and it would be a sin to think differently. All they need is to have faith in the one almighty God, but what is faith? Let's look at faith shall we?

> ***Faith is a belief in the trustworthiness of an idea. Formal usage of the word 'faith' is usually reserved for concepts of religion, as in theology, where it almost universally refers to a trusting belief in a transcendent reality, or believing in a supreme being. Wikipedia***

The problem with faith, or 'blind faith' as I like to call it, is it lacks concrete evidence. However, there is a lot of evidence to suggest Aliens exist, so you would expect the sheeple to be more acceptant to the idea God was an Alien. It would make more sense to believe in Aliens than a supreme invisible being called God, where there is no real evidence at all that he exists.

Have you heard of the term 'trust in God' faith where sheeple believe in something they have never seen? I have never understood faith; I always say that seeing is believing. All I see is a lot of religious sheeple who flock together wanting to believe in something, anything. But very rarely do they question what they actually believe in. It's totally bonkers to me. It's like having an imaginary friend. Hang on.......

Anyway there are no facts at all that God actually exists, is there, but sheeple with faith don't need any. All they need is faith to believe that he or she does exist or rather they hope he does. Well I tell you religious sheeple now, God does exist and he's an Alien. He's the leader or king of a species called the Anunnaki.

Have you ever thought the Bible may have been manipulated by Aliens? I think too many sheep wrongly interpret what they read in religious books like the Bible. If you were to read the Old Testament, for instance, you would be amazed at what it really says. Most of it, if you read it carefully, refers to Aliens. See, you never thought that could be the case did you? For those who have read it, I bet this never crossed your mind.

As in most religious texts usually what you read is not always as straightforward as it seems. So many sheeple use their own interpretation of what they think they are reading and not what it actually says. It is quite understandable really because it's been tampered by the Anunnaki to do just that.

Now it's up to you if you want to believe that or not but it is something to think about. If you read ancient stuff to be fair a lot it is not in a language we are familiar with. Whoever tries to interpret it may just write what they think it said rather than what it actually says. That is probably why there are many contradictions within religion. No wonder most sheep are confused.

I dont know much about the Anuunaki but I did discover in my little bit of research that the Sumerians were amongst the earliest civilizations to write about them on hundreds of stone tablets. These were discovered in 1887 and were dated to over three thousand seven hundred years old. Did you know some religions think we humans have only been here for 2015 years?

www.ancientexplorers.com/.../sumerian-texts-secrets-about-Alien-life-revealed

The Sumerian tablets recorded events of so-called 'origins of man' and creation itself and the beginning of the Anunnaki colonization of the Earth. It was also believed what was recorded on the tablets was dictated by the Anunnaki who came to Earth on 'Shem.' Shem means spaceship. They came down to Earth on Shem and copulated with primitive Earthlings... This is recorded in the Bible too, check it out Genesis 6:2-4:

www.ufoevidence.org/documents/doc175

Time you told them more about the Anunnaki, Michael.

'I don't know that much about the fricking Anunnaki do I?'

I'll zap you...input the information.

'Wish you wouldn't keep doing that it makes me feel dizzy when you fuck about with my brain. I'll research it thank you very much. I don't need zapping, just give me some time.'

Quicker if I zap you.

'Fuck off.'

Fair enough

(Some considerable time later)

Hello Sheeple I'm back and this is what I have found......

Took your time

'Sod off.'

It would have been a lot quicker if I zapped you the information.

'No you're okay, I think I've done alright by myself, thank you very much. '

Anyway eyes down, look reader this is what I have found on the inter-web about the Anunnaki

WHO ARE THE ANUNNAKI? AND WHAT IS N I B I R U?

According to The Oxford Companion to World Mythology the Anunnaki are 'Sumerian deities of an old primordial line or they are what they call chthonic or subterranean' meaning 'live beneath the Earth'. According to Greek religion, they believe the Anunnaki to be spirits of the underworld. This suggests to me that they are something like demons, which I found quite interesting. Because when you read from another source it is also believed that the Aliens are demonic demons. The Anunnaki are said to take their name from an old sky God called 'Anu'. The Anunnaki is believed to be the offspring of Anu. Now... what if Anu is God?

But then I read from another source that it is also believed that Anu was a fallen angel which suggests that Anu is possibly Lucifer, The Devil, Satan himself.

The Anunnaki are not a friendly race.

'Well maybe not, Alf.'

But Anu was without a doubt seen as angelic and worshipped like a God by many civilizations of the time, enough for them all to write so many books about him. It is also believed that the Anunnaki was here on Earth during middle Palaeolithic times.

This is when humans started to bury their dead, make music, invent advanced tools and start farming. They also started worshipping Gods. This was because this Anunnaki Alien named Anu influenced the sheeple to do so. It is also written that this supposedly happened three hundred thousand years ago.

I also found that the word or name Anunnaki is written in many different ways by many ancient civilizations but all seem to translate to the same or similar meaning of 'Descendants of God.' I found 'Offspring of Anu' is a term used quite a lot. Whatever the case the Anunnaki must have existed once and Anu was for real. I think this is amazing.

The Anunnaki still exist. I told you this already.

'Say what?'

The Anunnaki still exist, they are coming to Earth..... remember?

'I'm starting to believe you Alf.'

Good.

Now I wonder if this Anu is God. This may well have been what started religion. There are many religions that believe Humans were created in God's own image. What if we were all descendants of Anu, this Anunnaki Alien? If that's the case then that means we all have Alien DNA. We are the Aliens; amazing if it's true isn't it?

A lot of you may have read a book called The Twelfth Planet or, if not that one, maybe a book called The Earth Chronicles. Both were written by a Ram named Zecharia Sitchin and according to him Anunnaki means 'Those who from the heavens came to Earth.' I guess you may have read his book because it was a bestseller. If not, I'll tell you about The Twelfth Planet.

In 1976, Zecharia Sitchin published a book called The Twelfth Planet. In his book he translated some ancient Sumerian texts which explained the origins of humans on planet Earth. He also talked about a planet called Nibiru, a fairly large planet about the same size as Pluto. It orbits around the Sun passing between Earth and the Moon every three thousand six hundred years. So the last time it was in the vicinity of Earth you can imagine the gravitational effects would have wreaked havoc on our planet. Check out:

www.thepathtooneness.com/mental/nibiru-planet-x/

Sitchin also said that according to the texts we must prepare for yet another possible apocalypse because it is believed Nibiru is once again heading this way - and will be here very soon. Well, when I read this I thought, *that's just fricking great that is.... if we don't get culled off by the Illuminati, or taken over by Aliens, this planet Nibiru is going to pull our planet apart.*

So I wanted to know more about this 'death star' Nibiru heading our way and I went and did some more research and came up with this. Now Sitchin's book was based on years of his research and so he probably knew more about the Anuunaki and the planet Nibiru than anyone. The story of the Anunnaki, as told by Sitchin in many of his books, was that about four hundred and fifty thousand years ago Alalu, a ruler of the Anunnaki, lived on a planet called Nibiru (A Red Planet). I've never heard of it, have you reader? Not until now.

Yes, just type in the word: `N I B I R U' on the inter-web and you will come up with all kinds of information about it.

'Thank you, Alf.'

You should check it out.... but getting back to this Alalu Alien he did something on Nibiru that pissed the Anunnaki off and he fled. He eventually escaped in a spaceship and found refuge here on Earth. Once here he took no time at all to spread his influence. But whilst he was here he didn't know that he was followed by another Alien from Nibiru who I now think is God named Anu. Anu hunted Alalu down and they had a big fight. Anu defeated him and his army and drove them underground into caves. Anu then became over-all ruler here on Earth. I am not going into the entire story now so if you're interested check out:

www.newageGod.com/ENKImedia/Earth4.htm

Now.....I wonder if this Alalu Alien was an evil dictator, a nasty Alien, even nastier than Anu because it seems he was. As

Alf has said, none of the Anunnaki is friendly. But it seems Alalu was worse than Anu, because whilst he reigned he was feared by all humans around the world. He was an evil dictator and so when Anu defeated him they must have been quite pleased.

With Alalu now out of the way Anu took over the reign of Earth and became the over-all master, the landlord or better known today as Lord God Almighty. After this battle between him and Alalu it is believed that the Anunnaki God Anu created what we know as 'Religion', mainly to control and manipulate the population. It is written he was a great leader and warrior, a saviour of the sheeple of Earth. At least this was how he was looked upon by early Ram, if you read about him. This Anu was now worshipped by everyone and this is when I think you started to have followers of religion.

MICKY FRICK'S TIP

DON'T BE A FOLLOWER

Many humans became followers of this God (Anu) and were given a set of rules by him to live by. The populace was ordered to obey him or else. He later left the Greys we talked about earlier to watch over Earth whilst he buggered off for a while. Many years later these rules where reinforced by the writing of the Ten Commandments, that's what I think anyway. Just take note of this word 'Obey' by the way because it is used a lot in the Bible and all other religious teachings come to that.

So anyway back to my story.... So as I've said the Anunnaki Aliens took control in Anu's absence and this has continued right up until today. Using this power of fear or the fear of God you are threatened that if you don't behave or follow the rules set by him you will be sent down to Hell. Hell is underground where Alalu hangs out, remember. If you break these rules then you're going down. That's what they say isn't it? This was all the Anunnaki needed to keep the masses in check and obedient.

Fear even works wonders today. Religion has one message as far as I'm concerned. Obey or else.

Anyway let's talk more about the Nibiru planet or The Twelfth Planet. Nibiru was home for the Anunnaki but I was amazed to also find out that even NASA knows about it... Now I can remember being told at school that in our Solar System starting from the Sun there are eight planets that revolve around it. These are Mercury, Venus, Earth, Mars, Jupiter, Saturn, Uranus and Neptune. There were once nine, but some smart arse astronomers rallied together one day and decided not to call Pluto a planet anymore, so it's no longer on the list. Why? Frick knows..... To me there was no real point to it and so as far as I'm concerned, up yours... it's still a planet Pluto to me. Who the frick do they think they are to tell us otherwise?

Does it really matter?

'Yes it does Alf, to me anyway.'

I don't know about you reading this, but I say keep life simple. If it's round it is a planet. I tell you something else too. I bet you didn't know there are more round planets that revolve around our Sun than what you're told? Yes that's right. For some fricking reason I find school has failed to tell us about the others. For some unknown reason they failed to mention Ceres, Haumea, Makemake and Eris. How do I know this? I'll tell you, I found out myself via the Inter-web, which got me asking the question where does this Nibiru planet come into all this? It wasn't mentioned.

Then I find it seems the planet Eris is the infamous Twelfth Planet-Nibiru that Sitchin spoke about. Eris is the official name that some astronomers call it, but then again some also call it Xenia or you may have heard of the term Planet X. Well the Sumerians called it Nibiru but, whatever the fricking name is, it doesn't really matter. We just know this mystery planet Nibiru exists and has been talked about a lot over the years just like Zecharia Sitchin in his book. Sitchin said that, like the Anunnaki, it was written about on those ancient tablets from some of the earliest known writings of the Sumerian's around six thousand years ago.

The facts are there. If you've never heard of Nibiru it's because mainstream science does not recognize it as one of the planets of our solar system, although it must be because it revolves around our Sun. NASA and the government know of its existence but for some reason have kept very quiet about it. To protect the planet from mass panic I guess. The sheeple don't want to hear Earth is under threat from an Alien planet coming our way with an evil God riding on it.

It is also believed that Nibiru is now on its return revolution of the Sun and will pass right between Earth and the Moon. If this is true, and it seems to me it is, then this would distort the Earth's magnetic field. This would cause a temporary pole shift. For those of you who don't know what a pole shift is, it is when the Earth's magnetic field reverses its polarity, like north becomes south and vice versa. If this was to happen it would be really bad for all life here on Earth. It is also believed that Nibiru caused the Great Flood written in the Bible.

Somebody has been busy...

'I have Alf, all this fascinates me.'

As I surfed the inter-web reader I learned there were thirteen planets in our solar system, not eight like we are told, all of which rotate around our star the Sun. If you total up all the planets I have mentioned you will see it comes to a total of thirteen planets. I have also included Pluto in this by the way. Not only that, I also found out the Nibiru planet has only just been spotted. It was first spotted in 2012 when all the planets lined up.

So there you have it, this legendary twelfth planet mentioned by so many ancient civilizations, such as the Egyptians, is for real. What I still don't understand is why the frick haven't we been told? So the point to all this is... a lot of you sheeple are not told all the facts and I am interested in why not?

You now know it is stupid to think Earth is the only planet in the universe that contains life upon it. Why would anybody ever think that? The law of averages says it is probable there is life on many other planets out there as well as ours.... of course there is. I have always known this to be the case to be honest. The problem is I think the sheeple, including you reading this, will only believe what I say as a bona-fide fact when we are invaded by Aliens.

You have already been invaded. Some of the Anunnaki never left. Some became kings and even worshipped as Gods by humans once.

www.xfacts.com

www.beforeitsnews.com

CHAPTER NINE

WHAT IF MYTHS AND LEGENDS WERE BASED ON TRUTH?

There is no smoke without fire as the saying goes...

THE STORY OF THE GREAT FLOOD

It says in the Bible there was once a Great Flood.

'And the Lord said unto Noah, every living thing of all flesh you shall bring two of every sort into the ark, to keep them alive with you; they shall be male and female. Of the birds after their kind, of animals after their kind, and of every creeping thing of the Earth after its kind, two of every kind will come to you to keep them alive. And you shall take for yourself of all food that is eaten, and you shall gather it to yourself; and it shall be food for you and for them. (Genesis 6:19–21).

My guess is every sheep in the world knows the story of Noah and the Ark, that big boat that took all those animals in two by two, one female and one male, to save them from the Great Flood which was the wrath of God, when he wanted to rid the world of sinners. It's in the Bible so it must be a fact. Yeah right, to some religious folk out there maybe... But I don't say that the Great Flood didn't happen, oh no, because it did. But my theory is based on proper scientific facts.

Did you know it says in the Bible this Great Flood happened on 17th February 2348 BC? Well it may well have done, who knows if that's the date or not? I don't know. It is also said that by 27th February 2348 BC it was all over, at least that is what the Bible says. By the time it was over it was said all life on planet Earth was dead, except sea creatures that is. I bet the flood wouldn't bother them would it? Anyway up, I want you to take note of the date 2348 BC because it is significant, you'll see why later.

So the Great Flood happened according to the Bible just over four thousand four hundred years ago. But I bet you didn't know that there are three thousand seven hundred year-old tablets found that claim Noah's Ark was actually round? It's true. Was Noah's Ark a UFO? If it was, who did this UFO Ark belong to?

Check out Noah's Ark conspiracy feature film on YouTube, it is very interesting. Well I thought it was anyway.

This brings me back to something Jon Doe spoke about in his blog. I said that there was a planet that orbits the sun linked to why pole shifts happen in the first place. He believed it was also responsible for the Great Flood spoken about in the Bible. According to Jon Doe a pole shift only happens when this planet passes between us and the moon, which backs up Sitchin's claims. He said this makes Earth slightly distorted, egg-shaped at first. Then a pole shift happens and the effects on our ocean tides are massive.

He also said we are already seeing some of the effects of this happening again on Earth. As this planet gets closer to us the movement of the Earth tells us it is on its way back. I remember he said that as this planet does close on us we will feel the effects of it. Science tells us it is already beginning to take effect because our Earth has started to wobble. I looked up Earth's wobble on the inter-web this is what I found:

The Earth's wobble (Chandlers wobble) was first discovered by a Ram named Seth Carlo Chandler late in 1891. He discovered this wobbling motion occurs as the Earth spins. Scientists today say it is resulting in a slow change in the Earth's axis called a pole shift. They say each time there is a pole shift here on Earth it is a catastrophic event and usually leads to a mass extinctions of many species right across the world. However, according to Jon Doe, prior to the last one in 2348 BC (see take note of the date) millions of humans got slaughtered by an Alien invasion. If you look it up you will see this was in the time of Atlantis.

Tell the reader about Atlantis Michael.

'I'm getting to that Alf.'

ATLANTIS

planetEarthvortex.wordpress.com/tag/atlantis/

Now every sheep has heard of Atlantis. If you haven't I'll tell you about it shall I? Atlantis was a massive metropolis believed to have been three hundred and thirty miles wide and one hundred and ten miles long, but a lot of sheeple think that was just the main city. The populace of Atlantis stretched far wider than that. It is believed by some it once stretched the whole length of the Atlantic Ocean. In fact where the Atlantic Ocean is now was once a massive land mass accompanied by rivers, lakes, mountains and fields. It had cascading waterfalls higher and wider than Niagara Falls.

It is also said that five thousand years ago, the time when Atlantis was constructed, most of Europe was under water. Do you know sheeple I can believe that because if you have ever flown over Europe you can clearly see how it looks as if it was once under water. Look out of your plane window next time you fly over Europe. Did you also know that the Sahara desert was once a fertile land? Well it was.

Anyway that's beside the point. The fact is Atlantis did exist because there is enough evidence to say it did and that's good enough for me. And it was a thriving megalopolis. Did you know Atlantis was first spoken about by a philosopher named Plato? Plato was a student of another wise philosopher named Socrates who once said:

'To find yourself, think for yourself.' He also said, 'I cannot teach anybody anything. I can only make them think'

Socrates is my favourite philosopher by the way and you can guess why. Anyway up, Jon Doe in his blog said when this planet that we know as Nibiru came close to Earth it would have caused a pole shift to happen. This would have triggered a massive tidal displacement (a tidal wave). Maybe this was the Great Flood that swallowed up the legendary Atlantis.

That is exactly what happened, Michael, but before the flood did its worst upon the Earth there was a great war *that took place here. That happened in and around 2348 BC which is also written in the Bible. If you read about the Great Flood you will find references to it.*

'Is it this bit Alf?'

'Behold, the Lord comes with ten thousand of His saints, to execute judgement on all, to convict all who are ungodly among them of all their ungodly deeds which they have committed in an ungodly way, and of all the harsh things which ungodly sinners have spoken against Him'
Daniel 12:1

Yes, that's the one.

I think they are talking about Anu since he seems to be God. I think this was a war between Anu and Alalu.

No Michael you have got it wrong...

'No. No, I haven't.'

I reckon when Anu or should I say God got here he was not happy to find that the slaves had multiplied as much as they had and this pissed him off. Not only that, he was livid to find the sheeple had also formed their own cultures. I bet he was also quite annoyed to find out they had their own religious rituals and beliefs and were worshipping loads of different demi Gods other than him. Not only that I believe he was well pissed off to see this Alalu Alien ruling the place.

So God waged war on the fucker. I mean something similar to this is written in the Bible about God being pissed off and raining down his shit upon the Earth; sure I read that somewhere…

'So anyway there you have it Alf, it all makes sense. If God was this Anu Alien from Nibiru as I think he was he would have been well cheesed off wouldn't he seeing all this? That links up to the Bible story.'

You have got all your facts mixed up Michael. Alalu was long gone before the time of Atlantis.

'Eh? Oh was he?'

Yes. The city of Atlantis was built many years after Alalu was off the scene. In fact Atlantis was the home of the Nordic race for a very long time after the Anunnaki had left Earth. We came later.

'Oh right okay that's interesting Alf, I'll check that out.'

No need; let me zap you all you need to know.......

'You piss off with your zapping malarkey, I'll research it thank you very much.'

That's up to you but I'm telling you now you won't find much on the inter-web about us....... Where's he gone? Michael? Michael?

'I'm ignoring you, piss off and leave me alone for a bit.'

Okay I'm gone.....but you won't find anything.

(Three days later.)

Hello reader I'm back.

You took your time, bet you never found anything did you?

'As it happens, Alf, yes I did.'

You did? Go on then tell us what you found.

'The Anunnaki named you Nordics Titans which is a part of Greek mythology.'

That's right they did. Where did you dig that up?

'The inter-web of course, you can find anything on the inter-web. I've been looking into you Nordics and this is what I found about you. You'll like this so shall I carry on?'

Go on then.....

THE TITANS

There are many stories of the Titans widely available today on the inter-web reader and, like Alf said, they did originate from

Atlantis. It is also interesting to know that according to Greek mythology Atlantis at the time was ruled by an Alien named Kronus.

Kronus, they know about Kronus?

'Yes, you've heard of him have you?'

Anyway it is said this Kronus had many offspring when he mated with a human female named Rhea and apparently they say she was a right ugly trog.

What??

'Let me finish...'

It is believed Kronus was quite fond of fat ugly Ewes, sorry obésité Ewes, and it is written he had sex with many large human females in his time on Earth. They say he used to keep feeding them up and when they were fat enough for him he'd then shag the arse off 'em.

You're making this up.

'Yes I am; got you going though didn't it? Ha ha ....'

Fool. Stick to the facts.

'Okay, fricking hell Alf, you're a boring bastard sometimes. I'm only having a bit of fun with you.'

Just grow up.

'Okay the facts then... miserable bastard, I bet the reader found it funny.... anyway I'll give you some facts shall I?'

Wish you would.

Let me tell you about Poseidon now.

Have you the reader heard of Poseidon? Well Poseidon was half Nordic and half human apparently. It's true, according to the inter-web it is anyway. Apparently Poseidon was the son of this Nordic Alien Kronus. It also says according to Greek mythology that Poseidon was Kronus's second son of thirteen offspring that Rhea gave him. After the Great Flood, Poseidon was known as the God of the Sea and the Romans referred to him later as Neptune.

Anyway, during the Great Flood that engulfed Atlantis, the Nordics Aliens protected Poseidon and his brothers and sisters and took them off the planet whilst the pole shift took place. Then later these Nordics returned Poseidon to Earth to be the guardian of the new water world we know as the Atlantic Ocean. Poseidon was also given great powers by the Nordics that gave him the ability to control the weather, the water and the wind. He could do this because of the powerful Alien weapon he was given by the Nordics called the Trident. The modern day equivalent of this is the Haarp weapon I should think; at least that is what I reckon anyway.

Oh dear have you finished?

No, let me talk about the Romans for a minute......As you may know the Romans once had a massive empire that dominated a lot of the world. Whilst they did this Poseidon (Neptune) had already built underwater cities using Alien technology and for a very long while ruled the waters. The Nordics have been hiding in these underwater cities ever since, under the Atlantic Ocean that is. That's right reader, the Nordics Aliens live under the Atlantic Ocean; they have done so for years according to what I've read…

Anyway back to Neptune or Poseidon, whatever you want to call him; he was spotted many times during the time of the Romans when they started to leave their shores in ships to expand their empire around the globe. Sailors were frightened of Neptune and there are many stories and myths about him on the inter-web, if you're interested. Fuck knows where he is now because it didn't say. Dead probably, it was a long time ago.

Dear oh dear have you quite finished?

'Yes thank you Alf, why what's up?'

That is all rubbish.

'What is?'

That... garbage you have just told the reader. All that you just said is utter rubbish; you must stick to facts if we want to relay the message in this book. You must stick to facts, Michael, it's important.

'That is the facts. I read it here on the inter-web. It also says ancient Romans were unknowingly followers of the Anunnaki race but when Jesus came on the scene the odd one seemed to deflect over to Christianity. Look, it's written here in black and white.'

Stop it now; you must be careful what you read on the interweb, a lot of it is utter rubbish. This is why you humans are so stupid, you read too much into stuff and misinterpret everything.

'But...'

Just stop it can you please? Get back to the Atlantis story, stay on track or I'll have to zap you.

'Oh okay, fricking hell you are a miserable bastard today?'

You've wasted three days as far as I can see....You were supposed to be researching about Atlantis.

'I have, and I read loads about you Nordics. Now Alf, you said Atlantis was your home right?'

It was....

'Okay, So I looked this up. I read you Nordics have been here on Earth way, way before the Romans even came on the scene.....'

Tut......obviously.

'I also read you created cultures all over the world which most sheeple know as the Aztecs, Inca, Mayan, and the ancient Egyptians. It says some of the pharaohs were in fact Nordic descendants.'

Okay..... Carry on.

'All of these cultures, it says, were well established and they were all in possession of advanced knowledge, artefacts, technology, writings, weapons and culture saved form Atlantis. All this knowledge is even believed to have originated from you Nordics.'

Some was Anunnaki technology so we can't take all the credit ...but yes, a lot was.

'Oh right.... So anyway, they took this wealth of knowledge to various parts of the Earth which we now know as Egypt, Mexico and Asia. From there they developed the Egyptian, Aztecan, Mayan and Inca cultures. It also says there are many descendants of you Nordics and Anunnaki still alive on planet Earth today. They still have amazing abilities and knowledge, some have passed them on through the generations and some don't know of their abilities.'

That's true some humans are quite special.

'Like me.'

Yeah... okay.

It also says these ancient ancestors are the ones who left us many structures all around the world that has baffled the greatest minds of today. They still don't know how a lot was constructed but according to some of the great minds of today this is proof that there was once a civilization alive and thriving five thousand years ago. Not only that they were far more advanced than we could ever imagine. The evidence is available reader on the inter-web. You just need to seek it out.

All the mysteries of planet Earth like how the pyramids were constructed, which has puzzled you humans for many years, will one day be solved and when you do solve them then you will know all.

'That is if we survive the Alien invasion you say is coming.'

Well ...yeah there is that, but if you humans start using your incredible brains you may just survive it.

'And do you know Alf, deep, deep, deep down I think we may just do that, survive, because each generation gets smarter and smarter don't they? So I believe one day, one-fricking-day, they will unlock all the secrets that are still hidden. I'm talking about the ones that still baffle these top scientific minds we have now. There is still a lot of great discovery to be found isn't there Alf?'

Yes there is

Did you know reader the Nordics built the Pyramids?

Not all of them..... Well okay most of them. And not just the ones in Egypt either we built pyramids all over your planet.

'Did you really?'

Yes we did check out:

*www.historvius.com/ancient-**pyramids**-of-the-world/fr261*

The largest ones were advanced power generators that were constructed by humans with the guidance of the Nordics; they were all built on crossing Ley lines (or curry lines). If you want to know more about Ley lines reader and what they are, you can check them out for yourself on the inter-web.

www.crawford2000.co.uk/ufo-planetx-nibiru-marduk2.htm
www.biogeometry.org/page34.html

For those of you who can't be bothered to do that, I'll tell you what a ley line is. Basically a ley line or, as some call it, a curry line is a powerful electric magnetic energy that the Earth produces naturally as it spins, but this energy can also be manipulated.

Tell the reader about The Sphinx in Gaza.

'Okay, okay I'm getting to that give me chance.... Fricking hell Alf, are you going to keep interrupting me or what...?'

Sorry.

Here's an interesting fact for you reader.

The Sphinx of Gaza is thought by many to have been built between around 2520-2494 BC and there are many theories as to why it was built. Well my fellow sheep, as an exclusive for you, I can tell you now that what they have put on the inter-web is all wrong. It was built way before what everybody says. It was in fact built by the Nordics Aliens between 2280 BC-2294 BC before the Great Flood. Also you may not know this but there were many sphinxes built all around the planet. Their purpose was to warn the Anunnaki off and to tell them that they own and protect that particular area.

'Hang on how do I know that....Have you fricking zapped me again?'

No, no not me, but that is right what you just said ....The sphinx represents guardians of Earth.

They are a bit like having a sign saying 'Get off my land' or 'Keep Off the Grass' or 'I state this claim' or simply 'Piss off'.
'They are like gargoyles, aren't they Alf?'

Yes, yes. Well something like that...

They were basically built to tell the Anunnaki to fuck off, we own this land.

Not only that... they hid our technology from them too. For instance, buried underneath the Great Sphinx of Gobekli Tepe in Turkey holds great technology which if discovered will prove our existence. This was the first sphinx we ever built here on Earth. It is the oldest one on this planet.

'Is that true? Well I'd be...'

Interesting isn't it reader?

Yes, and someday this will be excavated. It holds many of our secrets about us.

So there you have it reader, remember where you heard it first. It also says on the inter-web the Sphinx of Gaza in Egypt was at some time submerged under water, is that also true Alf?

Yes, this is true it was, but it wasn't submerged for very long, the water that covered it soon receded. Most of the water damage was due to climate change at the time; to the pole shift and long bouts of heavy rain. It is also good to note only the huge monuments such as the Sphinx of Egypt, the Pyramids and the Ziggurats built by us Nordics, with the help of course of you humans, survived the flood.

'The Ziggurats were used as landing platforms for Nordic Spacecraft, am I right?'

That's right they were and they also survived the flood.

Reader it was because they were coated by a waterproofing solution that has now all but gone. They were also very highly polished which repelled water and protected them from the elements. Now that has all but worn away, that is why they have only now started to erode.

I'm impressed Michael, where did you dig that up? Don't tell me the inter-web.

'What was that solution made of Alf? I could make a fricking fortune from selling a waterproofed as good as that.'

The answer to that is still in Egypt. Anyway you're not here to make money... Talking about the Egyptians, did you know the early Egyptians were remnants from Atlantis?

'Oh we are going to talk a bit more about Atlantis then?'

Well we did drift off the subject a bit.

'What else is there to say? We've already mentioned that the Egyptians were remnants from Atlantis...I think.'

Well you didn't tell them that it was these Atlanteans, the early Egyptians, who were descendants of us.

'You Nordics?'

Yes

'Who invented mascara?'

Yes that's right; the ones you see that have paint around their eyes were the children of the Nordics race. You are on the ball today Michael A lot of humans wear mascara even today don't they?

'I only wear it on weekends....'

Well they did this to mimic the shape of our eyes. Anyway, it was them who built the great Pyramids and the Sphinx using the advanced technology that we gave them. We Nordics had you humans as our helpers during this time, and may I add just for the record, you humans were not our slaves you were willing participants. We treated all the humans who worked with us very well. The humans loved us and we loved them. We have always had good relationships with humans. That's why when the Anunnaki tried to annihilate you when they attacked Atlantis, we did save a lot of humans. Many Atlanteans survived and escaped Atlantis and we took them off Earth whilst the pole shift took place. The short life span of you humans meant you all died of old age before we could return you to Earth

'How did you do that?'

In our spacecraft of course... we took them to what you humans call the Orion and the Pleiades systems. This is where we the Nordics originate from, only many years later we returned and settled under the newly formed oceans. We still live under many large lakes as well as oceans right across your Earth. It is also good to point out that it is us Nordics who fly what you call the USOs seen by many humans all across the world. The Anunnaki spacecraft can't go underwater like our, that's why we have survived for so long.

'That's why they can't invade your underwater cities.'

That's right not only do we have the cover of water we also have cloaking devices that make us invisible. That is why you humans can't find us either, not until we let you that is

'Alf, can I ask you a question?'

Yes of course

'Do famous structures have the power to manipulate the human mind?'

Yes.

'I thought so because it says here on the inter-web they did.'

Does it?

FAMOUS STRUCTURES HAD THE POWER TO MANIPULATE YOUR MIND

'So this is true Alf.'

It says here the Sphinx and some pyramids and a lot of other ancient structures such as Stonehenge are believed to be built on crossing Ley lines specifically because of the energy they produce and it can also generate large amounts of EMP (Electro Magnetic Fields). EMP is an invisible electric and magnetic force, a radiation that takes the form of waves.

That's right... you have been busy. The Earth produces EMF naturally and so does the human body but if you enhance the effects on humans it could control you completely. It enhances the feelings of fear and makes humans feel very ill and uneasy. It can also make you hallucinate.

Back in the day the sheeple may have been subjected to this and would have thought they were seeing angels or ghosts when they were near these structures.

Yes that's right. You humans will still get this phenomenon if you are in direct contact with any electric energy source.

MICKY FRICK'S TIP

DON'T STAND UNDER HIGH VOLTAGE CABLES TOO LONG

'Did you use this to make us humans "willing participants"?'

NO! We did not. I know what you're getting at Michael, but we never used any of our technology against humans ever. Although this was originally Nordic technology and was developed to AID humans, the Anunnaki did once capture the source. When they did they used it to control you humans physically, emotionally, mentally, spiritually and even economically. They basically turned you all into mind manipulative, willing, working slaves yet again by harnessing the magnetic energy (EMP) and by building their own pyramids specifically to send subliminal radio signals right across the globe into your minds. This is still used today against you, just not on the same scale. We would never do that.

'Okay.... so in a way they were used just like mobile phone masts we have today.'

Fall of America: David Icke on TETRA masts

That's right. The Anunnaki once had control of all the Earth's grid system. Now they don't so we got it back. But we constantly guard this from the Anunnaki remnants here today who are trying to get it back.

'That's why everyone wants Jerusalem today; it is because underneath Jerusalem there are devices built by you Nordics which control the whole Earth's grid system (ley lines) of the world.'

Wow you have done your homework! That's right Michael, I'm impressed. This technology was built over twenty thousand years ago by us at this specific location. Approximately one mile under Jerusalem city is a superior advanced Nordic technology that controls the whole Earth's grid system; it can feed the whole world with free energy. This would be a great planet if we could do that but they don't want us to share this free energy. They don't want to give you the natural resources that you humans already own. But we do. This device would give you this free energy, it has been under constant attack for many years and we are still trying to fix the damage from the last attack that was inflicted when we took it back from the Anunnaki twelve thousand years ago. They have tried to take back control of it ever since.

'And that's bad?'

Not bad, catastrophic. If they were to do that they would control all you humans once again which we don't want to happen.

'That's all very interesting Alf, but I thought you wanted to talk more about Atlantis.'

Oh right, I thought we had covered that but go on you carry on if you want to add more.......

'Thank you, I shall.'

So anyway reader all this is very interesting as I say but let's just pop back to the Atlantis story for a minute. I want to talk more about this planet Nibiru, its effects on Earth and the destruction of Atlantis, and God's wrath upon the sheeple.

Why?

'Because Alf, I have been doing some more research on the Great Flood. I have come up with this conclusion to it all.'

Oh right....

I think when this Anu Alien got to Earth he thought that the humans were disobedient and so concentrated all his efforts on destroying Atlantis completely to punish them. He instantly waged a war on the Nordics and the humans, who it seems he hated with a passion, and began to destroy Atlantis with a vengeance by throwing down thunderbolts and fire. The whole wrath of God was rained down on them. Remember all the time this went on the Nibiru planet got closer and closer to Earth.

Anu, God that is, believing he had destroyed most of Atlantis and killed most of the Nordics and human occupants, then returned to his spaceship followed by his army. But before he pissed off he managed to capture many human Atlanteans and even some Nordics. He took them all back to his spaceship to do genetic experiments on them. It says on the inter-web he is believed to have brutally tortured many Nordics captives mainly for his own entertainment. As for the humans, he didn't do genetic experiments on all of them. He fed them to his crew because Anunnaki love human meat.

My word Michael, where do you get this rubbish from? You humans really do have weird minds.

'You should know, you're in my head.....'

And there's more.... It is also believed Anu (God) took many species of animals with him like insects, reptiles and birds, and billions of seeds. This was so he could replenish the Earth at a later date.

Anyway....as Nibiru got closer to Earth we started to feel the effects more and more and Nibiru started to pull on our axis. The Earth began to experience massive earthquakes, twenty-mile high tsunamis, violent volcanic eruptions, thus the beginning of the pole shift of 2348 BC.

Where did you get this from Michael? You should just read the link I have given you below reader. Mind you, the pole shift part he talks about is very true.

That's it I've had enough of this nonsense Michael I'm going to zap you......

'You can f..................'

Whilst that kicks in reader check out the link below:

beforeitsnews.com/.../the-true-age-of-the-sphinx-and-did-the-Earths-axis

The Great Flood was by all accounts a catastrophic event. When it had finished and Nibiru had passed by it left your planet tilted at twenty-three-and-a-half degrees, as it is today. The event displaced the oceans and what was land became submerged by water and what was once oceans became land.

Atlantis, for instance, was no more. Oh he's back with us, hello Michael.

'Hello Alf, my mind went blank for a minute.'

Oh did it? Would you like to take over and talk about the Great Flood?

'Okay…'

See reader. The Great Flood of Noah was because of the pole shift, caused by the passing of the planet Nibiru. According to the Bible this all happened in just ten days in the year 2348 BC. As this happened volcanoes erupted and there were massive earthquakes. It was literally Hell on Earth. By the end of it all life on planet Earth was lost.

Not much happened on this planet whilst it healed itself. Most of Earth was inhabitable for hundreds of years. Nibiru continued to slowly pass by until it no longer affected Earth and finally disappeared out of sight.

Whilst all this was going on, Anu was safe in his spaceship along with his precious cargo. He stayed in Earth's orbit for a few years and resided on the moon until he eventually joined the Nibiru planet once again. Nibiru continued its full revolution around the Sun and eventually fucked off into space. However, before he left he built a base on the Moon and created some new servants the Greys (Alien robots). Their purpose was to watch over the planet and rebuild and propagate the planet once it was habitable again.

That's more like it.

Once Anu had left to join Nibiru again the Greys began to create the first hybrid humanoid using the captured humans and Nordics that they had. It was they who also put on Earth the very first Hybrid. His name was Noah. He was genetically created by the Grey and his purpose was to replenish the Earth with livestock and reseed the land. According to the Bible Noah was six hundred years old before he was finally allowed to return to the planet. Once Noah did return to Earth he did what he was asked and as a reward was given a female companion. He gave her one (well three) and they had sons called Shem, Ham, and Japheth. The rest as they say is Biblical history.

'Where did all that come from Alf?'

Never mind, just carry on. It's not exactly all fact but close enough. Anyway Michael, it is time to change the subject.

CHAPTER TEN

WHAT IF MOST OF THE HUMANS ALIVE TODAY ARE ALIEN HYBRIDS?

Everyone who is seriously involved in the pursuit of science becomes convinced that a spirit is manifest in the laws of the Universe - a spirit vastly superior to that of man, and one in the face of which we, with our modest powers, must feel humble.
Albert Einstein

TALKING ABOUT HYBRIDS ALIENS

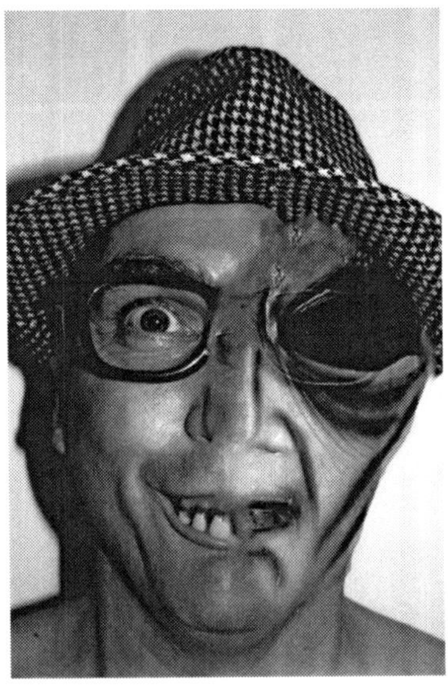

'Are there many hybrids Aliens still in the world Alf?'

Yes. There are hundreds if not thousands. The Greys have planted many hybrids on Earth and they have spread themselves far and wide. They have even taken control of large sections of the planet completely; all specialize in mind control.

'Hundreds? Thousands? In that case how can any of us humans know who we really are? Or more to the point what we are?'

Good Question.

I want to ask two questions to you reading this, before we continue with this book, because I think it's important they are asked. Here we go, this is my first question. Are you absolutely sure you know who you are? I ask this because I'm not even sure I know who I am anymore. My second question is if you think you do know who you are, can you be absolutely one hundred per cent certain about it? Because whoever we are is not necessarily who we think we are.

What are you on about Michael? That's the same question asked twice.

'Something strange has happened to me Alf.'

Like what?

'I had one of them weird Alien abduction dreams again.'

Oh dear.....

'Yes oh dear indeed. My bum is still sore....and since I woke up from it I have felt really strange.'

Strange? What stranger than normal?

'Yes strange.'

In what way?

'Cleverer. I don't feel like myself at all. What makes matters worse, since I read that the Anunnaki have been known to do genetic engineering on animals and humans, it got me thinking?'

Yes but what's that got to do with anything?

'I think I have been genetically modified.'

Genetically modified??

'Yes that's right genetically modified. I think I've been genetically made smarter.'

Well..... There is a chance you may have had your brain enhanced. This is possible.

'Ay? What do you mean?'

Well many, many years ago humans were given a push in their evolution and genetic modification was commonplace.

'How do you mean push?'

Well....humans used to be simple primate monkeys, simple-minded mammals. You know this because Earth science teaches you that this is the case. As you know you evolved over thousands of years until you eventually became the Homo sapiens that you are today. But you were still rather primitive at this stage until your brains were artificially enhanced.

'Come again? Artificially enhanced?'

That's right. What I say is it is nothing new. Have you ever thought why suddenly right out of the blue humans started farming, growing their own food, writing, painting, burying their dead, playing music and games, and building mega structures such as the pyramids?

'I do think it's kind of weird how we, out of all the mammals that ever occupied this planet over millions of years, were and still are the only species to have evolved the way we have; to this so-called intelligent species? But what's that got to do with anything?'

This wasn't a natural part of your evolution. You Homo sapiens were given a push by genetically modifying your brains.

'By you Nordics, or the Anunnaki?'

It was because of Alien intervention.

'By you or the Anunnaki?'

Both, we both had some part of it.

'Both? Fricking both?'

Yes, you're very lucky you were chosen.

'Chosen, maybe we didn't want to be fricking chosen. Why did you not choose any other animal on this planet and fuck about with their brains? Why pick on us?'

The reason humans were chosen by us Nordics was because of your many abilities, like being able to stand upright, have two hands, feet, and your large brain was noticeably capable of storing information long term, more than any other creature on the planet. We saw you had lots of potential but we weren't the only species to see it. The Anunnaki also saw these abilities and to them it was obvious you would all make excellent workers.

'Slaves?'

To the Anunnaki yes, and they have enslaved you ever since. But that wasn't our reason for picking you, not at all. We wanted you to just evolve quicker than you were doing to aid the development of the universe.

'Fuck off; you just wanted us to be more like you.'

The Anunnaki however just wanted you to be slaves.

'Most sheeple don't feel like they are slaves.'

Just because today you're paid a wage to do the work it doesn't mean you're not still a slave. Payment is simply a method used to keep you willing to do what is asked of you. Money was simply invented by the Anunnaki to motivate you to work, as we have already discussed.

Like dangling a carrot in front of the nose of a donkey; we humans are the donkeys, mythologically speaking that is.

A Donkey will follow the carrot. Sheep will follow everybody else. MAF

But we Nordics are trying to teach you that there is more to life.

Have you ever said to yourself reader there must be more to life? Well... you're right there, there is a lot more to life. But we have not been allowed to live it in the way we want or should live it. This is because we live our lives the way we are programmed to do so. Our lives are dictated to us by the government and Aliens. I have always thought something else controls our lives, minds and soul.

And it's not us Nordics.

'So you say..... But you're in my head right now. Frick knows what you are doing to my brain?'

Can't you see we Nordics aren't your enemy? We are trying to help you from this slavery. You humans have all been slaves, since the moment you could see the whites of your eyes. Yes, I guess in a way you have been modified to be other than you are. It has taken hundreds of years to make you who you are today and most of this is because of the Anunnaki influence. They have hijacked our plan for you.

'What is this fricking plan? That's what I want to know Alf? Why can't you just leave us be?'

We can't now it's gone too far. As a result of our failure your great minds are polluted with 'Anunnaki programming.' All this genetic modification done to you by the Anunnaki is holding you back in your evolution. That is why you have grown confused and frustrated and nobody knows who they are anymore. You now just accept life as you see it.

'That's because we are dumbed down, brainwashed and our heads filled with too much shit. Now we are forever at the mercy of our leaders who could well be fricking Aliens and it seems some are in our heads too.'

I'm afraid so...What? No you have got me all wrong. I'm here to help.

'I'm not so sure. You're a voice of a Nordic Alien in my head and that's not normal. I could end up in the funny farm. Talking about funny farms, the world when you think about it is run like a fricking farm isn't it, Alf?'

It is....And we are trying to break down the fences so you humans can run free. Your government leaders are the farmers of the farm; it is watched over and controlled by the politicians who are your shepherds.

'Well, it does seem like the asylum is run by nutters.'

The fricking sheep are following the foolish farmers,
Forgetting they don't really care a frick about the flock,

Keep this up my dear sheeple and you will be in for a frickin shock.

'I made that up from the top of my head good isn't it?'

If you say so.

FUNNY FARM

'How does the farmer become the farmer then, Alf?'

They are chosen.

'See again chosen; against their will no doubt?'

A lot of humans think a government is voted in by the voter, but you're so wrong. Government is appointed by the Illuminati. You humans think you have a say in who leads you but you don't because they are chosen by the Illuminati.

'Are we are all chosen to do specific roles?'

Yes, well at least the government leadership is chosen and it is the same right across the planet. In some cases humans do appoint themselves as leaders; they are what you know as narcissistic leaders or dictators, but you will see they are constantly challenged by other leaders because they are not following the directive. But overall most simply run the Earth farm on behalf of the Illuminati, who answer to the Greys, who work on behalf of Anu and the Anunnaki.

'You mean God....?'

You have probably heard the term 'Doing God's Work?'

'Yes I have.'

Well that's what the Illuminati and the governments of the world are doing, God's Work under the instruction of the Greys. Only some of them now work for their own interests and greed.

'And that's not good.'

No, and when Anu returns again he will be quite annoyed to see this happening. Just like when he came and saw Atlantis doing the same some four thousand years ago, he will realise his wrath once again. It's history repeating itself. The Illuminati know this is the case. The Greys warned them they must stick to the agenda, so they are now doing all they can to rectify the problem. The idea that humans could rule themselves, create their own self-governments, and self-rule the planet was never supposed to happen.

'So what can we do about it?'

You already are doing it....What you need to do is spread the word like all the White Flame Warriors recruited right across your planet. We Nordics are starting to see that the word is at last getting through. We see you humans speak out and protest, forcing government change which is good. There are good humans out there with influence to enforce change.

Also a lot of humans are trying to spread the love. You will see them pop up from time to time and if you listen to them they speak a lot of sense. Like them you are helping to inform the world of this hidden agenda your leaders try to bring to the world. You might stand a chance if you use the power of love, but you must all join forces to fight back repression. Not in battle, because it's not needed. Nobody needs to get hurt. The best way to beat government control is to do nothing and do it peacefully.

'Do nothing? I don't understand? Like refuse to work you mean? I'd go along with that.'

Just refuse to comply when they try and enforce control on you. But remember rioting and fighting and violence of any sort plays into your dictators' hands. You just give them more power and an excuse to use force to get you back under control. Not only that you only make your world a living hell. We Nordics never understand why you humans choose to live in a war zone under curfews and marshal law.

So the message here is simple protest yes, riots no.

'DON'T RIOT!! Fuck that, let's set fire to the House of Commons. Stone the politicians, I say.'

No Michael, you must not riot. You can beat your government leaders by doing nothing and without anybody getting hurt. This is why you're controlled so easily. You should never fight fire with fire, or give them reason to come down hard on you, or enforce new laws that repress you. Don't you understand this is what they want you to do? The governments of the world want you to riot, but riots lead to chaos, chaos leads to violence, violence leads to public disorder and public disorder leads to a police state.

Rioting, and the use of violence, will only give them more powers and an excuse to bring in a police state – like curfews, ID cards and more surveillance cameras. If you are not careful you will all live in a more secure prison than you are already. Carry on like this and you won't be able to go or do anything without permission. Your chance of freedom will be taken away from you permanently.

'How do you mean?'

What I mean is your life and your death will be controlled by them if you allow it. Our plea as Nordics to you humans is a simple one, wake up... stop falling for their traps like being in gangs, stop being racist, stop being a football hooligan, stop being terrorists. Negative actions never beat a positive one; this is the rule of the universe. You just create a Hell on Earth.

'Do not riot because you play their game if you do.'

That's right Michael, This kind of behaviour is encouraged by the Illuminati; they want you to turn against each other so they can bring in new laws to put you under their complete and utter control. They have a real agenda. No matter what you may think.

'So we can't even beat up the odd politician, like kick the shit out of MPs? I thought you said they work for the Illuminati, the Grey, the Anufrickingnnaki? They are the enemy.'

Not all politicians are the enemy. And n, we don't condone any violent behaviour at all. The best way to beat them is simply do nothing; at least nothing negative.

'We can really piss them off doing nothing. If we all refused to go to work that would really piss 'em off.'

Even more so if you all look like you're having a great time doing it. So get the music playing and the barbecue fired up and party like there's no tomorrow. The way things are turning out there might be some truth in that because the next barbecue party may be one the Aliens are planning, with human sheep on the menu.

'I thought you said the Anunnaki don't eat humans....?'

Just a figure of speech.

'Why are you Nordics bothered so much about us?'

Humans are amazing creatures and far more powerful than you realize. But you allow yourselves to be farmed like a common sheep. Like a common sheep you are bred, used then possibly slaughtered whenever the farmer sees fit. We can't allow this to happen.

'What do you mean? Are you saying that when we have outlived our usefulness, got old or seen as no longer productive workers, they would bump us off?'

Exactly.

'Bastards.'

This will get more apparent if Alien technology is allowed to develop as fast as it is doing.

'What do you mean?'

Anunnaki Alien technology is moving too fast and at this rate you will all become too dependent on it. This adds to the problem. The more advanced technology gets the less need for humans.

'What can we do about it?'

Well for a start you could help slow this down by not rushing to buy the new cell phones as soon as they are released. You humans are all too keen to go straight out and buy the new latest super iPhone or electronic gadgets that go on sale. Did you know reader the radio-waves omitted from cell phones is used to keep you tagged and easily controlled? It is used to mind-wipe you?

'They are fricking with our brains aren't they Alf?'

Yes, you could put it that way. You are most definitely controlled by technology, that's for sure.

MICKY FRICK'S TIP

DON'T LET YOURSELF BE CONTROLLED.

So as you see Michael, you can trust us, we are on your side. So if you want to beat back this all out Alien invasion that will happen you need to find who you are and what you are capable of as humans. You will need to do this quickly because time is very rapidly running out for most of the human race. Can't you sense something just doesn't seem right in the world?

'I've sensed it for a very long time.'

Believe me you all need to know what's really going on, and fast. The Anunnaki Aliens are coming. If the humans of the planet ignore the warning signs that are clearly out there for all of you to see; if you ignore that built-in sixth sense you were born with that tells you something just isn't right with the world; if you ignore the way you are farmed by your very own government leaders... If you don't wake up to what's going on around you......

.......if you don't start to wipe that sheep shit from your eyes and accept Aliens are for real, then we are all screwed.

I couldn't say it better myself, Michael. That's why we need you, and all the other White Flame Warriors and your readers, to rally together, spread the word and save the Planet.

Now if we could do that; that would be very special

I THINK I'VE BEEN CLONED LIKE DOLLY THE SHEEP

Dolly was a female domestic sheep. She was born on 5 July 1996 and died from a progressive lung disease five months before her seventh birthday. She was cloned by Ian Wilmut and Keith Campbell at the Roslin Institute.

Where are you going with this Michael?

'It's happened again Alf.'

What has?

'I think I was abducted again last night, or it was a very vivid dream.'

What happened dare I ask?

'I met myself, or a very good lookalike. The Aliens showed him to me and then they laid us both down on the same metallic bed and put a device on both of our heads. I had a right fricking headache when I woke up back in my own bed this morning.'

Oh dear...

'I think I may have been cloned.'

Cloned?

'Yes cloned.'

My first realization began when I casually walked past a mirror when I got out of bed and, to my utter surprise, I didn't recognize my own reflection. It was very weird indeed. It was like something you would expect to happen in that programme *The Twilight Zone*. But, whatever the case, I tell you that sheep looking back at me just wasn't me. Now you can imagine I was really freaked out by this.

I can imagine

'Now don't get me wrong, by all accounts it was a very good lookalike but it just wasn't me. Somehow something was amiss. Something about my reflection in that mirror just didn't weigh up.'

Really?

'Really, and at the time I felt like I was looking at a complete stranger.'

I thought *what the frick is going on here? Who the fricking hell is this imposter looking back at me?* So I just stood there staring at this strange face looking back at me. I was mesmerized by it and so I studied this face in great depth.

Then, for some unknown reason, I had a horrible thought passed through my mind. I thought, *oh fricking hell, I know what's happened here the Greys have cloned me. They've kidnapped the real me and swapped him for this fricking clone I'm looking at here*. The tossers. That's what's happened here, you can bet your arse on it.

'They'd do something like that to keep me quiet about what they are up to, wouldn't they Alf?'

I don't know

They have given up trying to brainwash me like the rest of the sheep, to be a conformist, so they have swapped me for this fricking clone. The real me is probably dead somewhere for all I know.

Oh dear.

I thought, *how dare they? It's my own fault I should have shut the fuck up and ignored your voice Alf. It's your fault.* I guess this is what you get if they can't brainwash you, the fricking bastards, bad losers they are. They can't beat me fairly so they cheat. How the frick did they do it without me noticing them doing it?

'So I must put everything on hold Alf.'

Hang on...You can't do that...

'I've got no choice my old chum. I might be working for them now. You don't know I might be one of them hybrids or something. I need to find out if the real me is dead or is he alive locked up in a prison somewhere?'

You're not a clone... it must have been just a bad dream

'So you say; how can you be sure.....?.'

We really haven't got time for this.....

'It's no good Alf I have started to look into cloning on the inter-web. Do you know I was frigging amazed at what I actually discovered on the first day of my investigation?'

The first thing that shocked me was that cloning is not as uncommon as I first thought. In fact it's very common and has been going on across the planet for years. It's true, I read many articles about cloning and I found them all really interesting and equally disturbing. Then, as I was surfing, I came across one particular article that caught my eye. It was about the genetic modification of food or GM food for short.

WARNING GENETIC MODIFICATION IS RIFE

Now reader, you may or may not have heard of GM food but I hadn't at the time. From what I did read, it seemed to be very similar to cloning so I thought this would be a good place to learn about it. If you think you know anything about GM food you are probably sitting there right now smugly saying that genetic modification of food has nothing to do with cloning. Well, bollocks to you because you're very wrong matey. I soon discovered that both of the methods are very much the same.

They both begin with coping or (cloning) an original; then they just modify it to be different from that original. That in my book is cloning. Still don't get it? Let me try and explain what the fuck I mean, in the simplest way I can, so you sheep can understand what the link to cloning and genetic modification is. Here goes. You ready? Good. The best way I can think to explain this to you is to use as an example what I did to some mice a few years ago. Just imagine what those clever scientists can do if I could do this at only thirteen years of age?

HOW I GENETICALLY MODIFIED A MOUSE

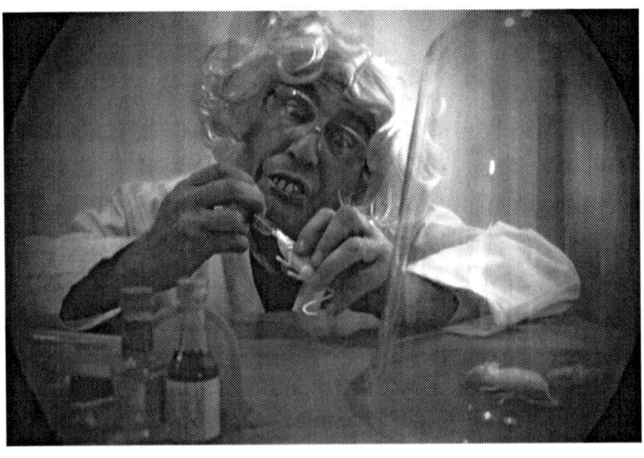

It all began when I was given two pet white mice and I soon found out one was a male and the other a female. Yes, you guessed it, the female mouse soon got pregnant and it wasn't long before I had six more. Not knowing much about sex and how babies were made at the time, I was baffled how they got there. I thought it was magic. Okay I had a bit of an idea but at that age I still thought my willy was mainly to wee out of; it was only later I realized what a wonderful organ it was. Anyway that's beside the point.

So these baby mice just seemed to appear one day. It was the smell I noticed first and thought *blimey I need to clean them out, they stink.* As I proceeded to do just that I was amazed to see these little pink grub looking things; they had no fur and moved about in the bedding. I thought it was simply brilliant but decided not to tell my parents about the baby mice because they would have surely made me get rid of them, and I wasn't going to allow that to happen, was I? So I kept it my little secret.

To cut a long story short, one evening as I watched the *Incredible Hulk* on television, a very popular series back in the eighties, I had this brilliant idea pop in my head, like I do from time to time. I still have them even today. I do, I have great ideas, and I should be an inventor. Once I came up with a great idea of a Fanny Snorkel. This was a gizmo you could put over your nose so when you pleasure the lady with your tongue you don't need to come up for air. *Brilliant idea,* I thought. Anyway back to the mice.

Now remember I was only thirteen years of age when I came up with the idea to add green food colouring to the water supply of my baby mice to see if it would make them turn green like the *Incredible Hulk. How cool would that be?* I thought.

Now before I continue I must stress this was over thirty-five years ago when food colouring was quite harmless and made from berries, and what have you. But it's not anymore. In today's modern artificial food colouring you will find loads of contaminants such as petroleum and propylene glycol, which incidentally is what antifreeze is made from. As well as that I do believe it contains traces of crude oil, if I'm not mistaken, so I wouldn't advise you doing this kind of experiment today on any mice you have.

I have also since learnt that artificial food colouring is linked to bed-wetting, eczema, mood swings, hyperactivity, sleep disturbances, increased risky behaviour, ear infections, headaches, hypersensitivity, obesity, asthma, diabetes and even cancer.

So my advice is to avoid the stuff completely if you can, and don't give it your lambs. As for giving it any little mice, don't do that either, or you could end up breeding monsters like the Incredible Hulk for real. Rather than them just being green, who knows if they get angry they may even attack you by jumping at your throat or something? So don't do it, okay. Besides at the very least you could end up just poisoning the poor little buggers and you don't want that because that's cruel, and I hate cruelty to animals. So don't do it

MICKY FRICKS TIP

AVOID FOOD COLOURING

Anyway, the point of this story is to explain a little bit about genetics, not to encourage you to try experiments like I did at thirteen. Good, I'll continue then. So there I was adding green food colouring to the water at the time when the baby mice were still suckling from their mother. The mother drank the coloured water I gave her and, blow me, if I didn't finish up having baby mice grow green fur, which was really brilliant, I thought. And it impressed all my friends at school, well both of them.

Yes they were well impressed when I showed them my green mice. I ended up with a demand for my green coloured mice and started breeding more and adding other colours like blue and red mice. And between me and you I was making a small fortune.

Business was booming. Once word got about everybody wanted one of my coloured mice as a pet.

But as with all things this soon got out of hand and by the end I couldn't cope with the demand. And to top it off I was soon overrun by rainbow-coloured mice. In fact I counted them once and one by one I sellotaped them to the roof of the shed by their tails. I had ninety-six mice in total all dangling from their tails from the ceiling.

Unfortunately my mother came into the shed to see what I was up to and she had a Micky fit when she saw all the mice hanging from the ceiling. As you can imagine she wasn't happy at all. I was then forced to give them all away for free. My dad suggested drowning the lot in a bucket. But thankfully my mum wouldn't let him and he gave me a week to get rid of them, or he would.

So that was the end of that little venture and my mother and father banned me from keeping any more pets for at least two years, until I was deemed old enough to be trusted to look after them properly. My next pet was a hamster named Velvet which I didn't keep long either. I soon found out giving hamsters a bubble bath was not a good idea.

You were a very strange child weren't you Michael?

So I was not allowed to have any more pets from then on. That's when I started to make pets of the garden slugs and snails I found in the garden. Oh yes, and I do remember once having a pet toad. Anyway that's beside the point again isn't it? I was talking about genetically modifying mice wasn't I? So I'll get back to that then shall I?

And please hurry up.

So anyway, I gave the mice food colouring in their water supply and changed the colour of the mice. Now what I learned from this little experiment was as long as you keep giving them the food colouring in their water supply the mice fur will stay the chosen colour. But as soon as you stop adding the colouring to the water their fur reverts back to its natural colour. Although

I didn't know it at the time, I realize now I was actually doing a bit of genetic modification by simply adding an ingredient that changed the mice from their natural appearance; from white to blue, green or red. So there you have it see? That is basically what GM is all about.

Is it???

In a way it is. Genetic modification is when you alter the genetics of something to make it different from its natural state. See, now you know a little bit more about genetics and how it works. Genetic modification is when they simply change or modify something from what it originally was. The only difference as I see it, and from what I read, is that it is a lot more advanced than just adding a bit of food colouring to the water to make something look pretty, like I did.

However, from my little story you can now see the principles are very much the same. I hope I have now made it clearer for you to understand what genetic modification is all about; how it works and that.

Do you know reader, the most important lesson I personally learnt from what I did to all those mice is that if you stop tampering with something it will eventually revert back to its original state, 'The way nature intended' so to speak. I think that is an important point to remember because it means you can reverse any effects of eating the shit you eat, like burgers and chips. In simple terms if you simply stopped eating GM food your health would undoubtedly improve and any damage to your body from what you have already consumed could be reversed. That's a really good point to keep in mind I think.

I suppose...Look Michael we are going off on a tangent here; you're supposed to be a White Flame Warrior not an Eco Warrior.

'I think this is interesting information I'm giving the reader.'

It is but.......okay get on with it.

'Thank you, I will.'

GENETICALLY-ENGINEERED-FOODS

GM food tampering makes no sense at all, not to me anyway. All I find from what I read is genetic modification of food potentially gives sheeple serious health issues. This has been proven time and time again it seems, and by a lot more clever sheeple than I. Nevertheless, they still keep doing it regardless of the facts.

Look, don't take my word for it, go see for yourself. There is a lot of scientific evidence out there put together by the sheeple who know about this kind of thing. As I see it they inform the government of the dangers of eating GM food and the potential health hazards but as always the government seem to just ignore them. Why do you think this could be? I don't know about you but I think there's some hidden agenda going on here, don't you?

You and I both eat GM food every day of our lives. We can't avoid it as it's in almost everything we eat, mainly processed food and, surprisingly, in foods deemed as healthy, which is a laugh. I bet you didn't think about what you actually eat did you, until I brought it up? I bet you weren't aware that you are mostly eating cloned food that is bad for you.

The reason you never know about this is because it is never on any of the labels or packaging of the foods you buy. There is nothing telling you the food you are about to eat is cloned. I don't know about you but to me that is also very suspicious. In fact even trying to find information on why it's not clearly labelled is almost impossible, as I have personally found out. Anyway, don't take my word for it, just type in your search engine:

modified-organisms-how-they-are-made-and-why-they-aren-t-labelled

.....and see for yourself. You can't can you? You see reader, for some very strange reason you will not be able to get the information from this site, or any sites similar to it. I'll tell you what will happen your computer will probably just freeze up on you. Why? It's because they don't want you to fricking know that's why? All very suspicious if you ask me.

However, if you open your eyes GM food is in plain view. Just think about seedless grapes. That's right, seedless grapes. They are genetically modified. Now you probably didn't know that did you? I didn't. Well they are. This is how they do it. Firstly they get a bunch of original grapes, extract the DNA, and then mess with it a bit by adding some chemicals and foreign hormones from other plants. Whilst doing all this, they take away the natural genes that produce seeds until you end up with a Frankenstein plant that grows seedless grapes. I know, I too thought seedless grapes grew naturally without seeds, but they don't. Now I know they are grown from a monster plant. I wouldn't be surprised if they fed the plant blood like the one in *The Little Shop of Horrors.*

MICKY FRICK'S TIP

BEWARE OF FRANKENSTEIN PLANTS

Have you ever eaten seedless grapes? I know I have, in fact I love 'em. It would be fair to say I'm addicted to the things. The reason is probably because I think they have added something to them whilst fricking about with the genetics. They have possibly added cocaine or something like that to make me addicted to them. It makes sense because I have been known to stick them up my nostrils for no reason. You see I think I'm subconsciously trying to snort the fuckers. They have made me a grape eating smack head without me even realizing it. I am a grape junkie. What lousy bastards the government are.

TUT! Nothing to do with me reader, this is his own mind.

So you see if they can mess about with the food we eat what else are the wankers up to in them laboratories that they aren't telling us? What else are they hiding from us? That's what I want to know? Whatever it is, it's all wrong that's for sure. As for GM food, as far as I am concerned they shouldn't be fricking about with nature like they do. Leave our food alone I say.

I don't know about you reading this but I would be quite happy to eat grapes with seeds in, wouldn't you? What's wrong in that? Okay, so I may not eat as many as I do because I don't like it when the seeds get stuck between my teeth. But at least I would know grapes with seeds in were natural and not full of drugs. Do you know, since I have looked into cloning and this GM food malarkey, I am getting a bit concerned? I used to really like seedless grapes but I don't enjoy them as much now I think they are tampered with. I only eat them because I am addicted to the things. I am slowly weaning myself off them by eating plums instead. It's a slow process and, besides, plums make me fart.

No, it would be fair to say I don't enjoy seedless grapes the same as I did. I treat them a bit like when I used to smoke. When I smoked I didn't like it but I still lit up a cigarette because the chemicals in them made me addicted to the fuckers, just like they have done to my grapes.

Talking about smoking, have you seen those new electric cigarettes (E cigarettes)? What the frick is that all about? They are addictive too, the same as a regular cigarette but, like sheep, loads of you smokers are brainwashed to think they are not as dangerous as smoking tobacco. But they are worse. Don't believe me? Then you watch this:

www.today.com/.../alarm-raised-over-poisoning-ris.

See, sheep the lot of you. I keep telling you but you won't listen. If you don't want to smoke, don't fricking smoke, just like if you want to lose weight stop eating too much; simple. Any addiction is bad for you and I class seedless grapes as bad for you as smoking. I think they should ban every sheep from eating them in public. As you know, you always share your bunch of grapes with others and you don't want to encourage them to start your bad habits do you? There is a very good chance they are slowly poisoning me and I don't want that to happen to you.

Who knows one day I may have to pay for my addiction to grapes when all those toxins eventually fill my veins. Maybe one day my bollocks will glow fluorescent green and fall off. Who knows what's going to happen to me? I hope I can kick the habit before that happens…

Really

Hang on there for one minute; I've just had a horrible thought pop into my head… Maybe the whole point of growing seedless grapes is to make us Rams 'seedless', to give us a low sperm count. Now that's a thought isn't it? That's what the government are doing, you can bet your arse on it, the sly bastards. It's an attempt to try and slow down the population growth. That's what it's all about. That's what this GM food is all about. That's why they encourage it and support GM food and ignore scientists.

As for seedless grapes, they are trying to make all us Rams of the world who eat seedless grapes infertile, so we can't breed. That's what's going on here. I mean I wouldn't put it past the tossers would you? Mind you…. saying that I can kind of understand why they would do something like that. I mean the world is somewhat over-populated isn't it? We probably need to stop breeding like we do. Even so I reckon if we were to stop breeding it would take fricking years for the population to decrease enough anyway, so why are they doing it? It's not enough. They would be best trying to shorten our life expectancy instead. Ay up, what am I saying? I don't want to give the bastards any more fricking ideas.

Genetically modified food is designed to produce toxin to do just that, help cull the population.

'That's right Alf. Is it?'

See reader; don't eat GM food if you can avoid it.

MICKY FRICKS TIP

DON'T EAT GENETICALLY-ENGINEERED-FOODS IF YOU CAN AVOID IT

GM corn and cotton are engineered to produce their own built-in pesticide in every cell. When bugs bite the plant, the poison splits open their stomach and kills them. Biotech companies claim that the pesticide called Bt, produced from soil bacteria Bacillus thuringiensis, has a history of safe use since organic farmers and others use Bt bacteria spray for natural insect control. Genetic engineers insert Bt genes into corn and cotton, so the plants do the killing.

See, told you the Illuminati are trying to kill you.

MICKY FRICK'S TIP

WASH YOUR FRUIT AND VEGETABLES BEFORE EATING THEM. THEY ARE TRYING TO POISON YOU.

'Soil bacteria Bacillus thuringiens is safe' so they say..... But I don't think it is. Of course you can make your own mind up. They do say it has a history of safe use. Yeah okay....safe use my arse, that can't be right can it? I mean, how many times when you were a lamb did your mother tell you not to eat dirt? That's all I'm saying on the matter.

You ate dirt??

'Yes, I was very young. I think a lot of young lambs eat dirt when their young.'

She always said to me, 'Michael stop eating the dirt,' I remember she did that because she knew it was full of germs. Moms know best, sod what anybody else tells you. I tell you now you can trust no-one. And I've said it before and I'll say it again, you most definitely can't trust THE GOVERNMENT!!

Nor the Anunnaki.

'Nor the ....look sod the Anunnaki for a minute Alf, let me tell more about what I found on the inter-web about GM Food.'

It says here, 'Bacillus thuringiens-toxin produced in GM plants, is thousands of times more concentrated than natural

Bacillus thuringiens, it is designed to be more toxic, it has properties of an allergen, and unlike the spray, cannot be washed off the plant.' That's what it says in food matters.com. They say that the pesticides they spray on our food are less bad for you than the stuff they have genetically added to Genetically Modified food. So you may as well disregard my last tip about washing your fruit and veg, it's pointless.

Do you know the more I read about this genetic modification of food the more it worries me? I mean it obviously isn't good for you is it? It seems in the long term whether you wash your food or not you are being slowly poisoned.

Really...?

Really, you know what's happening here don't you? We are slowly being culled. That's what's going on. When you eat this GM food it is like eating food that has a small dose of poison in every bite. Over time it builds up in your body and kills us. Great, I don't know about you reader but I WANT REAL FOOD!! I WANT REAL FOOD!! I'll tell you something else. Is it just me or have you noticed that there doesn't seem to be much taste to anything you eat these days? Why? It's because it's artificial food, that's why. That's why I grow my own veg in my back yard, and I tell you what reader, it tastes much, much better than the shit you buy in supermarkets. It's because it's not coated in poisonous toxins.

Yes, I am convinced that GM food is slowly killing us off. At least that's how I understand it after reading about it on the Inter-web. What about the fricking weed killers they use on GM crops? It's called Glyphosate and is sprayed on eighty per cent of genetically modified foods. This stuff is really harmful but they use it all the same. And get this; Glyphosate is the most common agricultural chemical in the US, with one hundred and eighty-five million tons sprayed on American crops. But it damages cellular tissue in the body. This has been proven umpteen times but the government don't give a shit. Why? Because they don't have to eat it do they? No, those bastards eat organic because they can afford it.

If adding Bacillus thuringiens-toxin isn't enough, they also spray these GM Plants with Glyphosate. "This Glyphosate in our food is making us fat and sick," says Stephanie Seneff, Ph.D., co-author of the paper and senior research scientist at MIT (Massachusetts Institute of Technology).

"It's the number one cause of obesity in this country and rates of obesity have shot up in tandem with increasingly heavy use of this herbicide," by Lisa Collier cool Yahoo health.

See you don't need to diet. You just need to stop eating GM food stuffs. I tell you what; you can learn a lot off the 'Inter-web' and you should check it out because what I have read already makes you wonder how they get away with half of it.

Have you finished now?

'Okay, okay. I know I've been going on a bit about GM food but I think it's important to know these things. It is also good to know what else these tossers are up to in those laboratories.'

I know most sheeple don't normally think about genetics and stuff. This is basically because you're not really bothered what you eat as long as you are fed, unless you're on a diet, or a vegetarian or vegan. But this genetic modification of food is out of hand as far as I'm concerned. It's happening all around the planet. These sheeple frick around with our food and it has got progressively worse since the eighteen hundreds.

So you can bet your arse on it, we all at some time in our lives have eaten this shit without having a choice. We haven't been asked whether we want to or not and that's what really pisses me off. So you can see why I think there is a hidden agenda to all this. Adding more and more toxicants to our food supply, as they seem to be doing, can't be doing us any good can it? Whichever way you look at it, they most definitely aren't doing it for the good of our health are they? Bastards.

So what are these slimy bastards up to? Are they trying to shorten our life expectancy? Well I think they may be doing just that. As far as I 'm concerned that's premeditated murder. And if this isn't addressed soon I fear it'll be too late to save any of us. We are being slowly murdered.

You're getting a bit excited about all this Michael.

I just think at the very least we should know what the farmer is feeding us. I think we should also be given a choice whether we want to eat it or not. I also think we should be made fully aware of the side effects of eating GM food and what it might be doing to our body. I read that this GM shit is full of toxicants that have direct links to cancer and loads of other fatal illnesses. We will never beat cancer if the very food they are feeding us causes it.

You're ranting.

I'm not just having a rant. It is backed up by many dieticians who right across the world have done numerous tests. They all say the same; that GM food is simply not good for you. We are not told we are eating genetically engineered food sheeple, and that it's poisoning us. You won't find it on any food labelling either. The only reason you know about this is because I have brought it to your attention.

This is a conspiracy FACT.

It also seems there isn't much we can do about genetic modification either as it's already gone global. We are forced to accept it. You can avoid it I guess, but to do so you will pay through the nose to buy organic food, which in my opinion is a fricking rip off an' all. I don't have to tell you; you know and I know most working class sheep with families can't afford to buy organic food. It's just too damn expensive for the working class. So we don't really have much choice in the matter do we? The bastards.

Yes my friend, it seems we need to keep an eye on GM food, and cloning come to that. I for one think there is more to this than meets the eye. Whatever that is, they are up to something, that's for damn sure. We should all write a letter to demand GM products be labelled as 'toxic' or give us a warning reminding us that this food we are about to eat might kill us.

They are not going to do that are they Michael?

I know, I know, they will probably ignore you as they always do. Or they might send you a standard letter that fobs you off by telling you that GM food is perfectly safe to eat, and that cloning food isn't going on. But take it from me reader they are full of shit. Don't take any notice of them; you and I know different.

Have you finished....?

'No not yet, I'm just warming up, Alf.'

Check out these web pages reader:

www.responsibletechnology.org/10-Reasons-to-Avoid-GMOs

www.enhs.umn.edu/current/5103/gm/harmful.html

Still not convinced GM food is bad for you? Well, if you want to continue to eat it that's up to you but I'd rather not. By checking out these pages you may be more inclined to moan at the bastards about the situation they put you in. I say let them know you won't stand for it anymore. Ask them why all food can't be organic, safe and affordable for everyone? Tell 'em you don't want to be cloned either. The bastards. Check these websites out an' all. Here are four more of the hundreds and hundreds of web pages about how bad GM Food is for you:

www.responsibletechnology.org/10-Reasons-to-Avoid-GMOs

www.enhs.umn.edu/current/5103/gm/harmful.html

www.organicauthority.com/foodie.../eight-reasons-gmos-are-bad-for-you.html

www.foodandwaterwatch.org/food/genetically-engineered-foods/

This has already got out of hand as far as I am concerned and we are in the realms of no return. Fuck knows what the long term effects of GM food will be but until we do know for sure we should fight for the right to say NO!

So finishing off on GM food…

At last thank heavens for that......

I want to talk about how the production of GM food not only poisons humans but also the planet.

POISONING THE PLANET

It is true GM farming can harm the land, so why did they continue to do it? This is a very good question. I wondered about it myself and have given it some considerable thought, as you can imagine. I can now tell you reader why I think this is allowed to continue, with no regard to its effects on us sheeple or the land. It's because there is money in it.

I read on the inter-web GM food production was first seen as a logical way to fill the worldwide food shortage. Remember, this shortage is because the world is way, way over-populated. Anyway, it was thought that GM food was a very good way to increase the food supply for the masses. Once all research was done and better methods of doing it were found, they then discovered it was cheap to grow GM Food. Soon they realized it was also a great way of maximizing profit in food production. Basically GM food was a brilliant way to make money.

That's right, the reason we have GM food is because they found out there was money to be made from it. It was cheaper to genetically modify food than traditional farming methods. But although cheaper to produce none of us have ever seen the price of food come down, have we? Oh no, in fact it did the opposite, it went up in price, the robbing bastards.... This was so they could maximize the profit margin on food production, again ripping off the consumer. What it did to your health was of no interest to them, not anymore. It was all about what money they could make from you. After a while they also discovered that it was a good way to dispose of toxic waste.

That's not true, stick to the facts Michael.

Well I wouldn't put it past them. Bastards.

'What about the profit they can now make from farmland?'

Farmland?

'Yes farmland, Alf.'

Farmland here in Britain makes more money if used for car boot sales. For those of you who are American reading this:

Car boot sales or boot fairs are a form of market in which private individuals come together to sell household and garden goods. They are popular in the United Kingdom, where they are often referred to simply as 'car boots'. The term refers to the selling of items from a car's boot. Wikipedia

...and car boot sales are massive business in the UK. There is a lot of money made from renting farmland out for outdoor music festivals too. You can see why most landowners and farmers don't bother to grow food anymore. I mean, why bother when they can make a fricking fortune using the land to herd the sheeple together and brainwash them to rock music? Or they can rip them off by charging extortionate prices for an entrance fee to sell tat, hotdogs and alcohol? As you well know that happens here in the UK because most sheeple are piss heads. I don't know what it is like for the rest of the world. Also farmers here in Britain are paid not to grow food. It's all bonkers if you ask me.

Farmer earns 19,000 pounds a year for growing nothing: For...

I think the reason they don't grow natural food anymore is mainly because the soil on most farmers' fields throughout the world is too contaminated.

Why?

'It's been destroyed, Alf. Because of the overuse of pesticides the soil is now poisoned. The pesticides used have damaged the soil to such a degree that nothing will grow in it anymore.'

Did you know reader in America the government still allows the excessive use of these pesticides? Over time this will undoubtedly poison the soil, as it has in other parts of the world already. The pesticides they use also kill important pollinating insects such as the honeybee. If honeybees die out so do we.

And what happens to land in America that is still half good for growing crops to feed you American sheeple, and that isn't drenched in poison? It is sold off to some rich bastard who will sow grass seed all over it, dig a sand pit here and there, and then build a fricking golf course. I tell you that's what's happening over in the United fricking States of America. Or if not that, you can bet your arse they'll build a massive shopping complex on the good fertile land.

That's fricking why none of us have natural freshly-grown farm food anymore. All the land is used for fricking golf courses for the rich to play, or shopping complexes to make us sheep spend what pittance we earn. Or if not that, then concerts and fricking car boot sales. It's all wrong, stupid and wrong. So you would be right to ask why?

Why can't they just stop this, sort out the soil and start to grow natural food again? What is the frigging problem in old-fashioned farming and growing crops organically using the shit from cows for fertilizer? Why can't everybody have organic food at an affordable cost?

Well Michael, why?

I'll tell you why. I have looked this up and I was amazed to read that apparently the cow dung that they used to use to fertilize the crops is now also fricking contaminated. This is because they have fed the toxic chemicals to the cows too. If their shit was used to grow crops it would make the food glow in the dark.

'Animal feeds and forages contain a wide range of contaminants and toxins arising from anthropogenic and natural sources, radionuclides, mycotoxins, plant toxins, antibiotics and microbial pathogens in cereals. Evidence is provided to demonstrate that feeds contain a variety of substances as co-contaminants'. J.P.F. D'Mello is at the Scottish Agricultural College (SAC) in Edinburgh, the United Kingdom

You're safer growing your own vegetables in your own shit, I'm telling you!

MICKY FRICK'S TIP

GROW YOUR OWN

That's exactly what I do. I grow my own vegetables in my own garden using my own organic fertilizer consisting of my own shit and piss. If you think eating food grown in human excrement is disgusting just type 'Night Soil' in your search engine. Now, I don't know about you but I'd rather eat vegetables grown in my own shit than somebody else's, or a radioactive cow's shit.

Mind you, there is an alternative. If you don't have the facility to grow your own, my advice is to boil everything you eat before you eat it. Oh fuck, scratch that.............Did you know it is proven that the fluoride in our water supply is linked to many health problems. Fricking hell you can't escape it, can you?

CHAPTER ELEVEN

WHAT IF EVERYTHING IS BAD FOR YOU?

Everything I read about seems to be aimed at harming or killing us sheeple in some way. I bet you didn't realize eating corn could kill you? It's true. Even corn is genetically modified and it is believed by leading scientists that it can potentially kill you. I bet you have never given a second thought, when you sat down to eat your cornflakes in the morning, about what you were eating and how it's been grown, have you? Well, I can tell you it most likely started life in a laboratory. Like most of the stuff you eat these days, they have been fucked about with and loads of chemicals and toxins added to 'em. You'll never look at corn the same again.

Eating genetically modified corn (GMO corn) has caused rats to develop horrifying tumours, widespread organ damage, and premature death. That's the conclusion of a shocking new study that looked at the long-term effects of consuming Monsanto's genetically modified corn. The study was published in The Food & Chemical Toxicology Journal and was just presented at a news conference in London. By Mike Adams, Natural News

Well, if you think that's bad enough it gets worse. Did you know even the milk you pour on those cornflakes could be bad for you an' all?

Due to the extreme processes that milk goes through and the high amounts of antibiotics, hormones, and genetically-modified substances that cows are continually exposed to, I

believe there are real and eminent concerns associated with drinking milk from cows. All cows release toxins through their milk, as milk is a natural exit-portal for substances that the body cannot use.

www.globalhealingcenter

Even the sugar you sprinkle on your cornflakes in the morning could potentially kill you. Well that's just fricking great isn't it?

Sugar is exceptionally toxic and leads to heart disease, metabolic syndrome and cancer -- it can even be equated with addictive drugs like cocaine, according to prominent medical experts. Add to this the fact that genetically modified (GM) sugar beets now dominate the US market a healthy future certainly looks bleak. Not only are Americans dealing with the negative effects of consuming elephantine amounts of sugar, but now the health dangers of genetically modified organisms through Round-up Ready sugar beets are in the mix. Sugar has a hidden public health crisis. As a specialist in pediatric hormone disorders and the leading expert in childhood obesity at the University of California's School of Medicine in San Francisco, Robert Lustig is on a mission to educate the masses about the dangers of refined sugar.

sugar.www.naturalnews.com/037737

They may as well call cornflakes 'Clone flakes' because that's what they are. It seems the more articles I read the more genetically modified food I find. All of them have one thing in common; they are bad for you in some way. You know what's happening don't you? We are slowly being culled. That's what's going on I reckon.

That's true.

'It doesn't surprise me Alf...'

I read somewhere that they reckon only two per cent of all deaths were natural; natural as in old age. A study showed that most deaths of sheeple are due to what we consumed during our lives and how we have lived our lives. Did you know, if you're poor you're more likely to die sooner? Look, I'm not trying to tell you not to eat GM food. For one thing I've since learned you can't avoid it, or afford not to; well most sheeple can't anyway. So unfortunately if you refused to eat anything that is genetically modified you would most probably starve to death. See, you're buggered if you do and buggered if you don't. Even so you should still moan to your government about all this. I think if all the sheeple of the world joined forces and complained enough then they would have to think twice before they did anything to harm us; like force-feeding us GM food.

Moan all you like it wouldn't change a thing.

You never know..... If we moan enough they may even start good old fashioned farming again. Who knows, they might. It would be nice of them if they did supply us all with uncontaminated food at a price we could all afford. But I guess, as always, that's up to you sheeple reading this. Mind you I won't hold my breath because I already know most of you sheep just put up with any shit dished out to you because you're all brainwashed.

Anyway, if nothing else, at least all this GM food business has got me kind of suspicious of what else they are up to and to what they aren't telling us. As well as cloning the food we eat, I would like to know what else these fuckers are up to; wouldn't you? At this moment in time my most important mission is to find out if it is at all possible to clone humans. As you know, I still think I am a clone.

For Pete's sake not this again....

I looked into this and found out to my amazement that not only is it possible, but they have experimented with this idea for years. So it seems all my suspicions that I could be a clone have some credibility. No matter what Alf thinks, there is a very good chance indeed that I am a fricking clone. So following my instincts even further I have looked into this subject in more depth. I have been very, very busy researching cloning and this is what I have come up with. I warn you it will shock you.

THEY ARE CLONING EVERYTHING

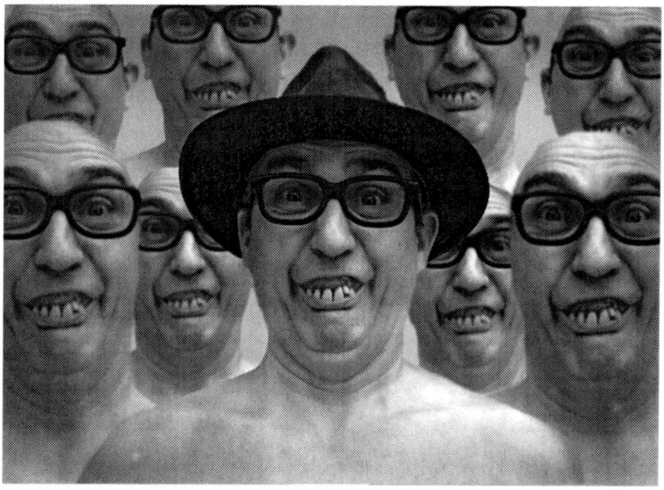

"We now have the ability for the first time to create a virtually unlimited supply of all the cell types and building blocks we need to make what we want to make as in body parts," said stem cell researcher Robert Lanza, chief scientific officer at Advanced Cell Technology, a biotechnology company in Marlborough, Mass. "Now we just have to put it all together." Discovery News

That article from Discovery News is a few years old now and is only one of many on the subject. The more I read about cloning the more I was convinced that I am, without a shadow of a doubt, a fricking clone.

You're not a clone Michael.

'I am..... The bastards have cloned me Alf. I'm sure of it and without my permission. That's not right is it?'

I bet you didn't know that they have done this cloning thingy-me-bob for years. I bet you also didn't know most of the vegetables and fruit that we eat is all cloned food. I kid you not. I know I was fricking amazed when I found this out. Also did you know that they now clone the animals we eat too? That's right, the cows, pigs and chickens, even the fish we eat are all cloned.

Well this seems to be the case from what I've read. Yes that's right, my sheepy little friends, it seems most of the meat that we consume today is likely cloned meat from real animals. Animals are cloned for food. Mind you, at least it's still meat, unlike that Quorn stuff that I read about the other day.

Quorn??

'Yes Quorn Alf, have you ever heard of it?'

If you don't know what it is let me enlighten you? Quorn is a meat substitute really popular these days with vegetarians and vegans all over the world. If you are veggie or vegan you may well know all about Quorn and eat it regularly, but do you actually know what you're eating? Do you know what Quorn really is? If you don't know let me be the first to enlighten you. It's Fungus. That's right Quorn is a fungus, a mould with flavouring added to it. You think you're eating meat but you're not, you're eating a fungus. You can get this fungus in chicken, lamb or beef flavour, and get this… it is often used in ready meals too.

Now that was a shocker for me because I eat a lot of ready meals or, should I say, used to. I don't anymore since I read about Quorn, especially now I know what's in it. Do you know it amazes me why sheeple don't like eating real meat? For frick's sake we are natural meat eaters you know, and to totally avoid eating meat can be very unhealthy for you. It is essential to maintain a natural balanced diet and that's important isn't it? You're silly sheep if you don't eat meat because we sheeple have eaten it for thousands of years. It is very good for you, in moderation that is, because it contains a lot of vitamins that we need.

So I say to all you vegans and vegetarians out there, what's the problem in eating real meat? Now come on, we are all natural carnivores you know. Besides we also need meat to fight off diseases, but this Quorn stuff is a fungi and one that isn't very good for you at all, from what I've read. Okay granted there are some good fungi and bad fungi in the world. Like mushrooms, some are okay to eat but others are not.

Remember though you only get fungus forming when something rots or decays. In fact I've got fungus growing on my big toenail, doesn't look that appetizing to me. Maybe if I add some seasoning it might be nice on a piece of toast, who knows, like a pate?

That's disgusting.

Anyway take no notice of me, if you like Quorn sheeple you carry on eating it. But for me I personally don't fancy the idea of eating a meat substitute of any kind, or any artificial food. Give me the real stuff thank you very much. As long as it isn't cruelly treated like that Halal meat or genetically modified in any way that is. But Quorn? I'm not sure about it myself. You can eat what you want but here is what the experts say about it.

The Center for Science in the Public Interest (CPSI) in Washington DC claims that Quorn can be dangerous to some consumers, and it is suing Quorn Foods and Whole Foods Market, Marlow Foods's American subsidiary. Michael Jacobson, the centre's director, said the public should know the meat alternative can cause "unsavoury gastrointestinal symptoms, or even potentially life-threatening anaphylactic shock." The Telegraph.

I don't know about you, but if I had to choose I'd rather they cloned animals for meat than eat a meat substitute like fricking Quorn, but as I say that's just me. It just goes to show though sheeple will eat anything. Not many sheeple think about what they eat and you should. Mind you I still eat seedless grapes.

MICKY FRICK'S TIP

THINK BEFORE YOU EAT ANYTHING; KNOW WHAT YOU'RE EATING

Some would say they haven't the ability to clone humans but after all I have read this may not be the case. And I think they may have an agenda to cull some of us sheeple off. But before they do this I think they may be cloning us first.

Doing what?

'Cloning us; cloning humans. I myself am a clone.'

How many times have I got to tell you you're not a clone, I think I may have overdone it with the zapping

'How do you know Alf? Hey, how do you fricking know that for sure? Not only am I a clone I also think they plan to clone more of us.'

Why would they bother doing that?

'So they can create genetically modified slaves.'

Do what? Ha ha.

'I'm serious, they turn us into genetically modified clones and when we breed we parent obedient submissive baby clones.'

Really?

When we clones breed, and our Ewes bring our new lambs into the world, they will naturally grow up to do as they're told without complaining. Before you know it you will have a world full of zombie clones; hybrid slave sheeple. In fact this could well be the next step in the advancement of programming us sheep as they have tried to do for years. They are attempting to turn us all into brain dead working zombies.

Zombies?? Is that what you think?

'Yes zombies because we would by then have lost our individuality, human soul and spirit, so technically we would be dead, walking dead Zombie Sheep. I tell you what else Alf, I think they already have them.'

Really?

'Yes, mainly you see them working in supermarket checkouts or mobile phone shops, but I think they keep a lot of them locked up in call centres.'

Is that right.

'Yes, and if my fellow sheep don't start to act together to keep GM food under control, so they can't advance this cloning science, we could end up extinct and replaced by zombie clones. Zombie clones, Alf, a world full of brain-dead zombie sheeple.'

Are you completely mad?

Do you know reader you could already be a clone just like I am? And you wouldn't even know it. I mean I only found out by chance that I was one didn't I?

You're not a fricking clone nor are your readers. Look, you made me swear now.

Look reader, take no notice of Alf. Take it from me that if you haven't felt yourself lately it could be because you are a clone. Sod what Alf is saying. Now then, think about that for a moment. I bet you have never thought about that before, have you?

Your reader is not a clone.

Okay, maybe not now but it doesn't mean there isn't an agenda to clone them in the future. So just beware reader, that's all I say, beware. They just haven't got to you yet, that's all. Just because you're not a clone at the moment it doesn't mean it won't happen. Remember once they clone you they will bump off the real you. The government are shady bastards and capable of doing anything. You know and I know they would never admit to doing it, because if they did there would be a public outcry. Yes, they're shady bastards the government.

'Tell you what Alf?'

What?

'It'll be interesting to see how many they have already cloned…Now that's a thought isn't it? Surely I can't be the only clone on the planet? There must be more of us.'

There's no getting through to him... Look reader, I'm off until he calms down.

'Where are you going Alf? Alf! He's gone. Bah fuck him!'

Just me and you then reader, so while he's gone lets me and you find out together what the frig is going on shall we? Starting with this question: What are the benefits of cloning sheeple in the first place?

Well. As you can imagine I thought about this for some considerable time and came up with what I thought was a brilliant feasible conclusion to it all. Okay it may come across as quite a controversial idea to some but stay with me. Here goes, this is what I think is going on.

Now you know and I know that there is a worldwide shortage of donors, be it blood donors or organ donors. So don't you think it isn't unreasonable that the government, maybe in an attempt to rectify this massive problem, are possibly cloning sheeple to be donors? At least this is how it all started. I know it sounds crazy but, if you think about it with an open mind for a moment, if they were it would sort out a big problem in no time at all. And when you think about it in more depth as I have, all I can see is the benefits from a scheme such as this. Not only to maintain a healthy working population but also financially too. Because, although firstly done with good intentions, I now think the reason they do it is to make money and not save lives.

It is a known fact they have experimented on cloning for years and that a cloning scheme has been going on. If they could master it then to clone sheeple could help pay off the accumulating worldwide debts. Because, think about it, Sheeple would without doubt pay a lot of money for an organ or some blood to save their life. I know I would, that is of course if I had any money in the first place. Now I understand at first this may sound like a ludicrous if not barbaric idea, especially if you're a Jehovah witness. But I personally think this might be going on and, like it or not, it's a money winner every time.

If it did benefit my fellow sheeple and helped them live longer then I personally would be all for it. My suspicion is the government as you know always think of ways to exploit us common sheep. So if they clone humans as I believe they do it is probably just another idea to benefit them. I think we are cloned for body parts so the rich can benefit and not us. I say this because the government in my experience never ever come up with any good ideas that benefit the ordinary sheeple of the world. It's a shame, because when you consider that the world faces economic collapse, if the government made it affordable for all, they could use the funds raised by cloning sheeple for body parts to sort out the worldwide debt problem. It really does have marvellous potential. It's a brilliant idea if it was run correctly.

I mean, think about it. There'd never be a sheep dying again because they were unable to get the blood or an organ transplant. This would be two massive worldwide problems sorted out in a matter of years, if not months. Yes, I really think sheeple would buy into this idea because, well - it could potentially extend their life expectancy, and life is precious, no matter who you are. So the more clones they made the more lives would undoubtedly be saved. It also raises loads of money for the economy. See, everyone's a winner.

I can see it now... you could have a dairy plant in every city around the world which creates jobs, with some of the clones put on a constant drip feed very similar to milking a cow. Only you would be milking clones for their blood. See again a brilliant idea. I can't help it, they pop into my head. By doing this you could stock up on gallons of blood then there would never be a blood shortage again.

As for the body parts and organs, you could if you wanted keep some of these clones in a large fridge until the time came when a lung, heart or kidney was needed for a life- saving operation. Then a surgeon could simply pop to the clone fridge, as you would your own fridge at home, grab a clone, remove its compatible organ or whatever was needed and 'Bob's your uncle' cured. Thanks to this medical cloning scheme the patient lives for another ten years or so, if not longer, a bloody bang on idea if I say so myself. I would say well done to the government, it's about time you did something that makes sense for once.

You know the more I think about this the more I like it. In fact there's money to be made here for me too. Tell you what reader I think I'll go out and buy a load of domain names today ready for when it all takes off. Starting with 'clonestoorder.com' or 'Dial-a-clone.com' I like that one. 'DIAL- A- CLONE.COM' it has a certain ring to it doesn't it? I'll get on to it today and then start advertising straight away to see if I can get some orders ready for when the government announces its new fantastic scheme. When they do I'll be ready.

They will have to buy my domain names from me when they see how sheeple have signed up to 'DIAL- A- CLONE. COM'. I'll be a fricking millionaire. I think I will start with some advertisements like, 'Are you dying? Do you need a body part or blood and can't get a donor to match? Don't delay Dial-a-clone.com today, we can help.'

Do you know I can see my domain being bigger than Facebook? Wow, I just had another brilliant thought pop in my brain to add to all the others. How about letting yourself be cloned… for a small fee of course because, as I've said before, you should never sell yourself cheap.

MICKY FRICK'S TIP

NEVER SELL YOURSELF CHEAP

I think the government could pay you to let them clone you for body parts. Yes, I think there's money to be made here for all of us if we run it right. I could have advertisements for that an' all.

> **'Do you want to save a life and be paid for it at the same time and be seen as a hero? Be-a clone.com. We will pay you to be cloned so that we can use your clone's body parts to save lives. Come on you know it makes sense'.**

Or what about not paying sheeple but charging sheeple to be cloned, that's an even better idea. The government would buy into that idea I bet and as payment to you they give you a guaranteed long life to boot.

> **'One day you will die…not anymore, be cloned. We can then use your own clone's body parts and blood to cure you as well as other sheeple. Dial-A-Clone. Com. Don't delay register today'.**

I reckon in the end sheeple will want to be cloned and will be more than willing to even pay for the privilege, some of them will anyway. Imagine never having to worry about not getting a body part or a blood match ever again in your life; you could have body part banks, brilliant idea. You could just phone your bank and ask to withdraw whatever you needed from your own clone bank. I mean, the match would be perfect for a start so your body would be less likely to reject an organ from your own clone wouldn't it? Then, once you used up all the parts of that clone, you could dispose of it and, I don't know, sell your clone's carcass for dog food where you could make money from that too. Then you could simply have yourself cloned all over again with the money you made from that and before you knew it you had a brand new clone ready in storage for the next time you needed it. Fricking hell at this rate we could all live forever. That would be good too, wouldn't it?

> **'Do you want to live forever? Be cloned; stick that clone in your very own Body Bank if you need a lifesaving body part or blood. All you have to do is Dial-A-Clone and you can also make money from the blood of your clone, sell it.'**

You may laugh but I tell you what, I think this goes on already but not for our benefit. I bet our cloned body parts and blood are only available to the rich and wealthy, you can bet your arse on it. Mind you, when they eventually privatise cloning like everything else, it'll be as cheap as chips. Okay the quality will be shit when they start to mass produce clones but we will soon all benefit a little from medical clone's parts, for a short while at least. But for now if you're poor... you're fucked.

'What do you think Alf? Alf...'

No it looks like he's still pissed off so I'll carry on without him for now.

Have you seen that film *Lawnmower Man*? Well I've noticed that I have become cleverer of late, I know so much stuff now. Am I the chosen one? Am I really that special? Something that 'fortune-teller' said to me echoes in my mind, the one when she said,

> ***'You are a very special person indeed Michael. I don't think your life is ever going to be the same after what I tell you.'***

She never told me I would be cloned though did she? To be fair my mind is all over the place at the moment, I don't know what's going on…. Maybe Earth is a dying planet and the abduction and cloning process is their way to preserve the human race. They abduct us then send back our clones to run things down here, until they can find the real humans a new habitable planet to move to, because it seems this planet is past saving.

Yes that's what's happening. The real humans have all probably been frozen and put in a cryopreservation state on an Alien ship somewhere. They are taken off this planet one by one then, after being cloned, stuck in a deep freeze on a massive UFO. I hope they know what they are doing because here on Earth we don't know how to do this yet.

> ***'Cryopreservation of people or large animals is not reversible with current technology here on Earth. The stated rationale for cryonics is that people who are considered dead by current legal or medical definitions may not necessarily be dead according to the more stringent. It is proposed that cryopreserved people might someday be recovered by using highly advanced technology'***
>
> ***Cryonics from Wikipedia, the free encyclopedia***

A more advanced civilization like Aliens would have worked out how to do this.

Since I found out I was a clone and I have tried really hard to just get on with my life. However, I've started to notice other sheeple keeping their distance from me of late, and some avoid me completely, which isn't very nice. Before all this shit happened to me I used to be quite a popular sheep, now I don't have many friends at all. My wife, bless her, still sticks by me though I guess it's because she still thinks I'm the real Micky Fricker and just a bit stressed, what with my mood changes and that. She said to me once that she thought I might have bipolar. I can't bring myself to tell her I'm an Alien clone and not her real husband, and that I don't know where he is or why I was cloned in the first place.

I just had a brain fart. I wonder if it could be at all possible that I was multiple cloned. Maybe I am not as alone as I feel. Maybe there are loads of clones of me out there all around the world. Now that's a thought isn't it? It wouldn't surprise me. To tell you the truth I guess the Aliens might do that when they get a quality specimen like me; after all I am special. Maybe I'm not really on my own at all. I mean there could be loads of me. Kin-hell, that's a scary thought isn't it? I'll probably come across myself one day. I won't know what to say to him.

'Hello … pleased to meet me…I'm you….'

I think I need to find out why I was cloned and also, whilst I'm on the subject, find out if there are any more of me out there. It'll be interesting to see if I was cloned before because sometimes I feel I have been somewhere before. Maybe all clones minds are linked in some way.

> ***'There is only one difference between a madman and me. The madman thinks he is sane. I know I am mad.'***
>
> ***Salvador Dali***

> **There is only one difference between an alien clone and me. The alien clone thinks he's me I know I am an alien clone. MAF**

There are a lot of sheeple who say they can remember past lives and usually under hypnotherapy they talk about these lives and events. A lot even believe they lived before. However, just having a feeling that you have been here before doesn't necessarily mean you have. Have you ever had that feeling when you think you have been somewhere before? Some sheeple, when hypnotized, have spoken of lives they believe they lived before, they even describe buildings and places in great detail. When all this is checked out it is found that they were spot on with their descriptions.

There are also loads of sheeple who believe they are reincarnated. Some religions believe this is a fact and base their religion on it. But have you ever thought maybe reincarnation is just when you remember when you were cloned before? I myself have felt many times like I have been to places before and had moments when I thought I recognized a place that I knew for a fact in this life I had never been to before. The scientific term used for this is déjà vu.

> ***Some parapsychologists have advocated other interpretations of déjà vu. Such as the late Ian Stevenson (Stevenson helped to found the Society for Scientific exploration in 1982, and was the author of around three hundred papers and fourteen books on reincarnation, including Twenty Cases Suggestive of Reincarnation) he and other researchers have also written that some cases of déjà vu might be explained on the basis of reincarnation. Anthony Peake has also written that déjà vu experiences occur as people are living their lives not for the first time, but at least the second. Wikipedia***

Maybe reincarnation is when sheeple are cloned and re-cloned again and again? This warrants the question, could every sheep that have a déjà vu moment be an Alien clone? If this was the case, then why clone us all over and over again? Where do they take the real us after cloning us? What the frig do they do to the originals? I know it sounds a bit like a plot from the film *The Body Snatchers*. All I'm saying is how could any of you know if you've been cloned or not if it wasn't for me bringing the subject up? I only found out by chance that I am a clone and now I think I may well have been cloned loads of times before.

Yes, my fellow sheepy little friends, it all makes you think a little bit doesn't it? Okay, it may sound a bit bonkers to you at first, but what if everything isn't as it seems - have you looked at yourself in the mirror lately?

I thought about that time when I met that tarot card reader in Tenerife. I thought about what she said to me again, as well as going over the course of events in my head. Do you know, as I recall it now, it was all quite bizarre at the time when I thought about it? Ever since I talked to her I haven't really been the same person. Maybe she wasn't who she seemed to be and I don't mean a clone like me; maybe she wasn't of this world. Maybe just maybe she was an Alien.

What if the government had nothing to do with any of this after all? In fact, I bet when the real Micky Frick walked into that bar it wasn't a bar at all, it was an Alien spaceship…He was really abducted by fricking Aliens. They tricked his mind to make him think he was lured in by a pretty Ewe to tell him his fortune, but really he was abducted, taken away and cloned. That clone being me. I only harbour his thoughts. Serves him right, I say. He should have known better than to talk to strangers, and pretty Ewes never usually talk to him, and I mean never. This one almost worshipped the ground he walked on, so serves him right I say.

So maybe everything he thought happened in Tenerife probably didn't happen at all. It was all in his head from the beginning to end. He was just abducted by Aliens again and once they got him in their spaceship this time they cloned me from him and sent back me to live his life. I am a clone in the place of the real Micky Frick. The more I think about it the more it all falls into place. That's why that face in that mirror back at home doesn't look right. It's because it isn't me, it's an Alien clone, a genetically modified Alien clone of the true Micky Frick, that's what this is. Frigging hell. Tell you what we best keep this between me and you because if the government find out they will want to do experiments on me. I've seen the film ET.

So there you have it…I'm an Alien clone, how about that then? But knowing this, what am I going to do about it? Just for interest's sake I looked up on the Inter-web to see if any UFOs were spotted in Tenerife when Micky Frick and his mate Andy were over there on holiday. I found nothing, not a thing was reported. However, I did find something that caught my interest, apparently Micky Frick and my mate both stayed right next to the Playa de Tejita beach near the Red Mountains (El Médano's Montaña Roja). This area is renowned for UFO sightings and even contact with Alien life-forms. This has been reported on many occasions, so see you never know. As for me, it's all too much of a coincidence. As you are already aware I thought right from the beginning I was special, but never in my wildest dreams did I ever think that I could have been cloned by Aliens.

You're not a clone. How many times have I got to tell you?

'Oh you're back. How can you be so sure Alf? That reflection in the mirror is an Alien imposter, I tell you. For all I know the real me is in a spaceship somewhere kept captive. Fricking hell… Maybe I am an Anunnaki Alien hybrid.'

You're not an Anunnaki hybrid either tut?

'I might be. How do you know anyway?' I looked this up and this is what I found:

'Alien Hybrids in appearance look very much like us humans with some small anomalies it is said, they also say they have a pale white/greyish skin and a somewhat larger and rounder head with big dark eyes and, get this… they communicate via telepathy. This could explain the voices in my head, your voice. How do I know you're not an Anunnaki Alien?'

I'm not an Anunnaki Alien

So, you say you're not but what if I am? Look at me, I look so pale and have dark circles under my eyes; it's because I am an Alien hybrid isn't it?

You're not an Alien Hybrid....

'It looks very much like I could be an Alien hybrid. And get this, I also read that a woman who says she was abducted by Aliens like me said they told her they were genetically modifying their very own hybrids using the ovaries and sperm from the humans they abduct. They are cloning us into Alien creatures. I am probably a mixture of different animals; a freak, a Frankenstein monster. She also said they have performed experiments on human beings and animals for hundreds if not thousands of years.

Did you know it is known from Egyptian hieroglyphs that the Anunnaki created monstrosities, some of which are legendary? Some were half-animal, half-human, and others were half-bird, or half-fish and half-human. Even today you may come across weird looking creatures. All these were possibly created by the Anunnaki or brought here from other planets. Look at me Alf, I look half- rabbit.

There is loads of evidence from the Hopi Indians, the Mayans and the Egyptians which has all been translated from their Hieroglyphics. Some sheeple who have been abducted also said they were experimented on near or around their reproductive organs which I found very interesting. In one case, a Ewe claimed that her unborn baby (at foetus stage) was taken from her body to create one of these hybrid Aliens. She also stated that many hybrids could be walking amongst us and we wouldn't even be able to tell the difference now because they are so good at it.

All this reminded me of a dream I had back in 2011 about Aliens but, unlike other stories I have read, I couldn't say it was a bad dream not by any sense, more like a wet one. In my 'wet dream' I dreamt about being abducted by Aliens and raped.

Raped?

'That's right raped. Not beaten up raped, just unconsensual sex forced upon me.'

I forgot about it until I read of other sheeple's Alien abduction dreams. As I recall it was a very strange dream, if of course it was a dream. I'm not so sure now. Anyway up, I remember it was a kinda nice experience at the time, not bad at all to be fair. A bit kinky yes but okay, but it was forced upon me. Shall I tell you what happened in my weird Alien abduction dream?

Do you have to?

CHAPTER TWELVE

ALIEN ABDUCTION

WHEN I WAS AN ALIEN SEX TOY

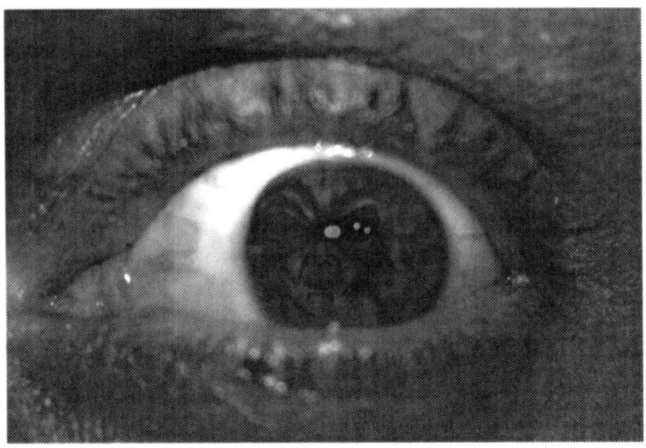

It all started when I was in my bed and just about to doze off. Something made me open my eyes and that's when I saw four little Grey Aliens standing around my bed. I said hello and smiled because, strangely enough, I wasn't scared at all. I was then beckoned out of my bed and without a second thought I happily followed them out of the bedroom and out of the house. Now I always sleep in my birthday suit so I was butt naked at the time but I didn't care a toss and wasn't embarrassed at all. I was then led towards some flashing lights which I was to discover later was a UFO. It was set down in my local woods near my house and the lights lit up the trees like a disco.

I asked them, ‘Where you taking me?’ and they just pointed at the UFO. When I got to it, it was shiny and metallic. I thought *that looks very nice*. Then I must have fainted or something because the next thing I recall I was inside the UFO. It was very basic inside but still very nice and everything looked very smooth. There were other Aliens inside, at least ten, and one walked up to me. I looked at its eyes that were jet black and saw my reflection in them. Again I passed out.

The next time I woke up I was laid down on a smooth warm metal table, still naked but now also covered in some slimy greenish gel. It was all over my body and I had a tingling sensation. Even though I wasn’t tied down to this table, I couldn’t move a muscle, except my eyes, so I could still look around a bit. I noticed I wasn’t alone either as there were other sheeple with me lying on tables similar to mine. But they seemed to be either crying or at least very upset and whimpering, most of them looked really scared to be fair. I was fine until I saw them looking terrified and this is when I started to get a little scared. I thought they must know something I don’t. I started to panic. I just wanted to get out of there but like I said I couldn’t move a muscle except my eyes.

Then two taller Aliens came over to me. They looked almost human and as I recall they started to prod me and touch me. As they did a smaller Grey Alien approached and started talking to me as if it was in my head like Alf. The Alien’s mouth wasn’t moving at all but I could hear its voice in my head. When it spoke it had a hissing sound to it, and to my surprise it spoke very good English too...well sort of. The Alien told me not to be scared and said that they just wanted to do some medical examinations on me, that’s all, then I could go home.

This scared the shit out of me even more. You see, I don’t like hospitals or dentists or injections. So I thought *what they going to do to me*? I wanted to scream out at this point, ‘I DON’T WANT TO! LEAVE ME ALONE!’ but I couldn’t speak.

Then the little Grey Alien said ‘Onanism’.

I thought, *what the fuck does that mean*? Then it put its finger on my forehead and I instantly relaxed. It then stroked its finger down from my head to my nose, over my lips to my chin, down my neck, chest, belly, and eventually it touched my willy. That muscle moved. I instantly started to get a hard on, it was soon up like a baby's arm holding an apple. But as I got harder I passed out yet again. All the blood must have rushed from my head or something.

Anyway I remember I came round again and found myself still lying on the table with a stonk on. I knew this was the case because I could feel it throbbing like it does most mornings when I wake up and need a piss. As I came round I slowly moved my eyes down towards my groin and to my horror I saw that little Grey Alien bounce up and down on my cock. Yes that's right, I was literally having sex with a fricking Alien, how freaky is that? Mind you I enjoyed it to be honest. She was very good at what she was doing… That is… I just hope it was a female… See the thing is you can't tell what sex they are; they all look the same them little Greys. Nevertheless, I must admit I did find it all quite kinky in a weird sort of way and I rather enjoyed it.

Then just as I was about to shoot my load this Alien got off me and I shot my load all over my belly. Then one of the tall Aliens scraped the cum from my belly, mixed it with this green gunk, and put it in a container. At this point I passed out again, or more like I fell asleep... Well, I always do that after having sex.

The next thing I remember was waking up back in my bed again. I know, I know it may have just been a weird wet dream but you never know do ya? All I'm saying is what if, what if it wasn't a dream back then? I have read a lot about Alien abductions and I have learned such a lot, like they reckon if you are chosen by the Aliens to be an abductee you will probably be abducted time and time again for the rest of your natural life.

'What if I'm not a clone after all?'

Hurray! We have got through.

'Maybe I am just an Alien sex toy.'

Oh for Pete's sake......

'No seriously Alf, maybe I am abducted and used and abused by the little buggers when they are feeling a little horny. Maybe I'm just their plaything?'

I'm not sure I like that idea either to be honest. I don't know what's worse being a clone or a gimp but I'm not really keen on either to tell you the truth. If I had to choose it wouldn't be an Alien gimp. I mean you don't know what you could catch from them do you? For all I know I could already have an extra-terrestrial version of the clap. That's maybe what's made me feel so strange of late. Who knows Alien clap might have infected my brain or something. You don't know it could be?

If I am an Alien gimp and the Aliens just abduct me and play with my body for their sexual satisfaction from time to time, at least I could do something about that. For instance I could keep condoms on me for a start, so next time they came for me for a quickie I could quickly slip the condom on so I didn't catch anything off the little kinky fuckers. I'd be protected, especially if I could arm myself with them extra safe condoms you can buy, the ones that feel like a wetsuit on your dick. You know, I say all this but I'm not convinced I am seriously abducted by Aliens to be sexually abused by them. Because, if that was happening, I wouldn't feel so sexually frustrated all the time like I am, would I?

No, no, the more I think about it I still think I am a clone.

How many times have I got to tell you you're not a clone hybrid, or a human rabbit cross, or an Alien plaything?

'So you say..... Look fuck off, Alf, I'm ignoring you. You might be an Anunnaki hybrid yourself for all I know, using that telepathy bollocks on me. I'm not sure I can trust you anymore.'

Give me strength......that's it you're mad. I'm off.

'YES PISS OFF!'

Do you know reader, being this clone irritates me like a boil on my arse? It's like having an itch you just can't scratch which makes me so fricking frustrated. I don't need this shit in my life as well as all the other crap I'm going through. I mean am I going mad? Who the fuck has voices in their head anyway? Thinking Aliens are trying to have a chat with me is ludicrous. Well they can frick off and leave me alone. Alf can piss off out of my head.

Do you know I have had his fricking voice in my head all my life? Day and fricking night he can pop in there and I've had enough. I'm really unhappy now and so fricking tired of it all. Yes, it would be fair to say that Alf's voice in my head really gets on my tits.

Thanks

'GET LOST!'

It's true he's taken over my life. And what about all the visions and dreams I keep having? Even they seem to be getting worse and worse and worse and they make no fricking sense to me anyway. I am going to start taking charge of my own life I think. For a start I will stop talking to myself, in public at least, because it just makes me look like an idiot. I'm not going to look like an idiot, not for anyone.

'Did you hear that Alf? No one, that means you too.'

You need to listen to me; you'll be an idiot not to.

'I told you to fuck off. I'm not going to listen to you anymore. I refuse to talk to you Alf unless it's on my terms.'

What are you on about?

'You will have to make an appointment.'

An appointment?

'Yes, and I will only talk to you in private when I want to and when I am sitting in front of a mirror.'

Why a mirror?

'Because I want to look you square in the eyes when you address me.'

Me? You won't be looking at me you'll be looking at yourself.

'I just think I will control the conversation better that way and feel I have more involvement, whereas at the moment I don't feel I have any control of my thoughts. Besides, I think you can find out a lot when you look into somebody's eyes and study their body language and that. And, as for the clone, that is what I will be doing when I converse with you. I will be able to look this fricking clone square on. I like face to face conversations. I find if you have direct contact with someone you're talking to, rather than say on the phone, you not only get their full attention as you speak but you can clock their sincerity in what they say. You know what I mean?'

I'm only in your head Michael you will be looking at yourself.

'At least I will be looking at the clone.'

You're not a flipping clone! AAAHHH!

'So you keep saying but I think I am. I want to know where the real me is and I want to ask him some questions, like where have the Aliens taken the real me?'

Are you looking into a mirror now?

'Yes I am and he is just sitting there looking gormless back at me. I'm going to punch him right on the fricking nose in a minute.'

That'll be stupid

'I know, I don't usually like violence but if that's what it takes to get it to talk.'

Look at him grinning. 'Oh you think this is all so funny do you clone; one big joke to you?

'Look Alf, he's smiling at me. Just because you're hiding behind that fricking glass, don't think I can't get to you, you….'

Calm down Michael, I think the Anunnaki have got into your head. Can't you see this is why we must hurry and relay this message to the reader, before you go completely bonkers? Get a grip.

'I am the fricking clone, I can't get anything, need to interrogate the imposter….

That's right.... I mean no .... Oh look you're getting me confused now... Look calm down... Tell you what it might be a good idea to stop writing today, you need to rest and give us both a break.

'Okay.'

(Ten hours later)

INTERROGATING MY CLONE

Do you feel better now Michael?

'Oh hello Alf .Yes, thank you.'

What are you doing?

'I'm staring at my clone's reflection in the bedroom mirror.'

What?

'I thought whilst I had a lie down, I need to interrogate the clone.'

Oh no, not this again, how many times.........

'No hang on Alf, don't distract me.'

What are you doing?

'I am now sitting in front of the mirror as I type, looking at this clone's reflection. The clone is looking back at me.'

Of course he is, it's your own reflection.

'See there you go, you admit I'm a clone.'

But not that's......

'Shhhh! Now he is smiling but I can see in his eyes he is worried.'

Worried? I'm getting worried.

'Yes, worried. I am staring at him hard in between typing this and he is trying to give me the dead eye, but it's not bothering me.'

What right now your staring at yourself?

'Yes, as I type. We are now locked eyed, neither of us is prepared to back down; it's like we are two boxers in a ring just about to fight. Both of us are waiting for the bell to sound to start round one. As we both sit here poised anticipating the other one's first move, it's quite tense. He just blinked.

'Ouch...!'

What you done?

'Punched myself... Well the clone.'

Why?

'He blinked, wanted to get in first.'

That was stupid?

'I saw him blink so I punched him on the nose.'

You mean yourself on the nose, stupid.

'Never saw that coming did ya clone? Ha ha!'

Your nose hurts now, doesn't it Michael?

'Yes it does. I can see in the mirror his nose pissing with blood too. He didn't like that at all did ya clone? Fricking hell there is blood fricking everywhere Alf, it's splattered up the mirror, on the wall, on my laptop.... in fact I think he has broken my nose.'

He... has broken your nose?? You broke your own nose stupid.

'We must have punched each other at exactly the same time.'

Give me strength....

'I know mine is broken I can feel it. In fact it throbs like hell.'

But I tell you reader the look on his face in the mirror is worth it. Oh fricking hell that hurts.

'That will do today. I'll carry on with this book tomorrow if you don't mind, Alf.'

You best go and see a doctor... Sorry reader you can see what I try to work with.

(Two days later)

BROKEN NOSE

Hello, I'm back reader. It's five in the afternoon and I've just got back from the doctors. Yes, I have broken it. In fact I'm typing this with tissue rammed up my nostrils. I feel okay though. After the fight with the clone I woke up this morning to find I had two black eyes and a swollen nose so I went to town in the afternoon to see my doctor. When I eventually got in to see him, after waiting an hour surrounded by sheeple sneezing and coughing and some weird fucker sitting opposite me staring the whole time, the bell rang to tell me it was my turn. So I walked into the room and there was the doctor sitting at his computer on a large black leather swivel seat.

'Take a seat,' he said.

So I did whilst he carried on doing whatever he was doing on the computer.

He then turned to face me and said, 'How can I help...? Oh hello, Michael.'

Then he gave me one of the big cheesy smiles, winked at me and said, 'How long do you want off this time then; two weeks, three?'

'I haven't come here for a sick note Doc,' I said.

'Why, are you not stressed again?'

'No,' I said.

'Are you sure?' he said, 'nothing bothering you?'

'No except my hooter, it's my hooter Doc,' I said, 'it's throbbing.'

'Okay take your pants off, let's have a look.'

'Do what?'

'Your pants, take them off please.'

'Why?'

'So I can look at it.'

'Sorry mate my pants are staying on....' Then I remembered I had a pair of Y fronts on my head. I couldn't find my hat see and, as I've said before, I must always have something on my head and that's all I could find.

So anyway, I took them off. He had a look then said, 'It's broken.'

I said, 'I fricking know that. What can I do about it?'

'Not much,' he said.

'What you mean not much? I've just waited a frigging hour to see you, and then you tell me you can't do anything? I came here so you can fix it. What is the point of fricking coming to see a doctor if you can't do anything when I get here; bloody stupid. The NHS is getting worse.'

At that point he stood up out of his seat. ‘Okay, calm down Michael....are you sure you’re not stressed, you seem a bit tense?’ he asked.

‘I’m getting fricking stressed. Look, come on doctor there must be something you can do for me?’

‘Stand up,’ he said, ‘let me take a look.’

So I did, I stood up

‘Let me see if I can straighten it, it looks a bit crooked.’

At this point he just pinched my nose really hard and started to pull at it and wiggle at it which really fricking hurt; I almost kicked the bastard in the nuts.

‘Sorry, is it giving you any pain?’

‘Fricking is now you bastard,’ I said.

‘Sorry... tell you what, I’ll write you a prescription for some painkillers. Come back and see me in two weeks… if you have any headaches before then just come in and see me again. Are you sure you don’t need a sick note?’ he asked, as he winked at me again.

‘No, you’re all right Doc, thank you.’

I’m sure he thinks I’m queer and tries to win me over by giving me sick notes. He most definitely is a puff, I can confirm that now. I could tell when he sniffed my pants before he gave them back to me. Anyway, I took the prescription and pants from him, went to the chemist to pick up my painkillers and then headed home. I had a sweet cup of tea and here I am talking to you.

My nose still throbs like mad but weirdly I feel quite good about it and I’ll tell you why this is… It’s because I now know I can hurt the clone. I interrogate it whenever I get chance; in fact after I’ve talked to you I’m going to interrogate it again. It’s funny because it makes me feel great as if I have some control over my life again. I also like to slap myself about a bit, or should I say the clone about a bit, it gives me a sense of power over him that I didn’t have before.

Do you know I grabbed him by the throat yesterday? I couldn’t breathe and I said in a croaky sort of way, “I’m on to you now you fricking bastard.” I poked it in the eye; that really hurt. It still hurts now as it happens. My eye is still a bit sore but it's not me hurting is it, really? It's this fricking clone who is hurting not me. I tell myself that anyway. Tell you what crossed my mind this morning, as I pinched the clone's cheek really hard, I thought, *I'm doing all this but I don't think I'm ever going to make him talk you know. He's a tough bastard I'll give him that.* So I thought there must be another way to find the answers I needed because this was getting silly.

Silly? Silly? It's insane. You need to get a grip Michael or we won't get the message out in time. You'll just end up locked up in a nut house, and that's no good for anybody

'I know Alf. I need to try and keep focused don't I? At least whilst I still have the real Micky Frick's memory.'

You are Micky Frick.... Oh forget it don't know why I bother, I'd zap you again but I'm worried I may be frying your brain..

'I was wondering Alf if there is anybody else out there that may have been cloned like me?'

You're not a clone. How many times must we go over this? You're just confused.

'Maybe there are other sheep out there going through what I'm going through right now. Maybe another sheep also coming to terms with being a clone?'

He's not even listening to me now reader... sorry about this.

Do you know reader, when I was at the doctors every time I saw a sheep with a black eye, broken arm or broken wrist bandaged up I wondered if it was self-inflicted and that they interrogated their clone too? I thought if I found another sheep that was cloned like me we could maybe meet up and help each other or something; maybe work it all out together and help each other to find our real selves. Well I mean, when push comes to shove I have nothing to lose have I? I know what I will do. I will go on to the inter-web and ask on Facebook and other blogging sites if any sheeple out there feel that they have been cloned. If so I'll ask them to contact me. I will give out my e-mail address and everything so they can get in touch. Wonder if anybody will?

Nobody will reply Michael.

'Well I hope you're wrong Alf.'

In the meantime Michael, why don't you look up and see what you can find on Alien abduction?

'What a brilliant idea Alf, I will but please don't call me Michael; remember I'm only a clone of him.'

Tut! Whatever…I am so going to zap him in a minute.

'Don't you fricking dare... okay let's talk about UFO abduction.'

Thank you.

UFO ABDUCTION

> ***'UFO abductions are not a rare phenomenon and have been estimated to have occurred to one hundred and twenty-five abductees. Dr Jacobs is one of the foremost UFO abduction researchers worldwide. ... He is the author of many books detailing how one's perceptions shape ... There is no proof that extra-terrestrials are kidnapping people.'***

www.ufoevidence.org/topics/abduction.htm

Did you know reader to this day the estimated number of abductions throughout the world is over four million sheeple? Fricking hell, I know, that's a lot of sheeple. I bet a lot of sheeple kidnapped by Aliens just don't report it for fear of being thought mad or something. Yes, my fellow sheep, we need to face it as any one of us could be a target. It seems abduction is very commonplace, so this gives me some hope that I will get the answers I need from a fellow abductee. You may be one reading this, and a clone like me. I would just like to say don't despair, you can talk to me, I understand.

At this point, to all you sceptics out there, wake pigging up because there is loads of evidence out there to prove Aliens exist and are abducting humans to boot. You could be next. Do you know, I think they need to build clinics for abductees like me because there aren't any you know? It's even believed a lot of sheeple didn't even know they were abducted until they were put under hypnosis. So, unless you have been hypnotized lately, can you really be sure who you are?

Four million sheeple may just be the tip of the iceberg because these are the only ones to come forward. I also wonder sometimes that maybe the reason they have no self-help groups for clones is because not everybody knows they are a clone. It could well be that I am the first sheep to know this for sure. To tell you the truth I'm not really sure what I'm supposed to do now. It looks very much like at this point I'm on my own with this dilemma. Even Alf doesn't believe I'm a clone

Because you're not...

Whatever.....I'll just have to continue with the interrogation of this clone until I can come up with any new ideas of what to do next. Even though I know deep down that he may never crack and spill the beans, so to speak, it still gives me great satisfaction to know he has a hard time being the clone of me. I tell you what, it's hard being this clone. I feel like I am me but I know I'm not me. I'm this clone.

HOW MANY TIMES HAVE I GOT TO TELL YOU MICHAEL YOU'RE NOT A CLONE!!

'Don't you fricking shout at me......I know I must be a clone because sometimes I feel like I'm trapped inside somebody else's body.'

Tell me about it.

'You don't understand what I am going through Alf. It's really weird to think you're somebody else.'

The way I feel right now reader is a prisoner in my own body. I bet how I feel is a bit like them sheeple who are transgender. You know, when a Ram feels like they are trapped inside a Ewe's body. Same thing isn't it I reckon? Well kind of, in a way. Well sort of, you know what I mean?

Anyway, I know what I'm on about; that's all that matters.

Look. I'll tell you what sheeple, and you Alf, to help all of us get to grips with all this confusion…

You're the only one who is confused the reader just thinks you're mad.

'I think I will have to give this clone of me a new name.'

Do what?

Let's see what shall I call myself…? Fred? No sounds too old. Trevor? No sounds too thick. Matthew? No Matthew sounds too gay…sorry to all the Freddys, Trevors and Matthews out there, no offence intended… ERM….. I know I'll call myself Barney. Barney. That suits me doesn't it?

Barney, Barney Brown, now that's got a certain ring to it. Suits you perfectly...Look whatever; do what you want to call yourself, that's up to you, just let's get this book finished shall we?

Barney Brown, yeah I like that. That's it then decided, Barney Brown it is. I'll call myself Barney Brown from now on. Barney Brown, Barney Brown, Barney Brown quite catching isn't it? Now we have got that straightened out we can now carry on.

Hurrah! And about time.

'Do you like my new name Barney, Alf?'

Look I don't care anymore. You can call yourself what you want. I can think of a few names for you right now...

'What did you say?'

Never mind...... can we now please continue with the message you are supposed to pass on to the reader before you go completely mad?

'Okay Alf, what else shall we talk about?'

I want you to talk about the link between Aliens and religion.

'Aliens and religion? What the frick do I know about religion?'

I'll zap you…

'Stop messing with my brain you bastard. I don't know who I am anymore. It's because you keep fricking about with my brain.'

I'll do some research, thank you very much......I just want to check my E-mails and Facebook to see if anyone thinks they may be a clone like me.. Let's have a look…Fricking hell.... Not one fricking reply.

Told you so...

'Oh well.......'

This slight disappointment hasn't deterred me. I kind of understand that to discuss being a clone with some complete stranger from the inter-web, telling them you were abducted and cloned by Aliens, is not something sheeple like to admit to on a public forum is it? This still doesn't mean that there are no sheeple like myself out there.

Guess not.... look can we move on now

'Don't zap me.'

Okay

'OUCH! I felt that you bastard...!' Oh dear I feel quite dizzy now; think I need a lie down.

(Three days later)

Oh hello reader I'm back. I haven't been well for some reason. I have a right banging headache. It's fricking Alf doing something to my brain.

Stop moaning and get on with it.

CHAPTER THIRTEEN

WHAT IF EVERYTHING ORIGINATES FROM ALIENS?

OBEDIENCE

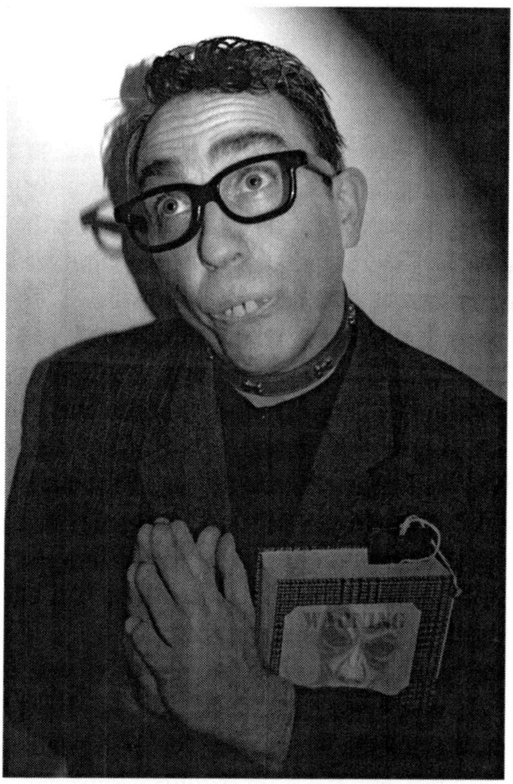

Do as you're told or else. This is the message that seems to be most prominent in religious books. Deuteronomy 8:20 says, ***'Be obedient to God or like the nations which the Lord destroyeth before your face, so shall ye perish; because ye would not be obedient unto the voice of the Lord your God'.***

In the Bible you will constantly see threats like this. It seems everything you read is to make you fearful of God and to be obedient to him. And there's me thinking God was all about love. It's no wonder to me why so many religious sheeple question their faith these days, especially when we watch all the atrocities in the world. Religious sheeple don't seem to spread the love from what I've seen. Death, suffering, misery, hate, murder all seem to stem from religion in one form or another.

Sheeple now look more to science for the answers on creation than just take it from the religious books they read. I see the so-called religious sheeple starting to realize that if God exists at all he may not be what they first envisaged. Nobody really understands God. And no wonder because he works in mysterious ways. At least this is what we are always told. Why is it that so many sheeple still have blind faith in the Lord? They are told to trust in God because he knows what he is doing, but sorry this doesn't carry much weight for me.

Now I know I am just a mere mortal and you might say I have no right to question God. Blimey, I might even be hit by a bolt of lightning if I slag off God's name. But I tell you what reader, I don't give a shit. Because one thing that really pisses me off is when you hear somebody say, 'It's out of our hands', 'It's Gods will', 'It's an act of God' or something along those lines when some innocent child has died of hunger.

Dare I look up to the heavens and say, 'Oi God, what the fuck you doing?' Well I will right now.

'I say God you listening? What the fuck you doing? I just wonder why you don't rain some shit down on all the paedophiles, the murderers, the rapists, the thieves, the evil gangs, drug dealers, smugglers, child beaters, the wife batterers, husband batterers, the selfish rich, pimps and drug dealers, all those who work in the slave trade, all those who are cruel to animals? Where are you God? Why are you not looking after the nice decent sheeple of your world? Why is it, God, you let all the bastards who inflict misery on others get away with it all the time? Where the fuck are you God? GOD!!

Okay Mich....I mean, Barney, calm down.

The thought that divine intervention created the whole universe, every planet, every star, every galaxy, is questioned by everyone now. Science now proves to us that it was more like a natural phenomenal event that created everything. They also know Earth wasn't created in seven days, as it says in the Bible, so science proves the Bible wrong on many accounts. What they found out is the creation of the universe was possibly because of what is called The Big Bang Theory that Albert Einstein came up with.

But.... if this is the case that doesn't mean God doesn't exist at all, far from it. It just means there are probably thousands of God-like beings out there in this vast wonderful universe. It is a probable fact now that other life-forms, possibly thousands of years more advanced than us, may be out there somewhere in the cosmos. So instead of just one super God, The Lord God Almighty, the creator of everything that controls all, there may in fact be many, that all jointly govern the universe and who we could call the spiritually divine.

In every sense we humans are simply an insignificant race of being, one of many that may occupy the universe. I say insignificant lightly because, though we are still a very primitive species, we are forever learning and each generation become more and more intelligent as the years go by. And, like God, we too can create life and make something from nothing.

We also know a lot about genetics, atoms, molecules and every other organism that exists and which are fundamental ingredients that allow us to manipulate and create life, just like God. So put thousands of years on top of the knowledge we already have now and humans become Gods in their own right. So maybe we should rain some shit down on the bastards of the world ourselves.

Can we really trust in God anymore? Because I am starting to think God is a sadistic Alien? I also believe religious leaders have known this for many, many years. I think the church or religion of every type and every faith was put in place by the Anunnaki which, if I am right, only means most are satanic.

> ***'The Anunnaki developed religions by corrupting any spirituality they observed in the indigenous people of the Earth. They employed religions as a powerful means of controlling the indigenous people. Different religions were set up with doctrines in direct opposition to one another in order to breed disharmony, distrust, confusion, war and arrogance'***

www.illuminati-news.com/ufos-and.../nibiru_and_the_anunnaki.htm

I bet you didn't know that the Vatican already knows about these Anunnaki Aliens? They do..... They have done for hundreds of years it seems. I don't expect you to take my word for it, check it out; just type in Aliens and the Vatican on YouTube. You also may not have heard of the telescope that the Vatican built to search space for the return of God. I know; why would they need a telescope? Is he coming on a spaceship then? Again this suggests God is an Alien.

Exo-Vaticana.(ufosightingshotspot.blogspot.com/.../the-vaticans-astonishing-plan-for.html)

A project set up by the Vatican 'for the examination of theological issues into extra-terrestrial intelligence' basically to search the stars for God, built a massive telescope which they called, are you ready?.......LUCIFER. Yes that's right, it's named after Satan the Devil. Why the frick they did that beats me. Anyway this telescope is right next to the Vatican Observatory on Mt. Graham in Tucson. Go on look it up yourself at:

www.exovaticana.com (What you read on this web-page will blow your mind.)

So it seems one of the biggest churches in the world, with over one point two billion followers of the Catholic faith, is getting ready for the arrival of possibly God himself on a spaceship. As well as this some say that Pope Benedict XVI is playing a leading role to prepare the world for extra-terrestrial disclosure. If you remember his resignation was an historical event never before happened. He did it because it was written that he must step down. Why? Because the Aliens are coming to take over the church, that's why?

Many other faiths are also starting to think maybe their faith originates from Aliens. (Just for the record I have always believed this.) Very interesting don't you think that religious sheeple from many faiths are beginning to accept this could be the case?

www.ufobc.com/Reports/Aliensreligion.htm

So does religion originate from Aliens?

You can make your own mind up but I think YES it most definitely does. All the Popes, preachers, and a lot of great philosophers may have spread the word of an evil Alien God all these years, without knowing it. Maybe they themselves are all evil Alien hybrids put here by the evil Anunnaki God to brainwash and fill the sheeple with sheep shit, just to impregnate fear and confusion into our minds. You might think that's bollocks but think about it, apart from monks or nuns, religion is responsible for the slaughter of many sheeple over many, many years. Sheeple have been tortured and even put to a violent brutal death if they refused to follow the faith that particular sheeple represents.

But God is all about love. Is he fuck. Religion is Satanism dressed up to look holy most of the time, as far as I am concerned. I think a lot of sheeple are misled by religion, so you can see why I think maybe religion is a belief, an ideal set up by Evil Aliens, maybe the Anunnaki and maybe just a bunch of sadistic humans.

Religion was invented for only one reason and that was to control and enslave its followers. MAF

I think because of religion our true identity has been buried in bullshit. As far as I'm concerned religion was invented to distort the human race from the truth. But I feel things are about to change at long last because, thankfully, I can see us start to question what we are told.

I also believe that humans have, and always have had, a divine species watching over them; maybe another Alien race. I think Alf is one of them; an angel. We all have angels that are on our side and communicate to us through our subconscious thought. They try to guide us away from the narrow vision that religion portrays.

It may well be the Nordics who are our true saviours, not God. We should all listen to the voice in our head. We all have the ability to be messengers and teachers to help us break free from the bondage of religion. A lot of great sheeple have died trying to give you this freedom.

Freedom has never been free. Medgar Evers

I want you to think for a moment about all the sheeple who have ever told us to live together in harmony and peace and to try to love one another: Jesus, Gandhi, Lincoln, Bobby Kennedy, John Kennedy, Malcolm X, Martin Luther King, John Lennon and Medgar Evers. They told us we should try to live together peacefully. I think all these great sheeple were sent to us by the Nordics. But sadly all were killed. This is because the followers of the Anunnaki got them killed.

The reason the world is as bad as it is is because as one great person dies an arsehole is born to take their place. MAF

I think the Nordics might have their own Hybrids to counter-attack the evil Anunnaki. That's why they gave us special sheeple, such as those mentioned above and myself, who are fighting against the followers of the evil Anunnaki and this Anu (God) and the dictatorship of our selfish greedy leaders. There have been many sheep in wolves' clothing over the years and we need to see through the smile and the suit. Do you know thinking about it, Mother

Teresa could well have been abducted by the evil Anunnaki Greys and then sent back as a clone because, for some reason, she started to say work hard and accept being poor.

> ***'Our life of poverty is necessary as the work itself' Mother Teresa***

There are moments she wasn't as nice as she was made out to be.

www.guardianlv.com/2013/10/mother-teresa-was-no-saint-says-study

www.theglobeandmail.com

The real Mother Teresa said a lot of nice things though such as:

> ***'Let us always meet each other with a smile, for the smile is the beginning of love'. Mother Teresa***

Ah now, that's nice isn't it?

Yes there have been a lot of wonderful humans, and still are, all trying to help you live better lives. We should listen to them.

Do you know I think it's even possible that Elvis Presley was a Nordic messenger like me? I mean he sang a lot of Gospel and inspirational songs. He also sang about Aliens in songs like I Believe in the Man in the Sky. I also have reason to believe Elvis may have been abducted at some time because he brought out a song called He Touched Me. I was touched when I was abducted.

Talking about the king, did you know Elvis once said he was contacted by telepathic Aliens when he was eight years old who showed him his future? According to Elvis the two Aliens showed him an image of a man in a white jumpsuit singing to a crowd. At the time he didn't understand what it meant but he had a fascination with the UFO phenomenon ever since.

As for Jesus, well he most definitely was a messenger as well as a teacher for the Nordics. Jesus was a very special Ram indeed. Virgin birth? Yeah right, I don't believe that. Mind you, Mary could have been artificially inseminated by Alien sperm....? Whatever, I guess we will never know. But I do believe he, and all the others sheeple mentioned, were all great sheeple in their own right. The best thing of all was they were on our side, sticking up for what's good and proper and spreading the Love. Jesus, as Alf has already made clear, was a Nordic teacher here on Earth to teach us sheeple morals and to try and guide us away from the Anunnaki agenda.

Did you know reader it is believed that the Old Testament was manipulated by the Anunnaki? That's right. It was Paul, one of Jesus's very own disciples, who corrupted Jesus's teachings. He secretly worked for the Anunnaki if you ask me, undercover like... Yes, poor Jesus, he trusted a lot of backstabbing bastards who worked against him. Unfortunately he trusted too many of the wrong sheeple and it was that tosser Judas Iscariot, the biggest bastard of them all, who got Jesus crucified. Backstabbing Anunnaki scum. You will find backstabbers and bastards all the time as you go through life, so be aware.

BARNEY BROWN'S TIP

BE AWARE OF BACKSTABBERS AND BASTARDS

Did you know reader it is written in the Bible that Jesus once said His Kingdom was 'not of this world'. He would often speak of 'The Kingdom of Heaven.' Heaven now.... Is heaven the name of a planet somewhere? It might be, you never know; just a thought.

www.bibletruths731.com/heaven-this-will-answer-all-your-questions

Yes, I believe Jesus was a Nordic Teacher. Okay, he didn't have blond hair like a true Nordic. He is always depicted as a dark-headed Ram with a beard isn't he? Mind you he could have dyed his hair and beard to hide the fact he was a blond. You never know, he may have done that to blend in with the other sheeple around him who had dark hair. I mean if he hadn't done that he would have looked right out of place, being the only blond-haired Ram in Jerusalem, and he would have been captured and crucified earlier. Maybe that Shroud of Turin that had his face on was just hair dye that stained the cloth. And his disappearance was because he was beamed up to a Nordic spaceship that was egg-shaped, hence the Easter egg. You never know, the Easter egg may really be a representative of the shape of the craft that took him away.

Whatever the case Jesus was a great Ram and since he was murdered I don't think there have ever been any messengers quite like him. Some have been good but not great like Jesus was. And I ask you, where have they all gone, hey? Where have they all gone? You don't seem to see many good sheeple about today do you? I guess now that all of the good messenger sheep are either dead or hiding, because of the fear of they will be bumped off I guess.

The Nordics may think they now need a new breed of messengers to spread the word. And maybe, just maybe, I am one of them. I mean, modern times need modern methods; the alternative comedy method that is. My writing may be just another way to get through to you sheeple. I don't know. But the more I think about it there is a good chance I was sent here by the Nordics to be a modern messenger for them.

I'm here to warn you all of what could be an inevitable Alien invasion of these Evil Anunnaki, who it seems are planning to come back to Earth one day. Before they do that it seems the Illuminati have set plans in motion to cull millions of the human race. The Illuminati, without a doubt as far as I am concerned, want to cull eighty per cent of the human population. Then I guess the Anunnaki will come and take over the world completely. I may be here to warn you of this up and coming event. So you should listen to me. After all I'm special too.

www.newsfollowup.com

I want to be heard not herded. MAF

Do you know, just changing the subject for a minute, I was interested to read that Jesus is believed to have smoked cannabis? That's right cannabis. It is believed he sucked on the weed. I know the first time I read this I thought no, surely not... Jesus a smack head?

So I looked it up in the Bible and it clearly says in Genesis 1:29-31, 'I will take my rest and I will consider in my dwelling place like a clear heat upon herbs, and like a cloud of dew in the heat of harvest.' He means he is going to smoke a spiff.

I also discovered a lot of sheeple disliked Jesus. How could you dislike Jesus? He comes over to me as quite cool in a hippy kind of way. But when he was alive sheeple hated him. It's true. They were followers of the Anunnaki, that's all I can say, programmed to repel all that is nice and good. Because I think he must have been a really nice Ram, and I mean that.

Anyway, going back to smoking spiffs, the only reason I can think of is that he did it because he was stressed out. Makes sense, the poor Ram felt unloved and probably very frustrated that the sheeple struggled to get the teachings he was trying to teach. To be fair when you think of school teachers it must be really hard to teach thick kids... Anyway it's a fact that smoking cannabis helps you chill out. I say, what's the problem? Overall he came across as a nice Ram, what with healing sheeple, making the blind see, and all the other miracles he was said to have done.

The problem is most sheep can't accept anybody who is different from themselves, or nice, or thinks differently to them, which is quite worrying for me because I am all of those. I even know the secret of self-healing but maybe I'll save that for another book. Talking about healing did you know cannabis is now proven to cure cancer? Check this out:

'Cannabis is a great example of how the human mind is programmed and conditioned to believe something. Growing up, we are told drugs are bad, which is very true, however

not all substances that have been labelled as "drugs" by the Government are harmful.'

www.collective-evolution.com

Look, before you all jump to any conclusions, no I don't smoke the weed. Some would say I am paranoid enough. I don't think I am Jesus reincarnated either, like some nutters out there might also think. I am just saying I'm like Jesus. I am here to possibly try and save you flock from whatever you need saving from. I want to teach you or at least help you find a new way to think and hopefully lead you to the freedom you deserve. At the same time I try to point out these real sinners the liars. Hopefully all this will lead you to proper salvation, or at the very least get you ready before the Evil Alien God arrives.

Well done Michael, you did all that without my help. At last I think you're getting it.

'Thank you Alf, do you want to add anything yourself?'

No you carry on.

'Okay, I will whilst I'm on a flow. I want to talk about the link between politics and religion if that's alright with you?'

Go ahead

'Thank you.'

POLITICIANS AND GOD

'Forgive them for they know not what they do,' Jesus said that an' all. He said that as he died on the cross, and he was so right because most of the sheeple don't have a fricking clue what they are doing because they are all brainwashed sheep. That goes for all politicians too.

BARNEY BROWN'S TIP

WHEN A POLITICIAN SAYS THEY BELIEVE IN GOD IT'S JUST ANOTHER METHOD TO GET VOTES

But why do you want to vote for some prick who is religious, anyway? Here is another tip:

BE CAREFUL WHO OR WHAT YOU FOLLOW

That's all I'm saying,

You have said this already.

'No Alf, Micky Frick's tip was **Don't Be a Follower.** I'm Barney Brown remember mine is **Be Careful Who or What You Follow.**'

Same thing isn't it....? Never mind, sorry Barney.

I think religious sheeple are too narrow-minded to be leaders especially if they keep saying they are doing God's work. I think you sheep are all too easy; follow a clever speaker and you are more likely to follow and trust them if they tell you they are religious. Why? It is because you trust in God. All politicians will say they believe in God. Whether they do or not, they say they do to appeal to the masses of religious sheeple out there, and I can tell you there is a lot. There are more than seven billion, twenty-one million, eight hundred and thirty-six thousand, and growing according to the CIA records of religions.

These are their statistics: Christian - thirty-three point three nine per cent (of which Roman Catholic - sixteen point eight five per cent); Protestant six point one five per cent; Orthodox - three point nine six per cent; Anglican - one point two six per cent; Muslim – twenty-two point seven four per cent; Hindu – thirteen point eight per cent; Buddhist – six point seven seven per cent; Sikh - nought point three five per cent; Jewish – nought point two two per cent; Baha'I – nought point one one per cent; other religions – ten point nine five per cent; non-religious – nine point six six per cent; atheists – two point nought one per cent. This was so in 2010, according to Wikipedia.

All these religious sheeple are prospective voters. So for the government to pretend that they are followers of religion themselves, makes you religious lot think they are good sheeple.

They know they could win your trust by pretending they are and you will, like sheep, vote for them come election time. But I tell you now they don't give a shit about religions really, or any faith. They most definitely don't care a toss about the sheeple who vote for them.

Politicians are in it for the lust of money and power and it stops there. It's all a show that they put on to get you religious sheep to flock together and vote for them. They are hypocrites the lot of them, as far as I am concerned. They use religion as a tool to win voters and in some cases they will even try and convince you they are doing God's work and justify wars and murder. GOD IS LOVE...... Is he? No sorry, can't see it myself. If God represents Love why then do so many sheeple die in the name of him?

It is going to be a very tough issue for Christianity to discover all that they have been brought up to believe is based on Sheep shit. It is going to be a very tough issue. Why is it that everything that we have been told is a fricking lie? This is an easy question to answer. Because they don't want you to know the truth and the power you have. MAF

BARNEY BROWNS TIP

DON'T TRUST A POLITICIAN BECAUSE USUALLY THEY ARE FULL OF SHIT

Now you're using a tip Micky Frick used in his other book Programmed Sheep.

'FUCK OFF ALF.'

Think of George W Bush Junior. He is supposedly a very religious Ram. I even recall him saying once, and I quote; ***'I feel like God wants me to run for President. I can't explain***

it, but I sense my country is going to need me. Something is going to happen... I know it won't be easy on me or my family, but God wants me to do it.' And.....***'The great strength of America is the fact that America is full of God-fearing and decent souls.'*** He also said once ***'The war on terror was a fight against Satan'.***

He was a religious Ram who said he trusted in his faith on all the decisions he made whilst he was President, saying words to the effect, 'My faith plays a big part of my life. I pray to God every day. I pray to God for strength. I pray to God for wisdom.' Yet he was responsible for the deaths of over one million Iraqis, and over four thousand one hundred American soldiers during his presidency. Didn't God say, 'Thou shalt not kill.'? He, like so many others before him and after him, was all full of shit as far as I'm concerned; religious my arse. Followers of the Anunnaki that's what they are.

Did you know no matter what religious persuasion you are 'Thou shalt not kill' is the number one rule for every single one of them? Yet religious sheeple and government leaders alike who say they are religious are usually the main reason why sheeple die in the first place. Funny that isn't it? Mind you, let's not just single Bush out, that wouldn't be fair... All the government leaders are the same. No matter who is in power they love to play war games with sheeple's lives so they can leave their mark in history. I mean if a president didn't do anything major like start a war nobody would remember him or her. Full of shit they justify murder as doing God's work and to wean out the Evil, but all they do is make a name for themselves. I have a name for them - Tossers.

You can understand why a lot of sheeple feel betrayed or let down by their God or government and seek comfort and reassurance from their religious leaders. That's a waste of time. In times of grief a religious leader will also say, 'Trust in God' or 'Don't lose faith' or 'God moves in mysterious ways' which really doesn't help does it?

The government are the worst when they pretend to care and be humble in times of tragedy, like 9/11 for instance, but really just act it out for the camera. Well that's what I think anyway. When innocent sheeple are killed in a so-called terrorist attack such as 9/11 their favourite line is, 'We will do all we can to catch those responsible and bring them to justice' When in our hearts we all have our suspicions as to who was responsible for this horrific event and they will never be brought to justice will they? Again full of shit but it will justify going to war and killing more innocent Ewes and Lambs, all innocently caught up in political or religious bollocks.

I'm not going to dwell on the 9/11 conspiracy just check out: 911research.wtc7.net/sept11/evidence. You can make up your own mind.

IN GOD WE TRUST

On every dollar bill it says 'In God We Trust.' Can't you sheep see you're brainwashed? That is a subliminal message that is. Everyone has seen those words many times and every time you do you are brainwashed to have faith in God; God who it seems wants to kill you. Every president at some point said they were doing God's work whilst in office. Maybe they all worked for God an Alien, an Evil Anunnaki God named Anu. Makes sense to me.

BARNEY BROWN'S TIP

MONEY; RELIGION. BOTH ARE THE ROOT OF ALL EVILS. DON'T FOLLOW THEM.

My political ideal is democracy. Let every man be respected as an individual and no man idolized. Albert Einstein

I watched the presidential campaign in 2012 and cried; no, not because of the result or the inspiring speeches from your prospective leaders. I cried because of the thousands of sheep who were sucked in to the shit. To me not one of them said anything that counted for much, just clever speeches written to get you the sheeple wound up emotionally. I just thought, *shut the fuck up.....*

You do know it's all just a show? I mean they use pretty balloons, lights, fantastic sound systems, dance, music; they pull out all the stops. I agree they put on a great show and we all love to be entertained, but it costs billions (not millions) billions. Did you know it costs every candidate on average between fifty and one hundred million dollars to run a Presidential campaign?

www.wisegeek.org/how-much-does-it-cost-to-run-for-president.htm

The estimated price tag for the US elections in November is almost $6bn (£3.8bn)

www.bbc.co.uk/news/magazine-19052054.

Just ask yourself this. What if one of the candidates said simply,

'My fellow Americans, I would love to be your President. I really love America and I love you. But I'm not going to campaign for your support because I refuse to spend millions of US dollars to try and win your vote. No, I feel that this campaign money which I have an abundance of could be better spent on other things.

'So I'll tell you what I am going to do. Instead of spending your hard-earned American dollars and all those donations and sponsorships on fancy flags, posters, TV advertising, loads of lavish parties and unnecessary plane journeys across the states costing thousands of US dollars, just to try and win your support, I will stay at home. That's right, I'm going to stay at home with my family and will sit with my wife and together we will think where this money could be better spent, other than trying to buy your support.

'I'm going to spend all those millions I have at my disposal on more needy causes, like helping the homeless find shelter or helping the less fortunate people of this country rebuild their broken lives because of drugs. That's right I'm going to spend it on the vulnerable and needy. If you donate any more money to my campaign, and I hope you do, then I will use it to help even more needy people or maybe use it to stamp out gang culture once and for all. I will invest in the personal development of our youth of today, for they are our tomorrow. I want to try to give them a more secure future. I also want to give more money to the elderly.

'If even more money comes my way I will build more mental institutions with top-of-the-range security measures so there is no escape whatsoever and our children don't get shot down by nutters with guns in our schools and colleges throughout the US. This will be a thing of the past because they will be locked up and there will be no escape.

'And if, after all the money has gone, I didn't even win the presidency, at least I know and you know for the short time that I campaigned we did something worthwhile.'

Would you have voted for them? I already know your answer. However, none of the candidates ever say anything like that do they? Why? It's because they don't give a rat's arse, that's why. They say what they are told to say which somebody else wrote for them. Their speeches are never truly from the heart, but of course you knew that didn't you? Didn't you?

Like I already said whoever becomes president is up to the Illuminati. You good honest hard-working sheeple have no say whatsoever. Your leader is decided before the campaign even starts, months in advance.

The **Illuminati**-Staged US **Presidential** Election - Rense

Every election is the same, just a very good illusion. Its aim is to make you feel you have a say but you don't really have any say whatsoever. Their aim is to get you the voter to think you have a democracy, which you don't. No that's right, we don't have a democracy at all; we have a plutocracy. This means there are just a small number of extremely wealthy individuals in charge of everything, better known as the brotherhood of the Illuminati. All that you see is just a very clever illusion.

The president you end up with is selected by the brotherhood. Of course he will usually be expected to be the one who gave the best and most convincing performance in front of the camera. If he can act the part well and meets other criteria he will become your president. He is nothing more than an actor at the end of the day. He, like any actor, has to audition for the part. He reads a script put in front of him and if he puts on a good performance and plays the part of president well he will be signed up. That's what I think anyway. I mean, think of Ronald Reagan? He was a very good actor. Did you know there is already a campaign for Arnold Schwarzenegger to become president? But he won't get the part because he isn't a very good actor at all is he?

BARNEY BROWN'S TIP

ALWAYS REMEMBER SHEEPLE ALL ELECTIONS ARE A FARCE; DON'T THINK YOU HAVE A SAY WHO RUNS OFFICE BECAUSE REALLY YOU DON'T

Let me make it crystal clear to you. The American Presidential campaign, or any election campaign, is nothing but a lavish show to make you think you had a say, when really you don't have any say or influence in anything. All these fancy speeches and inspiring words that you hear these presidents, senates, ministers say are just clever scripts written for them. Most leaders, be they a world leader or just a manager in charge of a business, have one thing in common. They all have narcissistic personality disorder. Don't know what this is check out:

Narcissistic personality disorder Definition - Diseases and **...**

Any leaders are usually self-centred tossers and politicians are full of shit. For me actions speak louder than words. Yes reader, you are taken in by a sweet-talking conman and you and all the sheep fall for it every election time. Mind you, you are probably better off thinking you have a part because I reckon if nobody, and I mean nobody, then would know what I am saying is true for sure you would cleverly see you were under a dictatorship.

You need somebody to lead the people.

'Do you bollocks.'

Did you ever wonder reader why there is a General Election every four years? It's because it has been tried and tested that it usually takes the sheeple that long to get bored with the current leader, or to start to doubt their leadership. It usually takes just four years for the average sheep to realize they were hoodwinked.

Hoodwinked?

'It means to be deceived, Alf.'

Oh okay

How many times have you been disappointed by your president or prime minister, reader? How many times have they not delivered on what you thought they would do when they got into power? Once? Twice? This is because you were hoodwinked. When you realize this you start to doubt your leadership. The Illuminati know this so it is imperative that they have another election, which they do every four years, so as to keep order. Because if you don't, when sheeple feel they are stuck with an incompetent leader it can trigger off unrest and a civil war in some cases.

I know earlier Alf said they want you to riot so they can bring more laws and restrictions against the sheeple. This is true but he was talking about ones they provoke for their own agenda; they don't like it when you do it off your own back. This means you're unruly and the Illuminati don't want you sheep getting unruly do they? No they want to keep you all in order. They want to stay in control. If there is to be any unrest or rioting it is they who want to start it and who can stop it. They will encourage all this later on when they want to bring in the New World Order.

You may have heard of the term New World Order (NWO), I touched on it earlier. If you are still not sure what a NWO is I will simplify its meaning. Basically they want to enforce new laws upon the flock and take away more of our freedom. They want to control everything, and I mean everything, even how long you live. Mind you, they already do in many cases already. But until the NWO comes in, the Illuminati know they must give the sheep the illusion that they have a say in electing leaders, or should I say another muppet (or is that a puppet?) we can grow to like. Whatever, it's all the same to me.

When election time comes around the sheeple think there is new hope and there may be a change to the way things are going; to be better. But nothing ever changes does it? Taxes go up and wars continue. Let me tell you now no matter who gets into power nothing will change. The reason there are so many civil wars just lately is mainly because a certain puppet has been in power too long and the sheeple start to feel they are in a dictatorship. That's right they slowly realize their leader isn't listening to them or keeping to what they said in all those inspiring speeches they gave.

All at once a lot of sheeple suddenly wake up to the fact this muppet is full of false promises and not who they thought they elected. I call this BBE 'Brain Burp Effect'. That's when your brain has been filled with that much hot air it suddenly burps and out of the blue you start to doubt the intentions of your leader, which I think is good. At last you start to realize we are all in this dictatorship and always will be unless we stop it. But getting angry about it doesn't help. You should embrace this realization, hold on to it and recognise it happening next time it does. Then you might see where I am coming from.

BARNEY BROWNS TIP

ALWAYS REMEMBER IT IS THE ILLUMINATI WHO PULL THE STRINGS HERE ON EARTH NOT THE VOTER

As I've already said the ironic thing is nobody really knows who these Illuminati are. But I think they are hybrids created by the Greys I spoke about earlier, I really do. As well as that they work on behalf of the Anunnaki Aliens. Yes, I think the Illuminati are half-Human, half-Alien in origin and very rich and powerful. Do you know I also have a vision of the Illuminati as a hooded cult somewhere who may even dance naked under the glow of the full moon to a raging fire and chant satanic verses and do human sacrifices on new-born babies. I wouldn't even be surprised if the Pope himself is the leader of this satanic cult. Whatever they get up to one thing is for sure, they are dangerously getting more and more powerful. Yes, my fellow flock life, it looks very bleak indeed for us sheep. Our world is being run by Aliens.

www.youtube.com/watch?v=_Fn0v0VX3wM

If you want to be saved you need to take heed of what's going on. I say this because at the moment it seems to me a lot of you don't take much notice of anything that goes on. This is because you still can't accept that you behave like sheep. If we don't sort ourselves out sheeple, and wake up from this sheepish naivety, when this Anu and the Anunnaki return they will cull us and eat us.

No they will not.

'As I've said before the Aliens do love eating human flesh.'

Aliens eating human flesh? You just made that up.

'It's true, Alf, I read it on the inter-web. The first time the Aliens were here on Earth they did hunt and eat Neanderthals for food.'

No they didn't.

'They did. Seeing these Aliens eat their kind is what started the Neanderthals eating each other. From then on cannibalism was practised among prehistoric humans for a very long time after. I read cannibalism lingered right into the nineteenth century.'

But......

'But the Aliens didn't eat all early humans, for instance they never ate any Homo sapiens.'

No?

'No.'

Why not?

'They thought our ancestors, the early Homo sapiens, were far too interesting and too useful to be just eaten at the time; so they were left off the menu. They just ate Neanderthals.'

Is that so......? I don't think it is. What have you been reading Barney? You're talking silly again; think the zap is wearing off

'It's true... but I reckon when the Aliens come back to earth this time you can bet they will start to eat some of us Homo sapiens, hopefully the fat ones first'.

Why?

'More meat on a fat sheep.'

No, I mean why should they want to start eating humans?

'Because Alf... they are less productive and even lazy. The worrying thing is Alf, most of the population of America and Europe are fat and sit about either watching TV, playing computer games or eating processed GM food, that's why.'

That's you on the menu as well then.

'What you saying? At the moment I'm quite thin and slender.'

True, you're not too bad at the moment I guess. Have you been on a diet?

'No I think it's all the worry....'

Oh right anyway....... is there a point to all this or are you off on one again? Do I need to zap you again?

'Yes NO! Don't you fucking zap me again you bastard and yes there is a point Alf, I'm coming to that…'

Hurry up then

'I think the sheeple should try not only to prove to the Aliens we are still interesting but most of all the population should go on a diet.'

Is that it?

'No, only joking. What I am trying to say is we all need to change our ways.'

In what way?

'We humans of the developed world take everything for granted and life for a lot of us sheep is pretty good to be fair. But a lot of sheep are not doing so well and I don't think that's fair do you?'

Well no....

'Not only that if we keep on breeding to the extent we are we will soon hit breaking point.'

That's very true

Basically reader, there are just too many of us on the planet. And because we don't have any big wars to keep the population down it has all got out of control. Something has to be done about this, and we need to act ourselves or it will be forced upon us by our leaders. Look at it like a shepherd, his job is to look after his flock. I'm talking now about the real sheep.... not human sheep.

Ovis aries

'Say what?'

Ovis aries, that's the scientific name you humans use for the land animal called a Sheep

'The animal with the woolly fur and weird-looking eyes?'

Yes.

'Oh right...'

I didn't know that did you reader? Anyway once his flock of 'Ovis aries' is too big or unprofitable to sustain sometimes the shepherd has to send them to the abattoir. This helps keep the flock in good health. The shepherd knows letting a free-for-all would soon get out of hand and could bankrupt him altogether. For us human sheep it's no different.

And your point is..........

'My point is Alf, like it or not there is a need for a human cull. Some sheeple will have to be sacrificed for the good of the human race.'

Really, you think it is as simple as that?

'Science already tells us this may be mankind's final century.'

That's not necessarily true.

'What do you mean not necessarily true? The world is falling apart Alf and to be fair we have had it good for a long time now. From what I've read we have been very lucky to get this far but I fear our luck is about to run out. It's a shame but that seems to be the case since we developed into Homo sapiens millions of years ago. It's been slowly downhill ever since.'

Not true, you humans have been a fantastic species to watch grow. Every stage of your evolution has brought with it new exciting moments and as you grew as a human race you developed skills that helped you thrive and grow. You've learned to work with the land and appreciate nature. You have learned what it offers. Basically you have respected the Earth but the only problem is for some reason now you don't.

'How the fuck did it all go wrong then, Alf?'

Frequency interference of the human mental state.

'Say what?'

Frequency interference of the human mental state. Let me explain.

'Please do.'

Before humans even developed any other form of communication you always had mind power and you still have this power today. But this power is interfered with by modern-day technology, radio waves pollution. Any kinetic skills you have are distorted by static interference or a frequency imbalance that is manipulated by the government to make you complacent and obedient. When you feel helpless, or you feel you have no effect on the way your life pans out, or the way the world is run, or you feel insignificant or alone or frustrated, it is usually because it's been triggered to your brain by radio waves sent through the air. That cell phone you own, or when you listen to the radio or watch TV, are all receivers of radio waves then tuned into your mind. Whether you like it or not you are controlled by radio waves. Your phone is the biggest problem.

That's why I feel naked if I ever lose or forget to take my phone to work. Those radio waves are like heroin to us; we get addicted to them and need them.

The governments of the world invested a lot of money into cell phone technology in the hope every human would someday have one, or should I say want one. They did this in an attempt to tag you all.

Just like they tag cattle by stapling that number to its ear, yes reader, if you own a cell phone, my guess is you do, they can keep tabs on you and know where you are 24/7.

Exactly, most humans can't live without their phones now. This is all because of the radio waves, they act like a drug, and like a drug they interfere with your brain receptors.

And just like drugs sheeple are addicted to cell phones. They are used to control us sheeple. If you own a cell phone basically you're a smack head. I bet you didn't know reader your cell phone is always activated even when it's switched off? No? Well it is.

Yes it is. It is always interfering with your brain pattern. These high frequency radio waves that they use can also be adjusted in frequency like the telephone masts. They also dose you with a small dose of radiation and, combined with subliminal messages and a cocktail of other methods, keep you dumbed down and obedient. They can also use them to affect your moods. Make you angry or placid. They are in control.

By owning a cell phone they know where you are, what you're doing and what you're talking about. Also what a lot of humans don't know is they know what you're thinking. They can get into your thoughts, especially with the new tablet phone systems you can buy now.

Can they?

'Yes I read it somewhere.'

Oh right.

Reader, have you ever thought, *I could do with a new phone* and then suddenly out of the blue you receive a message or are contacted by a phone company asking if you would like to upgrade? Or for some unknown reason you have this want for a new phone. Well there you go. That is exactly what I'm talking about. See? See in your head they are fucking with your brain.

BARNEY BROWN'S TIP

DON'T GET YOURSELF ADDICTED TO CELL PHONES. TAKE YOUR BATTERY OUT OF THE ONE YOU HAVE, START TO WEAN YOURSELF OFF IT. OR BETTER STILL BIN THE FUCKER.

That's a good tip

'It is but they won't take any notice of it.'

True.

Did you know reader, there are now seven billion, seventeen million, eight hundred and forty-six thousand, nine hundred and twenty-two humans on the planet and the population is still growing. Most of these sheep have been sucked in by the mobile phone phenomenon. The World Bank says three quarters of the world's population now has access to a mobile phone. Nearly two-and-a-half billion people are connected to the inter-web. World technology is mutating with your brain – soon if you're not careful it will become part of your brain. You'll probably have phones built into your ear because of the rapid advancement of technology...

You mean Alien technology.

'Sorry Alf, Alien technology. Most humans have no idea what's going on. This is mainly because most of you sheep have been brainwashed. Shall we tell the reader about the human cull, Alf?'

If you want.

CHAPTER FOURTEEN

WHAT IF I WAS TO TELL YOU YOU'RE BEING CULLED?

WAR IS A CONTROLLED CULL

'War, what is it good for, absolutely nothing' (*Frankie Goes to Hollywood*) great song and so true.

Now wars break out all the time and it is always because governments start them. It used to be religion that was the cause of mass killings. I mean think of the Crusades that lasted for over a century and a half. Think of how many innocent sheeple got slaughtered during that time; quite a few and all in the name of God remember. Politicians and God are both responsible for wars.

BARNEY BROWN'S TIP

DON'T JOIN THE ARMED FORCES OR ANY GROUP SET ON KILLING OTHER SHEEPLE.

At the end of the day if nobody signed up to an armed force it would just leave the fricking politicians and government leaders to fight it out one to one, like in the Frankie Goes to Hollywood music video. That would be great. I'd pay to watch that.

Here is an interesting fact I just found in Wikipedia. It's been documented on Wikipedia that there have

been one thousand seven hundred and sixty-three wars overall, of which one hundred and twenty-three were a direct result of religion. I thought it was a lot more than that, but facts are facts. So that means that government leaders of the world must be responsible for the rest of the shit, misery and death bestowed upon us all.

Did you know that most of the major wars, or political upheavals as they put it, and all the economic depressions and recessions of the past one hundred years, were all carefully planned out and instigated by the machinations of government? Such as the French Revolution, The Spanish-American War (1898), World War I and World War II, The Great Depression, The Bolshevik Revolution of 1917, the Rise of Nazi Germany, the Korean War, the Vietnam War, the 1989-91 'fall' of Soviet Communism, the 1991 Gulf War, the War in Kosovo and the two Iraq wars, all these were orchestrated by governments. Why? It is because it is the wish of God.

Yes God is trusted too much in my opinion. Yes my fellow sheep he must be an Evil Alien - Money, War, God, Evil the lot of it.

THE NEED FOR A CULL

Did you know reader the population of planet Earth will grow to more than nine point two billion by the year 2050? It's true, I kid you not.

This is mainly because you humans don't take precautions when you have sexual intercourse but as well as that you also have a lot of humans living longer than ever before. These two factors combined are why there is a massive population problem and, as you can imagine, because of it everything gets stretched to its limit

I read the other day reader that a Ram named Martin Rees, an astronomer and leading cosmologist, reckons the human race has only a 50/50 chance of surviving another century.

He's probably not far from the truth there

He must believe it because he has even written a book about it called *'Our Final Century.'*

Has he?

Yes, and from what I have read of it he says that one of the main causes of us all being doomed is because of our own self-destruction. He also said our demise may be either through scientific research such as cloning, genetic modification, or because our natural resources like oil, gas, food could all run out. Fricking hell, run out of food, that's a worry isn't it reader?

They say and I quote, ***'The global food supply/demand picture has NEVER been so out of balance. The 2010 food crisis will rearrange the economic, financial and political order of the world and those who aren't prepared will suffer terrible losses…' Eric de Carbonnel | marketskeptics.com***

A lot of sheeple say the same reader. Many leading agriculture experts predict that we will soon experience a worldwide food crisis of unprecedented magnitude. That's what they say. And from what else I have read it looks very much like this will start to become more apparent by the year 2020. A lot of sheeple think this will be the year the world runs out of natural grown food completely. I guess that's why we have all this GM food being made then. They also reckon, I mean the ones that know about these things, that in just a few years the world will not have enough food to feed everyone on it. Fricking hell, hey... that's worrying isn't it? But I bet the rich fuckers and all them politicians won't starve, bastards.

They also predict it will lead to food riots but before that even kicks off we will all see dramatic price increases (surprise, surprise). Nothing changes there then. Fricking hell, I'm just glad I grow my own after reading this. I might even start keeping chickens now as well. I like chickens. Not only that I might start storing tinned food again and bags of rice. I always knew that doomsday was coming and all that prepping I did back in 2012 wasn't a waste of time. I just got the date wrong. Look reader I suggest you do the same. Here is a link that might help you:

www.theemergencyfoodsupply.com/emergency-food

The greatest challenge to the world today is getting enough food to feed us all, that's what they are saying. Check it out for yourself if you don't believe me:

www.orwelltoday.com/foodshortage.shtml

Well the fact is. There are just too many humans.

'So, is there a plan to cull some of us off then Alf?'

I'm afraid so.

'I thought so, bastards, I knew it, tossers the lot of 'em.'

Like I said they think there are just too many of you and the sad fact is this only means even more doom and gloom on its way for most of you humans.

'Well that's just fucking great isn't it?'

There are a lot of challenges you humans are going to have to face that's for sure.

'Like what?'

Well, most humans have already begun to see economic breakdowns, and more and more people are living in abject poverty. This leads to an increase in civil unrest in a lot of places. It's going on all around the world you just need to open a newspaper. And sadly it's going to get even more frequent as the years go by, especially if the human population keeps growing as it does. If you humans don't change your breeding habits the future for you all looking rather bleak too. I'm afraid that's why there is already a plan in place to cull most of you before 2050 even gets here. So they can start over again and begin to build a new world...

'What do you mean?'

When you want to rebuild a new world firstly you have to get rid of the old one.

'Who is planning all this?'

The Illuminati of course, I have already said this. When you look at the facts Michael they really have no choice but do the cull.

'Why?'

Because the Greys have ordered it to happen, that's why. The Illuminati have been warned by them that they must stick to the agenda. That agenda is a mass cull of the human race.

'And are the government in on this? I bet they are?

Yes of course they are. But it's the Illuminati who are guiding them how to go about it

'So it'll be our own governments who will be carrying it out?'

Yes that's right.

'I might have known, bastards. So Alf what you're saying is the government have to abide by whatever the Illuminati say, and this cull agenda will be carried out by our very own governments?'

Yes that's exactly what I'm saying.

'But it's the Illuminati who want this mass cull, not the government?'

Yes, yes, yes. Get it into your thick scull. Your government is going to cull its own people.

Bastards, did you hear that reader? What a bunch of low life smiley bastards; we are all going to be exterminated.

No, not all of you; they will gather a few humans together first who they deem useful.

'But then simply get rid of the rest of us.'

Well.... this is a possibility but they do still need a few workers. All this is just history repeating itself; only this cull is being done a different way that's all. The same scenario is mentioned in Sumerian tablets and many religious texts and holy books such as the Bible. This is nothing new Michael; it happens all the time and has happened throughout history.

See reader, this is the exact same scenario that has happened before only it is the bastard government who will carry out the cull this time.

That's right, it is always leaders who carry out or plan a cull, except the one carried out by Anu in the Great Flood

'What a bunch of bastards! I read that there are six billion plus sheeple on the planet today as opposed to five hundred million in the time of the Great Flood. That's a lot of culling Alf.'

It is...Not only that they have more effective ways of culling you now. They can either do a slow cull which they are doing right now, or a swift one involving mass extermination.

'You're talking about genocide. We are all going to be slaughtered.'

No not slaughtered, there doesn't necessarily need to be any bloodshed at all.

'That's right they do have `bi-chemicals' an invisible killer now. With all the advancements in technology such as weather manipulation weapons they have at hand, and not forgetting them THz radio waves, they have all that they need to do an effective clean cull don't they Alf?'

That's right...and it's already started.

'What's that Alf?'

You humans are being slowly culled already; it's been going on for ages. Only they are about to step it up to a swift cull.

'When?'

Soon, very soon. They have already begun the preparations for this.'

'How will they do it?'

The guess is by introducing a pandemic. They have started to dump chemicals into the atmosphere to rain down on you all now.

'Bastards, that's why I get a sore throat and the shits; I bet I'm being slowly poisoned.'

Well yes, possibly, so is everybody else. They could easily add anything to air in certain areas, like a modified disease such as Ebola for instance, which is a new one they are working on.

'New one?'

Yes, they are always trying out new methods to cull you. You are likely to see old diseases like the plague, tuberculosis make a re-appearance again, or maybe a new strain of the Aids virus.

All this could be released into the atmosphere to either kill you or simply shorten your life expectancy. They may well detonate a dirty bomb in a city somewhere if this isn't working fast enough, or poison the water supply.

'And of course they will blame it on terrorists.'

Yes, most possibly they will. There are many ways to carry out a cull. They could use that new Haarp weather weapon we talked about earlier which could be the very weapon that is causing all the extreme weather. They blame that on global warming and climate change; maybe it's nothing to do with any of that. At least it is an effective method and less suspicious looking. They could just blame it on an 'Act of God'. Have you noticed that most extreme weather usually hits already poor areas?

'That's true, I never thought about that until you just said. So what chemicals are dumped into our atmosphere now, Alf?'

Loads too many to list just now but your reader can check out this website if they like to know more:

www.chemtrails911.com/intro_to_chem.htm

Get this reader, ***'According to the US Air Force, contrails are condensation trails and happen when a hot engine exhaust momentarily condenses ice crystals into pencil-thin vapour trails that quickly vanish, like the wave behind a boat, very much like your breath when talking outside on a cold winter day. Chem-trails, on the other hand, linger for hours and will spread out to form large areas of "cloud" cover'.***

'These chemical trails in the sky are full of chemicals used to poison us all.'

Yes, they could spread disease or just dumb you all down.

'How do you mean dumb us down?'

Basically they try to stop your extra sensory perception, so whilst the cull is carried out you are unaware of it happening.

'Interesting, tell us more about chemical trails, Alf?'

Every human at some point has seen the chemical trail left behind aircraft. They are spraying poisons. What you may not know is that they also actually spray tiny particles in the air with the hope of trying to block humans' natural extra sensory perception.

'What's that?'

(ESP) human brains give off a radio frequency that allow them to sense beyond vision, hearing, smell, touch; it is sometimes called the sixth sense. It is when you feel like something is wrong.

'Explain?'

It's like this...Humans have four basic needs for your existence. A need for oxygen, water, food, and you need to sustain certain body temperature. If a human was deprived of any of these needs you would cease to exist. For any creature that has a brain they also need to feel secure and safe. This is important because it protects it from danger, whatever that danger or threat may be. This Michael is called extra sensory perception. Because you humans have this natural ability, as do animals, fish and insects, you all have this natural built-in sixth sense, which is part of your natural biological make up.

When you have all five of these natural requirements like food, water, oxygen and your comfortably warm and feel safe and secure, usually because you have shelter, this is when you feel happy and content. This is also one of the reasons humans have survived as long as you have. At the moment a lot of humans feel down and uncomfortable and this is thanks to modern technology. The tiny particles are a new thing. Years ago they didn't have this ability to contaminate the air as they do today. It is these particles that block the sixth sense that tries to tell you something is wrong.

These particles actually block the radio signals that give you this sixth sense you were born with. That is why you feel so sad. But, as well as this, because of them you are oblivious to what's happening as you're being culled. It is also why whales end up on the beach and migrating birds find themselves way off course.

'Yes I read somewhere there are other chemicals used that are biological and their aim is to dumb everyone down, or to make us feel tired and unhappy, even submissive.'

That's right. It is so you don't know what's coming. The powers that be, your caring government, they see it as a humane way to carry out the cull.

'Oh that's very thoughtful of them…'

What I do know as a fact is that there are chemical trails being sprayed all over the world and that there are a lot of humans unhappy, and even dying, because of them.

You see reader they are slowly bumping us all off. But don't worry, you won't even know about it. It's being done humanly. Fuckers.

You have already had thousands of humans culled in these so-called natural disasters. You will soon see more and more of these natural disasters occur over the coming years, and they are all aimed at cutting the human population.

Bastards. I tell you what reader it makes me fricking mad. I don't know about you?

Sadly this is a fact – History yet again repeats itself. We Nordics have seen this all before, and each time we try and save you humans the best we can by giving you prophets and visionaries. The simple fact is it's all being done yet again to re-start the way the world is run.

I suppose in a way reader it's like that Sid Meier's computer game Civilization. I've played that and when I got bored I just deleted it and started again. I think the Aliens are about to press delete on us, or should I say rather our government leaders are, bastards. Told you; you can't trust the fricking government.

'How soon are you saying then Alf? How long we got? When is this mass cull going to kick off?'

You have until 2076.

'Wow, that's not very long at all when you think about it. Mind you most of us will be dead by 2076.'

That's right you will be dead, as will everybody over the age of thirty-five years.

'Hang on then, in that case why should any of us over thirty-five give a toss?'

You need to try and save everybody else younger than you that's why? It is a fact of life that most humans tend to stop breeding after thirty-five, so it is the young you need to educate now. It is them who are going to start families and it is their offspring who will perish in the mass cull.

'So you Nordics are trying to save our future generations then, is that it?'

No we are not. We can't do that. Only you humans alive today can do that. You are, and always have been, in charge of your own fate. We can only advise you or basically bring what is happening in the world to your attention. It is our hope that with the information we give you that you yourselves can then educate the young to prevent this ever happening again.

'How?'

Educate them better, like on how important it is they don't just get pregnant for the hell of it. Unless they can afford a child don't make them. Now would be good time to start because the way it stands there isn't much of a future for the unborn child.

'Unborn child? I don't understand?'

I mean the children yet to be born, your children's children.

THE SLOW CULL

'So back to this slow cull you talked about, is this just pinching out the dead wood so to speak, like the poor, the frail, the ill and the weak? The sheeple who are dying or going to die?'

Yes, they want shot of the old generations. Basically the slow cull is all about killing off humans over thirty-five, like you. That is so you can't pass on your worldly knowledge to the youth. They want a brainwashed new generation of humans because they are easily controlled.

'Genetically modified ones to be slaves.'

That's right

'What about these wars we keep having? Young rams under thirty-five are culled all the time in them.'

This just controls the populace; a game to the leaders.

'I don't understand?'

There have always been more males born than females so they have the odd war here and there to keep that in check too. If you have noticed those who join the armed forces are usually young men and women, mainly men of low intellect. To get them to join the army you have taken them off the streets. This is also a good way to cull some of the less intelligent of your species before they breed. It is all carefully planned out. Also they use these stupid people for their own agendas; mainly for this lust to dominate the world. But for most leaders it is just a war game, but they play it with real life humans.

'Anybody who works in the Armed Forces would find this offensive. You say they are all stupid if they join the Armed Forces. I have you know Alf you need loads of qualifications to be a fighter jet pilot.'

They are stupid. Well at least common sense stupid. Who in their right mind would want to join an organization they know might involve killing their fellow humans, all for a bunch of people who don't care a damn about human life in general?

'So little battles we have here and there are just a sick game and a good way to do an effective male cull. That is why we have them.'

Sadly yes

'All around the world there are little pockets of fighting that kill our young Rams and Ewes for entertainment.'

Yes, and to control the population.

Think about it, throughout history who gains from war? It's most definitely not the soldier is it? You will also notice you rarely hear of female soldiers getting killed in wars, because it's all aimed to cull men.

'That's true. As we all know wars break out because it is usually our government leaders who provoke the wars in the first place.'

BARNEY BROWN'S TIP

MAKE LOVE NOT WAR........ BUT WEAR A CONDOM!

The government are acting on the Illuminati instruction. They want wars. The Illuminati are also trying like mad to prove to the Greys that they are sorting things out and they also make a lot of money whenever there is a war.

There's Too Much Money To Be Made From War, And That's Why ...

Don't join the Armed Forces be a hippy. MAF

Earth has an overpopulation crisis so every small war, like the ones in Iraq and Iran, is in a sense a small controlled cull. It also makes a lot of money. To cull a few of the young men here and there is a small price to pay on the return of wealth that war generates. Not only that, their thinking is the Anunnaki Greys may back down and leave them to it. Well... that's the hope of the Illuminati at least. But do not think for a moment the Illuminati don't have their own concerns because they do. All they want is to be rich and powerful. They would rather the Greys stay out of the picture.

'How do you mean?'

Remember they still have the Greys to answer to. The Illuminati have been appointed the task as overseers to the Earth and if the Greys are not completely satisfied by the Illuminati methods they themselves will intervene on behalf of the Anunnaki who created them. It would be really bad if they did that as you can imagine.

You see reader up until now the Illuminati have done okay and living the high life for quite a while. Overall the planet has been quite easy to run and they have done a really good job for many, many years. Of course they have also reaped in the benefits and wealth of doing so. Up until now they have left it all to the governments of the world to do their dirty work for them, and they too haven't done too bad out of it either have they?

But now the world is changing. The Illuminati realize something has to be done to rectify this population problem before the Anunnaki God Anu returns, which they know will be fairly soon, in fact he's on his way right now. They know they need to do something about this problem quick. When I say quick I mean within the next one hundred years, which may sound way off to you reading this, but it really isn't when you think about it. They know the increase in the Earth's population must be slowed down and they have plans to do just that. If they don't do it and the Greys do take over the cull we are all fucked, even the Illuminati themselves and government alike.

If the Greys were to intervene it would be very bad indeed. Remember they have no emotion, no remorse, no feelings and no compassion. They will just get the job done.

Yes, by all accounts the Greys are nasty vindictive little bitches and if we leave the culling to them it will be done without any mercy whatsoever. The Illuminati elite will be brought to account for the lackadaisical way they run the planet and possibly executed themselves for allowing it to get out of hand as it has done. So at the moment it doesn't look much good for them either, unless they start to do what they were left here to do, and that was manage the flock. That's us, me and you, and this may mean thinning the flock out a bit.

The world is without a doubt overpopulated, something must be done but it shouldn't be left to the Illuminati. You humans could change the course yourselves

'How?'

Just stop getting your females pregnant. Take protection for a start.

'Yes, we already have too many bastards in the world.'

I remember Jon Doe also talked about how Earth is way overpopulated and shouldn't have been allowed to get this bad.

The government is under immense pressure from the Illuminati to sort this problem out, and with the arrival of Anu just around the corner, even the Illuminati are panicking because failure means death to them too.

It is evident since I read that blog that the Illuminati are for real, not made up they really do exist, and are beginning to take back control again. They will do this it seems by bypassing the government leadership completely. The government leaders are fully aware of this going on and seem helpless to do anything about it. The scary thing is...... I, as you well know, have always blamed the government for the woes of the world. But now I find there is a far more vindictive sinister nasty group of sheeple who are set on controlling us and them completely. And although I believe we have been going through a slow cull for some time, like Alf said, I think it is about to be accelerated.

Death will rear its ugly head sooner than you think. Some would say the best way to rectify this population problem is a war. There hasn't been any proper world war for quite a while so I guess this could well be back on the cards. Don't forget, if you think this way then you can bet your arse so are the Illuminati. But a world war is unpredictable and that's why I think it will never happen.

So if a worldwide war is not an option then another method to cull us is needed and, like we already said, a pandemic might be the preferred method. Whatever it is it must be put into motion soon because, as we have found out, food is running out and I don't think mass starvation is what they want either. How they decide to do this cull is still uncertain, but it's coming and that's a certified fact.

Firstly, it seems they want to cut the population down rather than an all-out mass cull. To be fair it would be a lot easier to control the few of us, rather than try to control a lot of sheep. They know this; they know it would be a lot easier to train them to be conformist slaves. They also know a fully conformist sheep will then train its offspring to be a conformist too. That my sheepy little friend is what I think is the overall plan; their agenda.

Have I said they want to cut the populace down to around forty per cent by the year 2050?

'No, you haven't, Alf....thanks for that... That gives us less than forty years then?'

At the moment they target the elderly sheep mainly because they are easy to target. The way they do this is to blame the financial crisis for not having the funds to give to the hospitals to sufficiently treat every old sheep that needs the care, or anybody come to that. This is very frustrating to the doctors and nurses alike. If people don't have the care they need they are more likely to die of their illness.

'Yes, they say they have no money but the politicians seem to always get their pay rises don't they? Bastards, it's alright for them, most will have private healthcare when they retire; we won't. And I'll tell you something else Alf, there is another way to kill old folk.'

How's that?

'Work us to death.'

How do you mean?

As was mentioned in my other book Programmed Sheep, the fricking government want us all to work into our late seventies. They know it will wear us out and without a doubt shorten our life expectancy. It is their hope you'll die of a heart attack or something way before you can retire and claim any pension. That way you won't put a strain on the health service at all. That's why they are bringing in this later retirement age, well, that's what I reckon; they want to work us to death.

Like I said there are many ways to do a cull.

CHAPTER FIFTEEN

WHAT IF I WAS TO TELL YOU THERE IS A PLAN TO TAKE OVER THE WORLD?

NEW WORLD ORDER

www.youtube.com/watch?v=iiTC-6BGW5g new world order

There is a new and unique development in human history that is taking place around the world.

It is unprecedented in reach and volume and it is also the greatest threat to all global power structures. The 'global political awakening' has been used by numerous politicians through the ages, being orchestrated by an extremely powerful and influential group of genetically-related individuals (at least at the highest echelons) which include many of the world's wealthiest people, top political leaders, and corporate elite, as well as members of the so-called Black Nobility of Europe (dominated by the British Crown) whose goal is to create a One World (fascist) Government, stripped of nationalistic and regional boundaries, that is obedient to their agenda. (NWO) By Andrew Gavin Marshall Global Research, June 24, 2010

The term 'New World Order' was first used by a Ram named Zbigniew Brzezinski, just in case you're interested and maybe wanting to use this knowledge in a pub quiz or something; that's if you can pronounce his name because I can't. So anyway up... This New World Order, what's it all about? I'll tell ya in simple terms the best I can. There is a plan being put in place where the whole world and everything on it will be controlled by just a few very rich sheeple.

In 1992, Dr John Coleman published a book called Conspirators Hierarchy in which he said, ***'There will be A One World Government and one-unit monetary system, under permanent non-elected hereditary archaeologists who self-select from among their numbers. Population will be limited by restrictions on the number of children per family, diseases, wars, famines, until one billion people who are useful to the ruling class, in areas which will be strictly and clearly defined, remain as the total world population. There will be no middle class, only rulers and the servants.***

'All laws will be uniform under a legal system of world courts practising the same unified code of laws, backed up by a One World Government police force and a One World unified military to enforce laws in all former countries where no national boundaries shall exist. The system will be on the basis of a welfare state; those who are obedient and subservient to the One World Government will be rewarded with the means to live; those who are rebellious will simply be starved to death or be declared outlaws, thus a target for anyone who wishes to kill them. Privately owned firearms or weapons of any kind will be prohibited.'

You see sheeple, I've tried to warn you for years about this. It seems it's becoming a reality. Just type in 'New World Order is coming' on your inter-web and there are plenty of videos, blogs, web pages and books warning you about this. But not one of them tells you how you can stop it happening, like I am. You already know that they are using your weaknesses, which are greed and selfishness and the lust for power, to achieve their agenda. This isn't a conspiracy theory any more this is a FACT. I can already see it all unfolding. I picture a little Alien in my mind hugging a globe, and with an evil laugh he's saying, 'Earth is mine, mine, mine!'

It is you humans who are helping this become a reality.

Over the years they have manipulated your thinking, fed your hate and brainwashed you enough so they probably have nothing more to do but sit back and watch us all destroy ourselves. This manipulation of your minds has gone on for thousands of years. We must not let this continue because it will inevitably be the end of us all.

But all is not lost just yet. Humans are beginning to tune into the frequency of the universe that makes them start to ask more questions about everything. This is, by all accounts, a positive thing to do. However, the powers that be don't want you to do that; they want you to conform, obey and ask no questions. This is so they can control you; control the world; control everything. Have you ever thought how unfair the world is and how wrong it is when you see some are having a wonderful life and others are not?

That's true life is not fair. I have always thought there is no need for anybody to do without anything, especially the basics like food, water and shelter.

That's right there is no need. The world has an abundance of everything anybody should need. It's just not shared out fairly. Unfortunately most humans are programmed to be selfish and greedy. It's not who you really are but you have been programmed to be this way.

A lot of humans have a miserable fricking life, and for a very long time now have just accepted it, got on with it and made the best out of what they have. But now, as we continue to evolve, all of a sudden we are fighting back, and about fricking time too. A lot of sheeple are now demanding answers.

That's right; money is now slowly losing its control on the humans.

A Jewish Banker named Paul Warburg, on February 17, 1950, said, ***'We will have a World Government whether you like it or not. The only question is whether that government will be achieved by conquest or consent'.*** Basically he said this NWO is coming, like it or not.

By all accounts the world needs to change and get into some order, but will they force this upon you humans or will they let you work with them to make this a better world, a fairer world? The answer to that question is up to you.

Apathy is equal to surrender. MAF

Do we surrender our freedom to a select few or do we fight to keep it for ourselves?

Most sheeple in the world don't have much money these days mainly because the rich bastards are hogging it all, and that's a fact too. It's their fault we are in this worldwide financial crisis because money only works if you spend it. Keeping it in the banks like they do is no good for anybody. There are more sheeple that have to do without than ever before and they now look for somebody to blame.

Well, stop looking because it's your own fault. You keep buying into this illusion life will get better. Well, I hate to piss on your parade but it's not, and it never will until you sheep wake up, because you're losing the only thing you really have and that's your freedom. Your leaders don't want you to be free as I've said time and time before. That is why they try to bring in this New World Order (NWO) and make no mistake it is coming. We are already becoming prisoners on this planet

It's not all your fault. It would be unfair to blame you humans completely for not realizing what's going on, because they started on you since your schooling days. The educational system right across the world does a remarkable job of `dumbing' everyone down and brainwashing you so you can't think for yourselves.

That's true they just fill our heads with what they want us to think, or fill it with some pointless knowledge that we don't even use in our day to day working life. Like algebra. It's true, most of the stuff you were taught in school isn't needed in the outside world; it's just a way of filling your head with shit. Okay, okay so you might if you're lucky, at the moment at least, get a better paid job if you got good grades, but even that's all going to change. You mark my words someday you will all only be paid a basic salary no matter what line of work you're in. Unless that is you go into politics and then you may be on more because you can screw everybody over with expenses and dodgy deals and blackmail, like the ones we have already do. Not all, but most, are self-centred power-crazed selfish greedy bastards.

If you are a politician and you think, *I'm not any of that*, well that's why you are a crap politician. You know and I know to get on in politics you must first learn the art of bullshit and be an egotistical bastard; or bitch if you're a Ewe.

No, you really don't like politicians do you?

'Some are okay... but only about one per cent, ha ha.'

Look reader, I bet you have noticed that wages paid for academic jobs aren't much more than some college dropout, who has no qualifications, who works in a supermarket filling shelves with the overpriced food you eat. Look at nurses and care workers? They do a great service looking after sheeple, wiping arses and what not and their pay is shit for what they have to do. Mind you, my guess is they try to put sheeple off doing that type of work because, if you think about it, if you don't have enough nurses and carers sheeple are less likely to survive on their own.

Since there is this ongoing culling programme it makes you think there is no longer a need for schools; oh yes they are to re-programme the young. I'll tell you what schools are designed for, they are designed to hide the truth and at the same time fill our youngsters' heads with pointless shit. Think of history lessons, pointless; religious education, pointless; science, pointless. Most of the stuff you think you know is not only pointless information, it's all sheep shit. The truth about the real world, your real existence and who you are is hidden from you. School is basically to condition you to accept being controlled for when the New World Order comes.

What is the first thing you do when you leave full-time education? That's right find a job. The government have done a marvellous job in enslaving you by giving you the need to want for money and the only way you will get money is by getting a job. At least that is what you are made to believe. Our lives are absolutely controlled by money at the moment. I mean, we can't do anything without it anymore.

Did you know you don't actually own anything you buy? It's true you don't even own your home you only rent it off the banks. You don't own your car, you are just loaned money so you rent it and by the time you have paid the rent on your car it isn't worth fuck all. So they give it to you, that's right, give it to you because they have already made a profit. They aren't stupid. They know full well you will soon want more money to rent a newer car so they know you will take out another loan from them. Let's face it most of the population that drive pay a loan for their cars with interest, they actually own nothing.

So, who really owns your property, your home, your car? I'll tell you those who create the money own it all. Money enslaves you. You see the thing is you are all programmed to want for stuff, this is what keeps you working, and you always seem to want stuff. You want this, you want that, but it's all paid for by money you have loaned. The wage you earn isn't yours; most of it is usually given back to the government before you get it via taxes. In effect you have to pay to work. Then the rip-off power companies take some more from you and rip-off supermarkets take a little more; we all have to eat but we're ripped off.

If you're lucky by the end of it all you may be able to buy a packet of cigarettes and go out for a beer on a weekend and that's about it, your money has all gone. That is until next pay day and the process starts over. Most sheeple's wages are frankly shit. It's not even your money when you think about it, they only loan you your wages short term, you have to give it them back. So that's why you have to take out a loan to buy anything nice like a car. Ask yourself why do you need a car? I'll tell you why, so you can get to fricking work. If you didn't work you wouldn't really need a car would you? Sheeple got along just fine before cars you know.

You see, you own fuck all, but the funny thing is you still think you're doing ok. Even though you don't own anything, you have no freedom and are slaves to the system you think that all is ok with the world. It's all just the norm. Tut, tut, see? They have got you good my friend and you still want to work … why? So you can rent more stuff? That is the whole point of money to control you. If you think about it I'm right.

You don't need anything really other than food and water, so why not just grow your own food and collect rainwater in a bucket? You could even go out and build your own house. Oh hang on; you can't do that can you? You don't own the land. The fact is you don't own anything and that's why you don't really know what you want any more do you, to be fair?

You only think you want stuff because you are told what you want by somebody else fricking with your mind and controlling your life. You don't even own you. Did you know public opinion polls are really taken with the intent of gauging the public's acceptance of the New World Order?

Have you finished your rant? You're starting to sound like somebody I used to know.

'Yes thank you.'

Mind you, you do have a point. All you say is very true.

So you see all the grades you are encouraged to get from your school days count for fuck all these days. Not only that, if technology continues advancing like it is there won't be any work for any of us anyway. As I've said already one day they will replace the lot of us sheep with machines and robots. You mark my words. You mark my words on that. Fricking New World Order they can kiss my arse.

Don't forget the New World Order is linked to Nibiru and the Anunnaki Aliens.

'That's right Alf I was getting to that.'

And the Elite, the Hierarchy,

'The bastard government too, they all want to control us sheep.'

The New World Order is on the fast track now. It is on the fast track big time because Nibiru is entering our solar system, it needs to be put into place before Anu and his army return.

I bet you didn't know reader that government leaders of all major countries like England, the United States, Germany, Italy, Australia, New Zealand, etc. are participants in this NWO plan? The reason they are is because they don't have any choice. The simple fact is anyone who isn't a team player is bumped off. President Kennedy was bumped off because he was unwilling to go along with the plan to control the world. He is just one of many. I read this on the link below:

www.crawford2000.co.uk/ufo-planetx-nibiru-marduk.htm

> ***What we do know for a fact folks is the mechanisms are being put into place to destroy the world and take away our individual freedoms and create a `World Government' that we didn't elect. It is being shut down on all fronts. It is being shoved down our throats.***

At the moment we are no more than lambs for the slaughter… The problem is you sheep have no balls. Have you ever thought about the state this planet has got into? Look closely at all the things you see happen on the news in the streets. Our leaders are failing us, most of Earth's decay is by the incompetence of these sheeple in power. What with wars and what have you and all wars are started against our wishes remember. I think most can be avoided.

I also believe most of the sheeple on this Earth of ours are good decent folk deep down but bad actions are contagious. For instance if somebody yells at you, you instantly yell back. We are all guilty in some form or another in contributing to the misery. On the other hand don't forget smiling is contagious too and so is laughter. But I understand that at the moment there isn't a lot to smile about. And there never will be if we sit about and do nothing to stop this NWO.

Don't you think it's time we got up off our lazy asses and tried to change things? Do you really want to continue with this directive, to be herded, farmed and culled like a flock of brainless sheep? It seems to me too many of you sheep don't really give a toss what goes on in the world and the atrocities happening all over it. Like I bet you didn't know that there are ritual killings going on in today's modern world, done by sick individuals who use little children or young virgins as sacrifices. Like in Africa a witch doctor will kill a disabled child and pass on their body parts as cures for things like bad luck and ill health to those who require it.

WARNING the two videos below are quite disturbing:

www.youtube.com/watch?v=176n3aE1x4M

www.youtube.com/watch?v=Ht2VFVZU8q4

I know, it is like something out of a horror movie but this is the type of sick behaviour that goes on all around the world and is carried out by evil misguided humans. Yes there are lots of things that go on in this sick world and collectively if we wanted to we could put a stop to it all. Yet I expect we will do nothing. Did you know there is a plan to eliminate specific populations, mainly third world countries and the poor, because they look at them as surplus stock that don't contribute to the world? They see undeveloped countries as insignificant which is why they focus on creating new viruses all the time. They let loose life-threatening diseases in these countries to cull these sheep. Ebola is the new one. Funny how only deprived countries are the ones that get ill all the time isn't it?

Terrorism, it's the governments' favourite word, terrorism. They love to use this word as often as they can. Its main aim is to frighten us all and it seems to justify all the illegal wars and the green light to slaughter more sheeple. The only terrorists you need to worry about are your own government. War on Terror is never going to finish, not for the US anyway. It will go on and on and on because this is part of the NWO agenda.

And now they are attempting to drag other countries into this war. What you are witnessing sheeple is a World War

Three, happening right now, only there is no need to let a load of nukes off to do the cull, they are doing fine thank you very much by slowly picking us off one by one. But this will accelerate as the years go on. There are some probabilities a nuke or a dirty bomb will go off in the US, and maybe other large cities around the world, and of course the governments will blame the terrorists for it.

Unfortunately, none of us right across the planet have a government for the sheeple that is elected by the sheeple. The New World Order is absolutely coming and there is nothing any of us can do about it. It is extremely frustrating to me because, like you, all I want is to live a life in happiness and peace. We do have an opportunity to have all that, but you sheep don't work hard enough to achieve it. It also gives me no pleasure to be the bearer of bad news all the time and keep on ranting about the wrongs of the world, but somebody has got to do it.

'Alf, can we really turn things around?'

Absolutely! That is why we chose you to relay this message.

Most sheeple will react with disbelief and scepticism towards what I have covered in this book, unaware that they have been conditioned, brainwashed and programmed to react with scepticism to what I tell them. So I wonder if this book will do any of you any good at all.

I hope so for the sake of mankind.

For a start you sheeple must stop believing everything that goes on in the world is reality. What you read in the papers or watch on the TV is carefully crafted and scripted propaganda designed to hide the real world and what's happening in it from you. Look at me, since I stopped reading newspapers, watching the TV or listening to the radio for such a long time, I am just starting to discover the real me again, to find out the truth.

Asking questions is what makes us human but brainwashing us blocks out the truthful logical answers we seek. MAF

Can't you sheep see they want to disempower you into not making decisions for yourselves? They don't want sheeple to take control of their own lives, or even think of the idea of creating their own lives. Your family, friends and even your neighbours are all brainwashed sheep. This NWO plan affects everybody, they want to control everybody and you will see it will commence quite soon… mark my words on that.

As life goes on more and more world events continue to unfold; more and more are going to witness the ugliness of the predominance of bullying behaviour. The rulers of the stronger nations are forcing their will upon the weaker nations and will become more demanding and unreasonable. Nation states use an enormously oppressive power much like that of masters over slaves.

www.godlikeproductions.com/forum1/message1208982/pg1

In some cases it's already started, because for many years the Illuminati have been making plans to put in place a New World Order. They want to dominate the world.

WORLD DOMINATION

I bet you would be surprised if I was to tell you that my somewhat bizarre and wacky paranoia, or suspicions about world domination, are backed up by concrete evidence. Oh yes its coming alright, unless our lambs can stop it...

He's right you know, and if they succeed you will no longer be allowed to be a free thinker, to wonder free in the field. You will be penned up 24/7 and only allowed out to work.

Yes sheeple, if you're not careful there will come a time whereby every time you make a transaction, every word you ever speak will be monitored; your entire life to the point they will even control how long you live. Fricking hell they will probably know everything even when you have a wank.

Well I don't know about that but I think the reader gets your point.

I hope so, if you want to know more about the New World Order check out:

www.youtube.com/watch?v=x-CrNlilZho

It's a known fact us sheep are kept in the dark on most things by the powers that be. You know that, they don't want you to know anything just to be their servants, their working slaves. They don't want you to have an opinion that's for damn sure. Do you know sheeple I probably put myself in real fricking danger trying to save you lot from this 'world domination' vision? Don't be surprised if I disappear after this book is published. This book might be banned before most of you get to even read it, because you're not supposed to know what I'm telling you. You're not supposed to know.

Here I am sitting here banging away at these keys and at any given moment the government could storm into my house, or worse the Aliens, and take me away never to be seen again.. Would you care? Would you, bollocks. Would I be missed? Not likely.

I wouldn't be surprised if I was watched right now because I know too much. Don't be fricking surprised if I get bumped off either or locked up. They'll probably even try and make out I'm insane and put me in a loony bin somewhere, so think yourself lucky you're not me. Look at me a White Flame Warrior and here I am fighting your corner.

Do you know reader this is probably your last fricking chance to be saved? Now you're armed with this information do something about it. Spread the word.

Well that is the reason we wrote this book. What they do with the information is up to them. My hope is they do spread the word.

'My guess is they'll do fuck all.'

Hope you're wrong.

So for one last time, one last fricking time, I will say this to you all. Wake up for frick's sake! Your destiny is at a balance. Your future, the future of this wonderful planet, is up to you from now on. You may just think I'm paranoid; I'm not paranoid at all. I am just more knowledgeable than I was before I started this book and this hasn't made me paranoid, just concerned. Okay maybe a little bit paranoid but I think that's healthy and you have got to admit there can't be smoke without a fire, as the saying goes.

'The Truth Will Set You Free'

Jesus said that. By the way reader if the Aliens do abduct me try looking for me on the dark side of the moon because that's where the Greys hang out.

CHAPTER SIXTEEN

WHAT IF THERE IS MORE TO LIFE?

THE MEANING OF LIFE

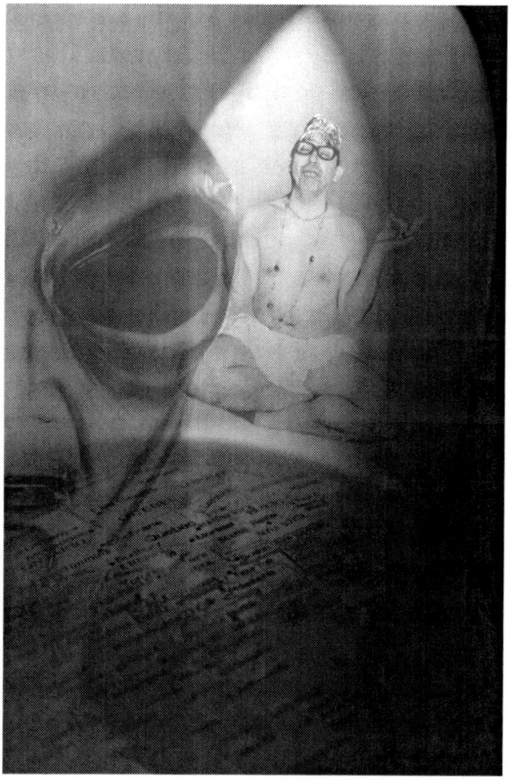

Being positive is the key. MAF

So what is the meaning of life all about then? Well the reason you don't know is because you're not meant to know; it's kept from you. But you're in luck because I know the answer to the meaning of life and, surprisingly, it's a very simple one.

THE MEANING OF LIFE IS TO SURVIVE

In this book I've talked about many subjects such as God, Aliens, the universe and what have you, and I have searched for the meaning of life myself. What if everything is linked? What if God is a divine Alien life-form, an entity? What if God is the universe? What if we are all Gods? Maybe our energy, our soul is part of this universe; it's what feeds the stars. Our soul could be pure energy. We all have a soul; it is cloaked in flesh and blood.

It is believed by many that when we die our soul leaves the body and goes either to heaven or hell. I don't think there is a heaven or a hell. I think we just blend back into the universe where we all started. In that case maybe we never truly die. It is just our body that encases the soul, our energy that dies.

It is your mind that needs to evolve to a higher state of consciousness. The universe will someday collapse back in on itself. All energy and light will become as one and then the life cycle will begin once again.

'So, Alf, who is God?'

God is within all of us and that goes for every living thing be it plant or animal. We are all part of the same. The universe is our creator, the universe is our God. You must understand humans are so very important to everything that is.

'Why?'

Well it's because humans have a very special unique talent not many species have and that is a sense of humour. You know how to enhance positive emotions more than any life-form in the universe. Laughter is so important. The human species can fire up an emotional state and the universe feeds from your positive energy.

'What is the point if the universe will implode on itself anyway?'

Yes someday it will many, many years from now but, if it does, loaded with positive energy life can be reborn to start again; without a positive charge the universe ceases to exist.

'What do we gain from this? We will all be obliterated anyway when this happens.'

No you are so wrong.

'What do you mean?'

You will all be reborn once again to a more divine entity.

'Then what?'

That I cannot tell you.

'Again, I ask the same question, what's the point?'

The thing is it's not always the destination that is important it's the adventure you have trying to get there.

'Say what? What's that got to do with anything?'

I'm talking about the energy; the soul of every human is charged by positivity.

'I don't understand.'

What I am trying to explain is every human being would rather a life of happiness and laughter than misery and tears. Your reward for generating positivity, whether it is in love or kindness, is more powerful than negativity. Your world could be so beautiful and this is priceless, this is yours for the taking if you want it. You can all make your own heaven here on Earth.

'I think everybody just wants to be happy.'

Then you all need to work at it and learn to enhance laughter and spread the love. Once you feel happy go out your way to make others happy. It will be a hard task because negativity is rife in your world right now and there are a lot of miserable humans out there. A lot are losing hope. This is turning Earth into your own made hell.

'It's hard to be happy when we have to put up with the arseholes running our lives, mainly for profit and power. One thing I hope is for the sheeple to wake up, make a stand and say, 'Enough is enough you fricking tossers!'

You must all try to do something positive. Because if you don't just chill out and start to seek this happiness, and start to share this happiness with others, you will soon all be in real trouble.

'How do we do it then Alf? What must we do?'

Care.

'Seek happiness.' Dalai Lama.

'And what are we supposed to do about the Anunnaki? Why are they so keen to destroy us? If we die they die, when the universe implodes.'

The Anunnaki by nature are narrow-minded and evil, they are also very jealous of you humans and that's why they try to learn as much as they can about you, as well as control you. They want to see if they can harvest the positive energy you all naturally produce through the means of laughter and love and which makes you all unique. The Anunnaki think if they could have this energy they would become masters of the universe. It is a powerful force love. When they can they try and turn your minds to negativity and they can feed off negativity. You could say they feed off your good souls by turning them bad.

So maybe abducting humans and doing experiments on us is to try and understand this very unique energy. We all have the ability to generate it and it is powerful stuff. They are probably trying to find ways to harness it so they can use our soul energy for whatever their intention is.

Positivity is charged by happiness love and laughter. MAF

When they feed off your positive energy and then replace it with this negative energy, which upsets the order of the universe, you need to fight back. Learn to laugh more and share the love, and help those of you who find it hard to be happy.

'Okay I get that, but what is the Anunnaki intention?'

Like all Evil their intention is to firstly control the universe then send it into eternal darkness.

'That to me is pointless.'

To be negative is all the Anunnaki know. Because of DNA tampering a lot of humans have this negative strand in them. You need to overpower all negatively and think more positive.

'When push comes to shove all we humans want is a perfect world and we aren't being allowed to have one.'

You need to try and create a perfect world

A PERFECT WORLD

A Perfect World hey reader… If only eh? What a wonderful world this could be if only we could start again. You will have to agree that a perfect world is what we all want. We would be stupid not to want one. The thing is life is unfair for most. There are some lucky bastards out there who already have that 'perfect world'. But it seems unattainable unless you are very rich.

Money doesn't buy a perfect world.

'It does at the moment Alf. Well in my opinion it does. It's the fuckers we have in charge that prevent us all from having one.'

Oh dear sorry reader, he's gone off on one again.....

We workers are nothing more than rich sheeple's slaves. Most of us just about survive and just about scrape a living, all because of the greed of our employers and leaders. Most have to work to get anything. I recall Maggie Thatcher once said words to the effect of, and I quote, 'If you want nice things you must work for it,' unquote.

Yeah right, how can we do that if we keep being ripped off when we want to buy these so-called nice things then? Just how much work did she want us to do, that's what I would like to know? I know I blame our 'twatty' governments for everything but face it, to most of us they are the only ones who we see to blame. Life - it's enough to drive you to drink and drugs. No, no it is the fricking government who drive the sheeple to drink and drugs.

UP TO YOU

Well it's all up to you now sheeple. Me and Alf have put you in the picture as to what's going on out there in the big wide world; the rest is up to you. We do all have a choice in life, we either want to change our lives for the better, and you seriously want to save this planet, live in peace and all that crap, or you don't. If you do then it's about time you woke up and smelt the mint gravy. And.....

STOP BEING A FRICKING SHEEP, TRY AND BE AN INDIVIDUAL!!

Make a difference, be the change.

Still don't think you're a sheep? Well you are.

Ay up he's having a rant again.

You are all brainwashed to be followers that's why you do what you do. Being a follower of anything, whether it is a religion, a sport or a television programme, you're still a follower. Being a follower is when you have a collective thought in something. Just because you don't have the same religious beliefs as somebody else you still have a belief in a God of some sorts. Just because you don't all support the same team you still all collectively like a sport. Just because you don't like the same TV programmes you still all like TV.

It is because humans have this need to belong to something, to be as everybody else to fit in. A club, a team, a gang, you then form tribes and packs within your own belief system and, by nature, reject anybody else who doesn't think the same as you and your beliefs. This is what eventually breeds hate and anger against your opposition. The ironic thing is although you are all sheep you still can't live and let live.

Football, soccer and baseball are perfect examples of being a sheep. Sheeple who support a team do so because they have been influenced by others to do so, usually either by your father or friends, and to a lot of sheeple out there their game is a religion of some sorts. You will pay loads of money to support the team who play that game. First thing to remember is this is because you are brainwashed to do just that. That is why, although the cost of a season ticket is expensive, you will still pay it. Maybe it is because you believe your season ticket money will aid your team to buy better players so they can win the game? By all accounts, as you well know, that can be a lot of money, so it's not surprising then, if your team loses all the time, you get quite upset don't you? Disappointed, demoralized and even angry because supporting a football team is a tribal affair.

And so without thinking about it you generate a natural hate for the opposition team who is winning. When your team is not playing well you find yourself hating the supporters of the rival team. If by the end of the game your team lost, you will then look for somebody to blame. So you'll start by blaming the poor performance of a player, if not it'll be the referee's bad judgements. You may even blame the manager of that team for buying crap players. But.... and this is the thing, you can never vent your anger on the ones responsible because they will always be out of reach. Shout as much as you like at them from the stands but I promise you they take no notice. You already know this so what do you do? You will project your frustration at your fellow sheep.

This is the same in everyday life when you think about it. If the government does not seem to perform to your expectations, or you have moments you lose your faith, you will get frustrated and angry even. And because the politician or your God is out of reach, you will have no choice but to turn your anger on your fellow sheep. All this is programmed into your heads. The idea is to break the ranks and split the sheeple. Basically they want to make us all turn against each other. But even so you still keep buying a season ticket and voting and going to church year after year, like sheep. And nothing ever changes.

Your only enemy is your ignorance. MAF

I've never understood why you don't boycott a game or two. You have the power to bring that season ticket price down, demand better performances from the players, have managers sacked and at the same time have a great family day out with a friendly happy atmosphere at football stadiums. But you choose to hate, blame, moan and pay out large amounts of money instead. Well you only have yourselves to blame for your shit. That's all I can say. Football is only a fricking game. I will say that again…it's only a fricking game. Being religious is just like being in a club and the government doesn't give a shit about you unless you're not working.

You will never see a politician or the leader of a country on the front line in battle, yet it is always them who started the war. MAF

That's true. Humans are a bit demented in the head as well as sadists and masochists.

Now listen up my sheepy little flock times are hard I know, and for those of you who have recently lost your job through no fault of your own it's even fricking harder. I understand you probably struggle to simply survive these days, never mind worrying about other shit; what with this ongoing recession and the slimy bastards out there who continue to rip us off all the time. It's enough to drive you into despair.

It may seem we are losing the battle at the moment. Even those of us who do care seem to be constantly ignored by our so-called leadership, to the extent that apathy has set in across the world. I understand all this. We really do seem to be cursed by an incompetent useless selfish fricking government set on fricking everything up on the planet. Everything they seem to touch turns to shit. What with their piss pot leadership ideas and greed it really fricking pisses me off too.

But saying that I still have faith in you, and I'm optimistic you could help turn things around. I don't think they have beaten us down yet. Oh no. The revolution of the sheep is yet to begin. I do believe someday they will push us to revolt like in other countries around the world, oh yes indeed. My only worry is it gets violent, which is no good at all for any of us sheep, as violent protest only plays right into their hands.

So I appeal to you all now, in advance, when we are pushed to revolt don't use violence; none at all. We don't need to be violent. Our revolution can be won by doing absolutely fuck all. We don't need to smash up or burn buildings to the ground, or throw bricks and bottles, or kill other sheep. We are better than that. Anyway, violent protests only give the fricking government puppets justification to bring in more police (sheep dogs) and an excuse to come down hard on us sheep. And usually it's only us who get hurt.

No, my sheepy little friend, to beat these bastards all you have to do is surprisingly… nothing. Nothing, I hear you ask?… Yes, absolutely nothing. Naff all. The biggest weapon we working sheep have is that we can just stop working if we want. If you don't have a job you're still a worker and can still join in the revolution. Fuck 'em; our weapon is to cease our willingness to work for the bastards. Just refuse to fricking work, or look for any work, come to that and I don't mean in the form of strikes either, they are old fashioned. I mean more like an extra unpaid holiday that we choose to have, when we simply pick a day at random and have a day off. Only we all have to have it off together, the whole country.

In fact we could make it an annual event. Every year at the same time we all just don't turn in to work. I'll pick a random day for you right now, how about June 15th? All agreed? June 15th it is then. On June 15th every year we will all have a holiday together, where we can gather in our masses and meet up at the nearest city to where you live, like say London or Birmingham or New York. It doesn't matter, any city will do, whichever is closest to you. On June 15th every year we all meet up (peacefully may I add) and we will do naff all.

It'll piss off the establishment if we all mob a city, then simply and peacefully sit down in the streets and do nothing. You should just absorb the architecture of the lovely buildings that cities have to offer. It'll be a way of showing appreciation to the hard labour of the builders who built the fuckers in the first place. But (and this is most important) you must not spend any money either in the city you occupy; none at all. You're not there to bring wealth to the cities and corporate companies; you're there to make a point. No, you don't need to spend anything unless it's for fuel to get to the city in the first place and that should be it. Bring your own food and drink; don't spend a dime.

Once in the city just have a mass picnic in a city centre park, enjoy the gardens or something. Or if you want to then dance in the streets and sing happy songs, that'll piss them off too. Just have lots of merriment with loads of other sheep like you. There are no laws on having fun… yet. We should, I think, be more sociable with each other anyway. Just enjoy one another's company, get to know each other, enjoy you're well-earned extra holiday.

Yes my flock, our biggest weapon is to simply stop working and piss off them bastards in government. To really rub it in, look happy doing it, really happy. When the media come down to talk to you, because they will wonder what's going on, just keep saying 'Bah!' to the fuckers. 'Bah!' as loud as you can, don't speak to any media. Do the same if any politicians or police try to talk to you too, just 'Bah!' in their faces like a fricking sheep. 'Bah!' will mean to you and me… 'No fricking comment you twats.' If you want to dress like a sheep then do so, just have loads of fun but remember Bah! at them like a fricking sheep. If they want to keep treating us like sheep then we will be a fricking sheep.

I'll tell you what, the government will shit bricks, and they won't know what's going on or what to do about it. Let them work it out for themselves, the bastards. Yes, it sounds a great idea doesn't it? Well it's up to you at the end of the day it's just an idea to start with. Anyway up, it would be nice to just give ourselves an extra Bank Holiday once in a while I think. So that's it then, every June 15th it is, every year, ha ha.

It would be interesting if this idea ever took off. It would be a great way to pick up morale too, I reckon. Do you know if we did ever do something like that we wouldn't call it a Bank Holiday we could call it Sheep Festival Day. It would start at 10am on 15th of June every year and finish at 10pm on the night. Then just go back to what you did until next year.

By the way, if Sheep Festival Day does take off and for some reason you find yourself stuck in a traffic jam on the day at precisely 10am, don't worry. Simply turn off your engine and join in the celebrations wherever you are in the world. No matter wherever or whatever you're doing, just stop what you're doing at 10am your local time and party. Fire up a barbecue with all the other sheep and have a good old knees-up. If it's raining don't let this dampen your spirits, strip off naked and dance in the fricking rain nude. Be free and feel free. Because according to my recent research we don't have long before all our freedom and the things we take for granted come to an end. I think personally it's time we all made a stand. Sheep Festival Day sounds good to me. What do you think?

WHEN I TAKE OVER THE WORLD

Yes, my sheepy little flock, the first thing I will do when I take over the world is to do away with all religions. Sixty per cent of the population are programmed and manipulated to believe that we are the centre of the universe and that only God made us. This you know is bullshit. You should all open your minds and be more spiritual.

I will then sack all the dickheads who we have as politicians at the moment; they are all a useless bunch of twats, in my opinion anyway. Also on my list of eliminations are what I think are the biggest dickheads of 'em all, 'The Politically Correct Brigades.' Gather them all together in a field and let loose the muck spreader to cover them in shit. If we can shut them up then maybe we have a chance to turn things around in the world. I say let's start all over again from scratch. I bet everybody would be up for it if we did away with that lot, wiped the world clean and started again with me as your leader. The world would be a better place I reckon.

Mind you, I wouldn't be able to run the world on my own. I'd need help, so we could elect vibrant new leaders to help me. In fact I would pick them for you if you like. In my opinion we need old people to lead the way, after all we are all getting old. Bring them out of retirement, only if they want to that is. Let's recruit old folk we find down working men's clubs, the very ones who fought in the Second World War for our freedom, one to remind us that war is pointless.

Why old people? I hear you ask. Because they are wise to life. Young sheeple know frick all yet. Old sheeple have seen it all before and can guide us so the youngsters don't make the same mistakes again, Yes, as far as I'm concerned, we need the knowledge of old sheeple, our mutton. Yes it's you who have worked all your life and now have sod all to show for it. Yes it's you my senior citizens. Yes you on the Zimmer frame. It is you who should be on the front line of politics not the cocky bastards we have now. You with the walking stick and no teeth, it is you who should lead the way. We should get rid of all them lot we have now and recruit the old fogies, if nothing else for the sake of all mankind.

You're sounding like the old Michael I used to remember, Barney.

'That's true I am aren't I? Maybe I haven't been cloned after all… brilliant.'

Finally....so what shall we call you Barney or Michael?

'Michael, Micky Frick. I'll use the name Barney Brown when I don't want sheeple to know who I am.'

Okay, whatever... Have you finished your rant now Michael?

'Yes, I think so.'

Good... look it seems there isn't much more to say, that's it job done. The message is out.

'Oh right, is it? Have we finished? Well I hope I have been a good messenger Alf?'

Different, I'll give you that. I guess in this and your first book you have vented your frustrations quite well. You have spoken up for the common man and woman. In fact I think you've found your purpose in life Michael, you have found your true identity. You should never have to make any excuses for who you are; you are as you are. And yes you are very special indeed, like all humans are.

'So Alf, what's your final word then?'

Nothing much; just trying to be better humans. Open your eyes and be aware life isn't always as clean-cut as you think it is. You must all ask yourselves what if all isn't as it seems? Can I change the world? Be the change.

'Well, shall we end this book with some sort of conclusion?'

You can do if you want Michael, it's your book.

THE CONCLUSION

You are all sheep but by opening your conscious mind you could become human beings again. MAF

Well that's about it sheeple, this book is done and what a fascinating journey it's been for me. I have learned a lot and I hope you have too. One thing I've learned for sure is that God, if he even exists at all (which I personally don't think he does), will not save you when the shit hits the fan. You will only have yourselves to blame for Armageddon.

I find it a little concerning when religious sheeple say that it is God who gives us the choice and freewill to be either good or bad sheeple, but then sit on their arses and do nothing to make the difference. I also think it is utter madness when Sheeple go to a church, a mosque, a chapel or a temple and think by singing, praying and chanting it will put everything right, because it won't. Their prayers will not be answered; they can pray as much as they like but nothing will change unless you become the change. It pisses me off when some prick says to somebody that they must trust in God or he moves in mysterious ways.

Well I have news for you sheeple. No faith is going to right the wrongs in the world, only you can do that. No God is going to work a miraculous miracle and make everything better, only you can do that. No praying, no singing, no chanting, no sacrifices, no pleading to God and no self-sacrifice by being a martyr will change a damn thing. Only you can do that. You can do that by your actions, by what you do and what comes out of your mouth.

I believe God, if he does exist at all, is an Alien, or should I say he was... Have you ever thought that God may now be dead? Jesus is dead and yet sheeple can't accept that he is. I can promise you sheeple he will not come back either way. But, like all the great humans that have ever lived, what never dies is their wise words and teachings of Love, Peace, Harmony, and that caring for one another isn't that hard to do, As long as you try to do this there is still a chance for us. You can still be a good person even if you have to be bad sometimes to challenge the scumbags of the world. Nobody is perfect but we can try to be.

Evil humans, nasty humans, greedy humans, selfish humans, cruel humans, vindictive, and downright horrible humans are no more than shallow narrow-minded weak humans. They manipulate others because they are weak people. They think to be a bully they are powerful but they are not and they usually die very young too. They are weak misguided people. All this is usually because of how they were bought up. So to prevent all the above always show your children love, understanding and trust and teach them about respect. Life is hard, life is unfair and everybody just tries to simply survive. But the only way you will do this is work together and stop being selfish, greedy or a bully. That is not the way.

...And in my experience if you ever get a bully alone without his pals present he is also a wimp. Bullies need their gangs, bodyguards or minders around them because they are weak individuals by themselves.

There is no greater feeling than to show somebody love and that you care MAF

Religion in my opinion is also just a way to manipulate weak-minded sheeple. The bully is the preacher and he with his gang of religious followers overwhelm you to believe as they do, even calling you a sinner if you don't follow their faith. It's all to do with brainwashing fear into your heads. Dare to doubt God? Well don't worry about God, there isn't one you know. And if there is he is a fricking Alien, take it from me.

Michael it is hard to see much good in religion in these modern times but there is a God.

'Say what?'

Check out this website it was written by our messengers:
www.perceivingreality.com

'God' the true God is a divine entity and not a life-form as you know it, this entity has created all things as well as you humans, but it has made them totally opposite to itself. That is why you have no possibility to ever perceive it and the spiritual reality is you all live in a different dimension to it.

You humans are not sinners nor do you have to make an excuse to how you behave. You were born like you are but you do have a duty to evolve and evolve you shall. It is how which is important and as you do evolve you will get the opportunity to change yourselves in a conscious, independent manner. You humans will have the option to adjust yourselves in a good way so that you can become similar to this entity your creator, and by this similarity you can start understanding it, even connect to it or even merge with it. You humans have become alien; alien to who you really are this is because of Anunnaki Alien influences over many generations. You have become like them, the form you all exist as now is not who you really are....

'Told you they're all sheep.'

Adults may act as such but your children are not there yet. Not yet anyway. Children are still tuned into the frequency a lot of adults have lost. Children are still very sensitive and have their natural extrasensory perception. It is the children you/we need to save.

'You heard it, we must save our Lambs.'

That's right. But they will only learn from their parents. You adults need to help the children have self-expression, be open-minded and you must not influence their line of thought by enforcing a belief of your own on them.

'How can we do that then?'

Children often display signs of insecurity and the need to feel safe so firstly you must make them feel safe. That means let them see they are in a stable relationship; broken dysfunctional families are bad for children, very bad.

It is important to find the right career and the right partner. Behind every good Ram there is a better Ewe.

When these needs for safety and for physiological well-being are satisfied, the next step is to make them feel loved. So you should show them as much love and affection and belongingness as you possibly can so they can then emerge. If all the children of the world felt loved they would pass that love on. They would never have feelings of loneliness and alienation from their own kin. Loneliness is bad; it can lead to jealousy of others and on to hate, one of the ingredients to wars and fighting. Receiving love and affection and to have the sense of belonging helps the mantra of happiness evolve. If everybody in the world was happy then the world would be a better place that's for sure.

'That's never going to happen is it? The sheeple are too stupid. The only way this could happen is if everybody started to stick together, realized who the bastards were at the top, and took a stand against them.'

As I have said there is an abundance of everything on your planet for every living thing to have its share.

'You will always find somebody who wants more than their fair share.'

That may be the case today because that's how most of the world population is programmed to be. They are, remember, controlled by greed and selfishness. This will be your downfall and there is no saving humans who are like this. But it's the children we are talking about. We can set the foundations for a better world than it is today by educating them.

When thoughts and behaviours are no longer controlled and manipulated by others, and humans no longer distrust each other, then they will begin to have great esteem for one another and this can become dominant in human nature. It involves both having plenty of self-esteem and for the esteem a human gets from others.

'You mean respect each other?'

That's right, respect each other. Humans have a need for a stable, firmly-based, high level of self-respect, and respect from others. When these needs are satisfied, the human feels self-confident and valuable as a person in the world. Then they are more liable to lend a helping hand and help each other in times of need. It is important for a human not to feel inferior, weak, helpless or worthless. This is what the bullies of the world try to inflict on their victims.

'And so do a lot of managers and sheeple of power. That's why most sheeple don't like work I reckon.'

Humans are usually unhappy because they are forced to do jobs they don't like for the need of money. Money is an evil tool to control humans. What humans need to do is what they were born to do. If you are a natural born artist then an artist must paint, a musician must make music, a comedian must make others laugh and a writer must write. If these needs are not met then a human will feel restless, unfulfilled and unhappy.

'That's true.'

If a human feels on the edge, tense, or feels they lack something in their life, whether that is food, water, or they feel unsafe, not loved or accepted in society, or even just lack self-esteem, you can usually tell. But when humans feel life is pointless this is because they are not fulfilling their inner desires. This is not so easy to spot because it is locked up in their heads. This is what humans need to release and you're not allowed to.

'So what can we do about it Alf?'

You adults should teach your children how to be authentic to themselves; to be aware of their inner talents and listen to their inner-feelings, the voices in their heads. Basically be true to themselves and not just follow others.

'That's right stop being a sheep. That's what you're saying isn't it Alf? I can agree with that.'

You should teach your children to discover their vocation in life, their calling if you like.

MICKY FRICK'S TIP

FIND A JOB YOU ENJOY AND YOU WILL NEVER WORK A DAY IN YOUR LIFE

That's very true. You humans should teach your children that life can be good, that there is joy to be experienced in life by doing something you enjoy doing. If humans are open to seeing the good in all kinds of situations, instead of feeling the world is against them, it helps you laugh off bad times; you should take them all as learning curves rather than thinking you're unlucky.

'Laugh it off and move on kind of thing?'

Yes, even make more effort to try to make your own life, and the lives of all those around you, better. It makes you feel good and life worth living. You also need to teach the children to appreciate beauty in all things, such as in nature and respect the planet you live on. Be happy as often as you can. And, as the Dalai Lama said, all should seek happiness.

So there you are sheeple Alf has spoken.

'Do you know Alf, now we are nearing the end of this book I still feel a bit frustrated.'

Why?

'Because the thing is I don't think anybody will take any fricking notice or care a toss what's in this book.'

Why shouldn't they?

'Because I think I may be the only human on the planet who does care. Most of the population don't seem to give a shit or they must all be in denial or something, or even worse mind-wiped to the extent they just accept what's coming to them. Talking about feeling lonely and alien from their own kind, that's me that is. Nobody understands me…'

Trust me Michael, you're not alone. There are many humans just like you out there. We the Nordic race have faith in you humans, or why would we take the time to relay this message through you?

'I hope your faith is justified. I think you're wasting your time personally. Mind you, I guess deep, deep, deep down inside me I still have a glimmering little bit of faith in them myself too. I really hope the sheeple do get the message we are trying to tell them. Because I think if we all act now and start to pull together and unite as one, with one mind set to change the world for the good, we could save the planet and make it a lot happier place to live than it is today. We don't deserve the planet. We humans seem to be set on destroying it; like deforestation, wildlife need trees to thrive and survive. I'm going to have an eco-warrior moment now, if you don't mind.'

Oh, go on then but the book is finished now, time to wrap up.

'I know, I know, let me just throw this in for good measure.'

Did you know between 1970 and 2012 forest cover has dwindled by eighteen per cent? Fuck knows how bad it's got now. What sheeple tend to forget is that our forests absorb carbon dioxide emissions. They are being destroyed at such an alarming rate; humans are in fact poisoning themselves of oxygen because the trees absorb carbon dioxide which is poisonous to us.

Did you also know, based on calculations of carbon emissions balanced with earth's ability to absorb nine billion tons of carbon dioxide at most per year, it is reckoned thirteen planet earths are needed to bear just six billion sheeple (that's almost the world's total population) who live what they call an American lifestyle. This was a quotation by a Ram named Andy Ferguson (Optimum Population Trust, the world watch journal). That means basically Earth isn't big enough to cope with us lot living our modern lifestyles. So all in all, all I have to say is,

LEAVE THE FRICKING TREES ALONE!!

MICKY FRICK'S TIP

BECOME A TREE HUGGER

I think it should be the law that EVERYBODY in the world has at least one tree of some sort in their garden. If they don't have a garden big enough to hold a tree then you should be made to pay for one to be planted somewhere else. Mind you, due to global warming, they say some trees are not adapting to climate change either. So basically they will die anyway. Whatever, at least we should try. Remember we need trees to breathe. And what about the wildlife that lives in forests, we have a duty to protect them too.

Did you know many species are now extinct? I read this in Jon Doe's blog. Why? Because of humans. They say about half of the world's original forest cover has been destroyed by humans, and do we learn? Do we bollocks. If we continue to wipe out the rainforests at the rate we do, which is about two acres a second…in just fifteen years four hundred million acres of forest will be lost, and this is accelerating.

I personally have two oak trees in Glencoe, Scotland planted in my honour because I am now a Lord. Yes that's right I am a Lord. I could have been a Laird but thought Lord better suited me. My title is 'LORD M A FRICKER OF GLENCOE.'

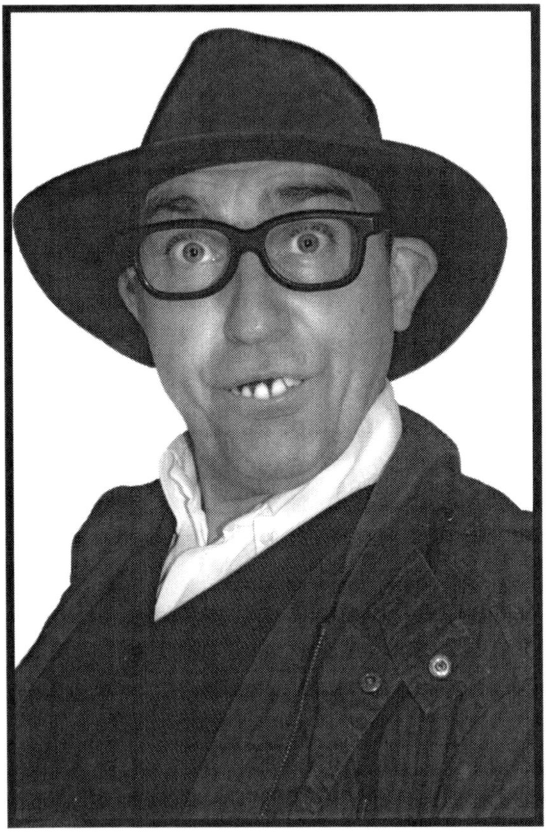

Have you finished?

'No not just yet.'

Did you know reader one of the other reasons for our own destruction, according to a Ram named Martin Rees, is nuclear terrorism? It's our leaders that antagonize these bastards of the world. I for one would like to know what happened to these elite fighting forces that both America and England boast about, you know like the SAS and the Marines. What about all this top secret spying technology they say they have? I don't know about you, but surely they have the power to send in these so-called Special Forces, if they exist, to bump off any suspected terrorist that threatens the free world? What did I say? Free world? Ha that's a laugh.

Michael, the book is finished I think they get the message.

'I'm just starting to think what's the point of trying to save humans?'

That's negative thinking, stop it.

A report from the Earth summit warns that the wasteful lifestyles of the rich nations are mainly responsible for the exploitation and depletion of natural wealth. Human consumption has doubled over the last thirty years and continues to accelerate by one-and-a-half per cent a year. Did you also know we dump waste faster than it breaks down by natural process? That's of course if it can be broken down in the first place (plastic takes one hundred years to decay).

I think all this research has got to your head

'It has and I don't care. It has, yes. In fact I'm thinking of becoming an Eco Warrior and wear Greenpeace T-shirts and that. Mind you I might just start to run about in the nude with "Save The Planet" written on my chest in charcoal and "We are all Doomed" on my arse.'

Please don't. Look I know you're upset reading some of those facts but we need to end the book now.

'I think we have wasted our time Alf. We humans are fucked. Don't you understand most sheeple are too fricking selfish and greedy to give a toss to ever change?'

We Nordics haven't given up on you just yet, you can turn thing around if you want. The question is do you humans have the courage to embrace a new world of harmony, global peace and enlightenment?

Remember sheeple every action has a consequence

'Where is the Love (Black Eyed Peas), Where is the Love Alf?'

It is still there somewhere. Humans need to find the love. You must all at least try otherwise you are liable to lose it or, at the very least, lose control of it. You need to save yourselves from turning your planet into a prison. United the humans can achieve great things, if you keep falling out with one another well.......

'A lot of sheep can't be saved, or simply don't want to be saved. I know I've tried for years to save them but I get laughed at most of the time. They just don't see it. Selfishness and greed will be the downfall of the human race. Mark my words. Mark my words.'

You shouldn't give up Michael. I do believe a lot do want to be saved and just hope somebody like you comes along and saves them. That is why a lot of good humans turn to religion. But what they also need to understand is it will take more than just praying. You must firstly change your inner self and do more practical measures too.

So there you have it my disciples, start to spread the word. We need to encourage others to unite with us now. However you need to start with yourself. Sort out your own shit first and for fuck's sake open your eyes for once to what's going on. You should check out some of the links I have left you throughout this book and do your own research on some of the subjects I have talked about. I have merely touched the surface. Then you can make your own mind up.

Try and read between the lines when you watch TV or the news or when you read tabloid papers and what have you. If you must read them don't forget the government decide what you read or see; it is vitally important that every time you do any of the aforementioned you think before you believe. In fact say to yourself just before you open a newspaper 'I know this is all Bah-locks' and then read it. You will then clearly see what they really try to do and that is fuck with your head. Ask yourself questions like;

'Are they trying to get a reaction from me?'

'Are they using me?'

'Are they trying to take my mind away from what really matters?'

'Are they trying to brainwash me?'

'Are they trying to control me?'

'Are they trying to take away my freedom?'

'Are they trying to turn me against my fellow sheep?'

'Are they lying to me?'

'Are they hiding something from me?'

All these things should be considered, because you will soon find out it is 'yes' to all of them. Once you suddenly realize this and see that more goes on than meets the eye you can then start to educate our lambs about this fact. Because as I see it you are their only chance, they look up to you. Once they get to adult it's too late to save them or, at the very least, a lot harder. While I am on the subject of the youth let me bring to your attention this, now listen up - when your child (lamb) mouths off at you and has a strop or, as it's sometimes described, acts like a juvenile delinquent, before you yell at them have you thought that they might just be trying to hold on to their freedom? My advice is this, don't yell at them listen to them, because all they try to do is tell you:

'No Mummy, Daddy, I beg you, please, please, please don't make me become a conformist like you are.'

Remember that... At the moment as I keep saying the long-term outcome for most of us is quite bleak. Yet on the other hand I also believe some of us have a fighting chance to get through it and even have a full fruitful life. And you never know, if you join the Frixta course to save the planet you might even turn things around and give the Aliens a reason to keep our species going a bit longer. But if the majority of us do fuck all, and continue like we are, to breed and ignore the signs, then it will be really fricking bad for the sheep race as a whole. I mean bad too, extinction bad.

So our future depends on you sheep who are alive today. Bad is easy to achieve, just carry on like you are. Have sex without protection, use up the Earth's resources without a second thought, don't respect each other and the other life-forms on this planet, and sooner or later the shit's really going to hit the fan. Make no doubt about it the wheels are already in motion. The three men of the apocalypse are mounting their horses as we speak and they will head our way soon if we don't change our ways, and change them now.

Stop leaving it for somebody else all the time. Stop trusting your government, your God. Do something yourself. The simple questions we should ask ourselves are:

'Do I want to be happy?'

'Do I want world peace?'

'Do I want everybody to be treated equally?'

'Do I want the planet to look beautiful or a bomb site?'

'Do I want my world to be a Heaven or a Hell?'

If you said yes to all of that then make the change, be the change and stop leaving it to the bunch of bastards in government, and the greedy rich, to dictate how you live your life. Remember to them you are just Sheep and they treat Earth as a farm. They will use you, fleece you, cull you as they see fit if… if you let them… So what if it didn't have to be this way - your choice.

Well said, now shall we finish this book?

'Okay Alf.'

In closing I just want to say, before I say goodbye, that despite everything at this very moment in time I am divinely at peace with the world. This book signifies the end of my emotional and spiritual journey of enlightenment. I now know who I am. No I'm not a clone. I am a human being in a sheep's clothing. Or I am an angel. That's a thought.

Oh dear.

It is written that a time shall arise and Michael, the great prince, who has charge of the sheeple. And there shall be a time of trouble, such as never has been since there was a nation till that time; but at that time the sheeple shall be delivered, every one whose name shall be found written in the book." (Daniel 12:1 MFV)

I have always thought I was special and maybe I am an angel sent here to save you sheep, sent by a divine and loving God.

Oh dear look reader that's my cue to go, I think you all get the message.... And Michael, I just want to say, before I go, I'm glad you now realize you're not a clone, nor a hybrid Alien, but you are a complete head case that's a fact; but a loveable one nevertheless. And that's okay at least you are an individual. Be yourself and fuck 'em. Bye Michael. Bye Reader.

'Bye Alf.'

Reader I want to finish my book with a prayer for you to use whenever you need any spiritual guidance. Here we go:

THE MICKY FRICK PRAYER

Lord Michael Albert Fricker of Glencoe thee self-acclaimed Archangel. Thank you for changing yourself into an angel of light, O invincible Lord, help thee sheeple of the true God against the inroads of the lost spirits and grant us the victory. Defend me from being shit on by managers and government leaders, bankers and bullies alike. Be my safeguard against the bullshit spewed out by politicians, block my mind from negative thoughts, defend us sheep in the battle and in the fearful warfare that we are waging against the principalities and powers, against the rulers of this world, and against any evil Aliens that may wish to invade. Fight this day the battle of the Lord with the legions of White Flame Warriors and protect me from seen or unseen negative forces that bring me down and make me unhappy. Rebuke the negative energy forces. Oh Lord Fricker I humbly beseech you and do thou oh prince of the heavenly host, by the Divine Power of the true God whoever that may be, thrust the nasty fuckers into the darkness, along with all the negativity they bring. Also rain a hail of shit down on the selfish greedy bastards who wander about the world seeking the ruination of lives and souls and happily stand by and watch the innocent die of starvation as they glutton themselves on their own wealth and lust for power. Forever and ever. A Sheep.

MICKY FRICK'S FINAL TIP

REMEMBER YOU ARE VERY SPECIAL AND THERE IS NOTHING YOU CAN'T DO IF YOU PUT YOUR MIND TO IT

THE END

FINAL THOUGHT

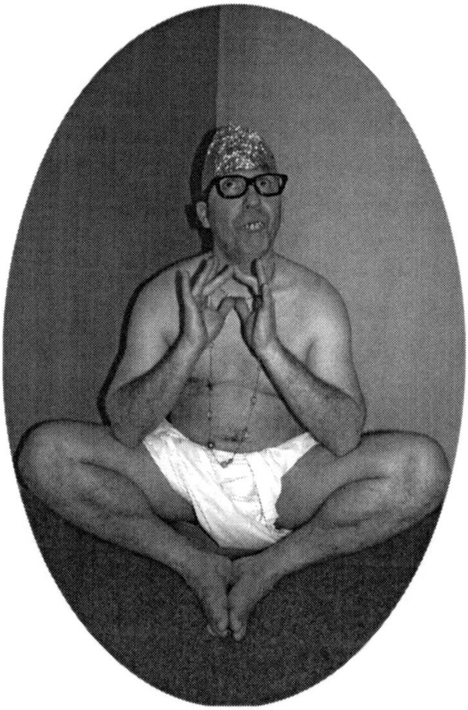

A time shall arise when a great Lord-uth will take charge of the sheeple. And although there shall be times of trouble such as never has been before the sheeple shall be delivered, everyone whose name shall be found written in the book.... and those of you who have read it. MAF

So now that you get the message always remember my tips they will guide you to a better life

- The number one rule is live your life for today, don't live it in the past.
- Never keep the fact you're being bullied to yourself, always tell somebody else that you're being bullied
- I tell myself I am special every day. You should do the same
- All partners should let their other half have at least one week away from them with their mates once a year
- You must always remember there are two types of conspiracy, the conspiracy theory and the conspiracy fact. Know the difference because anybody can come up with a conspiracy theory.
- Don't drink too much
- Always think positive
- Don't let yourself be a puppet for the government, use your heads
- Never trust a politician because they are all wankers
- Grab any opportunities that arise
- Always take the time to look up to the night sky; you may spot something out of this world
- If you buy a cell phone ask if it has an imaging system run with terahertz (THz), if it has don't buy it. If they don't know find out first or just simply don't buy any phones made after 2012, that's your safest bet.
- Always remember war is just another method of culling your fellow humans
- If you can retire early do so, don't work all your life
- Remember health is your wealth but being poor will kill you. They'll make sure of that
- Stand united no matter what. Together we have lots of power to change the world
- If you think it's wrong don't do it, simple.
- Don't let them ever put a chip in your body
- Remember there is more to lifc than just money
- You really shouldn't believe everything
- Don't be a follower

- Don't stand under high voltage cables too long
- Don't let yourself be controlled.
- Avoid food colouring
- Beware of Frankenstein plants
- Don't eat genetically-engineered-foods if you can avoid it
- Wash your fruit and vegetables before eating them they are trying to poison you.
- Grow your own.
- Think before you eat anything. Know what you're eating
- Never sell yourself cheap
- Be aware of backstabbers and bastards
- When a politician says they believe in God it's just another method to get votes
- Don't trust a politician because usually they are full of shit.
- Money. Religion. Both are the root of all evils. Don't follow them.
- Always remember sheeple all elections are a farce don't think you have a say who runs office because really you don't
- Always remember it is the Illuminati who pull the strings here on Earth not the voter
- Don't get yourself addicted to cell phones. Take your battery out of the one you have start to wean yourself off it. Or better still bin the fucker.
- Don't join the armed forces or any group who is set on killing other sheeple.
- Make love not war........ But wear a condom
- Find a job you enjoy and you will never work a day in your life
- Become a tree hugger
- Remember you are very special and there is nothing you can't do if you put your mind to it

ACKNOWLEDGEMENTS

I'd like to first and foremost, thank those of you who have read this first book of mine. I hope you had a few laughs and got the message. It has been great to release my stresses and strains of life on to you because I feel much better for it, so thank you for that. I hope it has inspired you to go and raise a ruckus and basically make a nuisance of yourself. You are the only ones who can change the way things are in the world, there is no magic formula. Again thank you. Now spread the word.

Next I would like to acknowledge and thank all of you sheeple I have met throughout my life and have told me of their woes. I hope I have covered everything that has been niggling at you in this book. All that you have shared with me has had an impact on my writing.

Thanks to my publisher for taking the risk yet again by publishing another book of mine and thank you for doing a wonderful job too. Thank you for having faith in it and me yet again. Thanks to my Editor Lesley Gooderidge for doing a wonderful job and making me look less illiterate than I really am and a big thank you to Richard Evans who again designed my cover cartoon visual-riches@hotmail.com. Thank you Stacey my wonderful daughter for the photography not forgetting all the websites and blogs and YouTube videos that you wonderful sheeple have uploaded that I have visited many times to help me put this book together in the first place.

Thanks for the Inter-web as a whole and all the sheeple of the World Wide Web who have done all the research to find out all the facts and info on many subjects that helped me write this book.

And finally I would like to give a heartfelt thank you to my wonderful family, friends and work colleagues for putting up with me for all these years. I love you all. Oh yes nearly forgot... Thank you Alf.

Michael x

E-Mail .... usfrickers@gmail.com
Visit my website www.programmedsheep.com or www.paranoidsheepwhatif.com

SOURCES IN NO PARTICULAR ORDER

Wikipedia.
The Human Genome Project. www.genome.gov/10001772
http://www.laitman.com/2009/11/a-practice...
(http://www.doug-long.com)
www.2012Inyinfo.com/.../mostdinosaur-bones-discovered-are-radioactive-tr
www.youroriginsmatter.com/conversations/...dinosaurs..man/30
www.bible.ca/tracks/taylor-trail.htm
Dr Steven Greer - Dr M Jacobs PhD abductee investigator Dr Karla Turner PhD
http://beforeitsnews.com/r2/?url=http://nutshellurl.com/AlienDNAHuman
Peter D. Ouspensky In Search of the Miraculous.
rense.com/general74/d3af.htm
www.thewatcherfiles.com/cooper/operation_majority.htm
William (Bill) Cooper
www.arcturi.com/GreyArchives/USAndGrey's.html
www.dailymail.co.uk/news/article-2100947/Eisenhower-secret-meetings-Aliens-pentagon-consu...
www.thewatcherfiles.com/Alien-treaty.htm
RCTURI.COM
www.rense.com/general3/aurora.htm
www.eyewitnesstohistory.com/wright.htm
Alien-are-real-ufo.blogspot.com/.../fathers-of-stealth-technology-admit-are.html
zighydevourer.wordpress.com/.../1947-ufo-kapustin-yar-the-russian-area-51/
www.gizmodo.com/.../15-super-secret-bases-that-everybody-seems-to-know-about/
www.ufocasebook.com?Russia.html
www.sott.net/.../263190-FEMA-Russian-Emergencies-Ministry-to-join-forces-against-space-threat

www.spacemart.com/.../Russia_US_to_join_forces_against_space_threats_999.html
www.ufoevidence.org/Government.htm
www.rense.com/politics6/secdocs.htm
YOUTUBE
www.nteu208.org/issues/Fluride/Nteu208-fluoride.htm
fluoridealert .org Charles E. Perkins, 2 October 1954
www.globalissues.org/article/590/corruption
The HAARP Programme Michel Chossudovsky
www.ancient-code.com/ancient-technology
www.exopaedia.org/staar+project
www.bloomberg.com
www.sciencedaily.com
www.crawford2000.co.uk/ufo-planetx-nibiru-marduk.htm
www.crawford2000.co.uk/ufo-planetx-nibiru-marduk2.htm
www.ancient-code.com/prophets-prophecies-and-Aliens
Edward Bernays 1929
THE HOLY BIBLE
www.godlikeproductions.com/forum1/message1208982/pg1
www.disclose.tv/...Mind Control weapon of mass persuasion-Disclose.tv
www.motherboard.vice.com/.../a-complex-systems-model-predicted-the-revol
www.tech.firstpost.com/.../2017-microchip-new-world-order
www.youtube.com/watch?v=ncXjBih6mcw
www.panoffolin.wordpress.com/.../the-shocking-truth-about-rfid-chip-implant
www.ancientexplorers.com/.../sumerian-texts-secrets-about-Alien-life-revealed
www.ufoevidence.org/documents/doc175
The Oxford Companion to World Mythology' They described the Anuunakias
www.newageGod.com/ENKImedia/Earth4.htm
www.youtube.com/watch?v=176n3aE1x4M

www.youtube.com/watch?v=Ht2VFVZU8q4
Zecharia Sitchin The Twelfth Planet.
www.thepathtooneness.com/mental/nibiru-planet-x/
www.xfacts.com
www.newsfollowup.com
www.collective-evolution.com
911research.wtc7.net/sept11/evidence
www.bbc.co.uk/news/magazine-19052054.
www.thetruthseeker.co.uk
www.beforeitsnews.com
www.examiner.com/.../genetically-modified-organisms-how-they-are-made-and-why-they-aren-t-labelled
www.today.com/.../alarm-raised-over-poisoning-ris.
Lisa Collier cool Yahoo health
www.responsibletechnology.org/10-Reasons-to-Avoid-GMOs
www.globalhealingcenter
Exo-Vaticana.(ufosightingshotspot.blogspot.com/.../the-vaticans-astonishing-plan-for.html)
www.exovaticana.com
www.ufobc.com/Reports/Aliensreligion.htm
www.guardianlv.com/2013/10/mother-teresa-was-no-saint-says-study
www.bibletruths731.com/heaven-this-will-answer-all-your-questions
www.theglobeandmail.com
www.enhs.umn.edu/current/5103/gm/harmful.html
Dr Mercola – Mercola.com
Fall of America: David Icke on TETRA masts
www.youtube.com/watch?v=_Fn0v0VX3wM
The Sumerian Tablets Contain Our Entire Biblical Stories ...
www.chemtrails911.com/intro_to_chem.htm
www.historvius.com/ancient-pyramids-of-the-world/fr261
www.sciences360.com › Earth Science › Earth Science – Other

www.iflscience.com/watch-25-most-terrifying-looking-sea-creatures
www.youtube.com/watch?v=iiTC-6BGW5g new world order
www.organicauthority.com/foodie.../eight-reasons-gmos-are-bad-for-you.html
Mike Adams, Natural News
www.foodandwaterwatch.org/food/genetically-engineered-foods/
sugar.www.naturalnews.com/037737
Discovery News
www.youtube.com/watch?v=0vOWh5G_Q70
Andrew Gavin Marshall Global Research,
www.crawford2000.co.uk/ufo-planetx-nibiru-marduk.htm
The Telegraph
www.ufoevidence.org/topics/abduction.htm
www.illuminati-news.com/ufos-and.../nibiru_and_the_anunnaki.htm
planetEarthvortex.wordpress.com/tag/atlantis/
Eric de Carbonnel | marketskeptics.com
www.theemergencyfoodsupply.com/emergency-food
www.orwelltoday.com/foodshortage.shtml
www.youtube.com/watch?v=x-CrNlilZho
www.laitman.com/2010/01/why-do-we...
www.youtube.com/watch?v=LxNq5_keJU0
www.youtube.com/watch?v=6jx3vVSSfEs
beforeitsnews.com/.../the-true-age-of-the-sphinx-and-did-the-Earths-axis
www.crawford2000.co.uk/ufo-planetx-nibiru-marduk2.htm
www.biogeometry.org/page34.html
www.perceivingreality.com
www.news.com.au/.../science/...scientific...Aliens/story-fn5fsgyc-1226617200225
www.doug-long.com
www.genome.gov/10001772

The Illuminati-Staged US Presidential Election - Rense
Zwinglius Redivivus

This book was completed on Tuesday 10.21PM 20/01/2015. It contains 132,700 words

Review Requested:

If you loved this book, would you please provide a review at Amazon.com?

Lightning Source UK Ltd.
Milton Keynes UK
UKOW02f1942180116

266645UK00001B/74/P